The Lunar Tao

Other books by Deng Ming-Dao

The Chronicles of Tao
   The Wandering Taoist
   Seven Bamboo Tablets of the Cloudy Satchel
   Gateway to a Vast World

Scholar Warrior

365 Tao

Everyday Tao

Zen: The Art of Modern Eastern Cooking

The Living I Ching

The Lunar Tao

Meditations with the Seasons

Deng Ming-Dao

HarperOne
An Imprint of HarperCollinsPublishers

dengmingdao.com
facebook.com/dengmingdao
twitter.com/dengmingdao

HarperOne

HarperCollins books may be purchased for educational, business, or sales promotional
use. For information, please e-mail the Special Markets Department at SPsales@harper
collins.com

HarperCollins website: http://www.harpercollins.com
HarperCollins®, ⛩®, and HarperOne™ are trademarks of HarperCollins Publishers.

Library of Congress Cataloging-in-Publication Data is available upon request.

ISBN 978–0–06–211688–8

HB 01.23.2023

For Alison Jade

Contents

12 The Last Moon 387

Festivals and Holidays at a Glance

Introduction

My grandfather emigrated from southern China to the United States at the beginning of the twentieth century. When he arrived in San Francisco, he bought a Seth Thomas Office Calendar Double-Dial Wall Clock. It had a windup mechanism and a pendulum. My mother kept it when he died. Now she's passed away too, and it hangs in my home.

The clock has two white faces set vertically in a carved oak frame. Slender black hands on the upper face point to twelve elegant roman numerals. Two revolving cylinders set in the lower face name the month and the day of the week, and a single narrow hand points to black numbers around the circumference to indicate the day of the month. My grandfather brushed a four-word phrase from the Confucian classics on a semicircle of red paper and glued it to the lower face above the cylinders:

Esteem virtue; accept everyone.

Whenever he looked at the clock, he saw these words in his own calligraphy. They expressed the ideal he observed for the rest of his life.

When my grandfather named me Dao, (the same Chinese character as Tao), he set the theme of my life as boldly as that black ink on red paper. I didn't know it as a boy, struggling to master the strokes of my own name, but Tao would become a lifelong passion for me. It has taken me into middle age to learn that Taoism is as simple as my grandfather's clock: set forth an understanding, observe it, and live it constantly throughout each year.

My grandfather used three calendars. He dated his diary by the reign year of the emperor then on the throne in Beijing, Emperor Guangxu (1871–1908). As the owner of a garment factory in San Francisco, he used the Western calendar. But he, his family, and the entire community tracked their significant holidays and seasonal observations by the lunar calendar.

When it was the Spring Festival, the shops sold oranges and quince blossoms, and the family came together to celebrate the year's beginning. During the time of the Clear Bright Festival, my grandfather spent the day on buses to and from the cemetery where he swept the graves. During the Dragon Boat Festival, my grandmother cooked special rice dumplings steamed in bamboo leaves. When the Moon Festival arrived—which coincided with my grandmother's birthday—the family shared moon cakes and watched the harvest moon rise. As the year came to an end, my grandfather was careful to settle all debts and clean the home to prepare for a fresh start. There were always plenty of people in the house—children, neighbors, factory workers, cousins visiting from afar. Each festival was a time of family reunion, and family meant even the most distant of relations or cherished friends.

Beginning with the first grade, I attended San Francisco public school during the day and then went to a Chinese school held in a church's classrooms at night. I sat at old oak school desks carved with graffiti. Fluorescent lights buzzed overhead, their reflections flickering on the dark windows. The smell of pine-soot ink and mulberry paper mingled with the odor of crumbling plaster, old varnish, and ammonia-washed linoleum floors. The lessons were historical, moral, or poetic—sometimes all three at once. The teaching method was the same as it had been in my grandfather's youth: memorization, recitation, and endless copying of words, idioms, and pages with a pointed brush. If we did not do well, the teachers ordered us to stand in a corner or dared us to cry as they hit us with chalkboard pointers, rulers, or yardsticks.

Occasionally, these harsh moments were tempered by sentimental reminiscences of China. At other times the teachers expanded on the folktales behind idioms such as "One bowl of rice is worth a thousand pieces of gold" (p. 128). Stories of the loyal hero Yue Fei (p. 53) or Song Hong's refusal to abandon his wife (p. 96) were far more vivid than the ancient utterances we memorized.

But the talks always returned to morality. A favored source was the *Twenty-Four Paragons of Filial Piety* by Guo Jujing (1260–1368). One of our teachers, Mr. Luo, gave rhapsodic accounts of one of the paragons, Wu Meng. The boy's family was poor and had no mosquito netting. Each night, Wu Meng lay in his father and mother's bedroom until the insects were too satiated to bite his parents. We scoffed at how dumb he was—which instantly brought more scolding.

Our skepticism was surpassed by puzzlement, however, because Mr. Luo—a short, slight teetotaler, with thinning hair and rimless spectacles, ever-dressed in a double-breasted suit and tie—enthusiastically praised the drunkenness of poets such as Li Bai (p. 264) and Tao Yuanming (p. 106), and artists such as Wang Xizhi (p. 85). He insisted that artists and poets needed wine to be free, to be creative, to become the greatest creators in all the centuries. "They had to be completely drunk before they would fling ink to make beautiful paintings or write words in masterly calligraphy. If they tried the next day when they were sober, they couldn't match the work from the night before." He delighted in our confusion, adding that we had no hope of comprehending these works, let alone becoming great ourselves.

Headmaster Tan, with shoulders like a gravestone, gray hair slicked to his skull, and age spots on his wrinkled face, wandered in whenever he pleased. Our strict teachers deferred to him without hesitation. The headmaster's message was unwavering: "The ancients were perfect. Preserve tradition and never compromise it. You are all duck eggs, but you must try!" Duck eggs were the shape of the number zero.

Nearly every student—even those who were already native speakers—wanted to quit Chinese school. We cheered each one who managed the feat as if he or she had escaped from prison. I went for nine years before my parents allowed me to withdraw. In a few years, though, I found myself returning to Chinese language, art, history, and religion during college and afterward. I soon began an intensive and ongoing study of martial arts and Taoism with private teachers.

I was driven by a mystery that appeared throughout the years. I kept running across the words Tao and Taoism. Maybe it began because it was my own name, but soon my interest in these scattered references went well beyond curiosity over a coincidence. Tao, I read, meant "the Way," and I encountered many books with titles beginning with *The Tao of—* or *The Way of—*. Mai-Mai Sze's *The Way of Chi-*

nese Painting began with a chapter titled "The Concept of Tao." To this day, a long list of words have been appended to *The Tao of—*, including dating, Jeet Kune Do, sex, leadership, equus, physics, travel, motherhood, nutrition, Montessori, health, meditation, sobriety, Willie (Nelson), and Pooh. *The Way of—* has been paired with shaman, herbs, shadows, master, sword, heart, energy, and Zen.

When studying the Chinese classics, I was fascinated with the varying meanings of the word Tao. Confucius said, "A filial son must not deviate from his father's way [Tao] for three years after his father has died." When discussing archery, he spoke of "the ancient method [Tao]." He said that a "scholar should set his determination on the truth [Tao]." He exhorted scholars to "be devout, studious, and keep an excellent course [Tao] for all your life. . . . The world has a way [Tao] whose laws can be seen. There is no path [Tao] whose laws cannot be seen." My inquiry into Chinese philosophy soon led to Laozi's book, the *Daodejing (Tao Te Ching—The Book of the Way and Virtue)*, but the wordplay in the first two lines only made the book seem more abstruse:

> The way [Tao] that can be spoken [Tao] is not the constant way [Tao]. The name that can be named is not the constant name.

I discovered Zen Buddhism. But Tao again appeared in the texts. D. T. Suzuki wrote in *Zen and Japanese Culture*, "Zen united itself to a great extent with Taoist beliefs and practices and with the Confucian teaching of morality. . . ." The scholar Okakura Kakuzo devoted a chapter to the subject, "Taoism and Zennism," in his *Book of Tea:* "Taoism accepts the mundane as it is and, unlike the Confucians and the Buddhists, tries to find beauty in our world of woe and worry."

How could Tao be a part of so many different subjects? How could it be so admired by people from Confucius to Bruce Lee, Laozi to Okakura Kakuzo? What in the world was everyone talking about? And what kept me looking?

The sentiment that Okakura Kakuzo hinted at—finding beauty in our world of woe and worry—appealed to me. After more investigation, I found that Taoism and Zen alike held meditation to be paramount. That was attractive—except I hated sitting still. After more searching, I read that Taoism had a method that began with physical training and proceeded step by step to the meditative.

Wen-Shang Huang wrote in *Fundamentals of Tai Chi Ch'uan* (Taijiquan):

> Tai Chi Ch'uan is also a synthesis or a crystallization of the philosophy of Confucianism, Taoism, and Zen Buddhism—Tao or Way of Chinese life. The mastery of this eminent art, based on natural laws as expounded by Lao Tzu [Laozi] and Tao Chia [Daojia], is the very key to happiness, longevity, and eternal youth. It also embodies meditation (Zen) in its movement, and one is likely to be rid of tension and disequilibrium, as well as to have one's physical health restored.

That appealed to me, and I went to a succession of teachers to painstakingly learn the system that began with stretching and progressed to spiritual practice (you can get an overview of this system in my book *Scholar Warrior*).

I found the culture of my Chinese school alive in martial arts teachers: memorize the movements, and then practice them daily for forty years to understand them.

And Chinese poetry teachers: chant poems every day and let their music and multiple meanings reveal themselves over time. And Taoist priests: read the scriptures morning and night, chant mantras to the gods, meditate daily, and give yourself over to good deeds for a lifetime, and someday you'll reach enlightenment. Everyone subscribed to Headmaster Tan's view: preserve the tradition and don't compromise it.

How does one learn about Taoism today without compromising it? Since my writing career began in 1983, many people have written to me asking about Taoism. The most common questions are, "How do I find a master?" and, "How can I learn about Taoism if I cannot find a master?" This book is one way to answer those questions—beginning with my grandfather's maxim:

Esteem virtue; accept everyone.

The Purpose of This Book

This book is written to help people follow Taoism until they find a master. As soon as I state this goal, Headmaster Tan's ghost appears: "Preserve tradition and never compromise it." I am preserving the tradition, not in a dry and dutiful way, but in a fresh and creative way. If you've glanced ahead at the sidebars, I've provided sources with original translations in support of the text. At the same time, I've written about Tao from my own experience. Taoism is the best tradition of wisdom I've found. This is my testimony to it.

When my teachers emphasized preserving the culture, I took it as one more arbitrary demand from annoying old people. Only after all this time do I see that the teachers were training me for myself and the generation after me. Their tradition had sustained people over thousands of years. If I'm passing on their tradition through this book, it's not because I'm trying to save traditional knowledge for its sake. No, I'm offering it for the sake of anyone who can gain by learning it.

The traditional rote approach has been replaced by better methods—all education strives to improve. But the original intention of the teachers was not that obtuse. It was meant to be a process of self-discovery. In the case of Taijiquan's forty years for realization, that meant a long time-frame, but the point was to reach an inner awakening.

Look at the three major figures in this book: they all exemplify self-discovery after long effort. Buddha reached his enlightenment only after he abandoned ascetic efforts, gave himself over to his own meditation, and trusted his own realization (p. 118). Laozi grew weary of the world and realized that he would not be able to advocate Tao in conventional settings; in leaving a book behind he ended up reaching a far greater number of people than he ever did as an archivist (p. xxx). Confucius is known to have been disappointed at the literal learning of his most beloved pupil, Yan Hui (p. 32), believing that if a teacher holds up one corner of a square, the student should be able to infer the other three (p. 281). Self-discovery is the goal of training, and self-discovery is the way to spiritual awakening.

We need Taoism that goes beyond dull lessons. We need Taoism that is daily life. The best way to find that is to return to the lunar calendar that has been embedded in the culture and shaped by centuries of spiritual and folk traditions. Providing something Taoist to consider each day for an entire year both imparts key concepts and models the importance of perseverance and constant learning. It may take decades for understanding to mature, but the initial meaning must be apparent right away.

The goal of understanding Tao is to discover a personal philosophy of understanding and self-reliance. All you need to do is to read each day and to consider how the idea presented might fit into your life. The small efforts of daily practice surpass grandiose declarations. There is no authority, no force, no threat of damnation, no guilt. Just an idea and an example from history, or a moving poem, or the example of someone's life. Consider each one. If it works, take it. If it doesn't work, move on. Out of all of the material presented, out of 365 days, there will surely be a good number of ideas to keep.

All the sources are collections of smaller essays, poems, or aphorisms. They are written in terse and poetic language, and they range wildly from the loftiest of cosmological outlooks to the most practical of minute advice. They can be read sequentially or at random. In the same way, this book invites you to enter it from where you stand and as you wish. The traditional, nonlinear model of writing has its advantages. This book is designed to be read in whatever way seems preferable. It can be read one page to each day, beginning at the beginning of the year. It could be dipped into by subject. One might simply follow the exercises, or one might refer to the sidebars only when necessary. Perhaps one enjoys the festivals and stories. Whatever your approach, this is a book that testifies to the tradition and experience of Taoism, and lets the reader choose how to approach the different dimensions offered.

This book is not *about* Taoism. It *is* a book of Taoism, and it's for everybody.

Esteem virtue; accept everyone.

Tao: Not Just Chinese

The concept and tradition of Tao happen to have their origins in China, but Tao is universal. People all over the world have embraced it and study it. Tao is a spiritual path for anyone who wishes to find understanding and contentment in life.

Imagine you were reading a French cookbook. You would want to know that the recipes were authentic, and you would enjoy knowing about the background of the dishes. But you wouldn't have to be French to cook the meals, and you certainly wouldn't have to be French to eat them! Taoism is the same way. Yes, it has a Chinese background; yes, it is thoroughly a part of its culture; and yes, it has thoroughly shaped that culture in return. Yet one need not be Chinese to be Taoist, and one certainly need not be Chinese to be nourished by Taoism. Especially when Tao's origins are dynastic Chinese, how can we remain both true to the tradition and true to who we are today? What does it mean when the gods are dressed in imperial robes and holding magic swords or peaches of immortality, looking nothing like what we see in our world today?

What matters is whether the ideas that the gods represent are useful to us. Over the past millennia important personages have given us vital ideas still unsurpassed today. Just as Newton gave us insight into classical physics, Darwin gave us the theory of evolution, and Beethoven gave us music no one else has come close to duplicating, great philosophers like Laozi, Zhuangzi, and Confucius have given us spiritual wisdom and insights into human existence. When we look for answers to our questions today, we can still learn from these figures who gave profound and ever-relevant responses to human dilemmas.

This book's many references to Chinese things therefore represent a grounding in tradition, a nod to authenticity, and an examination of the basis for the ideas—but nothing is true just because it's Chinese. We still need to take the ideas and find the right way to apply them to our own lives, regardless of who we are or where we live. There is no reason to meditate unless it works for you. There is no reason to try to be Chinese if you aren't. And if you are Chinese, there's no reason to dress as a medieval figure with a long beard and silken gown. Ideas are templates. If you find them useful, you are welcome to make them your own.

Esteem virtue; accept everyone.

Why Should We Study Taoism?

 Taoism (Daojiao) is China's oldest and only indigenous spiritual tradition. Buddhism (Fujiao) came from India, and Confucianism (Rujiao) is a system of morality, philosophy, and governance. Taoists believe in following Tao—the Way. They believe that there is a Way that all of nature and all human endeavors follow. Furthermore, they believe that everyone has a personal Way. The ideograph for Tao (Dao) illustrates this. On the right side is a face, representing a person. The left side and the bottom represent moving feet: Tao is a person—or people—on a path.

The dual sense of the English word "way" is true of the Chinese word Tao as well. When we say "way" in one context, we mean a path. When we say "way" in another, we mean a method, procedure, or approach, as in "there is a way to do it." Tao is the Way, as in the Way of all life, and it is the study of how to live and walk that Way well. Here are other reasons why studying Tao is worthwhile:

Antiquity. Taoism has been tested for centuries, and the doctrines that survive are the ones that are the most effective. Taoism definitely has had its share of mistakes, excesses, days of glory, and days of destruction. What is in the system now has been thoroughly examined—and has had to prove itself against other systems.

Nature. Taoism patterns itself after nature. It looks to the cycles of day and night and of the seasons for its truths. It points to what all of us can see and experience, and it does not need to say that its laws were given by a god to be valid. Instead, it asks us to look in the world around us for the answers to our spiritual questions.

Open Theism. Taoism is polytheistic. Any of us can find a god that is most resonant with us. However, Taoism is also the perfect system for the doubter, the agnostic, or even the atheist. The masters freely admit that either the gods are not the highest beings in the world, or they don't exist at all independently of human belief. One need not even worship a god to be a Taoist, because one can concentrate wholly on Tao itself. Taoism is the spiritual tradition for anyone, from someone who wants only to worship a special god to someone who does not want to worship a god at all.

Health. Taoism has a wide variety of health techniques. It asserts that being healthy and living a long and happy life are vital to spirituality. There is no mind-body duality. There is only a mind-body continuum.

Moderation. Taoism advocates the middle path: no extremes, no fanaticism, no campaigns against other people or other religions.

Individuality. Taoism is nonconformity. Due to the enormous social pressures of Confucian society, there had to be some sanctioned relief. Taoism was the system for the eccentrics, the artists, the poets, the musicians, and the hermits.

Inquiry. Taoism is skeptical. The most cursory reading of Zhuangzi (p. xxxi) reveals his dry wit, his criticism of the established Confucian order, his skewering of the rich and powerful, his mockery of rationalist philosophers. Many of us today question religion, authority, and power. Taoism has been doing that for more than 2,500 years. Taoism addresses the political—except its stance is that people in power are usually abusive and seldom try to benefit the people.

Philosophical. Taoism is practical. While it addresses every level of reality from the beginning of the universe to the meaning of death, it is not inclined toward speculation or intellectual intricacies. It tries to get at reality directly, and its teachings are intended to lead the student to the source of all things. That doesn't make it easy to master, but it does show that Taoism is a complete philosophy.

Mysticism. Taoism is unabashedly mystical. That doesn't appeal to every person. On the other hand, for those who intuitively believe in the need to accept mystery, and even account for it in one's outlook, Taoism is perfect.

Community. Taoism believes in community. It believes in supporting the masses, not propping up the ruling elite. It believes that government exists to feed the people, keep them happy, and protect them from conflict. How many governments really live up to those simple goals?

Peace. Taoism believes that each individual deserves peace, and it believes in peace for every country.

Taoism welcomes anyone who comes to it.
Esteem virtue; accept everyone.

The Lunar Calendar

The lunar calendar that provides the structure of this book has been used in China since at least 500 BCE. It was first used for farming. The calendar's Chinese name is *nongli*, meaning "agricultural calendar," and it incorporates both lunar and solar features. Generations of farmers followed it to plant crops and predict when rain, sunny days, and snow were most likely to occur. As the centuries passed, farmers added folk customs to the calendar and tracked the rituals and festivals that fit with the seasonal rhythms of their lives. Their spiritual concerns had to match their cycles of work.

When harvests were good, the farmers were more likely to give thanks to the God of the Local Land at a roadside shrine than to trudge to a temple. They brought offerings such as fruit, rice, flowers, and cooked foods, and these offerings evolved into the foods associated with today's festivals. The calendar eventually filled with celebrations ranging from the first day of spring to thanksgiving for plentiful crops, remembrances of special myths, memorials to heroes, and the observance of key days such as the summer solstice.

China's three great spiritual traditions—Taoism, Buddhism, and Confucianism—also contributed holy days. While there were some conflicts, an open acceptance of all gods and beliefs developed among the populace. If a story was compelling or if a person was worth honoring, people placed them in the calendar.

The three systems address different aspects of spirituality. Generalization is risky, but the rough differences are these: Confucianism addresses propriety, morality, social organization, scholarly understanding, the dominance of family, and worldly accomplishment. Buddhism is visionary, otherworldly, compassionate, and advocates devotion. Taoism is nonconformity, creativity, physical health, and lifelong integration with nature. Needing all three, people wove the profundity of these great spiritual traditions into the lunar calendar.

The effort to integrate society with nature by observing the moon was by no means exclusively Chinese. Other cultures use the lunar calendar as well. Easter falls on the first Sunday after or on the first full moon following the spring equinox (northern hemisphere) or autumn equinox (southern hemisphere). Islam uses the Hijri calendar. India uses a Hindu calendar. The Jewish calendar is used to determine religious and ceremonial observances as well as agricultural dates. While all the world uses the solar calendar, billions of people all over the world keep parallel traditions of living with nature and celebrating with the seasons by following the moon. The lunar calendar fits a deep-seated need in us. It keeps us in tune with the seasons and the rhythms of the sun, moon, and tides. It ties us back to simple childhood observations of the moon crossing the night sky.

Esteem virtue; accept everyone.

The Festivals

The lunar calendar has seven major festivals.

Spring Festival begins with the first day of the lunar new year (which occurs during a four-week period centered around February 4) and extends over fifteen days. There are many observations and celebrations, but the central theme is family reunion.

Lantern Festival is a night for beautiful lanterns in many shapes, fireworks, and feasting. It closes the fifteen-day spring celebration.

Clear Bright Festival occurs roughly around April 4 or 5, shortly after the spring solstice, and is a day to visit the cemeteries, remember the dead, and focus on our ancestors.

Dragon Boat Festival is observed on the fifth day of the fifth moon. It features competitive rowing races to honor Qu Yuan, a patriotic poet who lived nearly 2,300 years ago.

The Double Seven Festival is held on the seventh day of the seventh moon. Sometimes called Chinese Valentine's Day, it is a day for lovers and romance.

Moon Festival occurs on the fifteenth day of the eighth moon. It is also known as the Mid-Autumn Festival, and it celebrates the time when the full moon appears largest.

Double Nine Festival is held on the ninth day of the ninth moon, celebrating the harvest, chrysanthemums, and the elderly. It's been adapted in China as Senior's Day.

Smaller festivals, birthdays, and holidays focus on Taoist gods such as the Three Pure Ones, the Gods of the Five Sacred Mountains, or the God of Literature; Buddhist figures such as Buddha, Guanyin, or Bodhidharma; and Confucian figures, including Confucius himself, the poet Qu Yuan, and the legendary emperor Fuxi. Since the lunar calendar varies, these birthdays aren't literal; rather, they are observation days. Furthermore, there are regional and sectarian variations on some of the dates of observation.

Chinese families are relaxed about the dates of these observances. They use them more as rough guides; the important thing is that family members come home, the old stories get shared, and bonds get renewed. Nobody is terribly dogmatic, every good philosophy is preserved, and basic ideas are adopted as one's own.

Esteem virtue; accept everyone.

How This Book Is Organized

Twelve lunar months, with thirty days each, make a year. Each month begins with a new moon. Since a lunar month is 29.530589 solar days, an intercalary, or leap, month added every two or three years synchronizes the lunar and solar years.

The first day of the lunar new year falls on the second new moon after the winter solstice. This day may be as early as January 21 or as late as February 20. The actual day is determined by astronomical data that vary according to one's position on the globe. The original calculations that fixed the calendar were based on the position of the stars as they were observed over the east coast of China thousands of years ago. Not only do the stars' positions appear different from different places on the globe, but the speed and orbit of the earth have changed since as well. Local calculations therefore are required each year; information about the moon for specific areas is available in newspapers or online.

Furthermore, the meteorological aspects of the calendar may be perfectly attuned to northeast China—but they don't hold completely true for the rest of China or for any other place in the world. In subtropical southern China, for instance, it does not snow, rendering terms in the calendar like "Great Snow" symbolic. Using the lunar-solar calendar requires numerous local adjustments according to the season, longitude, and latitude of the place where we live.

While the months are calculated by the moon, dates based on the sun are also incorporated—most notably the two solstices and equinoxes, the first day of spring, and the festivals of Clear Bright and Winter Solstice. The solar year is divided into the Twenty-Four Solar Terms, consisting of fifteen days each, for a total of 360 days.

This book matches the 360 days of the lunar calendar and the 360 days of the Twenty-Four Solar Terms to show the ideal structure and to give a universal organization for coming years. However, in any given future year, these two sets may not match exactly, and minor adjustments will be necessary to tally with the true solar year of just over 365.25 days. To provide five more days to make up 365, the Five Phases that appear at the end of the book can be used as "spacer" days. Since the Five Phases are also keyed to the seasons, they are also ideal to round out the year. For greatest accuracy, map out the lunar calendar for your exact location.

Each of the Solar Terms opens with the exercise prescribed for it. These are meditative *qigong* (vitality training) exercises rather than athletic ones. The key to this training lies in the breathing instructions, in the visualization coupled with swallowing, and in how we are encouraged to sit in meditation when the exercises have been completed. It should be obvious that these exercises cannot treat serious illnesses. They are included here for cultural and historical reasons, to demonstrate the idea of bodily integration with the seasons, and to consider exercise as a prelude to meditation. They are not literal prescriptions for therapy.

Swallowing is a classic Taoist technique. First, Taoists consider saliva the body's own medicine. It's called the Jade Elixir and the allusion to the legendary elixir of immortality is wholly intentional. Second, each time we're asked to swallow, we inhale and then exhale to the *dantian*—the center of energy deep in our bellies. Not only does the breath charge this center with vitality, but the swallow opens the channel to the dantian so more qi can flow to it. This is a boon to the circulation of energy fundamental to Taoist meditation—and a bodily way to integrate ourselves with the days and seasons.

Twelve part-openers appear with the number and literary title of the moon, a poem, and the two solar terms within that month.

Each one of 360 entries appears with a sidebar of source information beside a meditative essay for that day.

The Five Phases round out the lunar year to the 365 days of the solar year. The sidebar details the many meanings related to each phase.

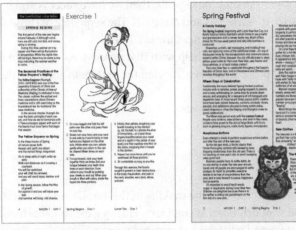

The exercises to the Twenty-Four Solar Terms divide each month, with the Yellow Emperor's seasonal advice appearing once per season.

Festivals, gods, and important people are highlighted in pages interspersed throughout the book.

Therefore, the overall structure of this book divides the years into moons; divides each moon into its two solar terms; gives the exercise for each solar term; and includes interspersed pages focusing on festivals, important gods, or personages, accompanied by daily meditations supported by factual examples or explanations. The sidebars and the highlight pages for festivals and biographies note sources and give possibilities for further exploration; when one is learning Taoism from a teacher, the explanations and cultural references range from religious to academic, from historical to anecdotal, and from the profound to the practical with no distinction between "high" or "low" culture.

Following Those before Us

When my grandfather moved to the United States, he left a life of poverty. The house he fled had dirt floors, no indoor plumbing, and rooms so small that their four walls could nearly be touched with outstretched arms. Nevertheless, he needed great determination to face the unknown future as he embarked on a monthlong sailing over the Pacific Ocean.

He worked the rest of his life in his garment factory, but he kept up his scholarly pursuits. My grandfather kept diaries and records in beautiful calligraphy, and many of the woodcut illustrations you'll see in this book come from his collection, kept in the wooden trunk that held them when he crossed the seas. As a community, business, and religious leader, he maintained his ties to China, working in the early twentieth century to contribute to the establishment of the Nationalist government. His experience suggests the importance and possibilities of maintaining and enlarging one's beliefs even in difficult circumstances.

We can set goals each morning and we can work to achieve them. If we can reflect at night and say we've met those goals, then we have success and happiness. Each night, we return to ourselves and our path. The sequence of those days and nights forms movement. And movement means Tao.

This book is an offering to help with that process. As the moon is constant, so too are the words of those who have traveled the path before us. Let their example be an inspiration to us all.

Esteem virtue; accept everyone.

Acknowledgments

Many people contributed to the making of this book, and I am grateful for their guidance and support. Pearl Weng Liang Huang gave valuable insights into Chinese texts and culture and edited the translated poetry. Shao-Nian Bates was an important source of information, sometimes writing to contacts within China to confirm certain points. Andrea Cochran-Pastel read a number of passages, commenting on the text and the use of illustrations. Donna Mekis discussed the role of fables and myths. Saskia Dab provided dates for some of the festivals as well as a great deal of information about contemporary Taoism in China and the building of new temples.

I am grateful to Jacqueline Berkman, Xiaolin Chang, Jeanette Perez, Betty Gee, Lynn Golbetz, Shannon Kong, and Susan Riley for editorial and production work.

Many of the pages are enhanced by photographs from andelieya, Kathy Bick, Saskia Dab, Bernard De Poorter, Ying Fry, and Peter Pynchon. I thank them all for their contributions.

Romanized Chinese

The Chinese language is based on ideographs. Each one has a single-syllable sound, but words may be combined for complex subjects. For example, the word for computer is the compound: "electric-brain-machine." Thus, a term that may seem to be multisyllabic is always a combination of single words. The name Laozi, for example, is a combination of the words "old" and "master." Naturally, language has evolved over thousands of years, many meanings have been added, and translation is complex.

Since the Chinese language is not alphabetic, different systems to approximate its sounds in English were established. The task was not easy. First, there are sounds in Chinese that no English sounds can duplicate. Secondly, and confusingly, there can be five different tones to any given Chinese sound, with each tone signaling a completely unrelated meaning. While there are about four thousand syllables in English, there are only about forty in Chinese, so each basic sound must have its five different tones (flat, rising, falling, falling-rising, and neutral) to gain a large enough number of words. A sound like *ma*, for example, can mean "mother," "hemp," "horse," "scold," or it can be a question-particle—all depending on the tone.

One prominent method of transliteration, established about 1867, was the Wade-Giles system, and that is where Tao spelled with a "T" originates. In 1958, the People's Republic of China adopted a new method of romanization, known as pinyin, that became the prevailing system throughout the world. Pinyin utilizes diacritics to indicate tones for language learning and pronunciation, although these diacritics are seldom employed in publications and scholarly works. The majority of the Chinese words in this book are romanized according to pinyin.

Exceptions to Pinyin Romanization There are some exceptions to pinyin in this book when a word has entered the English language under an earlier spelling. Tao, Taoist, and Taoism are the major examples. In pinyin, Tao is properly spelled Dao (which is a better indication of its pronunciation—a hard "D" sound rather than a hard "T" sound). However, especially in search engines and popular references, "Tao" has far more recognition than "Dao." Examples of other words left in non-pinyin spelling are *I Ching (Yijing)*, Confucius (Kong Fuzi), and Buddha (Budai).

How to Read Chinese Names Chinese names are written with the family name first. For example, Zhang Lang is from the Zhang family and his personal name is Lang. When someone has a two-word personal name, the personal name is made into a two-syllable word. For example, Zhao Gongming comes from the Zhao family and his personal name is Gong combined with Ming. A few people have compound family names, such as Sima Qian and Zhuge Liang.

Many of the gods mentioned in this book have descriptive titles. Taishan Laojun means the Great Supreme Old Lord. In these cases, the translation of the title is used with the pinyin in parentheses.

Major Sources

Many sources have been utilized in writing this book, but most of the references come from the core texts of Taoism, Confucianism, and Buddhism. Their titles and alternate names can be confusing, so a brief overview of naming conventions and the names of the key texts will be helpful. All translations are original.

Naming Conventions

In order to standardize the translations of book titles, the designation *jing* is translated as "classic." For example, the *Shijing* is translated as *Classic of History*. The word jing means a classic, a sacred book, scripture, or canon. Any book that has the appellation jing is highly revered.

A *ji* is a record. Examples are the *Record of Rites (Liji)* and the *Records of the Grand Historian (Shiji)*.

Some books are named after their author; one might refer to an author's name and then refer to the book title by the same name in the same paragraph. For example, Zhuangzi is both the name of the author as well as the title of the *Zhuangzi*.

In most cases, the title is given in its English equivalent, but there are three notable exceptions. The *Daodejing* and the *I Ching* are given by their Chinese titles, since they are widely known by those names. The *Zhuangzi* is also left as it is, in part because it is familiar by that name, and in part because it means no more than "Master Zhuang" and there would be nothing illuminating about referring to it in English.

Daodejing and *Zhuangzi*

The majority of Taoist quotations are drawn from the *Daodejing* and the *Zhuangzi*.

Daodejing The *Daodejing (The Classic of the Way and Virtue;* also spelled *Tao Te Ching)* is Taoism's premier holy book. The authorship of the book is constantly debated in scholarly circles, but tradition holds that an ancient sage named **Laozi** (p. xxx) wrote this book in the sixth century BCE.

The text is central to philosophical Taoism and it has strongly influenced other schools such as Legalism and Neo-Confucianism. Religious Taoists chant the text as a devotional act and they worship Laozi as the **Great Supreme Old Lord** (p. 5). Chinese Buddhism has also utilized the book, taking its terms to translate Buddhist texts brought from India. In addition, many commentators have asserted that Chan Buddhism, which is known as Zen in Japan and the West, represents a melding of Buddhism and Taoism.

The traditional text consists of eighty-one short and poetic chapters in language so variable in meaning that many simultaneous understandings are both possible and valid. The *Daodejing* is one of the most frequently translated of Chinese spiritual books.

Zhuangzi The book, dated to the fourth century BCE, has also been known as the *Nanhua Zhenjing (The True Classic of Nanhua)*, because it's believed that **Zhuangzi** came from southern China *(nan* means south). As is the case with the *Daodejing,* scholars dispute the idea that a single person wrote the entire book. The academic view is that Zhuangzi wrote the first seven chapters, called the Inner Chapters, and that others wrote the Outer Chapters. In traditional contexts, however, all parts of the *Zhuangzi* are considered important.

Where the *Daodejing* is terse, brief, and poetic, the *Zhuangzi* is largely prose, utilizing essays and fables to make its points. Zhuangzi satirizes the arguments of other philosophers with exaggerated logic that leads to absurd conclusions, and imagines dialogues between Laozi and Confucius, or between Confucius and his students. Sometimes he uses Confucius as an exemplar of wisdom, and at other times, he shows Confucius rebuked by others. He also makes use of dreams, dialogues with skulls or trees, and shows the native wisdom of fishermen or butchers to be superior to sages. Zhuangzi is the skeptical, absurdist, argumentative, and humorous counterpoint to Laozi's mysticism.

Confucian Texts

Analects *(Lunyu)* A compilation of speeches and record of discussions between **Confucius** and his disciples. Most of the text was written by Confucius's students thirty to fifty years after his death. The date of publication is estimated around 500 BCE.

Mengzi *(Mencius)* A collection of conversations between Mencius and the kings of feudal states regarding the proper philosophy of ruling.

Additional material is drawn from the canonical texts of Confucianism known as the **Five Classics** *(Wujing)*. All were

The *Daodejing* inscribed on a wall on Zhongnanshan.
© Photo by Peter Pynchon

supposed to have been in some way compiled, edited, or commented on by Confucius himself.

Classic of Poetry (Shijing) A collection of 305 poems consisting of 160 folk songs, 105 court ceremonial songs, and 40 hymns or eulogies used in sacrifices to gods or the royal family's ancestral spirits. The poems date from the tenth to seventh centuries BCE.

Classic of History (Shujing) Also known as the *Classic of Documents (Shangshu),* the book is a compilation of documents and speeches written by the rulers and officials of the Zhou dynasty. The majority of the texts are thought to have originated in the sixth century BCE.

Record of Rites (Liji) Rites are a central component of Confucianism. They are rules governing rituals; court ceremonies; and social conduct around filial piety, ancestor worship, and funerals. The original work was reputedly edited by Confucius, but the present version is probably from about the third century BCE.

I Ching (Classic of Changes) The proper transliteration of this book's title is *Yijing,* but the book is better known under this older spelling. It is a book that can be used on many different levels. Based on sixty-four hexagrams—graphs consisting of six lines—the *I Ching* is a deep study of change. The core texts go back to at least the twelfth century BCE, and it has been studied as a book of divination, strategy, and philosophy ever since. Its core thesis is that all is constant change propelled from within by yin and yang.

Spring and Autumn Annals (Chunqiu) Also known as the *Linjing,* the book is a historical record of the state of Lu, Confucius's native feudal state. Diplomatic relations, alliances, military actions, the affairs of the ruling family, as well as natural disasters from 772–481 BCE are chronicled for both their historical and moral significance.

These are the first lines of the *I Ching,* incised into one of the Kaicheng Stone Classics (Kaicheng Shi Jing). The 114 massive rock slabs preserved at the Forest of Stone Steles Museum in Xi'an contain twelve Confucian classics including the *Classic of History,* the *Classic of Poetry,* and the *Analects.* The monumental "books" were carved by order of the Tang Emperor Wenzong (809–840) in 833–837 as an indisputable reference work for scholars.

Poetry

The primary source for most of the poems quoted in this book is *Three Hundred Tang Poems (Tangshi Sanbai Shou),* an anthology of poems from the Tang dynasty (618–907), first compiled around 1763 by Sun Zhu (1722–1778). There are actually over three hundred poems, perhaps emulating the 305 poems in the *Classic of Poetry.* Many people consider the Tang dynasty the time of China's greatest poets, with Li Bai, Du Fu, Wang Wei, Li Shangyin, Bai Juyi, Han Yu, and Meng Haoran among the most notable.

Records of the Grand Historian

The *Records of the Grand Historian (Shiji)* was written by **Sima Qian** (c. 145–90 BCE, p. 46), who is considered China's foremost ancient historian. His history covers some two thousand years from 2600–91 BCE. While modern historians may debate some of the details of the text, Sima Qian had the advantage of being closer in time to the events he was writing about.

Chan Buddhist Texts

A number of Chan (Zen) Buddhist koans *(gong'an)* are referenced in this book. All of them are drawn from two sources, the *Wumenguan* and the *Blue Cliff Records.*

Wumenguan (The Gateless Gate) As is the case with the *Zhuangzi,* the book is named after its writer, the Chan Buddhist master **Wumen Huikai** (1183–1260). Each koan recounts a dialogue or situation that reveals an understanding of Chan Buddhism. Wumen wrote a commentary and verse to each one of forty-eight cases. The name *Wumenguan* itself is ambiguous and lends itself to multiple interpretations. It can be translated as the *Gateless Gate,* the *Checkpoint With No Entrance,* the *Pass With No Door,* and many other possibilities.

Blue Cliff Records (Biyan Lu) A collection of Chan Buddhist koans first compiled in 1125 by the Chan master **Yuanwu Keqin** (1063–1135), which he later revised and expanded.

The Twenty-Four Solar Terms

The woodcut illustrations and basic text of the exercises to the Twenty-Four Solar Terms are taken from *The Beverages of the Chinese,* by John Dudgeon, The Tientsin Press, 1895. Dudgeon (1837–1901) spent nearly forty years in China as a doctor, surgeon, translator, and medical missionary. According to editor William R. Berk, the exercises were taken from *Zunshen Ba Jian,* written by Gaolian Shenfu in 1591. Other sources name the exercises' creator as **Chen Tuan,** also known as Chen Xiyi (871–989), a legendary Taoist sage associated with the western sacred mountain, Huashan.

These movements are a subsection of qigong classified as *daoyin*—movements to lead energy. The instructions are modified according to contemporary training. ◗

Laozi and Zhuangzi

What is the most basic knowledge we have about **Laozi** and **Zhuangzi,** the two most influential writers in Taoism? We have two books, the *Daodejing* and the *Zhuangzi,* and we know that both are highly regarded works of spirituality and singular wisdom. In the case of Laozi, he was deified, revered by every sect of Taoism, and given attributes that reflect the concerns of the worshippers: the religious consider him one of Taoism's highest gods, the alchemists portray him as a maker of the elixir of immortality, and the philosophical consider him the source of Taoism's naturalistic and visionary philosophy. In contrast, Zhuangzi was not deified, and any mythologizing of his personality came from his own stories. Depicting Zhuangzi asleep and in the act of the Butterfly Dream has become a motif in itself, and phrases from the *Zhuangzi* have entered the culture in the form of proverbs, idioms, fiction, opera, and comic books.

It is impossible to say with certainty who Laozi and Zhuangzi really were and the dates we have for them are educated guesses. However, we can understand the stories around them, keep a working knowledge about their lives, and absorb the intent of the beliefs about them.

Laozi

Laozi literally means, "The Old Master." According to the *Records of the Grand Historian,* he was a native of Chu

(p. 150), which places him in southern China. There is no clear knowledge of his exact dates, but he is often placed about the sixth century BCE. His surname was Li, his given name was Er, and he was also called Lao Dan. Laozi served as the keeper of the royal archives for the court of Zhou until he saw the decline of the dynasty and resolved to leave it, mounting a water buffalo to ride beyond the western border. When he reached the pass in Zhongnanshan, an official named Yin Xi asked him to put his teachings into writing. The result was a book of some five thousand characters—the *Daodejing.*

The *Records of the Grand Historian* recounts a meeting between Laozi and Confucius (551–479 BCE), where Confucius asks Laozi to give instructions about the rites. Similarly, the *Record of Rites* portrays Confucius quoting Lao Dan on proper funeral rites. The *Zhuangzi* also contains stories of encounters between Laozi and Confucius, but it's impossible to tell whether these are historical or allegorical episodes.

Over the centuries, Laozi was venerated for many reasons, and the sum of all these efforts elevated him in Taoism and Chinese culture in general. The first organized Taoist religion in the second century, called the **Way of the Celestial Masters** (Tianshidao), made Laozi the personification of Tao itself. During the Tang dynasty (618–907), the imperial Li family traced its ancestry back to Laozi as Li Er. In the third–sixth century, the intellectual movement known as the **Mysterious Learning** (Xuanxue), also called Neo-Taoism, made Laozi the center of their thought. As a result, Laozi's philosophy influenced literature, calligraphy, painting, and music. In 731,

The speaking platform on Zhongnanshan, marking the place where Laozi gave his first discourse on the *Daaodejing.* © Photo by Peter Pynchon

the Tang Emperor Xuanzong (685–762) decreed that all officials should have a copy of the *Daodejing,* and he placed the book on the list of texts to be used for the civil service examinations.

The religious Taoists made Laozi one of the gods of the highest trinity, the Three Pure Ones, with the title Great Supreme Old Lord (p. 5).

The *Daodejing* was translated into Sanskrit in the seventh century. By the eighteenth century, a Latin translation was brought to England. There are some 250 translations of Laozi, with more than one hundred in English, and more being added each year.

Whether there was an actual person named Laozi is academic at this point. The figure of Laozi has become the nexus for concerns from the philosophical to the political to the religious. Merely to reduce him to normal biographical parameters is to miss much of his importance. On the other hand, the lack of solid evidence about him makes him as mysterious as his own writing—and in the end, we are left with what we started with: one of the world's greatest books of wisdom. Regardless of who Laozi may have been, it is his gift to us that truly matters.

Zhuangzi

The name Zhuangzi means "Master Zhuang." His personal name was Zhuang Zhou. Much like Laozi, we cannot be certain of his dates, but he is usually placed in the fourth century BCE during the Warring States Period (475–221 BCE). He is believed to have come from Meng City (Meng Cheng) in what is now Anhui. Scholars dispute whether he is an actual person or whether the *Zhuangzi* is a text constructed by a group of writers. Perhaps he's fiction. Perhaps he's simply a person following Taoist philosophy of self-effacement and modesty. Certainly, there are pseudo-autobiographical references in the *Zhuangzi* itself. The picture of a witty philosopher emerges.

People today ask, "What is it like to live as a Taoist?" Zhuangzi's sketches of himself help answer that question. Here are just a few of them:

Huizi (380–305 BCE; a philosopher and representative of the School of Names famous for ten paradoxes of the relativity of time and space) told Zhuangzi that he had been given seeds and had grown a large gourd. But then he didn't know what to do with it. When filled with water, he could not lift it. He cut it in half to make drinking vessels, but the pieces were too big and unstable. He threw the gourd away. Zhuangzi reproached him: why didn't he use the gourd to float over the rivers and lakes?

Huizi compares Zhuangzi's words to a big tree that is large, but so knotted and crooked that no carpenter can use it for straight timber. Zhuangzi retorts: "If so, why don't you plant this tree in the barren wilds? Then you could saunter idly by it or sleep under it. No axe would shorten the tree's existence. Why should uselessness cause you distress?"

Huizi asks: "Can a person be without desire?" Zhuangzi replies that this is possible. "Tao gives a person appearance and ability. Heaven gives bodily form. You subject yourself to toil. Heaven gave you the form of a person but you babble about what is strong and white."

Zhuangzi was fishing in a river when the king of Chu sent two emissaries to say: "I wish you to rule all within my territories." Zhuangzi continued fishing and without looking around said, "I have heard that in Chu there is the shell of a divine tortoise who lived three thousand years ago. The king keeps it in his ancestral temple, covered with a cloth. Tell me, was it better for the tortoise to die but be so honored? Or would it have been better for it to live, dragging its tail in the mud?"

"We suppose that it would be better for it to be dragging its tail in the mud," replied the officials.

"Go away, then," said Zhuangzi. "Let me drag my tail in the mud."

When Zhuangzi's wife died, Huizi went to express his condolences. He found Zhuangzi squatting on the ground singing, and pounding a basin like a drum. "When a wife lives with her husband, brings up his children, and dies in old age, to wail for her is not even enough expression of grief. Instead, you drum on a basin and sing. Isn't that improper and strange?" Zhuangzi replied that he was indeed affected by the death, but then, reflected, "Before she was born, she had no life, no bodily form, and no breath. In the intermingling of the waste and dark chaos came a change. Then there was breath; another change, and then came a body; another change, and thus came birth and life.

"There is now a change again, and she is dead. The relation between phases is like the sequence of the four seasons from spring to autumn, from winter to summer. She lies with her face up, sleeping in the great chamber. If I were to fall sobbing and wailing for her, it would mean that I didn't understand what is meant for us all."

Zhuangzi dreamed that he was a butterfly, flying about, enjoying itself. He did not know he was Zhuangzi. When he awoke, he found that he was Zhuangzi. He did not know whether he had been Zhuangzi dreaming that he was a butterfly, or if he was a butterfly dreaming that he was Zhuangzi. ◗

1

The First Moon

Spring Festival

Thoughts on a Still Night

Moonlight so bright before my bed
I took it for frost on the ground.
I raise my head to the moon,
then lower it and think of home.

—Li Bai (701–762)

The two solar terms within this moon:

SPRING BEGINS

RAIN WATER

Spring Festival

A Family Holiday

The **Spring Festival** (Chun Jie), beginning with Lunar New Year's Day, is a family holiday. Family members return home to see parents and grandparents and to renew family ties. For many, it may be their only opportunity of the year to go home. Much of Asia closes for this two-week period, and most businesses close. The Spring Festival is the busiest time for the transportation and communications systems in China.

Nowadays, e-mails, text messaging, and mobile phone calls are replacing some of the traditional travel. However, the old attitude prevails: every person should go home for the Lunar New Year, see friends and close relatives, or at least make contact.

The Lunar New Year is celebrated throughout the People's Republic of China, elsewhere in Asia, and in Chinatowns and Chinese and other Asian communities throughout the world.

Fifteen Days of Celebration

Traditional Spring Festival practices include visiting temples, praying, paying respects to parents and in-laws, withdrawing on some days for private observances, and arranging for a succession of rich banquets and vegetarian days. In more recent times, joyous public celebrations have been added: fireworks, concerts, acrobatic shows, parades, and exhibitions abound in many communities. Lavish fireworks in cities like Beijing and Shanghai make for grand celebrations.

The fifteen-day period ends with the **Lantern Festival** (p. 19). People carry lanterns, view lanterns, and stroll in the streets. Lanterns have grown to the size of large floats with glowing dragons, crabs, birds, figures, and pagodas.

Auspicious Actions

Every attempt is made to perform auspicious actions before and after the start of the new year.

As the old year ends, a family cleans house thoroughly, symbolically sweeping away lingering misfortunes from the old year. There is no cleaning on New Year's Day to avoid sweeping away good luck.

Businesspeople hurry to settle debts, for no one wishes to enter the new year encumbered, and all people are encouraged to settle grudges. As much as possible, everyone wishes to be free of any problems from the past, and to look forward to peace, happiness, and prosperity.

It's important to avoid harsh words, anger, or arguments during Lunar New Year. Children are delighted because there is neither scolding nor punishment on the first day of a new year.

Windows and doors are decorated with paper cuts and couplets with good wishes for happiness, prosperity, and longevity. In particular, one can see the word "happiness" *(fu)* everywhere. This word is often displayed upside down, symbolizing happiness pouring into our lives.

On Lunar New Year's Eve all the members of the family gather for a rich feast. Traditional dishes include roast pork, duck, chicken, fish, and sweets. All the food must be perfect in appearance and taste, and poultry and fish must be served whole—having "a head and a tail" symbolizes being thorough and complete. The night ends with firecrackers to drive away evil spirits.

Early the next morning, children greet their parents and wish them a happy new year. The parents hand out red envelopes with "lucky money" inside. The envelopes are decorated with wishes for happiness, long life, wealth, success, and the fulfillment of all wishes.

Married couples also give these red envelopes to the elderly, to unmarried family members, and to children. Even numbers are favored for the amounts. The number eight is popular because it sounds like the word "wealth," and the number six is popular because it sounds like the word "flowing."

Many things having to do with the Lunar New Year are red, which is considered a lucky color. (By contrast, white is avoided as sorrowful since it's worn at funerals.) Red represents joy, virtue, truth, sincerity, and the heart.

New Clothes

The new year is a time to start fresh. Accordingly, people get their hair cut before New Year's Day to avoid "cutting off their prosperity," and they buy new clothes for the coming year. Red is a popular clothing color, especially for women and children.

The Nian Monster

There was once a mythical beast named **Nian**. *Nian* is the actual word for "year" and is a pictograph of a person carrying the harvest home. But in this legend, the Nian came on the first day of the new year to devour livestock, crops, and villagers, especially children. People were forced to put food in front of their doors on New Year's Day so the Nian would not eat anyone.

One year, though, the Nian was scared away by a child dressed in red. Thereafter, villagers hung red lanterns and red scrolls on windows and doors and used firecrackers to scare the Nian away.

The beast was eventually captured by a Taoist monk named **Hongjun Laozu,** who rides the Nian to this day.

Greetings

There are two predominant greetings at the new year: *xinnian kuaile,* "happy new year," and *gongxi facai,* which means "congratulations and prosperity." It's not clear why one expresses congratulations: some say it's because one has survived the harsh winter, others say it's because the bad luck of the old year is over, and still others harken back to the story of the Nian and are happy that misfortune has been avoided.

Meals with Symbolism

On New Year's Eve and a number of other days during the fifteen-day period, scrumptious banquets are held. The food is delicious, and the dishes are made to look like lucky objects or chosen because their names are homophones for auspicious events.

Among the dishes that are important for their symbolic appearance are:

dumplings shaped like ancient gold ingots *(youjiao)*

mandarin oranges (because the name sounds like "prosperity"; they are gold; and they have many seeds, representing many children)

melon, pumpkin, lotus, sunflower seeds as wishes for many children

uncut noodles to symbolize long life

Some of the dishes whose names sound lucky are:

fish (the name sounds like "surplus")

a New Year pudding made from glutinous rice (sounds like "prosperous" or "high year")

a vegetarian Buddhist dish with a black, hairlike alga (sounds like "prosperity")

dried bean curd (sounds like "happiness and wealth")

bamboo shoots (sounds like "wishing all will be well")

a hash of oysters and other meats wrapped in fresh lettuce (sounds like "good tidings")

Flowers

Most families decorate their homes with flowers, and each kind has its own meaning. Plum blossom, quince, and kumquat symbolize luck and prosperity. Narcissus bulbs symbolize prosperity and perfume the home beautifully. Chrysanthemums symbolize longevity. Azaleas symbolize good luck.

The Family Altar

Devout Buddhists and Taoists keep altars in their homes. The gods on the altar are usually selected with the guidance of a master or temple priest.

The statue of a god is not simply bought at a store and brought directly home. Rather, it is taken to a temple to be consecrated and "awakened" by a priest. Afterward, the god is invited to come to the home, brought in as one would welcome an important personage.

For those less fortunate, the god or gods can be represented by a picture or even just the god's name brushed in elegant calligraphy.

Like the home, the altar should be cleaned and prepared prior to New Year's Day. Any decorations from the old year are burned before the start of the new year, and new decorations are put up.

Though it varies with the customs of the family, the altar is usually carved rosewood and has an incense burner, two ever-burning candles (electric candles have become normal and are safer), two vases of fresh flowers, cups of tea and sometimes wine, rice, chopsticks, and soup spoons. For the new year, offerings of pomelos and tangerines are common.

Devout families offer meals to the altar before sitting down themselves.

The Lion Dance

In many communities, especially those with ties to southern China, the **lion dance** *(wushi)* is a frequent sight. While there are northern lions and Taiwanese lions, the southern lion is distinct in its elaborate head and multicolored body. The lion dance is performed by two people, and lion dance clubs are nearly always associated with martial arts schools, since the dance requires great athleticism. While gongs and drums keep a martial beat, the lion dancers mimic all the movements and moods of a lion, from sleeping, to playful, to aroused, to hungry. The lion dancers often dance at businesses during this time, and their presence, drumming, loud cymbals, and firecrackers drive off bad luck. The merchant reciprocates with a red envelope of money, which is often donated to charity.

There are many legends surrounding the lion dance. In one story, there were many calamities and a monk prayed for guidance on how to dispel them. The gods answered that a lion would protect the people from evil—except that no one in China had seen a lion. So the monk made a combination of all the mythical animals he knew, and that accounts for the lion's fantastical appearance. Others say that the lion is really a representation of the Nian monster (p. 2). Regardless of its origins, the distinctive beat of the drums and the powerful movements of the lion dance are significant symbols of the new year.

Visiting Friends

While the Lunar New Year is predominantly a family gathering, one also visits friends, bringing gifts and oranges. These are not only sweet to eat, but symbolize your bringing gold into their homes (the friend always gives you an orange to take back with you, symbolizing the mutual flowing of good fortune). ▶

Exercise 1

SPRING BEGINS

This first period of the new year begins around February 4. Although conditions may still be cold, dark, and snowy, spring arrives.

During this time, warmer air may already be felt as the temperature fluctuates. While the nights may still be frigid, some sunny days are the harbingers of warmer weather.

The Seasonal Practices of the Yellow Emperor's *Neijing*

The **Yellow Emperor** (Huangdi, 2696–2598 BCE) was one of the Five Legendary Emperors of China, and authorship of the *Classic of Internal Medicine (Neijing)* is attributed to him. This classic established the earliest and most basic assumptions about Chinese medicine and is still used today in traditional Chinese medicine.

In the second chapter, the Yellow Emperor discusses the basic principle of each season, and how we are to harmonize with it.

The Yellow Emperor on Spring

In the three moons of spring,
all nature issues forth.
Heaven and earth are reborn
and the myriad things invigorated.

Go to sleep early at night, wake up
    early.
Walk vast distances as if crossing a
    courtyard.
You will be revitalized,
your will shall be renewed,
and you will avoid injury, decline, and
    pain.

In the spring season, follow the Way
    of growth.
Act against it and you will injure your
    liver
and summer will bring cold disease.

This exercise is best practiced during the period of 11:00 P.M.–3:00 A.M. (The exercise can be done any time, but this is the time when the natural energy is highest. The times vary for each solar term.)

1. Sit cross-legged and fold the left palm over the other and press them on your lap.

2. Slowly turn your torso and your neck to one side as if you're trying to look behind you. Keeping your legs and palms in the same position, repeat on the other side. Inhale when you turn; exhale gently when you return to the center. Repeat fifteen times on each side.

3. Facing forward, click your teeth together thirty-six times. Roll your tongue between your teeth nine times in each direction. Form saliva in your mouth by pushing

your cheeks in and out. When your mouth is filled with saliva, divide the liquid into three portions.

4. Inhale; then exhale, imagining your breath traveling to the *dantian* (the field to cultivate the elixir of immortality—at a level three fingers-breadths below your navel and at a depth in the center of your body) and then swallow one-third of the saliva, imagining that it travels to the dantian.

5. Repeat two more times until you've swallowed all three portions.

6. Sit comfortably as long as you like.

Through this exercise, ancient Taoists sought to prevent or treat obstructions in the body; rheumatism; and pain in the neck, shoulder, ears, back, elbow, and arm.

1 | The Old Child

Great Supreme Old Lord

The Great Supreme Old Lord (Taishang Laojun) is the deified **Laozi** (p. xxx) and one of the **Three Pure Ones**. Laozi (sixth century BCE) is the author of Taoism's best-known text, the *Daodejing* (p. xxviii).

The Three Pure Ones

The **Three Pure Ones** (Sanqing) are Taoism's highest trinity. The first of the three is the **Jade Emperor** (Yu Huang; p. 13), the present ruler of heaven. Taoists conceive of heaven as an imperial bureaucracy; every god reports to the emperor, and the **Kitchen God** (p. 8) and the **Gods of the Local Land** (p. 40) report human activities to him as well. He is supported by the **Heavenly Lord of the Primal Origin** (p. 12), the former ruler and now advisor, and by the Great Supreme Old Lord, who acts as the emperor's teacher.

Maitreya Buddha

Maitreya, or Budai Luohan, is a bodhisattva (p. 58) who will appear in the future, achieve complete enlightenment, and teach the pure law of Buddhism. He is to be the successor to Sakyamuni Buddha (p. 117).

The Chinese form of Maitreya is often shown as an enormous laughing monk with his chest and big belly bare. His laughter represents a happy future and his girth symbolizes the wish for plenty.

Hold the old and hold the new.
Be the elder and be the child.

The name Laozi means "Old Master." The second word in the name, *zi*, also means "child." There can be a right understanding out of an unusual translation.

On the first day of the new year, we take care to act as positively as we want to act for the rest of the year. We learn from our past experiences, and we optimistically resolve to do our best in the coming year. We are literally *lao* and *zi*, elder and child: we carry the wisdom of the old but look forward with the innocence of youth.

When the ancients placed the birthdays of both Laozi and Maitreya on this day, they looked forward to a young future. Each time we come to the first day of the year, this double sense of being old and young energizes us.

Take this journey through this year. Move through all four seasons, and through the festivals and memories generations have left behind for us. If, as a child, you imagined that the moon "followed you" when you traveled at night, you can keep that same image here, and have the moon as your companion; to follow the lunar calendar is to literally follow the moon.

The same moon has been seen by every generation since the first human being, and it will be seen by every generation to come. We'll take what's useful from the past to guide our spiritual efforts in the present. Let us be the old, embarking on a journey toward the new. If the way seems hard to see at first, we need only remember that new sprouts are under the snow and the moon shines every night, encouraging us to seek enlightenment.

Be the elder and be the child; come together with the seasons, gods, family, and us.

2 | The Cord

- Pray to ancestors and gods
- A married daughter visits her parents
- For Cantonese businesses, a day to "open the year" and hold ceremonies to bring success in the coming year
- Honorary birthday of dogs

Wives, Parents, and In-Laws

A married daughter returns to visit her parents on this day, and her husband accompanies her.

In the past, when a woman married, she became a part of her husband's family and was no longer considered a part of her birth family. A woman's name was not written into the records of either her birth family or her husband's family.

These negative attitudes are fading, but many couples still visit their in-laws on this day or at some other time during the Spring Festival to maintain their extended family ties.

Seasons, gods, family, and us—
We are tethered on the same cord.

Each of us is an individual, but each of us comes from an unbroken line of parents, ancestors, and gods. It is a line that threads through every season. Your umbilical cord may have been physically cut after your birth, but the spiritual connection is never severed.

This is a day of joining with others, a day of acknowledging our family. We add to that cord and its sequence grows longer.

If we acknowledge the seasons, the gods, our ancestors, our parents, our in-laws, our spouses, our children, and our community, then we strengthen our ties and benefit from them. The respect we show to others always returns to us. The love we give to others comes back with greater force.

We had a mother and father. We had a divine ancestor. They all shared the seasons. Our living family sustains us. Our spiritual ancestors sustain us. The earth and the seasons sustain us.

Family knows us in every intimate way possible—and embraces us just the same. Family is there when we are in trouble. Whether we "deserve it" or not, family rescues us. Family is there to celebrate the joys of life with us. Family is there to comfort us when life is dark. Family is the greatest model of loyalty we know.

We are tethered on the same cord, and must care for one another when the red mouth opens.

3 | Dodge Danger

- **Crimson Mouth** or Crimson Dog Day—considered by some an unlucky day to visit family and friends
- Honorary birthday of pigs

The Honorary Birthdays

During the first ten days, there are observations or "birthdays" for everything from chickens to barley. All of the subjects celebrated are central to human life, and it's a good opportunity to express gratitude for them.

When the red mouth opens,
good fortune means we dodge.

All through the New Year's festival, you'll hear people wishing each other good luck. But the wise know that this is wishful thinking. Misfortune is inevitable. Otherwise, what would there be to sweep away at the end of the year?

Following Tao is as easy as being present to receive the good and being skillful enough to dodge the bad. This day is a reminder of misfortune's crimson mouth. When that maw opens, we should get out of the way.

So many people bemoan "bad luck." Bad luck comes to everyone, but misfortune is not an automatic condemnation. It can't be eradicated, but it can be avoided. If you have to face bad luck, the next best thing is to keep calm and focused. The worst mistakes are to compound our problem by missing opportunities, being so rattled that we make more mistakes, or being so distracted that we don't notice another *worse* danger heading our way.

Good fortune and bad fortune alike come to us. It's how we respond that determines whether we accumulate more luck and safety than disaster and danger.

In fact, one might argue that a great deal of civilization arises from the mastery of doing dangerous things safely. We do many risky things each day: light fires, use knives, drive cars, cross streets, work with big equipment. A thousand times a day, we actually hold danger in our hands, but we've learned how to keep ourselves safe and continue our work. It's worth considering how much of our "bad luck" is not some mysterious and malevolent force but avoidable carelessness.

In fact, it is only by risking danger that we ever accomplish anything. The secret is to put safety measures in place and to evade danger whenever the unexpected arises. As a new year begins, this has to be our central resolution.

Good fortune means we dodge—we avoid our downfall when we burn arrogance in humility's flame.

4 | Humility's Fire

The Kitchen God

The Kitchen God (Zao Jun—"Stove Master") protects the family and reports its activities to the Jade Emperor at the end of each year. The Kitchen God's picture, or his name on a plaque, is placed near the stove.

More elaborate portraits include his wife, who records everything that has been said in the home, and two servants, who hold rewards and punishments stored in jars.

On the twelfth moon, twenty-third day, the Kitchen God reports on the good and bad deeds of the family. The family smears his mouth with honey so he will only say good things, and then sends him to heaven by burning his image. The family places a new picture in its home and the god returns to the home on this day, the first moon, fourth day.

The Kitchen God was originally a man named **Zhang Lang**. He was married to a virtuous woman, whom he abandoned during an adulterous affair. Heaven blinded him as punishment. When his lover left him, Zhang's fortunes declined until he was reduced to being a beggar.

One day, he went begging at a house, not knowing that it belonged to his remarried ex-wife. She recognized him, but since he was blind, he did not know her. As she cooked him a meal, he described his folly. When she heard his remorse, she told him to open his eyes, and his vision was restored. However, he was so ashamed to see his wife that he threw himself into the hearth and burned to death.

In pity, the Jade Emperor reunited the couple in the afterlife, deified them, and gave them their kitchen duty.

Burn arrogance in humility's flame.
Go from the lowly to the highest god.

Humility is the greatest virtue, and yet few people are humble. Most people try to assert their will in every situation: the infant pounds toys while screaming, the general orders entire cities leveled, the king wantonly invades other countries. Without exception, comeuppances follow, although some seem not to suffer until the end. Those who are truly lucky suffer mildly from their mistakes and learn early.

Arrogance must be burned in the flames of disappointment and shame. In the parable of Zhang Lang, redemption was possible only when he confessed and his wife forgave him. Nevertheless, he was still overcome with anguish and was unable to live with himself. He was not humble enough to accept his own faults or to accept forgiveness.

As a god, though, Zhang Lang must have understood the truth well, for he chose to dwell in the kitchen by the stove. How apt that must have seemed to him. The fire of the stove is necessary for life. The flame of experience is necessary for humility. The Kitchen God is content to stay in people's homes all the time, not on a high altar, but down on the kitchen floor. It happens to be the central place in the home.

We claim the center by being humble.

Go from the lowly to the highest god, but don't be enslaved by wealth.

5 | Wealth

- People stay home to welcome the **God of Wealth**
- In the north, people eat dumplings (*jiaozi*)
- Some people avoid visiting with family and friends on this day
- Honorary birthday of cattle

The God of Wealth

Families and businesses keep a statue of the God of Wealth (Cai Shen). Some businesses reopen on this day, with offerings, lion dances, and firecrackers.

There are several different gods of wealth. One is shown as a kindly man with a black beard, rich brocade robes, and a scroll or scepter in his hands. Another is **Bigan** (p. 148). A third is **Zhao Gongming**, shown riding a black tiger and holding a golden rod.

Zhao Gongming used magic in battles to support the collapsing Shang dynasty (twelfth century BCE) and hurled pearls that exploded like grenades.

His enemy, **Jiang Ziya**, on the side of the subsequent Zhou dynasty, made a straw effigy of Zhao. After performing twenty days of rituals, he shot the effigy through the eyes and heart with peachwood arrows. Zhao was far away but died instantly.

Later, Jiang Ziya persuaded **Yuanshi Tianzun** (p. 12) to release the souls of the great heroes from the underworld, and Zhao was named to head the heavenly ministry of prosperity.

Don't be enslaved by wealth.
Make those riches serve you.

Unless you have resources, you can't look after your health, you can't eat, you won't have adequate shelter, and you can't do anything to help others who are in need. You need some wealth to get by in this life.

Even spiritual people like monks and wandering renunciates depend on wealth. They are supported by their religious orders or they live on the generosity of laypeople.

However, wealth, like many other things, is best in moderation. Too little wealth is ineffective, and too much wealth weighs you down. If you're comfortable and you can use your wealth for positive actions, then you are rich enough.

The God of Wealth doesn't merely dole out riches. While people make offerings to him in their homes, and businesspeople keep him in their stores, everyone still has to work. Great wealth is earned.

To be wealthy, we have to work hard and we have to be smart. The God of Wealth may accept the offerings on the altar, inhale the incense, and thrill to the firecrackers, but the real offering he requires is hard work.

Make those riches serve you: give to others as you press your palms together and bow.

Altar in the Gods of Wealth Palace, Changchun Guan, Wuhan. From left: Guan Yu (p. 17), Zhao Gongming, and Bigan (p. 148). © Saskia Dab

6 | Prayer

- A day to visit with family and friends (sixth to tenth day)
- Visit temples to pray for good fortune and health (sixth to tenth day)
- Honorary birthday of horses

Taoist Pantheon, Buddhism, and Confucianism

The lunar calendar combines Taoist, Buddhist, and Confucian observances, and a short explanation of the differences will be helpful.

Taoism is the primary indigenous religion of China. Buddhism originated in India but became a part of Chinese culture, and Confucianism is a system of statecraft, etiquette, and ritual.

Taoism has many forms that encompass sorcery, ritual, worship, internal alchemy, and martial arts. Every sect has absorbed some aspects of the others.

Taoism is pantheistic and incorporates hundreds of gods, local deities, and spirits. The highest gods are the **Three Pure Ones** (p. 5).

Buddhism centers around the teaching of **Sakyamuni Buddha** (c. 563–483 BCE; p. 117). His teaching of compassion and enlightenment to transcend suffering merged with native Chinese sensibilities, eventually evolving into a system of worship, monasticism, sutras, service, and meditation.

Buddhist and Taoists maintain temples, but there are also combined Taoist-Buddhist temples.

Confucianism is a doctrine of social organization. Confucius (Kong Fuzi) articulated the Chinese family structure. He advocated a system of **benevolence** (ren), ritual (li), and filial piety (xiao) to unify both the family and the nation. Confucians maintain ancestral halls, and while they're solemn places, they can't be strictly categorized as religious.

Press your palms together and bow.
The gods will instantly appear.

Prayer is simple.

Pressing your palms together is a universal gesture of prayer, benediction, gratitude, and humility. It signals that you are unifying all aspects of yourself and that you are completely present. No one can pick up a weapon or form a fist with palms pressed together. In prayer, there can be no aggression.

Some people doubt prayer. They declare that there are no gods to listen. Prayer works—because that higher part of ourselves is listening—and it works instantly: the very act of prayer is its own truth and its own reward.

We have to free ourselves of childish expectations; we must not pray like children whining to our parents. We must also reject any latent feudalism in our hearts: we still call our gods "lords" and act like serfs begging for consideration. Neither infantile wailing nor medieval supplication is the prayer we need.

Without a doubt, we all have problems. We all have misfortunes. We all face times that try us to our souls. Nevertheless, we cannot go to a temple and order up a solution by bargaining on our knees. In all of history there has *never* been a single person that the gods raised to float above the earth. Every person has had to walk on the ground, experiencing both good and bad.

We say "I need to pull myself together" when we're frazzled. If we look at that statement literally, we can see how helpful it is to put our hands together. Press palm to palm, breathe deeply.

When you pray, there is no brand on you that says "Taoist," "Buddhist," or "Confucianist." Don't worry about what kind of prayer you're making. A sincere prayer is far more important than a crafted or dictated one.

You're you, a whole person. Give yourself some time to be quiet at the end of each day. If you're faced with a big decision, take refuge in silence. Put your hands together. Trust yourself to do the right thing. You'll know instantly.

The gods will instantly appear because we came from One and remain part of One.

7 | Unity

- A day to visit with family and friends (sixth to tenth day)
- Visit temples to pray for good fortune and health (sixth to tenth day)
- Honorary birthday of human beings
- Farmers display their produce
- Eat noodles to symbolize longevity; eat raw fish to symbolize success (the word "fish" is a homophone for "success")

No Place for Death to Enter

In Chapter 50 of the *Daodejing,* Laozi writes of life and death:

> To be born is to go toward death.
> For the followers of life, there are three in ten.
> For the followers of death, there are three in ten.
> For those who let their lives proceed toward the place for death,
> there are also three in ten.
> Why? They use their lives to pursue life's grossness.
> Now hear how the excellent arrange their lives.
> They do not encounter rhinoceroses or tigers on the road.
> They join the army but are not hurt by armor or weapons.
> The rhinoceros has nowhere to thrust its horn.
> The tiger has nowhere to put its claws.
> A weapon has nowhere to show its blade.
> Why? Because there is no place for death.

We came from One and remain part of One,
we live as One, and we return to One.

Each of us is connected to everyone and everything else. All existence came from One, and therefore all existence continues to be a part of the One. We may have a sense of great diversity, but if we look, we can discern ties in every part to every other part—and we can trace all those ties back to one origin. Each scale of a pinecone faces a different direction and has its own place on the cone—but each one joins to a central core.

Habit makes us see ourselves as individual and separate. We usually do not think of ourselves as being part of a greater whole, even if we inwardly want to be. We fear being "alienated," or being a "social outcast," or being "lonely," "not fitting in," "having no place to go," or being "without a home." Instinctively, we are frightened of being separated, but we don't try to understand or take comfort in the unity of all things.

Something had to arise from primordial chaos for this world to appear. The sun, the earth, and the moon—and all that we experience in our human existence—sprang from a single source. We are kindred with all and we remain a part of all.

Therefore, we need not fear death because we cannot be destroyed: we are only returning to the One that was there from the first. Death is mere appearance because One may seemingly be divided, but the whole is always One. One can never die.

We live as One, and we return to One: when drinking water, think of the source.

8 | The Source

- Birthday of the **Heavenly Lord of the Primal Origin**
- A day to visit with family and friends (sixth to tenth day)
- Visit temples to pray for good fortune and health (sixth to tenth day)
- Day to eat **Labazhou** (Soup of the Eighth Day), a porridge of millet, maize, sorghum, glutinous rice, barley, and other ingredients that honors **Sakyamuni Buddha** (p. 117)
- A night designated for family reunion dinners
- Last day of celebration for businesses
- Honorary birthday of rice and grains
- Fasting day

The Heavenly Lord of the Primal Origin

One of the Three Pure Ones, the Heavenly Lord of the Primal Origin (Yuanshi Tianzun) is the child of Pan Gu (p. 338). He set the stars and planets into motion and was the main god until he retired and the Jade Emperor (p. 13) became the celestial ruler.

He represents the origin of all things and the first principle. At each new **kalpa** (every 129,600 years), he imparts the mysterious doctrine of immortality and anyone who learns it will become immortal—even if he or she is still on earth.

According to one sage: "If you would know Yuanshi, you must go beyond the boundaries of heaven and earth because he lives beyond all limits. Ascend and ascend until you reach the sphere of nothingness and of being— the plains of luminous shadows."

When drinking water, think of the source.
When your spirit flies, return to the source.

"When drinking water, think of the source" is an old saying. It is a reminder of a much greater philosophy: there is a universal source, and Taoist spiritual practice seeks that source. When Laozi speaks of returning to the source (p. 34), he speaks of the goal of all Taoist practice.

Knowing the origin means unwinding all of our connections and complex states of mind back to when all was primal, simple, and wordless.

The Heavenly Lord of the Primal Origin is a personification of this idea. People had trouble contemplating the abstract notion of an impersonal and mysterious beginning to all things, although the more sophisticated sages saw the logical necessity of it. So they personified the idea of a source and made it part of the very ruling trinity of heaven. Today, we should try to think of the source in its abstract sense. The Heavenly Lord points beyond himself.

Drinking water and thinking of its source is an example of how the immediate can be connected back to the distant. We need not make up a myth to guide us. When you drink water, think of its source. When you contemplate the cosmos, think of its source.

When you hear the story of the Heavenly Lord of the Primal Origin, you can ask: what if you were the original being? What if you lived beyond the boundaries of heaven and earth, beyond all limits? What if you dwelt in the sphere of nonbeing and being on the plane of light and shadow? The Heavenly Lord points beyond himself.

Remember that the Heavenly Lord also gives out the doctrine of immortality: each human being has the possibility of finding him and learning his treasured secret. The Heavenly Lord points beyond himself.

When your spirit flies, return to the source—whether you lead the world or leave the world.

9 | The Leader Sage

- A day to visit with family and friends (sixth to tenth day)
- Visit temples to pray for good fortune and health (sixth to tenth day)
- Birthday of the **Jade Emperor**
- Honorary birthday of fruits and vegetables

The Heavenly Lord of the Divine Treasure—the Jade Emperor

The Jade Emperor (Yu Huang, Yu Di, Lingbao Tianzun) is one of the **Three Pure Ones** and the emperor of the heavenly government. Here is one story of his origin:

There was once a king named Jing De whose queen, Bao Yue, could not bear a child. Taoist priests held intense ceremonies, and Laozi, riding a dragon and holding a little boy, appeared to her. She asked him to help her conceive, and he blessed her. Soon afterward, Bao Yue became pregnant. She gave birth to a son who grew into a handsome prince.

The prince was compassionate and generous to the poor. Although he reluctantly ascended to the throne when his father died, he felt the pull of spiritual concerns. After some years, he abdicated in favor of his chief minister and became a mountain recluse. He spent the rest of his days meditating, engaging in spiritual practice, curing illnesses, and helping the poor.

After 15,500 kalpas, he became a Golden Immortal. After another one hundred million years of cultivation, he became the Jade Emperor.

Whether you lead the world or leave the world:
See all. Sit still. Breathe deep. Care for the ill.

The Jade Emperor symbolizes the Taoist ideal of leadership. He is kind and compassionate, concerned with the sick and the poor. When put in a position of great responsibility, he performs his duty well, but he is indifferent to power. Devoting himself to spiritual practice, he is content to withdraw into nature. Later, when he is again called upon to lead, he accepts the role, but he also accepts the regular and dispassionate advice of the other two members of the Three Pure Ones, the Heavenly Lord of the Primal Origin and the Great Supreme Old Lord.

The Three Pure Ones symbolize everything one needs to be a Taoist:

Be good and pure, engage in spiritual practice, be disinterested in power, and heal and care for the poor—like the Jade Emperor.

Be deeply learned, be master of an entire archive, have insight into Tao, and be compassionate enough to transmit your insights to others—like the Great Supreme Old Lord.

Return to the source, for you are the source who knows the secrets of never dying and dwelling beyond all limits—like the Heavenly Lord of the Primal Origin.

See all. Sit still. Breathe deep. Care for the ill. Kneel down, open your heart and hands. Give.

10 Offering

- A day to visit with family and friends (sixth to tenth day)
- Visit temples to pray for good fortune and health (sixth to tenth day)
- Invite friends for dinner (tenth to twelfth day)
- Honorary birthday of corn and barley

Record of Rites

The *Record of Rites* describes sacrifice and worship:

> When people make sacrifice and worship, three things are of great importance. In offering, nothing is more important than being austere. In music, nothing is more important than measured song. In dance, nothing is more important than performing *King Wu's Night Before Battle*.... This is how the noble person makes sacrifice, exerting to the limit and giving clear meaning to these important things.... It is Tao of the sages.

Kneel down, open your heart and hands. Give.
Only emptied hands can then receive.

We live in such cynical and self-conscious times that we are embarrassed by simple, unabashed, and honest moments. Saying thank you, telling someone you love them, cradling a child—there are a thousand genuine expressions that others ridicule.

Kneeling down, quieting ourselves, giving of ourselves, and bowing are true, heartfelt actions. We have to free these feelings from the prison of social inhibition.

Consider whether religion may not be the imposition of prescribed rite but actually the openness to show how we really feel. If we are open-hearted, then the act of offering is powerful.

The best offering is made with no thought of return. Paradoxically, when we offer without any ulterior motives, good fortune comes to us ten times over. But an offering made selfishly diminishes us ten times over.

Offer. Use both your hands and open your palms heavenward. Only when your hands have been emptied can they be open to receive.

Only emptied hands can then receive, so bow when asked, "Have you eaten rice yet?"

© Saskia Dab

11 | Have You Eaten Yet?

• Invite friends for dinner (tenth to twelfth day)

Dali

大利

One of the phrases written on New Year's decorations and red envelopes is *dali*, which means "great benefit."

The first character, *da*, is a picture of a man in a big stance with his hands stretched out.

The character *li* combines the character for "grain" on the left and the character for "knife" on the right. This image of harvest is extended to mean "benefit." When we eat and share food with others, we extend the benefits that came from the hard work of planting and harvesting, and from the blessing of nature itself.

Have You Washed Your Bowl?

This Chan Buddhist story is recounted in the *Wumenguan*.

> A monk said to Zhaozhou, "I have just entered this monastery. Please teach me."
>
> Zhaozhou: "Have you eaten your rice porridge?"
>
> The monk: "Yes, I have."
>
> "Then you had better wash your bowl," said Zhaozhou.
>
> With that, the monk gained realization.

Zhaozhou Congshen (778–897) was a Chan Buddhist master noted for his longevity and his challenging methods of teaching. He was a student of Nanquan Puyan (747–834) and studied until that master died. After three years of mourning, he traveled throughout China before settling in a ruined temple in northern China, where he taught monks for the next forty years.

"Have you eaten rice yet?"

"I have—and you?"

That was the way people greeted one another a generation ago. In today's urbane style, they simply say hello.

The old greeting reflected the widespread awareness of hunger. A generation ago, many people still experienced famine, starvation, and poverty. Asking whether someone had eaten reflected a natural concern. If people had not eaten, then it was important to feed them.

On this day to visit others, and especially to have a family reunion dinner, the centrality of eating is important. We share our table, we share our meals. We talk about the past and make plans for the future. Shared dining fortifies us. If you are what you eat, then you are shaped by what you share as you eat. Sharing the same meal reaffirms kinship.

The traditional family table is round. No corners. No sides. No head. No tail. Everything is smooth. The food is in the center, and each family member reaches over the same distance. Someone you love is next to you on each side, and no one is last or at the end. The person farthest away from you is also the person facing you.

This planet is also round. There is no "head" position on a sphere. All parts of the surface are equal. And yet, at the "round table" of our planet, there are still people who go hungry. There is more than enough to go around. If we share the food at our family table with abundance and joy, we should also take the time to see those who are not at our "small" family table, but who are silently sitting hungry at our "large" family table.

Have you sat in your place in the circle today? Have you eaten yet?

"I have—and you?" My gratitude is high as a mountain, flowing like water.

12 | Friendship

- Invite friends for dinner (tenth to twelfth day)

High Mountain, Flowing Water

This story, recounted in the *Annals of Lu Buwei* (completed 239 BCE by a group of scholars), is often used to epitomize friendship.

During the Spring and Autumn period (770–476 BCE), a diplomat named Bo Ya traveled on a mission near present-day Wuhan. When he stopped for the night, he took up his *qin* (a seven-string zither) and played freely, thinking of the sacred mountain Taishan (p. 44). A poor woodcutter named Zhong Ziqi chanced by and commented, "How splendidly you play—lofty and majestic as Taishan." When Bo Ya played more, Zhong Ziqi said, "How splendidly you play—like flowing waters."

Although the two men were of different classes and from different countries, a great friendship began. Each year, when Bo Ya's duties brought him back again, he met Zhong Ziqi and played the qin for him.

One year, Bo Ya returned, but his friend did not meet him. Zhong Ziqi had starved to death.

As a wealthy diplomat, Bo Ya knew that he could have saved the poor woodcutter, but he saw that Zhong Ziqi had refused to exploit their friendship. Despondent, Bo Ya smashed his qin and declared that he would never play again, since no one was left who could truly hear his song.

Idioms

"High mountain, flowing water" is a *chengyu,* meaning "set phrase." Usually four-word phrases, these have meanings beyond their literal ones. Many of them refer to myths, historical events, or allegories. There are some five thousand of them, and by loose definition, as many as twenty thousand. Since they represent wisdom embedded in the popular culture, they appear periodically in this book.

High as a mountain, flowing like water.
Friendship is lofty, and can flood the world.

The story "High Mountain, Flowing Water" has been embellished many times in poetry and song. Whenever someone utters the title phrase, now a common idiom (chengyu), people instantly recall the story behind it.

The tale originates with the *Annals of Lu Buwei.* Alluding to a ruler's need to find worthy people to serve him, the *Annals* state that a good person will not serve a ruler unless offered courtesy, support, rapport, and trust: "A fleet-footed horse will not willingly go a thousand *li* [about five hundred kilometers] if the rider is not skilled."

There are three kinds of friend, according to traditional belief. The first kind is the friend with whom you have a cordial speaking relationship. The second kind is the friend with whom you'll share a meal. The third and rarest kind is a friend whom you trust to give criticism: the deepest exchanges make us better. Whether you're a ruler of a country or an ordinary person, it's important to find someone whom you trust to tell you the truth. It's equally important that each of us be a good enough friend to be truthful with those who give us their trust.

A ruler and a worthy person who don't connect, a musician and a listener who don't find one another, or two potential friends who never meet all lose. Those who are blessed with friendship are as lofty as the mountain and flowing as the water, gaining a precious and rare rapport.

Friendship is lofty, and can flood the world, reaching the child with stick in hand.

13 | Warrior Loyalty

- Celebration of **Guan Yu**, the Warrior God, protector of businesses, god of wealth and success
- Plain rice soup (rice porridge, congee) and vegetables are consumed as compensation for the rich banqueting of the previous days

The Warrior God

Guan Yu (162–219), also called Guangong, lived just before the Three Kingdoms period (220–265). He was an enormously strong warrior, skilled on horseback and ferocious with a halberd, yet he was also a learned scholar who could recite the *Spring and Autumn Annals* and the *I Ching* from memory. His story is featured in the *Romance of the Three Kingdoms.*

The Han dynasty had fractured first into the Six Dynasties and then into three states—Wu, Shu, and Wei. During this period of decay, worsened by famine and natural disasters, local rebellions broke out. The greatest of them was the Yellow Turban Rebellion, led by three Taoists.

Patriotic and righteous, Guan Yu swore a chivalrous oath of brotherhood with two other men, Zhang Fei and Liu Bei, to oppose the rebellion. Together, they fought many battles.

Eventually, Guan Yu was captured and beheaded. Nevertheless, generations after him revered him and made him a god.

Guan Yu, one of the most popular deities, is worshipped by Buddhists and Taoists, soldiers and scholars, policemen and gangsters, shopkeepers and private citizens. For all of them, he is the epitome of righteousness, justice, loyalty, and courage.

Reaching the child with stick in hand:
there stands a warrior, sword in hand.

Many a mother is horrified when her tender baby boy begins to chase others, wrestle, swing sticks, and build forts. Being a warrior is natural.

We are all against war. That doesn't mean that being a warrior is unnecessary. Guan Yu's example is clear: being a warrior is about being both a scholar and a fighter. A warrior upholds righteousness, justice, loyalty, and courage. Those values, not swinging sticks, are always needed.

A warrior stands in the midst of a crisis and risks body and soul to defend and win. A warrior grapples with dangers impossible for an ordinary person and emerges with victory. In order to do this, however, a warrior must first have trained away personal weaknesses: cowardice, fear, reluctance, laziness, ignorance, and temptation. This is why everyone can benefit from warrior training—every person should overcome these vulnerabilities. If we must go to war, let us go to war against our own shortcomings, and if we should strive for victory, let it be the victory of shining character.

Loyalty was Guan Yu's greatest virtue. Loyalty requires commitment and is the ultimate standard for a trustworthy, reliable person to work toward. Loyalty tested and maintained even in the most terrible circumstances is rare but powerful.

The impulse to be a warrior is inherent even in children. It takes a strong, grown, and mature person to conquer childish faults and become the champion of loyalty.

There stands a warrior, sword in hand, who yet knows that winter is death that brings rebirth.

14 | Preparation

- Preparation for the Lantern Festival
- Fasting day

Daughter Wine

Made from glutinous rice and wheat, Shaoxing liquor is famous throughout China for its splendid quality. In the past, when a daughter was born to a family in Shaoxing, her father buried many large ceramic jars of wine. The jars were retrieved and the well-aged wine was served when the daughter married.

The ceramic containers themselves were elaborately decorated with flowery motifs and were gifts in their own right. The wine was called *huadiao jiu* (flowery-carving wine) or simply *nu'er hong* (daughter-red).

This is an example of farsighted preparation.

Winter is death that brings rebirth.
Winter is death that brings each spring.

This is the day that people prepare for the Lantern Festival. While the festivities are important, we shouldn't lose sight of where we are. We are nearing the end of the first of the Twenty-Four Solar Terms. We won't have a celebration tomorrow if we don't get ready today. On a more subtle level, we wouldn't even have the opportunity to enjoy spring if nature hadn't prepared for it all winter.

Any moment is just one point on a circle. We may notice features of that circle, pick out certain days, and assign charming stories to them, but they are only points on a circle. Nature has none of our intellectual or sentimental inclinations. It is pure action with no consciousness. We may embed our philosophies within mythological figures, but nature simply continues to revolve without any regard for the feelings of human beings. It simply is.

Thus, it is we who describe winter as death. Yes, animals hibernate and trees go dormant. Lakes freeze and little grows. But these are all necessary for the rebirth of spring. Spring may be the time when we rejoice that we survived the harsh winter—and yet winter is the inevitable season that prepares the way for spring.

Getting ready for a massive celebration on the next day is easy. We do that with great anticipation and happiness. What is hard is remembering this day the next time we are plunged into despair, illness, and death. It is then that we must remember the deeper meaning of this moment: without the prelude of grim times, we can't have the celebration of happier ones.

Winter is death that brings each spring, just as the night, stars, and full moon bring the next day.

Lantern Festival

The **Lantern Festival** (Shangyuan Jie or Yuanxiao Jie) ends the fifteen-day period of the Spring Festival. Traditionally, children went to the temples on this night carrying paper lanterns. Nowadays, cities in China and abroad hold elaborate festivals with glowing parade-float lanterns shaped like dragons and other large animals. People enjoy outdoor concerts and fireworks. There are thousands of smaller lanterns, too, either carried by people or, as in Taiwan, sent floating up into the sky. Many lanterns have riddles on them, with the solutions being wishes for good luck, family reunion, abundant harvests, prosperity, and love.

In keeping with those wishes, families gather to share a favorite dish—*yuanxiao* (a sweet, glutinous rice dumpling). The Lantern Festival is also a night for lovers. In olden times, young people were chaperoned in the street to glimpse a possible mate.

Here are three legends about the Lantern Festival, all of which feature emperors being deceived.

The Jade Emperor and the Lantern Festival

A heavenly crane once happened to alight on earth, only to be killed by villagers. The Jade Emperor angrily ordered the village burned on the fifteenth day of the first moon.

The Jade Emperor's daughter took pity on the villagers and warned them. The people were frantic; no one could think how to escape the wrath of the Jade Emperor. Then an old man suggested that every family hang red lanterns around its house, light bonfires, and set off firecrackers so that the village would appear to be on fire. The celestial troops were deceived and reported that the village was already ablaze. Mollified, the Jade Emperor stopped all further attacks—and the tradition of lanterns and fireworks on this day was established.

Sweet Rice Dumplings

During the Han dynasty, a young palace maid named **Yuan Xiao** was despondent because she missed her parents. One winter's day, the emperor's chief advisor, Minister East, was walking in the garden when he heard sobbing: Yuan Xiao was about to jump into a well to kill herself.

When he stopped her and asked why she was so troubled, she cried that she had not seen her family since she had been taken into the palace. Minister East promised her that he would help her see her family again.

Leaving the palace, he set up a fortune-telling table in the street. Every person who asked for a prediction received the same answer: *a disastrous fire on the fifteenth day of the first moon would destroy them all.*

Rumor, then panic spread. The frightened people begged Minister East for advice. He said that the God of Fire would send an envoy dressed in red astride a black horse on the thirteenth day of the first moon to bring a condemnation to the city. He said their only chance was to beg for mercy.

Minister East arranged for Yuan Xiao to play her part, and when the people asked for leniency, she held out a decree of execution, purportedly from the God of Fire. She ordered the people to take it to the emperor. As soon as the scroll was read, he turned to Minister East for counsel.

Minister East reasoned aloud that the God of Fire liked to eat sweet dumplings and that he might be dissuaded with offerings and a grand display of fire. He recommended that a palace maid named Yuan Xiao lead every house to cook dumplings, light red lanterns, and set off firecrackers. Furthermore, the palace should be opened and every citizen should carry lanterns into the streets and watch fireworks. This might placate the God of Fire.

The emperor eagerly accepted these recommendations. He declared a grand holiday and ordered lanterns hung throughout the city. On the fifteenth day of the first moon, people walked happily with hand-lanterns, lit firecrackers, and watched fireworks. The palace had the most impressive lanterns and decorations of all, and the citizens came to view them. Yuan Xiao's parents were thus able to enter the palace among the other revelers and reunite with their daughter.

Since Yuan Xiao cooked the best dumplings, the people named the dumplings after her and have enjoyed them ever since. Some people even call this day the **Yuan Xiao Festival** (Yuanxiao Jie).

Little Golden Dragon

Little Golden Dragon was bored during a celestial banquet lasting three days and nights. Curious about the human world, he stole to earth, only to see that people were suffering from a three-year drought. He returned to heaven, filled with sympathy, and determined to help the people.

But the Dragon King, who was in charge of the rain, was drunk at a banquet, and the guards would not permit Little Golden Dragon to see him.

Little Golden Dragon was worried. One day in heaven was a year on earth, and he grew desperate. Thinking hard, the little dragon went to the gods of thunder, lightning, wind, and clouds and persuaded them to put on a harmless show. Then he evaded the guards, roused the Dragon King, and told him that he was late to a storm already in progress! The Dragon King rushed out and poured rain from his magic vase.

The Jade Emperor was furious at the little dragon's deception and ordered him executed by burning on earth. But the grateful people sheltered him, shooting off fireworks to fake the execution. Ever since then, dragon dances are held during the Lantern Festival to pray for good crops and to celebrate Little Golden Dragon. ▶

15 | The Lantern

Official of Heaven–Great God and the Three Festivals Dividing the Year

This is the birthday of the Official of Heaven–Great God (Tianguan Dadi). He is one of the **Three Officials** (Sanguan), the other two being the Official of Earth (p. 231) and the Official of Water (p. 336).

Together, the Three Officials grant good fortune to the deserving, send punishment to the wicked, and help those who are lost. According to legends of their origins, the Three Officials were once vast epochs of time that gradually became gods. Even now, the Three Officials preside over sections of the lunar calendar: first to sixth moon (heaven), seventh to ninth moon (earth), and tenth to twelfth moon (water). Each of them has his birthday and festival day on the fifteenth day of the first moon in his period:

The **Early Year** Festival (Shangyuan Jie), first moon, fifteenth day

The **Midyear** Festival (Zhongyuan Jie), seventh moon, fifteenth day (p. 231)

The **Later Year** Festival (Xiayuan Jie), tenth moon, fifteenth day (p. 336)

Since the Official of Heaven likes entertainment, people prepare all kinds of merriment and events for the sake of winning good fortune. In the temples, the devout chant sutras to the Three Officials to petition for good fortune.

The night, stars, and full moon bring the next day.
The red lantern in your hand lights the Way.

Lighting a fire was one of the first things that primitive people learned to do. Until people found a way to light the darkness, they could do little once the sun went down. After they learned to light fires, people could cook and work at night.

Now entire cities blaze throughout the night, and some places, like airports, are never dark. We have an excess of light. We are able to turn lights on instantly, and all our computers and media devices operate on light. We are surrounded by light—yet we rarely stop and really appreciate it or absorb what it means to us.

So once in a while, perhaps on this night, turn out all the lights, or go out into the wilderness where there is no artificial light, and consider what it would mean to live in a world that is dark after the sun goes down, where there is no other light but the Milky Way and the moon. Take the time to absorb some of the magic that the stars and the moon give to us, the magic that is so often lost in our own blaze of lamps and flashing images. Feel the darkness. Feel the earth moving beneath you. Gaze up at the stars that fired the imagination of your ancestors. In that darkness, in that quiet, you can hear your heart beat and your breath move.

After you let time pass leisurely, light one lantern—that lantern that welcomes the spirits, that is brave in the darkness, that welcomes people home. That light is the beginning of the human. It also represents spirituality: enlightenment.

Then put that lantern out again. Consider what it's like. Look within. Perhaps you can see the glow of your own inner light, and realize that you are the lantern.

The red lantern in your hand lights the Way to show: the demon's gnashing teeth are really ours.

Exercise 2

The air grows warmer, the snows begin to melt, frozen rivers and lakes begin to thaw, and rain is plentiful.

This posture is identical to Exercise 1 except that this one begins with the right hand over the left.

This exercise is best practiced during the period of 1:00–3:00 A.M.

1. Sit cross-legged and fold the right palm over the other and press them on your lap.

2. Slowly turn your torso and your neck to one side as if you're trying to look behind you. Keeping your legs and palms in the same position, repeat on the other side. Inhale when you turn; exhale gently when you return to the center. Repeat fifteen times on each side.

3. Facing forward, click your teeth together thirty-six times. Roll your tongue between your teeth nine times in each direction. Form saliva in your mouth by pushing your cheeks in and out. When your

mouth is filled with saliva, divide the liquid into three portions.

4. Inhale; then exhale, imagining your breath traveling to the dantian and then swallow one-third of the saliva, imagining that it travels to the dantian.

5. Repeat two more times until you've swallowed all three portions.

6. Sit comfortably as long as you like.

Through this exercise, ancient Taoists sought to prevent or treat obstructions in the body; rheumatism; and pain in the neck, shoulder, ears, back, elbow, and arm.

16 | Who's Guarding?

• Celebration of the **Door Gods**

The Door Gods

In traditional homes, people put up fresh prints of the Door Gods (Menshen)—two fierce generals in full armor with long-handled battle-axes and swords. They are placed facing one another on the double doors of Chinese houses and temples. The Door Gods honor **Qin Shubao, Yuchi Jingde,** and **Wei Zheng.**

The story harkens back to Tang Emperor Taizong (599–649), who was ill and could not sleep because he heard demons. Generals Qin and Yuchi stood guard outside his door, and the dreams went away. Even after their ruler recovered, the generals maintained their posts every night. Finally, to spare their constant vigil, the emperor had their images painted and posted in their stead. That seemed to help—until the demons returned. Then Minister Wei Zheng volunteered to guard the single back door, and the emperor recovered for good. Thus, one will often see images of these three guarding the front and rear doors.

> The demon's gnashing teeth are really ours.
> The guardian's mighty hand is also ours.

Every religion guards against demons, reassuring us with specific stories and detailed lists of a particular guardian's abilities, powers, and deeds. There is often far less detail about the demons and monsters.

That's in large part because our real demons are fear and trauma. We are afraid of death, our own anxieties, or the attacks of others, and we are disfigured by the injuries inflicted upon us in the past. Our own private demons, not random ones that might happen upon us, are our greatest threat.

How can guardians stationed at the door protect us from what has already reached the inner chamber? Qin Shubao and Yuchi Jingde never fought any attackers, and yet the emperor recovered. The problem was internal, and the solution was internal. Our struggles are inside us—and so are the remedies.

Everyone needs to feel safe and secure. Pasting up the images of the Door Gods each year is a ritual to seek safety. Through this act, we reinforce the cordon of protection around us. Our homes need to be our sanctuaries. Even if we have been haunted by demons, a happy refuge is the best defense.

The guardian's mighty hand is also ours: lock the gate, and not even a breath can pass.

17 | Gates and Locks

Taoist Internal Alchemy

Some sects of Taoism pursue "immortality" (or at least good health) through exercises. *Qigong* (breath training), which literally means to train the breath, or *qi* (p. 63), is part of that system.

Qigong's basic assumption is that the body is naturally capable of health. Health is defined as equilibrium within oneself and with one's environment. Illness and decline occur when balance is lost. Imbalances occur when blockages prevent the energy from flowing freely through the body, parts of the body weaken or stagnate, or problems in one's environment keep the "universal qi" (outer energy) from nourishing the body.

The key to reopening these blockages, then, is to find the gates in the body and open them again. Qigong and Taijiquan (Tai Chi Chuan), two of the best-known exercise forms, excel at reopening and balancing the body.

By understanding the locks of the body—bending joints, squatting, holding the fingers in various positions—a practitioner can temporarily direct larger amounts of energy to force the gates open again. Conversely, using locks also prevents the energy from damaging certain areas during practice. Therefore, any practice of qigong or Taijiquan can be enhanced by understanding how the forms open the energy channels and how they control the flow of energy by locking and unlocking gates.

Lock the gate, and not even a breath can pass.
Open the gate, and all of heaven flows through.

If we put mighty gates on our cities, palaces, temples, and homes, making them so strong that every anticipated enemy will be kept out, then we also have to have locks on them to keep them shut.

Those locks must have bolts that will not break, but they must also be designed to prevent others from picking them or making keys for them.

We use a gateway as a metaphor for many things: gateway to knowledge, gateway to the future, gateway to new ideas. We use a lock as a metaphor as well: locking away our memories or locking our data. If we look inward, we can use the gate and lock as metaphors for spiritual techniques.

Within the body, there are gates that lead to spiritual understanding. Taoists believe that these gates exist simultaneously on the physical, energetic, mental, and spiritual levels: to act upon them physically is to also act on them on the other levels as well.

Therefore, you can use body positions as locks to direct the flow of energy. Taijiquan, for example, consists of a series of postures, with each movement locking one area of the body while opening another. If you bend the elbows or wrists, it inhibits the energy from going through those joints. Conversely, spreading one's arms or turning the waist opens those areas, encouraging the energy to flow and expand. This process of constantly opening and closing is how Taijiquan circulates energy.

If Tao is the flow of all life and all life is energy, then we direct the flow of Tao by using gates and locks.

Open the gate, and all of heaven flows through, as imaginary lines between stars guide us to new harbors.

18 | Vanishing Point

▸ Celebration of the **Star Gods**

▸ Fasting day

The Three Stars: Happiness, Prosperity, Longevity

There are a number of gods associated with stars, and this day celebrates all of them as a group.

The most prominent of these gods are the **Three Stars**. They are commonly seen in homes, businesses, and temples. The **Star of Happiness** (Fuxing) is dressed as an imperial official holding either a scroll or a child—passing the examinations or having a child symbolizes great happiness. The **Star of Prosperity** (Luxing), also in imperial robes, is a smiling, bearded man who holds the Wish-Fulfilling Scepter *(ruyi)*. The **Star of Longevity** (Shou Xing) is an old, bald man with a large head and white beard, often depicted leaning on a gnarled staff and holding the peach of immortality.

The Star of Happiness is the planet Jupiter. The Star of Prosperity is Mizar in Ursa Major. The Star of Longevity is Canopus, the South Pole Star in Chinese astronomy.

Imaginary lines between stars guide us to new harbors.
Imaginary points on the horizon anchor our path.

Some people say it's fanciful to think that constellations form pictures. They are simply stars in the sky, and it's only the imaginations of primitive humans that see pictorial meaning there. On the other hand, think of the sailors over many centuries who learned to navigate by the stars. Using stars as reference points helps us achieve practical effects. In both cases, the stars that are in the night sky stimulate our imaginations. What we see in nature inspires us and helps us direct our thoughts.

Living in harmony with nature means integrating our decisions with grand movements and cycles. We just have to make the right distinctions and align ourselves with nature in a practical rather than fanciful way.

Setting points in the vastness of infinity to structure our lives is important. The universe is infinite, but it doesn't follow that we should wander without purpose: we have to set a destination for our personal voyages in order to traverse the vastness of this existence.

In perspective drawing, we designate a point on the page and connect all our perspective lines to it. In the classic example of railroad tracks, the two lines are far apart in the front of the picture and converge onto the vanishing point. In the same way, we choose stars as the points toward which all our roads travel. When we are faced with the enormity of Tao, how do we move within it? By connecting to the glimmering points.

Imaginary points on the horizon anchor our path: to know someone's purpose, look where they steer.

19 | Inclusion

- Celebration of the **Hundred Gods**
- Birthday of **Qiu Changchun**

The Hundred Gods

On this day, all the gods in heaven pay their respects to the Jade Emperor, and people contribute with offerings of food, burning incense, and spirit money. In a private home, the head of the household might hang pictures or place statues of **Guanyin** (p. 58), **Guan Yu** (p. 17), the **God of Wealth** (p. 9), the **Three Stars** (p. 24), or any other gods the family reveres. In order to avoid omitting anyone, a bundle of pictures representing all the gods is placed on the altar. Among the representative gods included are gods of heaven and earth, dragon kings, city gods, fire gods, Confucius and his disciples, star gods, gods of the weather, warrior heroes such as **Yue Fei** (p. 53), and the gods of trades, such as **Lu Ban** (p. 193), the patron of carpenters.

Taoists and Genghis Khan

Qiu Changchun (1148–1227), also known as Qiu Chuji, was the founder of the Dragon Gate sect (Longmen).

In 1220, **Genghis Khan** (c. 1162–1227) was interested in learning from other religions, and he invited Buddhist monks, Muslims, and Christians to give discourses to him. Although he was far from China in the Hindu Kush mountains in present-day Afghanistan, he wanted to learn from Qiu and sent an envoy with an invitation in the form of a golden tablet.

Qiu accepted and traveled with eighteen disciples, the khan's emissaries, and an armed escort. It took two years to reach the khan in 1222.

A tent was raised for the discourses and all the lectures were recorded for later study. Eventually, it took Qiu four years to return to China.

Genghis Khan gave some former imperial grounds in Beijing to Qiu Changchun for the building of the **White Cloud Temple** (Baiyun Guan).

To know someone's purpose, look where they steer.
To judge a religion, see what it offers.

Some religions believe in one omnipotent god. Some religions believe in many gods who are omnipotent in sum. The results are the same: the divine is perfect and boundless in its diversity, the human is imperfect and limited.

Taoism is a decentralized religion. There is no single authority, and there are numerous local cults, regional beliefs, and practices originating outside China. It is a religion that exists on a folk level, with the common people keeping the beliefs that best suit them. It is a religion that has grand rituals suited to emperors. It is a religion that has deep and abstruse mysticism and rigorous philosophy. The lunar calendar combines nature worship, Taoism, and Buddhism.

The celebration of the Hundred Gods alone shows that no deity or hero is to be excluded.

How much do we attack others in a pathetic effort to define ourselves? We should accept all others, and we don't need to build ourselves up by belittling others. Our religion should not only reflect inclusiveness, but inspire it. If

Sticks of burning incense at the White Cloud Temple, Beijing. © Saskia Dab

Genghis Khan could ask to learn of spirituality from a Taoist many thousands of miles away, and if he was open-minded enough to consult with all religions, how can we do less?

Qiu Changchun's primary advice to the khan was to give up killing. One day, Genghis Khan was hunting a boar when he was thrown from his horse. Inexplicably, the boar did not charge the fallen khan. Qiu seized on this as a sign, telling the khan that it meant he should give up killing. Genghis Khan responded that hunting was his way of life, but he promised to minimize it.

If, like the khan, we keep an open mind to all religions and all gods, who knows what transformations might be possible?

To judge a religion, see what it offers, for the gateway is found only after a long search.

20 | Gateway to Mystery

Laozi's Gateway

In the *Daodejing*, Laozi refers to *wu*—meaning "no," "not," or "nothing." Chapter 1 states the relationship of nothingness to existence:

> These two issue forth together, but have different names;
> Together, they are called mysterious.
> Mystery upon mystery:
> the gate to all marvels.

At the end of Chapter 40, Laozi is even more explicit, using just four words: "Existence comes from nothingness."

The *Wumenguan* and Zhaozhou's "Wu!"

The first case in the *Wumenguan* is known as "Wu."

A monk asked Chan master **Zhaozhou Congshen** (p. 15), "Does a dog have Buddha-nature?"

Zhaozhou answered, "Wu!"

On face value, this answer says, "No!" But the masters teach that this would be an erroneous interpretation. Contemplating what "wu" means here is often the entrance to a beginner's Chan.

The gateway is found only after a long search,
and the long search is a spiral going inward.

With so much multiplicity—a pantheon of gods, the orbit of the earth around the sun, the orbit of the moon around the earth, the spinning of the earth, day and night, minute after minute—how do we discern the Truth? Maybe we find small and relative truths, but is it important to find the one, big, ultimate Truth? Physicists, for example, are seeking a unified theory. The search for a single truth is a powerfully intriguing journey.

Even Taoists want to know the first cause, the first principle, the first origin. For all the mythology surrounding him, that is exactly what the Heavenly Lord of the Primal Origin (p. 12) represents: that there is a single fundamental truth that gave birth to all the universe—and that this source is benevolent.

Taoism teaches that there is both a relative truth and an absolute truth. That is why Laozi says, "These two issue forth together, but have different names." The relative truth can be reached by science, deduction, reasoning, discussion, and observation. The absolute truth is reached by mystical perception.

Chief among that which we try to perceive is the gateway to all mysteries.

And the long search is a spiral going inward, to where breath flows through nine openings without cease.

21 | Exchange

Breathing and Meditation

Taoism, Buddhism, and the Yogic traditions all incorporate breathing methods as a foundational spiritual practice. Taoism, qigong (p. 23), and fundamental meditations such as the **Microcosmic Orbit** (p. 68) feature "guided breathing." Buddhist meditation techniques extend qigong with chanting and sutra recitation. The Yogic traditions have **pranayama, mantra,** and other advanced breathing techniques.

Here is an example of a nearly universal breathing method:

Sit calmly.

Inhale deeply through your nose, imagining that the breath travels deeply into the depths of your abdomen.

Exhale gently and steadily through slightly parted lips until you've expelled all your breath.

Repeat until you've completed a cycle of ten.

Then start over for as many cycles as you like.

Chan is Zen is Meditation

The word **Zen** has entered our culture as a catchall term for the mystical and the spiritual, yet how many people really know what it means?

Zen is the Japanese pronunciation of the Chinese word *chan*. **Chan Buddhism** originated in China around the sixth century and spread from there to Vietnam, Korea, and Japan. Today, it's spread all over the world.

At base, the word "chan" simply means "meditation." This now sophisticated and deep spiritual tradition is simply—and most profoundly—meditation.

Breath flows through nine openings without cease.
In; out. We are the world; the world is us.

We breathe in, and we breathe out. We drink water, and we pass water. The microbes in our bodies, so essential for life, were not with us when we were born, and yet they are an integral part of us now. We hear sounds, and we speak. When we walk in the fields, we leave footprints—but the dust also clings to us.

We are not isolated and independent entities in this world. We are a part of it. This world makes us who we are just as much as our genetics might. Food, air, water, sunlight, night, the weather, our families, and our communities—all these are absorbed into us, and all of these receive small parts of ourselves in turn.

We learned about world explorers when we were schoolchildren. That gave us the idea that people were the initiators and that there was an endless but passive expanse for us to travel. The very name "wilderness" implied that there was only dumb nature, waiting for us to traverse it and build upon it. Later, conquerors of continents and corporate executives alike acted as if the world was a passive background waiting to receive the initiatives of strong people.

The more subtle truth is that the world changes us as much as we change the world. There is no set and static body or mind tied to our name. We are changing constantly in ways both great and tiny, in ways we register and in ways we have not learned to track. But by being aware of our exchange with the outside world, we learn more of our true natures.

In; out. We are the world; the world is us. Therefore, the first order of practice is to become pure.

22 | Purification

Breathing Exercises

The **Taoist Canon** (Daozang) gathers some 1,400 texts into one collection and forms the basis of Taoist scripture. The *Daodejing* and *Zhuangzi* are included. Many of the books impart qigong and health practices. Central to them all is the swallowing seen in the exercises to the Twenty-Four Solar Terms.

The *Classic of the Yellow Court* (*Huangtingjing*) was written by Lady **Wei Huacun** (252–334), the first leader of the **Supreme Clarity** sect (Shangqing). Her book leads the reader in a revelatory meditation, as if we are journeying through the human body as a landscape or paradise. We receive explicit descriptions of gods we meet along the way. In this sample of Wei Huacun's observations about breath and purity, she imagines the end of the journey to the "person in the Yellow Court" located in the brain:

> The person in the Yellow Court is dressed in vermilion. Shut the gates, secure the lock, and close the doors.
>
> Breathe to the dantian. Let the clean and clear Jade Pond water the Divine Root. Whoever nourishes this carefully will enjoy a long life.
>
> Renounce lusts and desires and guard your essence.
>
> Bathe and groom yourself and take care not to be sullied.
>
> When you are quiet and calm and have nonaction (p. 215) the spirits stop and dwell, and the energy travels to tend each pass. Once the seven openings are clear, one will not age.
>
> When inhalation and exhalation become nonexistent, then form manifests. Guard it day and night and your spirit will be bright . . .

The first order of practice is to become pure:
simply start by controlling what goes in and out.

If we are sum of minute-by-minute exchanges, it follows that both good and bad go in and out. Disease, for example, often comes from outside of ourselves. It enters our bodies, we get sick, and we can become contagious. As a consequence, disease travels around the world faster than we can eradicate it. Various kinds of flu arise each year, and more serious diseases like AIDS spread by way of our constant process of exchange.

Just as basic hygiene helps us control or even prevent disease, the way to establish basic spirituality is by controlling exchange. Learning meditation begins by observing one's breath. Qigong, the art of breath training, not only uses breathing, but emphasizes the importance of breathing in clean air. By the same thought, we can enhance spiritual progress by eliminating distractions and stress and by emphasizing good activities such as reading inspiring texts.

It's easy to look at great masters and sigh over their accomplishments. While they have reached high levels of success, they all had to start from nothing. Perhaps they had talent, or the chance to study with a great teacher, but one thing is certain: they would not have attained their great success without long examination of the process of exchange and the striving for purification.

At this time of the year, the weather is unstable, and great cold can alternate with sudden warmth. There might be snow or ice on the ground, there might be harsh winds. The entire world is purifying itself, cleansing away the dead and dirty and moving toward balance. Shouldn't we do the same?

Simply start by controlling what goes in and out: one raindrop, a hundred ripples.

23 | A Drop Starts a Cycle

› Fasting day

"Clear Evening after Rain"

The sun sinks toward the horizon,
the light clouds blow away.
A rainbow shines on the river,
the last raindrops spatter the rock.
Cranes and herons soar in the sky,
fat bears feed along the banks.
I wait here for the west wind
and enjoy the crescent moon
shining through the misty bamboo.

Many consider the Tang dynasty poets the greatest in Chinese history. Among those exalted poets, **Du Fu** (712–770), the author of this poem, is one of the most beloved.

As a young man, he attempted to follow the tradition of becoming a civil servant, but failed the examinations twice. The An Lushan Rebellion, a fifteen-year period of war that began in 755, devastated the country and severely traumatized him personally. An estimated sixty percent of the population—some 36 million people—died. Much of Du Fu's poetry deals with the injustice and suffering he observed.

As a poet, he was not immediately accepted by literary critics, who pronounced his innovations too daring and bizarre. Over the centuries, however, his writing influenced Chinese and Japanese poetry, has been extensively translated, and has influenced poets in many other countries. Nearly 1,500 of his poems have been preserved.

One raindrop, a hundred ripples.
One raindrop, a hundred seeds sprout.

This is the time of Rain Water. Without rain, the earth is dusty. Grass, animals, and people die.

When rain falls, green blades spring up from the dark earth. Plenty is everywhere. The bare branches of the peony that looked withered and lifeless all winter suddenly put forth red buds like hands unfolding after prayer. Sprouts are all around us despite the snow and rain. We may curse some plants as "weeds," but nature has no labels—only life in abundance.

The rain brings life. Just see where the rain fell, perhaps just beyond a roofline, and you'll see thicker sprouts. Just a drop starts an entire cycle of life—sprouting, growing, flowering, and putting out seed before dying. The plant may be picked for eating or used as an herb. An animal might eat it. Perhaps a spider will attach a web to it. Maybe the plant's roots will crowd out another plant. No matter what, the plant born of cycles grows more cycles.

If you want to know the future, you need not do anything more complicated than watching the cyclical nature of things. If you want to know the cyclical nature of things, just look at a single drop of rain.

One raindrop, a hundred seeds sprout; see that and question. Test. Use every sense you have.

24 | Verify

› Fasting day

Buddha on Verification

The *Kalama Sutra (Qielanjing)* recounts Buddha's (p. 117) teaching to the Kalama people that each person must verify what he or she learns before practicing it:

Do not go by revelation.
Do not go by tradition.
Do not go by hearsay.
Do not go by the authority of sacred texts.
Do not go by the grounds of pure logic.
Do not go by a view that seems rational.
Do not go by reflecting on mere appearances.
Do not go along with a considered view just because you agree with it.
Do not go along on the grounds that the person is competent.
Do not go along simply because "the recluse is our teacher."
...Kalamas, when you know for yourselves that something is wholesome, that something is not blameworthy, that something is praised by the wise, then undertake and observe. If these things lead to benefit and happiness, then undertake them and abide in them.

Question. Test. Use every sense you have, and yet still believe that dawn will come.

We must be able to look critically at any religious belief we hold and, if necessary, modify it. There is no religion that is practiced today the way it was practiced five hundred or a thousand years ago. Every spiritual tradition evolves.

People get confused on this point. In the effort to ensure that their beliefs are valid and true, they try to make sure these are as close to what their founders taught as possible. Taoism is no different. More often than not, the answer to a student's question is, "This is what our ancestors taught." The implication to such originalism is that there should be no questioning.

However, we *must* question. We must not believe blindly: that is stupidity and not devotion. Unless we can prove every belief against our own experience, there is no reason to keep it.

Admittedly, a belief may take years to confirm fully, but there should still be an initial and instant benefit, however small, when we first adopt it. Whether it's an exercise, a meditation, or a philosophy, what we learn has to make immediate sense. Anything that seems useless, or superstitious, should be viewed skeptically.

This process of verification is a prelude to building a strong sense of spirituality. As the *Kalama Sutra* indicates, we want to find what leads to benefit and happiness. Once we do that, we can undertake these actions and abide in them.

And yet still believe that dawn will come, for the spirit is wrapped in reason.

25 | Reason and Spirit

Zhuangzi

After Laozi, **Zhuangzi** (c. 369–286 BCE) is considered one of Taoism's great writers. Many of the stories in the book named after him are marked by wit, skepticism, logical argument, humor—and unique insight.

Zhuangzi and Master Hui strolled across a bridge that spanned the Hao River. "The fish are out and swimming," observed Zhuangzi. "This is the joy of fish."

"You are not a fish," chided Master Hui. "How do you know the joy of fish?"

"You are not me," Zhuangzi answered. "So how would you know that I don't know the joy of fish?"

"I'm not you," said Master Hui. "So I don't know what you do. But you're not a fish, so it's irrefutable that you do not know the joy of fish."

"Let us go back to the root of the question," said Zhuangzi. "When you first asked, 'How do you know the joy of fish?' you asked because you already knew that I knew. I knew it by strolling over the Hao."

The spirit is wrapped in reason,
and reason is wrapped in spirit.

As human beings, we use both reason and spirit. These two are sometimes pitted against one another in discussions, as if one is better than the other.

Falling into the trap of having to choose between the two is dangerous. If we ignore either one, we deny part of our inner natures and part of what we need to live successfully. Although some rationalists declare the spiritual to be superstition and a psychological crutch, and though some spiritualists declare the rational to be stiff and limited, we need both.

Reason and spirit really cover two different territories in our lives. When we are in the realm where reason holds sway, it would be absurd to turn to mystical means. Likewise, once we enter into the realm of mysticism, reason is of limited use. Far better to be rigorously logical and rational when the situation calls for it and to be mystical when that is called for. The versatility of such a personality will always be advantageous.

And reason is wrapped in spirit—even if the faithful still have doubt.

26 | The Edge of Doubt

Confucius and Doubt

Yan Hui (521–490 BCE) was the first of Confucius's seventy-two primary disciples. He has been described as coming the closest to being like his master in learning and personality. When he died at the age of thirty-two, Confucius was so bereft that he cried out, "Heaven is destroying me! Heaven is destroying me!"

However, Confucius makes this rare complaint about his favorite student, as recorded in the *Analects*: "Hui was not any help to me. He accepted everything I said." Confucius wanted devoted students, but he did not want unquestioning ones.

The faithful still have doubt.
The doubtful still have faith.

When we inquire deeply, we will inevitably come to borders. There is the border between certainty and uncertainty. There is the border between belief and doubt. There is the border between true and false—and perhaps some of what is called false is merely not yet proven. There is also the border between our every faculty and what remains mystery.

Human knowledge is infinite. No one person can master all that is known. Yet all that we know is powerless to explain so much. Birth and death, two borders through which we must each pass, cannot be explained by any of our knowledge. Yes, we can explain that the borders are there. We can describe their biology and chemistry, but that is mere testament to what is left behind. We can wrap these events with our best rituals, but to explain what makes someone live or die is still not something we can precisely explain or understand.

There are many other spiritual questions that similarly cannot be answered by our intellects. Religion crafts provisional or tentative answers. All of them require leaps of faith. None of them go beyond a charming story. So if you're intelligent and you're a searcher, you inevitably come to these borders. Perhaps you even dwell along those edges. Having doubt is not a sign of being faithless. It's a sign that you are confronting the important and most difficult questions in life.

The doubtful still have faith—that is why you are the perceiver and the perceived.

27 | Two Ways of Learning

Two Ways of Learning

There are two ways of learning.

The first is summarized in the Confucian classic, *The Great Learning (Da Xue)*:

> Those who want to rectify their hearts first integrate their thoughts. Those who want to integrate their thoughts first perfect their knowledge. The perfection of knowledge comes from investigating things. Once things are investigated, one attains perfect knowledge.

However, there is a second mode that is just as important. Zhuangzi makes this explicit:

> Who can climb the sky, wander the mists, whirl into the limitless, living by forgetting others beyond endings or terms?

In another passage, he says:

> There is nothing that one does not forget, nothing that one does not have. Serene and limitless, all good things come to one.

You are the perceiver and the perceived,
and the knower of the unknowable.

We love to examine things, play with them, try to figure out how they work. Our cities stand because of the arts and sciences that sprang from simple examination, experimentation, and the compounding of knowledge. Engineering, electricity, planning, laws—all the knowledge that made our society originated with the examination of our world and ourselves.

There is something else, though. There is a different kind of perception that is inward, not outward. It is introspection, it is reasoning, yes, but eventually, this inward attention gives way to a meditation that is all-absorbing. It is a state where the perceiver and the perceived are one.

You know what this absorption is, don't you? You knew it as a child. You still know it now, on the occasions where you are so involved in something that you don't even hear someone call you by name. This is not the esoteric and mysterious practice of some bearded sage on a distant mountaintop. This is a natural ability you have—as does everyone.

Our society doesn't name it and cannot sell it, so it is not known by any common name. But you know it, don't you?

And the knower of the unknowable will tell you: if you're uncertain, return to the Way.

28 | The Goal of Returning

‣ Fasting day

Returning

反 The word for "return," *fan,* shows a cliff on the left with a hand below it. The word has three meanings: "reversal," "opposition," and "turn back." This word is used with all these meanings throughout philosophical writings.

In Chapter 40 of the *Daodejing,* Laozi says: "Reversal *(fan)* is the movement of the Way." This is a reference to polarity—the opposition of yin and yang animates all movement.

Zhuangzi observes in Chapter 17: "East and west oppose *(fan)* one another yet cannot do without one another."

The *I Ching,* Hexagram 24, uses returning *(fan)* in this sense: "Returning is its Tao. In seven days, returning comes."

One of the most explicit reminders of returning to one's own life path is in the *I Ching,* Hexagram 24, line 1: "Return to your own way. How can this be wrong?"

Mencius (p. 63) said:

If you try to love others and they don't respond, return to benevolence. If you try to rule others and they resist, return to wisdom. If you try to honor others and they don't accept, return to respect.

When actions fail, turn inward for the reason. Correct yourself and all under heaven will return to you. The *Classic of Poetry* says: "Forever strive to accord with heaven's will and you will find much happiness."

If you're uncertain, return to the Way.
If you're on the Way, return to the Source.

No matter how far we wander, no matter how much the storms of our lives blow us off course, no matter how confusing our daily stresses, no matter what kinds of injuries are inflicted on us, there is always one action that Taoists would have us remember: return to the Way.

We are born in the circle of a womb. We enter this world through a round birth canal. We are nursed in the circle of our mother's arms. We are protected by our father's embrace. Every year, we complete our own special circle and mark it as our birthday. Every year, the earth orbits the sun, and we mark that by our calendar. Every month, the moon orbits the earth, while every day, the earth makes a full revolution.

The direction of Tao is a circle. The cycles of the weather move in circles. The shapes of flowers, cells, and atoms are circles. Our own personal trajectory is a circle too. There is a path that we each are on. If we lose sight of what that is, if we fly away and become lost, or if we are pushed off by circumstance, then we return to our Way to regain ourselves.

Each night, as dusk falls and the moon rises, we see swallows returning to their nests. If we forget where we should go, nature provides us with so many examples each day.

If you're on the Way, return to the Source and study the gods, strengthen your values.

29 | Values

Taoist Gods

Every god has a role. Every god represents some quality that is admired or seen as a necessary part of human experience. No god is without attributes. Each god is an affirmation of our ideals and what we find holy.

The pantheon of Taoist gods takes the enormous diversity of existence and personalizes what we wish to embody ourselves.

With a little thought, we could look beyond the gods themselves to their abstract qualities and discover the values we most admire—and we can rely on those values precisely when the future becomes uncertain.

A home altar. © Ying Fry

Study the gods, strengthen your values.
Fall back on values to face the unknown.

There are many gods. What matters is to absorb the values that the gods embody. If we simply list commandments and precepts, they are difficult to recall, much less adopt. We more readily absorb images, symbols, and stories.

Why do we need values? We need them because we are often faced with the unknown. A variety of decisions will be possible, and no one decision will seem better than the next. There is no science, there are no statistics, there is no system of prediction that will help us make unthinking decisions.

We rely on our values because they help us make more successful choices. Having learned lessons by studying the gods, we are better equipped to handle decisions that must be made in the face of a vague future.

Following the gods is akin to play acting, or role playing. The Chinese opera tradition of Guan Yu (p. 17) sets an example for us. It's said that an actor who plays Guan Yu has such a solemn responsibility that once he puts on his makeup, he can no longer speak to anyone until his role is over and he has taken his makeup off. Once he's in character, he makes an offering at an altar so the spirit of the god will enter into him. Then he plays his role. Needless to say, the actor must be good at singing, drama, and martial arts; he has to be a deserving vessel for the god to inhabit.

Isn't it likely that acting the part of Guan Yu changes a person? The body language, the ideals, the way he responds to trouble—all these become values that the actor absorbs. In the same way, when we study and cherish the gods, we become their willing vessels, so that their values become ours. From the sterling masculinity of Guan Yu to the merciful compassion of Guanyin, we can embrace many values that will serve us well for years.

If we pray to a god, we're not really asking for someone to come over and fix things for us. Rather, we're concentrating on what that god represents, and with our minds thus focused, we can better make the decisions that can only be sustained by belief in our values.

Fall back on values to face the unknown; that is the only way that the swimmer rises.

30 | Riding the Tide

Change

> When the sun rises, the moon sets.
> When the moon sets, the sun rises.

This comes from the *I Ching* and is one of the most succinct statements on the cycles of life.

> The swimmer rises
> when ebb turns to flow.

When one month ends, the next one begins the very next day. There is no gap, no effort needed. The next month follows naturally.

In the same way, we experience many different kinds of endings in our lives—but like the months, they all lead immediately to the next stage. Sometimes we have problems because we don't *like* what is coming next, or we *fear* what is coming next, but this doesn't alter the momentum of the cycles: every ebb is followed instantly by a flow. If we aren't taking advantage of the tide going out, we won't benefit when the tide comes in.

You can be powerful simply by identifying the next crest and riding it. So much of success in life is "being in the right place at the right time." If your personal goals coincide with the tide of the times, you will be highly successful. But if your aims go against the tide, you will go nowhere.

This is the time when the first month continues into the second month. Contemplating the power of this transition yields advantages to last a lifetime.

> *When ebb turns to flow, it reveals the power that makes all things begin and end with the sun.*

2

The Apricot Moon

Moonlit Night

Deep in the night, moonlight half-floods my house
The North Star rises above the railing, the South Star
   falls.
Tonight I feel the warm spring air keenly:
new insect song through the green window screen.
—Liu Fangping (eighth century)

The two solar terms within this moon:

INSECTS AWAKEN

SPRING EQUINOX

Exercise 3

INSECTS AWAKEN

Insects and animals awaken from hibernation. Thunderstorms occur. Signs of spring are everywhere. As insects increase in activity, so too does the pace of the countryside grow quicker.

This exercise is best practiced during the period of 1:00–5:00 A.M.

1. Sitting cross-legged, close the fists tightly, with the thumb inside the fingers.

2. Turn the head from side to side, moving the elbows up and down like the wings of a bird each time for thirty repetitions.

3. Facing forward with your hands resting on your lap, click your teeth together thirty-six times. Roll your tongue between your teeth nine times in each direction. Form saliva in your mouth by pushing your cheeks in and out. When your mouth is filled with saliva, divide the liquid into three portions.

4. Inhale; then exhale, imagining your breath traveling to the dantian and then swallow one-third of the saliva, imagining that it travels to the dantian.

5. Repeat two more times until you've swallowed all three portions.

6. Sit comfortably as long as you like.

Through this exercise, ancient Taoists sought to prevent or treat toxins and relieve back pain; obstructions in the back, lungs, and stomach; dry mouth; yellow eyes; swelling; loss of sense of smell; and darkening of vision.

31 | The Sun

- Festival of the **Sun God**
- Fasting day

The Sun God

The **Sun God** (Taiyang Xingjun) visits the Jade Emperor on this day to discuss plans for the coming year. The Sun God is honored as the bringer of warm weather, and because the sun shines on good and bad alike, it is the symbol of impartial benevolence.

The Sun God's actual birthday is on the nineteenth day of the third moon (p. 94), and he is also honored with a third festival on the nineteenth day of the eleventh moon (p. 375).

All things begin and end with the sun:
the sun makes us the sun of our lives.

Even before people understood that our earth revolves around the sun, they understood that the sun was central to our existence. Without the sun, we would have no warmth, no heat, no day, no light, no growth. Life would be impossible, and our planet would be a dark, icy lump, untethered and doomed.

Our calendar is a record of the sun. Even the moon, which defines the phases of the calendar, would not have light and would not have a planet around which to revolve. Taoists understood that there are many things worth our reverence, but the sun held so much reverence that it was given festival days in three different periods of the year. This shows the enormous importance that the ancient people placed on it.

Besides being the maker of life, the sun also symbolizes understanding. So much of our knowledge depends on examination "in the light of day." We call understanding enlightenment, and since the sun is our primary source of light, we associate it with seeing the truth.

With understanding, we can see that each of us is the center of his or her life, just as the sun is the center of our solar system. We must accept that our worlds revolve around us, not in an egotistical sense, but as an acknowledgment of responsibility. The sun exerts the gravity that holds the earth in the safety of its orbit.

If we are truly enlightened, if we have the light of the sun in our hearts, then we also know that we hold innumerable worlds and lives by the sheer force of our presence.

The sun makes us the sun of our lives in the same way that you are the child of the land where you were born.

32 | The Local Land

- The Spring Dragon Festival
- Birthday of God of the Local Land

Spring Dragon Festival

The Spring Dragon Festival (Chunlong Jie), or the Second Moon, Second Day (Eryue Er), calls the **rain dragon** to lift his head and send rain. In olden times, families in northern China drew water before dawn and returned to offer sacrifice in a ceremony called "attracting the dragon in the fields." Then they ate noodles, symbolizing "lifting the dragon's head," and shared fry cakes, which meant "eating the dragon's gall bladder" (symbolizing courage). Popped corn represented "golden beans" to attract the dragon, encourage rain, and bring plentiful crops.

The God of the Local Land

Every place has its own God of the Local Land (Tudi Gong), and there are thousands of altars by roads and canal banks, and on the floors of homes and businesses. Along with the Kitchen God, he dwells with us on earth. The god is depicted as a kindly old man with a white beard, and his wife, the **Goddess of the Local Land** (Tudi Po), often appears next to him.

The God of the Local Land aids and protects the residents and helps travelers in need. If there are disasters or other significant events, he reports them to the Jade Emperor.

The God of the Local Land has an unusual story. The Song Emperor Taizu (1368–1399) once arrived at an inn to find all the tables occupied. Seeing the image of the God of the Local Land on an altar table, he ordered it moved to the floor, saying to the god, "Give me your place." After the emperor departed, the innkeeper was about to restore the God of the Local Land to his rightful place, but the god appeared in a dream and said, "I dare not defy the emperor." From that day on, the God of the Local Land preferred to remain on the floor with no stand or table.

You are the child of the land where you were born.
You belong to the land where you choose to live.

Tudi specifically means the local or native land. Taoists believe that there are gods of the land in every local area, in every district, in every village. This goes along with worship of nature spirits, because there are also gods of trees, rocks, streams, flowers, plants, and every other part of nature. Nature is alive; nature has spirits worth reverence; nature has a consciousness that is responsive, beneficial, and active.

Every person is the child of his or her tudi. It's your home territory, the place you love, the place that stays connected to you, the place that nourishes you like no other land.

We all understand that inside. Many times, we'll ask a new acquaintance where he or she was born because it reveals something unique and important. We talk about going back to our roots. The land exerts a powerful pull on us. It is our own personal gravity—our special home.

We could not exist without the land. All our food and water comes from the land. The air we breathe is renewed by the breath of plants. We belong to the land and the land belongs to us, and we must never forget to honor that.

If we take care of the land, the land will take care of us.

You belong to the land where you choose to live, just as words last as if written on the body.

33 | Words in the Sun

▸ Birthday of the **King of Literary Glory**

Literary Glory

The King of Literary Glory (Wenchang Wang), the God of Literature, appears as a bearded scholar riding a white horse. Two grooms whose names imply discretion stand behind him—**Deaf Heaven** (Tianlong) and **Mute Earth** (Diya).

A demon balanced on one foot atop a carp (a homophone for success), **Kui Star** (Kui Xing), stands in front of the king as his vanguard and as the one who bestows literary degrees. His body and limbs form the word *kui,* as shown on the right, and he's standing on the calligraphic *ao,* the name of a mythological sea turtle. His left foot supports the word "ladle" *(dou)*—a reference to dispensing degrees to the Big Dipper; Kui is believed to be the four stars of the body of the Big Dipper.

There is a fourth attendant as well: **Red Robes** (Zhu Yi), who helps those who have a *poor* chance of passing the examinations.

All the attendants can be depicted holding various symbols of the cultured life: scrolls, books, and three-legged bronze vessels from the Zhou dynasty *(ding).*

Wenchang

文昌 *Wen,* the word for "literature," also means "culture." The ideograph was derived from a picture of a tattooed chest. The second word, *chang,* or "glory," also means "to prosper" or "flourish." The character combines the sign for "sun" above the sign for "word."

Words last as if written on the body.
True words must be pure as brightest sunlight.

By contemplating the name Wenchang, we can think of how important literature is. Words should be as meaningful and lasting as something we would choose to tattoo on ourselves. Words should be true enough that they can be uttered openly in the light of the sun.

Being literate is a basic and necessary skill in this world. Unless you can read, write, and express yourself, you won't get far. Worse, you can easily fall victim to those who manipulate language, the news, contracts, and laws.

The most wonderful aspect of being literate is the ability to read the words of the greatest thinkers yourself. We approach the author as peer, giving the words all the consideration we can—we read

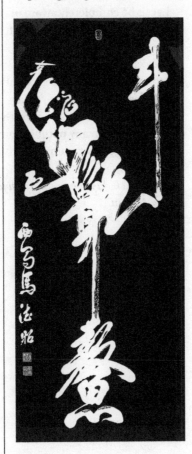

them by the light of our own sun. No one needs to filter the truth for us. No one needs to interpret for us. No one can bar us from the instant and searing understanding that comes from the direct impact of great words.

If we are literate, then we can also express ourselves and speak words charged with the power of our own souls. We give testament to our existence, and we convey our truth to others. When we do that, then we truly are expressing literary glory as bright as the sun.

True words must be pure as brightest sunlight; only then can you enjoy each day without rush to grow old.

34 | The Pattern

Pattern Leads to Principle

理 *Li*, the word for "pattern," originally indicated veins and grain in jade. It also means "principle" in the most profound philosophical sense.

When people speak of reason and principle, they combine the word Tao (*dao*) with li: *daoli*.

In the "Great Appendix" to the *I Ching* we find these words:

Look up to contemplate the patterns of heaven. Bend down to examine the principles of earth....

and ...

Knowing that change is easy and simple, one can obtain the principles of all under heaven.

Enjoy each day, without rush to grow old—
make each day the foundation for the next.

There is a pattern to the seasons. There is a pattern to the year. One day passes after the next in perfect and unvarying sequence.

Our lives move in the unvarying sequence of the days and within the larger cycles of the calendar such as the four seasons. It is by such cyclical alternations that our lives ratchet in even measure.

Given that process, we need not rush to grow older. It's impossible: one day is the same length as the preceding one, and to wish for anything other than that is to divorce ourselves from today. It's just as foolish to wish that we were younger: who we are today is the result of all the days that have gone before. Not only is it unrealistic to unwind our days, but to even think of that invalidates and dishonors who we are.

Let us be completely aware of who and what we are today. Let us embrace it, make the best of it, celebrate it, and see how this day will lead to tomorrow.

We celebrate birthdays every year, but we should look beyond the counting of years to the counting of days. At the age of eighteen, you've been alive 6,570 days. Before the age of twenty-eight, you have exceeded 10,000 days. By fifty, you have reached 18,250 days. Standing on any of those sums is cause for gladness and cause for confidence: your foundation is deep.

Make each day the foundation for the next, and always avoid the greatest sin.

35 | No Separation

Pushing Hands

Taijiquan, a Taoist martial art, takes an unusual approach to fighting. Instead of attacking from a distance with overwhelming force, the Taiji fighter establishes a relationship by touching the opponent lightly throughout the match. The Taiji fighter does not separate from the adversary.

With that contact, the fighter can sense the opponent's movements and intentions and thereby "arrive before the opponent." The fighter easily deflects or dodges and can take advantage of any opening. That is why the *Classic of Taiji (Taijiquanjing)* speaks of "deflecting a thousand pounds of force with only four ounces of strength."

Students of Taijiquan learn this skill through a controlled sparring exercise called Pushing Hands (Tuishou).

The Unity of a Ruler with the People

The *Guanzi*, a collection of ancient writings attributed to Guan Zhong (c. 720–645 BCE), has this passage about a ruler's heart:

Taking the heart of the hundred clans as his own heart is called "one body." When a state is of one mind, the myriad people have one heart.

Avoid the greatest sin:
Avoid separation.

Taoists are seldom absolute about anything. It's understood that all is relative, and that something bad in one context may be perfectly good in another. However, a Taoist will nearly always avoid separation for several reasons.

First, there is Tao itself. A Taoist doesn't wish to be separated from Tao. It may happen occasionally, perhaps because of illness or some egoistic decision on the part of Taoist, but the immediate goal is to get back in touch.

Second, there is the social context. While Taoists advocate withdrawal into contemplation, something that by necessity is usually done alone, very few people can live in complete solitude and provide for all their needs without anyone else. People need other people, and so a Taoist avoids alienating others or falling into paralyzing isolation.

Third, a Taoist realizes that all is relationship. Some are minor, some are profound, but all are relationships nevertheless. Even conflict requires engagement: when a person attacks another, a relationship occurs, however temporary.

If a Taoist is to deal with conflict, the worst thing is to lose touch with the other person. In a martial arts match, for example, whenever an opponent attacks there must be a lowering of defenses. If an attack is to be met, there can be no separation, for the moment of attack is exactly when a chance for counterattack opens. The Taoist avoidance of separation means always being in touch.

It is by keeping in touch with all around us that we keep in touch with the Way.

Avoid separation and make pilgrimage to your sacred mountains.

- Birthday of the **Great God of the Eastern Peak**

The Five Sacred Mountains

The Five Sacred Mountains (Wuyue) in China are believed to have been formed by the body of Pan Gu (p. 338). They are:

Taishan (Tranquil Mountain), the East Great Mountain (Dongyue), Shandong. Considered the first of the five mountains.

Huashan (Splendid Mountain, p. 360), the West Great Mountain (Xiyue), Shaanxi

Hengshan (Balanced Mountain, p. 404), the South Great Mountain (Nanyue), Hunan

Hengshan (Permanent Mountain, p. 260), the North Great Mountain (Beiyue), Shanxi

Songshan (Lofty Mountain, p. 93), the Central Great Mountain (Zhongyue), Henan

In this book, each mountain's ancient graphic symbol appears on the page describing it.

The Great God of the Eastern Peak

The **Great God of the Eastern Peak** (Dongyue Dadi) exorcises evil spirits and receives the souls of the dead, which float to Taishan. He determines people's fortunes, the success of officials, and the length of lives. He also administers the Eighteen Levels of Hell (p. 115).

Make pilgrimage to your sacred mountains.
Find the vantage closest to your heaven.

Each of the Five Sacred Mountains is a center of history, spirituality, art, and poetry. Pilgrimages to the sacred mountains are highly valued as inspiring, reverent, and beneficial journeys. Pilgrims believe that they can absorb the power of the mountain and the divine power of heaven. The makers of the lunar calendar wanted to encompass the entirety of human existence: by preserving observation days for each sacred mountain, the lunar calendar incorporates both time and place.

What are the sacred mountains in our own spiritual landscape? That can be a literal question—are there mountains near where you live that are special to you? It can be a metaphorical question—what are the peaks of your inner landscape? In either case, they are mountains to be discovered. They are mountains to be climbed.

In the past, people ascended mountains to be closer to heaven and far from the corrupt human world. Such Taoists are called "immortals" or *xian*—the word combines the character for "person," on the left side, with the character for "mountain," on the right side. Retreating from the world for spiritual practice, it was called to "ascend the mountain."

Some Taoists believed that the Eastern Peak was the actual home to gods—therefore, it *was* heaven. Others believed souls flew to the Eastern Peak upon death—which places paradise on the mountain. All these examples show mountains as symbols of greatness and as places for spiritual cultivation.

Each of us has Five Sacred Mountains inside us. Ascend them, and you are closer to your heaven. Be a "person on a mountain," and you are on your way to becoming an immortal.

Find the vantage closest to your heaven to discover that each pilgrimage is a circle.

37 | Pilgrimage

Many shrines and temples exist in virtually every city of China, other Asian countries, and abroad—including temples in the United States.

The North God, Zhenwu, on Wudangshan. Note how he sits in his own alcove and how he's draped with an actual cloak.

© Bernard De Poorter

*Each pilgrimage is a circle
we travel to return transformed.*

Pilgrimage is honored the world over. In the ancient world, there were Karnak, Thebes, Delphi, Ephesus, Jerusalem. In Buddhism, there were Lubini, Bodhi Gaya, Sarnath, Kusinara; in India, the caves of Sanchi, Ellora, Ajanta; in Tibet, Lhasa; in Indonesia, Borobudor. In Hinduism, there are dozens, beginning with the four sites of Char Dham: Badrinath, Dwarka, Jagannath Puri, and Rameshwaram. In Islam, there are Mecca and Medina. In Judaism, there is the Wailing Wall. In Christianity, there are the Holy Land and cathedrals and churches throughout the world. And the many sites of Taoism show how the ancients viewed the land as sacred.

We may also go on personal pilgrimage, to places where a poet, musician, or artist once lived; to pay our respects to a historical battlefield; to stand where a famous peace activist once stood; or simply to see what the first explorer must have seen.

The key to pilgrimage is to embark on the trip with a heightened intention. We are not just tourists. We're going to honor someone or something. By honoring what is sacred to us, we make it more real in our lives. We join with it.

Inevitably, we return from pilgrimage, and this is an essential part of the meaning as well. We're *supposed* to return to our normal lives, except that we return transformed, carrying the experience with us forever, having touched the reality of what we love, having walked in the same dust as the thousands who also have the same beloved.

Finding something sacred in our lives, traveling there in devotion and commitment, humbling ourselves, sharing the experiences with others, and coming back transformed—all these are human expressions, human necessities. Pilgrimage is spiritual human migration. A sacred place makes us sacred.

We travel to return transformed, even if we face stress and mutilation each day.

38 | Greater Than Shame

▸ Commemoration day for **Sima Qian**
▸ Fasting day

The Grand Historian

Sima Qian (c. 145–90 BCE) is considered China's foremost ancient historian. His work covers over two thousand years (2696–87 BCE), from the Yellow Emperor to Han Emperor Wudi. He completed his *Records of the Grand Historian* under considerable tribulation and is remembered for clear writing and great determination.

Beginning at the age of twenty, Sima Qian traveled across China, collecting information and verifying as much historical detail as he could. After he entered the imperial service, he was assigned to reform the calendar and advise the emperor. Sima Qian created the Great First Calendar (*Taichuli*), which defined a year as 365.250162 days (quite close to the current duration of 365.242199 days).

Sima Qian's father, Sima Tan (c. 165 –110 BCE), had begun writing an ambitious historical record. He asked Sima to complete the enormous task as he was dying.

However, in 99 BCE, Sima Qian addressed Emperor Wudi (156–87 BCE) in defense of General Li Ling (p. 407), who was blamed for a disastrous defeat. This enraged the emperor, and he ordered Sima executed. The condemnation could only be commuted by money or castration. Sima Qian had no money. Desperate to complete the responsibility his father had given him, Sima Qian endured the pain and humiliation of castration and imprisonment. Upon his release in 96 BCE, he worked to complete his masterpiece.

His tomb and memorial temple are in Han Cheng, Shaanxi. The story here is taken from Sima Qian's "Letter to Ren'an."

We face stress and mutilation each day.
Since we only die once, what's right to do?

Sima Qian was deeply committed to righteousness and duty to posterity, but he was shamed for it. His predicament is repeated every day for millions of people at the hands of government, bosses, or family members. For all of us, Sima's story is important in five ways.

First, Sima Qian spoke out against injustice. General Li Ling commanded five thousand troops against the Shanyu, part of the Xiongnu (from areas that include present-day Siberia, Mongolia, and Manchuria). Vastly outnumbered, the Chinese troops fought to the death. Li Ling was captured, and Emperor Wudi condemned him to death in absentia. When Sima Qian was told to state his opinion, he spoke honestly.

Second, not a single person interceded on his behalf. No one spoke for him or offered the money that could have spared him.

Third, suicide was considered more honorable, and yet Sima Qian wrote that had he committed suicide, people would have assumed that he had had no other alternative. He was determined to finish his father's work. If not, he wrote, he could never have been able to visit his parents' graves, and he declared that "a man has only one death."

Fourth, the castration was physically, mentally, and socially devastating. Sima Qian stated that there was "no greater defilement" and that he would "not be considered a man anywhere," since eunuchs were universally detested. Sima described himself as a mutilated wretch, fit only for serving in palace women's apartments, whose only hope for vindication was for his histories to be read after his death.

Fifth, he recovered his sanity after being bound, stripped, beaten, imprisoned, and castrated. He gasped with fear, he wrote, having been overawed and broken by force.

Sima Qian, a great man in world history, reminds us to study the past diligently because the injustices he endured and recorded are constantly repeated in every country around the globe. The powerful humiliate us every day, but our forbearance must be stronger than the oppression that would crush us.

Since we only die once, what's right to do? What is your Work?
What do you leave behind?

39 | What Do You Leave?

What is your Work? What do you leave behind? Do you choose slashing sword or freeing brush?

How many tourists on the Great Wall ever stop to consider the fate of the general who was ordered to build it? How many people who write with brushes are aware that the same general influenced the form of the brush we still use some 1,800 years later?

When General Meng Tian was ordered to commit suicide, he said that his family had loyally served the dynasty for three generations. As the head of 300,000 troops, he could have ordered a revolt. He did not do so because he could not bear to disgrace his ancestors or forget his debt to the late emperor. He was not trying to avoid death, he said, but to make it a remonstrance so that the emperor would return to the Way. When the envoy demanded that the decree be carried out, Meng Tian decided that in building the Great Wall, he had cut the arteries of the earth, and for that, he had to atone. Then he swallowed the poison.

Sima Qian (p. 46), in recording this, did not agree with Meng Tian. He himself toured the northern border and traveled the roads that the general had built. Yes, he had cut through mountains and valleys, but he had done so by the forced labor of millions of people. Sima Qian concluded that Meng Tian had not remonstrated with the emperor forcefully enough, that he had not relieved the ills of the common person, the elderly, and the orphaned.

We ask what we should do in this life, and we ask what we should leave behind. Do we choose the path of power at the expense of others' lives? Or do we choose the path of obscurity, and thereby preserve lives? Meng Tian wielded both the sword and the brush.

He chose the sword.

Do you choose slashing sword or freeing brush? Why not put both aside and, beginning at the bottom, climb a mountain path?

40 The Inner Landscape

The *Internal Classic Diagram*

This is a rubbing of the Internal Classic Diagram *(Neijing Tu)*. It was made by Liu Chengyun, whose Taoist name was Suyun Daoren—the Plain Cloud Taoist. This carving has an estimated date of the nineteenth century and shows the path of energy from the base of the torso to the crown.

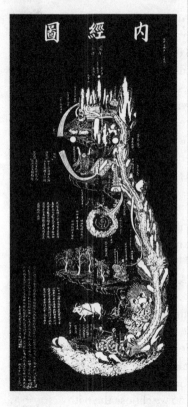

Beginning at the bottom, climb a mountain path.
Meet the sage at the peak, and find that it is you.

This depiction of Taoist inner landscape shows the path to enlightenment because, for Taoists, enlightenment requires the transformation of physical energy. Starting at the base of the torso, the practitioner raises raw energy up the spine—shown as a rocky mountain path—to be refined and cultivated at each of the three dantian (fields of cultivation). The agrarian imagery is unmistakable.

Finally, the energy reaches the crown, where one discovers Laozi. The wisdom that one reaches by this spiritual journey is one's own. The refinement of energy and the activation of important centers power realization.

Some Chinese landscape paintings don't depict an actual place but, instead, a "mind-journey." The artist began in one place and painted in a spontaneous and continuous exploration. The painting became a record of meditation, of movement in some inner space. Likewise, the *Classic of the Yellow Court* (p. 28) reads as one long ecstatic journey through what is at once body and landscape.

Taoists make no separation between the body and the mind. They are one. The body can be used to raise one's spirituality. The spirit can be used to heal the body. All is continuous.

Meet the sage at the peak, and find that it is you; then descend to wander the rivers and lakes.

41 | The Outer Landscape

The Ten Continents and Three Islands

Beginning in the Warring States period (475–221 BCE), Taoists believed that gods and immortals lived in special places on earth. They imagined palaces of gold and silver, and places where the elixir of immortality might be found. Numerous naval expeditions were sent to find islands in the Pacific where immortals dwelt, but none were found. Nonetheless, people continued to believe in the **Ten Continents** and the **Three Islands**.

Chief among the mythical islands of immortals was **Penglai**, and there are many references to it in Taoist literature. This island was thought to be on the eastern side of the Bohai Sea.

Taoists also believed that there were places where mortals could go to become immortal, and that heaven intersected with the earth at certain points. These were called the **Ten Greater Grotto Heavens**, the **Thirty-Six Lesser Grotto Heavens**, and the **Seventy-Two Lesser Realms**. All of these places have actual locations in China. Most have unique and beautiful scenery—inspiring people to believe in "heaven on earth."

Wander the rivers and lakes.
Chase after the divine breath.

Just as a Taoist tries to raise spiritual energy up the spine to the crown as if climbing a mountain trail, so all of nature is seen ecstatically as a spiritual place. The Five Sacred Mountains are one manifestation, but Taoists believe that there are special places and energy spots everywhere and that there are meridians of power, or places of the divine breath, just as there are acupuncture meridians in a human body. Taoists literally see microcosm and macrocosm as one.

Many Taoists love nothing better than to wander the world to chase after this divine breath. This breath might be found by looking at the contours of the land. For example, the "spine" of a mountain is believed to be a "dragon meridian." Walking that line will allow a person to feel the energy of the land.

The divine breath moves. A place can become stagnant and uncomfortable. Another place can seem beckoning and stimulating to one's vitality. There are no set rules for this. One simply has to chase it, dancing spontaneously with nature's relentless process of change and renewal.

In ancient times, people believed that heaven was rooted in several places on earth. The Ten Greater Grottoes, the Thirty-Six Lesser Grottoes, and the Seventy-Two Lesser Realms were all places where heaven or immortals lived on earth.

Heaven is not separate from earth. Spirit is not separate from the body. A human being is not separate from the earth. Heaven and earth exist within us.

Chase after the divine breath—beyond where the flock of black wings cross the sky.

42 | Where Do the Birds Fly?

The Universe

宇宙 The modern Chinese term for "universe" or "cosmos" is *yuzhou*. *Yu* has the sign of a rooftop and eaves on top and therefore alludes to the rooms and the structure of a building. *Zhou* means "time," including the concept of infinite time. Thus, the word for "universe" alludes to infinite space and infinite time.

The *Masters of Huainan* (*Huainanzi*)—a second-century BCE philosophical classic that was the result of discussions between the prince of Huainan, Liu An (177–122 BCE), and scholars in his court (p. 124)—states: "Going back to the past and coming to the present is called 'zhou' [time]. The four directions and above and below are called 'yu' [space]."

Flock of black wings cross the sky.
Birds are not afraid of direction.

The sky is infinite. Its blue is unblemished. Beyond our atmosphere, we know that the sky is part of a black space that is endless in all directions and that there is neither up nor down, east nor west in it. The limitlessness of space is far more than we could ever measure by any human scale.

The measurement of a light-year was invented to cope with this overwhelming space. We used the distance it takes for light to travel one year. We took the enormity of our travel around the sun and used it to measure a space billions of times greater. In ancient times, distances were measured by the length of the king's thumb. We are only a little more sophisticated today in comparison to the enormity of the universe around us.

The birds think nothing of such speculations. They fly to seek food or better weather, or to build a nest. The endless expanse of space is there—perhaps we could even call it their home—and yet they choose their directions and fulfill their lives. They are not undone by infinity. They simply use infinity in all that they do.

Birds are not afraid of direction, and neither must we be, even if we must all sail upon vast floods.

43 | Sage of the Flood

▸ Festival day of **Hung Shing**

Sage Hung

Hung Shing (Hongsheng), also known as Grandfather Sage Hung and Tai Wong (Daiwang), was originally Hung Hei (Hong Hei), a government official of the Tang dynasty who served in present-day Guangdong. While in office, he promoted the study and use of astronomy, geography, and mathematics, and established an observatory. After he died at an early age, he was granted the title Sage King Hung Great Benefactor of the South Sea. People believed that Sage Hung continued to guard them against storms and other disasters, and there are many temples to him in Guangdong and around Hong Kong. He is especially revered by fishermen, sailors, sea traders, and boat people.

We must all sail upon vast floods—
with our knowledge, wisdom, and faith.

The literal translation of Hung is "flood." Although this is simply the sage's surname, it seems strangely apt that a god who protects against the dangers of the oceans has a name that literally means "Sage of the Flood."

Just as the sky is infinite, so too are the oceans. They are the greatest of floods, covering much of the earth. One can sail upon them forever without stopping. But to sail on such an expanse is as treacherous as it is exhilarating, and so it makes sense that people turned to divine help.

Those who live on the oceans may have the greatest of skills. Boat people live their entire lives on boats and fishermen have to navigate and find food too. Hung Shing encouraged the use of astronomy, geography, mathematics—all good forms of knowledge for those who would sail the seas. Yet even after all that we do, we sometimes need something extra to face the unknown. Some call it luck. Some call it the protection of the gods. Whatever you call it, it means faith in the end.

We all must navigate vast floods during our lifetimes. We must all find a way to set a course by the stars, even as all that we see around us seems to be wave upon wave. We don't know what is beneath us—opportunity, like fish to catch, or danger, like dangerous currents or rocks? Yet like the sailors, we must continue on even if the ocean is deadly. We must go on, knowing that divine help will come.

With our knowledge, wisdom, and faith, let us awaken to this dream! Then keep dreaming.

44 | Awaken

• Fasting day

The Butterfly Dream

One of Zhuangzi's most famous parables is this:

> I, Zhuangzi, dreamt that I was a butterfly flitting about and enjoying myself. I did not know I was Zhuangzi. Then I woke up and I was Zhuangzi again. But I could not tell if I was Zhuangzi dreaming that he had been a butterfly—or if I was a butterfly dreaming that he was Zhuangzi. However, there must be some difference between Zhuangzi and a butterfly. We call this the transformation of things.

Awaken to this dream! Then keep dreaming.
Be the dreamer who's aware of the dream.

This is the time of Insects Awaken, when the insects that have been dormant during the winter return to activity as the weather warms. Living creatures accord with the seasons, entering dormancy when necessary and awakening when the season changes.

The greatest awakening is spiritual awakening, that profound insight into the truth of our existence and the nature of the world. Having such an awakening dispels all doubts.

All of us have had the experience of nightmares, and all of us understand the relief of waking up and sighing, "It was all a dream!" Since so much of meditation and Taoist practice is internal, this makes an interesting question. How do we distinguish the trap of our inner anxieties from the capacity of our minds to awaken to the great truth?

We join with Zhuangzi in his ambiguity.

Be the dreamer who's aware of the dream, even if you struggle to say: "The Way that . . . the name that . . ."

45 | Constant

- Festival day for the **Three Pure Ones**
- Birthday of **Laozi**
- Birthday of **Yue Fei**
- Fasting day

Laozi

The opening lines of Laozi's *Daodejing* have even become a proverb:

> The Way that can be spoken is not the constant Way.
> The name that can be named is not the constant name.

Image of Laozi, Yuanming Palace, Qingchengshan. © Saskia Dab

Yue Fei

Yue Fei (1103–1142), a general of the Southern Song dynasty, fought against the invading Jurchen. Four words meaning, "Serve the nation with utmost loyalty," were tattooed on his back.

In 1126, the Jurchen took the Song capital of Kaifeng and captured Emperor Qinzong (1100–1161). After several years' war, Yue Fei was on the verge of retaking the capital. Fearing the return of Qinzong, Emperor Gaozong (1107–1187) plotted with Chancellor Qin Hui (1090–1155) to recall Yue Fei, who returned because he felt that his duty was to be loyal to whomever was emperor. Qin Hui had Yue Fei imprisoned and executed on false charges.

Yue Fei was a famous martial artist, poet, and calligrapher, and remains a paragon of loyalty. His temple stands in Hangzhou.

The Way that . . . the name that . . .
Then what does everlasting mean?

Laozi refers to the "Way that can be spoken" and the "name that can be named," contrasting them with the "constant Way" and the "constant name."

The word "constant" is the word *chang*. It also means "always," "ever," "often," "frequently," "common," "general," "rule," or "principle." The lower half of the word represents a cloth, as in a banner of a lord held up for all to see.

常

Tao that can be spoken is provisional and relative. It cannot encompass the constant Tao beyond words. In the same way, our name or classification for things cannot describe the ultimate truth. Our names are limited and finite. Tao is limitless and infinite.

In using the clumsy translation "not," we can miss what Laozi meant. He avoided several other words meaning "no" or "not" and used a word, *fei*, that implied *opposites*. Look at the word, which was originally a picture of two wings. We cannot discard either side of the equation. Both sides are important. We need speaking and words, and we need to perceive the constant Tao that has no description for its eternal character.

非

The hero Yue Fei gives us a different sense of constancy—constancy of character. He was fixed on being loyal, patriotic, and merciful to the weak. When we read of the constant Way, we may ask how we can be constant in our own lives. Yue Fei's determination to be brilliant, brave, and steady is one answer. That steadiness cannot be named, it cannot be categorized, but it is real and profound nevertheless.

Go beyond words to see the constant Tao, and then you will learn what it is to be constant yourself.

Then what does everlasting mean if we do not wish for spring?

Statue of General Yue Fei, Hangzhou. His own calligraphy appears above him: "Return my rivers and mountains," meaning "Give back my nation."

Exercise 4

SPRING EQUINOX

The spring equinox is one of the two occurrences a year when the days and nights are of equal length. From this point to the summer solstice, the daylight hours increase.

Weather continues to grow warmer and more pleasant. Farmers plant rice paddies, corn, and trees in this period, and life in the countryside becomes more active.

This exercise is best practiced during the period of 1:00–5:00 A.M.

1. Extend your arms, with one palm pressed on the back of the other. Extend one leg.

2. Turn the head to the left and the right twenty-one times. Then switch legs and palms, turning to the left and the right twenty-one times. Inhale on the turn, exhale in the center.

3. Sit cross-legged and face forward. Click your teeth together thirty-six times. Roll your tongue between your teeth nine times in each direction. Form saliva in your mouth by pushing your cheeks in and out. When your mouth is filled with saliva, divide the liquid into three portions.

4. Inhale; then exhale, imagining your breath traveling to the dantian and then swallow one-third of the saliva, imagining that it travels to the dantian.

5. Repeat two more times until you've swallowed all three portions.

6. Sit comfortably as long as you like.

Through this exercise, ancient Taoists sought to prevent or treat weakness; poison in the chest, shoulders, and back; tinnitus; feverishness; and pains in the upper torso.

46 | Eternal Spring

Spring Song

Spring winds move a spring heart,
Flowing eyes gaze at a mountain forest,
a mountain forest of exquisite splendor.
Bright birds sing clear sounds.

This is a *yue fu,* a poem written in a folk song style. "Yue fu" literally means "music bureau," a reference to the imperial agency charged with collecting and recording folk songs. This poem dates from the Northern and Southern dynasty period (420–589).

"Late Spring" by Han Yu

Han Yu (768–824) was a scholar, a teacher, an official, an essayist, and one of the poets anthologized in *Three Hundred Tang Poems.* He advocated a strong central authority in government and orthodoxy in culture. Noted as one of China's finest prose writers, he is considered the foremost member of the Eight Great Prose Masters of the Tang and Song.

The grass and trees know spring is not
    far from returning.
Red and purple blooms, fragrant and
    lush, vie with each other in a hundred
    ways.
But poplar flower and elm seeds have no
    poetic feelings;
they only feel the flying snow fill the sky.

We do not wish for spring.
Spring gives life to wish.

Spring comes back each year—and we welcome it joyously. Even if it is stormy on this day, we know that the storms will pass. Even if it is dark on this day, we know that daylight will grow steadily longer.

There are often references to a second spring in one's life. Can we reclaim our youth? There are also references to eternal spring. Can we stay forever young? Perhaps these ideas were not wishful thinking. Perhaps they were uttered by those who saw spring return each year, and who thought it was natural that we should have spring return to our bodies each year as well.

And so it does. We find renewal in our lives constantly. Every morning when we wake, we are reborn. Every time we recover from illness, it is like spring following winter. Every time we begin a new venture, start a new friendship, nurture a newborn, or undertake any number of other kinds of new efforts, it is spring again.

Our bodies consist of millions of cells. Some of them die each day, others are born each day. Winter and spring happen within us on an ongoing basis. There are cycles within cycles within cycles, and organization emerges from that. Coherence, identity, and meaning spiral out of the ongoing alternation of birth and death.

But on this day, the power of life asserts itself again. Growth buds, bursts, prepares itself for bloom. Blue skies and the welcome warmth of the sun are on their way, and for that we are both happy and grateful. Life quickens, and we quicken with it.

Spring gives life to wish, and we labor on, even if hidden roots and rocks block our plow.

The *Classic of Poetry*

This portion of one of the works of the *Classic of Poetry* gives a vivid picture of agrarian life thousands of years ago.

> They join to cut the brush and plow the ground,
> clear a thousand areas, pulling roots up to the marshes and dykes.
> The master, his eldest son, his younger sons, and their children all work.
> When they rest, there is the sound of many people feasting; more food must be brought.
> The men think lovingly of their wives, the wives stay close to their men.
> Methodically, they plow the southern acres
> and sow hundreds of seeds with such effort and work. . . .

Pull the Roots

"Cut the grass and pull the roots" is a famous idiom. Its connection to the farming life is obvious, but its implication is to take care of a matter once and for all, so that there can be no recurrence.

Hidden roots and rocks block our plow.
Sweat. Pull waste now and clear the way.

When a field is cleared, farmers cut down weeds, grass, and brush, and they dig up roots, rocks, branches, or the ruins of long-forgotten homes. All of these must be put aside in large piles until expanses of clean earth are left.

Look at the heaps: tangled stems, withered leaves, gnarled roots stained and pungent with damp earth. The pile is left to dry, and then it's burned. The ash that's left goes back into the soil.

The spiritual life is like that too. If we are to have any chance of gaining spiritual freedom, we need to clear our fields. When we do that, we will dig up traumas and injuries deep in our subconscious. All of these must be pulled out and then discarded with the diligence of a farmer clearing the field.

It's hard work. When we survey the expanse of the field we must clear, the extent may be daunting. As we bend to the task, we may well find that the amount that we accomplish in a day is discouragingly small. But each bad thing dug up will never bother us again.

Dig up and discard the bad things in your past. Pile them up. Let them sit in the sun so that they wither and dry. Burn them, for you will be doubly free afterward. Your field will be clear, and it will be enriched by the very ash of what were once hidden obstacles.

Sweat. Pull waste now and clear the way. Then pause, as a farmer rests when his buffalo stops.

48 | The Water Buffalo

• Fasting day

The Golden Water Buffalo of West Lake

West Lake (Xi Hu) in Hangzhou is one of the most beautiful places in China and perhaps in the world. The ample history and charms of the area have made it rich in folktales and legends.

During the Han dynasty (206 BCE–220), there was a golden water buffalo who lived at the bottom of the lake. Whenever the lake dried up, the water buffalo spewed water until the lake was full again.

The local officials wanted to present this marvelous animal to the emperor, and they ordered the people to drain the lake with foot-powered water-wheels. When the buffalo appeared, the officials dashed forward, vying with one another to capture it. But the water buffalo bellowed angrily and spewed water so quickly that the officials were drowned as the lake filled rapidly. Since then, West Lake has never run dry.

A farmer rests when his buffalo stops.
Which end of the reins is really guiding?

There are two classic scenes of the water buffalo on a farm. One is the buffalo pulling a plow. The other is the buffalo at rest, languishing contentedly, half-submerged in water and mud. Domesticated for some five thousand years, the water buffalo can survive on poor food sources, yet is strong and well suited to plowing muddy fields and rice paddies. A single buffalo can weigh as much as two thousand pounds.

As powerful as it is, a water buffalo cannot work all day. The plowman has to rest and feed the animal. Naturally, the farmer can also rest, or turn to other chores, accepting the limit to how much plowing can be done. Now we have machines that run on gas and electricity and that never get tired. We exceed what a single man and animal can do, when we use our engines rated in the hundreds of horsepower; our trucks, trains, and planes that need only a quick refueling; and our computers that we never power down.

Yet in our "advancement" over the single plowman, we have paid a price. We, the operators of our machines, are now driven to keep up a tireless pace. We do not bother to extend the consideration we show for a water buffalo to ourselves. Nuclear fuel, the combustion engine, ubiquitous electricity, computers and mobile devices drive us to work far longer hours than those lowly farmers.

Meanwhile, the water buffalo wallows in the mud.

Which end of the reins is really guiding, after compassion opens us to others?

Guanyin

Guanyin was originally a Buddhist deity who was also adopted by Taoists as an immortal. She represents compassion, and her full name is Guanshiyin—the Hearer of the World's Cries.

Guanyin is a **bodhisattva**—an enlightened being who is eligible for **nirvana** (liberation from suffering) because of exemplary living, great wisdom, and self-cultivation. However, like all bodhisattvas, she delays accepting this lofty status of becoming a Buddha to help all other sentient beings gain nirvana first.

Buddhism originated in India, and Guanyin began as an Indian and male bodhisattva named **Avalokitesvara**. He made a vow to help all sentient beings in distress. In the *Lotus Sutra (Miaofa lianhua jing,* or *Fahuajing),* Avalokitesvara has thirty-three manifestations—including a female one—so that his different forms can be suitable to a range of people. All the manifestations have the same purpose—to listen to the cries of those suffering and to help them.

Knowledge of Avalokitesvara came to China through the travels of **Faxian** (337–422) and **Xuanzang** (c. 602–684; featured in the epic novel *Journey to the West*), two monks who traveled to India on pilgrimage and who returned with Buddhist scriptures.

Miaoshan

Guanyin is widely known today as female, and there has been much scholarly speculation as to how this happened. It is probable that there were local deities similar to Guanyin who were absorbed into the worship of Guanyin. One likely example is the story of **Princess Miaoshan**.

In this story, the king wants his daughter, Miaoshan, to marry a wealthy man. She replies that she will consent only if the marriage can ease three misfortunes. When asked to explain, she replies, "The first misfortune is the suffering of people as they age. The second misfortune is the suffering of people when they fall ill. The third misfortune is the suffering caused by death. Unless my marriage can alleviate all three sufferings, I would prefer to take religious vows."

Her father asks if anyone could do such things. Miaoshan replies that a holy person could address all three misfortunes. The king declares that he wants a man of wealth and power for a son-in-law, rather than some poor holy man. As punishment, he forces Mioashan into hard labor and reduces her food and drink. But Miaoshan will not yield and begs every day to become a nun.

Frustrated, her father sends her to a temple—with instructions that she be given the hardest chores to discourage her. She must work day and night, but the animals see that she is a good person and help her do her work. Then her thwarted father orders the temple burned down, but Miaoshan smothers the fire with her bare hands and isn't hurt. Finally, her father orders her put to death.

Philip Lange/Shutterstock

As she is about to be killed, a tiger appears and carries Miaoshan to the underworld. Upon seeing the suffering of those in hell, she plays music, and blossoms shower down around her. Through her compassion, the suffering souls are liberated, and her presence begins transforming the underworld into a paradise. The king of hell hurriedly sends her back to earth to prevent the collapse of his realm.

Miaoshan returns to earth and lives in solitude on the island of Putuoshan (she is sometimes depicted calming a storm on the seas), where she continues to try to relieve the suffering of all the people on earth.

Guanyin with a Thousand Arms

Guanyin is depicted in many different ways—sometimes seated, sometimes standing in white robes, sometimes with her teacher Amitabha Buddha (p. 91). But there is one distinct depiction: **Guanyin with a Thousand Arms**.

As the legend goes, Guanyin vowed to free all sentient beings from the suffering of reincarnation. The effort was strenuous, and after some time, she realized that there were still many more beings yet to be saved.

The struggle to comprehend the needs of all beings in the world was so intense that her head split into eleven pieces. Amitabha Buddha saw her plight and transformed each piece to give her eleven heads.

Now she could better hear the cries of the suffering, but she wanted to reach out to all whose cries she heard. Her two arms shattered into pieces from the strain. Once again, Amitabha came to her aid, transforming her broken arms into a thousand arms. ▶

49 | Compassion

- Birthday of **Guanyin**, Goddess of Mercy

Guanyin in Popular Belief

In popular belief today, many people ascribe even more attributes to Guanyin than her compassion for all people. She is regarded as the embodiment of unconditional love and mercy and as the protector of women and children. Women hoping to become pregnant pray to her or visit her temple. She is also seen as the champion of the sick, the disabled, the poor, and the unfortunate. In some coastal areas, she's regarded as the savior of sailors and fishermen, and some have even modernized her to be the protector of airline travelers. In this role, she is very close to **Mother Ancestor** (p. 98), and some blend the two goddesses.

Compassion opens us to others:
Each self is a gateway to the world.

Compassion is a noble virtue, and it takes on its greatest power when it arises naturally. There's a level of compassion that is deeper than moral practice, deeper than mere empathy. The greatest compassion comes because we are the world and the world is us.

Perhaps this gives the greatest resonance to the bodhisattva vow—that one will refuse one's own nirvana (liberation from suffering) until each person is the whole world and the whole world is us. There is no true liberation for any one individual while others are suffering. In reality, *we* will continue to suffer as long as one sentient being suffers.

The practical will say, "But there will never be an end to suffering." The wheel of reincarnation will continue to turn. The very nature of existence is predicament.

What do you say? If you abandon all effort, then suffering becomes damnation. If you work to liberate all sentient beings, then the work can seem futile. Perhaps that's why the masters teach that there's a third point of view: that we must transcend duality. In the face of overwhelming odds, the enlightened person *still* chooses compassion. Every day. Every moment.

Each self is a gateway to the world we try to sweep clean, but no matter how soft, the broom wears down.

© Kathy Bick

50 | The Worn Broom

Shide Holds a Broom and Talks to Hanshan and Fenggan

Shide (c. 9th century), whose name means "The Foundling," was a Tang dynasty Buddhist poet who lived on Tiantaishan. He was a lay monk, worked most of his life in the Guoqing Temple, and is frequently depicted in Chinese and Japanese paintings holding a broom.

A number of paintings also show Shide with two older friends and fellow poets, Hanshan and Fenggan.

Hanshan (Cold Mountain, p. 391) was an eccentric Buddhist hermit who lived on Cold Cliff in the Cold Mountains from which he took his name. The mountains were a day's travel from Shide's temple. Hanshan wrote a famous collection of poems, the *Cold Mountain Poems,* which have been extensively translated, and which show many Taoist influences.

Fenggan (Big Stick) also lived at Guoqing Temple. According to legend, he was a tall monk with an unshaven head (Buddhist monks traditionally shave their heads) who rode a tiger. He was probably the oldest of the trio.

No matter how soft, the broom wears down.
How can you sweep and yet be preserved?

If you use a broom for a while, the ends start to round and wear. Soon, the broom is no longer straight across the end: it's shaped by the habit of the user. In time, it's worn to a nub, and then it must be replaced.

One of the main tenets of Taoism is softness. Be soft, it is said, and your body will be preserved and you will live long. But no matter how much the bristles of the broom might flex, they are sacrificed in order to fulfill their purpose. Is the same true of us as well?

All of us must work, but work wears on us. The work may be necessary—certainly the work of the broom is needed—but no one escapes work without being worn out. In theory, monks left the world to avoid the entanglements and problems of an ordinary working life—but they still had to work in the temple.

There is only one way out: work must be devotional. Then the sacrifice is worth it. What we sweep is as important as how we sweep. We sweep to clear away. We sweep because we know that cleanliness is the prelude to the serenity needed for spiritual advancement. In the end, sweeping away the dead leaves and dirt of our bad habits and ignorance makes renewal possible.

With renewal, there is no wearing out.

How can you sweep and yet be preserved, knowing what the body is to the spirit?

51 | The Temple

Kaiguang

When a person takes a Taoist or Buddhist figure into their home for a personal altar, it has to be consecrated. This is called *kaiguang*—"opening the brightness."

A temple priest will hold a ceremony and invite the deity to empower the statue, filling a material proxy with divine presence. The statue is then considered "alive" with the power of the deity. A personal god, once consecrated, is carried like a living person and placed in a position of honor on an altar.

Consecrating a Temple

Consecrating a temple is even more elaborate. The site has to be properly chosen according to geomancy; a qualified priest has to preside over the rituals; statues, scriptures, altars, and all the implements of worship must be installed; and perhaps there will be other holy relics to be venerated. Hours of ceremony are involved, and the rituals must be precisely timed to the cycles of the sun, moon, and seasons. Taoists will then consecrate every statue in the temple. Thereafter, it's believed that the gods themselves occupy their images.

The body is to the spirit—
what the earth is to heaven.

The body is the temple for the spirit, and it makes sense to keep our temple clean and pure. In every culture, we have made holy places so that the divine can enter into our lives.

Think about a temple, though. If you go to a temple and look in one corner or the other, you won't see the spirit. If you take the building apart beam by beam and post by post, you won't dismantle the spirit. If you burn down the temple, you won't destroy the spirit. *Those people who dissect the body looking for the spirit won't ever find it, but it's still here.*

On the other hand, build a fine temple, consecrate it, and the spirit enters it immediately. *Those people who say that we don't need to respect holy places won't ever find the holy, but it's still here.*

The spirit enters into this world through a body, and the body is the vessel for the spirit. The health and purity of the body have to be preserved, even as we understand that this bag of blood and bones, breath and tears, milk and semen, this body wired with a mind that can be crazed or sublime, this body is the temple for the spirit. *Those people who say that the human can never be divine will never find the divine, but it's still here.*

Where is heaven? Is it far away? Out there? Up there? Heaven is here, with us, now. Just as the invisible spirit is rooted in the body, heaven is interwoven into this world. *Those people who search for heaven outside of this world will never find it, but it's still here.*

How simple it is to be holy. We are in the temple already.

What the earth is to heaven, the journey is to Tao, and a journey of a thousand miles begins with . . .

During the consecration process, various materials to empower the statues are prepared.

The materials are blessed and bundled in red cloth before they are sealed inside the statues.

The Three Pure Ones remain covered with cloth before consecration. Xianling Guan, near Wuhan. © Photos by Saskia Dab

52 | The Way

Tao: Dao

道 The word Tao (dao) is a picture of a person on a path. The "v" shape on the right side represents two tufts of hair, and the rectangle with the two parallel lines inside indicates a face. The zig-zag shape on the left that extends into a long stroke at the bottom represents the movement of feet.

The word is used by Taoists, Confucians, and Buddhists, but with slightly different meanings.

- Taoists use Tao to mean the great cosmic way, the movement of the universe as a whole, one's personal life path, and the way of living that is right for each person.

- Confucians use Tao to mean the law and a proper way of living that is moral, ethical, socially responsible, and cultivated.

- Buddhists use Tao to refer to the principles and law (dharma) of the Buddha.

A journey of a thousand miles begins with . . .
After a thousand miles, we find ourselves in . . .

Tao means the Way. That seems simple enough. Everything in the universe follows a way, and our lives will be smooth if we follow that way too.

A way implies a direction, and a direction implies a goal. There is direction to the universe—the sum of countless complex and constantly changing smaller directions—but the universe isn't traveling linearly toward some destination. The universe is starting point and destination in one. Nevertheless, within its expanse, there is movement, and hence, there is a way.

Taoism means to follow Tao. Following Tao means that one can find direction but not necessarily a final destination. That would mean an ending; Tao is unending.

We speak of a personal Tao, and it's tempting to think of our lives as having a goal and direction. This isn't ultimately helpful either. Is the "goal" of our lives old age and death?

We must look beyond the limitations of our own small lives toward the infinity that surrounds us. The scale of what holds us is difficult to imagine. The life span of a redwood, the expanse of our planet, the age of our sun, the sheer distances to other stars: all these are immense in scale.

Shall we think of ourselves as dwarfed by such magnitude? Should we speak of our life span as the goal and the ending of our way? No, we are of the Way, and the Way is us, and the Way continues unendingly. We too go on forever—if we aren't stunted by the smallness of our own thinking.

After a thousand miles, we find ourselves in a place of power: great energy makes action possible.

53 | Energy and Intention

› Fasting day

Mencius on Qi

The philosopher **Mencius** (Mengzi, 372–289 BCE) was a key interpreter of Confucian thought (some accounts state that he was tutored by Confucius's grandson). Like Confucius, he traveled throughout China in a long and mostly fruitless attempt to advise rulers on better governance.

Mencius asserted that human nature was innately good. Like other Chinese philosophers, he felt that moral character was connected to natural truths and even physical phenomena. Thus, he articulated a view of qi (breath, energy) and its intimate relationship to the will, to morality, and to heaven and earth. Among his points:

› The will is the general of the qi, and the qi is the fullness of the body . . .

› When the will is concentrated, it moves the qi. When the qi is concentrated, it moves the will.

› He said: "I carefully tend my surging qi . . . Like all qi, it is great and firm. It is tended by rectitude and cannot be harmed, yet it fills all within heaven and earth."

氣 The character for "qi" is taken from vapor rising from rice (the cross at the bottom with the slanted lines in each quadrant represents rice). Qi means gas; air; smell; weather; vital breath; get angry; to be enraged.

Jing, Qi, Shen

Taoists are explicit in connecting the physical to the spiritual. **Jing** (essence, vitality), the basic strength of the body including all its chemical functioning, is transformed into qi (breath, energy). Qi is transformed into **shen** (spirit). Thus, for Taoists, there is no spirituality without physical health—and vice versa.

Great energy makes action possible,
and intention makes action effective.

Taoists have extensively studied human energy, which is called *qi*. The word "qi" nominally means our breath, but it also means our life force, the basic energy for movement.

Furthermore, Taoists (and martial arts derived from Taoist theories, such as Taijiquan, Baguazhang, and Xingyiquan) teach that our energy follows our intention. On the most exaggerated levels, this leads to colorful tales of superhuman feats by mysterious heroes who spend a lot of time meditating to generate extraordinary energy. The legend is that people with accomplished attention command unusual power.

This sensationalism overshadows a truth we can use in our daily lives: our energy flows towards our focus. The more we focus, the more constantly our energy flows. The more we safeguard and build our energy, the more energy we have at our disposal. And when we put our energy and our intention into synchronization, the more we are capable of great accomplishments. The more we establish patterns of activity, the more our bodies and minds conform to those patterns: we become what we do the most.

Taoists know this. There is no mind-body separation for a Taoist. Mind and body go together, and when they do, then the legendary abilities of a Taoist become ordinary.

Taoists connect the spiritual with the physical. Since jing becomes qi and qi becomes shen, all our different kinds of energy flow into one another and support one another. Mencius connects this three-part process to the will, to morality, and to the universe as a whole. Great intention requires great energy; great energy supports great intention.

And intention makes action effective, even if you fly to the edges of the universe.

54 | Confronting Limitations

‣ Fasting day

Wuji, Taiji, and Yin and Yang

Wuji, Taiji, and yin and yang are key cosmological principles in Taoism.

Wuji means to be "without limit." This means all infinity and comprises all that we know and cannot know.

Taiji means the "ultimate limit." This means all that is known or knowable and includes all of heaven, earth, and humanity.

Yin and yang are the duality that make up Taiji. All energies and substances can be understood in terms of yin and yang.

The two graphics here are derived from the *Diagram of the Supreme Ultimate (Taijitu shuo)*, written by Zhou Dunyi (1017–1073). The open circle represents Wuji. There are no limits, but because there are none, there is nothing to be distinguished.

Wuji transforms into Taiji—the Supreme Ultimate. Now things are distinguishable, and because there is differentiation, things can be understood through yin and yang. The lower diagram shows that yin and yang—represented by intermixed black and white—are subsets of Taiji.

Zhou's diagram shows Taiji transforming into the Five Phases (p. 422).

Fly to the edges of the universe
and then you can only fly back.

No matter how far our journey goes, we must turn back home at some point. No matter how magnificent our energy, it will reach a point where it can go no farther. The surface of the earth is infinite anywhere along the two dimensions of its surface, and yet it cannot jump even one millimeter into the sky. The sun is mighty enough to drive all life on our planet, and yet it cannot outshine even the star beside it. All things have their limit, and when limits are reached, there must be return.

We live in a time where people mouth the grotesque exhortation to "go beyond our limits." Our athletes speak weekly about how they broke a record, achieved a personal best, found a way to wrest triumph from bleak defeat. A season later, the athletes have retired. What was once transcendence has to be accepted as limitation.

Without a doubt, we should not accept our limitations—especially the ones that exist because of ignorance, laziness, and indifference. These attitudes must always be challenged. But in the daily struggle to do better and to learn more, we have to be wise about what we choose to do. A globetrotter circumnavigating this globe can go on endlessly. But if he seeks to leap into the stars, he will not be able to do it. We must consider what's possible as a prelude to challenging ourselves.

Confront your limitations. Be better today than you were yesterday. Learn something new each day. Discard a fault each day. All these things are good. But understand what you cannot do, too.

It is from this very limitation that the limitlessness of creativity springs.

And then you can only fly back, accepting that this is a life of poverty.

55 | Ask

The Foolish Old Man Who Moved a Mountain

This fable originally appeared in *Liezi,* a Taoist text attributed to Lie Yukou of the fifth century BCE. The story is known in a number of contexts, from its abbreviation into an idiom to its use by Mao Zedong in a 1945 speech.

There was an old man of ninety who lived between the ocean and two seven-thousand-foot mountains. It vexed him that the peaks blocked his view, and that it took days to journey around them. He called his family together and proposed that they move the mountains.

His wife objected. "You are old and weak! Besides, where will you put all the dirt and stones?"

"In the sea."

Together with his sons and grandsons, the old man began to break the stones, and everyone carried away the dirt and stones in baskets. A neighbor boy even joined them.

Another old man mocked them. "You are too old to even bend a blade of grass. What can you do with stones and dirt?"

The foolish old man said, "Your mind is too set for me to penetrate it. When I die, my sons will survive me. My sons will have sons and grandsons, and those generations will have sons and grandsons. My descendants will go on forever, but the mountains can grow no bigger. What difficulty should there be in removing them?"

The mountain spirits were afraid and reported this to heaven. The heavenly king was impressed and ordered the mountains magically moved away.

This is a life of poverty:
You must ask for riches to come.

It's surprising how many requests are denied in the world. This begins in childhood. Parents must deny a child in order to be protective or to teach, but they must not deny a child simply out of tiredness or impatience. That can too easily progress to wrongful denials: the parent doesn't know the answer, the parent is projecting his or her own negativity on the child, or the parent simply can't envision fulfilling the request. No! No! No! A child hears that dozens of times a day.

In school, small-minded teachers and administrators continue this pattern. "There's no budget." "If I do this for you I have to do this for everyone else!" "What makes you think *you're* so special?" "You just don't have the grades." It's surprising that we aren't all curled up, catatonic and drooling.

We have to keep getting up every day. We have to keep trying. We have to envision what we want, and we have to work for it. When we have an idea, however, the ghosts of those parents, relatives, and teachers reappear like a flock of filthy birds and chant: "Who do you think you are? What makes you think *you're* so special?" We are defeated by these ghosts before we can take a step.

Ask. Open your mouth and ask. Yes! You are special! Yes, you will create something new! Yes! You are spiritual! It may take some time to realize this completely. But every time you *ask*, you deny those who denied you.

Every single moment of asking silences the noisy flock.
Every single moment of asking opens possibilities.
Every single moment of asking makes the vistas more clear.

You must ask for riches to come—after all, is there destiny, or is there none?

56 | Destiny

Dream of the Red Chamber

Dream of the Red Chamber (Hong Lou Meng) is one of China's major classical novels. Written by Cao Xueqin (c. 1715–1763), it is also known as the *Story of the Stone (Shitou Ji)*.

The novel opens with a stone that has accidentally received consciousness. One day, a Buddhist monk and a Taoist priest happen upon it, and the stone begs to be sent into the "world of red dust" to enjoy the pleasures of earthly life.

The two holy men try to dissuade the stone, but it is insistent. The Buddhist monk transforms the stone into a piece of jade and takes it to earth.

"You shouldn't have interfered with the destiny of the stone," the Taoist says. "What are you going to do with it?"

"Don't worry," the monk replies. "The stone is involved in a drama that must be enacted on earth. I am not interfering with its fate—I am facilitating it."

"So another group of spirits has brought the curse of incarnation upon themselves! Where did this drama originate, and where is it to be enacted?"

Is there destiny, or is there none?
How you answer determines your fate.

Destiny is a term in many classic writings, and it can be a charming attitude. "Oh, I was destined to meet you today." Certainly many couples in love would like to believe that they were destined for one another. At the same time, plenty of people use predestination to explain their misfortunes, and they reconcile themselves to their lot in life by sighing that "it was just my fate."

But can you say what will happen tomorrow? Can you say what will happen in ten years? Of all the world's disasters and calamities in hurricanes, tsunamis, famines, genocides—not one has ever been accurately predicted. If these gigantic events cannot be detected, how can the minute events of one person's life be preordained? Use your own sense. Why believe someone who wants you to accept a predestination that you can't confirm?

What will happen on the last day of this year? You can't answer that. Why? Because tomorrow, and the day after tomorrow, and every other day are *created* by the events of today. There is no predestination because the future is made by the present.

However, to some degree, we can set down plans that will act *as if* there is predestination. If you save money today, it is likely that you'll have money tomorrow. If you invest in your education, it is likely that you'll live with more awareness and perhaps even comfort and health. There is no predestination, because there is uncertainty. But we can consider probabilities, and we can influence them.

This road we travel is not there until we step on it, and with each step, the road stretches on, just ahead of our walking: it is our walking that makes the Way.

How you answer determines your fate; the riddle is that the universe moves—that is Tao.

57 | Nothing Is Static

These passages about change are from the "Great Commentary," an appendix to the *I Ching*.

Images are perfected in heaven, forms are perfected on earth. Thus, change and transformation may be seen. . . .

Of change and its implementation, none is greater than the four seasons. . . .

Movement and stillness are constant . . .

Zhuangzi says:

Spring and summer come first and autumn and winter follow. This is the sequence of the four seasons. The ten thousand things are transformed . . . and pass through the stages of growth and decline . . .

The universe moves—that is Tao.
All is change—movement in movement.

All of life is change. Nothing is static. On one side, one thing grows. On the other side, another thing dies, but nothing is ever lost: transformation after transformation marks every moment, and this dynamic process never ceases.

The same is true of us too. We may think, "It's just the same old me," even as we are astonished at a new gray hair, wonder about that wrinkle that wasn't there yesterday, or worry about the needle on the scale trembling beside a higher number.

The more subtle and more challenging view is that every part of us is changing—from the cellular level to our thoughts—that inexorable change surrounds us as ocean currents surround a fish. Nothing is static. Everything is movement. That's why the essential task of being a Taoist is to understand how all things—including ourselves—are in constant motion. It is possible to be aware of this. It is necessary.

Great freedom follows this understanding. Since nothing is fixed, we are not condemned to being a certain way. We have hope. When we are up against the seemingly intractable realities of our lives, we know change is not only possible, it's inherent.

All we need to do is reach out to influence and direct that process of change.

All is change—movement in movement—so why do we learn that stillness is meditation?

• Fasting day

The Microcosmic Orbit

The **Microcosmic Orbit** (Xiaozhoutian) is one of the fundamental Taoist meditation methods.

Here is the procedure in brief:

1. Keep the tongue pressed to the roof of the mouth and clench the anus.

2. Inhale, then exhale while you visualize energy traveling from the dantian to the perineum.

3. Inhale, sending your energy up the meridian that follows the spine. Travel over the crown to the upper palate of the mouth.

4. Put the tongue to the lower palate and exhale down the front of the body to the perineum, relaxing the anus.

5. Repeat the cycle by inhaling up the back again from the perineum.

Notice the similarity to the Neijing Tu (p. 48). The Microcosmic Orbit follows the same route up the spine and into the head. However, it also joins the energy in a circle, thereby affirming Taoist principles of returning, circulating, continuity, and movement.

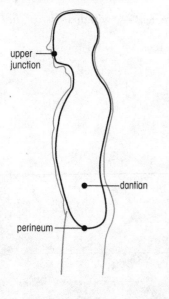

upper junction

dantian

perineum

We learn that stillness is meditation.
Still, meditation is constant movement.

The central training of Taoist endeavor is the daily practice upon which we build ourselves and our perceptions, binding together our own internal process of change in meditation. However, even while meditating daily for years, one must look beyond the classic teaching.

The classic teaching is this: Still yourself to perceive Tao. In the stillness of meditation, the ordinary chatter of one's mind becomes calmed, and one can see one's own inner nature.

And then what? That's when the masters merrily tell us to try it, adding that to say more is interference.

But perhaps it would help to point out that certain kinds of meditation are *not* stillness. While the outer body is held still, the inner body and the mind are constantly moving. Our heart beats, our nerves fire, our blood flows, and our mind moves. We are not trying for cessation. We are directing that movement to achieve healing, power, and spiritual presence.

There are places where the body intersects with the spirit, just as Taoists conceive of places where heaven has a footing on earth (p. 49) or as Mencius connected our breath to the universe (p. 63). Moving our energy to those places is how we move from the physical to the spiritual. It isn't a matter of imagination. Meditation is the movement of energy—and it begins by charging certain places in the body with qi.

Only when the traveler steps from earth into heaven does the presence of the sojourner light heaven.

Still, meditation is constant movement; we use that calm and see that to follow Tao is to respond to it.

59 | Change the Feedback

• Fasting day

Feel Movement in Stillness

The *Song of the Thirteen Methods* (*Shisan shixing gongxin jie*), one of the texts of Taijiquan, has this passage:

Attend to the changes between empty and solid,
Ensure that qi flows freely through the body.
Feel movement in stillness and seek stillness in movement,
Fill your opponent with wonder at your unpredictable responses.

The text is traditionally ascribed to a man named Wang Zongyue. According to what is traditionally taught about Taijiquan, Wang learned the art from a Taoist named Zhang Sanfeng (c. twelfth century).

To follow Tao is to respond to it.
Yet Tao also responds to us.

The classical teaching about Tao is that we should respond to it and follow it. Each day, a person tries to be more open and sensitive to the movement of all things, and should thereby find the day easy and positive.

At the same time, Tao responds to us. Whatever we do changes all that we encounter. There is a wide latitude for our actions. If you don't like how your life is going, try something different today. It doesn't have to be enormous. Just try a little thing and see how different the reactions are. Approach the people in your life differently, exercise differently, eat something different, try a new route home. Whatever you do that's different is sure to change what you experience.

When some people hear that Taoism includes martial arts, they are confused. They fear martial arts as violence. However, there is much more to martial arts than its fighting aspects. Over the centuries, Taoists have inverted the aggressive aspects of martial arts and have instead made them a vehicle for spiritual cultivation. The discipline, the physical training, the stamina, and the philosophical demands of martial arts have all been sublimated into a spiritual pursuit. Unless you learn how to work with an opponent, how will you work with the myriad of other entities around you? The totality of that working with others is Tao.

Our relationship to Tao is dynamic and open. Following Tao is not about determinism or fatalism. Nothing is preordained. We are not victim to any heavenly script. Every single part of Tao—uncountable as they are—contributes to an ongoing dance that is improvised each second.

Yet Tao also responds to us, for Tao is mother to all under heaven.

60 | We Are All Children

Don't Lose the Child's Heart

Mencius (p. 63) said: "The great person does not lose having the heart of a child."

If One Discovers the Mother

In Chapter 52 of the *Daodejing*, Laozi wrote:

> All under heaven have a beginning
>   that acts as the mother of all under
>   heaven.
> If one discovers the mother, one can
>   know her children.
> If one can know her children, one can
>   again preserve the mother:
> Through the end of life, there will be
>   no harm.

Tao is mother to all under heaven.
We become children again to find her.

There's something comforting about having the same patterns of one's childhood. That is one of the great advantages of the lunar calendar's festivals, observations, and even its foods. Each detail is easy to follow, and the accumulation of those details forms a pattern that is comforting to return to each year. When all is change, the regularity of cycles can be reassuring.

We live in times marked by self-consciousness, self-analysis, and worship of the ironic. We are afraid to be seen as mere repetition of the previous generation. We want to be new! Revolutionary! Unprecedented!

Yet we ask what to do when it's time to marry. We search for the right actions whenever a family member dies. We may have turned away from the last generation's rites, but we need rites nonetheless.

The lunar calendar's current state reflects many revisions over the years. The turnover of dynasties alone have tested it. What emerges millennia later is a pattern born of consensus. The practices have changed, but they have changed slowly enough that each generation can take comfort in them. And our generation will continue to modify the calendar, and that is as it should be.

Even so, we don't need to reinvent everything. In observing the changing of the seasons, the divisions between cold and warm weather, the shifting of the sun, and the need to strengthen family ties, there is a reassuring ease. In organizing our spiritual inquiries and efforts into the lunar calendar's time and space, there is a freedom to give our full energy, knowing that our efforts fit into a greater whole.

We become children again to find our mother.

We become children again to find her, and then, after the clouds of winter, the sky is clear and bright.

3

The Peach Moon

Spring Sailing on Ruoye Brook

Unending serenity fills my thoughts,
The evening breezes blow my bobbing boat
through a flowery path to a deep pool.
At night's ending, I turn toward West Valley,
see the Southern Dipper beyond sheer peaks.
The lake mists fly up, then dissolve, dissolve.
The moon sinks lower toward the thick forests.
Worldly matters are so overwhelming:
I'd be an old man with a bamboo rod!

—Qiwu Qian (eighth century)

The two solar terms within this moon:

CLEAR BRIGHT

GRAIN RAINS

Clear Bright Festival

The **Clear Bright Festival** (Qingming Jie) occurs on the fifteenth day after the spring equinox and is the first day of this solar term. People travel to visit and maintain the graves of their loved ones. The traditional burial places in old China were in the hills and mountains, where the view, scenery, and drainage were better. Whether by design or practicality, this left the flat land for agriculture.

How to Visit Graves

Perhaps the easiest way to understand the Clear Bright Festival is to learn the tradition of visiting graves. This is a lifelong endeavor. Young and old go without exception; no child is considered too young, and no person too old.

If there is a God of the Local Land at the cemetery or near the burial place, then one makes obeisance and offering at his shrine. Then one finds the resting places of loved ones and sweeps them clean. Weeds are pulled, and tombstones are washed. If one has to step across other people's graves, one asks for forgiveness, always showing respect for the graves of others as well as those of one's own family.

Many families bring food. Traveling to the graves in olden times was often an all-day affair because the burial sites were far away and most people had to walk. It's common to see entire roasted pigs and cooked chicken as well as many accompanying dishes. Tea, wine, and incense complete a full offering.

Bowls and chopsticks are set out at each grave. Special treats are served to the dead according to their preferences. If the deceased liked to drink, wine is poured on the ground. If he or she liked to smoke, a cigar or cigarette is lit and left on the grave. Whatever the person liked while alive—candies, sweets, favorite foods—is offered to him or her in death.

Many people also burn "spirit money" or "hell notes" so that the dead will have money in the afterlife. People keep up with changing times. Burning elaborate offerings made of paper and bamboo—including clothes, luxury automobiles, computers, and mobile phones—provides for ancestors' well-being.

Finally, people bow three times to their ancestors in respect and honor. Along the way, stories are told of those who have passed, and since children grow up with these annual pilgrimages, they have a clear understanding of who their ancestors were.

The family then either stays at the tombs or goes to a nearby park. The cemeteries often require a long journey; there is food that should not go to waste, and so the offerings double as a picnic.

History

The festival is tied to the **Cold Eating Day** (see next page), but as its own festival, the Clear Bright Festival has a tradi-

tion dating back at least 2,500 years, established in 732 by Tang Emperor Xuanzong (p. 136). The wealthy were holding an excessive number of extravagant and expensive ceremonies to honor their dead—sometimes as often as every two weeks. In order to curb this, the emperor decreed that formal respects should be observed solely on the day of the Clear Bright Festival.

Cold Eating Day

The day before the Clear Bright Festival is Cold Eating Day (Hanshi). This day commemorates **Jie Zitui**, who died in 636 BCE during the Spring and Autumn period. He was a loyal retainer to a young feudal prince named **Chong'er**.

Chong'er was the second son of Duke Xiao, the monarch of Jin. However, the duke wanted the son of his favorite concubine to inherit the throne and he ordered Chong'er and his brother killed to avoid any barrier to succession. Learning of the plot, Chong'er fled into the wilderness, where he lived some nineteen years with only a small group of supporters.

Once, Jie Zitui served soup to his lord, even though there was no food to be had and the small group was hungry. Chong'er enjoyed the soup and wondered where Jie could have gotten it. Jie had cut a piece from his own thigh.

As soon as Chong'er became **Duke Wen of Jin,** he rewarded all the people who had been with him in exile—but he inadvertently overlooked Jie. Offended, Jie disappeared to lead a hermit's life. Realizing his error, the duke sent men to search for him.

Learning that Jie had moved to a remote mountain forest with his mother, Duke Wen traveled in person to apologize and to ask Jie to rejoin his court. But Jie retreated farther into the forest with his mother. The officials suggested setting a fire to flush Jie out—but the resulting blaze killed both Jie and his mother. According to one legend, Jie's body was found in the position that he had been in as he died—carrying his mother on his back. A note written in his own blood read: "I cut off my flesh to dedicate to you, in the wish that my king will be clear and bright (*qingming*)."

In remorse, Duke Wen ordered workmen to build a temple and decreed a memorial day without fire and the eating only of cold food in remembrance of Jie. Others say that the people did not need any command. They themselves remembered Jie's loyalty and principle and began a tradition of visiting his tomb every year.

Some Joyous Clear Bright Festival Practices

Not everyone is strict and solemn about the Clear Bright Festival. The day is also known for kite flying and as a time for couples to start courting. There are family outings, picnics, singing, dancing, and firecrackers. Agriculturally, it's a time to begin plowing, and in the tea world, it's an important time of demarcation. Pre-Qingming tea is highly prized and is considered the best quality because it consists of the earliest and freshest shoots of the year.

Along the Bian River at Qingming Festival

A section of the handscroll *Along the Bian River at Qingming Festival,*1736, National Palace Museum, Republic of China, appears below. A copy of the twelfth-century original by Zhang Zeduan is in the Palace Museum, Beijing; the painting has been copied a number of times and is highly popular.

In 2010, the twelfth-century version was animated for the Shanghai World Expo and projected on a screen 110 meters long and six meters high—thirty times larger than the original handscroll. The ink painting was brought dramatically to life, with traveling people, running water, goods for sale, boats moving on the water, and lighting changing from day to night.

An exhibition of the Palace Museum, Beijing, painting at the Tokyo National Museum in 2012 attracted 40,000 visitors willing to wait eighty minutes in line on the first day. ▶

Exercise 5

Clear Bright occurs around early April. Plants are growing in full force. Green is everywhere, but there can still be much rain.

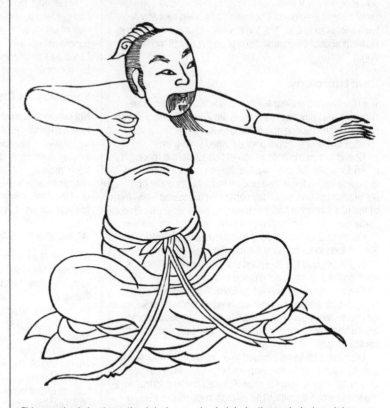

This exercise is best practiced during the period of 1:00–5:00 A.M.

1. Sit cross-legged and raise your arms as if holding a bow.
2. Pull back with your cocked arm as if drawing a bow. Repeat on the other side. Inhale when you pull; exhale gently when you relax as you change sides. Repeat fifty-six times on each side.
3. Facing forward with your hands resting on your lap, click your teeth together thirty-six times. Roll your tongue between your teeth nine times in each direction. Form saliva in your mouth by pushing your cheeks in and out. When your mouth is filled with saliva, divide the liquid into three portions.

4. Inhale; then exhale, imagining your breath traveling to the dantian and then swallow one-third of the saliva, imagining that it travels to the dantian.
5. Repeat two more times until you've swallowed all three portions.
6. Sit comfortably as long as you like.

Through this exercise, ancient Taoists sought to treat weakness and pain in the legs, kidneys, intestines, and stomach; difficult swallowing; decline in hearing and pain in the ears; neck and shoulder pain and mobility problems; and pain and weakness in the arms and legs.

61 | Clear Bright

After the clouds of winter, the sky is clear and bright.
After the clouds of mourning, we will be clear again.

"Clear Bright," by Du Mu

Du Mu (803–852), regarded as a major poet of the Tang dynasty, wrote a poem that has become deeply linked to this festival. People make every effort to go home during the Clear Bright Festival, and tending the family graves is as much a tie to home and family as it is an obligation. Thus, the assumed background of the poem is that someone traveling at the time of the Clear Bright Festival is already far from home, separated from family, and lonesome. Here, the traveler is sad and melancholy, without even the possibility of wine for comfort.

> It's the time of Clear Bright: rain swirls and scatters.
> On the road, this traveler's heart is close to breaking.
> He politely asks where the nearest wine shop might be.
> A shepherd boy points to far-off Apricot Blossom Village.

The name "Clear Bright" is probably a reference to the weather at this time. The clouds of winter are gone, and the light is clean, still, and radiant. This is the time for people to tend graves and bring offerings to the dead. Winter may have been harsh, and attending to the dead is just as important as tending to the living.

This is hardly some practice isolated to the ancient Chinese. People all over the world remember the dead and tend graves. The festival of Clear Bright encourages the regular practice of honoring the dead. It is an important human ritual worth every person's consideration.

The dead are still with us. The blood of family still runs in us. The memories of close friends live on in our hearts. The spirits of those who have been powerful in our lives stay on in us.

So at the time of Clear Bright, we may follow the traditional rituals, or we may have our own way of honoring those who have passed. However, for all of us, remembering the dead is part of being human. Remembrance does not extend grief, but it acknowledges a true and important part of being human: You did not come from nowhere, you are here because of others. And those who have died are *not* forgotten but live forever in us.

After the clouds of mourning, we will be clear again, determined that we never leave our dead abroad.

62 | Returning the Dead Home

Mourning Loss

We first became husband and wife seventeen years ago.

We couldn't look at each other enough then.
Now being without you goes on endlessly.

Already, my temples are nearly white, yet my body won't come to its end.

Someday we'll lie together again in a grave—
but death hasn't come yet, and I'm left sobbing.

This poem is by **Mei Yaochen** (1002–1060), a poet of the Song dynasty. He had a minor career as an official. Many of his later poems focused on ordinary life and mourned his first wife and several of his children.

We never leave our dead abroad.
We bury them in their homeland.

In every war, we bring back our dead. We do not abandon them on the battlefield. Even in hostility and war, both sides understand this and send the dead back to the other side.

War or not, it's a familiar wish for people to be returned to their native land. Every place has its own God of the Local Land (p. 40), the god of one's native locale, or, more intimately, the god of one's home soil. When people want to be buried in their native land, they want to go back to the place where their God of the Local Land will oversee and protect them.

We pray for our dead. We pray for their salvation from suffering. That is exactly why we bring them back to be close to us.

We are tied to place. We love where we came from, we want to go back there. The earth is our home, our cradle. It is part of our very bodies, and we want to return our bodies to it.

We bury them in their homeland, for wherever you go, your gods go with you.

- Birthday of the North God
- Third Moon, Third Day Commemoration for the Yellow Emperor
- The Spring Purification Festival
- Day of the Orchid Pavilion

The North God

The North God (Bei Di), also called Beihai Zhenren, or Zhenwu, is a prominent Taoist deity who is especially popular in southern China. A warrior general dressed in black with a gold breastplate, and who goes barefoot, he is often seen with his allies, a gigantic tortoise and an enormous serpent.

The North God has been worshipped widely and for many centuries to control flooding and for the protection he extends openly to any person.

The Yellow Emperor

Third Moon, Third Day Commemoration (San Yue San) honors the Yellow Emperor (p. 4), the legendary ancestor of all Chinese and of Chinese civilization. He taught people to build shelters, carts, and boats; make clothing; domesticate livestock; and grow grain. His wife, Leizu (twenty-seventh century BCE), taught people how to make silk. At his request, his minister Cang Jie (c. 2650 BCE) created the first written script. The Yellow Emperor is also considered the maker of the earliest calendar.

Spring Purification Festival

The Spring Purification Festival (Shangsi Jie) was an ancient festival for picnics, picking orchids, dispelling bad luck, and ritual cleansing.

The Orchid Pavilion

In the year 353, forty-two literati gathered at the Orchid Pavilion (Lanting) near Shaoxing on this day (p. 86).

Wherever you go, your gods go with you.
In a strange land, your gods will protect you.

The Bok Kai (the Cantonese pronunciation of "Beihai") temple in Marysville, California, was dedicated in 1854. The Chinese who came to work in the gold fields built the shrine on the banks of the Yuba River to protect both against flooding and against hostile people. Bok Kai was also known by a number of other names, including God of the Mysterious Heaven and God of the First Heaven.

The temple burned down and was replaced in 1880. It is still open by appointment and on festival days, and people go there for divination or to pray for good fortune. Many couples who have gone there to pray for children say that they had their wishes fulfilled.

Marysville is more than 120 miles from San Francisco's Chinatown, and more than forty miles from Sacramento's Chinatown. There were no cars during the nineteenth century, and the distance must have been isolating for Marysville. From the gold rush days into the early twentieth century, Chinese were bullied, expelled from their own homes, or killed outright throughout California. The temple was maintained to keep a sense of pride and homeland, to keep their gods with the Chinese, and to appeal for divine intervention. Building a temple to the North God—invoking his martial heroism, celestial power, ability to control flooding, and openness to any person—must have been deeply comforting.

In the same way, we carry our gods with us wherever we go. Our gods aren't trapped in one place. What good would that do for us or them? They go with us, and even in a strange land, they protect us.

In a strange land, your gods will protect you, for traditions keep people alive.

64 | Customs

Maintaining Customs in Another Land

The *Record of Rites* describes how a person should preserve culture and customs even when living in another country. Few of the Chinese immigrants over many centuries would have read the book since many were illiterate. However, this passage shows how Confucianism, as extensive and complex as it was, saturated the culture thoroughly.

The passage was probably meant for officials serving in other feudal states, but it articulates the expectations and customs practiced by generations living away from China.

> When a superior person practices the rites [in another country], he does not change his own customs. His sacrifices and worship are proper. His dress when mourning and his posture in wailing and weeping will accord with the customs of his home nation. He will carefully study the rules, and practice them exactly.
>
> Even if he has been away from the country for three generations, if his title is still accorded to him at the court, and his activities are still reported to the state, if his brothers, cousins, and clan remain, he should continue to send reports about himself to the head of the family.
>
> Even if he has been away from the country for three generations, even if his title is not accorded to him at the court, and even if his activities are not reported to the state, it is only on the day of his establishment [to a rank in the new nation] that he should follow the customs of his new country.

Traditions keep people alive.
People keep traditions alive.

What does it mean to have customs and rituals? Are they merely familiar behaviors or are they powerful in their own right? The Clear Bright Festival has been a custom for hundreds of years, and even in the twenty-first-century United States, far from the villages and hills of China, people keep it alive.

Or do traditions keep people alive?

The early Chinese who died in the United States were buried, but after a time, relatives, friends, or members of their family association would gather the deceased person's bones in a solemn ritual, wrap them carefully, store them in an urn, and send the remains back to the deceased's home village. That rarely happens now. People have been born and have died without ever having gone back to China. America is their local land, but the rituals like Clear Bright still comfort them. If it's the job of an ancestor to protect subsequent generations, then the ancestors have to be nearby. If it's the job of the descendants to keep the ancestors happy, then they need to remember them, visit them, and communicate with them.

The bodies of the dead are gone. The native land of the Clear Bright Festival is not this land. The people who immigrated here came from another place. Yet we should not be distracted by any of this. The observances of the Clear Bright Festival are important because they fulfill human needs.

All this land is still the Earth. Any sky is still Heaven. And the people still have need to express themselves and shape their feelings by custom.

They keep tradition alive because tradition keeps them alive.

People keep traditions alive: we know what to do when a leaf falls and the cherry blooms.

65 | Leaf, Bird, Song

Cold Eating Day

This is an anonymous poem included in the anthology *Three Hundred Tang Poems.* Again, the reference is to people unable to go home for the Clear Bright Festival. The cuckoo's cry is a poetic motif referring to home- or lovesickness.

As Cold Eating Day approaches, rain
　makes the grass luxuriant and full.
Young wheat waves in the wind and
　the causeway gleams through the
　willows.
But I cannot yet return to my family
and the cuckoo won't stop crying at me!

A leaf falls and the cherry blooms
while the birds sing madly in flight.

The brittle leaf on the pile, browned of all its green, blows with the breeze, but is not alive.

Sometimes, when we're sitting with someone who's just died, we imagine that they've moved. The body is settling, pulled by gravity. But the force that once made that body strong enough to jump free of gravity is gone forever. It was only our perception, perhaps our deepest wish, that the person we lost was returning to be with us.

Oh, of course the sages tell us words to comfort us, tell us that death is a transition and not an ending, that the world goes on, and that the soul of our loved one does not die. True, our loved one stays in us, and as long as we are alive, we will carry that loved one with us.

Yet we still have to face the death, as we have to face the browned leaf settling to earth. We bow our heads to the silent ground beneath us, where the roots dwell in silence and darkness.

In the meantime, the cherry tree above it is bursting with flowers, each petal pristine in the sun, each flower adorning its bare gray branch with a galaxy of beauty. A bird perches on the branch and sings madly.

While the birds sing madly in flight, they flee before death
so dark and dreadful.

66 | Before and After

"Song Written on Yuzhou Lookout"

Chen Ziang (661–702), a poet of the Tang dynasty, helped to revitalize the poetry of his time by looking back at ancient models. He was an advisor to Empress Wu Zetian (624–705), and he advocated poetics that reflected real life. Unfortunately, he was persecuted by Chancellor Wu Sanshi (d. 707) and was imprisoned several times before his death.

> Before me, I do not see the ancients.
> Behind me, I do not see the coming
>   generations.
> Pondering heaven and earth, vast and
>   endless,
> my tears fall in sad loneliness.

Chen's poetry was highly influenced by Taoism. This is his only poem in *Three Hundred Tang Poems*.

Before: death so dark and dreadful.
After: there is solemn knowledge.

There are two stages to a person's maturity: before and after the experience of death.

Before a person has experienced death, he or she is an innocent child. If the person has witnessed death from afar, or heard about it, or read about it, or seen it in movies, it has a somewhat abstract quality. It's a mere literary element. It can still be terrifying, yes, but that's because death is naturally frightening to children. It threatens all that they find secure. It goes against their natural joy, hope, and ambition.

The experience of death, especially the death of parents, irrevocably alters a person's sense of the world. Mourning and grief, and then the attendant duties, destroy every shred of childish innocence. There is only *knowing* afterward, the knowing, on one level, that all our actions matter now because we are the leaders and deciders now—and on another level, that our actions matter not one bit—we're all going to die.

Before and after. Once you're in the after stage, the question is whether you can alloy your somber knowledge with the levity of youth again.

After: there is solemn knowledge that there are worse things than death.

67 | Worse Things

Sai Weng Loses a Horse

This famous idiom recalls Sai Weng, who lived along the border and raised horses.

One day, a horse of his ran away. His neighbor tried to console him for such bad luck, but Sai Weng said, "Who knows if it's good or bad?"

The horse returned, accompanied by another beautiful horse. The neighbor congratulated him on such good luck, but Sai Weng said, "Who knows if it's good or bad?"

Sai Weng's son liked the new horse and rode it frequently. One day the son fell from the horse and broke his leg. The neighbor tried to console him for such bad luck, but Sai Weng said, "Who knows if it's good or bad?"

The king declared a war, and hundreds of young men from the area were conscripted. Sai Weng's son was passed over, and few of the other men ever returned.

There are worse things than death.
What we most prize is choice.

We dread death. It is dark and terrifying, and appears to be the complete opposite of everything we hold dear. No more laughter, no more joyous days in the sunshine, no more embraces from someone we love.

Yet we hear that some people want death. The old, the infirm, those sick with chronic pain want to die. Death, for them, is a release. So it appears that there's something worse than death—when misfortune takes all that we hold dear *while we remain alive.*

Those of us who are well and yet still fear death must listen to the experiences of those who would welcome death. Not only does that lend more value to our healthy lives, and not only should it awaken compassion for those who are suffering, it also shows us that the fear of death is far from universal. Contemplating death is not fun—but it is beneficial.

Death is not the complete vanquishing of the human as long as we keep the ability to choose. Then death is not an ending of the human but the exercise of choice. If we know we can no longer savor life's pleasures, if we know that joy will never come again, we value having the choice to leave rather than to suffer.

If we cannot have life, then we choose to die. What we most value is our will—we define "quality of life" as our standard. If we must lose body to illness, we at least want to be conscious, aware—and ready.

What we most prize is choice: we gain that power once we realize the child is not the parent.

68 | Inheriting Power

Spiritual Lineage

The Chan lineage goes back from master to master to the very first transmission of Chan in a wordless exchange between Buddha and one of his disciples, Mahakasyapa.

As Buddha was about to give a discourse at a gathering of thousands of disciples, he silently raised a flower in his hand.

In that instant, Mahakasyapa was enlightened and smiled. It was this silent transmission that began the Chan lineage, and every Chan master to this day traces his or her line of transmission from one generation to another back to that moment between Buddha and Mahakasyapa.

The child is not the parent
until the parent is gone.

Is this too outrageous to say? Sometimes you don't become powerful until the people older than you die. It's as if they hold onto their power until they expire and only then does it pass to you. This is true of parents. It's true of teachers. It's true of anyone with whom you've been deeply involved.

Every one of our elders had abilities that we do not possess. Every one of them lived a life saturated in their own thoughts, their own fortune, their own talents. Many times, we're in awe of what they accomplished. They might have tried to coach us or give us advice, pass on knowledge, give us a business, or leave us an inheritance. But they cannot and would not make us them, and we cannot ever be them. Strangely, when they pass, we can do what they used to do, even if we might only have done it imperfectly before.

People give material bequests. Why can't there be spiritual bequests too? An heir to the throne never becomes sovereign until the old ruler passes away or abdicates.

We know that, and we try to soak up the powers from the past. We go to where Buddha was enlightened. We go to a cave where a Taoist gained realization. We visit relics of saints. We want to know the lineage of masters. We want to be initiated into a tradition and be eligible to receive the "direct transmission." All of these are examples of the same thing: when one generation dies, its power transfers to the next.

Bamboo shoots are already growing when the tallest bamboo are still green.

Until the parent is gone, the parent worries about children.

69 | Filial Piety

Filial Piety from the *Analects*

The *Analects* records this exchange:
When asked what **filial piety** was, Confucius answered: "Parents are anxious that their children not have shortcomings."

At another time, he said, "When living, parents should be served according to propriety. When they die they should be buried according to propriety. And the sacrifices to them should be made according to propriety."

Filial

Xiao means "filial piety" and "obedience," and also "mourning clothes." It shows a picture of an old person being carried by a younger person. Xiao is often paired with *shun*, a word that means "to obey," "to follow," "to arrange," "to make reasonable," "to go along," and "favorable."

The parent worries about children.
Children honor parents in life and death.

Children are asked to be filial—*xiaoshun*. They are taught to respect their elders, and older adults show respect for those who are older still. Adult children look after their parents and provide for them, mirroring how they were provided for as children. Rarely do people talk about Confucius, although he articulated filial piety and made it the cornerstone of his school. People don't verbalize what is always there. They regard it as normal.

Today, we might not learn about Confucianism unless we make a scholarly inquiry into his writings. We encounter filial piety in his texts, and we can hold it at arm's length and contemplate it. But that's like saying we want to hold out a heart to examine it. We can't: it's a part of the body and has to stay there.

During scholarly analysis we can overlook the emotional basis for the doctrine. Filial piety is too often propounded as something Confucius invented as an *obligation* and a mechanism to reinforce his envisioned social order. But what if Confucius was only articulating and formalizing the emotions that already existed?

When one reaches an older age, one realizes the importance of relationships. Filial piety becomes not indoctrination but expression. When Confucius said, "Parents are anxious that their children not have shortcomings," it was a deep insight into the parents' worries. They understand that life ahead is filled with troubles and that the worst of these arise from shortcomings. In raising and educating children, then, they are anxious to help the children overcome as many of their own faults as possible.

If we look at the *Analects,* we see that filial piety is really rooted in feeling: parents worry about their children, and children want to honor their parents. That's what filial piety is really about. When we're children, our parents carry us. When our parents are old, we carry them.

Children honor parents in life and death: if you say men don't cry, you don't know men.

70 | Tears

A Saying about a Man's Tears

A man is a man:
He may shed blood,
but never his tears.

Lines from the *I Ching*

Riding a team of horses: Sobbing and weeping blood.—Hexagram 3, line 6

Weeping and running tears as if in mourning and grief: fortunate.
—Hexagram 30, line 5

Exclamations, tears, and sniveling. No fault.—Hexagram 45, line 6

"Qiang Village"

Red clouds tower in the west,
the sun sinks below the plain.
A sparrow chirps on the wicker gate.
This wayfarer returns from a thousand
    miles.
Wife and children, shocked to see me,
try to calm themselves and wipe away
    pouring tears.

I have floated through this disordered
    life,
and by chance managed to return alive.
My neighbors lean over the wall
with much sighing and sobbing.
Deep into the night, we still hold candles,
and face each other as if in a dream.

This poem was written by Du Fu (p. 29) in 757. The An Lushan Rebellion had begun two years earlier, forcing the emperor to flee the capital and abdicate the throne. Du Fu was a member of the new court, but he was imprisoned, though later pardoned, for defending a friend. It was after his release that he was granted leave to return to Qiang Village, where he stayed for a few months.

If you say men don't cry, you don't know men.
Only men who cry truly know themselves.

It's good to cry. Crying means release. Crying means letting go.

When we pick up a weight that is too much, our bodies will reflexively drop it. Our subconscious overrides our ambition and releases our muscles. The same is true of weeping. The tears of an actor or a liar are not genuine. Real tears are unmistakable and understood around the world. Real tears are our bodies (and a deep part of our minds) letting go. Such tears are always true and right.

Tears remind us that much of us is, after all, water. Water cleanses, water flows, water falls. Water does not work to hold anything up. If something floats on water, it's only because the object has buoyancy, and while the water is there, it does not *exert* itself to make something float.

Water does not fear death: it cannot be killed. Boil it, and it vaporizes. Freeze it, and it will eventually thaw again. If you have a glass of water, have you captured it? Can you imprison all the water in the world? It does not matter if you have a drop or an ocean—because no matter what the quantity, you still have water.

When we're sad over loss, it's good to cry. The tears running down our face are a reassuring reminder of what's true: there is no loss, just as water can never be forever separated from itself. There is no loss, because our one drop will eventually rejoin the whole. In the same way, there is no true loss in our lives. Just as all water is water, we are kin to all kin, and the whole family can never be lost.

Only men who cry truly know themselves—they weep even for a person's handwriting.

71 | Handwriting

Wang Xizhi

Wang Xizhi (303–361) was so skilled with the brush that he's called the Calligraphy Sage. The Tang Emperor Taizong (599–649) so prized Wang's work that he reportedly wanted to be entombed with the *Preface to Poems of the Orchid Pavilion* (p. 86). Sadly, none of Wang's original works remain; we only know of his writing from copies and stone rubbings. His calligraphy is so powerful that even these inadequate reproductions are superior to the majority of calligraphers in all of Chinese history.

The sheer power of Wang's calligraphy is the inspiration for the idiom "Pressed into wood by a centimeter." The saying arose when Wang was asked to write a phrase to be carved into a wooden board. Wang laid paper over the wood and wrote so forcefully that when the carver took the paper away, the stroke had already been impressed into the wood by a centimeter! While this is undoubtedly a tall tale, it underscores the reputed vigor of Wang's strokes.

A person's handwriting:
trace of the vanished hand.

Finding a letter from a loved one, or perhaps reading correspondence between our parents after they're both gone, or seeing the signature of someone who is no longer here holds a mysterious importance. The tangibility of the handwriting is immediate; the way that the strokes testify to the personality of the writer is moving in ways beyond description.

We are led to ask, "Did they know that someone would read this after they were gone?" "What confidence did they have to write what they did?" "Were they aware of the finality that their own death would give to their words?"

When we read back over someone's letters, we view his- or her life in a way that the writer could not have glimpsed. We see a life completed. There are no more possibilities, no more exceptions, no more aspirations. The trajectory has ended. The momentum has stopped. We see a life framed by birth and death. We honor it. We learn from it. We are moved by the profundity and glory of it. We see faith that communicating across distance and time was worthwhile. Faith that recording thoughts would be meaningful. Faith that the individuality of everyone's hand truly matters.

Trace of the vanished hand may be all that lingers when, whether long or short, life comes to an end.

Preface to Poems of the Orchid Pavilion

Wang Xizhi wrote this when he collected the poems of those who gathered at the Orchid Pavilion.

In the ninth year of Yong He, at the time of Gui Zhou, it is late spring. We gather near Shanyin, Huiji, at the Orchid Pavilion during the Purification Festival. Illustrious men young and old join together. We are among majestic mountains, high peaks, lush forests, tall bamboo; clear streams and rushing torrents, with bands of sunlight shining left and right.

We sit in a line, drinking from wine cups floating down the twisting stream. We have neither wind nor string instruments, yet with each drink of wine someone recites a poem—enough to fully pour forth our deep feelings.

What a day! The sky is clear, the air is pure. Favorable breezes blow gently. We raise our heads in admiration: how immense the universe is! We look down and notice: how abundant all things are! Let our eyes wander and our hearts quicken, watching and listening to our utmost pleasure. True joy!

When people gather to discuss life, some talk privately, while others want a large audience. Some prefer rooms, some a multitude of activities. Some prefer quiet, others prefer voluble exchanges. Yet once we find happiness and contentment, we all forget growing old with its weariness.

Feelings follow shifting events, trailing pangs of regret. Before we know it, delights are gone, leaving us sorrowful. Whether long or short, life must end. The ancients said: "Great indeed are death and life!" How poignant that is!

Every time I read the words of the ancients, I feel a strong bond to them. I sigh and lament, but cannot express more. I know death and life may come to naught, and that between long life and death there may be no difference.

We in the present look at those in the past; those in the future will look back on us in the same way. Therefore, I make a record of my contemporaries and their words. Times will change, yet our feelings will linger. What will those in the future feel when they read these words?

Whether long or short, life comes to an end:
so take the wine cups from an endless stream.

The servant boy said: "On the Third Moon, Third Day, I went with my master to the Orchid Pavilion. More than forty esteemed men had gathered—statesmen, artists, calligraphers, musicians. All could write and recite their own poetry. It was the day of the Purification Festival, the day when we washed everything to bring good luck and to keep illness away. It was fitting that men of talent and insight took up places by the clear stream. The other servant boys and I busied ourselves pouring the finest wine into porcelain cups before sending them bobbing down the watercourse.

"One guest took up a cup, drained it to the cheers and laughter of the others, and recited one of his poems. Enraptured, the others sighed and nodded in appreciation. Then another took up a cup, urged everyone to drain their own cups with him, and then he poured forth his own poetry. Soon, they vied to outdo one another: the next master might answer the previous one, or one might follow another by imitating his rhymes to fashion an entirely new poem. Scribes bustled to record the rapidly spoken poems until there was quite a collection.

"Master Wang was drunk when he wrote a preface to the recorded poems. Sober the next day, he tried to make a neater copy. He couldn't. As great a calligrapher as he was, he could not outdo himself. Besides, why should a man try to improve sober what he has already done better drunk?

"I was fourteen then, and not that able to read, but I had a sharp mind. Since I saw the preface several times over the years, I had ample opportunity to contemplate its meanings. In addition, I often heard my master talking to others, so I came to understand his view well. Today, my hair is white and sparse, my spine bent, and my eyes dim. My master's words come back to me: 'Whether long or short, life must come to an end.' I don't know what others will feel in the future when they read his words, but I do know that every generation will sigh over the brevity of its dreams."

So take the wine cups from an endless stream, and contemplate the tall mountains and winding rivers.

73 | No Longer an Outsider

Tall mountains and winding rivers:
you wake up in your own homeland.

The Poetry of the Orchid Pavilion

The poetry of this collection is part of a shift toward nature poetry. Look how Wang Xizhi combines details of the landscape with more abstract feeling when he says:

> The sky is clear, the air is pure. . . . We raise our heads in admiration: how immense the universe is! We look down and notice: how abundant all things are!

During Wang's lifetime, the ideal of creative people living in nature to enjoy and express themselves became popular. These thinkers felt that the mountains and rivers were themselves Tao, so to be in nature was therefore to be with Tao.

Here is one work from the *Poems of the Orchid Pavilion,* written by Zhan Fangshen (fourth-century) and titled "Sailing Back to the Capital."

> Lofty mountains ten thousand feet high.
> Long lakes a thousand miles clear.
> White sand for an entire year clean.
> Pine forests from winter to summer green.
> Water uninterrupted never stops flowing.
> Trees a thousand years old still lasting.
> Waking, I write a new poem.
> Suddenly, I no longer feel like an outsider.

Traveling down a great river like the Yangtze is to experience the wonders of nature and human history at the same time. You admire the cliffs, marvel at the inexorable current, glimpse the picturesque farms and towns along the banks. You are brought to feel the superiority of nature as you are carried on a mighty current. You're made acutely aware of your flimsy boat as you hear of other vessels that have broken on the very rocks you are now gliding past. You see the markers of the high flood lines, you know that millions have died when the river overflowed every levee and plain, and you know that no bank has ever contained these waters for long.

You pass the places where great battles took place. You hear the stories of how kings built grand cities on the shores, cities that have now been long washed away. You recite the poems written by someone who looked at this very scene one thousand years ago, and you recall famous paintings that captured the charm of these shimmering waters.

This is your land. These are your mountains. You may be here no longer than any of those whom you recall, but you are here now, intoxicated with the beauty of all around us.

The philosophers talk of Tao. The priests chant of Tao. The singers cry of Tao. But those are words. Where is Tao to be seen? Where is Tao to be felt? Tao is in these mountains and streams.

And when you are in the mountains and streams, you are also home.

You wake up in your own homeland, and you must never become a man who is both killer and poet.

74 | Villain and Poet?

Cao Cao

Cao Cao (155–220) was a warlord and chancellor of the Eastern Han dynasty. He paved the way for what would become the state of Cao Wei (220–265) during the Three Kingdoms period. Some portray him as a brilliant ruler and military strategist, skilled in poetry and martial arts, and author of many war journals. Popular culture remembers him as merciless and canny. In the historical novel *The Three Kingdoms,* as well as in opera and films, Cao Cao is portrayed as ambitious, cruel, and villainous. Here is one of his poems, "View of the Blue Sea":

> Facing east from a great cliff,
> I view the blue sea.
> How the water roils and rolls
> around upthrust mountain isles
> clustered with dense forest
> and grass growing in profusion.
> How the autumn winds sigh.
> Great waves surge upward so
> the trails of the sun and moon
> seem to rise out of them,
> and the glittering Milky Way
> seems to emerge from them.
> What a fitting time
> to sing unending aspiration.

Cao Cao lives on in a popular saying. In an expression equivalent to "speak of the devil," people say: "Speak of Cao Cao and Cao Cao arrives." He is an ongoing character in film, television, video games, and even a sliding block puzzle, shown to the right.

In this seemingly easy ten-piece puzzle, Cao Cao is blocked by nine other tiles. The object of the game is to slide the tiles until Cao Cao can escape through the mountain pass—a slot in the front of the frame—a process that takes a minimum of eighty-one moves.

A man who is both killer and poet—
sword and words remain tools of ambition.

It's fascinating that Cao Cao has been considered both a great villain and a great poet. When people discuss him historically or as a character in opera or the novel *The Three Kingdoms,* his gifts as a poet are rarely mentioned. Likewise, when he is studied in poetry circles, we rarely take into account the tens of thousands of people killed in his wars.

We tend to think that people can only be great at one thing. If Winston Churchill, for example, also painted watercolors, we think of that as a mere hobby and not part of his entire persona. In the case of Cao Cao, he was certainly known as a fierce warlord, a man who pursued his vast ambition with cruelty, violence, shrewdness, and ruthlessness. At the same time, he holds a place in the history of poetry for his innovation in pastoral poetry. How is it that a man can be both an unmerciful conqueror and a major poet?

Recently, we have fallen into a related controversy. When we somehow disapprove of someone's behavior as a person, we then express the same disapproval of that person's art: we assume that a bad person cannot make good art.

Sword and words remain tools of ambition: better a sword in one hand, gourd in the other.

75 | Warrior Goddess

- Celebration of the **Mysterious Lady of the Ninth Heaven**
- Fasting day

The Mysterious Lady of the Ninth Heaven

The Mysterious Lady of the Ninth Heaven (Jiutian Xuannu) was a woman warrior and teacher of the Yellow Emperor.

When the Yellow Emperor was fighting a rebel, the Mysterious Lady gave him a seal, a sword, and a drum with eighty sides to use in battle. Only then was the emperor able to overcome his adversary. She is depicted with an upraised sword and a gourd (Taoist symbol of immortality, healing, longevity, and good fortune).

A sword in one hand, gourd in the other:
the warrior goddess both fights and gives life.

Why is a warrior goddess such a compelling image? She's an inversion of what we think is normal—men go out to hunt and fight, women stay home to cook and care for children. But is it also because a woman is a much different kind of warrior than a man is?

The legends suggests that by the time a woman goes out to fight, she has had to overcome all her natural reluctance. She goes to battle only when necessary: her cause must be both urgent and moral. Thus, she must win because the situation is dire. Indeed—as in the case of the Mysterious Lady of the Ninth Heaven coming to the aid of the Yellow Emperor—only the woman's entrance into a conflict will bring victory.

There's no question that women lack the brute force of men. Therefore, a woman warrior has to rely on superior intellect, strategy, weaponry, and perhaps even subterfuge. Throughout history, women warriors have often bested men, taking advantage of the men's assumptions that strength and power were supreme. They are not. The person who is better prepared and who has greater determination will win.

The Mysterious Lady holds both a sword and a gourd—that symbol of healing and immortality. The warrior goddess takes life and gives life. That is sometimes necessary, and none of us should shirk when we must—perhaps when there's no other choice—go into battle.

The warrior goddess both fights and gives life, and urges us to show kindness to strangers.

Exercise 6

GRAIN RAINS

This period is named for the plentiful rains that fall. Grains—rice, wheat, millet, barley, sorghum, maize, and others—must be grown in great quantities. They are the staple of everyone's diet.

Cotton and other spring crops are also planted at this time, and peonies, China's national flower, come into bloom.

This exercise is best practiced during the period of 1:00–5:00 A.M.

1. Sit cross-legged and raise one hand overhead, palm facing upward. Bend the other arm across the body with the palm also facing upward.
2. Alternately change position, pushing upward with the raised hand, while bringing the other arm in front of your body. Inhale when you push upward; exhale gently when you relax and change sides. Repeat thirty-five times on each side.
3. Facing forward with your hands resting on your lap, click your teeth together thirty-six times. Roll your tongue between your teeth nine times in each direction. Form saliva in your mouth by pushing your cheeks in and out. When your mouth is filled with saliva, divide the liquid into three portions.
4. Inhale; then exhale, imagining your breath traveling to the dantian and then swallow one-third of the saliva, imagining that it travels to the dantian.
5. Repeat two more times until you've swallowed all three portions.
6. Sit comfortably as long as you like.

Through this exercise, ancient Taoists sought to prevent or treat obstructed blood in the spleen and stomach; yellow tint to the eyes; nosebleeds; swelling in the cheeks, neck, and arms; and excessively hot palms.

76 | Be a Liberator

• Celebration of the **Buddha of the Western Land**

The Buddha of the Western Land

The Buddha of the Western Land (Amituo Fo) is the Chinese name for Amitabha Buddha, the central figure of the **Pure Land Sect**.

Amituo Fo began as Dharmakara, a king who renounced his throne after hearing Buddhist teachings. He made forty-eight vows, and he is especially popular for his eighteenth vow: Should anyone wish to be reborn in Amituo Fo's paradise, they need only call his name ten times—even if they haven't been especially devout prior to that.

His nineteenth vow stipulates that he will come in person, together with all of his bodhisattvas and cultivated persons, to receive the soul of any person who calls his name before dying.

Show kindness to strangers.
Be as kind to yourself.

There are many choices we can make at any moment of the day, and necessity forces us at times to be calculating. However, there are many times when we have a wide latitude of choices. One of our primary goals should be to free others of misconceptions and suffering.

If we can relieve others of a mistaken notion, then we have gained a small victory over ignorance. Who among us wouldn't answer a question from a stranger asking for directions? Why can't we bring that same innocence and directness to all that we do?

If we can be kind to others, there is no reason we should not do it. If by saying something kind we relieve others of a little pain, that is good. Who among us would refuse to give an aspirin to someone with a headache? Why can't we bring that same innocence and directness to all that we do?

Finally, can you liberate yourself? It's amazing how we drive ourselves with all the ferocity of a demon whipping victims in hell. We have business ambitions, we are embarrassed by our self-perceived faults, we obsess over why others don't like us, we think ourselves stupid. We don't even show to ourselves the consideration we give to a stranger asking directions.

Should we leave everything up to the last moment? Should we leave all responsibility to the Buddha of the Western Land? If we envision our world as paradise, we have already liberated ourselves and everyone in it.

Be as kind to yourself as you are when you feed every mouth the grain of life.

77 | Grain

Prince Millet

Millet and rice were grown in China as early as 7500 BCE. **Prince Millet** (Hou Ji) was the god of harvests. His story appears in the *Classic of Poetry*, which praises Prince Millet as the partner of heaven in bestowing the gift of millet, rice, wheat, and barley, and for teaching humanity how to cultivate and harvest these important crops. The poem about Prince Millet is titled "The People's Livelihood," and here are excerpts of it:

> . . . He planted beans.
> The beans grew sturdy and tall.
> His millet flourished.
> His hemp and wheat grew thick.
> His young gourds teemed. . . .
>
> He gave us auspicious grains.
> The black millet, the double-kernel,
> the red millet and the white.
> Far and wide the black millet and the
>   double-kernel,
> Field after field he reaped;
> Far and wide the red millet and the
>   white,
> he carried in his arms, bore on his back,
> brought home to offer in worship. . . .
>
> We heap the offerings on wooden
>   stands,
> on wooden stands and earthenware
>   vessels.
> When the fragrance rises up,
> God above is well pleased.
> What smell is this, so good and strong?
> Hou Ji founded this sacrifice
> to propitiate the gods,
> And it has come down to this day.

Feed every mouth the grain of life,
bind our communities like sheaves.

Nearly every person in the world eats grain on a daily basis. Without grain, there is no settlement, no nation, no civilization. Whenever a new community was built in the wilderness, people quickly planted grain in order to feed themselves.

Grains are grasses. We eat the seeds because they are nutritious and because they grow in such abundance. We are used to sacks and sacks of grain, great piles, huge silos.

The seeds are what regenerate the plant. Left to go through their entire cycle, new plants would sprout. We live by eating the most powerful and regenerative part of the plant. When we eat, it's as if we sow those seeds in ourselves, and benefit from the energy of growth.

Grain made our world possible. First we needed grain to feed many people. People then specialized in farming to grow and harvest grain. The need for grain and the work of farmers became the basis for community.

When the farmers saw the sheaves in the field, they could have seen them as the perfect metaphor for community: richness came from unity. Unity was only possible with hard work and the patient nurturing of grain through its entire life cycle. People working in cooperation, meshed with the growing cycles of grains, made the future possible.

With our sophisticated lives, it's easy to overlook how fundamentally we are tied to the most basic ways of living. You can lose all your electronics, but you can't stop eating grain. You can lose all your fancy restaurants, but you can't do without cereal, rice, and bread. Just as we should remember the source of our water, we should also remember the source of our grain: our very world is built upon it.

Bind our communities like sheaves—as heaven, earth, and hell are one land.

78 | Heaven, Earth, and Hell

- Fasting day
- Birthday of the **Great God of the Central Peak**
- Festival day of the **Mao Brothers**

The Great God of the Central Peak

The Central Peak of the Five Sacred Mountains (p. 44) is **Songshan** in Henan. Besides being the sixth of the Thirty-Six Lesser Grotto Heavens (p. 49), the mountain is also famous for the Shaolin Buddhist Temple, (Shaolin Si) associated with both Bodhidharma (p. 325) and Shaolin martial arts. The Great God of the Central Peak (Zhongyue Dadi) determines people's fortunes, the success of officials, and guards an entrance to the underworld.

The Mao Brothers

The eldest Mao brother is said to have ascended to heaven on this day in 97 BCE. Celebrations begin in the first moon and culminate on this day at the temples on **Maoshan** (Mao Mountain). Maoshan is the eighth of the Ten Greater Grotto Heavens and the first of the Seventy-Two Lesser Realms.

The eldest brother, **Mao Ying** (c. second century BCE), learned supernatural skills at Hengshan (p. 260). He later moved to practice on the mountain that would be named after him and became powerful enough to ascend into heaven.

Once this happened, his two brothers, both officials, resigned their posts, went to Maoshan, and, after practicing three years, became immortal and rode to heaven on yellow cranes.

Heaven, earth, and hell are one land,
with Tao flowing through everywhere.

The Great God of the Central Peak is a deity, yet dwells on earth in one of the grottoes that connect heaven and hell. The Mao brothers began as humans, practiced austerities in another grotto of heaven, and ascended to heaven itself. The borders between heaven, earth, and hell are not firm.

Heaven is rooted in the earth in the form of the Ten Continents, the Three Islands, the Ten Greater Grotto Heavens, the Thirty-Six Lesser Grotto Heavens, and the Seventy-Two Lesser Realms. Hell is not far away, but has entrances right here on earth. What is mystical and spiritual is not distant, but intermingled with earthly existence in the here and now.

Thus, every part of our spiritual world is present. The spiritual world is not relegated to an afterlife but is here and now. The Great God of the Central Peak has to guard the entrance because it's a usable passage. One can stand in heaven anywhere in the above 131 places—or, in fact, anywhere on earth. Gods live among us, from the Kitchen God to the Local Land to the gods of the Five Sacred Mountains.

Each human being is a microcosm of the greater whole. Heaven, earth, and hell are in us. Gods and demons alike are in us too. Every day, we should resolve not to travel the passages to hell, but to dwell in the heavenly grottoes, and to practice to become immortal.

With Tao flowing through everywhere, nothing destroys hope— not even in darkest night.

79 | Sunrise

• Birthday of the **Sun God**

Worship of the Sun God

The Sun God (Taiyang Xingjun) can be greeted at dawn with incense and ceremony wherever one happens to be, but a grand ceremony is also held on this day in his temple. He is also celebrated on the first day of the second moon (p. 39) and the nineteenth day of the eleventh moon (p. 375).

The Ten Suns

In the time of **Emperor Yao** (2357–2255 BCE), there were ten suns in the form of large birds. They roosted in a mulberry tree in the eastern sea, and each day Xihe, the mother of the suns, carried one of the birds in her carriage.

One day the birds decided to come out all at once. The crops shriveled, the lakes and ponds dried up, and humans and animals alike were nearly burned to death. Yao asked **Hou Yi**, a great archer, to shoot down nine of the suns. According to some legends, the tenth sun fled and had to be coaxed back by the intriguing sound of a cock's crow—which is why the rooster still greets the rising sun to this day.

Even in darkest night
a new dawn is coming.

Every one of us has been discouraged, depressed, frustrated, and defeated. We strive for an entire day and yet, despite all our best efforts, everything falls apart. Each hour of the night lets in new demons howling with doubt and visions of failure.

But every night ends.

It doesn't matter how discouraged we are. The next day is a new day. Go outside and look at the morning. The branches are green. Birds cross the sky. Whatever confusion we may have, the flight of birds shows that there is still intention, still will, still a way to find direction in vast uncertainty. The sparrows swoop down and perch momentarily before flying off. If they can find direction, so can we.

Why speak of some distantly future reincarnation? Every dawn is the reincarnation of the entire world and us along with it. Whatever happened yesterday is done and gone. Today follows yesterday, but today need not be completely determined by yesterday: today is always our chance at the new, the glowing, the brilliant.

Ten suns were too many. Ten possibilities, ten ambitions, ten directions, ten tomorrows—perhaps those are too many as well. Each day is new—one day, one opportunity, one life. There is only one sun, one target, one Way. Aim for that with all the might of an immortal archer and you will be the sun god.

A new dawn is coming, and a bowl of rice warms both our hands.

80 | A Bowl of Rice

Filling Bellies

In Chapter 3 of the *Daodejing,* Laozi writes: "This is why the sage's rule empties the people's hearts but fills their bellies." (The early part of the chapter indicates that he means to empty hearts of envy.)

Decrease

The statement of Hexagram 41 of the *I Ching*:

Decrease. Have confidence. Great fortune. No fault if one can be upright. Gain by having a place to go. How should one act? Two square bamboo baskets can be used in offering.

Even when poor, we keep our sense of virtue and offering. Hexagram 29, line 6, makes this clear:

A bottle of wine, a bamboo basket, and two bowls offered simply through a window. In the end, no fault.

Compare this to Confucius commenting on Yan Hui (p. 32):

How admirably virtuous Hui was! He had one bamboo dish of rice, one gourd of drink, and he lived in a narrow lane. Others could not have endured such deprivation, but his joy was unaffected. How admirably virtuous was Hui!

Eating from the Bowl While Eyeing the Pot

This depiction of someone eating from his rice bowl and all the while gazing at the pot for more food is the picture of greed and anxiety.

A bowl of rice warms both our hands.
A pot of rice can feed many.

A bowl of rice is a fundamental thing, not just in Asia, but in many other parts of the world. Having a bowl of rice means the difference between starvation and health.

A bowl of rice is comfort food to millions of people. Many of them hold the bowl and bend to the food. It's intimate. The rice is cupped in their hands. They savor the aroma and are grateful.

Rice can't be cooked in single portions. It would burn. That means that rice is inherently communal. A big pot of rice becomes the center of a shared meal. It means that there's plenty, too. If one more person comes to the table, there will still be enough rice for everyone to eat.

The person who eyes the pot even as he has a full bowl in his hands is greedy. Can you live this life with one eye on the afterlife? Should you worry about all that is going on in the world when you haven't even taken care of your own affairs? Why worry about all the gods in heaven if you haven't attended to your own body and mind? Isn't this all like "eating from the bowl while eyeing the pot"?

Everything becomes so simple with a bowl and the rice to fill it. Instead of worrying about whether we'll get more, we focus on what we have.

A bowl is empty. A bowl is made to be filled and then emptied again. A bowl that is always full cannot have any more added to it. A bowl that is always empty cannot fulfill its purpose either: it cannot nourish. The life of a bowl is the rhythm of filling and emptying with regularity.

When we hold rice in our hands we are assured that we will have enough to eat. When we give a bowl of rice or another helping to someone, it means we want that person to have enough to eat too. A bowl of rice makes all this compassion possible.

A pot of rice can feed many, so think of others as we scoop rice out of our pots.

81 | The Rice Paddle

As we scoop rice out of our pots,
we recall when we had little.

Everyone, from the most jaded king to the lowliest beggar, understands privation. The king is fearful of it; the beggar knows nothing else. There are plenty of people all over the world who have suffered starvation and hunger. Just because some developing nations are now facing obesity issues does not change the global reality of hunger. Too many of our brethren have no rice in their pots.

Don't think that any country, even the wealthiest in the world, is immune to hunger—if for no other reason than that no nation is immune to calamity. Every nation undergoes natural disaster on an annual basis. Hurricanes, blizzards, typhoons, earthquakes, tsunamis, floods, volcanic eruptions—every year nature topples our proud civilizations. These disasters quickly leave our fellow citizens homeless and hungry, and they add to the numbers of poor in every country who are hungry every day.

The rice paddle is such a common implement that it's seldom noticed. The handle is shorter than that of a cooking spoon. A paddle shape scoops the sticky rice more easily. And a rice paddle is excellent for one more task: scraping the sides of the pot so we don't waste anything.

Each time we eat, we remember when we too were poor and hungry. We don't waste. Not a grain gets overlooked, because we know what it's like to search madly even for one grain. Paradoxically, we don't hesitate to share, either—since we know hunger, we can feel sympathy for someone else who may be lacking what we can give.

Maybe you've been treated badly in the past. Maybe you held your hand out as others turned their backs. But don't repeat the cruelty that may have been inflicted upon you. All our bowls are the same. All our bowls measure out our rice and keep us alive. A person with a full bowl one day can easily have an empty one tomorrow. We all share in the human dilemma—and we all share in giving human kindness. We are kind, because we remember privation.

We recall when we had little, when offering a bowl of rice.

82 | Both Hands

Receiving with Both Hands

掬 The word *ju* means "to receive with both hands." The left side of the character is the sign for "hand." The right side is a wrapping around rice. "Ju" is often used to mean "wholeheartedly."

Confucius and Rice

The *Analects* describe Confucius's behavior as sparing:

> He did not eat much.... When eating, he did not converse.... Although his food might be coarse rice and vegetable soup, he would offer a little of it in sacrifice with a solemn and respectful air.

Chopsticks

Chopsticks *(kuaizi)* originated in China as early as the Shang dynasty (1600–1046 BCE). A pair of bronze chopsticks has been excavated from ruins dated to 1200 BCE.

When offering a bowl of rice,
make offering with both your hands.

Every child is taught this:
When offering a bowl of rice, offer it with both hands.
When giving a gift, give it with both hands.
When receiving a bowl of rice, receive it with both hands.
When receiving a gift, receive it with both hands.
When greeting someone, clasp both your hands in greeting.
We use both hands because it shows that we are being respectful and that we are giving all our attention. The worst thing is to give or receive carelessly, impolitely, or negligently.

Using both hands opens the way to reverence.

Chopsticks come in pairs. The two need to work in concert to be effective. Neither is longer than the other, and they need to be evenly matched in the hand to work properly. Isn't this the very lesson we need in working together? One chopstick is not useful. Two chopsticks are useful only if they are equal. The very model for cooperation is in our hands every day.

We give, we receive, and we bow using both hands. We don't emphasize the left more than the right. Both hands work equally. The same is true when we clasp our hands to pray: from basic sustenance to the highest spirituality, the lesson is simple, direct—and right there in our hands.

Make offering with both your hands, before the sea of life storms and death swells.

Mother Ancestor

Mother Ancestor is the literal translation of the name **Mazu**. Her worship began in Fujian, spread to the adjacent provinces of Zhejiang and Guangdong, and eventually extended to other coastal places such as Taiwan, Vietnam, Japan, Malaysia, and Singapore. She is the protector of sailors, fishermen, and the boat people who live their whole lives on floating vessels. She is known as Heavenly Empress (Tianhou), Heavenly Goddess (Tianfei), or simply Goddess (Niang Niang). Mother Ancestor has many names because her worship spread widely and because emperors over some eight hundred years added more titles, including State-Protecting Sage, Protector of the State and People, Prodigious Goddess, and Saintly Goddess.

According to her legend, Mother Ancestor was born in 960 to a fishing family on Meizhou Island, Fujian. Her birth name was Lin Moniang.

Moniang wore red clothing and sometimes stood on shore to guide fishermen home. She was an excellent swimmer and rowed a boat over stormy seas to rescue people thrown overboard.

One day a typhoon arose while her father and brothers were fishing. Moniang fell into a trance while praying for their safety. In her trance, Moniang saw her father and brothers, and took them one by one to safety by taking their small figures into her mouth. But her mother, thinking that Moniang had fainted or had died, tried to wake her and broke her concentration. Moniang had to make a slight sound to reassure her mother.

When her father and brothers returned, they said that they all had been saved by a miracle, except for one brother who had drowned—the one whom Moniang had been saving when her mother shook her.

There are at least two versions of Moniang's death. In one, she climbs a mountain at age twenty-eight and ascends to heaven. In the other, she dies at age sixteen after swimming into stormy seas and saving the ten-person crew of a merchant ship.

After her death, fishermen and sailors began to pray to Mother Ancestor for protection. They were moved by her courage in saving others from the perils of being on the ocean.

Zheng He and Mother Ancestor

Zheng He (1371–1435) was an admiral, explorer, diplomat, and Chinese Muslim who led fleets comprising hundreds of ships from China to Southeast Asia, India, Africa, and the Middle East.

While his expeditions are historical fact, a legend tells of his fleet being caught in a great storm in the Pearl River Delta of Guangzhou. The ships survived miraculously to continue their voyage. That night, Mother Ancestor, as Tianhou, appeared to Emperor Yongle (1360–1424), saying that she had saved the fleet and that she wanted a temple built at the site. The emperor obeyed, and a temple was built in 1410.

The Widespread Worship of Mother Ancestor

When emigrants left China by sea, they prayed to Mother Ancestor for protection. Once in their new homes, they gave offerings and erected temples to her in gratitude for their safe passage. There are about sixty Tin Hau (a variant spelling of Tianhou) temples in Hong Kong alone.

Mother Ancestor is both a Taoist and a Buddhist goddess. Some have asserted that she is a manifestation or reincarnation of Guanyin (p. 58). Mother Ancestor is often depicted with two guardian generals: Thousand-Miles Eye, a red demon with two horns, and With-the-Wind Ear, a green demon with one horn. It is said that Mother Ancestor conquered and subdued these two demons, and they became her guardians. She is depicted in red robes and sometimes as a full empress on a throne.

Mother Ancestor May Bring International Peace

Meizhou, Mother Ancestor's birthplace, is across the straits from Taiwan. The Republic of China on Taiwan regards itself as an independent nation, while the People's Republic of China regards Taiwan as a province. However, people from both sides of the straits gather in Meizhou to worship Mother Ancestor by the tens of thousands, establishing cooperation and paving the way for possible reconciliation and reunification. ▶

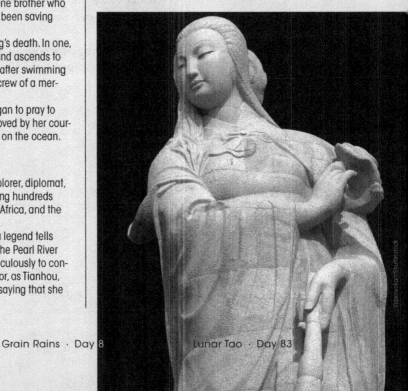

83 | Goddess of the Sea

▸ Birthday of **Mother Ancestor**
▸ Fasting day

The Worship of Mother Ancestor in the Qing Dynasty

Worship of Mother Ancestor during the Qing dynasty (1644–1911) was elaborate. In the city of Tianjin, where a rich merchant built a magnificent temple to her, elaborate festivals were held on this day. Each year, a statue of the goddess was borne in an imperial carriage from her temple to the Fujian-Guangdong guild hall in the northern section of the city. During the procession there were lion dances, flower drums, acrobatics, and music. The goddess stayed for three days of celebration, after which she returned to her temple in another elaborate procession.

One year, the Qing Emperor Qianlong (1711–1799) came to watch the celebration. He was so impressed that he awarded yellow jackets and festival banners as a sign of his approval (yellow clothing was normally worn solely by royalty). Due to this honor, the Goddess Festival was renamed the Imperial Festival.

Before the sea of life storms and death swells,
kneel and ask for your crossing to be blessed.

Living on the sea takes a special kind of person. There are some people who are born to be on the water, just as there are some people who lack that talent altogether. Certainly, the great expanse of the oceans draws the seafarer in an overwhelming way. The possibilities, the adventure, the exploration, the thrill of sailing toward a new horizon are so powerful that many people spend a lifetime on the seas.

Those who live on the seas learn to find support from the water. The oceans support the boat and provide fish. Currents can carry a ship hundreds of miles. The winds, so much a part of the seas, can fill a ship's sails for days at a time. For those who live on the ocean, everything can be gotten from it.

The seafarer respects the oceans too; the waves can crush a person in an instant. That's why those who live on the seas worship Mother Ancestor. Even if they are wise in the ways of the ocean, they know they have no control over the sudden storm, the rogue wave, the submerged rock, the behemoth from the depths. People can be as careful as possible, but that won't account for everything. Sometimes, they need divine intervention.

Crossing the oceans, whether as a long-term sailor or as a traveler, has an element of danger. The port where one lands, often as a stranger, can be dangerous too. Isn't this true of all our crossings? We can try to be safe, but we need divine help too.

All of us sail into the unknown nearly every day. May the goddess protect us, and may we in turn help others.

Kneel and ask for your crossing to be blessed, then travel from the Middle Kingdom.

84 | Not the Middle Kingdom

• Fasting day

The Middle Kingdom and Under Heaven

Early references to China in literature simply used the term **Tianxia**—literally, Under Heaven. The name Zhongguo—Middle Kingdom—appeared as early as the *Classic of History* (parts dating from 300 BCE) with the meaning of "Center of Civilization." The earliest known appearance of the name was on a bronze vessel of the Zhou dynasty that is more than 2,700 years old and is currently stored in the Baoji Museum in Shaanxi.

The Silk Road and International Trade

The **Silk Road** is a network of overland trade routes. Some of the routes lead from the north of China across the Middle East to Europe. Southern routes lead to India. Maritime routes lead to Korea, Japan, Southeast Asia, Ceylon, the Philippines, Arabia, the Mediterranean, and Africa. Thus, ancient China, India, Tibet, Persia, Egypt, Arabia, and Rome were interconnected, exchanging goods, culture, and religious beliefs.

Zhang Qian (200–114 BCE) was a diplomat and explorer and is one of the key figures in the early history of the Silk Road. His missions opened China to many countries and to trade from many parts of the world previously unknown. Details of his explorations are preserved in the *Records of the Grand Historian*.

Travel from the Middle Kingdom.
Under Heaven touches heaven.

It's said that China is called Zhongguo, the Middle Kingdom, because the ancient Chinese regarded themselves as the center of the world and China was closed to foreign influence.

If we stop our considerations there, we will miss a greater truth not only about China but about spirituality. China did not always close itself off to the world. The voyages of Zheng He (p. 98), centuries of trade over the Silk Road made possible by Zhang Qian, the spread of Buddhism from India, and the arrival of Islam in cities like Xi'an show that there were many links to other countries and continents. Chinese musical instruments like the *pipa* (lute) and *yangqin* (hammer dulcimer) can be traced to the Middle East; the broadsword *(dan dao)* is derived from the scimitar. Look at how places in China are believed to be part of heaven (p. 49), and suddenly China is not an isolated, inwardly looking kingdom at all.

Spiritually, we should not isolate ourselves and say that we are only of one tradition, or that we are uninterested in other spiritual systems, or that we deny that heaven can be a part of our current and everyday lives. The borders of the Middle Kingdom weren't completely closed, just as it turns out that the borders between earthly and heavenly life are not closed.

Under Heaven touches heaven, so wherever you are is under heaven.

Most of the major territory of the Silk Road. The Middle East is on the left, India below, and China on the right. NASA Earth Observatory

Tianxia

The term **Tianxia** appeared during the Zhou dynasty, some three thousand years ago, and in texts like the *Chronicles of Zuo (Zuo Zhuan,* c. 369 BCE) and the *National Discourses (Guoyu,* c. fifth century BCE). **Qin Shi Huang** (p. 159), declared that he wanted to unite all under heaven. The term appears widely in Confucian and Taoist texts, and is still used to this day.

Sun Yat-Sen

Sun Yat-Sen (Sun Yixian, 1866–1925) sparked the revolution that toppled the Qing dynasty and led to modern government in China. He wrote the famous phrase: *tian xia wei gong* or "All under heaven is for the people."

Sun Yat-Sen, a doctor, revolutionary, and political leader, was born in Zhongshan, a district of Guangdong, and hence is also popularly known as **Sun Zhongshan**. He worked long to establish Nationalist China, traveling to Singapore, Malaysia, England, Canada, Japan, Hawaii, and the mainland United States to gather crucial support among overseas Chinese. He was the first president of the Republic of China and the founder of the Chinese National People's Party (Kuomintang). However, a longer period of unrest and warfare followed, and stability did not return until the establishment of the People's Republic of China in 1949. Sun Yat-Sen may be the only political figure honored by both the People's Republic of China and the Republic of China on Taiwan.

Wherever you are is under heaven.
You are the heart of the Middle Kingdom.

China—Zhongguo—was not as isolated or closed as the name implies. People traveled the maritime routes to other continents with little more than wooden ships, compasses, maps, and human fortitude. Thousands of people traveled the Silk Road by donkey, horse, camel, or foot. The country benefited by this exchange. Modern China might not have come into being without support from its own emigrants and others outside its borders.

We must detach ourselves from rigid notions of race, cultural purity, location, and spiritual singularity. The history of exchange between China and other lands shows us far more flexible and far more open-minded meanings. There is no such thing as pure Chinese and there is no such thing as pure spirituality. We follow not the individual utterance of a single prophet, but thousands of years of joyous exchange.

No matter how far we travel, no matter if we have moved from our original birthplace, no matter if we are living in our birth country or "abroad," we must affirm our global allegiance and not be confined to nationalistic ones. We must affirm our human connection and not let our commitment to spirituality divide us. We must honor who we are, even if we live continents away from where we were born.

All the sojourners over millennia never escaped this: they were still under heaven. We are the center of wherever we are.

You are the heart of the Middle Kingdom, there when heaven sends down all its goodness.

The Silk Road traverses the Hindu Kush, a mountain range that stretches from Afghanistan to Pakistan before continuing to China.

Jeff Schmaltz, MODIS Rapid Response Team, NASA/GSFC; Visible Earth

86 | The Earth

Heaven, Earth, and Humans

Heaven, earth, and humans (*tian, di, ren*): This phrase summarizes basic cosmology. Consider this passage from the *Luxuriant Dew of the Spring and Autumn Annals (Chunqiu Fanlou)*, by Dong Zhongshu (179–104 BCE):

Heaven, earth, and humans are the source of all creatures. Heaven gives birth to them, earth nourishes them, and humans complete them. Heaven endows creatures at birth with kinship and loyalty. Earth nourishes them with food and clothing. Humans complete them through ritual and music.

A passage in the *Classic of History* states:

Heaven and earth are the parents of all creatures, and of all creatures, people are the most highly endowed.

And the commentary to Hexagram 1 of the *I Ching* gives us this passage:

Heaven's way is to send beneficial influences below, where they are brilliantly displayed. Earth's way, lying low, is to send its influences upward and to act. Heaven's way reduces the full and builds the humble. Earth's way undermines the full and replenishes the humble.

Tao is still behind both heaven and earth. The *Masters of Huainan* (p. 50) states: "As for Tao, it covers heaven and holds up the earth."

Heaven sends down all its goodness.
The earth sends up all its goodness.

Our feet must touch the ground. None of us float. We have to walk on the earth. Heaven is above. Earth is below. People live in between. There is no separation between heaven and earth. Heaven touches the earth everywhere. The earth rises to touch heaven everywhere. Therefore, we must all have our feet on the ground and our bodies and heads in heaven.

Furthermore, there is not one thing about us that is not of heaven or earth. The air we breathe is of heaven. The earth provides us with every material aspect of our lives. Everything we use, everything that shelters us, everything that feeds us is of the earth.

When we die, we return to the earth. Whether we are buried or cremated, in time, every single particle will go back to the earth. Everywhere, and in great and constant profusion, we see what happens next: the earth receives all the wastes and all the dead and brings forth miraculous life. Grass grows on the tombs by the next rains. The earth never stops transforming the dead into the living.

The earth sends up all its goodness, for you're in heaven and heaven is in you.

Inside Knows the Outside

How Heaven, Earth, and Humans are Macrocosm and Microcosm

Taoists view a human being as a microcosm of heaven and earth. This view is not simply an assertion, but is accompanied by theory intricate enough to command entire schools, lifetimes of study, and many volumes of writing. In addition, this theory forms the basis of traditional Chinese medicine.

Yin and Yang: Every aspect of heaven, earth, and humans can be viewed as either yin or yang. Furthermore, the power that animates them and every one of their actions also results from yin and yang.

The Five Phases (Wuxing, p. 422): All substances and all phenomena can be viewed according to the Five Phases Theory: fire, earth, metal, water, and wood. These five interact, generating and destroying one another in constant interplay. The Five Phases describe both substance and action—for example, fire is energy moving upward, while water is energy flowing downward. The Five Phases literally indicate macrocosm–microcosm in the human body: wood–liver; fire–heart; earth–spleen; metal–lungs; water–kidneys.

The Inner Gods: Some schools of Taoism believe that there are 36,000 tiny gods in the human body, each one corresponding to some part of the anatomy. These gods must be retained through moral and healthy living—or else they will gradually abandon the body in disgust.

You're in heaven and heaven is in you—
so you know heaven by knowing yourself.

We are heaven and earth in miniature. What happens in heaven and what happens on earth also happens inside us. We are not discrete entities isolated from what is around us. We stand in exact miniature correspondence to all that is larger than we are.

We breathe, we drink, we eat, we are anchored by gravity, we need the light and warmth of the sun. When it's about to rain, our joints swell.

These questions still imply outside and inside: Do we feel the rotation of the earth? Do the positions of the stars matter to us? Do the phases of the moon affect us? The Taoist response is that the full moon is *in* us. We are the full moon and the full moon is us.

If you would know the way of heaven, then you don't need to go to heaven. You only need to go within. By understanding yourself, you can understand heaven itself.

Some might wonder about all the different individuals in the world. How can they all contain the outer world too? The Taoist view is that all the great plurality, when multiplied by itself, yields a single reality: one.

So you know heaven by knowing yourself: take away from it, and nothing is lost.

© Ying Fry

88 | Neither Lost nor Gained

Zhuangzi on Heaven and Earth

Zhun Mang was on his way to the ocean when he met Yuan Feng, who asked him where he was going.

"I am going to the ocean," said Zhun.

"Why?"

Zhun Mang said: "It is the nature of the ocean that the waters which flow into it can never fill it, nor can those that flow from it drain it. I will enjoy myself, rambling by it. . . ."

Yuan Feng asked, "I should like to hear about the government by spiritual people."

Zhun Mang replied: "Men of the highest spirit-like qualities rise up on the light, and their bodies vanish. This is what we call being bright and ethereal. They carry out their powers with which they are endowed to the utmost, and not a single attribute goes unexplored. Their joy is that of heaven and earth, and all embarrassments of their affairs melt away and disappear. All things return to their proper nature. . . ."

Take away from it, and nothing is lost.
Add one speck to it, and nothing is gained.

We like to say that a human being is "just a speck" in the vast universe, but we don't really mean it. We still want to think of ourselves as significant, celebrate our ambitions, and thrill to the feelings of being human.

It's no accident that Taoist hermits of old lived on mountaintops. For one thing, there were fewer people to bother them. For another, civilization becomes tiny when viewed from a mountaintop. Even fields that cover many acres look like postage stamps. How much more insignificant are human beings?

And say one of those human beings died down in one of those distant fields. What difference would it make to infinite heaven or vast earth? On the cosmic scale, would anything be lost?

Then let's say that a baby was born in one of those distant fields, invisible from the mountaintop, yes, but let's say one was born anyway. On the cosmic scale, was anything added?

No soul was lost and no soul was added. Why?

What joins heaven and earth is the spiritual essence, Tao. Tao is infinite in width, length, and depth. The movement of one speck in one part of Tao affects every other speck. The slightest tremor in one particle makes every other particle vibrate too. Change upon change occurs. But no part of Tao is ever diminished and no part of Tao is ever augmented.

We are Tao.

Add one speck to it, and nothing is gained: and still you learn who you are by working.

89 | Work and Strive

• Fasting day

The Great Yu

The **Great Yu** (2200–2100 BCE) is one of China's legendary emperors. At that time, the land was plagued with floods, and Yu organized the dredging of the streams and rivers. He is still honored to this day for his engineering service. His temple and mausoleum are in Shaoxing.

This passage is from the *Classic of History:*

> King Gao Yao spoke: "Come Yu, and speak well."
>
> Yu bowed and said, "Oh my king, what can I say? Each day I have tried to be as diligent as possible."
>
> Gao Yao sighed: "How so?"
>
> Yu then replied: "Floods overflowed the sky, vast torrential floods deluged mountains and washed away grave mounds. People were left stunned and overwhelmed.
>
> "I drove a four-horse chariot around the mountains and cut down trees. With Yi, I taught the people how to get fresh fish and meat to eat.
>
> "I surveyed the nine provinces, gauged the distance to the seas, and dredged canals and streams to the rivers. Along with Ji, I showed the people how to sow grain—I can report that it has been difficult for people to find fresh food. I showed them how they could trade for whatever they needed. As a result, everyone had enough grain to eat, and the myriad states are well governed."
>
> Gao Yao said: "Excellent! We shall learn from your good speech."

You learn who you are by working.
Only challenge reveals limits.

Is this all there is to life? Are you satisfied with where you are? Or do you still need to work harder to achieve what you want?

This is not a matter of being richer or more accomplished than the next person. This is a matter of looking deeply at your life and asking if there is more that you need to do. If you're satisfied, then that's fine, and you should consider yourself lucky. But if you look at yourself and at the endless suffering all around you, then you may well feel that there is much more effort to be applied.

No divination will reveal the contours of your life. Only hard work and daily contemplation will. As when a farmer clears fields, only working will reveal how much can be cleared and how fertile the soil can be. How far will you go in life? Only by clearing the fields, planting, and working will you find out.

The Great Yu did not sit complacently. He saw the suffering of the people when the land was flooded and he set out to remedy it. When he was first called to the task, he had only been married four days, and the resulting campaign took him thirteen years. During that time, he passed his home three times but never went in, saying that since other people had no homes, he could not rest in his.

Yu saw the floods and worked to channel them. He traversed the nine provinces to do so. In putting limitations on floods, he found his own limitations. In putting limitations on floods, he made the limitless feeding of his people possible.

Only challenge reveals limits—that was why the hermit failed to find Peach Blossom Spring,

▸ Fasting day

Tao Yuanming

Tao Yuanming (365–427), also known as Tao Qian, is one of China's greatest and most beloved poets. (Note that his name is *not* the same word as Tao, the Way.) His great-grandfather had been a famous general and governor, but Tao Yuanming's family fell into poverty. Although Tao served in a series of minor government posts, the official life did not suit him and he lived in retirement for his last twenty-two years to concentrate on poetry, wine, and growing chrysanthemums. In addition to his poetry, Tao is known for the prose work "Preface to the Poem on the Peach Blossom Spring." Here is a brief version of the story.

Peach Blossom Spring

During the Taiyuan era of the Eastern Jin dynasty (376–396), a fisherman named Wuling was sailing upstream and lost track of how far he had gone. Suddenly, he came to a forest of peach trees in full flower on both banks. The air was dense with drifting petals.

Astonished, the fisherman rowed farther to see where the exquisite forest would end. He found a spring at the head of the stream—and a small opening in the adjacent hillside through which he could see light. He crawled through, and after twenty feet, he came to another land with farms, homes, and people strolling about.

The residents were startled to see the fisherman. They had retreated into that hidden valley during the upheaval of the Qin dynasty (p. 159) nearly six centuries before. After remaining for several days, the fisherman went home. He told the governor, who promptly sent soldiers to investigate—but they could not find Peach Blossom Spring.

A man of refinement named Liu Ziji planned to search himself, but he died before he found it, and no one has made any other attempt.

The hermit failed to find Peach Blossom Spring. Unsuccessful, he died of a sickness.

The ghost of Liu Ziji said: "I heard the story of Peach Blossom Spring, and I went in search of this paradise. Where else would I ever find a group of people who had found a refuge from this corrupt world and who still lived according to the ways of the ancients?

"I traveled the length of the stream. I searched in vain for the opening that the fisherman had found. I hiked over the mountains—surely the valley had to be on the other side. How gloomy I felt when I found nothing. It was a rebuke, a sign that heaven reproached me for my arrogance. Heaven struck me with illness.

"Now I lie in bed, listless, weak, and sad. It's not that I failed to find paradise, it's that I succumbed to the folly of attempting to find a utopia. There isn't one. I wanted a pure land, when deep down, I already knew that there is no land but this, and that purity exists not in some sequestered place, but grows from filth in the same way that the radiant white lotus is rooted in mire.

"In my fever, I dream that I'm in the boat, still searching. Suddenly, I sit up, astonished. It was not the opening that I should have been searching for! All around me the air was swirling with peach blossoms. The trees were right there, only I sailed right by them, intent on the story, blind to the reality. Could those trees have borne the peaches of immortality? The blossoms were falling on my face, sticking in my white beard. The message couldn't have been more clear. I already was in paradise, only to miss it because I was deceived by words.

"Such is the foolishness of an old man. Such is the danger of learning. Such is the confusion that springs from listening to others instead of seeing with one's own open eyes and open heart.

"I, Liu Ziji, hermit who has lived for centuries, hermit who was already learning when those villagers fled the Qin dynasty, now lie dying, with all my efforts for naught.

"But what's this? A peach blossom floats through the window . . ."

Unsuccessful, he died of a sickness, muttering, "If you want to pray, let go of your sword."

4

The Plum Moon

Returning to Live in the South

I sow beans under the south hill—
flourishing weeds, meager bean sprouts.
Rise at dawn to clear tangled brush.
Lift my hoe and lead the moon home,
my trail narrow with grass and trees.
The evening dew dampens my clothes,
but wet clothes are of no concern
as long as my hopes aren't thwarted.
—Tao Yuanming (365–427)

The two solar terms within this moon:

SUMMER BEGINS

GRAIN FILLS

Exercise 7

SUMMER BEGINS

Depending on where in the world you are, this time may still be late spring. Certainly the hot weather of extreme summer is still approaching. The amount of rain that falls at this time will determine the size of the harvest.

People are traditionally careful of their diet at this time, emphasizing low-salt, low-fat, and high-fiber foods. Eggs are also customary. There is a saying, "If you eat eggs at the time of Summer Begins, paving stones will break beneath your feet."

Huangdi on Summer

In the three moons of summer,
all nature flourishes handsomely.
Heaven's and earth's energy
    intermingle.
The myriad things are glorious and
    fruitful.

Go to sleep later and rise early,
but be mindful of the next day.
Be determined, but avoid anger.
Be splendid, brave, successful, and
    elegant.

This exercise is best practiced during the period of 3:00–7:00 A.M.

1. Sit with one knee up, foot flat on the floor, hands clasped around the leg just below the knee. Close your eyes.

2. Pulling in gently, turn your head to look backward. Inhale as you pull; exhale gently when you relax and change sides. Repeat thirty-five times on each side.

3. Sit cross-legged and face forward. Click your teeth together thirty-six times. Roll your tongue between your teeth nine times in each direction. Form saliva in your mouth by pushing your cheeks in and out. When your mouth is filled with saliva, divide the liquid into three portions.

4. Inhale; then exhale, imagining your breath traveling to the dantian and then swallow one-third of the saliva, imagining that it travels to the dantian.

5. Repeat two more times until you've swallowed all three portions.

6. Sit comfortably as long as you like.

Through this exercise, ancient Taoists sought to prevent or treat wind (excessive pressure or movement) and dampness in the acupuncture meridians and capillaries; swelling in the arms and legs; and excess heat in the palms.

91 | Disarm

▸ Fasting day

**From Chapter 31 of the
Daodejing**

Men's weapons are inauspicious tools.
All creatures loathe them.
Therefore, those who have Tao do not
    wield them.

When the noble one stays home, he
    emphasizes the left,
but if he uses weapons, he emphasizes
    the right.

Weapons are inauspicious tools.
They are not the tools for a noble
    person. . . .

Later in this same passage, Laozi
states that "in auspicious times, value
is placed on the left, and in harsh
times value is placed on the right." In
the above passage, the noble one staying peacefully at home is auspicious.
Moving to the right represents the
harsh and inauspicious.

If you want to pray, let go of your sword.
If you want to bow, unstrap your armor.

Ordinarily, we strive to be more clever and powerful every day.
That is necessary and understandable. We live in a competitive
world, and those who win are admired and rewarded.

However, cleverness and power form an armor that is useful for
battle but useless for spiritual life. The sword of professionalism
may lay waste to your competitors and make you enormous sums
of money, but it will not help you pray.

Living a spiritual life means being completely open to heaven
and earth. If you want to be completely open to heaven and earth,
then you don't want any blockages. There are no greater blockages
than the armor and weapons we use in our daily lives.

From the grimmest corporate raider to the most ordinary
householder, we are all in competition and striving in one way or
another. There is no one who lives in the ordinary world who does
not wear armor and swing a sword. Therefore, if you want to meditate and be spiritual, you need to disarm. You need to put down
your sword, unbuckle your armor, clean yourself, and dedicate
yourself to the holy.

Spiritual people dedicate themselves to the sacred in everyday
life. When we disarm and join them, we can breathe easily and
freely. When we walk a holy path, we will find the spirit—and with
the spirit, there will be peace.

*If you want to bow, unstrap your armor, then close your eyes if
you want to see the spirit within.*

92 | Let Go of Fear

The State of the True Person

A **True Person** (Zhenren) is one name for the ideal Taoist. Zhuangzi wrote:

> How do we speak of the "True Person"? The True Person of old did not disdain being among the few; they did not try to be accomplished heroes; they did not engage in the plans of scholars. Even if they made some mistakes, they had no regrets. If they had success, they did not try to take credit for themselves.
>
> Therefore, they could climb the highest heights without trembling. They could dive into water without sinking. They could enter fire without being burned. It was because of this that they rose to be with Tao.

If you want to see the spirit within,
then let go of the fear that turns your head.

It's easy to say, "Let go of fear." It's not that easy to do. In fact, fear is a necessary, and it has its usefulness. But like many things, fear is only useful if it's kept in its proper place. When there's no use for fear, then it must not operate.

Some people are afraid to meditate, or to acknowledge their own power. They look within, they engage in spiritual practices, but upon having any actual results, they are frightened and stop. It's an odd dichotomy, isn't it? We practice to gain a result, and when the result comes, we're so shocked that we stop.

Alternatively, sometimes it's fear that keeps us from getting spiritual results. Inevitably, spiritual practice will uncover repressed feelings and memories. After all, spiritual practice is a process of self-examination and cleansing. Well, if we have problems in our past that need to be cleansed, it's obvious that we're going to encounter them in our practice. That's when some people turn away, because they're too afraid to confront the pain that they carry inside them.

If we can be safe when we meditate, then we can let go of our fears. No one is going to hurt us. That takes care of the fear of outside threats. Then we have to dedicate ourselves to practice. We *want* to improve our lives. That takes care of the fear of results. Then all we have to do is look wide-eyed at our demons. They are frightening, yes. But they are ghosts, without power. It turns out that the real demon is fear itself.

Then let go of the fear that turns your head, without worrying whether the doors open either inward or outward.

The Doors of Laozi

In the *Daodejing*, Chapter 47, Laozi writes:

> Without going out of the door,
> know all under heaven.
> Without peeking from the window,
> see heaven's Tao.
> The farther one travels,
> the less one knows.
> Therefore, the sage doesn't move, but
> still knows,
> does not see things but can still name
> them,
> does not act but still completes.

Doors open either inward or outward.
Just understand whether to push or pull.

We control our lives by doors. Every building has doors. Every room has a door. Our cars have doors, our elevators, our toilets, our closets. Castles and palaces have enormous thick doors meant to hold back armies for months, while a tiny playhouse door is meant to give a child the chance for privacy and fantasy.

With the exception of swinging doors, the vast majority of doors open in only one direction. Perhaps that seems obvious, but the truth is that if you want to open a door, you have to move it in the direction that it's made to open. If you don't know whether to push or pull, you'll stand beside it in frustration. The same is true of anything in life. There are many times when the difference depends simply on perceiving whether to push or pull.

We also have doors in our bodies: the nine openings. The obvious ones are the eyes and the mouth. Spiritual people train themselves simply by knowing when to open and close these doors. Open your eyes to see the outer Tao. Close your eyes to see the inner Tao. Close your mouth to breathe in the divine breath through your nose, open your mouth to release exhaust. Simple.

We have doors around our souls. Some are there naturally, boundaries to pass on the way to freeing our spirits. Some have been put there by circumstance: doors of fear and trauma. All these doors have to be open if the spirit is to be free. Use these doors. The challenge is no more than knowing whether to push or pull.

Just understand whether to push or pull, if you would see that form is emptiness.

94 | Form Equals Emptiness

▸ Festival day for **Manjusri**

Manjusri Bodhisattva

Manjusri Bodhisattva (Wenshu Pusa) is believed to live on Wutaishan in Shanxi, a holy mountain also revered by Taoists. He is said to grant visionary experiences on the peaks and in the caves.

Manjusri has been called the oldest and most significant bodhisattva in Mahayana literature, and he symbolizes the embodiment of transcendental wisdom. The *Lotus Sutra* (p. 307) places him in a pure land called Vimala, one of the best paradises in all the past, present, and future.

Manjusri is depicted with a double-edged sword (symbolizing logic and analytic discrimination) in his right hand and the *Prajnaparamitra Sutra (Bore Boluomiduo)* in his left hand.

There is another *Prajnaparamitra* called the *Heart Sutra (Xinjing)*. It has become embedded so deeply in the culture that it appears inscribed on teapots, and Hong Kong pop singers have set the sutra to music to raise money for charitable causes. The thesis of the sutra is contained in these lines:

> Form does not differ from emptiness; emptiness does not differ from form. Form itself is emptiness; emptiness itself is form. So too are feeling, cognition, formation, and consciousness.

Form is emptiness.
Emptiness is form.

Form is emptiness. Emptiness is form. Mathematically speaking, form equals emptiness, and the reverse is equally true. But what does emptiness mean here?

One way to think of this emptiness is to accept that all meaning is provisional. Nothing has any inherent or independent meaning. Money that is a delight to a city person might be of no value to someone dwelling in a forest. A car that might seem to be a luxury vehicle in the city would be useless in a desert. Or just look at what happens in a natural disaster: people abandon everything in an instant to flee. Emptiness means that no object has inherent value. Therefore, we should not depend on the material world as if it has any particular value to us.

Yet where do these forms come from? Ultimately, they must come from emptiness. If we want to look back for the "ultimate cause," we must search for a nonmaterial source. Any material source raises the possibility of what created it. The only possible source for the material is the nonmaterial—emptiness. Something

comes from nothing, and something returns to nothing. This is not limited to a one-time event, like the Big Bang. It's happening all the time on levels both grand and subatomic.

The sutra goes on to say that our feelings, cognition, formation, and consciousness are also empty. We are empty too, meaning that our thoughts and feelings don't have inherent or lasting value. We are emptiness as form, and the truth lies in perceiving that.

Emptiness is form; once known, even a householder can surpass a Buddha.

95 | The Householder

The Vimalakirti Sutra

Vimalakirti (Weimojie) was an elder who lived in the town of Vaisali. Although he was married and had children, he observed all the Buddhist vows and became more highly accomplished than bodhisattvas.

Once, Buddha was about to give a discourse to five hundred disciples, 32,000 bodhisattvas, and hundreds of other spiritually advanced beings. Vimalakirti pretended to be ill and did not attend. Buddha asked someone to inquire about the elder's health. However, because each of them had been dumbfounded in previous encounters with Vimalakirti and had been unable to match his eloquence in expounding the dharma, all the disciples and all the bodhisattvas were afraid to go. Only Manjusri (p. 112) agreed to go.

The encounter that follows forms the body of the *Vimalakirti Sutra,* and records the great teaching that emerged out of the discussions between Vimalakirti, a layperson, and Manjusri, the great bodhisattva. When they heard that this exchange was about to take place, the hundreds of thousands of attendees all miraculously fit into Vimalakirti's house to hear the discourse.

Manjusri asked why Vimalakirti was ill and the elder replied: "Since all living beings are subject to illness, I am ill as well. When all living beings are no longer ill, my illness will come to an end. Why? A bodhisattva, because of his vow to save living beings, enters the realm of birth and death and is subject to illness . . . a bodhisattva loves all living beings as if they were his sons . . . when they recover, he is no longer ill."

A householder can surpass a Buddha: everything is empty, even a name.

Vimalakirti appeals to the popular imagination because he is a householder—someone who lives a lay life—and yet demonstrates himself to be wiser than the disciples of Buddha and thousands of bodhisattvas. Not only is it possible for a layperson to be enlightened, it's possible for that person to understand spiritual truth in an unusual way. The encounter between Manjusri and Vimalakirti, a dramatic moment to be sure, was popular enough to become the subject of a number of Chinese paintings, including several of the frescoes at Dunhuang (a major stop on the Silk Road with many richly decorated cave temples) and a number of surviving ink paintings.

What counts is insight, not official titles. What counts is independent thinking, not mere study of doctrine. What counts is understanding, not the supernatural power that many of the attendees at Vaisali manifested.

We who worship at temples and who consult with priests and teachers should remember this: we are not supposed to simply be religious clients the rest of our lives. We are actually trying to reach the level of bodhisattvas, Buddhas, immortals, and gods. We are not supposed to be like them, no matter how impressive they are. We are supposed to be like ourselves, except that by observing the precepts and relying on our own insight, we transcend our worldly illness. Like Vimalakirti, we can love all living beings, nursing them back to health, and "when they recover," we will no longer be ill.

Everything is empty, even a name, yet we still see how a mother carries her child.

96 | What We Carry

The Migration of the Zhou

Early in the history of the Zhou people, a leader known as the **Ancient Duke** (Gugong Danfu; c. twelfth century BCE) led them away from a nomadic life into an agricultural one. No sooner did they prosper, however, than the other nomadic tribes made raids to plunder and enslave the Zhou.

The people wanted to fight, but the Ancient Duke said, "The people want to fight, but I have no heart to see fathers and sons slaughtered for my sake." So the Zhou migrated, moving all their things, supporting the old people, and carrying their children. They crossed the Qi and Ji Rivers, climbed past the Liang Mountains, and settled at the foot of Mount Qi. The site today is Qishan County in Shaanxi.

A mother carries her child,
A sage carries the relics.

When you see a mother carrying a child through the streets, the love is unmistakable. The child is precious to the mother, and the child is nurtured and taught by the mother's unconditional giving. The child too is relaxed and feels completely safe. If there's any doubt that human beings have tangible examples of great love and devotion, one need only see the simple sight of a mother carrying her child.

Holy people carry their relics and their scriptures too. The people who traveled the Silk Road in both directions included religious people. Buddhist monks traveled the Silk Road, a route of more than 1,600 miles, from India to Kashgar (now in the Xinjiang Uyghur Autonomous Region) to the then capital of Xi'an (then known as Chang'an). They carried their scriptures, relics, and teachings with the same tenderness and devotion as a mother carrying her child.

What we carry is what we hold precious. We hug it to our hearts, we protect it with our arms, we are moving it because we are willing to risk the dangers of the road for a greater good.

The world is a harsh place. It's good to remember that the commitment of the carrier is as beautiful as what is being carried.

A sage carries the relics, silently showing that accounts of hell are bad fiction.

© Saskia Dab

97 | How Dull Hell Is

Dongyue Temples

The Dongyue temple is located on the mountain of Pu Xian in Shanxi. Its earliest history isn't known, but it was already famous as early as 1205.

The temple honors the **Great God of the Eastern Peak** (Dongyue Dadi), the god of Taishan (p. 44). The temple is notable for its depiction of hell. The **Eighteen Levels of Hell** occupy fifteen caves beneath the temple, with life-sized clay statues of all five gods of the Sacred Mountains, the kings and officials of hell, other gods and demons of Taoism, and scenes of punishment: people having to climb a mountain of knives, being boiled in oil, being dismembered by a mill or saws, and so on.

Beijing has another Dongyue temple, with a hundred life-sized, fully colored plaster statues depicting seventy-six departments and eighteen layers of hell. Punishment is amply illustrated in the Life and Death Department, the Final Indictment Department, and the Department for Implementing Fifteen Kinds of Violent Death. One can also seek assistance at offices such as the Department for Good Fortune and Longevity or the Department for the Cure of Deep-Rooted Disease. The temple is especially busy on festival days such as the Spring Festival or the Moon Festival.

Both the temple in Pu Xian and the one in Beijing are far from Taishan, located in Shandong. The fact that the Great God of the Eastern Peak is worshipped from so far away shows the reverence in which he's held.

Accounts of hell are bad fiction—
the crises of inner visions.

When you have the time, do a little research and read accounts of hell. It actually doesn't take long, and you can probably even cover a couple of different religions in one sitting. Review the scriptures, the literature, the horror movies. In old China, there were even temples with life-sized re-creations of hell complete with luridly painted statues of tortures.

But if you look at this with any discrimination, you'll see well-intentioned people threatening you with universal fears: pain, torture, loneliness, retribution, and a merciless bureaucracy. If, as Buddha said, all of life is suffering, then all of hell is extreme suffering—intentionally inflicted for eternity.

Is there a hell? If so, and if it looks like the accounts given to us, what an awful deal existence is. But the implausibility of hell raises questions about the rest of the afterlife. If a good afterlife is a time of endless bliss without unpleasant consequences, does that make any sense? Existence becomes one sliver of time on earth leading to either extreme pain or extreme bliss. That doesn't really seem consistent with anything we truly know.

The stories of hell are dull and unconvincing. The tales of the afterlife seem to be wishful thinking. Better to concentrate on the here and now.

The crises of inner visions were only broken when Buddha remembered his father plowing.

Cheung Chau Bun Festival

The **Cheung Chau Bun Festival** (Changzhou Taiping Qingjiao) is held solely on the island of Cheung Chau near Hong Kong. It is an important example of how the Taoist *jiao* (ceremonial offering and sacrifice) festival is still being held today and how a festival can be the centerpiece of its community. The festival honors a number of gods we've already seen: the North God, Mother Ancestor, and Guanyin. The celebration draws tens of thousands of visitors to its colorful procession and the unique tower of buns climbed by skilled athletes.

In the eighteenth century, the island of Cheung Chau was devastated both by plague and by invasions of pirates (caves on the island were ideal hiding places). Local fishermen brought a statue of **Pak Tai** (the North God, p. 77) and carried the god through the streets at the head of a procession. According to legend, both the plague and the pirates were driven away.

Ever since, the festival has been repeated annually. Today, it has developed into a seven-day festival that culminates on the eighth day of the fourth moon. Many of the island's people observe a vegetarian diet during this time. During a grand procession led by colorful flags, gongs, drums, musicians, and lion dancers, the North God's statue is carried in an elaborate gold and red palanquin. He's followed by a parade that includes people dressed in the vivid colors of medieval warriors, monks, priests, and famous heroes, more lion dancers, martial artists, gongs, musicians, bikini-clad dancers, local dignitaries, and marching bands.

The highlight of the procession is the Parade in the Air, where children appear to float above the heads of the marchers. They are dressed in the lovely traditional costumes of famous heroes, folk figures, or gods. Some of them appear to be standing on the tips of swords, flowers, or fans. Others float above another child, balanced upon an upheld object—anything from a miniature tower of buns to an abacus. In actuality, the floating child is safely braced by a hidden steel framework bolted to a rolling cart. The streets are packed with spectators, with residents peering out windows or leaning from balconies in the heat of the tropical sun.

The North God is worshipped not only because people believed he subdued the original plague and pirate problems, but because he is believed to protect fishermen and sailors, and because he will ensure that the fishermen catch plenty of fish.

The other gods included in the celebration all have to do with the lives of the people: they protect from the dangers of the oceans, hear the prayers of the people, grant good fortune, and help women conceive. Mother Ancestor (p. 98), known locally as Tin Hau, protects sailors, fishermen, and boat people; gives warning of imminent storms through dreams or intuition; and helps to save people from shipwrecks. Guanyin (p. 58) is worshipped for her mercy and protection, and Hung Shing (p. 51), the God of the South, grants wishes and also protects from the perils of the sea.

The Bun Snatching

The major event of the festival takes place in front of the Pak Tai Temple. In the past, there were three bun towers, known as *baoshan* or "bun mountains." These sixty-foot-high bamboo towers were covered with steamed buns, each one stamped with red characters reading "Northern [God] Society." Young men raced up the towers to snatch a bun from as high on the towers as possible. The higher the bun, the more good fortune was supposed to accrue to the family of the climber. However, in 1978, one of the towers collapsed and more than one hundred people were injured.

Since then, a steel tower anchored by cables has been erected, the buns are made of plastic, and the climbers are selected in earlier competitions. The competitors are safely secured with belays as they race up the tower. Once at the top, they fill sacks tied behind their waists with as many buns as possible—steadied by the belays, they do this with both hands—and then rappel as quickly as possible back to the bottom. This all takes place in a raucous carnival atmosphere, with cheering crowds, tourists, and television news cameras. ▶

Benjwong

Laszlo Ilyes

Sakyamuni Buddha

Sakyamuni (Sage of the Sakyas, 563–483 BCE), born as Siddhartha Gautama, is known around the world as **Buddha** (Enlightened One). He was born in what is now Nepal and taught mostly in eastern India. Buddhism is estimated to be the fourth-largest religion in the world.

Siddhartha Gautama

Siddhartha was born to King Suddhodana and Queen Maha Maya. Sadly, Queen Maya died shortly after giving birth. The child was named **Siddhartha,** meaning "he who achieves his aim." At his birth celebration, the hermit seer Asita prophesied that the infant would become either a great king or a holy man. During the naming ceremony, eight Brahman scholars gave the same dual prediction.

King Suddhodana did not want his son to become a holy man and therefore made every effort to have the young prince raised in comfort and luxury. Siddhartha was married at sixteen to Yasodhara and fathered a son.

At the age of twenty-nine, Siddhartha left the palace to meet his subjects. Despite his father's attempts to prevent exposure to anything that might turn the prince toward the holy life, the prince had a series of experiences that led to his spiritual questioning.

When Siddhartha first saw a frail old man, he did not know what he was seeing. His charioteer explained that all people aged. Eventually, the prince ventured farther from the palace, and he saw a diseased man, a decaying corpse, and an ascetic.

Deeply affected, Siddhartha left the palace and became a mendicant. He wanted to overcome aging, sickness, and death through an ascetic life. He studied with two teachers, both of whom wanted him to be their successor, but Siddhartha was not satisfied and moved on. He then joined a group of five other ascetics, and together they tried to take their austerities further. They gave up all worldly goods, restricted their food drastically, and even practiced self-mortification.

But Siddhartha collapsed from such extreme practices, and he reconsidered asceticism. As he remembered a time when he was watching his father plowing, he entered a deep meditation.

Realizing that asceticism was not for him, Siddhartha perceived the **Middle Way**—a spiritual path of moderation that steered clear of both self-indulgence and self-mortification. Starved and weakened, he accepted milk and porridge from a village girl who mistook him for a spirit due to his emaciated appearance. His five companions abandoned him because he had forsaken the vows of asceticism.

Fortified again, Siddhartha seated himself under a bodhi tree and vowed not to leave until he had found the truth. After forty-nine days of constant meditation, during which he was tempted by Mara, a demon who tried to distract Siddhartha

Sculpture of the seated Buddha from the Longmen Grottoes, south of Luoyang. Carved for the Empress Wu Zetian (p. 419) in 676.   Alex Kwok

with visions of beautiful women, he became enlightened and was thereafter known to followers as the Buddha.

The Four Noble Truths

Upon his enlightenment, Buddha understood and eventually taught four truths:

1. All of life is suffering.
2. The cause of suffering is craving (for delight, lust, identity, existence, and extermination).
3. There can be an end to suffering.
4. The **Eightfold Path** can lead to the end of suffering.

The Eightfold Path

1. Right view
2. Right intention
3. Right speech
4. Right action
5. Right livelihood
6. Right effort
7. Right mindfulness
8. Right concentration

Further Concepts

Some additional concepts are: mental and physical dissatisfaction with life causes suffering; teachings should only be accepted if they match our experience and if they are praised by the wise; all things must come to an end; and nothing can really be called "I" or "mine." ◗

98 | Plowing to Bliss

‣ Fasting day
‣ The **Cheung Chau Bun Festival**
‣ Birthday of **Sakyamuni Buddha**

Dhyana, Jhana, Chan, Zen

Dhyana is the Sanskrit term for a meditative state of deep stillness and concentration. **Jhana** is the Pali, **Chan** is the Chinese, and **Zen** is the Japanese version. (Thus the very name Chan or Zen means "deep meditation.")

Saccaka was a Jain and follower of Nigantha Nataputta—another spiritual teacher contemporary to Buddha. The *Maha Saccaka Sutta* (the *Longer Discourse to Saccaka*) is based on two interviews Saccaka held with Buddha.

Buddha recounted how the practice of austerities did not lead him to a superior human state or special knowledge. He had been practicing many austerities in an effort to detach himself from sensual and worldly attachments. Finally, he asked himself if there might be another path to awakening. He recalled sitting in the cool shade under a rose-apple tree to watch his father plowing. As he thought of this memory, he entered into a great calm. It was his first moment of meditation.

Understanding that it was meditation and not asceticism that was the path to awakening, Buddha broke his fast and ate some porridge. His five fellow ascetics were disgusted that he would abandon the path of self-mortification and left, thinking that he was reverting to a life of indulgence.

Thereafter, Buddha entered additional levels of jhana.

Buddha remembered his father plowing
and he entered a fresh meditation.

Siddhartha (Sakyamuni Buddha, p. 117), growing disillusioned with the established spiritual traditions, first tried asceticism, but then realized that it would not be the right path for him. He collapsed in a river while bathing and almost drowned. When he remembered watching his father at the start of the plowing season, he entered a deep meditation. (Note that this story either is symbolic or showed Buddha's father ceremonially plowing, since his father was a king.)

It's instructive that Siddhartha's early breakthrough was triggered by a memory of his father and was tied to working in the fields and the seasons themselves. This is the very logic of what we are exploring: that the seasons lend us the circumstances for spiritual growth, that we are tied to our family—even if we are wandering mendicants— and that the act of plowing symbolizes our spiritual training. Just as there will be no crops without the initial step of plowing, so too will we miss out on a spiritual harvest if we don't take the right steps and work hard.

And he entered a fresh meditation when Buddha attained his enlightenment.

99 | There Is a Way

The Eightfold Path

The Eightfold Path (p. 117) can be divided into three parts.

The first two paths, right view and right intention, form the path of wisdom. Right view begins with the perception of our own inner nature as well as the truth about the world in which we live. Right intention is the commitment to a full Buddhist practice.

The next three paths are right speech, right action, and right livelihood. Together, these make up the path of ethical conduct. We control how we speak, act, and make a living in order to cultivate wholesomeness in ourselves.

The final three paths are right effort, right mindfulness, and right concentration. These join into the path of mental discipline. The key to this is to work toward spiritual growth in the right way, to cultivate awareness, and to practice meditation.

Both Taoists and Buddhists would agree on the basic ideas of the Eightfold Path. Taoists believe in an overall path. In this case, the detailed practices of the Buddhists form a concrete approach to joining the Way.

Rosemania

When Buddha attained his enlightenment
he found the way that halted suffering.

The Four Noble Truths (p. 117) include the declaration that a path can lead to the end of suffering. This is known as the Eightfold Path, but it's important to see that this path is synonymous with the Way—Tao.

Now, there are definitely differences between Buddhism and Taoism. There is no reason to try to impose Buddhism on Taoism or to try to assert that Taoism is inside Buddhism. Historically, some Chinese tried to assert that Buddha was a reincarnation of Laozi, but that was obviously a political attempt to reconcile the native Laozi with the foreign Buddha.

We can learn from both Buddhism and Taoism—as millions of people have done and continue to do. There are remarkable similarities, which is why the two traditions can be compatible, but each one must be given its own due respect.

Both Laozi and Buddha speak of a path or way. Buddha may have referred to an Eightfold Path, and Laozi might simply have said that "the Way that can be told is not the constant Way," but both great sages were pointing to the same way.

What's remarkable is that there is a way, and we can find it and walk it. We often find ourselves in spiritual wastelands. We sometimes feel lost. It's important to remember that there is a way we can follow to find a better way of life. And if we're persistent, that way can lead to jhana and beyond.

He found the way that halted suffering, accepting that the spirit dwells in your body.

100 Body and Spirit

He Xiangu

He Xiangu is the only woman among the **Eight Immortals** (p. 124). She is depicted with a lotus leaf or bamboo ladle filled with the mushroom of immortality, peach, bamboo, pine sprigs, and narcissus flowers (all symbols of immortality).

When she was about fifteen years old, a god appeared to her in a dream and instructed her to eat powdered mica. Along with other alchemical practices, this made her immune from death. Lady He pursued immortality and vowed to remain a virgin.

She grew so light that she could travel over the hills and valleys as if she had wings. Each dawn, she would wander the countryside and then bring mountain fruits back to her mother. Eventually, Lady He gave up ordinary food altogether.

He Xiangu ascended to heaven in broad daylight in about the year 707. She was seen again in 750 standing on rainbow clouds. In 772, she reportedly appeared in the flesh in Guangdong.

The spirit dwells in your body.
Can you train them at the same time?

Buddha's final realization came after he had meditated for forty-nine days. After that, he gave discourses in great detail. The religion that originated with him developed an extensive canon, and meditation remained a part of what it means to be Buddhist.

Worship is important. Reading the sutras is important. Compassion and service to others are important. All of those things, however, are bound up in dhyana, jhana, Chan, Zen, meditation. Spirituality may be devotional and intellectual, but it also requires sitting down, stilling oneself, observing the breath, and entering into stillness.

Taoism is the same. Countless immortals have learned meditative techniques as well as intellectual ones. They realized that physical transformation is just as important as mental and spiritual change. Taken metaphorically, the tale of He Xiangu has all the hallmarks of Taoist practice: controlling one's diet to transform oneself, vowing to remain pure, and wandering in nature.

Therefore, to be spiritual is not to dwell in one aspect or another, but to practice all of them at the same time.

Can you train them at the same time, and yet remember that the spirit is not pattern or colors?

101 | Culture

"A Day Without Work . . ."

Baizhang Huaihai (720–814) was a Tang dynasty Chan master. He is an example of how Chan Buddhism changed to suit the Chinese mentality.

Where Buddha and his followers in India begged for their meals (allowing others to support their spiritual calling, showing their nonattachment to material things, and practicing humility), Baizhang Huaihai established monastic rules that emphasized farming, work, and self-sufficiency. This willingness to be self-supporting helped the sect survive anti-Buddhist persecutions.

Many asserted that the Buddhists were a financial burden on society (because they begged and didn't work), that they were otherworldly (and therefore irresponsible), that they were anti-Confucian, and that Buddhism was a foreign religion.

The emperor at that time was a Taoist. It may well be that the blending of Taoism, Buddhism, and Confucianism that we see today was brought about by the various persecutions that happened (sometimes, it was the Taoists or the Confucian scholars who were persecuted). The religious sects and beliefs had to bear up to governmental and social pressures, had to fit with the culture, and had to reconcile themselves to one another. In short, the more similar Taoism, Buddhism, and Confucianism could become, the more deeply rooted they could remain in the culture and the more likely they were to survive.

Baizhang Huaihai understood the Chinese belief in work and deep loathing for "freeloading." He is famous for the phrase "a day without work, a day without eating."

The spirit is not pattern or colors
but we enter through patterns and colors.

There is no such thing as cultural anatomy. Every human being's inner anatomy is the same. There is no such thing as cultural spirituality. In the deep states of contemplation and absorption, there is no language, no pattern, no color, no sound.

However, we need to go through culture to get to the spiritual practice. Culture consists of integrated patterns of knowledge, beliefs, learning, and lifestyles. It consists of shared attitudes, goals, values, and social practices. The culture around us is as vast as the ocean, and like fish, we depend on that ocean to support us, to give us oxygen, and to bring us food. When Siddhartha began his search, he first learned the holy ways of his culture. When he taught, he taught in the context of learning and spirituality that was indigenous to eastern India.

When Buddhism came to China, it changed. In part this was because it had to reconcile itself with Taoism, and in part it was because the Chinese mind was different from the Indian one. When Buddhism spread to Korea and Japan, it changed again. And now, as it spreads to the United States and Europe, it is changing yet again.

The Taoist and Buddhist temples and festival days surround us with the culture of spirituality. We borrow history, folktales, poems, songs, and ways of worship to spring into spirituality, just as Buddha did. This is necessary, but these are all ultimately outer things. In time, we enter into the temple. And from the temple, we enter into our inner temple—ourselves. The deeper we go, the more the cultural trappings fall away until we reach purity.

But we enter through patterns and colors, becoming a delicate vessel: a cup can break or last thousands of years.

102 | Fragility

Cups and Bowls

Mencius (p. 63) wrote:

> Can you respect the character of the willow if you use it to make cups and bowls? Don't you have to kill it to make cups and bowls? If you must injure a willow to make cups and bowls, then don't you also injure humanity in order to establish your principles of humaneness and righteousness?

The *Classic of Rites* gives another view on the value of objects such as books or bowls, in a deeply emotional passage that anyone who's lost a close relative will recognize:

> When his father died, he could not read his father's books—the faintly damp touch of his hand still seemed to remain. When his mother died, he could not drink from her cups and bowls. The faintly damp touch of her mouth and her breath still seemed to remain.

A cup can break or last thousands of years.
One can be vulnerable yet still strong.

A cup can last for thousands of years, be perfectly useful, and then be shattered in an instant.

A person can be beautiful and kind, and a gift to all the world, and then be killed in an instant.

A butterfly on the ground can be barely moving, raising our impatience, and be squashed in an instant.

The most beautiful and ancient temple can be revered for generations, and yet defiled and torched in an instant.

The fact that we can ruin anything in a moment does not change its value. In wars and revolutions, men go to holy places, defile them with blood and feces, murder people before the gods, and tear down the walls. They laugh and demand, "Where are the gods now?" But all that they're really showing is their evil, not the weakness of gods. Rape, genocide, murder, torture, slavery—these are proof of humanity's perversity and not the nonexistence of gods.

The very fragility of the holy means we treasure it more. The very fact that we can lose our spouses and our children to accident, madmen, and sickness makes us more vigilant and loving. The very fact that we can break a cup in a moment makes us more appreciative, sensitive, and careful.

Nothing lasts. The sages are right. But what we hold that is fragile, we hold more dear because of that very fact.

One can be vulnerable yet still strong: to know a person, see how he cares for children.

103 | Caring for Children

The Sage Treats All as His Own Children

Chapter 49 of the *Daodejing* speaks of the sage's attitude:

> The sage does not set his mind to be unchanging,
> but takes the ordinary people's heart as his own.
> If the people are good, then I am good to them.
> If people are bad to me, then I am still good to them.
> Virtue is good. Trust is also good.
> If people trust me, then I trust them.
> If people do not trust, then I still trust them.
> Virtue is trust.
> When the sage is under heaven, he draws back;
> when he acts under heaven, he obscures his own heart.
> The common people all keep their ears and eyes on him,
> and the sage treats them all as his own children.

To know a person, see how he cares for children.
To know a nation, see how it cares for children.

There is nothing more precious than a child.

A child is life. A child is the future. A child is innocence. A child is hope. A child is faith. A child is soft. A child is observant. A child is open. A child is the cure for every cynical thought. A child is a test to see if we can be selfless and empathetic. A child is the opportunity to give without reservation to another. A child gives back all the unconditional love you offer. A child is the chance for you to give a better life than you had yourself. A child is the chance to give to another all the beauty you've experienced. A child is reincarnation—in this world and without the necessity of death. A child is a reaffirmation of all the truths you had forgotten. A child screams, laughs, shouts, and burbles with the sound of life. A child is the embodiment of all ancestors. A child is inspiration. A child is joy. A child is tenderness. A child is all that we want but were afraid to ask for. A child is the brilliance of human potential. A child is the triumph of education. A child is the glory of the spirit. A child is a god.

Caring for children negates ordinary mathematical thinking. When you truly love children, you might first think, "How can I love them all?" Ordinary mathematics says that you can only divide the love you have among the children around you. But once you care for children, you realize that you can love every child one hundred percent, and that you can love an unlimited number of children—and give one hundred percent of your love to each one.

Caring for a child is sacred.

To know a nation, see how it cares for children: their lives can end while the yellow millet simmers uncooked.

The Eight Immortals

The **Eight Immortals** (Baxian) are a group of Taoist deities. Each immortal represents a different aspect of human existence and has unique powers, represented by implements with magic powers that they hold as emblems. Any one of the immortals can aid the pursuit of immortality or confer long life. They live on Penglai (p. 49), the island of immortals, in the Bohai Sea.

The immortals are:

He Xiangu (p. 120) is the only woman of the group. Lady He holds a lotus leaf or bamboo ladle filled with the mushroom of immortality, peach, bamboo and pine sprigs, and narcissus flowers (all symbols of immortality). She represents women.

Cao Guojiu (p. 322) is the uncle of a Song emperor and is always shown in royal robes. Cao is shown holding either castanets or the plaques required for admission to court. He represents the nobility.

Li Tieguai (p. 225) is a disfigured and disabled homeless man. He was originally a handsome Taoist adept who went spirit-traveling, but he was forced to take the body of a nearby beggar when his own body was burned. Li leans on an iron crutch and carries a gourd that emits a mystical mist. He represents the sick.

Lan Caihe (p. 207) is usually shown as a young boy, but the legends state that Lan is of ambiguous gender. Lan carries a hoe and a flower basket filled with the mushroom of immortality, peach, bamboo and pine sprigs, different kinds of plums, chrysanthemum, and red berries. He (or she) represents carefree youth.

Lu Dongbin (p. 125) is an older scholar, sorcerer, and internal alchemist. He is the most well-known of the group and has many temples dedicated to him as an individual. Lu carries a double-edged straight sword. He represents scholars and internal alchemists.

Han Xiangzi (p. 398) is known as a philosopher, flutist, and magician. He tried to convince his uncle, the famous statesman, essayist, and poet Han Yu (p. 55), to give up being an official, but his uncle was too much of an orthodox Confucian. Han carries a flute and castanets. He represents the musician and happy person.

Zhang Guolao (p. 331) is the eldest member and is known as an alchemist, necromancer, and qigong practitioner. Zhang holds a fish-shaped bamboo drum (*yugu*) that is used by Taoist priests. He is also known for his white donkey that can be folded up like a piece of paper at the day's end and then reconstituted with a sprinkling of water. He represents the elderly.

Han Zhongli (p. 126) is a teacher, former general, and, along with his student Lu Dongbin, the leader of the group. Han holds either a feather fan or a palm-leaf fan. He represents the military.

The Eight Immortals, first described in the Yuan dynasty (1271–1368), may have been patterned after the **Eight Immortals of Huainan**, the scholars who wrote the *Masters of Huainan (Huainanzi)* under the patronage of Liu An (p. 50).

The immortals are sometimes described as the Drunken Eight Immortals, and this may be a melding with another famous but unrelated group called the **Eight Immortals of the Wine Cup**. These real-life men of the Tang dynasty, such as China's foremost poet, **Li Bai** (p. 264), and **He Zhizhang** (p. 334), were all celebrated and prodigious drinkers.

The Eight Immortals are favorite subjects for the decorative arts, appearing as sculpture, in paintings, and in dramas and movies. They appear in literature as well—the most prominent being the **Yellow Millet Dream** (p. 125).

In a Ming dynasty (1368–1644) story, "The Eight Immortals Cross the Sea," the Eight Immortals arrive at the Eastern Sea during a dreadful storm. Lu Dongbin suggests that each immortal show his or her powers. Each immortal casts his or her own implements on the water—Lu his sword, Han Zhongli his fan, and so on—until all can cross the sea using their emblems as stepping-stones. Today, when people accomplish something difficult through cooperation, they invoke the idiom: "The Eight Immortals cross the sea: each shows supernatural power to get through." ▶

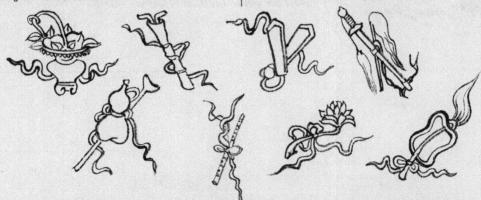

104 | Yellow Millet Dream

• Fasting day
• Birthday of Lu **Dongbin**

Lu Dongbin

The most prominent member of the Eight Immortals (p. 124) is Lu Dongbin, a dignified older scholar who carries a double-edged straight sword. He is worshipped in temples of his own as the patron and protector of jugglers, magicians, and barbers. Lu represents the scholarly life and internal alchemy.

The Yellow Millet Dream

The story of his conversion is the stuff of legend, literature, movies, and operas.

When Lu was still a baby, Patriarch Ma predicted that Lu would be extraordinary. As a youth, Lu met the Taoist Huolong in the mountains and learned swordsmanship from him.

But Lu could not pass the imperial examinations. At the age of sixty-four, around the year 841, he was still trying for academic and worldly success. He was on his way to another attempt when he met a Taoist priest in an inn who turned out to be **Han Zhongli** (p. 126). Han remarked how weary Lu looked, and he gave him a magic pillow so he could take a nap. As Lu fell asleep, millet was cooking on the stove.

Lu went on to pass his examinations. He married and was eventually promoted to prime minister. But he became corrupt and was stripped of all he had and banished. Just then Han woke him. The millet had not yet finished cooking! With that, Lu took Han Zhongli as a teacher and gave himself over to the Taoist life.

The yellow millet simmers uncooked,
while you travel to the land of dreams.

These are the lines Han Zhongli uttered to Lu Dongbin when he awoke from his dreams. The story fits well with Zhuangzi's butterfly dream (p. 52). An entire life can pass in less time than it takes millet to cook. Both incidents are metaphors for the Taoist assertion that life is ephemeral and that our perceptions and the value we place on it can change or vanish in a moment.

On the other hand, becoming an immortal is very much like cooking a pot of millet: all must be gathered and prepared, the grain and water have to be good, and the required amount of time for the pot of grain to be fully cooked must pass.

Can we realize the vanity of a lifetime in less time than it takes for the pot to simmer? Can we then go through the arduous process of getting "cooked" ourselves, boiling away our impurities and misgivings until all that remains is not yellow millet but a golden embryo?

While you travel to the land of dreams, when will you, the warrior, retire?

105 | Warrior, Retire

• Fasting day
• Birthday of **Han Zhongli**

Han Zhongli

Han Zhongli, one of the leaders of the Eight Immortals (p. 124), is easily recognized: he is an older man, wears his hair in two buns atop his head (only one shows in the picture below), he has a large beard and a big belly (sometimes bulging through an open robe), and he holds a feather or palm-leaf fan. His father was a prince who ruled over a small fief. When Han was born during the Han dynasty (206 BCE–220 CE), he did not make any sounds until the seventh day, when he sprang up and declared:

> My feet have walked in the purple
> palace of the xian [immortals, p. 44].
> My name is recorded in the capital of
> the Jade Emperor [p. 13].

Han became a general and was sent to fight in Tibet. However, he was defeated and fled alone through the wild and mountainous countryside. He came to the abode of a foreign priest—the legends specify a "blue-eyed foreigner"—who led the general to the home of Master Donghua.

The old master appeared wearing white deerskin and leaning on a black-thorn staff. "Are you not Han Zhongli?" he cried. Surprised, Han Zhongli decided that it was time to learn the ways of Tao. He stayed with the master to learn the Taoist arts of immortality, and eventually went on to study with other masters. After discovering secret texts in a jade casket on a mountain-top, he ascended to heaven.

When will you, the warrior, retire?
Will you leave killing for long life?

Throughout Chinese history, there were many formidable warriors. They did what all proper warriors must do. They obeyed their lords, they protected their country, they were loyal to their comrades and the men they commanded, they never abandoned their principles, they risked their lives, they defended the weak—and they killed.

It was just as much a part of the tradition that they retired. Many of the warriors became Buddhist monks or Taoist priests and spent the rest of their lives atoning for their sins. This is also how martial arts came to be a part of the holy life, because these retired warriors taught their fighting arts to the other adepts—a reasonable thing to do, since wild animals, bandits, and invaders regularly attacked monasteries and temples. But the warrior life vividly shows the need to leave the conflict of the world to seek the spiritual life. Han Zhongli was fleeing defeat. That was no shame. For the spiritual person, *all war is already defeat.*

It's simply realistic to accept that many of us must fight in one way or another in the first half of our lives. Because of circumstance or ambition, we strive, we fight, we risk our lives. A few of us manage to be true heroes, and we accomplish many things out of sheer will and might. But the sage would remark that even victories that save lives or establish dynasties are hollow.

If you find the way to learn Tao, if you stumble on the trail in the mountains trodden only by immortals, then leave your conflicts and go without hesitation.

Will you leave killing for long life? All things are done, one by one.

Exercise 8

GRAIN FILLS

Summer crops like horsebeans and wheat ripen, and this is the optimal time for planting seedlings in rice paddies. Plentiful water is crucial for such farming, and so people say: "A flooded paddy promises a full granary. A drop of water saved is a grain of rice ensured."

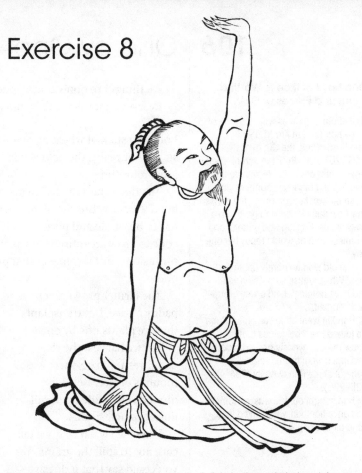

This exercise is best practiced during the period of 3:00–7:00 A.M.

1. Sit cross-legged and raise one hand overhead, palm facing upward. Press the other palm on your lap.

2. Alternately change position, pushing upward with the raised hand, and pressing downward with the other hand. Inhale when you push; exhale gently when you relax and change sides. Repeat fifteen times on each side.

3. Facing forward with your hands resting on your lap, click your teeth together thirty-six times. Roll your tongue between your teeth nine times in each direction. Form saliva in your mouth by pushing your cheeks in and out. When your mouth is filled with saliva, divide the liquid into three portions.

4. Inhale; then exhale, imagining your breath traveling to the dantian and then swallow one-third of the saliva, imagining that it travels to the dantian.

5. Repeat two more times until you've swallowed all three portions.

6. Sit comfortably as long as you like.

Through this exercise, ancient Taoists sought to prevent or treat obstruction in the liver and lungs; feeling of fullness in the chest and ribs; discomfort and palpitations of the heart; flushed faces; yellow eyes; depression; and excessively hot palms.

106 | One by One

One Bowl of Rice Is Worth a Thousand Pieces of Gold

That idiom originates with the story of a boy named **Han Xin** (d. 196 BCE), who lived during the Qin dynasty (221–207 BCE). Both his parents died, leaving him destitute. He went to the river to fish but rarely caught anything.

An old washerwoman on the banks saw how thin he was and gave him a bowl of rice. Han Xin was grateful and promised that he would repay her one day.

The old woman gently upbraided him. "Why promise something when you have nothing? Find a way to support yourself."

Han Xin went off to seek his fortune. He joined the rebel forces that overthrew the Qin dynasty and eventually became a wealthy and respected general of the Han dynasty (206 BCE–220).

Han sought out the washerwoman and gave her food, wine, and a thousand pieces of gold.

All things are done, one by one.
Everyone matters, one by one.

Look at a stalk of wheat or rice. True, in a field there are many stalks, but really, the field is filled with one plus one plus one to a great multitude.

The tip of the stalk has many seeds, so heavy that together they bend the stalk. But the plant has to grow each seed, and each seed has to be whole and perfect. Indeed, each seed has within it the code to grow an entirely new plant. Nature displays itself in grand profusion—but it achieves that profusion by building things one by one.

The farmer grows an entire paddy of rice, but transplants the rice plants one by one. When we harvest the rice and thresh it, true, there are mounds of rice. But those mounds are made up of millions of single grains.

When we wash rice, we take care not to spill the grains. Yes, you could say that it doesn't matter whether you lose a grain or two, but how long can you keep that up before the loss is significant? A child is told not to waste even a single grain of rice, a practical attitude in a country that was shaped by famine and drought for thousands of years.

If the old woman had not given Han one bowl of rice, he might have died. Had he not worked hard to accumulate his wealth and power one occasion at a time, he would never have repaid her.

Oh, it's fabulous to be grand, to be sweeping, to be a powerful ruler commanding thousands of square miles! But no matter how grand and powerful you may be, remember that your power is built up one grain at a time, that every grain matters, and that wisdom is to be able to see both the single grain and the loftiest mound at the same time.

Everyone matters, one by one, yet there is just one meditation.

107 | One Meditation

The Girl Comes Out of *Samahdi*

This story is from the *Wumenguan.* Samahdi *(sanmei)* is a Sanskrit word meaning a high level of meditation.

The Bodhisattva Manjusri (p. 112) arrived late at the assembly of Buddhas to find that everyone had already departed. Only Buddha and one girl remained. She sat in samahdi near Buddha's throne.

"How can this girl get close to your throne while I cannot?" Manjusri asked Buddha.

"Bring her out of samahdi and ask her yourself," Buddha replied.

Manjusri walked around the girl three times, snapped his fingers, transported her to the Brahma heaven, and exerted all his spiritual power, but he could not bring her out of her meditation.

Buddha told the frustrated Manjusri that down below them, past lands as innumerable as the sands along the Ganges River, there was Bodhisattva Wangming, who could rouse her from meditation.

Upon the mention of his name, Wangming emerged from the earth. Buddha ordered him to rouse the girl.

The bodhisattva snapped his fingers and the girl came out of her samahdi.

Wumen Huikai asks why Manjusri, the teacher of the Seven Buddhas, was unable to rouse the girl, while the lowliest beginning bodhisattva was able to do it.

There is just one meditation,
as there is only one journey.

It's a mistake to think that there are different kinds of meditation. It's an error to say that one meditation is better than another. It's wrong to say that there are failed meditations.

If you still yourself, let your breathing calm, and are mentally engaged in what you're doing, then you are meditating. The masters teach that there are stages to meditation, and that there are preliminary exercises to prepare us. They do this to help us, but it becomes easy for students to think, "Oh, I'm not *really* meditating *yet*." This thought is a barrier—like wondering whether you're really in love or not.

Thus, it's better to dispense with this question. If you're trying, then you *are* meditating. A journey of a few steps can lead to a walk of a mile, and a walk of a mile can turn into a trek that traverses a continent. As soon as you take the first step, you *are* on the journey. We don't say, "Oh, your journey isn't real until the first mile." Who could make such a distinction?

Thus, anyone can begin meditation and return to it again and again. In the same way, anyone can hum a tune and therefore be making music. It's quite reasonable to have the ambition to play more music or become better at it, perhaps even to compose. But when you first hum that tune, you are making music, however simple it may be.

Just close your eyes, sit straight, breathe naturally, and look within. Listen. Be aware. There's no better way to understand yourself and to ground yourself.

As there is only one journey, flowing water never stagnates.

108 | Moving Exercise

Hua Tuo

Hua Tuo (c. 140–208) was a physician who lived during the struggle for the Three Kingdoms era (the struggle began in 184; the official dates of the period are 220–265). He was the first person credited with using anesthesia during surgery, and he was skilled in acupuncture, moxibustion, herbal medicine, and daoyin (a form of qigong; p. xxiv) exercises. He is considered the creator of the **Five Animal Frolics** (Wuqinxi)—exercises that improve health by imitating the movements of the crane, bear, deer, monkey, and tiger. Sadly, he was executed by the warlord Cao Cao (p. 88). Just before his death, Hua Tuo burned the records of his medical techniques when his jailer was too afraid to accept them.

Flowing water never stagnates.
A well-used door hinge will not rot.

These observations are attributed to Hua Tuo and are the rationale for his Five Animal Frolics. Like all Taoists, he observed that everything in the universe moves and changes. Health exercises logically follow the same philosophy, using movement to maintain health.

Where others might approach exercise by stretching one muscle after another, rotating the joints systematically, and running to build stamina, Taoists take a different approach. They look to nature as the template. Hua Tuo did not want to simply create exercises based on the human body. By copying the movement of animals, he followed the Taoist habit of patterning after nature. He would have wanted not simply to have people exercise, but to have exercise *return* them to nature itself.

Each animal form has a purpose: the crane is for the qi, the bear for the liver and kidneys, the deer for the hormonal system and sexual organs, the monkey for lightness, and the tiger for the bones and muscles. Practice in this way, and one can indeed stave off stagnation and rot.

A well-used door hinge will not rot; fear is instinct, but can turn to madness.

109 | Teaching Fear

Standing Alone Without Fear

These words, attributed to Confucius, appear with Hexagram 28 of the *I Ching*:

> The lake overwhelms the trees: great excess. The noble one stands alone without fear, and can withdraw from the world without sorrow.

Laozi on Fear

Laozi takes a different approach to fear in Chapter 13 of the *Daodejing*:

> Favor and disgrace seem frightening, but suffering should be considered a part of life.
> Why is it said that favor and disgrace seem frightening?
> Favor leads to inferiority.
> Gaining it seems frightening, losing it seems frightening.
> So it's said that favor and disgrace seem frightening.
> Why is it said that suffering should be considered a part of life?
> The reason I experience great suffering is because I have a body.
> If I didn't have a body, how could I experience suffering?

Fear is instinct, but can turn to madness.
Fear can be advisor but not the king.

Every family wants to do well by its children. Most do very well, guaranteeing that the younger generation has greater and fresher advantages. Every family is also concerned about safety, and so children grow up with cautions and admonitions.

This process can go awry. A families overemphasizes caution, or the children apply the maxims too strictly. The family doesn't teach safety; it teaches fear.

Fear of fire and sharp blades and wild animals, fear of poisons and falling off heights, fear of being hit by a car or train—these are reasonable fears. When we start to teach the necessary fear of strangers and abduction, then it's harder to calibrate. When we come to the far more subtle issues of how to meet other people who might become friends or associates, when we talk about traveling safely or starting new ventures, when we talk about how to reach our aspirations, then it's not at all clear how much caution to mix with the encouragement.

What does a parent do with his or her own disappointments? These engender fear too. Some want their children to achieve what they themselves could not. Some think they are helping their children by destroying the aspirations that led to their own disappointment. Fear of failure and fear of success are both destructive.

If we are the child saddled with fears, we must exert a considerable amount of effort undoing what has been done to us.

Fear can be advisor but not the king; proclaim! For what is repeated becomes real.

110 | What's Repeated

Practice

練 Everything about Taoism, martial arts, and all of Chinese culture in general is based on the word *lian*. The word is defined as "to practice, to train, to drill, to perfect one's skill." Repetition is integral to that—like the many turnings of a wheel.

The Wheel in the *Daodejing*

In Chapter 11, Laozi declares:

> Thirty spokes share one hub;
> the empty space makes the cart useful.
> Clay is shaped into a vase;
> the empty space makes the vase useful.
> Cutting doors and windows makes a
>   room;
> the empty spaces make the room useful.
> Therefore, what exists gives benefit.
> What does not exist makes usefulness.

What is repeated becomes real.
It's bold to choose what to repeat.

If all of Tao moves in cycles, we can imagine it as one big wheel. Buddhism chose the wheel as the symbol of Buddha's teaching—the Wheel of the Law. Laozi stated in the *Daodejing:* "Thirty spokes share one hub; the empty space makes the cart useful." So if both Buddha and Laozi say that all turns around us like a circle, what shall we declare the center to be?

Our mind is the center around which our world turns. That means that whatever we accept or decide is going to determine how our world revolves.

Furthermore, what is repeated in our minds takes on a greater significance. The spouse and children we see every day are going to be more significant than the stranger across an ocean. What is repeated shapes us and shapes our lives: where the wheel rolls each day is where the Way is most worn.

We know repetition already: we memorized our multiplication tables, we chose a career, we practiced something—whether it was sewing, basketball, or a musical instrument. We also need to be wary of what is unintentionally repeated—the repetitive movements that lead to chronic pain, repeated abuse, even the daily stress of our jobs. Being a Taoist means being aware of what is repeated each day, compounding our abilities through positive repetition, and preventing the problems of negative repetition.

By directing and enhancing positive repetition and minimizing negative repetition, one can become an immortal.

It's bold to choose what to repeat: that's why the ocean of knowledge is without shore.

111 | Renounce "Sageliness"

Chapter 19 of the *Daodejing*

Renounce "sageliness," abandon
    "wisdom,"
and people will benefit a hundredfold.
Renounce "benevolence," abandon
    "righteousness,"
and people will recover filial piety and
    kindness.
Renounce "opportunity" and
    "advantage,"
and there will be neither bandits nor
    thieves.

Taking these three as parts of our
    culture is not enough.
We must make them actual and
    integrated.

See the plain. Embrace the simple.
Lessen selfishness, reduce desires.
Renounce learning and there will be no
    worries.

The ocean of knowledge is without shore.
To give up learning is also learning.

An old attitude describes learning as sailing on a vast ocean that has no shore (p. 327). Learning is infinite and as pleasurable as the adventurous discoveries of the best sea voyages.

When Laozi says that we should "renounce sageliness" and "abandon wisdom," he is railing against the conventional learning and knowledge that was used to oppress people. When he says to abandon benevolence and righteousness—two key components of Confucianism—he is declaring that there will be recovery of a *natural* filial piety and kindness if false and forced propriety are first discarded. When he says to abandon (the drive for) opportunity and to reject (the calculation of) advantage, he is saying that the accumulation and power of one class over another invites banditry and thieves.

In another poke at Confucianism, Laozi says that learning (or scholarship) leads too many to wants and schemes. Instead, we should "see the plain and embrace the simple, lessen our selfishness and reduce desires."

Learning is important. Learning keeps us young and keeps our minds fresh. Learning is the way to lessen our selfishness and to reduce our desires. For the more we know, the more we see that mere selfishness is meaningless in the vastness of the ocean of knowledge. The greatest lesson to learn is to abandon the learning of artificiality and instead learn natural innocence.

To give up learning is also learning: there is light, even behind dense clouds.

112 | Clouds

Smallness Tames

Part of the text for Hexagram 9 of the *I Ching* reads:

> Smallness tames.
> Persevere.
> Dense clouds, no rain at my western
> border.

Contrast that with this poem from the *Classic of Poetry,* entitled "Xinnan Mountain":

> The skies above are joined in cloud:
> rain and snow, mist and fog.
> The fine rain is good.
> It already soaks the land,
> it already soaks enough
> to grow us abundant grain.

Even behind dense clouds,
The sun is always there.

There are stormy days and there are sunny days. Sometimes, it's cloudy and we don't see the sun all day. But the clouds glow with the light of the sun behind them, and the sun is always there. It's simply covered for the time being.

In the same way, the gods, spirituality, and Tao are always there. Something might be obscuring them, but that doesn't mean that they've vanished. They're always there.

We experience happiness and sadness throughout our lives. If we hold the thought of the sun behind the clouds, we can see that the unhappiness we experience is only temporary—like the clouds.

No matter how fierce a storm, it cannot last long. Even a hurricane must come and go. No matter how destructive it may be, it must pass. Having the knowledge that the sun is behind the clouds and the forbearance to know that storm clouds cannot cover it forever is the key to wisdom.

The sun is always there, so why worry: Whatever you hoard, put it down.

113 | Small Fasts

• Fasting day

Some Historical References to Fasting

The *Classic of Rites* has a number of references to **fasting**. For example, it prescribes "seven days of vigil and three days of fasting" in its instruction for one ceremony. It also states that worship, in the form of "serving the spirits," requires extensive cleansing:

Vigil and fasting are required in matters of the spirits. Select a day and month to see the ruler. Do not let the people fail in their reverence.

Fasting is also a part of filial duty:

Does a filial child make offerings? Does the child fast? There is no way to keep the image of the ancestors from fading and being lost except by fasting. Therefore, a filial child must fast, so that the vision of the parents will continue. That is why the child receives no guests during the time of offering. Those who do not make offerings to their ancestors are rapacious animals!

Zhuangzi has his own perspective on fasting. In a fictionalized dialogue with Confucius (here identified by his courtesy name, Zhongni), his beloved first student, Yan Hui (p. 32), says that he doesn't have enough to eat—can that be regarded as fasting? Zhongni answers:

"That is the fasting of worship and sacrifice, but it is not the fasting of the mind."

"What is the fasting of the mind?" asks Hui

Zhongni answers: "Have a single purpose.

"Don't listen with your ears, but listen with your heart.

"Don't listen with your heart, but listen with your breath.

"Stop the hearing of the ears. Stop the heart from dwelling on concepts.

"Then slow the breath too.

"Empty yourself from taking anything in. Only Tao collects in emptiness. If you find emptiness, then that's the fasting of the mind."

Whatever you hoard, put it down.
Whatever might tip, put it down.

Today is a fasting day, one of many throughout the year. We already learned from Buddha's example (p. 117) that harsh asceticism is not the way. However, sometimes engaging in small fasts can heighten our appreciation of what we have.

The most common form of fasting is to give up a particular food. This doesn't mean that you must go hungry. Just try voluntarily foregoing something. It could be for a day, it could be for longer.

Fasting as a spiritual exercise does several things. First, it creates independence. If you're able to give up a food you would normally crave, you gain greater discipline and freedom to give up anything else you might choose. Second, it allows you to observe what your life would be without something you thought essential. Sometimes that means you can give an indulgence up entirely; sometimes you come to value that thing even more. Either is useful. Third, when you give something up temporarily, you're able to see its true place in your life. Without it, you have to rebalance everything. When you add it back in, you have to balance again, and these observations are educational. Fourth, while you are fasting, you can see the state of your body, mind, and spirit. There is the chance for cleansing. In short, fasting is a welcome respite that will teach us a great deal about ourselves.

Fasting can be extended to many other things too. Television, music, our digital devices, entertainment, sex—fasting need not be long, and it should never be obsessive, but it can be a way of self-knowledge.

Recently, social scientists have told us that a child's ability to defer gratification is the single biggest predictor of maturity as well as academic and career success. The sages sensed the same thing when they adopted fasting: the ability to defer, to be patient, to master one's drives for immediate gratification establishes a person's vital power.

Whatever might tip, put it down. Or are you addicted?

114 Addictions

▸ Fasting day

Zhong Kui

Zhong Kui, the Demon Catcher, is worshipped on the fifth day of the fifth moon. However, in 1757, people put up Zhong Kui's picture to counter a plague. They recovered, and from that point on, Zhong Kui was invoked throughout the year for his ability to fight illness and demons. Eventually, that came to include the illness of addiction.

According to legend, Zhong Kui lived on Zhongnanshan in the early Tang dynasty (618–907). He was extraordinarily ugly, but he was a man of integrity and righteousness.

Emperor Xuanzong (685–762) ascended the throne in 712 and Zhong Kui took the imperial examinations that same year. He ranked first out of all the candidates. However, a minister named Li Qi found him so ugly that he persuaded the emperor not to give any award to Zhong Kui. Despondent, Zhong Kui dashed his head against a palace pillar and died.

Later the emperor became ill and dreamed that he saw a demon steal the imperial consort's purse and one of the emperor's own flutes. Before it could get away, however, the ghost was captured by a fearsome man in official robes. The rescuer introduced himself as Zhong Kui, the Demon Catcher.

When the emperor awoke, he described his dream to the court portraitists, and paintings of Zhong Kui have been popular ever since. People still display his picture to chase demons away.

Are you addicted?
Can you give it up?

Addictions are powerful. There is no doubt about that. We can empathize with anyone who is suffering from addiction because most of us have experienced that kind of pull in one form or another. It's unnecessary to condemn those who are suffering from addiction. How can one soul look down on another?

However, if you are suffering from addiction, there is only one question: do you want to give it up? And if you want to give it up, why not today? Why not right now?

After all, addiction is powerful enough to kill a person. There is no more jealous lover, no more parasitic demon, no more life-sucking devil. We let that addiction in. We can eject that addiction too.

Drugs, drink, gambling, sex, power, food—we human beings are able to turn nearly any activity into an addiction. Perhaps the worst thing about addiction is that we surrender our own independence and let a substance or activity dictate our lives.

The essence of driving a car is to steer it, to accelerate, and to brake. The problem with addiction is that "someone else" is driving our car. We can neither steer nor stop—there's only a headlong acceleration down a hellish highway. You can't have two people driving a car. It just doesn't work. So if you're going to drive the car of your life, you have to kick the demon out of the driver's seat.

Just as there's no halfway in driving a car, there's no halfway independence from addiction. Just do it. Destroy your addiction and you'll discover a will and power that no wine or smoke could ever give you.

Can you give it up? Or does your sickness come from outside?

115 | Recovery from Illness

All the Earth Is Medicine

Yunmen Wenyan (c. 862–949), a Tang dynasty Chan Buddhist master and founder of one of the five major schools of Chan Buddhism, is the subject of a number of koans. In the *Blue Cliff Records,* he said:

"Medicine and illness go with one another. All of earth is medicine. Where is your true self?"

Yunmen also said:

"I do not ask you about the days before the fifteenth day of the moon. But what about those after? Come give me a word about those days."

Then he answered for them: "Every day is a good day."

Obviously, he was attuned to the lunar calendar. The fifteenth is the middle of the lunar cycle, when the moon is full. This parallels his statement about illness—on a subtle level, he is commenting on sickness and health, waxing and waning, and the right attitude for facing the cycles of life.

Does your sickness come from outside?
Is it medicine that cures you?

We've all had that feeling of getting better after an illness. We announce that we feel better. Perhaps we throw ourselves back into work, or we go out and find something fun to do. As wonderful as getting well is, there are a few things worth considering about it.

First, medicine may have played a role, but the most common treatment for every affliction is rest, plenty of water, and good nutrition. Medicine can only play an intervening role, and true recovery depends on the power of one's own body to heal. For that, there is no medicine. There is only the body's natural ability. Plenty of people die in spite of medicine simply because their body's own natural healing ability has given out.

Second, every illness is mentally oppressive. We just aren't our natural selves when we're sick. We all have learned that, and we've all learned forbearance as we get through recovery. We learn that we cannot make major decisions or call upon our natural abilities. So we wait until we're better. That alone is a valuable lesson: we need to take care of ourselves and watch over ourselves, and we need to acknowledge when we're unable to do our best.

Third, recovery is joyous. Coincidentally, the Chinese word for "medicine" combines the symbols for "grass" (as in medicinal herbs) and "joy." This combination is merely for the sound, and yet it hints at the satisfaction recovery can be. We also celebrate having learned something from the process. We continue our Way.

Is it medicine that cures you? Or is it the force of one hundred tendrils?

116 | The Vine

From the Tiniest Sprout

Chapter 64 of the *Daodejing* states: "A tree that a person can put his arms around grows from a tiny shoot." Laozi takes this philosophy of understanding the small and applies it to human affairs. Here is the full chapter:

Peace is easy to maintain: what has not been portended can still be planned for.

The fragile is easily broken, the minute is easily scattered.

Act before anything occurs, control before there is disorder.

A tree that a person can put his arms around grows from a tiny shoot.

A nine-level terrace begins by piling up earth.

A journey of a thousand miles begins by putting a foot down.

Those who act on things ruin them; those who hold onto things lose them.

That is why the sage does not act, and so is not defeated.

No holding—therefore no losing.

When people pursue their undertakings, it is always when they're at the point of near success that they are defeated.

If they were as careful at the end as they were at the beginnings, then their undertakings would not be defeated.

So the sage wants what others do not want,

ignores rare treasures,

studies what others will not study, and returns to where the masses have gone away.

Thus, the ten thousand things are supported in their nature, but the sage has not dared to act.

Of one hundred tendrils,
one grows through the fence boards.

The vine has no plan. Unlike humans, it has no consciousness. It cannot see, nor does it have a brain. Yet it grows according to the patterns it naturally embodies, and it prospers.

The vine grows in a tangle. One tendril grows over another, seeking light. It climbs over whatever is nearby, whether cliff face, tree trunk, other plants, or a fence. It doesn't search or explore. It simply goes by touch, warmth, and light, growing into the openings favorable to it.

A vine might cover the entire side of a fence, but if a tendril finds a crack between two fence boards, it grows through it. Slender at first, it sends out a long stem. In time, it will sprout leaves and spiraling strands to support itself until the stem is too thick to withdraw itself from the crack. It has found new territory, a new way to the sun, and it will continue until more vines follow.

In the same way, we have to grow true to our own natures. We should not do only one thing in life, but many. We cannot always predict where our initiatives will go, but we can let each one grow as it will. It is only in profusion that we prosper. If we do things one at a time, we can never achieve the diversity of growth necessary to do well. If we want to have a rich future, we need only follow the young tendril of a vine.

One grows through the fence boards, whether from the past or from the present.

© Ying Fry

117 | Best Practice

The Salve

Zhuangzi tells the story of a man of Song. He made a salve that prevented chapped hands. His family had been in the business of bleaching cocoon-silk, and the salve was their family secret and great asset.

A stranger heard of the salve and proposed to buy the method for a hundred ounces of silver.

The family met and considered the proposal. "We have been bleaching cocoon-silk for generations, and yet we are still poor. Now in one morning we can sell our formula for a hundred ounces of silver! Let him have it."

The stranger left with the formula. He was an advisor to the king of Wu, who was then at war with the state of Yue. The king gave the stranger command of his fleet, and in the winter they went to battle. The soldiers used the salve to protect themselves from the cold and were able to fight nimbly while their foes were stiff and clumsy. Yue suffered a great defeat and lost a large amount of territory.

Zhuangzi concludes: the method of keeping hands from getting chapped was the same in both cases. In one case it led to the rapid advancement of a stranger, and in the other it only enabled a family to continue bleaching. The different results were due solely to the different ways that the old art was used.

Whether from the past or from the present,
don't hesitate to choose the best practice.

What's the point of going back through ancient things? Why study what some long-dead Chinese sages wrote? The only reason is if it helps us find the best practice.

In the same way, it's useless to cling to tradition if tradition is no longer relevant. It's just as silly to be limited by your family, your hometown, your ethnic group, or your gender. All of these can be sources of guidance and advantage, but when they cease to be beneficial, then they must be discarded for something better.

Consider this: even if one looks back into ancient times, the practices were different a thousand years ago than two thousand years ago. Basic health and awareness around the world today are superior to what they were even a hundred years ago. True, there are still many problems and atrocities, but overall, we are better off. A hundred years from now, people will look back on our time as one of pitiable savagery.

So if the past still offers the best practice, use that. If you find a new way to do something better, do that. Never hesitate to evaluate and adopt a better way of doing things. Only then can constant progress become your tradition.

Don't hesitate to choose the best practice; be elite, but do not be elitist.

118 | Elite

‣ Fasting day

Su Shi

Su Shi (1037–1101) was a writer, poet, painter, calligrapher, pharmacologist, and official. He is also known as **Su Dongpo**, which means "Su of the Eastern Slope," after the name of a place that he loved. He is considered one of China's greatest poets.

Although he was an official in various capacities, it was his time as governor of Hangzhou for which he is best remembered, and the causeway he ordered built across West Lake still bears his name. However, his political views twice led to banishment.

Su Shi was popular with the common person, as this folktale relates:

News reached Hangzhou that there would be a new governor named Su Dongpo. The city prepared a celebration and readied cannons to salute the high official. But the new governor did not arrive for many days.

One day, two men went to court, demanding that it settle their dispute. The guard told them the new governor had not yet taken office, but the two men insisted on waiting. Just then, a tall, bearded man wearing Taoist robes rode in on a little donkey, strode to the governor's chair, and sat down. The guard objected: "You can't sit here! You'll be put to death!"

"Why? Who's allowed to sit here?" asked the man.

"Only someone with a gold seal!"

"Oh? Like this?"

Su Dongpo ordered the cannon fire dispensed with and began the hearing right away.

Be elite, but do not be elitist.
Be the best, but always be generous.

It's hard to be good at what you do. But if you are good, never doubt it, and keep trying to be better. No matter what the field, there will always be someone better than you. So why not keep trying to be better?

In the field of calligraphy, there have only been a few truly great calligraphers over the past thousand years. Of course, everyone has to write, and everyone has something to express, but that doesn't change the singular fact that only a few calligraphers are truly celebrated. Among poets, some feel that Li Bai, Du Fu, and Su Shi were among the best—and Su Shi died more than nine hundred years ago. The same is true in Western literature, in music, in physics, in mathematics. The truly great are rare. Therefore, we must all strive to be better and better—we may not overtake the greatest, but we must act every day as if we will. We must constantly strive for excellence.

People sometimes worry about being "elitist." They are aware that they are outstripping their peers, that they are interested in higher levels than other people. But there is nothing wrong with being elite. There is only something wrong with being elitist.

As long as we are trying to be the very best for the sake of being better people, there is no mistake. As long as we do not use our skills to take advantage of others, there is no mistake. As long as we are compassionate and humble enough to use our knowledge to better others for their sakes, there is no mistake.

And to be a person who makes no mistakes is to be elite.

Be the best, but always be generous. Innovate and resolve problems.

119 | Innovate

• Fasting day

The Case of the Folding Fans

The first case that Su Dongpo heard concerned a loan that needed repayment. The first man, Li, had saved ten ounces of silver. His friend Hong asked to borrow it to start a business. After a time, Li wanted to marry and asked for repayment, but Hong did not have any money. Su Dongpo asked why.

"I borrowed the money to start a business selling folding fans," Hong related. "But this year was unseasonably cold and it rained constantly. My fans turned moldy and no one bought them."

Su Dongpo smiled. "Bring me twenty fans and I will settle this case."

When the fans were spread before him, Su Dongpo studied the mold spots on each, and then painted the fans with superb renderings of rocks, mountains, or flowers, obscuring every spot.

He gave ten fans to Li. "Go on the street and call out, 'Fans painted by Su Dongpo, one ounce of silver each.' You will be repaid."

Then he gave the other ten fans to Hong. "Sell these fans and use the capital to start a new business. Case dismissed."

Innovate and resolve problems.
Don't hesitate: be different.

Let's say you can paint like one of the Impressionists. It won't get you much farther than selling paintings in tourist galleries or making greeting cards. What was radical and innovative in one era quickly becomes decorative in another.

We don't celebrate those who are merely skilled duplicators. If you really wanted to, you could make calligraphy, or paint, or play music in skillful imitation of the masters, and no one would consider this a great accomplishment. There's little use copying the art of the past if you don't go on to create the art that is right for *your* time.

So be the best that you can be, but don't spend your time making your best *imitation* of someone, no matter how great your heroes might be. You have to be different.

That's terrifying, isn't it? It seems easier to be someone who works with sure things, because to be creative is to live the riskiest life possible. When Su Dongpo painted the fans, he relied on his skill and his fame, but he improvised something completely new. He made great art and he also solved a dispute. We all should take risks. Taking them is exhilarating and lets you know you are alive. Whether you become the next classical master is beside the point: to dare to be different is to innovate your true self.

Don't hesitate: be different; after all, classic and fundamental aren't equal.

120 | Discern the Fundamental

‣ Fasting day

One Treasure

Yunmen Wenyan (p. 137) said:

> Between heaven and earth, within the universe, is treasure hidden in a body. You take the lantern, enter the Buddha Hall. You take the temple gate and put it on the lantern.

The paradoxical last sentence means that words are simple, but action is difficult.

Lanterns and gate of the meditation hall at Yunmen Temple near Shaoguan, Guangdong.

Yunmen was himself a treasure:

> A monk asked: "What is the road of Yunmen?"
> "Personal experience!"
> "What is the way?"
> "Go!"
> "Where is the road? Where is the way?"
> "Start walking!"

Here is his counterbalance to concerns about patriarchs and ancestors:

> "Do you want to meet the old Patriarchs?" Yunmen pointed his stick above the monks: "The Patriarchs are jumping on your heads!" Then he asked, "Do you wish to look them in the eye?" He pointed to the ground and said: "They are all under your feet!" After a moment, he muttered to himself: "I made a great feast in the temple, but the hungry gods are never satisfied."

Classic and fundamental aren't equal.
The classic is merely a high standard.

Classical culture exists in every country in the world. Classical music, classical literature, classical art, and more form a high standard and the people's collective identity. But as difficult as it is to achieve, the classical is merely a point of view. Bach, for example, has both ardent adherents and detractors. For every admirer of the calligraphy of a Wang Xizhi (p. 85), plenty of people are more moved by the styles of other calligraphers.

Underneath it all, there are even more fundamental forms in life: children growing into adults; people falling in love and choosing to marry; parents raising children; drinking water; eating; sleeping; wanting to travel; working; buildings that give us shelter; the lever and the wheel—there are entire strata to our existence that are deeper and beyond classical.

You can only be who you are, and whether your work becomes classical is a matter for posterity to judge. Grounding yourself in the fundamental is the right way. Yunmen had no thought that he would be remembered a thousand years later. He simply grounded himself in the fundamental.

If we base our lives on the fundamental, then we find that we become people of classical cultivation. Yunmen asked what the one treasure was. But he was not talking about a static thing—like the lantern, the Buddha hall, or the temple gate. He was talking about movement and action. What movement and action?

Yunmen answered: "Go!"

The classic is merely a high standard—when you choose, choose life.

5

The Pomegranate Moon

Night Mooring on Jiande River

I moor my wayward boat in the isle mist.
As the sun sets, my sadness starts anew.
Earth is vast, heaven descends to the trees.
In the clear river, how close the moon seems.

—Meng Haoran (689–740)

The two solar terms within this moon:

EARS OF GRAIN

SUMMER SOLSTICE

Exercise 9

EARS OF GRAIN

During this busy time, wheat is ready to burst and ripen. Farmers harvest wheat and plant rice.

The monsoon season begins south of the Yangtze River. The rains at this time are called Plum Rains because of the ripening fruit, but the excessive moisture can also lead to mold—explaining the less glamorous nickname, Moldy Rains.

This exercise is best practiced during the period of 3:00–7:00 A.M.

1. Stand with feet shoulder-width apart. Arch the body back, head facing upward. Push the palms up as if hoisting a great weight. Hold the push momentarily, then relax, slowly lowering the palms to shoulder level, but still keeping them facing upward.

2. Inhale when you push upward; exhale gently when you relax. Repeat thirty-five times.

3. Sit cross-legged and face forward. Click your teeth together thirty-six times. Roll your tongue between your teeth nine times in each direction. Form saliva in your mouth by pushing your cheeks in and out. When your mouth is filled with saliva, divide the liquid into three portions.

4. Inhale; then exhale, imagining your breath traveling to the dantian and then swallow one-third of the saliva, imagining that it travels to the dantian.

5. Repeat two more times until you've swallowed all three portions.

6. Sit comfortably as long as you like.

Through this exercise, ancient Taoists sought to prevent or treat weakness in the kidneys and legs; dryness when swallowing; pains in the chest and ribs; yellow eyes; excess thirst; heat in the torso and thighs; pain in the head and neck; red face; cough; diarrhea; seminal emission; and depression.

The God of Longevity

The **God of Longevity** (Shou Xing) is also known as the Star of Longevity because he is identified with the Southern Pole Star (Canopus). Qin Shi Huang (259–210 BCE), the First Emperor, established sacrifices to the Old Man of the South Pole in 246 BCE. The god appears as a smiling, elderly man with an exaggeratedly large bald head, a long white beard, and a stooped back—which explains the large staff carved with a dragon's head upon which he leans. A gourd dangling from the staff contains the elixir of immortality, and the peach in his hand also confers longevity. The god is often shown with a deer (homophone for "prosperity") and a bat (homophone for "happiness").

Nineteen Becomes Ninety-One

One story associated with the God of Longevity is the legend of Zhao Yen. When Zhao was born, a physiognomist predicted that he would only live to the age of nineteen. However, he was told that he might escape this fate if he went to a certain field on a certain day far in the future, bringing dried meat and a jar of wine with him. If he found two men playing checkers, he should offer the meat and wine but take particular care not to answer any questions.

On the appointed day, Zhao Yen did as he had been told. He found two men dressed in rich silk playing checkers under a mulberry tree. When the men had finished the meat and wine offered to them, they asked the boy how they might thank him for his hospitality. Zhao Yen remained silent.

"I can see that you are only fated to live until the age of nineteen," said one of the old men. He happened to be the God of the North Pole, the determiner of the day on which people are born. His even older companion, a man with an enormous bald head and a white beard, who was the God of the South Pole (and who, in this version of the legend, determined the length of people's lives), proposed to reciprocate the boy's generosity by reversing the numbers in the book of life. Thus, the boy's predicted life span of nineteen years became ninety-one.

In some versions of this story the two gods are the gods of birth and death, and Zhao Yen is first granted the ninety-one years, then made immortal to become the God of Longevity himself.

The Symbols of Longevity

Longevity is a major goal of Taoist practice and a central part of Chinese culture. One gives a scroll of the God of Longevity on the birthday of any relative sixty years (or older) to wish a long life. Chinese art is filled with dozens of symbols of longevity to convey these good wishes in various ways:

- **The One Hundred Ways to Write Longevity** There are one hundred different characters meaning "longevity."
- **Bamboo** A homophone for "congratulations," it is evergreen and bends in storms without breaking (symbolizing humility and integrity).
- **Crane** Its white feathers are like white hair on an old person, and it was believed that a crane could live up to a thousand years.
- **Deer** It was believed that a deer could live a long time and find the mushroom of immortality. Its name is also a homophone for "prosperity."
- **The Eight Immortals** (p. 124) Any of them could grant immortality. ▶

The character "longevity" inscribed on Wudangshan. © Bernard De Poorter

121 | Long Life

- Fasting day
- Birthday of the God of Longevity

Vignettes of the God of Longevity

The image of the God of Longevity (p. 145) is frequently seen in homes and at birthday celebrations.

He appears in the famous novel *Journey to the West*, holding the mushroom of immortality *(lingzhi)* and offering it to Buddha to preserve life.

In the Chinese opera *Lady White Snake* (p. 227), Lady White travels to the South Pole to steal a magic herb that will save her husband, Xu Xian, but the God of Longevity stops her.

The *History of the Later Han Dynasty (Hou Han Shu)* describes a ceremony to the God of Longevity where those seventy years and older are awarded a gnarled and carved staff just like the one that the god uses.

Choose life.
Live long.

Choose life. Death and suffering are always at hand. Simply stop breathing and you choose death. Death is easy. Nurturing life takes effort.

Live long. This world is so filled with wonder that it takes a lifetime to appreciate it.

Choose life. Let us be moved to reverence, for reverence calls for our heart, mind, body, and breath to be one.

Live long. As we grow older, we don't look at the world as we did when we were younger. We need to give ourselves the chance to look anew.

Choose life. For joy is fleeting and happiness seldom flutters into our days.

Live long. For you have gathered wisdom unique to yourself, and the people still in darkness need the light you have.

Choose life. For the way is eternal and every road needs travelers to walk it.

Live long. For you have your own place in the universe that no one in history could fill—and no one in the future can ever take away.

Choose life.

Live long. Give thanks for your long life.

122 | Gratitude

"A Year of Abundance"

This poem is from the *Classic of Poetry*.

> It's an abundant year, with much millet
>   and rice.
> Our tall granaries are filled
> with millions and millions of grains
> for wine and sweet wine,
> to offer to our forefathers and
>   foremothers
> in numerous ceremonies:
> all good fortune descends on us.

Give thanks for your long life.
Give thanks for the tall grain.

No matter what your age, be grateful for all that you have received. If you have the strength to work, and you planted your fields, then give thanks when the grain is up to your ears.

Plunge into those clean and waving stalks. Let them surround you in windblown waves. All the richness of life is yours. All the blessings of life are yours. All the gratitude for what you have is yours too.

The largesse of this life is constant: the sun keeps shining, the grain keeps growing. While we were experiencing the ebb and flow of our emotions, the world goes on in constancy. As we mature, we must take on that same constancy—and we should be most constant in our gratitude.

Give thanks for the tall grain. Reap when the heart and the mind are one.

Christopher Elwell/Shutterstock

123 | A Sincere Heart

The Heart of a Sage

Di Xin (r. 1075–1046 BCE) was the last emperor of the Shang dynasty. In his early years, he was bright enough to win all arguments and strong enough to hunt wild beasts bare-handed. In his later years, however, he gave himself over to liquor and sex and neglected the affairs of state. He was enamored with his consort, Daji (eleventh century BCE), spending most of his time with her. The two were reportedly aroused by watching men being tortured.

His advisors tried desperately to get Di Xin to reform and lead his country. **Bigan** (eleventh century BCE), dubbed the most faithful minister in history, said, "To fear death and not remonstrate is cowardly. Only to go on remonstrating until stopped by death is true loyalty."

Bigan went to the emperor and began remonstrating. Di Xin ignored him and continued his vicious pleasures. Bigan stood and remonstrated for three days. Finally, the drunken Di Xin said, "I have heard that an ordinary man's heart has five openings, but a sage's heart has seven. The way Bigan talks, he must be a sage. Let's see whether his heart has five or seven openings." He ordered Bigan killed where he stood, and his heart cut out to be examined.

The temple to Bigan, built in 494 BCE, stands in Weihui, Henan. It is near the site of the Battle of Muye, which ended the Shang dynasty. Some people identify Bigan as the God of Wealth (p. 9).

When the heart and the mind are one,
the fullness of life is complete.

It's good to study anatomy. It's good to know all we can about ourselves. Understanding how we're made helps us maintain our health.

The heart is one of the chief components of our health. Like breathing and thinking, its function has to be constant: we need to keep our blood circulating to keep living.

Yet in every culture, the heart is the place of emotions we cannot possibly determine anatomically or by dissection. When we're sad, we speak of heartache. When we're happy, we speak of joy in our heart. When we're excited or stressed, our heart beats harder. When we're relaxed, our heartbeat slows. If a person lives a life of constant frustration and disappointment, that person's heart is weakened. If a person lives a life of overconsumption, that person's heart is strained. If a person lives a healthy life of exercise, good diet, and good rest, that person's heart is strong.

Interestingly, in Chinese "heart" is synonymous with "mind". This is important to realize when reading translations of the old texts. Frequently, a line such as "The mind of the sage . . ." could just as easily have been translated "The heart of the sage . . ." It's hard to know whether this double meaning is the wisdom of the language or not, but to contemplate it brings guidance nevertheless.

The fullness of life is complete when standing amid the golden grain.

124 | Golden Serenity

"A Place for a Joyous Outing"

The Tang dynasty poet Li Shangyin (c. 813–858) was a moderately successful civil servant, although he never was promoted to a high position.

Toward evening, with restless thoughts,
I drive my carriage onto the ancient plain
The setting sun is boundlessly beautiful
until trembling dusk draws near.

Standing amid the golden grain,
you'll have the peace of your right place.

This is the time of Ears of Grain, a time of ripening. Grain turns golden when ripe, and that is the symbolic color of the earth.

Usually, the explanation of that symbolism is that the earth in northern China is yellow. But another possible explanation is that grain and some fruits turn yellow when ripe and full. Yellow is the color of fullness. Yellow is the color of plenty. In this time of grain ripening, we can look out over our fields and sigh with satisfaction.

There's something comforting in that simple response. There's time enough to be learned, sophisticated, and discerning. There's a place for action, a place for organizing, a place for striving for grandness. But there is also a place—notice that word, "place"—for taking stock of what we have, celebrating the joy of the earth giving us grain to eat, taking pride in our labor, and reflecting that, yes, we have a place in this world, and that place is good.

The sun shines down on us without discrimination. The earth grows our crops without reservation. The rivers quench our thirst without limitation. The days follow nights without separation. The air gives us breath without deviation. Nature gives us all this from its vastness.

So we should take the time to appreciate that, to take comfort in it, and to allow serenity to come to us as the sun shines down on the acres of amber grain. There is no serenity like the serenity of a place. There is no serenity like the serenity of belonging. There is no serenity like the serenity of having grain as high as your ears.

What you hear is the serenity of what is right.

You'll have the peace of your right place when the sage has two eyes and opens a third.

Dragon Boat Festival

This festival is known as the **Fifth Moon, Fifth Day Festival** (Duanwu Jie) or the **Dragon Boat Festival** (Longchuan Jie) Most people associate this festival with dragon boat races, the rice dumplings called *zongzi*, and the poet **Qu Yuan**.

The dragon boat is constructed of wood and looks like a long, low canoe. It is often brightly painted with a fully carved dragon head at the prow.

The standard crew consists of twenty paddlers facing the bow, a drummer at the bow facing the paddlers, and a sweeper at the rudder. However, some boats have as few as ten crew members while others have as many as eighty. When the boat is large, the drummer stands at its center.

The drummer is the leader of the boat. The drummer signals the crew with drum beats, hand signals, or calls for the crew to do their best during the race.

Dragon boat racing developed into a modern sport in Hong Kong during the 1970s. According to the International Dragon Boat Federation, the sport is thriving in more than sixty countries with the sponsorship of many colleges, corporations, and community organizations.

windmoon/Shutterstock

Zongzi, Sachets, Lucky Strings, and Tiger Head Shoes

Called rice dumplings or Chinese tamales, zongzi consist of glutinous rice and various fillings wrapped in bamboo or reed leaves in pyramidal or cylindrical shapes. They are cooked by steaming or boiling. Each family has its own recipes, but common ingredients include mung beans, red bean paste, jujubes, pork, chicken, sausage, black mushrooms, salted duck eggs, chestnuts, cooked peanuts, green beans, dried shrimp, dried scallops, and taro.

Increasingly, people buy their zongzi in stores and even online. In China and Taiwan, the price and sale volume of zongzi are used as economic indicators.

Another custom is to hang calamus (a fragrant wetland plant) and mugwort *(moxa)* on one's door and to give pyramid-shaped silk sachets to children. This emphasis on fragrant plants is reminiscent of Qu Yuan's poems. In "Lady of the Xiang" ("Xiang Furen"), there are repeated references to fragrant plants and flowers. White sedge, duckweed, lotus, irises, perfumed pepper, cassia, orchid, lily, peonies, fig leaves, sweet clover, and wild ginger enrich his imagery, and he is extravagant in his love of scent:

> Combine a hundred plants! Fill the courtyard!
> Let fragrance build! Scent the halls and gates!

Baisuo—five colored strings, sometimes with little bells—are given to children to wear around their necks, hands, and legs for good luck. Tiger Head shoes—embroidered red cloth shoes—are also popular for small children.

Qu Yuan

While there are a number of explanations for the origins of the Dragon Boat Festival, most people associate it with Qu Yuan (339–278 BCE), of the feudal state of Chu (roughly the south-central and eastern part of China today). Chu was one of seven feudal states that formed after a larger state collapsed.

Qu is one of China's earliest and most revered poets, visionaries, and patriots. He was a descendant of the Chu royal house and an official of the court.

When King Huai (r. 328–288 BCE) decided to make an alliance with the neighboring state of Qin (roughly centered around present-day Sichuan and Shaanxi), Qu voiced his opposition. He was accused of treason and banished.

In the years that followed, the ruler of Qin, King Huiwen (d. 311 BCE) and his strategist, Zhang Yi (d. 309 BCE), undermined Chu through various diplomatic plots and a relentless series of small military raids across the border. Chu suffered many defeats and was slowly forced to cede territory to Qin.

When King Huai finally attacked Qin, Zhang Yi manipulated King Huai into offending his other allies politically. As a result, they joined the war on Qin's side. In 299 BCE, King Huai was lured to Qin for a diplomatic meeting, where he was captured and held hostage until his death.

Thereafter, Qin conducted a succession of military campaigns against Chu, until General Bai Qi (d. 257 BCE), a man known more for his brutality than his strategy, captured the Chu capital of Ying. Qin would eventually conquer all the other feudal states, uniting their territories under a single rule. The Qin ruler who did this was none other than Qin Shi

Huang (p. 159), known as the First Emperor, and the man whose terra-cotta army in Xi'an became a world-famous archaeological discovery in our own time. The name we use today, "China," is derived from the word "Qin."

When the capital of Ying fell, Qu Yuan hefted a large stone in his arms and drowned himself in the Miluo River on the fifth day of the fifth moon. The dragon boats reenact the urgent attempts of the people to rescue the heroic poet. According to legend, the people beat the water with their paddles to frighten away the water dragons and threw lumps of rice into the river so the fish would not eat Qu Yuan's body. This gave rise to the practice of making zongzi.

Dragon Boats in Qu Yuan's Own Poetry

One of the best ways to understand that dragon boats existed in Qu Yuan's own time is to turn to a reference in his poem, "Lady Xiang" ("Xiang Jun").

In this poem, Qu describes searching for the goddess herself. Here is a portion of the poem:

> The goddess does not come, she holds back.
> What keeps her on her island?
> I would look upon her elegant beauty.
> Plowing through the water in my cassia boat,
> I command the waters of the Yuan and Xiang to smooth their
>   waves:
> Oh great rivers! Calm your flow!
> She waits for the lord who has not yet appeared.
> Who does she think of while she plays her reed-pipes?
>
> Sailing my flying dragon, I head north,
> and I steer a course to Dongting Lake.
> Evergreens, lychee, cypresses, and orchids in silk.
> Irises on my paddle, orchids on my banner,
> I reach Cen Yang mooring.
> I've crossed a great river, and my soul swells!

The flying dragon in the second stanza refers to the boat Qu used—a boat with a dragon carved on its prow. Dragon worship must already have been long established. The poem also shows how the mighty paddling of a boat and ecstatic emotions were part of Qu Yuan's life. The Dragon Boat Festival of today not only reenacts the drama of searching for Qu Yuan upon his death, but also recalls his life.

The *Songs of Chu*

The "Lady Xiang" is one of many poems preserved in the *Songs of Chu (Chuci)*, an anthology of poems in the Chu style. The collection begins with "The Sorrow of Parting" ("Li Sao"), Qu Yuan's most famous poem.

The Chu songs differ from the *Book of Poetry*, abandoning the regular four-character verses and allowing verses of varying lengths. Moreover, its pronunciations, and therefore its rhymes, are based on the Chu dialect. The *Book of Poetry* was northern in its structure, sentiments, and pronunciation. The Chu songs were distinctly southern in their open emotion, ecstatic visions, vigorous actions (racing over the waters),

and love of extravagant imagery ("evergreens, lychee, cypresses, and orchids").

Incidentally, the *Songs of Chu* has had several revisions, and one of the key figures in collecting the poems was the Prince of Huainan (p. 50).

"The Sorrow of Parting"

The poem "The Sorrow of Parting" is commonly known by its Chinese title, "Li Sao." It is also known as "Encountering Sorrow" or "Encountering Trouble." The entire poem is long—372 lines and about 2,400 characters. It is worth a read and repeated study. Here are some of its major themes.

Qu Yuan's Background The poem opens with Qu Yuan stating his own background:

> I'm descended from the High Yang god.
> My father was Bo Yong.

Ecstatic Exclamation Most of the poem's lines consist of six words followed by *xi,* a breathing syllable that lends emphasis to the middle of the line. This structure creates a feeling of ecstatic utterance and vigorous emotion.

> In the morning I forded the white water; I scaled Lang Feng and
>   tied my horse.
> I turned to look back suddenly and began to sob; I was sad that no
>   woman was with me on that hill.

Shamanistic Imagery He invokes a spirit journey. The places in the excerpt below are legendary: the Hanging Gardens are in Kunlunshan (on the northern edge of the Tibetan Plateau), Lake Xian is a constellation, and the Fusang is a divine tree that grows in the east where the sun rises.

> My team of four jade horses pulls a phoenix chariot; I rise steeply
>   in a whirlwind into the heights.
> In the morning I unchock my wheels, and leave Cang Wu; by the
>   evening I reach the Hanging Gardens.
> I want to rest a little by its spirit gate; but how quickly the sun
>   plunges. . . .
> I water my horses at Lake Xian; I tie their reins to the Fusang tree.

Disappointment in the King He clearly spells out the king's refusal to listen, and the intrigues in court.

> He does not see my inner feelings; heeding slander, he turns on
>   me in a rage.
> I know my bold speech brings me trouble! But I must endure and
>   abide.

Despair The poem is famous for the sadness it expresses, but it also demonstrates the poet's determination to keep his integrity.

> I am bitter, forlorn, thwarted; why am I alone and poor? It's the
>   times.
> Better to die quickly as an exile; I cannot bear to live like them.

Qu Yuan was a great poet. He leaves us a lasting challenge to be spiritual, politically vital, highly principled, and true to ourselves for a lifetime. ▶

125 | Spiritual Politics

"Elegy for the National Martyrs" from the *Songs of Chu*

This poem is from the suite of poems called "Nine Songs" (which actually consists of eleven songs).

> They gripped the halberds of Wu, wore rhinoceros-hide armor.
> Chariot hub crashed, short swords clashed.
> Banners blotted out the sun, their foes charged like clouds.
> Volleys of arrows answered each other, warriors vied to be first.
>
> The enemy broke their ranks, trampled their lines.
> The horse on the left died, the one on the right was slashed.
> Chariot wheels seized in the dust, teams of horses fell tangled.
> Raising jade drumsticks, they shouted and beat their drums.
>
> Yet heaven's season was against them, the powerful gods were angry!
> Our staunchest men were slaughtered, left scattered on the field.
> They went out, did not come back, will never return.
> The plains lie empty, the roads stretch on.
>
> They buckled on their long swords, raised their Qin bows.
> Although their heads were hacked from their bodies, their hearts held no regret.
> They were truly brave, such great warriors.
> Strong and powerful to the end, they were never cowed.
>
> Their bodies may be dead, but their spirits have become gods.
> Their souls are transformed, they are our ghost heroes!

The sage has two eyes and opens a third.
Both demons and gods alike are seen.

Qu Yuan represents the combination of the political with the poetic and spiritual. He served in the court, advocating policies that he thought beneficial for his country. He wrote poetry that became immortal not only in his native language but in other languages as well. He came from a shamanistic culture and his poetry spoke of ecstatic visions of gods and goddesses and of spirit travel. He saw the warfare of his time and paid tribute to the heroes who bravely fought to defend their country.

Nowadays, we don't usually think of being political, poetic, and spiritual at the same time. We like our political leaders to be conventionally religious, but we don't want them to profess ecstatic visions of the divine. We want our leaders to be good orators and writers, but we don't expect them to be poets. Yet Qu Yuan's example shows us the importance of being both political and poetic.

We should look back on all that we've examined so far and really see how much of Taoism and Confucianism is both political and spiritual. The *Daodejing, Zhuangzi,* the *I Ching,* and of course all the Confucian canon contain plenty of political advice. The tendency to read all of Qu Yuan's poetry not as poems of ecstatic love but as allegories of ruler and subject is another way to meld the political and spiritual. The real issue is this: when we open our eyes after sitting on our meditation cushions, how can we not see the suffering of the world? And if we see the suffering of the world, how can we not become politically involved?

Both demons and gods alike are seen, but nobody sees that heroes do not fail in failing.

126 | Failure

The Young Marshal

Zhang Xueliang (1901–2001) was known as the Young Marshal. He is famous for the **Xi'an Incident** (Xi'an Shibian) and is regarded as a patriotic hero.

Imperial rule ended in China in 1911. However, no stable government emerged and many factions vied for domination, including warlords, the Nationalists, and the Communists. From 1927 on, the Nationalists and Communists fought a civil war. The situation became more complicated when Japan invaded and occupied neighboring Manchuria in 1931.

Toward the end of 1936, the military commander and leader of the Nationalists, Chiang Kai-Shek (1887–1975), flew to Xi'an to monitor the campaign against the Communists. During that same period, a Japanese backed Mongolian army invaded China, but was turned back by the Nationalists.

Zhang and others urged Chiang halt the civil war, but Chiang refused. On December 12, 1936, the Young Marshal kidnapped Chiang to force the Nationalists to join forces with the Communists against the Japanese. The Young Marshal was right: Japan invaded the following year.

Although Chiang agreed to unite with the Communists, he kept the Young Marshal prisoner for forty years. Zhang Xueliang, true to his name (Study Excellence), spent his time reading literature and the Bible; collected fan paintings, calligraphy, and other works; and became a famous artist himself. The Young Marshal was finally allowed to emigrate to Hawaii in 1993, some fifty-seven years after his courageous act. He died at the age of one hundred.

Heroes do not fail in failing
to keep the ruler from failing.

Was Qu Yuan a failure? After all, he failed in persuading his liege to listen to his advice. He failed in his policies (although history ultimately vindicated him). He failed to save his country from ruin.

Qu Yuan was a paragon of righteousness. He kept to his ideals, even through his ruler did not listen to him. We are urged to do the same. But it's hard to live a life of disappointment and apparent failure. It's hard to be banished and to die feeling that none of what you did mattered. If it were not for his poetry, we wouldn't know of Qu Yuan at all. There were thousands of people like him who were exiled or executed for standing for the ideals that the entire country should have been following. We happen to know about Qu Yuan because he recorded his thoughts in timeless and gorgeous verse.

Hidden inside this question is another one about the emperors of every dynasty: why did so many get it wrong? Was it personal failure? Their failures are different from Qu Yuan's. Their failures are condemned by history. Emperor Huai did not listen to Qu Yuan and banished him. Di Xin had Bigan killed (p. 148). If we look at the record, we can see that every emperor who destroyed a hero ended up destroying himself and sometimes even the country. It seems inevitable that a ruler of a country will be prone to error, intrigue, corruption, personal foibles, and excess.

Today we've turned away from dictatorships, tyranny, and imperial governments. Yet the dynamic of being wrongly rejected still exists today in governments, corporations, academia, and sometimes even clubs and families. Someone's in charge. Someone gets it wrong, but won't listen to advice. Then, if we're in the position of Qu Yuan, we repeat the same drama: we stand up for what we are responsible for, and we are punished for it.

Is that failure? Or does the failure lie with those in power?

To keep the ruler from failing, stand up even if all seems against you.

127 | Speak Up

Criticism and Dissent

Two streams run through Chinese tradition. One is the exhortation to be loyal and obedient to one's ruler. But the other is a sharp observation of the wrongs of society. Qu Yuan's position against injustice had ample precedent.

Confucius describes four evils in the *Analects*:

> To kill people without teaching them is called oppression.
> To demand that work be completed without any prearrangement is called tyranny.
> To be slow in issuing orders and then suddenly demand a severe deadline is called betrayal.
> Finally, when it comes to rewarding people, to be stingy in compensation is called being a petty official.

Mencius said that a ruler could only follow two courses—benevolence, or its opposite:

> A ruler who is greatly brutal to the people will be slain himself, and his kingdom will be destroyed.

In the *Daodejing*, Chapter 17, Laozi writes of a bad ruler, "People fear him." Of the worst ruler, he writes, "People scorn him. If a ruler is not sufficiently trustworthy, then there will be no trust."

Even if all seems against you,
speak up! Win or lose, just speak up!

People are starving. Tyrants are wiping out entire provinces. Rich people bully the poor into working like slaves. Corporations regard children as customers to be groomed for profit. The drive for ruthless efficiency has ruined our farm systems and loaded our foods with unhealthy additives. When natural disasters strike, not enough people give aid. Our taxes diminish our personal wealth while we watch government inefficiency fritter public money away. The gap between the highly educated and the marginally educated increases. Immigrants are made the scapegoats for social ills. Sickness is rife in our country and we are still fighting epidemics. Women face the fear of sexual assault.

On an individual level, the problems are no lighter. Our managers are unfair to us. We cannot get decent wages for the amount of work we do. We are driven to work harder for less money while bosses gobble expense-account meals that cost more than we are paid in a day. Workers who become too old are forced out of the company. Jobs are outsourced. Jobs are eliminated. Unemployment continues. We don't have enough money to support ourselves or our families. We can't find places to live. We lose our houses and are forced onto the streets. We argue with our spouses. Our spouses abuse us. Our children abandon us.

Injustice happens every day. Yes, we have to work against it. But the first thing we have to do is to speak up! No matter what it is, say something! You can argue that Qu Yuan was unsuccessful in rescuing his country, but at least he spoke up.

And in the poetry that has outlasted both his home country and his country's conquerors, he is still speaking up!

Speak up! Win or lose, just speak up! For a foot cannot count what is short.

128 | Without Diving

▸ Fasting day

"Divination" from *Songs of Chu*

In this part-prose, part-poetry piece, Qu Yuan consults with Great Diviner Zheng Zhanyin. The diviner prepares his instruments of divination—turtle shells and yarrow stalks—and waits for Qu's inquiry. Instead, Qu Yuan asks many questions. Here are a few of them:

Is it better to be sincere, genuine, honest, simple, and loyal—or should I labor and exhaust myself in endless service without end?

Is it better to condemn injustice as if plowing up grass and weeds—or should I travel in search of a great patron and fame?

Is it better to be correct in speech without hiding—even if it's at risk to my own life—or should I follow the manners of the vulgar and wealthy just to secure a life?

Is it better to reach for lofty ideals and safeguard the truth—or should I serve the king's consort, flattering, chattering, and grinning with the other scholars?

When Qu Yuan had blurted out all his questions, Zheng Zhanyin stopped and excused himself, saying:

Sir, a foot cannot count what is short, and an inch cannot count what is long. Things can be counted, but without any basis. Knowledge can count without revealing. Numbers can count without reaching an end. Divination can count without clearing things up. Use what you understand of your ruler's heart to carry out your ruler's will. Such things cannot be foretold by turtle shells and yarrow stalks.

A foot cannot count what is short.
An inch cannot count what is long.

The ghost of the Zheng Zhanyin said: "I made my comments to the poet as succinctly as possible. Whatever calculations we use to make our decisions, we have to use what is appropriate. If we measure what's short, a foot-long ruler is too big. If we measure what is lengthy, the span of an inch will not be long enough. We have to tailor our method of inquiry to the situation.

"What can you say when confronted with the infinite? Things can be counted without any basis. Knowledge can count without enlightening. Numbers can count without reaching an end. We can calculate all we want in the immensity of things and still not arrive at a concrete or usable understanding. If we're tangled in calculations, we will never be able to make reliable decisions.

"Who among us has not been faced with the same questions as Qu Yuan? And yet we are afraid to make mistakes. How can we choose to live rejected and alone for the sake of what we know is right? Numbers won't give the answer.

"Only our own heart and will answer all questions—and reach the right conclusions."

An inch cannot count what is long; when the waters are clear, wash your tassels.

129 | Qu Yuan's Fisherman

"The Fisherman," from the *Songs of Chu*

After Qu Yuan had been banished, he wandered, reciting poetry while walking alone by the rivers and marshlands. His face was emaciated, his appearance haggard. A fisherman saw him and asked, "Are you not the leader of the Three Great Clan Districts? What has brought you to such a dire state?"

"All the world is muddy," Qu Yuan replied. "I alone am clear. All men are drunk. I alone am sober. That is why you see an exile."

"The sage is not blocked by anything," said the fisherman, "but instead moves as the world moves and shifts. If the world is muddy, why not dredge the mud and disperse the waves? If all men are drunk, why not eat up their dregs and drink their lees? Why get exiled because of your deep thoughts and lofty policies?"

Qu Yuan said: "I have heard that one who has just washed his hair should brush off his hat. One who has just bathed should shake out his clothes. How can I go along with the accusations and schemes of others? I would rather throw myself in the river waters and be interred in the bowels of fish than to submit my shining light to this dirty world of ignorance and vulgarity."

The fisherman first smiled, then laughed. He struck his oar in the water and departed, singing:

> When the cold waves are clear,
> I can wash my tassels in them.
> When the cold waves are muddy, I can
> still wash my feet.

With that, he was gone down the waterway without speaking further.

When the waters are clear, wash your tassels.
When the waters are muddy, rinse your feet.

The *Songs of Chu* recounts this encounter between Qu Yuan and a fisherman. It's difficult to know if the story is factual or allegorical, but in either case it provides a frank, Taoist response to Qu Yuan's personality.

The fisherman is a well-known symbol for Chinese culture in general and Taoism in particular. A fisherman represents freedom—he isn't tied to serving in court or beholden to a taskmaster's schedule. He spends all his time in nature, and although fishing is work, the fisherman has to develop a certain relaxed attitude toward life: sometimes he'll catch many fish, sometimes he won't, but he'll view a sparse haul with forbearance and even cheerfulness.

In this story, then, the fisherman represents someone more attuned to nature, someone more practical, flexible, and accepting. Qu Yuan, acknowledged to be a great leader and patriot, has his single position, which he asserts with great determination. He does not want to be sullied by the dirty world of ignorance and vulgarity. In contrast, the fisherman does not take such a rigid position. If the world is muddy, why not do something about it? If people are deluded, why not work with that delusion?

Qu Yuan's response to the world is to hold himself apart from it, to keep his integrity and purity, and to rail against the corruption of his time. The Taoist response is to work with whatever one is given, to look for the advantages in every situation, and to never allow oneself to be destroyed by others. As admirable as Qu Yuan is as a hero, a Taoist has a far more subtle approach.

When the waters are muddy, rinse your feet: take your law from heaven and act with that truth.

130 | Confucius's Fisherman

Confucius and the Fisherman

The *Zhuangzi* describes a scene with Confucius and a fisherman. The story is lengthy and worth reading in its entirety, but here is a brief summation:

Confucius and his disciples were on an excursion in the woods when a fisherman stopped his boat and approached them. His beard and hair were white and his sleeves long and dangling. He asked the students who Confucius was, and they replied that their teacher was a sage.

"Is he a ruler?" asked the fisherman. "Or does he serve a prince or king?"

"No," the students replied.

The fisherman turned, laughing. "Benevolence is benevolence, but I'm afraid that he will not escape the evils that all humanity bears. He is embittering his mind, straining his body, and endangering his true nature. How far he is from a proper way of life!"

When Confucius was told of the fisherman, he went to him. The fisherman reproached Confucius for his interfering efforts by naming four evils:

Conducting great affairs, altering what is long-established [practice], to obtain for oneself a reputation for meritorious service is called ambition. Claiming all wisdom, intruding into affairs, encroaching on the work of others and representing it as one's own is called greediness. Seeing one's errors without changing them, going on more resolutely even if one is corrected is called obstinacy. Approving when another agrees with oneself and disapproving when no one agrees is called boastful conceit. These are the four evils.

Confucius begged to learn more from the fisherman to "finish my learning of the Great Way."

The fisherman refused: "I have heard. . . . If you cannot walk with someone who does not know Tao, do not associate with him and you will not be responsible! Do your best, but I must leave you now!" And with that, the fisherman rowed away.

Take your law from heaven and act with that truth.
Then you will not meddle, though you still act.

Qu Yuan advocated independence and righteousness for his country and was banished. Confucius advocated benevolence, propriety, and just government and never found a ruler who would follow his advice. Both men are rebuked in symbolic stories. The Taoist view advocated by the fisherman in each tale is not to interfere with the world but to work with it as it is.

Zhuangzi's fisherman tells Confucius the truth as he understands it. One must possess truth, for without pure sincerity one cannot move others. Confucius advocates propriety, but the fisherman rejects those who "force themselves to wail if they do not feel real sorrow, or who force themselves to be angry without exciting awe in others, or who force themselves to be affectionate when there is no reciprocation." Instead, "true grief can be silent yet sorrowful. True anger may have no outward sign, yet awaken awe. True affection may not show outwardly by even a smile, yet will elicit a harmonious reciprocation." It is inner truth, not outward spirituality, that the fisherman values. He allows for filial duty, loyalty and integrity, pleasant enjoyment, sadness and sorrow—as long as they are genuinely felt. What he rejects is Confucius's insistence on form, on prescribing behavior for every activity from joy to sorrow.

"A person's proper truth comes from heaven and it operates spontaneously and steadily," the fisherman explains. "Therefore the sages take their law from heaven, prize their truth without bowing to the restrictions of custom. The stupid do the opposite. They do not take their law from heaven and follow the influences of others. They do not prize inner truth, but are dominated by ordinary things and waver according to customs."

Then you will not meddle, though you still act when you question heaven.

131 | Questioning Heaven

"Questioning Heaven" from the *Songs of Chu*

This piece consists of 172 questions ranging through heaven, the cosmos, astronomy, weather, heroes of antiquity, and kings and princes. They indicate Qu Yuan's searching mind and his view of the world and society around him.

Here are some of those questions:

Who can tell us of the beginning of the remote past?
Who can prove what it was like before high and low had taken shape?
Who can penetrate to the most obscure limits of dark and light?
Who can recognize the fastest-moving shapes?
There is the brightest of the bright, and the darkest of the dark, but what comes of them?
Yin and yang combine in three ways. Where is their root and what are their transformations?

. . . .

Who set down the Eight Columns and why were they too short in the southeast?
Where are the boundaries of the Nine Heavens and how do they join each other?
They have so many turns and corners, who can account for them all?

. . . .

What happened when Peng Keng poured pheasant broth to the gods?
What lengthened his already long life?

. . . .

Bees and moths have short lives, yet why are they be so strong?
When the maiden was startled while picking ferns, why did the deer protect her?
Why was she happy, going north to the gushing waters?
Her elder brother had a hunting dog. Why did his younger brother want it?

When you question heaven
the act is the answer.

It takes a brilliant but also exasperated mind to pose Qu Yuan's questions to heaven. Needless to say, these are not the questions of the dull, the unimaginative, the vulgar, or the mediocre.

Maybe Qu Yuan's point was that no one could answer these questions and that he was ridiculing conventional learning. Or maybe he was being truly Taoist and indicating that the only real answer to these questions was the single word "mystery." Daring to question heaven is a dangerous thing. Qu Yuan knew he was standing on the brink, facing the sky, and challenging the supreme power of the universe.

Or, if he heard no answer, was that his point? Was he trying to ridicule heaven, shaping it into mute nature, dumb happenstance, a mere accidental reality only appearing to have some semblance of order and reason?

If he was a good Confucianist, he may have been humbly asking the questions, expecting no answers, saying that he understood, as a small person, that he could never expect to have them resolved, and that he was only begging for the slightest favor.

Or he may have been flirting with the temptation to find the answers by any means—after all, he lived in a shamanistic culture where people sought gods or sought to have the gods enter into them. Might he have been tempted to enter into some Faustian arrangement to learn more?

We have to question heaven. One might say our entire lives are a question to heaven. No matter what you think of Qu Yuan's reasons for questioning heaven, the very questions are in themselves signs that heaven answers.

The act is the answer when a good poem can block a sword.

132 | A Poem's Power

The First Emperor

Qin Shi Huang (259–210 BCE), whose name means "The First Emperor," established the Qin dynasty by conquering six other feudal states and creating a unified China in 221 BCE.

Qin Shi Huang was concerned with reformation. He set a daily quota of reports to read himself—measured by

the pound. He standardized weights, measures, the width of chariot wheels, and money. Where there were smaller walls of defense in the conquered states, he ordered Meng Tian (p. 47) to join and enlarge them, forming the Great Wall of China. His chancellor, Li Si (p. 47), created the first standardized written Chinese language based on a variety of previous scripts.

Burning of the Books

Qin Shi Huang ordered the burning of most of the books in his realm at Li Si's recommendation. There were so many scholars using history books to voice dissent that they were called the Hundred Schools of Thought, and this annoyed the emperor.

The only books exempted were those on war, medicine, agriculture, and divination. Even the *Classic of Poetry* and the *Classic of History* were to be destroyed. We only have some of these texts today because they were hidden away or reconstructed by memory (in those days, a scholar was expected to memorize, recite, and expound on entire books).

Qin Shi Huang also ordered hundreds of scholars buried alive, along with alchemists who had failed to produce the elixir of immortality.

A good poem can block a sword.
The right poem should stop a war.

What power does poetry have? Written on a scrap of paper, a poem can be crumpled, burned, shredded. If it's committed to memory, every mind that knows it can be scrambled, brutalized, extinguished. The poet can be starved, ridiculed, tortured. The listener can be reeducated, persecuted, brainwashed, exterminated.

Qin Shi Huang, who destroyed the state of Chu, ordered nearly all books burned and the scholars buried alive. Irritated by dissent, annoyed with plurality of opinion, and scornful of those who tried to assert the lessons of history to question his imperial will, he reached the same conclusion as he had when he first gazed at the feudal states: destroy all that was different and unite the world under his own rule.

Qin Shi Huang was a warrior. His armies were formidable and brutal. Killing women, scholars, poets, and people of other states was easy. What did their gods do to protect them? Nothing. What did their wisdom do to guide them? Nothing. What did their poetry do to preserve them? Nothing. How thoroughly Qin Shi Huang must have disregarded the passions and hopes of mere peasants. How useless he must have found poetry. He would have said, "I can kill any of you by the thousands and your poetry cannot save you in the least."

When Qin Shi Huang died, he was buried in a tomb that has not been opened to this day. He was guarded by terra-cotta warriors with real weapons. However, the empire did not last. His palaces were burned and the dynasty fell within four years after his death. Qin Shi Huang, who asserted the supreme judgment of the sword, faded away, while Qu Yuan (p. 150), a man banished by his own king, a citizen of a country that was obliterated, left poetry that has lasted to this day.

"What good is a poem?" ask pragmatists, tyrants, and killers. It cannot stop a bullet. It cannot build a country. It cannot manufacture products. It cannot be used to gain large profits. But a poem inspires, and people then stand against despots. A poem inspires, and people then stop wars.

The right poem should stop a war, as you feel your place in your generation.

133 | Ancient Cities

- Birthday of **Guan Yu**
- Birthday of the **City God**

Guan Yu

Guan Yu (p. 17) is celebrated on more than one day in the lunar calendar, indicating his popularity. He is one of the most revered generals in Chinese history, a fighter of such skill, bravery, loyalty, and righteousness that he was proclaimed a god. His titles include prince, duke, marquis, and, posthumously, "Saintly Emperor Guan the Great God Who Subdues Demons of the Three Worlds and Whose Awe Spreads Far and Moves Heaven." One can see statues of him everywhere, from homes to businesses, police stations to gangster headquarters.

The City God

A City God (Cheng Huang) is in charge of protecting each city and its inhabitants. There are ongoing ceremonies in his honor, and people often pray to the god for help and support. He is worshipped on his birthday with offerings, firecrackers, and celebrations.

Each city has its own god, and most of the gods are deified former officials known for their righteousness. For example, the City God Temple in Shanghai honors three gods: Huo Guang (d. 68 BCE), a Han dynasty chancellor who helped depose an emperor; Qin Yubo (1295–1373), who served as the imperial examiner in the Ming dynasty; and Chen Huacheng (1776–1842), a Qing dynasty general who died defending the city during the First Opium War.

---

*You feel your place in your generation
knowing an ancient city outlasts you.*

Living in an ancient city has a special feeling. You can feel the past strongly. There are monuments, old buildings, a hundred stories about the streets, squares, and places of worship. The architecture is old, worn, in a style no longer in vogue, but still dignified, lavish in its own terms, and sturdy in a way that would be impractical to build today. Even ordinary buildings have their own significant history. A composer lived in this apartment four hundred years ago. A famous scientist lived in this house and charmed the children of the neighborhood. A leader who changed world history attended this little school. Ancient cities have also been plunged into war, and the memories of battles, massacres, and triumphs are still tangible even amidst the traffic and the rushing footsteps of businesspeople.

Where ancient cities have catacombs, you can sense how their very foundations are built upon the lives of those now long gone. In the meantime, you can see the children playing in the parks above. You can see the hospitals where babies are born on one side and the dying depart on the other. You are of your generation. Many came before you. Many will come after you.

An ancient city offers ample benefits. You take your place in that city and you take advantage of all the trade, the social exchange, the work, the entertainment, and the culture that it offers. Living in a city gives you a sobering but valuable perspective. The shortness of life is on continuous display, but this encourages you to take advantage of all that is there, to decide to make a contribution to others by leaving some good behind. You can then set your mind at peace, knowing that you may well pass away in that city, but that you are forever part of how the world works. We may not become immortal, but we can accept being mortal by living in an ancient city.

Knowing an ancient city outlasts you tells you that we cannot afford city walls.

134 | All Within the Four Seas

▸ Fasting day

All Are Brothers

This famous saying is taken from the *Analects:* "All within the four seas are brothers."

We cannot afford city walls.
We cannot color-code people.

A city is a place of exchange. Thousands of people go in and out each day. Some are commuting, some are traveling, some are going about the business of moving and delivery. In the past, we walled our cities. Most of those walls have since been torn down. In our modern world, ease of exchange has become far more important than the clumsy security of ramparts; we've learned to apply security more skillfully. With digital firewalls, encryption of information, privacy practices, and even more flexible means of national defense, we've adapted our security to guard against specific dangers, all in the service of allowing the greatest freedom of exchange.

However, in other ways we remain coarse enough to use medieval means to judge others. We still have a walled-city mentality, judging others by whether they are "us" or "them." In the past, we could distinguished someone who lived in our walled city by looks, accent, or dress. Nowadays, however, no one lives in a walled city; people come and go from many places all over the world, men and women are free to mix, and people bring their food, their festivals, their gods, and their families with them.

We look at where people live, how old they are, how educated they are, how well they speak, what sports teams they like, and so on. Perhaps we make decisions based on their race. Not one of these factors is a foolproof standard for judgment. We cannot say that a person of one race is automatically good or bad. We cannot say that either men or women are automatically good or bad.

We live in a diverse world. That demands that we use subtle means of living with others, not the coarse means established when our cities were still walled. The four seas contain us all, and our attitude is that we live inside them, rather than inside a city wall. Within the four seas, all are brothers.

We cannot color-code people if we want to be approaching the zenith.

135 | Approaching the Zenith

› Fasting day

Plentiful

Hexagram 55 of the *I Ching* has this divination:

> Plentiful.
> Progress.
> The great king arrives.
> Do not grieve.
> All is right as the midday sun.

Approaching the zenith
we approach the splendor.

Today is not yet the zenith. Tomorrow is. In a way, however, the greatness of any extreme is just before the peak. Once the ultimate point is reached, decline is imminent.

The essential philosophy of yin and yang expressed in the *I Ching* states that when anything reaches its extreme, it inevitably begins to change into its opposite. As soon as we reach the highest height, we must descend. As soon as we reach the darkest depth of the night, we begin to move toward dawn. As we approach the summer solstice, the longest and brightest day of the year, we begin to move toward winter.

Nevertheless, brightness is great, and valuable, and welcome. Any one phase in life may be undercut by its opposite, but the phase itself is no less valuable because of that.

So let us celebrate the triumph of the light. The summer solstice must have its place in the circle of days. In fact, each one of our 365 days is valuable. We may notice some days by their astronomical significance or name them festival days or days of remembrance, but every day is good. For the circle to be whole, it needs the summer solstice just as it needs every other day. Extreme brightness may last one day, but that brightness is unique and worth honoring.

As the summer solstice approaches, we should arrange our lives to accord with it. As good fortune approaches us, we should prepare for it and welcome it. The summer solstice is not just a single day, but the gateway to the glory and splendor of summer.

We approach the splendor of when spring and summer lead.

Exercise 10

SUMMER SOLSTICE

The time of the longest days is the true start of summer. Temperatures will continue to climb and crops grow rapidly with the maximum amount of sunlight.

This exercise is best practiced during the period of 3:00–7:00 A.M.

1. Begin from a cross-legged position. Raise one foot in front of you and clasp your hands around the sole. Slowly extend the foot until your knee is straight, then bend the leg again.

2. Exhale as you push; inhale as you bend your leg. Breathe normally as you change sides. Repeat thirty-five times on each side.

3. Sit cross-legged and face forward. Click your teeth together thirty-six times. Roll your tongue between your teeth nine times in each direction. Form saliva in your mouth by pushing your cheeks in and out. When your mouth is filled with saliva, divide the liquid into three portions.

4. Inhale; then exhale, imagining your breath traveling to the dantian and then swallow one-third of the saliva, imagining that it travels to the dantian.

5. Repeat two more times until you've swallowed all three portions.

6. Sit comfortably as long as you like.

Through this exercise, ancient Taoists sought to prevent or treat arthritic and rheumatic pains in the knees, ankles, and arms; painful and excessively hot palms; pains in the kidneys, back, and legs; feeling of heaviness in the body; and general pain.

136 | Summer Solstice

- Summer Solstice
- Festival of the **Union of Heaven and Earth**
- Celebration of the **Three Pure Ones**

Celebrating Summer

Summer Solstice (Xiazhi) combines a number of festivals. People sought to escape the heat and went to the temples to worship. Celebrating the union of heaven and earth was a way to pull all observations together at this time of culmination and to celebrate the creation of the universe. The Three Pure Ones are worshipped, as they are on several occasions throughout the year.

Naturally, food plays a big part. Shandong people eat cold noodles. Guangdong people have all sorts of soups, porridges, and teas, as well as cooling soy milk, herbal beverages, and plum juice.

From the "Way of Heaven"

In this chapter, Zhuangzi articulates how Taoists seek to pattern human life after heaven and earth.

> The ruler leads, the minister follows. The father leads, the child follows. The older brother leads, the younger follows. The elder leads, the youth follows. The male leads, the female follows. The husband leads, the wife follows.
>
> It is from the movement of heaven and earth that the sages took their pattern. Heaven is high, earth is low. The gods are established in their brilliance. Spring and summer lead, autumn and winter follow. The four seasons are set in their sequence.
>
> The myriad things change and flourish. Every bud and place has its proper form. Abundance declines and decays, yet all transformations flow. Thus, heaven and earth are divine in setting forth high and low, leading and following—so should people follow that as their way!

When spring and summer lead,
fall and winter follow.

There are two solstices and two equinoxes in a year. We fix the start and the end of a year. We divide the year by the moons, the twenty-four seasons, and the days. By measuring and tracking, we give a sense of proportion to all that we do. It's necessary.

The essence of Tao is to pattern our lives after nature. This helps us accord with the larger movements of life. Taoists believe this to be more reliable than strictly following the laws and theories created by people. Looking back at history and seeing the mistakes of emperors, alchemists, philosophers, and generals alike, who can blame them for such a view?

There's beauty in following the natural way. This world is bountiful and good. We travel in it. We find food and medicine and all our raw materials in it. We climb mountains, sail rivers, soar in the sky, and go spelunking into the earth. We are awestruck by the world's peaks, its deserts, its waterfalls, its forests, its rainbows, and its stars. We photograph nature, paint it, compose rhapsodies to it, and write pastorals. Nature moves us, and so it is right that we find spirituality in it.

Nature always returns to balance. It may have extremes—the waters can bring us drink and food or they can wipe us out in a flood—but there is always calm after a storm, always day following night. When we pattern ourselves after nature, we try to achieve balance in ourselves and all we do.

Nature is not a person. It responds to our work—like our planting of fields—but it does not respond to our requests. In the search for a philosophy that is detached from our own greed, subjectivity, and ignorance, nature is the best template: we should strive for a philosophy untainted by our own wishful thinking. That is truly natural.

Fall and winter follow, so don't count the paintings thrown away.

Giving Up Halfway

The saying "Give up halfway" really means that one should *not* give up halfway, as the story behind it attests.

A scholar named Le Yangzi, who lived during the Eastern Han dynasty (25–220), went to study with a teacher in a faraway place while his wife remained at their home weaving silk. When he returned a year later, she was still weaving, and she asked him, "Have you finished your studies?"

"No," he replied. "But I missed you so much I came home."

His wife picked up a pair of scissors and said, "I gather silkworm cocoons to spin thread, then I weave one thread at a time to form cloth. It takes months to finish just one bolt of silk. If I carelessly cut the bolt with scissors, all the work I did will be wasted.

"It is the same with your studies. Learning must be accumulated day by day and month by month. If you give up halfway it's like cutting the cloth with scissors."

Chastised, Le Yangzi went back to his teacher and did not come back until he had finished his studies seven years later.

Don't count the paintings thrown away
because good ones arrive in time.

An artist has an entirely different attitude about mistakes than the normal person. An artist only cares about continuing the work. It's a given that some, maybe even most, of the pieces will fall short of the maker's standards, but that's not even a consideration. The artist paints, knowing that one painting must follow another. In that sequence, no one can predict which painting will be the "masterpiece." Will it be number seven? Number twenty-three? Number 1,101? No one knows. Even more important, the artist might not even recognize whether a painting is good when it's first finished. A good painting is alien, original, unexpected. Even the artist should be surprised.

Good artists throw away more than they keep. It's the same in every art form. The musician practices for hours away from people, never pretending that every song will be worth hearing. The potter scraps imperfect bowls, letting them dissolve again in water. This is automatic, a part of the process. The artist knows that many mediocre paintings have to be made to arrive at the good ones.

Industrialization has given us the attitude that everything should be perfect and manufactured in mass quantity. Business practices are meant to eliminate waste: templates, machines, robots, computers, electric eyes are all used to eliminate the risk of error as much as possible. The artist, on the other hand, is not a factory. Every piece is an experiment, an attempt to single-handedly bring something into existence from the unknown. Perhaps art is more akin to mining, where there is massive digging to uncover a scattering of gems.

So the artist keeps painting, striving to make each painting perfect, accepting it immediately when one is unsuccessful. However, none of the paintings are failures. Each one is necessary, because without finishing a painting, one cannot arrive at the next one. Who knows where the great painting is in the future? Unless the mistaken paintings continue to be made, the right painting will never arrive.

Because good ones arrive in time, know how to loaf.

138 | Do Nothing, Do Everything

• Fasting day

No Action Is Left Unacted

From the *Zhuangzi*:

> Heaven does nothing and yet is pure. Earth does nothing and yet is serene. Neither does anything and yet together achieve union and the ten thousand things are transformed. How vast and imperceptible! How without an image! Yet each of the ten thousand things has its role and part. So it follows that doing nothing can be productive. It is said: "Heaven and earth do not act, and yet no action is left unacted."

The words translated as "does nothing," "do not act," and "no action" are *wuwei*. Wuwei is normally translated as "nonaction" (p. 215).

Loaf.
Smile.

So many of us today drive ourselves relentlessly. We understand competition. We laud the winners of everything from track competitions to political campaigns to Best Picture awards to literary prizes. We don't understand loafing because it raises the suspicion that we are slipping toward the mass of losers we secretly deplore.

Even spiritual people take on competitive attitudes, boasting of the teachers with whom they've studied, or noting how long they can sit in meditation, or how much better they think their lives have become since they've embarked on the road to enlightenment.

We need time to loaf, to do nothing, to rest. We need to get away from the need to beat everybody else, to up our game, to raise the bar. "Faster, higher, stronger" is a great motto, but we need the yin to that yang. There's a great need to play, because in playing there is exploration and discovery. There is a great need to wander, because wandering renews our ties with the world around us. There is a need to acknowledge that who we are at this exact moment is exactly who we are supposed to be and that there's absolutely nothing wrong with that. We need to loaf, wander aimlessly, and play—just *be.*

After all, should we define ourselves by who we *are,* or what we *do?* If heaven and earth "do not act," and yet leave nothing "unacted," what does this mean? It means that heaven's and earth's effects do not come from motivated action, conscious intention, or intellectualism. Heaven and earth "act" because "acting" is a part of the very nature of heaven and earth: action results from their existence. Force comes from their form.

No individual consciousness directs their movements. Heaven and earth *are* movement. If we manage to simply *be* who we *are,* then *doing* is merely an outcome of who we *are.*

Smile. Know what is enough, and avoid disgrace.

139 | The Charm of Loss

Laozi on Life and Loss

This is from Chapter 44 of the *Daodejing*:

> Fame or life—which is valued more?
> Life or property—which is valued more?
> Gain or loss—which is more harmful?
>
> Those who love to extremes certainly pay greatly.
> Those who hoard much will certainly lose substantially.
>
> Therefore, those who know what is enough will not be disgraced.
> Those who know when to stop will not be harmed.
> They will be longer than long.

In Chapter 48, Laozi describes a process of reduction:

> For learning—increase daily.
> For Tao—decrease daily.
> Decrease and again decrease until one arrives at not-doing.
> No doing but doing without doing.

Know what is enough, and avoid disgrace.
Know when to stop and you will avoid harm.

If you really take a critical look at imperial history, you will see that the vast majority of people were utter failures. Emperor after emperor fell into debauchery, kings were overthrown, and countless aristocrats and officials died in murderous intrigues.

The life of the scholar was no better. Chief among the spectacular failures was Confucius himself, who never succeeded in finding a liege who would put all his recommendations into practice. A cursory reading of his biography reveals repeated rejection and even hostile attack by different leaders.

Then there were the imperial examinations—one had to pass these difficult tests in order to qualify for civil service, the most prestigious career possible, a system that lasted for thousands of years. Those that failed were condemned to lives of shabby poverty, scrounging for jobs as tutors, letter writers (most of the population was illiterate), or scribes.

Military heroes fared no better. Two of the great warriors we admire today, Guan Yu (p. 17) and Yue Fei (p. 53), were killed ignobly—Guan by ambush, Yue by intrigue and betrayal.

Among Taoists, we can argue that Laozi gave up in frustration and fled the world. Numerous seekers of physical immortality poisoned themselves experimenting with minerals and plants. The Boxer Rebellion failed in its assumption that spiritual techniques could stop a bullet.

A culture that lauded achievement instead produced a mass of loss. This led thousands to embrace the Taoist idea of idleness, spontaneity, and freedom. Rather than be affected by a lack of "success," they accepted who they were and went on their way, happy.

We may not be on the wealthy, lauded, and accomplished levels of society, but a joyous life can be enjoyed by anyone. Sitting in the sun, having something to eat and drink, and talking to friends takes little money. Traveling can be as simple as getting up and walking. Having the mind to write poetry, paint a picture, or hum a tune takes no gold. Sitting quietly as a child of nature requires no fee. Wandering in this world is free.

Know when to stop and you will avoid harm. Love only what is simple and plain.

140 | Intensity

A Child of Heaven Is Like the Sun

This passage from the *Book of Rites* is often translated as calling the emperor the "son of heaven." But the term can also be translated as "child of heaven." We can therefore apply the term to ourselves because each person is a child of heaven.

> The child of heaven follows heaven and earth. Hence, his virtue matches heaven and earth. He joins and brings benefit to all the ten thousand things. His brilliance is equal to the sun and moon, and he enlightens all within the four seas without excluding the minute and small.

Zhuangzi on Fame

Zhuangzi urged purity and simplicity over the pursuit of ambition and fame:

> There is a common saying: "The multitude emphasize gain, the upright scholars emphasize fame; the talented emphasize ambition even more, and the sages emphasize unusual purity."
> In contrast, plainness is unalloyed. It is pure and clean. It cannot be damaged. It is divine. Only those who can embody such purity and simplicity can be called True Persons.

Only what is simple and plain,
Pure and bright, is called summer's sun.

How hot the summer sun is! The best life is an intense one.

Our life span is fixed, although we aren't privileged to know (or perhaps tortured by knowing) its measure. Just as summer in a given year can be long or short, the brightness of our lives is limited. It is better to live that time with intensity than with slack disinterest. If you value life as most of us do, it's important to take advantage of it, to honor it, to fulfill yourself, and to enjoy yourself.

Only a life of brilliance lights up our days. This brilliance, however, need not be the socially defined incandescence of a celebrity star. That is transitory too, and others can share it only through a distant voyeurism. Chasing after fleeting fame is exhausting and likely futile for most of us. Not only are we unlikely ever to grasp the shining trophy of worldly glory, we are most likely to miss all that we were supposed to have been.

The sun doesn't care what it shines upon. It doesn't choose where its beams fall and where they don't. It exists in its own presence, and whatever light it gives is unquestioned and unreserved. In the same way, we need only look at the world and shine. Just as the sun does not define itself by what it lights, neither should we take our meaning from our lot in life. We are here. We shine.

A life of intensity is not realized through a life of toil. Neither is it realized through a life of suffering and pain. Toil, suffering, and pain are intense, but the intensity of a life lived on one's own terms and guided by one's own insight is the right one. What resolves the intensity of pain and the intensity of insight is spirituality: the wisdom to see as far as the sun shines, and to act every day upon what one sees and feels.

Pure and bright, is called summer's sun. Not catching fish is part of catching fish.

141 | The Straight Hook

The Great Man

Jiang Taigong (also known as Jiang Ziya; d. eleventh century BCE) was a man of lofty ambition and great ability who found no position in the last years of the Shang dynasty (1600–1046 BCE). He hoped to serve the leader of the vassal state of Zhou, **Prince Ji Chang** (1152–1056 BCE), but he could not make himself known. So he went fishing every day and waited.

One day, the prince was out hunting and encountered Taigong fishing from the bank of Sandy Rock Creek. When the prince saw the bearing of the seventy-year-old Taigong and noticed that he was fishing with a straightened hook, he questioned him and found the old man so wise that he took him immediately into his court. Taigong became the prince's key general and advisor. In time, Prince Ji Chang became **King Wen** (p. 358).

Later, Taigong became a god in his own right. In the Tang dynasty (618–907), he was given the title Prince Wucheng. Sacrifices were offered to him and many temples were built to him. Pictures of him were posted everywhere because people believed his mere image would dispel evil spirits.

Taigong is in charge of granting titles to other gods. Since he ranks so high above other gods, he is placed on the roof beam high above the floor instead of on an altar. When a new house is built, carpenters place a banner there reading, "Jiang Taigong is here; good luck to you." When a house is vacant for years, a red piece of paper is posted reading, "Taigong is here; all other gods stay out of the way!"

Not catching fish is part of catching fish.
Fishing with a straight hook catches a prince.

How admirable fishermen are. They keep their tackle clean and tidy, plan each fishing trip, and seek the best spots. Whatever their favorite fish are, they search for the right places, whether rocky mountain streams, tule-lined lakes, or open ocean. They might lose bait or lure, or face the treacherous open water, but the risk is part of the effort. If the fish aren't biting, the fishermen move on.

They are the epitome of acceptance and patience; the perfect blending of initiative and passivity; the right way to work in nature with enjoyment.

When there is enough fish to cook—whether by steaming, pan-frying, or deep-frying in golden oil—the fisherman is jubilant, as if the gods themselves have handed down the bounty. When the catch is small or nonexistent, the fishermen accepts with little frustration: not catching fish is part of catching fish.

King Wen was one of the great shapers of the *I Ching*. He determined the order of hexagrams we use today, and he wrote the portion of each hexagram's text called the Statement. According to legend, the prince asked for a divination on the day he met Taigong. The divination was: "Neither a dragon nor a serpent, neither a tiger nor a bear, but something far more useful to a prince." So the prince went hunting not for game, but for something more valuable. And the wise man, Taigong, waited not for fish, but for a destiny that would change a nation.

A prince in need of a general. A general in need of a prince. A nation in need of leadership. Each of us— in need of opportunity.

What a simple lesson fishing is.

Fishing with a straight hook catches a prince; why bend your back for five bushels of rice?

142 | Five Bushels of Rice

Tao Yuanming's Resignation

Early on, Tao Yuanming (p. 106) took on a minor official job to support his parents, but he soon resigned and returned to farming. Poverty was never far off. One day, he asked his relatives and friends if it would be acceptable for him to become a minstrel singer to pay for his garden's upkeep. Aghast, his friends arranged for him to have a position as a magistrate. The office came with an official home, a stipend, and five bushels of rice a year.

Once in office, Tao ordered that all the fields belonging to the local government should be planted with glutinous rice—the ideal grain to make the wine he so loved. Only after his wife protested did he allow one-sixth of the land to be reserved for the more staple variety of rice.

One day an imperial official was scheduled to visit. Tao's secretary suggested that he should dress in an official gown and prepare to meet the official deferentially. Tao declared, "I will not bow for five bushels of rice," and he promptly resigned.

Tao Yuanming's words became an idiom, still used today by people who find the demands of career or government demeaning.

Why bend your back for five bushels of rice?
Bend your back writing a poem.

If it weren't for money, why would we work for petty, small-minded bureaucrats and buffoons bent on self-glorifying ceremony? And once you get to a certain point in life, even the money isn't enough to make you grovel before those who, in spite of their obvious incompetence, have managed to get into positions of power.

Tao Yuanming retreated to his farm and spent the rest of his life in simplicity, growing the flowers he loved, drinking wine, and composing poetry. Perhaps, by the measure of being gainfully employed by the emperor, he was a failure, but as with Qu Yuan, nobody remembers the people with whom Tao Yuanming worked, or even remembers very well who the emperor was at that time. However, people remember Tao Yuanming, and they remember his poetry.

Far more importantly, Tao Yuanming points us to the value of a life that isn't spent chasing after fame and power. He shows us that tending to our own garden, living in quiet far from the frantic concerns of others, and looking inward to express the honest truth of being human are wonderful and healthy ways to live. Tao Yuanming was perhaps even more of a Taoist than the priests and monks in their robes and their elaborate temples: he needed no trappings, no title, no adoring congregants. He merely lived his life as the spirit moved him each day. What could be better than that?

Bend your back writing a poem—because a caged bird misses the forest.

143 | Escaping the Net

▸ Fasting day

"Home to Farm"

This poem by Tao Yuanming expresses his feelings about leaving worldly striving for the pastoral life that is more suited to him. The words "dusty net" symbolize the entanglements of ordinary society with its striving and scheming.

> Since youth, the crowd's pace did not suit me;
> my first instinct was always to love the hills and mountains.
> Mistakenly, I fell into the dusty net, and was trapped for thirty years.
> A caged bird misses the old forest, a fish in a pond misses the old waters.
> I'll till wasteland on the edge of the southern wilderness,
> stay rustic, and return to my garden farm.
> There are some ten acres around my house,
> eight or nine other thatched rooms.
> Elms and willows shade my back eaves, peach and plum trees line the front.
> I hardly see anyone; they're so far away
> I only know faint village smoke.
> Dogs bark in deep lanes,
> roosters crow from the tops of mulberry trees.
> No dust swirls into my door or house; the empty rooms promise quiet leisure.
> For too long, I was shut in a cage.
> I only hope that my wishes won't be thwarted.

A caged bird misses the forest.
A captured fish misses the sea.

We could all have a place that we feel the most free and content. However, most of us do not live in that place. Sometimes, we leave to follow a career, or glory, or another person. Sometimes, we are caught in the dusty net of worldly activities and find it nearly impossible to free ourselves.

A bird is a creature of the forest, and is best left in the forest. A fish kept in a pond still rushes to the open waters if released. One charming Buddhist practice is to buy fish, birds, turtles, or other live animals from markets and release them back into the wild. This is a tangible way to save others from the dirty nets that caught them. But we humans are no less likely to be ensnared by this difficult world.

A captured fish misses the sea; follow the Way, for the method of Tao surpasses all art.

144 | Zhuangzi's Cook

• Fasting day

Nourishing Life

Zhuangzi tells this story: The ruler Wen Hui, saw his cook cutting up an ox. After the most seemingly minor of cuts, the cook reached forward with his hand, leaned with his shoulder, planted his foot, and pushed with his knee, and the skin and membranes of the carcass tore audibly. His knife continued moving with a regular rhythm. The cook worked as if dancing; the sound of his work was like music.

"You have perfected your art admirably," said Wen Hui.

The cook put aside his knife and replied: "Your servant loves Tao, which surpasses any art. When I first began, I only thought of cutting up an ox. After three years I saw the ox as a whole. Now I use my spirit, and I rarely rely on my eyes. My spirit moves as it will. I rely on the natural lines, slip through the seams, and follow the large openings.

"A good cook changes his knife once a year. An ordinary cook changes his every month. I have used my knife for nineteen years and have cut up several thousand oxen, yet my blade is as sharp as if it had come newly from the whetstone.

"There are spaces between the joints, and the edge of the knife has no thickness. When my knife enters those spaces it moves along easily. If I come to a complicated joint, I proceed carefully, not turning my eyes away, and move slowly. Then with the slightest stroke of my knife, the part quickly separates and drops like a clod of earth. Then I stand up easily and satisfied, wipe my knife clean, and sheath it."

Wen Hui said, "Excellent! I have heard the words of my cook, and learned from him how to nourish life."

The method of Tao surpasses all art.
Free your spirit! Find guidance in the seams.

Zhuangzi's famous story of the cook is the ideal way to understand how one can be leisurely and yet effective. How can one know the right way to act, but still not act contrary to Tao?

All that the butcher did was discern and make use of emptiness. He searched for the openings between joints and used a knife that tapered down to a width of near nothingness. When he needed to apply force, he applied it at the right time and in the right place, using the leverage and weight of his body rather than pushing only with his arms. Zhuangzi's cook shows how a person can be one with Tao and yet do practical work.

In our own lives, we have the same task as the cook: we have to find the seams and lines and we must hold a honed knife. Following Tao is more than sitting on a meditation cushion. We must see our openings and take the initiative to act.

When we're done, we put away our knife. What counts is not our tools, or even our profession. What counts is the untrammeled freedom of the spirit. A person who has that can rule a single life or, in the position of a Wen Hui, rule an entire country.

Free your spirit! Find guidance in the seams! All of us should listen if a butcher knows right from wrong.

145 | No Butcher

The Sheep-Butcher Who Would Not Go to Court

The tale of a ruler who wishes to gain the wisdom of an innocent commoner is told a number of times in the *Zhuangzi*.

King Zhao of Chu lost his kingdom to invasion and fled. Many of his citizens became refugees, including a sheep-butcher named Yue.

Later, the king regained his domain, and Yue returned home. The king wanted to reward all who had remained loyal to him. However, the sheep-butcher refused the reward: "When the Great King lost his country, I lost my job and home. When his majesty regained his kingdom, I got my job back with its income and status. Why reward me further?" When the king was told this, he ordered that the reward be given by force. Again, the sheep-butcher demurred.

"I committed no crime to lose the kingdom, and did not accept death when the capital was lost. I rendered no service to regain the kingdom, so I am unworthy to receive a reward."

The king then summoned Yue to court, but the butcher refused: "An audience in court is a great honor, but I was neither wise enough to save the kingdom, nor brave enough to die defending it. When the armies came, I ran in fear with no thought of loyalty. The king should not violate propriety and invite me to court."

The king said, "A sheep-butcher is a lowly profession, and yet what he says is correct and high-minded. Let me appoint him to be a distinguished advisor." Hearing this, the sheep-butcher again declined, saying: "Although this rank is far higher than mine, and although its salary is far greater than my meager earnings, it would be greed to accept and it would make the king's gift unlawful. I dare not accept, but will return to my stall as a sheep-butcher."

If a butcher knows right from wrong,
no ruler should be a butcher.

Butchering is a necessary job. Regardless of how you feel about killing animals to eat, we need butchers.

Butchering is killing, and yes, it's important to consider its place, but for now, what is worth considering is the unnecessary killing of people. Killing an animal to feed people may be a sin, but at least we can do it humanely, not waste any of the body, and have a sense of gratitude that we are not hungry. None of this applies to the wanton killing done by tyrants. They kill for the sake of consolidating their power and imposing their ambition upon others. They look upon the rivers and mountains and lust to possess them. Sons and daughters of others are mere pawns to them; future children will be brainwashed into new worshippers. Any impediments to their ambitions must be removed, and if that means erasing people from some book of life, well, they are ready to rend the pages and drench them in blood. That kind of killing is to be abhorred.

In traditional times, the position of a butcher was a lowly one. Yet the sheep-butcher of Zhuangzi's parable was capable of displaying greater virtue than a king. Doesn't this show that one's position in life need not determine how good a person one is? The sheep-butcher was honest, did not pretend to be someone he was not, and asserted the simple morals deep within him. The king, on the other hand, sought to buy his subject's loyalty, and his only thought of how to be involved with a virtuous man was to try to enslave him in the court. The king sought to exploit good people, and to serve a king often makes a good person bad.

No ruler should be a butcher; follow the way of the simple rustic.

My Retreat at Zhongnanshan

Wang Wei (699–759) was a Tang dynasty poet, musician, painter, and statesman. His paintings, which survive only in copies by other artists, influenced all of Chinese painting that followed him. His poetry is so well respected that twenty-nine of his poems were included in *Three Hundred Tang Poems*. Wang Wei was a devout Buddhist and a vegetarian, and he established a monastery on his own property after the death of his wife.

Zhongnanshan is south of Xi'an in Shaanxi. According to legend, it is the place where Laozi was asked to write the *Daodejing*. In his poem on Zhongnanshan, Wang Wei uses a number of allusions and idiomatic phrases. "I've walked to the waters' end" means that he believes he has worked futilely and has been a failure. "I sit to watch the rising clouds" refers to meditating, reaching clarity, and ascending to higher levels of cultivation. When he says, "I don't want to go back," he means that he'd never go back to the ordinary world where, as he says in the fourth line, he found success to be empty.

> In middle age I'm quite fond of the Way.
> Lately, I've lingered at the foot of Zhongnanshan.
> When the mood comes, I wander there alone.
> I found gratifying success to be empty;
> I've walked to the waters' end.
> I sit to watch the rising clouds.
> By chance, I meet an old woodcutter:
> talking and laughing, I don't want to go back.

Follow the way of the simple rustic.
Live by the earth's gifts, and give to others.

In traditional times, woodcutters went into the forests. Sometimes they gathered fallen wood, sometimes they had to fell trees. They brought their loads back to fuel the stoves in their own homes and sold the rest. There was a limit to how much wood they could cut, because they carried it on their backs. The weight they could bear, the distance they had to walk, the amount of wood available, the amount they could chop, and the roughness of the terrain were all limiting factors. These limits determined the extent of what was possible, and human existence fell into equilibrium with what the forest could provide.

Many of these woodcutters carried out their task well into old age, and the scene of the woodcutter walking back into the village with a bundle of wood is easy to imagine. Invariably, the woodcutter had to do one thing at the end of his trek: he put down his load, undoubtedly with a sigh of relief and the satisfaction of knowing that his family would have enough to eat.

We are no different today. Each of us is like the woodcutter, going out to forage for what will sustain us and our families, and straining against the limits of what we can do. We have a particularly modern problem, though: many of us cannot or will not put down our loads—the psychological burdens, the sticks that have been hurled at us, the bundle of our responsibilities.

Let us put down our burdens at the end of each day, so that we are at least free at night. And, if we understand, we can burn what is in our bundles to provide warmth and light.

The woodcutter lives simply, works hard, knows how to stop working, and shares the benefit of his work with others. Is there any better pattern for living?

Live by the earth's gifts, and give to others, just as the flower made Mahakasyapa smile.

147 | Loving Flowers

The Beginning of Chan

Chan traces its transmission back to Buddha holding up a flower, with Mahakasyapa (p. 82) being the only disciple to understand and smile.

Symbolism of Flowers

Many flowers are associated with auspicious meanings. Here is a partial list:

- **Plum** The first flower to bloom after winter represents renewal. It is a symbol of vigorous old age, and the five petals symbolize the Five Blessings—old age, wealth, health, virtue, and peaceful death.
- **Osthmanthus** Homophone for "noble" and "distinguished"; symbolizes literary success
- **Hibiscus** Homophone for "wealth and glory"
- **Lily** Symbolizes harmony and unity
- **Lotus** Symbolizes purity, continuity
- **Cymbidium** Symbol of friendship and the wish for many grandchildren
- **Apricot** Symbol of spring and passing examinations successfully
- **Peony** Symbolizes wealth, honor, official position, and high status; considered the king of flowers
- **Poppy** Homophone for "brocade"; symbolizes being clothed in brocade, wealth, and honor
- **Wisteria** Its purple flowers are used to allude to the purple sashes and cords of official seals, symbolizing honor and rank
- **White Magnolia** Symbolizes purity
- **Chrysanthemum** Symbolizes longevity and recluses
- **Day Lily** Known as "the plant that dispels grief"; a metaphor for one's mother
- **Marigold** Symbolizes longevity
- **Narcissus** Represents good fortune, prosperity, and Taoist immortals
- **Peach** Symbol of longevity
- **Rose** Represents eternal youth

The flower made Mahakasyapa smile.
Even a sage is transformed by a bloom.

What joy flowers give us! They open to the morning sun, and as we walk along the dew-drenched paths where the shadows are still long and the petals are edged with gold, we can't help but feel privileged and uplifted. There is no room for brutal or loutish instincts. In the appreciation of beauty, we understand the simple truth of opening.

Whether in joy or in sadness, we choose flowers to be our companions. We have flowers on our tables, we hold them as we sing or dance. We offer them to lovers and adorn our marriages with them. We put them in our children's hair.

Likewise, we instinctively reach for flowers in our moments of sadness and pain. We bring flowers to the sick and dying. We have flowers at our funerals and burials.

What altar is without flowers? We ask flowers to convey our highest spiritual aspirations. We bring flowers to our temples and offering tables. Flowers even provide the central metaphor in meditation: we imagine a lotus opening within us as an aid to visualization.

There is something savage about picking flowers. If possible, enjoy them in their native habitat. Yet flowers will wilt before long, and plants left unpruned will not grow well again. The peony needs to die in winter and be cut back in order to bring forth its glory. So cut flowers with reverence, put them on your altar, and in the worship of flowers, worship beauty and all that is higher in this life.

Even a sage is transformed by a bloom—rejoice in the source of blessings.

148 | Regal Wealth

The Well

The well appears as one of the fundamental symbols of the *I Ching*. Hexagram 48 states:

> Well.
> A city may change, but the well does not.
> It does not lose, it does not gain.
> In spite of all who come and go from a well, it remains a well.
> But if the rope cannot reach, or if the well's vase is upended: misfortune.

Rejoice in the source of blessings.
What a miracle a well is.

Taoism does not overlook the life of regal wealth. That may mean monetary abundance, it may mean great fortune meeting others, it may mean talent, it may mean the knack for winning soccer games. Wealth may come and go for some, but it comes to us all at least sometime in our lives. Wealth can be constant and overflowing—like having a well that never runs dry.

If your Tao is to have great plenty, then the dangers are no different than those of poverty: being fat is as unhealthy as being thin. If you are rich, then use those riches responsibly. Sustain yourself and your family, enjoy what life offers with moderation, and then use your wealth to help others. If you have more than enough water, then give the thirsty water to drink rather than spilling it carelessly. The greatness of a rich person is to remember poverty and to have empathy with those who are poor. The greatness of a poor person is to be in touch with all of nature and Tao that does not require money to access. The greatness of a person is to define him- or herself not by material possessions but by compassionate actions.

Who among us wouldn't like to try a royal life? Yet looking back at history, how many among the royalty have been truly good? Be different. If you gain your own version of the royal life, then show grace when moving along that Tao.

What a miracle a well is: water comes, just as you can bring a god into your body.

149 | Spirit Mediums

▸ Fasting day
▸ Celebration day for the **Jade Emperor**

Spirit Mediums in Taoism

There are three major kinds of spirit mediums in Taoism: the oracular medium; the medium that temporarily acts as the god or spirit itself; and the spiritual fighter, who believed that he or she brought a god or spirit into the body when fighting.

The oracular medium allows the spirit to enter into this world, usually for the purpose of answering questions or providing guidance. The medium will fall into a trance and then either speak in the voice of the god or write out answers, spelling words in a basin of sand set nearby (p. 244).

The medium possessed by a god often acts wildly, speaking in esoteric languages and performing strange feats such as burning or piercing him- or herself to show this can be done without harm. Mediums can claim to be possessed by any number of gods, including the **Jade Emperor** or even non-Taoist gods, such as Jesus.

Finally, the spiritual fighters summoned gods into themselves when they fought, believing that this gave them supernatural powers. Many of these fighters were part of the **Boxer Rebellion** (1898–1901; p. 369) and believed—wrongly—that their spiritual training made them invulnerable to bullets.

Bring a god into your body.
Do all you can to be holy.

Mediums still exist in parts of Taoism. On this celebration day for the Jade Emperor we can ask two important questions about mediums. The first is whether the gods are separate entities that exist somewhere else but can be brought into our world through a host body. The second is whether all of us in an ordinary sense can benefit from metaphorical or imaginary "possession." The two questions are linked.

There is no evidence that there are gods existing as separate personages in some other dimension, waiting for us to contact them or wanting to come into our world. Certainly it doesn't make any sense that someone is sitting inside a star, dressed in ancient robes and ready to dispense good fortune to us. Therefore, it doesn't seem possible that some spirit is going to travel to earth and speak in a host body. Notice, by the way, that philosophical Taoism does not rely on gods or spirits but explains everything by the impersonal workings of the universe.

That being said, can we still benefit from worshipping gods and *imagining* that the gods can enter into us? If we take the gods as the personification of certain values, then we can still benefit. The gods may not be real in a literal sense, but when we're motivated to celebrate, give presents, and nurture the innocence and goodness in others, the gods certainly have real effects. When someone dresses up as one of the gods during a street festival, in a temple, or in a shopping mall, it's our version of spirit possession. Who's to say that the spirit of the divine doesn't really enter into that person?

So on this day, let us imagine that we can let gods into our bodies. What would that mean? It would mean purification. It would mean acting as if we were gods. It would mean that we take on the best of what it means to be a human being.

Do all you can to be holy, for the True Person covets nothing.

150 | The True Person

The True Person

A person who is well versed in Tao is called a **True Person** *(zhenren)*.

A True Person ranks above an **immortal** (xian). Buddhists also use "zhenren" to designate a *luohan* or *arhat* (highly accomplished Buddhist adepts). The term first appeared in the *Zhuangzi*:

> The True Persons of old did not know to explain life, nor did they know to be unhappy about death....
>
> The True Persons of old did not eschew the modest. They did not seek heroic accomplishment. They did not scheme like scholars and warriors. They had no need to repent mistakes, nor did they covet anything for themselves.
>
> They could mount lofty heights without trembling. They could go into water and not be soaked. They could enter fire and not be burned. From all this they had the knowledge to overcome all falsehoods and reach Tao.
>
> The True Persons of old did not dream when they slept. When they woke, they were not melancholy. When they ate, they were not carried away by sweet flavor.
>
> When they breathed, they breathed deeper than deep: the True Person breathes from the heels, while the common person merely breathes from the throat.

The True Person covets nothing.
The True Person breathes from the heels.

Can you stand on the highest precipice without trembling?
Can you dive into water and not get soaked?
Can you walk into fire and not get burned?
Can you accept a modest life?
Can you not yearn to do heroic deeds?
Can you avoid scheming and cunning?
Can you avoid the cruel strategies of the warrior?
Can you sleep without being bothered by dreams?
Can you awaken without yesterday's stress?
Can you eat without gorging?

If you can do all this, then breathe from your heels. Avoid the shallow breathing and, by extension, the shallow living of the common person. If you can be a True Person, then breathe deeper than deep. You live because you use the emptiness within you.

Be neither bothered by your birth nor bothered by death. Then you will be like the True Persons of old.

The True Person breathes from the heels, so it's useless to worship gods.

A Taoist priest preparing for an outdoor ritual. The elevated altar table—here simply accomplished by stacking tables upon one another—are typical of Taoist ritual.
© Saskia Dab

6

The Lotus Moon

To the tune of "Sand-Washing Creek"

Ill, try to rise. Wretched. Both my temples gone gray.
Lie down. Watch the waning moon climb the window screen.
Boil cardamom tips into a strong brew
and take it like tea.
Poetry books on my pillow, their words always good.
The scene before my door: lucky rain approaches.
All day long facing much fragrant comfort—
flowers amid thorns.
—Li Qingzhao (1084–1151)

The two solar terms within this moon:

SLIGHT HEAT

GREAT HEAT

Exercise 11

Depending on one's latitude, full summer may already be in progress, and the weather can become quite hot. In southern China high wind and rain are common, threatening some crops. Typhoons are likely, and yet this is still a busy time for farming.

This exercise is best practiced during the period of 1:00–5:00 A.M.

1. Begin from a kneeling position, supporting yourself by pressing your hands on the floor behind yourself. Raise one leg and slowly stretch it in front of yourself until your knee is straight, then bend the leg and pull it back toward your chest.

2. Exhale as you push; inhale as you bend your leg. Breathe normally as you change sides. Extending each leg counts as one round. Repeat for fifteen rounds.

3. Sit cross-legged and face forward. Click your teeth together thirty-six times. Roll your tongue between your teeth nine times in each direction. Form saliva in your mouth by pushing your cheeks in and out. When your mouth is filled with saliva, divide the liquid into three portions.

4. Inhale; then exhale, imagining your breath traveling to the dantian and then swallow one-third of the saliva, imagining that it travels to the dantian.

5. Repeat two more times until you've swallowed all three portions.

6. Sit comfortably as long as you like.

Through this exercise, ancient Taoists sought to prevent or treat rheumatism in the legs and knees; excessive phlegm; asthma, cough, violent sneezing, and pain in the sternum; feelings of heaviness; loss of memory; and conflicting feelings of joy and anger.

151 | Declaration

• Fasting day

If You Meet a Buddha

"If you meet a Buddha, kill that Buddha!" said the Chan master and founder of the Linji (Rinzai) Sect, Linji Yixuan (d. 866).

> Followers of the Way: if you want to get an understanding that accords with the dharma, never be misled by others. Whether you're facing inward or facing outward, whatever you meet up with, just kill it! If you meet a Buddha, kill that Buddha. If you meet a patriarch, kill that patriarch. If you meet an arhat, kill that arhat. If you meet your parents, kill your parents. If you meet your kinfolk, kill your kinfolk. Then for the first time you will be emancipated, you will not be entangled with things, and you will pass freely anywhere you wish to go.

It's useless to worship gods.
It's useful to worship gods.

Let's be honest. If you look with any objectivity at religion, it just doesn't seem to make sense. How can the gods be dressed in imperial Chinese robes? How can a particular god have a long black beard, while another one is clean-shaven? How can a god be living in a well, or a tree, or your kitchen, or inside a mountain? What does it mean that one god is a woman and another a man and another of unknown gender? None of it stands up to serious examination.

If you put out a basin of water on the night of the full moon, how does it become blessed? If you burn a bamboo-and-paper model of a car, how does your ancestor receive it? Where are your ancestors anyway? Where are the gods? Where are heaven and hell? How does incense carry prayers? How does a statue of a god stop floods? The fact is that this is all blind belief or superstition at best. Let us declare: the gods are fictitious.

Yet being fictitious does not necessarily equal being untrue. Fictional literature exists in all major cultures, and we value it not only for entertainment but for what it reveals of our lives. We reach universal truths through the channel of fiction, finding that a great work of literature, drama, music, or art can express truths that journalism or science cannot.

Following Tao means taking the seemingly awkward position of respecting and absorbing all that religion has to offer, going so far as to study it, celebrate it, and protect it, and yet knowing that none of it can be taken literally. It all has to be taken as a grand text, a way to read back into the beliefs of our forebears, a way to see what is archetypal about our psyches. It's a way to acknowledge that we want to be pious and reverent—with the same strength and power with which we want to have friendships and fall in love—and that we find benefit in the act of worship.

It's useful to worship gods—until you throw everything from your circle.

152 | Throw Everything Out!

Nanquan Draws a Circle

Case 69 of the *Blue Cliff Records* gives this story:

Nanquan, Guizong, and Magu traveled together to pay their respects to National Teacher Zhong.

Stopping halfway through the journey, Nanquan drew a circle in the dirt and said, "If you can say a word, then we will go on."

Guizong sat in the middle of the circle.

Magu bowed from the waist.

Nanquan said: "Then I will not go!"

Guizong said: "What's going on in your mind?"

Throw everything from your circle!
Tao remains when else is gone.

Draw a circle around your life. Then throw everything out of it. Your computers and mobile devices, your televisions, radios, books, magazines, and newspapers. Throw out your clothes, your car, your latest beloved gadget.

Throw out your awards, your money, your aspirations—and your demons and devils too. Throw out your gods, throw out your history, throw out your culture, throw out your ethnicity, throw out your ancestry, throw out your parents and your children, throw out your pets, throw out your friendships, throw out your most treasured memories—and throw out the injustices and hurts and hatreds that have been hurled at you and that cling to you like gigantic leeches.

Throw out the pride in your body, throw out that image in the mirror, throw out your need to survive, throw out your hunger—and throw out illness, injury, accident, fear, and death.

Throw out your language, throw out your dance, throw out your science, throw out your groping and your touch—and throw out lies, deceit, mistakes, clumsiness, awkwardness, stupidity, and ignorance.

Draw a circle around yourself and throw everything out. Throw everything out and then throw yourself out of the circle too!

What remains?

If we say "something" remains, we are wrong. How language betrays us! How language wants us to talk about *things!* What remains is not solid, not subject to time, not confined to location, and yet we sense it in our circle, sense it with a perception that is not one of our senses.

We sense because we are that which we sense, and that which we sense has, without senses, awareness of itself. That self is what the universe is and is not. That self is what there is, and there is nothing else.

The circle is drawn in a place—but both sides of that line are one and the same.

Tao remains when else is gone, so throw everything away.

153 | The Rivers and Lakes

Rivers and Lakes

The phrase "rivers and lakes" (*jianghu*) means to travel around the country. It also means a vagrant, a wanderer, or an itinerant professional.

Wuxia

Recently, the phrase has been used in martial arts movies and in the martial-literary genre known as **Wuxia** (Chivalrous Heroes).

Earlier Appearances of the Term

In the Song dynasty, **Fan Zhongyan** (989–1052) used the term in his essay commemorating Yueyang Tower in Yueyang, Hunan. (He was also the teacher of Ouyang Xiu, p. 196.) After Fan criticized the chief councilor, he was demoted and his proposed reforms failed.

Fan wrote of the ancients he admired: "When in a high position in court, they were concerned about the people. When living by distant rivers and lakes, their concern was for the emperor."

The *Zhuangzi*, which dates to the fourth century BCE, has a parable in which Zhuangzi reproaches a man who did not know what to do with the large gourds he had grown: "Why did you not think of making them into large vessels, so you could have floated over the rivers and lakes?"

Throw everything away:
Mountains and streams remain.

Stay, if you will, in this state where you have thrown everything out of your circle. What you cannot throw out is whatever was outside your circle. What is outside your circle is Tao.

Stand at the base of a mountain and see how its greatness was thrust up in a mass our cities could never accumulate. Absorb the mountain's lesson of stillness, of presence, of lasting.

The rivers flow forever from the highest ground to the lowlands by the sea. Poets have written tributes, but the poets are gone. Warriors shed blood fighting over the river, but the water runs clear. Nations set boundaries by the river, but no one remembers those names while standing in the current.

We have perpetuated disappearances: we have polluted the waters and destroyed our fellow creatures. The Baji river dolphin lived only in the Yangtze River. Today, it's extinct. Rivers all over the world have been polluted by factory wastes and made sluggish by the dregs of our civilization. One can almost see the winter floods as angry attempts at purification.

Let us stop polluting the world and each other with our carelessness. Let us see how nature gives us all that we need, and that the right response is reverence and respect. The lakes brim every year. The surrounding streams run into them. The hillsides sink toward them. The animals all come to drink. The fish swim and spawn. And no matter what, the surface of the lake is always one way: level. The wise person needs no other remembrance.

Throw away everything. Then go outside. The mountains and streams remain.

Mountains and streams remain part of a cycle, like the snake turning to bite its tail.

The First Trigram of the *I Ching*

The *I Ching* includes eight basic symbols called trigrams. The first of these trigrams consists of three unbroken lines and is called Heaven (Qian). The *I Ching* explains the qualities associated with it:

Qian is
the sky,
a circle,
a ruler,
a father,
jade,
metal,
cold,
ice,
deep red,
a good horse,
an old horse,
a thin horse,
a piebald horse,
the fruit of trees.

The trigrams are arranged in either of two circular formations:

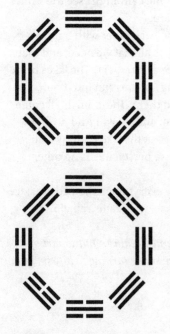

Thus, heaven, which is circular, takes its place in a greater circle. The overall patterns are called the **Eight Trigrams** (Bagua).

The snake turning to bite its tail.
Reject Tao and you will find Tao.

What of that circle you drew? What of that line, which has a presence but has no width, no depth, no solidity? Follow that line around again, follow it and walk it around and around. You've found Tao, and yet, when you follow Tao for an entire lifetime, you find that Tao turns back on itself, that the end is the beginning, that the beginning is the end, and that, in actuality, there is neither beginning nor end.

We are on this journey through a lunar year, but the statement that there is a new year and an old year is a mere concept we use to shape our understanding. The moon doesn't care what phase it's in. It hasn't kept tally of the number of times it's turned since the beginning, and it doesn't number where it is in relation to the sun and the earth. The moon doesn't know of the seasons that we experience here on earth. The moon revolves and follows its orbit, and its Tao that is part of the great Tao. It completes its circle, and its circle is constant and eternal.

It's we who measure and mark and seek repetition. We take comfort in that. Primitive humans stuck poles in the ground and learned to understand when the sun and moon would seemingly return in fixed patterns. Slowly they formulated the ideas of day, month, and year. We discovered cyclical movement, and we learned to depend upon it. If not for the circle, both our minds and our civilization would collapse.

Tao is the greatest circle of all. Try to escape it, and you cannot, for it is the knowable and the unknowable. Study it and you find that Tao is the circle that connects everything. Try as you might to get off the circle, you will only find yourself on it again.

Reject Tao, and you will find Tao when you add things back in.

155 | Add Back In

Mountains Were Mountains . . .

Chan master Qingyuan Weixin
(c. ninth century) said:

> Before I studied Chan for thirty years,
> I saw mountains as mountains, and
> waters as waters.
>
> When I gained a more intimate
> knowledge, I reached a point where I
> saw mountains not as mountains and
> waters not as waters.
>
> Now that I have gotten to the
> substance, I have reached a point like
> before: I see mountains merely as
> mountains and waters merely as waters.

When you add things back in,
Their meaning will be clear.

Once, an artist said to the admirers visiting his studio that everything should be orderly and not a single extra thing should be in that room. "Take everything out of the room," he advised, "and then only bring in, one by one, what you absolutely need." His studio was indeed a model of order infused with the vitality of minimalism.

We should do the same thing with our lives. In fact, we are like that artist's studio—a sacred space, scrupulously white, bathed in light, at once a shelter and a launching pad, at once a temple and the entire universe, at once defined dimension and endless possibility. For we, like the artist's studio, are located in this infinite cosmos, and yet we are the cosmos entire.

How the glittering stars fill our night skies with the very image of profusion—and yet how the stars occupy their own set places at vast distances from one another. It would seem that all that is there is meant to be there, as if "given" its own proper place. We can arrange our lives in the same way, and it is up to us to bring back into our sacred space only what we need, only what pleases us, only what makes us whole and strong.

Space itself is pure, clean, the stuff of possibility. As we move things—not necessarily the material but the defined—back in, let them meet the criteria of space itself. Let every thing we put back in our lives be pure, clean, and the stuff of possibility. Then we will never lament that our lives are meaningless, because we will have filled them only with meaning.

Their meaning will be clear, so clean your house, invite the gods in.

156 | Refuse the Gods

Observances of the Sixth Day of the Sixth Moon

There is no single large celebration for this day, but there are several small and local observations.

The Basking and Bathing Festival (Xishai Jie) is a day to air bedding, clothes, and books in the sun.

Heavenly Bestowal Day (Tiankuang Jie) originated with Qin Shi Huang (p. 159) and the tradition he began of making sacrifice on Taishan (p. 44). During the reign of the Song dynasty Emperor Zhengzong (968–1022), Taoist scriptures appeared that were said to have come from heaven, and the emperor marked the occasion with imperial sacrifices at Taishan. He later decreed the deification of the Jade Emperor (p. 13) as the highest ruler of heaven.

Airing the Sutras Day (Fanjing Jie) is a Buddhist observation. Sutras in the temples are aired to prevent mold. According to legend, when Xuanzang (p. 269) returned from India with Buddhist sutras for translation, some fell into the water, and he rushed to dry them.

Clean your house, invite the gods in,
all is at peace, all is now clear.

On this day, monks and temple caretakers put the sutras out to air, preventing mold and must.

Then they take the sacred books back inside.

In the same way, take your cherished books out too. Bring them into the sunlight both literally and figuratively. Air them, for to leave a book on a shelf unopened is a travesty. Review them too, for to slavishly keep books you've outgrown is equally wrong—why not pass them on so that others may find the same way you did?

We value books. Yet the author is not there with you. If you accept that point, then can we dare to say that we can have the gods in our lives—even though the gods are no more with you than the authors of your books?

Su Dongpo the poet, Beethoven the composer, Laozi the sage, Homer the bard, Guan Yu the god of martial loyalty, Einstein the physicist, Gautama the Buddha, Shakespeare the playwright, Wang Xizhi the calligrapher—all of these people are dead and nowhere to be found physically, psychically, or mystically in our lives today. Not a trace of their bodily lives is present—yet they affect us nevertheless. What do you call that?

We forget things all the time. As our world changes, we also change and adapt, discarding what is no longer useful. Clearly the ability to forget is of vital importance as we either let go of traumas or distill them into vital strands of wisdom painfully won. Perhaps, in the same way, you no longer believe in the gods you embraced during your youth. You see them now as fairy tales, or mere habits passed down by your parents. The question is, what knowledge and what gods serve you now?

So take our your sacred books and air them today. Take out your gods too, and make sure they still have a place on your altar.

What's important is what remains.

All is at peace, all is now clear: why reject filial piety?

157 | Reject False Filial Piety

Zhuangzi on Confucius

Zhuangzi portrayed a fictitious situation where Confucius went to see a person named Dao Zhi, who rebuked him:

> The more you talk, the more nonsense you utter. You get your food without plowing and your clothes without weaving. You wag your lips and move your tongue like a drumstick. You arbitrarily decide what is right and wrong, leading the princes throughout the kingdom astray, and distract scholars from their proper business. You recklessly set up filial piety and fraternal duty, and curry favor with the feudal princes, the wealthy, and the noble. Your offense is great; your crime is extremely heavy. Go home at once!

Reject filial piety
and you will find your family.

You might think it's a trick by now. "Sure, throw out everything but then take it back in. It's just the bait to get us to accept the same old traditions." But no, the real point is this: we should only keep that which is necessary to our lives. We cannot keep the moribund traditions and exhortations of our elders. We keep what is fresh, alive, and needed.

The lunar calendar is built on agriculture, but it is also built on family. Do we really need family? For many of us, family, like religion, has been dysfunctional.

Every day we hear news about families torn apart by divorce, infidelity, poverty, mental illness, and ignorance. Every day, we also hear stories of noble sacrifice, of a husband who dies shielding his wife against a tornado. Or a mother who works three jobs so her children can go to college. Or a sibling who becomes the parent to orphaned brothers and sisters.

What keeps family together is the power of blood, the power of love, the power of acceptance. That power is mysterious. That power is spiritual. That power connects us to a force and a magic greater than just who we are as individuals. That power sustains and protects us. It is that power that we want to get in touch with.

If you have a good family, value it. If you have a bad one, leave it and build a better one. The duties that Confucius prescribed were merely guidelines, dry form to surging and vital force. Throw out all the lessons of Confucius and yet there is still that living, breathing, pulsing energy that is family. And that spiritual energy is what must be honored.

And you will find your family vital—the more times change, the more we need wisdom.

158 | Spirituality Now

> Fasting day

Chinese Inventions

In ancient China there was constant invention and innovation. The spiritual systems we view as traditional today were also developing and evolving, as they continue to evolve today. Here is a partial list of innovations known in ancient times:

> paper; printing with movable type; bookbinding; ink
>
> gunpowder; bombs; chemical warfare; crossbow; flamethrower; land mines; trebuchet catapult; coffin
>
> plowshare; cultivation of rice, soy, millet and other grains; heavy moldboard iron plow; horse collar and harness; wheelbarrow; winnowing fan; stirrups
>
> noodles; tea; tofu; toilet paper; silk; porcelain; lacquer; celadon
>
> calendar; compass; armillary sphere; seismometer
>
> bellows; belt drive; blast furnace; borehole drilling; chain drive; crank handle; finery forge; rotary fans; trip hammer
>
> acupuncture; inoculations
>
> matches; fireworks; flares; rockets
>
> fishing reel; rudder; oar; leeboard
>
> bell; tuned bells
>
> chopsticks; fork
>
> automatic doors; mechanical theaters; mechanical cup-bearers and wine-pourers
>
> cast iron; steel
>
> contour canal; suspension bridges using iron chains
>
> archaeology
>
> kites

The more times change, the more we need wisdom.
When we need wisdom, we need the spirit.

The contrast between the antique imagery of all the world's religions and our everyday life of computers, phones, cars, airplanes, televisions, and industry is obvious. The China from which Taoism came was as filled with innovation as our world today. Dozens of inventions came out of ancient China—all while the spirituality that we now study was developing. In fact, we wouldn't even know about much of Taoism were it not for the inventions of paper and printing with movable type. We are conversing at this very moment via the latest developments in technology and communication; we are conveying ancient ideas and old calligraphy by way of pixels.

So there need not be any contradiction between modern life and spirituality. We dress, eat, work, and raise our families using all our current lives have to offer. Ignoring that is simply to be out of step with the times. We use all we have to support our spirituality too: we have to understand modern nutrition and sanitation, avail ourselves of all that medicine has to offer, use technology to find the ideas that will sustain us. There may be drawbacks to modern life—by definition, there are drawbacks to everything. However, drawbacks are not negations or reasons to refuse progress.

The great innovations of one era become commonplace in the next. No matter how much we innovate and invent, we use our inventions to point back to ourselves. It's the wisdom and spirit that are paramount. The innovations are mere means.

When we need wisdom, we need the spirit, so grasp a sword to cleave ignorance.

159 | Grasp a Sword

Delight in the Sword Fight

Zhuangzi speaks to a king about three kinds of swords:

> The King's Sword has Yanqi and Shicheng as its point; Qi and Daishan as its edge; Jin and Wei for its back; Zhou and Song for its hilt; Han and Wei for its sheath. The wild tribes protect it; the four seasons encircle it; the Bohai Sea surrounds it; the enduring hills belt it. The Five Phases regulate it. Its principles are punishment and virtue. Its unsheathing shows yin and yang. Grasp it in spring and summer; move it in autumn and winter. Thrust it—nothing stands before it. Raise it—nothing is above it. Lay it down—nothing is below it. Swing it— nothing escapes it. Above, it cleaves floating clouds. Below, it penetrates to the foundation of earth. Use this sword just once and the princes will be reformed and the kingdom will be rectified. . . .
>
> The Feudal Lord's Sword has wise and brave officers for its point; pure and honest officers for its edge; worthy and good officers for its back; loyal and sage officers for its hilt; valiant and eminent officers for its sheath. Thrust it—nothing stands before it. Raise it— nothing is above it. Lay it down—nothing is below it. Swing it— nothing escapes it. Above, it takes its law from round heaven and obeys the three lights; below, it takes its law from the square earth and accords with the four seasons; inside, it is in harmony with the will of the people, and it brings peace to the four quarters. Use this sword just once and thunder will peal and shock. Within the four borders no one will fail to respectfully submit and obey the commands of the ruler. . . .
>
> The Commoner's Sword is used by those with tangled hair, bristling whiskers, slouching caps with long and dangling tassels; who wear coats cut short behind; who have glaring eyes and speak hatefully. They clash together before you. Above, they chop at necks; below, scoop at liver and lungs. These are the swords of the commoner. They are no different than fighting cocks. Every dawn brings death. They are of no use in affairs of state.
>
> Now your majesty stands as the Child of Heaven. Approving of the Commoner's Sword is unworthy of a great king.

Grasp a sword to cleave ignorance.
One thrust—the heart comes to a point.

Not many people are interested in swords these days. Perhaps you've seen one in a museum, perhaps you've watched movies where fantasy characters wield outlandish blades. Maybe you've played a digital game or two with sword fighting. That may be the extent of it. Taking up an actual sword is unlikely. You might even be horrified by the idea of holding a sword, thinking of it only as an instrument of slaughter, a tool of savagery that should be left behind in medieval times.

Yet the sword is a constant theme in spiritual imagery. Lu Dongbin (p. 125) is depicted with a sword. The Door Gods (p. 22) are shown with swords. Statues of guardians with swords adorn many Buddhist temples. Here we are in this modern world, where people don't engage in personal combat with swords, yet we still use them as symbols.

Using a sword as a spiritual implement is an exercise in mental focus. Think of someone writing calligraphy—in midair, without ink. The swordsperson tracks the path of the sword as a means of contemplation, projecting mental concentration beyond the body and mind into the outside world. The sword makes many movements that together form small paths. Following those small paths leads you to the grand path that is Tao.

A sword is a weapon, and a weapon is for killing. Any implement for killing is inauspicious and should only be used as a last resort. It is said, "A sword is never unsheathed without tasting blood." Therefore, if you would not kill, your sword should not be unsheathed, and of course, killing is evil and wrong.

Put down the sword of killing. Renounce it completely. But don't overlook the sword of spiritual practice that we use to discipline ourselves. A sword used in this way is not a weapon. It has been purified into a tool of meditation. Where the killing sword is fed by blood, a spiritual sword is purified by the essence of its user.

One thrust—the heart comes to a point, and we slay ignorance with the sword.

160 | The Blade Leads the Breath

A Taoist practicing the sword on Wudang-shan. The words on the temple wall—*fu, lu,* and *shou*—mean "happiness," "prosperity," and "longevity," and represent the Three Stars (p. 24). © Bernard De Poorter

We slay ignorance with the sword
and face our opponents: us.

The theory of the sword speaks of leading the breath. The breath—qi (p. 23)—follows the movements of the sword. One uses energy to move the sword, and also feels one's energy following the sword.

We say that we feel energetic. We say we have to eat well in order to have enough energy. We might appreciate the visible energy of an athlete or dancer. But in our common terms, we don't go much further than that.

The swordspeople and the sages, however, not only speak of energy as a force but believe that force can be increased, channeled, and concentrated to do extraordinary things. Whether it is used for the graceful wielding of a sword or the powering of meditation is a matter of a person's preferences. The energy is the same.

In practicing with a sword, then, it takes energy to thrust, parry, slash, and cut. But one learns to direct one's energy precisely into those movements. As with any other skill, the more one practices, the more efficiently one's energy moves in those patterns.

We don't use swords as weapons anymore, but working with them is still valuable as a way of practice. What the sword truly teaches is courage, precision, positioning, movement, and grace. Who among us does not need these?

When the sword cuts, it parts yin and yang. Practice that each day and you open the road to profundity.

And face our opponents: us. Our ambition is to act with great force.

161 | Sinking

Our ambition is to act with great force—
when great force is already under us.

Zhuangzi on the Full Understanding of Life

Zhuangzi tells the story of a drunken man falling from his carriage. He might be hurt, but he will not die. Although his bones and joints are the same as those of other men, his spirit is whole.

The drunk is unaware of getting into the carriage or of falling from it. Thoughts of death or life, alarm or fear, do not occur to him. He meets danger without shrinking from it and emerges unscathed because he is completely relaxed and at ease.

Zhuangzi asks how much better it would be if the man was not drunk but imbued with heaven: the sage who is filled with heaven cannot be injured.

Falling can be the simplest act. Perhaps we should make use of it. In good martial arts schools, falling—yes, there are sophisticated techniques for it—is taught before punching and kicking. It makes sense. If you're going to fight, you're probably going to meet good opponents, and if you meet them, they're going to knock you down or throw you. You have to know how to fall.

After that, it's important to know how to stand. Martial arts places great emphasis on stance—but what is stance but a skilled way of "falling" too? The masters talk about being "rooted" to the ground, but what they're really talking about is being solid, with a low center of gravity. The most stable thing is what has already fallen and sits there without resistance. The key to a good stance is to be relaxed and low—using gravity instead of resisting it.

Thus, the teachers will constantly urge their students to "sink." This not only means squatting deep into a stance, but it also means letting all your strength and intention sink down, making yourself heavy and stable and not betraying yourself with fearful tension and flighty apprehension.

But what about kicking, hitting, moving? Why not let gravity help? After all, even the most gigantic man is weaker than gravity. Instead of going our own way with our own puny force, it's better to avail ourselves of the great forces. We generate force from the floor, using gravity not just for stability but to push against.

If we understand the dynamics of falling, then we can make our opponents fall. If we understand the importance of sinking, then we can remain standing.

When great force is already under us, we hold both the tool and template.

162 | Early Tools

Carving an Ax Handle

This is a poem often quoted from the *Classic of Poetry*:

How do you carve an ax handle?
Without an ax it cannot be done.
How do you gain a wife?
Without a matchmaker it cannot be
done.

Over the centuries, this poem has taken on a number of interpretations. The most common one is that the pattern for anything we need to do is close at hand. Being unable to carve an ax handle without using an ax means that all the knowledge we need to do our work and live our lives is already at hand.

Another implication is clearly one of process: one uses an ax to make another ax handle. One needs a matchmaker to organize the process of marrying. This refers again to the understanding of fundamental patterning, the need to make something new from that pattern, and a subtle recognition of professional ability.

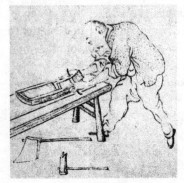

We hold both the tool and template
and we reshape our minds' pattern.

The earliest woodworking tools were not much different from knives and swords. In fact, one of the first planes was like a spearhead, and knives are used to mark and whittle. Axes were used to fell trees, and they were also used to shape the wood. Eventually, this led to the adze, and perhaps the adze led to the chisel. A plane is nothing more than a thick blade set in a block, and even a saw is arguably a set of tiny chisels set in a line.

At first the role of blades was general and undifferentiated. Specialization came later as needs and ingenuity evolved. We needed spears and swords to hunt and fight. We needed blades to skin animals and cut the meat. We needed ax heads to chop wood and shape the most basic supports for shelter.

Therefore, it is natural that we use tools. And it is natural that as these tools developed, they took on our spiritual intentions as well. The swordmaker used ritual purification and engaged in ceremonies to empower the sword. The blacksmith who made tools did the same. The *Classic of Lu Ban* (p. 193) mentions charms and spells a carpenter can use to bring either good or bad fortune to the occupants of a house.

There is an interesting contrast in Western and Asian tool use. Western woodworkers *push* their saws and planes. Asian woodworkers *pull* theirs. In the end, it's a matter of the woodworker's skill. Neither pushing nor pulling in itself provides greater advantage. But doesn't it show that how we use tools proceeds from our minds?

The sword develops and leads our energy. All the tools we use develop and lead our energy. They express our minds.

And we reshape our minds' pattern, saying, "I am the Dragon King."

God of Carpenters

Lu Ban (507–440 BCE) is the God of Carpenters and Artisans. He was also an engineer, philosopher, inventor, strategist, and statesman. His wisdom is collected in the *Classic of Lu Ban (Lu Ban Jing)*.

Lu Ban was a contemporary of **Mozi** (c. 470–391 BCE).

Mozi was a philosopher who opposed both Confucianism and Taoism. He was also a carpenter and inventor who created mechanical birds and siege ladders with Lu Ban.

The *Classic of Lu Ban* discusses all forms of carpentry, giving design and construction details for nearly every conceivable carpentry need. Houses, palaces, temples, furniture, small objects, and farm items ranging from sheep pens to foot-operated waterwheels are all detailed. The book integrates the practical knowledge of craft and design with geomancy, talismanic writing, the correct selection of auspicious days for all phases of building, and the ways to curse or bless the occupants of a newly built house. There is advice on how owners can neutralize any sorcery by the builders, how they should move into the house, and how they should consecrate their altar to best invite the gods into their new home.

Lu Ban's biography gives special mention to his wife, Lady Yun. Her skills are described as "heavenly," and the objects she made are reputed to have been even more beautiful than Lu Ban's. "Husband and wife helped each other and thus were able to enjoy great and everlasting fame."

Lu Ban frequently asked his wife to help hold pieces of wood on his workbench. She showed him how a stake of wood (bench dog) set in the bench could take the place of her hands, and this stake is still called *ban qi*—"Lu Ban's wife." He also asked his mother to help hold the other end of his ink line until she suggested a wooden hook, and today this part of the tool is still called *ban mu*—"Lu Ban's mother."

There are still temples to Lu Ban, such as the Lo Pan Temple in Hong Kong. As one of the two ministers of public works under the administration of the Jade Emperor, Lu Ban continues to be worshipped by carpenters and varnishers today.

The Lu Ban Rulers

Lu Ban stated that roundness was the shape of Heaven and squareness was the shape of Earth. However, the "ten thousand generations all over the world" could not match his understanding. Therefore, he advocated use of the compass, the square, the level, and the ink line to help in the building of palaces, houses, ships, carriages, and other projects.

Two rulers shown in the *Classic of Lu Ban* are drawn below. The shorter ruler forms one leg of the carpenter's square (*quchi*) and is divided into ten units named after colors. The longer one is called Lu Ban's True Ruler (Lu Ban Zhenchi), measures about forty-three centimeters, and is divided into eight units whose names have good or bad meanings. The rulers were primarily used to measure doors, but they were also used in all other areas.

Carpenters still keep this square and ruler as ritual objects. Taken as symbols, they express the wish for all tangible things to be aligned with spiritual principles.

Feng Shui

The carpenters of the *Classic of Lu Ban* were thought to have extraordinary powers. When building a house, they had to choose auspicious days for every act, from cutting down trees to beginning the building to raising the ridgepole. The book also gives instructions on how to curse the occupants of a house with hidden charms and talismans, how to bring fortune using other charms, and what rituals to use during construction and when the house is completed.

Furthermore, the very siting, direction, and architecture of the house could be either auspicious or inauspicious, and the book gives a catalog of both types. This was geomancy—feng shui—as design from the ground up. ▶

白	紫	白	赤	白	黃	綠	碧	黑	白
White	Purple	White	Red	White	Yellow	Green	Blue	Black	White

吉	害	劫	官	義	離	病	財
Propitious	Harm	Plunder	Official	Righteousness	Parting	Sickness	Wealth

163 | I Am the Dragon

The Dragon King

The dragons of Chinese belief live in pools, wells, rivers, lakes, and seas. They are considered the kings of animals, and so became emblems for the emperor. Furthermore, dragons bring beneficial rain and are regarded as the embodiment of nature's fecundity.

A dragon has been described as having the head of a horse or camel, the horns of a deer, the ears of an ox, the eyes of a devil, an abdomen textured like a cockle, the scales of a carp, the tail of a snake, and wings on its sides. It has four legs with feet that combine the claws of an eagle with the soles of a tiger. An imperial dragon has five talons on each foot, while an ordinary one has four.

Since there are dragons everywhere, there is no single dragon king, although there are many stories about and many temples to individual local dragon kings. A dragon king has a human body, robes like an earthly emperor, and a dragon head. He can take full human form or change completely into a dragon.

Dragon kings live in palaces deep underwater, commanding ministers, generals, and soldiers that are human sized aquatic animals like fish, shrimp, and crabs.

I am the Dragon King:
human and animal.

The voice of the Dragon King said: "I am every animal combined with the human. You aren't like me, but you are in awe of me. All animals submit to me because I am all of them combined. All humans are in awe of me because I live in every body of water, I am the veins in mountains, I bring the rain. I am everywhere—acting, creative, fecund, powerful, and eternal.

"I am the Dragon King. At one time, I was worshipped everywhere. Now people think of me as a myth. That's how a king should be. A king is not common. A king is not seen every day. Laozi says that 'the greatest ruler is one that people don't know exists.' You say you don't know if I exist. Yet I lead everything. You make effigies of me for your parades and your celebrations. You decorate your buildings, paintings, and clothes with my image. You dub your sports teams after me. You name companies, games, movies, stories, restaurants, and heroes for me. Have I ever ceased to fire your imaginations?

"I am the Dragon King. You, sitting there in your garden, by a pool or a well—I am right there with you. You, on the parched plains yearning for rain—you ask me to come save you. You, trembling as the thunder rolls, cowering in a cellar as the lightning strikes—you fear me. You, standing at the beach, looking at the waves, wondering what is under the surface where your mortal eyes cannot see—you sense my empire.

"I am the Dragon King. I am animal made human. Human made animal. In so many ways, you fantasize about being just like me. It is possible. That's a secret few know. But I am a king and I can only leave you with this pronouncement, this challenge: can you, woman or man, child or elder, find the day where you can stand against the swirling sky and declare: 'I am the Dragon King'?"

Human and animal, even if you unify your entire being, what you learn in art can never be used.

164 | On Art

Dong Qichang

Dong Qichang (1555–1636) was a painter, calligrapher, connoisseur, critic, and Chan Buddhist. He led a group of scholars and artists that formulated the principles of literati painting, and whose works had a lasting influence on the Chinese and Japanese art that followed. Dong Qichang is considered one of China's great painters, and his landscape paintings and his calligraphy are justly famous.

Tokyo National Museum

Dong Qichang believed in tradition and in mastering the styles and techniques of the masters. However, he warned against "studying the ancients without being able to change."

> What you learn in art can never be used:
> if you give in, it's called imitation.

It's maddening to be an artist. Learn mathematics, for example, and you can reliably memorize your multiplication tables, postulates, theorems, formulas, and proofs. Then you can build upon them, never again wondering what the sum of one plus one might be. Music is the same. You learn the scales, the chords, the rhythms, and while there are infinite variations, the notes never alter.

Not so with art. As soon as you get good at it, the teachers immediately mock what you do. "Oh, so you've learned to paint like so-and-so. What are *you* going to paint?" Writing is the same. If you use the same phrases or rhymes as another poet, you're ridiculed as derivative or clichéd. It was fine for the first person to use a brilliant metaphor, but nobody else attempting to use the same words receives any admiration.

Art is a Tao. It is a way of exploration, creativity, and searching. You have to work at it every day. Write every day. Sing every day. Paint every day. Whatever your art form, you have to do it every day. Most of what you'll make will be unusable. If you're really searching and probing, you will have many failures. Making a lot of beautiful things that are like a lot of other beautiful things is manufacturing, not art.

Your mind is a wilderness. You're an explorer along the frontier. You run into dead ends, box canyons, sheer cliffs. You try mining, and the vein runs out. You drill for water, and sand runs through your fingers. You hack at the weeds, only to find stone. You keep trying, sweating under the sun, woozy, feeling abandoned—bitterly noting that even the vultures aren't willing to circle you. And yet, you will never abandon the effort.

Art is its own Tao. All that counts is staying on the Way. If you keep going, day after day, sooner or later, you'll cross that wilderness and find a paradise. And it will be yours alone.

If you give in, it's called imitation; be creative and use anything, whether it's old or new.

165 | Honor of Ownership

The Three Zithers of Ouyang Xiu

Ouyang Xiu (1007–1072) was a noted leader of literary stylists who revived the ideals of ancient writing. He was one of the Eight Masters of Tang and Song Prose.

In this famous essay, he writes about the seven-string zithers (qin) he

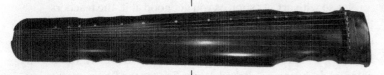

is fortunate enough to own. Each one shows exquisite craftsmanship and is well constructed. They are old. The lacquer on each of them is reticulated, a pattern he says only develops after a hundred years.

He knows the makers. The zither with gold studs was made by Zhang Yue and has a tone that is "rich and penetrating." The one with stone studs was made by Lou Ze and has a sound that is "pure and gentle." The one with jade studs was made by the Lei clan and has a tone that is "harmonious and resonant." Ouyang Xiu writes: "At present, anyone who owned a single one would treasure it. I now own all three."

These zithers were fretless, and the studs helped the placement of fingers. "It is hard for an old man with failing eyesight to place his fingers on those studs," he writes, adding that since the stone studs do not shimmer, "stone-studded zithers are best for old men."

"One need not learn many zither pieces," he concludes. "The important thing is to enjoy playing. Likewise, it's not necessary to own many zithers. But since I have come to own this many, it would be foolish to worry about having too many and to let some go."

Use anything, whether it's old or new.
Honor it and pass it on after you.

If you're both fortunate enough and so inclined, you have antiques in your home, things made by craftspeople long gone. Your mother's china, perhaps, or a wooden chair; an old piano or old books.

All these things were made by craftspeople who intended that the objects they made outlive them.

Take an antique chair, for example. The wood is probably of a kind that can no longer be found—dense, hard, old growth. The joints were put together to take the weight of a person, even someone rocking on two of its legs, or standing on it to hang a picture. Probably the joints are mortise and tenon—the same kind found in the oldest Egyptian furniture. These joints are archetypal, universal, used the world over. They have no ethnicity, no culture except the culture of the craftspeople who make things that challenge mortality.

If you have such things, *use them.* Keep them out of the cabinet or warehouse. Let children play with them. Sit on the chair, cradle the silver knife in your fingers, make the piano sing, use the book to go back in time.

If you don't use these things, then you dishonor the craftspeople who made them.

What if they break? What if they wear out? That's the challenge that the craftspeople took on. What if they don't break? Then you have had the honor of being the caretaker of beloved things, and you hope that they outlive you too.

Honor it and pass it on after you; carefree, you'll plant trees and build your own house.

Exercise 12

GREAT HEAT

These are likely to be the year's hottest days. Wind may be slight and in some areas the humidity may be high, making the weather stifling.

Those farmers who plant two crops of rice must quickly harvest the early rice and plant the late rice. A delay in planting can mean a smaller yield or a failed crop.

Health problems from the heat are a danger for the young, the weak, and the elderly, so it's important to keep these populations cool.

This exercise is best practiced during the period of 1:00–5:00 A.M.

1. Sitting cross-legged, close the fists tightly, with the thumb inside the fingers and rest them on the floor before you.

2. Turn the head from side to side, "like a tiger," for fifteen repetitions on each side.

3. Facing forward with your hands resting on your lap, click your teeth together thirty-six times. Roll your tongue between your teeth nine times in each direction. Form saliva in your mouth by pushing your cheeks in and out. When your mouth is filled with saliva, divide the liquid into three portions.

4. Inhale; then exhale, imagining your breath traveling to the dantian and then swallow one-third of the saliva, imagining that it travels to the dantian.

5. Repeat two more times until you've swallowed all three portions.

6. Sit comfortably as long as you like.

Through this exercise, ancient Taoists sought to prevent or treat rheumatism in the head, neck, chest, and back; cough and asthma; thirst; feeling of fullness in the chest; pains in the arms; excessive heat in the palms; pains above the navel or in the shoulder and back; hot and cold perspiration; diarrhea; and depression.

The Humble Administrator's Garden

The Humble Administrator's Garden (Zhuozheng Yuan) is the largest garden in Suzhou, a city famous for many lovely gardens.

The garden was originally the residence of a Tang dynasty scholar, Lu Guimeng (d. 881). In the Yuan dynasty, it became the monastery garden for the Dahong Temple. In 1513, Wang Xiancheng, a poet and imperial envoy, appropriated the temple and retired there after long persecution by the East Imperial Secret Service.

He began work on the garden in collaboration with the Suzhou artist Wen Zhengming (1470–1559). Wang took Tao Yuanming's (p. 106) rejection of official life as one of his principles. The garden's name was inspired by Pan Yue, a writer of the Jin dynasty: "I enjoy a carefree life by planting trees and building my own house . . . I water my garden and grow vegetables to eat . . . such a life suits a retired official like me."

The garden was completed after sixteen years, in 1526. Unfortunately, Wang lost the garden gambling, and it changed hands many times thereafter.

The painter, poet, and novelist Cao Xueqin (p. 66) lived in the garden as a teenager, and it is believed that the famous novel *Dream of the Red Chamber* takes its garden settings from the scenery Cao knew so well.

Carefree, you'll plant trees and build your own house,
water the garden and grow your own food.

Having a garden is a beautiful dream. If you have a garden—even if it's a few potted plants on a balcony or patio—you know its pleasure and tranquility. If you have a larger garden you can walk in, so much the better. Or perhaps you're one of the lucky few who has a big garden, and professional gardeners, and who knows the passion of planning and the hard work of planting—and also the grand feeling of sitting in your own retreat, sighing in relief, and letting the hours dribble away without concern.

The Taoist reverence for nature takes on its own form in a garden. Although someone may call him- or herself an owner, a garden may well outlive its owners. In fact, the great gardens are almost never achieved in a single generation. It takes many generations to make a garden—the wealth required is significant—and many of the trees won't even come to maturity in the lifetime of the first owner. Each owner is merely caretaker of a dream.

The owner ends up being owned by the garden—the plants must be watered and fed, tree limbs must be staked up, ponds must be cleaned, glorious rocks must be searched out and brought in at great labor and expense. The owner almost becomes a worried slave—but a few moments in the garden, perhaps in a vine-covered arbor where the shade is cool, always convinces the gardener that every bit of toil was worth it.

Water the garden and grow your own food, and put aside all contrivances.

167 | The Garden Gate

Zhuangzi's Gardener

Zhuangzi tells the story of the scholar Zigong, who met an old man tending a section of a vegetable garden.

He had dug his channels, gone to the well, and was bringing water in a jar to pour into the ditches. He toiled and expended a great deal of strength, but accomplished very little.

Zigong said: "You could use equipment and thereby soak a hundred fields in a day. With little effort you could achieve a great result. Would you, master, like to try it?"

The gardener looked up and asked, "How does it work?"

"It is a wooden device, heavy behind, light in front. It draws the water as quickly as water boiling over. It is called a *gao* [shadoof or water pulley]."

The gardener stood up angrily, then laughed. "I have heard from my teacher that where there are machines, there are sure to be machinations. Where there are machinations, there are sure to be scheming hearts. When pure simplicity is impaired, the living spirit is unsettled and cannot be with Tao. It is not that I do not know what you're referring to; I would be ashamed to use it."

Zigong looked down abashed, hung his head, and said no more.

Put aside all contrivances:
open the gate; open your heart.

There's something especially attractive about a garden gate. It is magical. It hints at the occupants—who cared enough to make a special place. The gate beckons.

A garden is beautiful not just for the loveliness of what's planted there, but because it represents the mind and spirit of the designer. Each garden is a meaningful response to nature. Each garden reflects care.

Zhuangzi's gardener rejected the water pulley—the point was not to be more "efficient," the point was to work in the garden honestly, with a unit of human effort matching a unit of nature.

Entering into a garden, then, is to witness human care in conjunction with nature. It is a circular system: as much as the garden may "benefit" by the attention lavished upon it, the gardener is nourished too, and the garden's occupants find renewal and revitalization in all that is put into that garden.

Open the gate, open your heart, and let your flag stand as the highest standard.

168 | Flags

▸ Fasting day

The Sixth Patriarch: Why Does the Temple Flag Wave?

Case 29 of the *Wumenguan* tells of a debate between two monks:

> One said: "The flag moves."
> The other said: "The wind moves."
> They argued repeatedly but could not reach a conclusion.
> The Sixth Patriarch said: "It is not the wind that moves. It is not the flag that moves. It is the mind that moves."

Sunzi and the *Art of War*

Sunzi (c. 544–496 BCE) was a general, strategist, and philosopher and the author of the *Art of War (Sunzi Bingfa),* a book of military strategy studied today around the globe and utilized in business.

Sunzi described five important points for strategy:

> First is Tao.
> Second is Heaven [nature, weather].
> Third is Earth [situation, terrain].
> Fourth is the General [leader].
> Fifth is Art [strategy].

A good general was the one who "had Tao."

> If you know the enemy and you know yourself, one hundred battles will not be dangerous. If you don't know the enemy but know yourself, even winning once will be burdensome. If you neither know the enemy nor know yourself, then every battle will end in your defeat.

Sunzi discussed the use of flags during battle in this way:

> Words can't be heard, so we use gongs and drums. We can't depend solely on ordinary sight, so we use banners and flags. We use gongs, drums, banners, and flags so we can see and hear as one. The brave will not advance alone, the cowardly will not retreat alone. This is the art of mobilizing a large army.

Let your flag stand as the highest standard.
When it waves, it shows the invisible.

How beautiful flags and banners are. They add so much to a house or garden. They display colors that are a joyous statement to the world.

All flags and pennants are symbols. Like words, they communicate. Sunzi's *Art of War* states: "When fighting at night, make much use of signal-fires and drums, and when fighting by day, use flags and banners."

Flags show us the unseen. The wind is normally invisible—if we can see the wind, in the form of tornados or waterspouts, we are in real trouble. A benign wind is a different matter. Like the sage, it is invisible. Flags let us know that the wind is there.

A flag reveals the unseen wind, so it also symbolizes the unseen principle. A master holds up a standard to us. We are meant to behold it and to take heart from it as if it were a flag waving in the wind, and to strive for what that flag means.

A flag is just colored cloth. Yet people live and die for those colors, not because of any literal value, but for what they represent. How amazing that people will unite around such a symbol in every culture even though the material from which the symbol is made has no intrinsic worth. That's something to remember when we wonder if gods and religion have value.

We fly flags, banners, and pennants over our gardens because the gardens themselves are important to us. Like the flag, the garden is a standard of how we want to live and how we want to live with nature. We cultivate it, nurture it, care for it. Living in a garden is a standard to which we aspire—and the flag is just the start of understanding that.

When it waves, it shows the invisible in the garden: temple and retreat.

169 | Solitude

• Commemoration of the day **Guanyin** became a bodhisattva

When Confucius Went to See Lao Dan

This parable is from the *Zhuangzi*. Lao Dan is another name for Laozi. The story should be taken as an allegory rather than a description of an actual historical meeting.

Confucius went to see Lao Dan, arriving just as Lao Dan had finished washing his head and was letting his uncombed hair dry. Lao Dan was motionless, as if he were not a person.

Confucius waited quietly. When he was introduced after a short time, he said: "Was I confused? Is it really you? Just now, sir, your body was like dead timber. You seemed as if you had abandoned all things, as if you had left the human world and were standing in solitude."

Lao Dan replied, "My heart had roamed to the beginning of all things."

© Kathy Bick

The garden: temple and retreat.
In solitude, open your heart.

We retreat, like the sages, to remote caves on windswept and mist-shrouded mountains to contemplate the Way without other human presence. We visit priests, nuns, and monks in gilded temples to learn more about the Way, marveling at the architecture dedicated solely to the otherworldly. We learn of the wandering seekers who traveled the length and breadth of China, who traversed the Silk Road, who climbed the Himalayas, and who visited the civilizations of India, Persia, and Europe in their quest for understanding.

Yet not all of us can have long access to the experiences of immortals, holy people, and spiritual seekers. Not all of us can live on mountaintops or in temples or on the road to enlightenment. But we can all have gardens—and those of us who do not possess our own can have an even grander experience in public gardens.

Just as a bonsai (*penzai*—"to grow in a basin") represents a great tree, we are not slaves to scale. The universe can exist in a speck of dust. A speck of dust can be infinite in size. The important thing is that our gardens are retreats from the turmoil of the outside world, allowing us to renew our ties with nature and therefore with ourselves. In that place of retreat, not only can we enjoy the beauty of what surrounds us, we can also enter into a meditative state. We can pick a flower or rock to gaze upon and all of Tao opens to us. We can listen to the trickle of a stream and all of Tao opens to us. We can inhale the breath of the trees and all of Tao opens to us.

Today is the day commemorating Guanyin's becoming a bodhisattva: that means that spiritual transformation is possible for any of us. Guanyin's legend is also a simple way of understanding what the essence of spiritual transformation might be: to contemplate, to listen, to understand the suffering of others. When Guanyin returns to earth after nearly turning hell into paradise, she lives in solitude on the island of Putuoshan to listen to the cries of the world (p. 58).

In the end, we may retreat to the solitude of our gardens, but the goal is neither escape nor selfish withdrawal. The goal is to become more attuned to nature and to ourselves—and there, in that solitude, to become more attuned to the entire world.

In solitude, open your heart: accept how a thicket grows, and "pattern" comes later.

170 | Rubble, Stumps, and Thicket

Pu and the Daodejing

樸 The word *pu* appears in the *Daodejing*. The left side of the ideograph shows that the word is in the category of wood, and the right side means "thicket." It has been frequently translated as "a block of wood." Wood in its natural state represents a human being as a plain and simple person.

In Chapter 15, Laozi describes the sage as "sincere, like plain wood."

A thicket grows, and "pattern" comes later.
Let us grow simply as nature allows.

Most people can find the beauty of a garden self-evident and breathtaking. How many look at the heap of plucked weeds, the rubble and stumps of the areas being cleared? How many look at the fallow fields, or the storm-wrecked fallen tree? How many look at the dense hedges and thickets that have been left to grow as they will? These areas are no less beautiful than the tenderly cultivated flower bed simply because they are not accomplished in the glory of perfection. Rather, they are perfect in the glory of possibility. In them is a single basic lesson: that earth is constantly fecund; that earth takes back anything, no matter what it is; that earth is the receiving ground for every aspect of nature and human life.

There is a beloved Taoist word, "pu." We take it today to mean "plain," "simple," "honest," or "rough." The rubble on the ground is like that. Stumps are like that. A thicket is like that. Nature has its own patterns. Perhaps they are "determined" in advance by the inherent nature of the plant: a bamboo will not grow to look like a pine. And yet, even though we know the seedling of a plant will grow into what it must be, we cannot know in advance how that plant will look, exactly how tall it will be, precisely what branching will occur.

If we look at any leaf, we will know reliably what kind of tree it comes from. And yet, if we look more closely at the leaf, we cannot find that its pattern of veins is like that of any other leaf.

In the same way, each of us may be a human being, each of us may have an inherent genetic and mental character with which we were born, and yet each of us will be unique. We don't need to "make" ourselves into something! We don't need to "be" anyone else! We can only be who we are, and accepting ourselves just as we accept what's in our garden is plain and simple. And if we accept what is plain and simple, then we in turn become who we are, plain and simple.

Let us grow simply as nature allows; we are the whole, just as one rock is a whole mountain range.

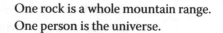

171 | Trees, Rock, and Moss

Appreciation and collection of rocks has a long history. Rocks were placed in gardens at least as far back as the Han dynasty (206 BCE–220). Among the types of rocks are small ones that people keep personally, medium-sized rocks that scholars keep as indoor sculptures, and large rocks placed in gardens. The four principal aesthetic qualities of rocks were set down in the Tang dynasty (618–907): thinness *(shou)*, openness *(tou)*, perforations *(lou)*, and wrinkling *(zhou)*.

Among the most famous and prized rocks are the ones from Taihu, a lake near Suzhou. The most valuable are those that were naturally formed—with wave-carved patterns and perforations worn through by the lake. Today, artisans partially sculpt and carve stones to hasten the erosion process before submerging them in the lake. The sculpted rock that is retrieved, sometimes decades later, commands high prices.

One rock is a whole mountain range.
One person is the universe.

The trinity of rock, tree, and moss is one of the most charming features of a garden. The varying combinations of just those three elements form an endless variety of poems—wood, green, and stone "rhyming" with more possibilities than words can offer.

Shadows alone are a fascinating theme. Shadows on tree trunks show roundness, interrupted by the texture of bark—the smoothness of the maple, the roughness of the pine. Shadows on moss are a fine stipple, any highlights on the moss muted to the green of new growth. Their fine stems and branches reach for life, as we all do, but in their own way—with profusion yet modesty. Shadows on rock are jagged, forceful, broken in facets too unpredictable to allow boredom. Gardeners in the past have spoken of finding inspiration in these three elements and seeing wordless instruction in how to be human. Can we weather life like the rock? Can we cling and accept a humble position like the moss? Can we be rooted, yield to storms, and yet prosper like the tree?

One person is the universe: let the sun burn leaf shadows everywhere.

172 | Light

God of Fire

The Fire God (Zhu Rong) has a number of origin stories. Here are two of them.

The first story centers around the deification of Lo Xuan, who was a minister to the last king of the Shang dynasty, Di Xin (p. 148). In the legend, Lo was a Taoist priest whose face, hair, and beard were bright red; he had three eyes and wore an ornamented red robe. His horse snorted flames and shot fire from its hooves. While fighting for the dynasty, he changed into a giant with three heads and six arms, each with a magic weapon: a seal reflecting heaven and earth, a wheel of fire dragons, a gourd with ten thousand fire crows, two swords, and a column of smoke containing fire swords. (Zhao Gongming's story, p. 9, is from the same time.)

The second story of Zhu Rong's origin as the Fire God dates from even earlier (2698–2598 BCE). He was a legendary emperor who taught people how to use fire for many things: to drive predatory animals away, to smelt, to forge, to weld. His tomb is on the southern slope of Hengshan (p. 44).

Let the sun burn leaf shadows everywhere.
A lantern at night reclaims all vision.

Light is an indispensable part of a garden even beyond the obvious need for the growing power of sunlight. White garden walls are a perfect screen on which to watch the movement of shadows from morning to night. The noon sun shines down in great shafts, punching bright patterns through leafy branches. Sparkles dance across the pond where the orange, black, and white carp come to the surface.

At night, we still want light in our gardens. Perhaps we have a bonfire or fire pit to keep warm on chilly nights. Or perhaps we want the mellow glow of a single candle set in a stone lantern deep in the shadows among the maple and camellias.

A lantern at night doesn't simply light the way. It beckons. It reminds. It says "Welcome home" to the weary traveler. It says, "I remember," even when the night is dark. It says, "I love the spirit," for the spirit is like that: a solitary light burning in the dark.

In lighting lanterns, we remember fire. Every legend of the Fire God goes back to the earliest times because fire is that fundamental to our lives. We may seemingly have tamed it to fine proportions with our glowing monitors, our forced-air heaters, our stainless-steel stoves, and our firefighters. We need fire, and it is always wild, captured for the moment, never truly domesticated.

So even in a garden at night, we light a fire. We don't take it for granted—that's why it's housed in bronze or stone—and we approach it humbly—that's why we commit only to a wick. It is not the candle that is small. It is we who dare not approach fire in a way that overwhelms us. We cannot look directly at the sun. We cannot approach fire in its full might.

We are single spirits, alone in our gardens. We embed ourselves in the glory of nature. We light candles to remember the centrality of fire and light.

A lantern at night reclaims all vision; we follow the light to ride day and night.

173 | Horses

▸ Fasting day
▸ Birthday of the **Horse King**

The Horse King

The Horse King (Ma Wang) is mostly worshipped in the north because the horse was in greater use there and because Mongolian horses were particularly prized. Horses were significant in transportation, travel, commerce, and warfare even into the early twentieth century. The horse remains a symbol of speed, perseverance, and quick-witted youth.

In some images, the Horse King is shown as an ogre with three eyes and four hands holding various weapons. Often shown with the **Bull King** *(Niuhuang)*, the Horse King was a god for ranchers and all those who raised horses and livestock.

The Mare

In the *I Ching,* one of the central symbols is Earth (p. 211), and earth is specifically tied to the image of a mare: "Gain by the purity of a mare."

We follow the light to ride day and night,
riding with the purity of a mare.

Horses have been a part of human development throughout the world. The horse was a means to work, to travel, and to fight. Domesticating wild horses meant learning to communicate with and ride an animal that was many times stronger than any person. Riders are devoted to their horses, and many horses are loyal to their riders.

The Horse King is an extension of that relationship. Worshipping him expresses reverence for that special bond between human and animal. It also acknowledges that we have harnessed another living creature in order to extend our wills.

A farmer had to work together with family and other farmers. A general had to work with soldiers. A rider had to work with horses. There was the need to be aware of other people and animals. Now, we don't work so intimately with others: our machines only reflect our own visages, and we are the poorer for it.

The horse is mighty, vigorous, and spirited. Don't we imagine our heroes on horses? That symbol is still potent today. But the image of the mare is also important: the mare represents fecundity, docility, and forbearance. If we could have the power and spirit of a stallion and the gentleness of a mare, we would be complete. Only by honoring how we've domesticated animals can we domesticate ourselves.

Riding with the purity of a mare, pure as when the lotus grows from filth.

© mariait

174 | The Lotus

The Thunder God

The Thunder God (Lei Gong) has the face of a monkey, a long and pointed jaw, feet like eagle talons, and a muscular body. He holds a wedge in his left hand and a hammer in his right, ready to beat any of the five drums around his waist or the drum under his foot. He is a god of justice and often appears to punish—and even execute—the wicked.

"After the Lotus Flowers Have Opened"

This poem was written by Ouyang Xiu (p. 196).

> The lotus flowers on West Lake have
>   opened well.
> It's time to bring the wine!
> There's no need to wave signal flags
>   when all around us are red curtains and
>   green canopies!
>
> We punt our painted boat where the
>   flowers are thick.
> Aroma floats from our golden cups.
> Misty rain is light and fine,
> with a bit of pipe song I go home drunk!

The lotus grows from filth,
yet the muck rolls right off.

The lotus is a much-beloved flower. It is the symbol of purity because it grows in bogs and marshes and yet rises pristine and pure. Rain and mud roll off of flowers and leaves. The Confucian scholar Zhou Dunyi (1017–1073) wrote: "I love the lotus because while growing from mud, it is unstained." No wonder that the lotus has become the symbol of spirituality—to the point where meditators imagine energy centers in the body as opening lotuses.

You can see the entire cycle of life in one lotus pond. The shoots are like the beginnings of life. The flowering is the glory of life. The lotus pod with its many seeds is the reproducing of life. And when the leaves wither and decay into brown lace, we see the seeming decline of life—but with a hidden power in the seeds that means that life will come again.

In the water and mud, the lotus roots are rhizomes running in long sections. If one cuts them open (every part of the lotus is used as a food, tea, or soup), one sees that tuberous roots have hollow channels. The roots have become the symbol of continuity because of their length, and their hollowness represents the open mind to which wise people aspire.

The entire world's wisdom can be found just by contemplating the lotus.

Yet the muck rolls right off, so live unstained by the dirty world.

175 | Carefree

‣ Birthday of Lan Caihe

Lan Caihe

Lan Caihe, one of the Eight Immortals (p. 124), is of ambiguous gender and is varyingly portrayed as a youth, an old man, or a girl. One early play depicted Lan as a man, while another showed her as a woman. Chinese names and pronouns are not necessarily gender-specific, and the situation has remained undefined.

Lan carries a flower basket containing various plants associated with longevity: the lingzhi mushroom, sprigs of bamboo and pine, plum flowers, chrysanthemum, and a red-berried plant called "ten thousand years green." He often goes about with one bare foot, carrying castanets and a string of cash. In summer, Lan wears a padded wool gown. In winter, Lan sleeps in the snow, exhaling breath like steam.

When drunk, Lan likes to sing and dance in the street, not caring whether his string of cash breaks, is given away to the poor—or is used to buy more wine.

Live unstained by the dirty world.
Live without care and you live long.

No matter who we are, we should embrace that.

But some of us struggle to embrace ourselves. We find it painful to embrace our flaws and appearance, our age and failures. We find it painful to check back on our goals and see how we've fallen short. We find it painful to look at what both Eastern and Western societies say success means and realize that we are never going to be celebrities or world leaders or champions. Today, on the birthday of Lan Caihe, it's important to look at who this immortal was: he was positively nonconformist, unique, and contrary to everything that was socially acceptable. Note that he was not nonconformist because he hated society. No, he was who he was *first*—and the labels came afterward.

In a time when every person aspired to success in the examinations, civil service, wealth, power, position—in short, to being as close to the throne as possible—Lan Caihe was contrary in every way. He was indifferent to money; he didn't care where he lived or how he dressed. Yet he enjoyed singing and dancing in the street—and he possessed the secret to immortality. That trumped power and wealth.

We should be who we are, even if that doesn't fit society's categories—including, in Lan's case, those of sexual identity. Was Lan of ambiguous gender? Was he gay? Was he indifferent to sexuality? Perhaps it's worth considering that he did not define himself by gender.

Nothing about Lan fit what was conventional, but he became a god. The real secret shown here is not necessarily the secret to immortality, but the secret that being true to oneself is in itself a path. This leads to one's own personal Way. We are at the beginning of Lan Caihe's song. We need to sing it as we dance through the streets. Only then can we find the sweet themes that belong to us alone.

Live without care and you live long— if things aren't right, what are you going to do?

Erlang

The name Erlang means "second son."

Erlang was the son of Li **Bing** (c. third century BCE) and a disciple of Taoist Li Jue. When he was appointed prefect by Emperor Yangdi (605–617), Erlang learned that a river dragon flooded the land every year. When another flood occurred during the fifth moon, Erlang led ships and soldiers onto the waters and dove into the depths with a sword. After a fierce underwater battle, he returned with the dragon's head.

Erlang was deified a mighty celestial warrior, with his spiritual third eye opened. Wherever he goes, he is accompanied by a hound named Eagle Dog, and he carries a magical mirror that reveals hidden demons.

People still claim to see him in stormy weather, riding the river waves on a white horse and accompanied by his dog. Erlang is also the god of stage artists and acrobats.

The Dujiangyan Irrigation System

The **Dujiangyan Irrigation System** was built on the Min River in the state of Qin in 256 BCE. It is still in use today and is considered an outstanding example of good water management, controlling flooding and providing for the irrigation of over 2,000 square miles (5,180 square kilometers).

The effort was led by the Qin governor Li Bing. He wanted to avoid a dam to keep the waterway open for troops traveling to the frontier, so he ordered a levee constructed and a channel cut through Yuleishan, bringing excess water to the dry Chengdu Plain. The Two Kings Temple (Erwang Miao) houses a statue of Li Bing, and the Dragon-Taming Temple (Fulong Guan) memorializes Erlang, Li Bing's legendary son.

If things aren't right, what are you going to do?
Will you dive with your sword to do battle?

Some Taoists say that we should accept everything as it is. Why do they then busy themselves with so many things? Practicing exercises, chanting scriptures, digging in their gardens, traveling the world, healing the sick. For people who are supposed to simply rely on Tao, they really are quite contrary.

A Taoist does not depend solely on doctrine. All is meant to be revised and changed. As soon as you say what a Taoist is, a thousand exceptions can be found. As soon as you say what a Taoist isn't, you'll meet a person who isn't like any of the classical descriptions and yet demonstrates the insight and character of a Taoist. You'll never pin a Taoist down. You'll never define one. And if you are one, you delight in being yourself. Every rule is meant to be broken, and every broken rule only proves the rule in the first place.

Sometimes, Tao is out of balance. Sometimes, things are wrong and people are suffering. Is it Tao to act? Or is it Tao to retreat? Tao is not to fall into the trap of choosing between extremes, but rather to act spontaneously as is right at the moment.

If an evil dragon is hurting the people year after year, and the Taoist has a great sword, then let that Taoist act and save the people. If a person has the ability to save others and does not—then that person is the true evil dragon.

The great flood of life is constantly upon us. If you can, like Li Bing, relieve suffering by diverting the waters, and sustain others by bringing water to them, that's a superior way of life. People help in the ways that are most suitable to them. For some, the way might be fighting dragons with swords. For others, it is designing practical flood management. Everyone is the sage-king according to his or her particular circumstances.

Will you dive with your sword to do battle? Stop: wine will bring a moment of clarity.

177 | Enjoyment

"Written While Drunk in Lake View Pavilion on the Twenty-Seventh Day of the Sixth Moon"

This is a good day to remember Su Shi (p. 140) and his carefree appreciation of nature.

> Black clouds fly like ink but can't cover the mountains.
> White rain hits the boat like jumping pearls.
> A sudden wind sweeps the earth, then is gone:
> Below me, the lake mirrors the sky.

Wine will bring a moment of clarity.
This wine is a lake mirroring the sky.

Fling one drop of ink onto an expanse of white paper, and a whole world springs forth. That black spot is alive, growing, spreading. The ink is made of water and pine soot with a skill greater than that of the most famous alchemist. It lives, breathes, and spreads with a life even a god in the throes of creation could not match.

Take up the wine. In that clear liquid there are infinite worlds. Let the poets worry about their lake. Here is a lake greater than the most picturesque of theirs. We need no poetry to tell us that this lake of wine is beautiful. We need no official to worry about building a causeway across it. We need no lovers strolling around the shores. We take this wine in our hands, more powerful than any god, more joyous than any lover, more knowing than any sage, and we drink. We drink down all the waters of West Lake, exhale the vapors of the origin, and laugh to shake the earth and stars.

This porcelain wine bowl is bone-white yet translucent. It's thin as a lotus petal. It's round, the shape of heaven. Its circumference is heaven, its foot is the earth. This is the entire world! This is infinity. Tell me, if an ant were to travel that rim, would it ever reach the end? It would not! To hold this wine bowl is to hold infinity.

A sudden wind sweeps the earth and is gone. Even something as powerful as the wind cannot last, so how can the works of people ever attain permanence? Far better to cast our worries aside and revel in what is simple and close at hand. Far better to idle by this lake of wine, draining it to view the priceless treasures at the bottom, then refilling it again.

Sitting here at the pavilion, setting the empty bowl on the railing, sloshing it full again: "Below me, the lake mirrors the sky."

This wine is a lake mirroring the sky, and this bowl of tea can be shared with everyone.

178 | Tea

› Fasting day

Lu Yu

Lu Yu (733–804) is the personification of tea, and his thoughts are preserved in his *Classic of Tea (Chajing)*.

Legend states that Lu Yu was walking in the wilderness chanting a poem when he was suddenly overcome with feeling. He went home and wrote the *Classic of Tea,* which recorded all the important details of the art of tea as he had come to know them. Divided into three parts, the book includes the beginnings of tea; tools and manufacturing methods; proper equipment for making tea; the way of brewing and drinking tea; history, folklore, and famous persons associated with tea; a survey of the best tea-growing regions; and ways of extracting the book's content for scrolls and quick reference.

While tea leaves are the essential ingredient, Lu Yu placed great emphasis on the water used. He preferred mountain streams, reluctantly accepted river water, and avoided well water or waters that came from gushing and turbulent sources "as if nature was rinsing its mouth."

He said that the first cup should have a "haunting flavor that is strange and lasting."

Tea can be shared with everyone.
Any of us can sip from Tao.

The value of tea, gardens, and Tao can be understood through a single wonderful word: harmony. (This word also means union and peace.) The word combines the picture of grain (on the left)—such as rice, still on the stalk—and a square (on the right) that represents a mouth or gate: peace and harmony exist when we are at one with nature, we accept nature's gifts, and everyone has enough to eat.

Tea, gardens, and Tao all represent the beauty of nature. When all of us can enter the gate, when all of us can have enough to eat, then we know harmony and peace. In our gardens, we can partake in all of these: there is a unique pleasure in savoring tea in a tranquil garden. To sit quietly with a single cup of tea is to awake to the beauty of Tao. Even if we sometimes find meditation elusive, even if we are sometimes bewildered by the words in the classics, even if we still feel that we have many years of exploring the spiritual ahead of us, we can enjoy a complete moment of peace by sipping a cup of tea in a garden.

Lu Yu is the personification of the way of tea. Although he sometimes is called the God of Tea, the Patron Saint of Tea, or the Sage of Tea, he is not really worshipped in a ritualistic way, nor are there stories of any responsibility he might have in the heavenly bureaucracy. He is credited with no mythologized powers, no magic feats, no tales of mounting to heaven in broad daylight. No, Lu Yu represents the ideal of tea culture—a relaxed informality heightened by personal sensibility. No titles. No worldly role. No granting supplications or making requests. We brew a cup of tea, bring it to our mouths, and the Way opens to us.

The next time you have the chance to enjoy a moment of quiet and a cup of tea, think of Lu Yu, and think that a lifetime of Tao is just like this.

Any of us can sip from Tao; any of us can see that Earth gives birth to ten thousand things.

179 | Earth Takes Back All Ruins

The *I Ching* Hexagram for Earth

The second hexagram of the *I Ching* is **Kun**, which means Earth and represents the female as a cosmic principle:

> It gives birth to the ten thousand things.
> It accords with heaven.
> Kun is the substantial support for all things.
> Its virtue is to join all things within limitless borders.
> It holds enormous expanses in bright greatness.
> It makes all things progress smoothly.
> The mare is of the earth and roams the limitless ground.
> Gentle. Compliant. Beneficial. Pure.

The three split lines forming the symbol for Earth, cast onto a bell on Wudangshan. Note the mountain's height, shown in the background, and the offerings of locks to the left. © Bernard De Poorter

Earth gives birth to ten thousand things.
Earth makes new life of all dead things.

Once some people find the doctrines that resonate with them, they expound them all their lives. How admirable that is! How enviable that is! The rest of us go out onto the path, seeking elusive understanding. The Way? Tao? For some of us, our Tao is formed by the lifelong pursuit of a truth that seems so maddeningly dim, so enormously high, so impossibly wide, and so profoundly deep. We have reached our insight by the hardest way possible: trial and error. Yes, we have studied. Yes, we have visited the holy people and the sacred sites. Yes, we have even learned to move in dances choreographed by the ancients. And yet, still we search, not because we are dissatisfied, but because there is more to learn.

In the forest we stumble on the foundations of some forgotten home and imagine it was once the place of laughing children, a mother setting out fresh fruit on the kitchen table, a father coming home at dusk from a day in the fields. Sometimes we find a ruined temple, the gods gone, the doors hanging from their hinges, the red dust of the world blown into every crack. Sometimes we step upon broken ramparts, the fortifications for which men died angrily, exerting their utmost power to resist what they knew was evil. Gone. All gone.

Whether noble accomplishment or wretched effort, whatever we make and then abandon still stands upon this earth, and the earth accepts it. Whatever we make and can no longer sustain, the earth takes back. All that we have ruined, the earth turns into new life: grass sprouts, vines grow, water dissolves, and the soil eventually moves to cover it all.

Seeing this, we see ample reason for reverence. Seeing this, we see a great example for our character. Seeing this, we come to understand our *place* in this world.

Earth makes new life of all dead things: how beautiful the garden path.

180 | The Garden Path

▸ Fasting day

A Chan Buddhist Retreat Behind Broken Mountain Temple

This poem was written by Chang Jian (fl. 749).

On a clear dawn, I go to the ancient temple.
The sun's first rays glow at the top of the forest.
A crooked path winds through a secluded grove
to a Chan retreat deep in flowers and woods.
Here, birds delight in the mountain brightness.
Deep reflections; an empty heart.
Ten thousand sounds completely quieted—
except for the ringing of the temple bell.

How beautiful the garden path
where we walk with our own two feet.

A garden path is truly a lovely thing: a simple way leading into the distance, full of the promise of tranquil delight.

How lovely is a line of stepping-stones over dark and placid waters, placed so that we can be practically walking on water, surrounded by the smooth surface that reflects light and reveals its depths at the same time. The stones have the texture of the ancient. Their gray faces accept the sunlight with the same equanimity that they accept the shadows, the nights, the moonlight, or the rain that still puddles in tiny pools.

A gardener put all this there for only one reason: our enjoyment. In setting down a completely unmoving path, in sinking heavy stones in an irregular line, the gardener was nevertheless anticipating one thing: movement. The gardener knew that people would be walking along the path, watching the different views change, feeling the texture of the stone beneath their feet, catching different fragrances as they passed from mossy shadow to sunlit peonies.

Isn't this all we need in life too? All we need is to follow the path that we find, delighting in all that comes our way, realizing, in the end, that we are the final element that makes the garden what it is.

Where we walk with our own two feet, Heaven and Earth move without intentions.

7

The Orchid Moon

Looking at the Moon, Thinking of One Far Away

The bright moon rises from the sea:
sky and cliff join in one moment.
My love's so distant in this dark,
all night I think how we're apart.
Lamp snuffed, I gaze at the full moon
and drape my cloak as the dew grows.
Unable to share what I feel:
to bed to dream of better times.
—Zhang Jiuling (673–740)

The two solar terms within this moon:

AUTUMN BEGINS

LIMIT OF HEAT

Exercise 13

AUTUMN BEGINS

The sweltering heat of summer begins to fade, and the weather will slowly turn cooler from here.

There may still be a brief period of high heat and an Indian summer, but autumn will inevitably follow.

Crops in this period show tremendous growth and fruit begins to ripen. Farmers have to ensure adequate irrigation at this time as they anticipate a good harvest.

The Yellow Emperor on Autumn

In the three moons of autumn,
all nature is fulfilled.
Heaven's energy becomes hurried,
earth's energy becomes manifest.

Go to sleep early, wake up early
with the chickens.
Set yourself on being calm and
peaceful.
Don't rush, and you will avoid
autumn's injuries.
Hold back from releasing your
essence,
receive the divine energy,
and make autumn placid.
Don't express willfulness.
Keep the lung's energy pure.

In the autumn season, follow the Way
of harvest.
Act against it and you will injure your
lungs
and you will have digestive problems
in the winter.
Cultivate storing energy to stay young.

This exercise is best practiced during the period of 1:00–5:00 A.M.

1. Kneel, lean forward, and press your palms on the floor in front of you.
2. Keeping this position, jerk your body slightly upward by contracting your muscles. Exhale when you jerk, inhale when you relax. Perform this fifty-six times. The traditional instruction is to hold your breath for the entire exercise, but this should only be attempted with caution by experienced qigong practitioners.
3. Facing forward with your hands resting on your lap, click your teeth together thirty-six times. Roll your tongue between your teeth nine times in each direction. Form saliva in your mouth by pushing your cheeks in and out. When your mouth is filled with saliva, divide the liquid into three portions.
4. Inhale; then exhale, imagining your breath traveling to the dantian and then swallow one-third of the saliva, imagining that it travels to the dantian.
5. Repeat two more times until you've swallowed all three portions.
6. Sit comfortably as long as you like.

Through this exercise, ancient Taoists sought to prevent or treat weakness in the body; feelings of trapped air in the body; pains in the heart and ribs; feelings of being unable to turn; headaches and pains in the jaws; bulging eyes; swelling in the chest and arms; and cold sweats.

| # Acting Without Acting

Understanding Wuwei

Wuwei is normally translated as "non-action," and it is a central concept of the *Daodejing* and the *Zhuangzi*.

In Chapter 3 of the *Daodejing*, Laozi describes the sage as "acting without acting" *(wei wuwei)*.

Acting without acting does not mean refraining from action. Rather, it means to act naturally and without intellectualized plans. Heaven and earth, for example, seem to have neither intention, advanced planning, nor partiality to any person. All events result from heaven and earth's simply existing and interacting.

Laozi advocates that human beings similarly act from their natures and not out of conscious scheming or desire.

The passage below is tricky because it uses the word for action in several different ways. Note the word "wei" in parentheses.

> Not rewarding the capable ensures that the people will not contend.
> Not valuing the rarest commodities ensures that the people will not act (wei) as thieves.
> Not seeing desirable things ensures that the people's hearts will not be confused.
> That is why the sage's rule
> empties people's hearts but fills their bellies,
> weakens ambitiousness but strengthens bones,
> always ensures that the people don't know too much and or have too many desires,
> ensures that the intellectuals will not dare to meddle (wei).
> Acting (wei) without acting (wei),
> yet nothing goes ungoverned.

Heaven and earth move without intentions.
Nature acts from nature and does not act.

A knot tied in a rope does not alter the diameter or length of the rope, but pulls tight: acting without acting.

The button inserted into the buttonhole doesn't change the button, the hole, or the garment: acting without acting.

The hairbrush pulls through hair without altering its shape or diminishing the hair: acting without acting.

The chain never breaks its links, never stiffens, never loosens, but still anchors the heaviest of ships: acting without acting.

The vase keeps its shape and remains open, allowing itself to be filled and emptied countless times: acting without acting.

The spool is the core without which soft thread would have no shape, no order, no stillness: acting without acting.

The hose is emptiness enclosed in a soft tube, channeling water without losing a drop: acting without acting.

The hat gives shelter from rain and sun without weight or mechanism: acting without acting.

The writing brush gathers ink without grabbing, deposits ink without hesitation, keeps nothing for itself, and yet communicates volumes: acting without acting.

The abacus keeps its beads in rows without deviation, moves in its prearranged patterns without error, and yet can calculate infinity: acting without acting.

The hook holds its shape and can secure anything from a cable to a jacket, never losing its shape, never distorting: acting without acting.

The magnet never changes shape, never needs to rest, and yet attracts or repels as needed: acting without acting.

The sages speak of acting without acting and we are confused by the term, yet all around us the most ordinary of things confirm that acting without acting is not only possible, but effective.

Nature acts from nature and does not act: thus, you can read Laozi and become Laozi.

On Study

Confucius said: "A noble person studies knowledge broadly, lives in accord with propriety, and therefore does not exceed boundaries."

From the *Classic of Triple Words*

As its name implies, this work on learning is built on three-word phrases. Two groups of threes make a sentence, and two sentences make a complete thought.

The *Classic of Triple Words* (*San Ji Jing*), was written in the Song dynasty by Wang Yinglin (1223–1296). It is a child's primer of Confucian learning, and it was popular until the end of the nineteenth century. Its triword format made the book easy to recite, teaching vocabulary, grammar, history, and morality at the same time.

It's impossible to translate the text into English while keeping the triword structure intact. To give some sense of the triwords, the words are highlighted in bold.

> **Dogs guard** the **night**,
> **roosters preside** over the **dawn**.
> If **carelessly** you **don't study**,
> how can you **be human**?

> **Silkworms secrete silk**,
> **bees make honey**.
> A **person** who **doesn't learn**
> is **not** even **equal** to **animals**.

> When **young, then learn**,
> when **grown, then achieve**.
> **Above, advise** the **king**,
> **below, benefit** the **people**.

Read Laozi and become Laozi.
Follow the old Way and become new.

Whenever we read the words of a sage, we become the sage. Rather than experiencing the messiness and contradiction of any person's life, you are experiencing the distillation of that person's experience.

That's true of the sage's words. It's also true of the work of the poet, the musician, the painter, the martial artist, the doctor, the potter, the knife maker, and the furniture maker. It extends to what anyone does, even the cook and the housekeeper. If you are sensitive enough, you can change places with anybody for a time, and experience the best that they have to offer.

The ancient people knew this, and so they urged us to memorize the great poems, scriptures, music, and martial arts movements, to internalize them by memorization and study.

Yet generations of students have balked at tedious memorization. Besides, generations of scholars failed the examinations, so how good a system was it? However, there is great benefit from trying to master something every day until it becomes a part of us. We can even be much more relaxed about it since we're not trying to pass the imperial examinations. We're merely trying to go beyond our own limitations.

Keep at it. Great learning changes every day. The ideas or words that are puzzling at first sometimes take on new meaning later. The movements in a martial arts set that seem odd at first later become easy as our bodies adapt. The music that seems challenging becomes a vessel for our own feelings as our hearts overflow.

Follow the old Way and become new, for a master comes from truth.

183 | True Masters

Practice Begets Skill

"Practice begets skill" is a popular idiom. Here is the story behind it.

Chen Yaozi was a famous archer. As he practiced at an archery range before a crowd of admiring people, his every arrow struck the bull's-eye. Chen proudly reveled in the crowd's reaction—until he noticed a nearby oil vendor who merely looked on politely.

Feeling slighted, Chen confronted the man: "Are you an archer?"

"No, I'm not," replied the vendor. "But in my opinion, there's nothing special about your archery. Your skill comes from practice."

"Outrageous! You just sell oil! How can you criticize me?"

"It's true that I'm just an oil vendor. Here, I'll show you something."

The old man put a hollow gourd on the ground and placed a copper coin over the narrow mouth (in those days, a Chinese coin had a small square hole at its center). Raising a ladle high over the coin, he poured a steady stream of oil through the hole without spilling a single drop. The crowd was impressed. Chen's mouth dropped open.

This story comes to us from *Records of Returning to the Fields (Guitian Lu)* by Ouyang Xiu (p. 196).

A master comes from truth
and all that's done is truth.

People are confused about what the word *shifu* means. It's translated as "master," and martial arts teachers as well as Taoist masters are often addressed by that name. But in reality, a shifu can be any skilled master of any particular art. When you hire a carpenter, you use the title "shifu." When you address a chef, you use the title "shifu."

Most of the time nowadays, the preparation and serving of food have become careless. They've been subjected to corporate "efficiency," scientific "health practices," and the need to provide food as cheaply as possible. If you have the chance to travel widely, however, you'll realize that there are still people making excellent food. It's not necessarily expensive, because the cook doesn't have to support a glamorous restaurant. It isn't trendy, because the food is of the earth, the soul, the people. The recipes have been shaped by generations, not the cleverness of someone who has to market a unique product. It is food in the classic sense, food that reflects the people, the land, and local sources.

The raw ingredients are selected by the cook. There is no delivery truck. The traditional seafood cook, for example, goes down to select the fish himself each day. The vegetable cook goes to check the available harvest each day. The making of the food starts with the growing and choosing of the food, culminates in the preparation and cooking, and only ends with the serving.

No matter what the culture, food is part of offering. No matter what the culture, food is part of ritual. No matter what the culture, we understand that the preparation of food must be universal. Everyone needs to eat: but the one who can take this necessity and turn it into art—only that person can be a shifu.

Traditionally, we don't distinguish the status of a master cook from that of a spiritual master. An artisan who can weave baskets at an expert level may be more powerful than a sorcerer. A fisherman can be wiser than a scholar. It's not what people do that makes them masters: it's how true they are to what they do.

And all that's done is truth. That's why the gulls soar past the skyscraper windows.

184 | The Gulls

Written at Whirling Stream Villa After a Long Rain

Wang Wei (p.174) wrote this poem at Whirling Stream (Wangchuan) Villa, a rambling estate and famous garden in the hills outside of present-day Xi'an (then called Chang'an). In the last line, Wang Wei says that the seagulls won't fault him because he's left the world of social ills and so has the innocence not to frighten off representatives of nature.

> The empty woods have filled with rain; smoke from the cooking fires rises slowly.
> Smells of steamed pigweed and cooked millet drift over the east fields worth a soldier's pay.
> Languid, languid is the water by the fields, flying is the white heron.
> Shrouded in shadow, the golden orioles sing in the summer trees.
> Deep in the mountains I practice stillness and watch the morning glories.
> Under the pines, I break my pure fast and discover a sunflower.
> I'm a rustic old man who no longer fights for position.
> How can seagulls fault me?

The gulls soar past the skyscraper windows:
it's the people who are in the birdcages.

Where the gulls fly, the trees seem more green. Where the clouds swirl around the mountains, the mountains are more lofty. Where the deep aqua of the waves breaks over the black rocks, the foam is more white. Where the land slopes to the sea, the tiny strip where humans live is more precious.

The gulls fly, mostly in pairs, circling, soaring. There is no obvious path, there is no apparent plan. There is only improvisation and interaction and the sheer joy of flight.

Let man put up tall towers. They do not impede the gulls. No matter what man does, there is no significant encroachment on the sky.

The gulls take fish from the sea. They land wherever they please on the earth. They float as long as they wish on the waves. The gull soars over earth and sea, rises to any height, traverses any breadth, and is free.

In the meantime, we labor away in a room that is one of hundreds, stooped over our computers and phones, rushing into meetings that we insist are "very important" for bosses as arbitrary and fallible as any mandarin; we huddle in steel cars amidst honking bumper-to-bumper traffic, get turned away from streets that are blocked off, all the while telling ourselves that we are doing all of this to be free.

The gulls fly by our plate glass windows and we don't even notice.

It's the people who are in the birdcages—go to an old grove and sing with others.

© andelieva

185 | The Grove

The Seven Sages of the Bamboo Grove

The Chinese empire fractured into the **Three Kingdoms** in the third century. In Wei, one of those three kingdoms, generalissimos of the Sima clan forced the emperors into figurehead status. War, intrigue, murder, and corruption followed.

Against this backdrop, a group of men known as the **Seven Sages of the Bamboo Grove** (Zhulin Qi Xian) retreated with their leader, **Xi Kang** (224–263) to live Zhuangzi's ideals. They met in a grove outside the capital of Luoyang, where they were free to converse, admire nature, immerse themselves in Tao—and drink wine in prodigious amounts. Their admiration of Zhuangzi was unmistakable: one of the sages, **Xiang Xiu** (223–300)—who held a high military rank, and practiced alchemy—wrote a profound commentary about the *Zhuangzi*.

Liu Ling (221–300) traveled with a servant who not only supplied him with wine at all times, but also carried a shovel—so that Liu Ling could be buried wherever he fell dead. Liu Ling went about naked when he was home. This shocked a prudish official who came to visit, but Liu replied that the whole universe was his house and his room was his trousers—so what was the official doing in his trousers?

Liu's only preserved writing is the *Ode to the Virtue of Wine (Jiudesong)*:

[The Great Person] travels without
  wheels or tracks,
and wanders without house or hearth.
He makes heaven his curtain and earth
  his seat,
indulging as he pleases.
Pausing, he holds his wine cup and
  maintains his goblet;
walking, he carries a casket and holds
  a jar.
His only obligation is to wine,
which he knows in abundance.

Go to an old grove and sing with others.
Sing a children's song of the earth and trees.

In traditional stories, the sage teaches in a forest. Buddha, the Seven Sages of the Bamboo Grove, the participants in the Orchid Pavilion—all these had their settings in forest groves. We lose something today when gatherings are in meeting rooms or by video feed. There is something remote and divorced about wisdom passed on in this way. Yes, the words are the same, the texts studied are the same, and the intentions are the same. But we must notice that the "how" influences the "what."

A forest grove is far more than a charming setting, much more than a place for people to gather if they couldn't manage a grand building. The grove has its own power, its own energy. Just go into any grove to sense the other lives that have crisscrossed that space: people, animals, birds, and insects.

A grove is a living place so much older than any of us. Walk in the grove and you'll feel the age of the trees. Feel how the ground has been trod for hundreds of years. Archaeologists and geologists can show us the age of the place and the complexity of the human history there. A power emanates from the ground and gives everyone the opportunity to inhale the breath of the earth, that crucial force that unites all beings.

Electricity and atomic energy: we consider them to be real forces. Dealing with spiritual questions: we think of this as mere routine, psychology—and some people would even label it unreal fantasy. But do we have to keep justifying the spiritual? Our aim is not to sell the spiritual to those who do not want it, but to state the truth of spirituality for those who need it.

If we sit in the grove, we can feel all of this. In feeling all of it, we can partake of it. In partaking of it, we can find a wellspring of power that will alter the wisdom exchanged here. The words will be the same as those spoken in a city, but the effect will be altogether different.

Sing a children's song of the earth and trees, soar beyond vastness without bounds.

186 | The Great Person

Xi Kang and the Seven Sages of the Bamboo Grove

Ruan Ji (210–263) a poet, drinker, qin player, famous whistler, and maker of guzheng (a zither with between twelve and twenty-five strings), was another member of the Seven Sages of the Bamboo Grove (p. 219). In his *Biography of Master Great Person (Xiansheng Daren Zhuan)*, Ruan Ji wrote that the ideal Taoist:

> Soars without a steady perch
> beyond vastness without bounds.
> Raises a comet like a banner
> and strikes like resounding thunder.

Ruan's nephew, **Ruan Xian** (234–305), was a poet, a musician, and the inventor of the *ruanxian* (a four-stringed lute with a circular body). Both men drank wine from enormous vats—it is said that they did not even bother to wave the pigs away when the animals wanted to drink too.

Two high officials were among the remaining sages: **Wang Rong** (234–305) and **Shan Tao** (205–283). Wang Rong was the youngest of the Seven Sages, and Shan Tao rose steadily in rank, surviving to join the next dynasty.

The most famous of the Seven Sages of the Bamboo Grove was **Xi Kang**, a poet, philosopher, painter, blacksmith, and qin player. He is best known as the author of one of the greatest writings on music, the *Prose Poem on the Qin (Qinfu)*.

Xi Kang studied Laozi and Zhuangzi in his youth, came from a wealthy and prominent family, and was well educated. He engaged in the alchemical pursuit of the elixir of immortality. He often trekked through the mountains in search of special herbs, wandering for long periods and seeking conversations with recluses and sages.

Soar beyond vastness without bounds:
you are a thundering comet.

Xi Kang was pressed to become an official, but he refused. The generalissimos pressed again, but Xi Kang refused a second time, saying he rejected worldly life. His attitude offended a general named Zhong Hui (225–264).

When Xi Kang visited prison to help a friend named Lu An, Zhong Hui arranged for Xi Kang's arrest and charged him with treason: "Xi Kang does not loyally serve the emperor above and does not serve the kings and princes below. He is overbearing, thinks himself too good for this world, and does not work for the common good. Not only does he do no good, he also corrupts good morals. Such things must not be tolerated. They must be eliminated from the beginning and so purify the morals of the public."

The generalissimo was persuaded. Xi Kang and his friend Lu An were executed. Xi Kang was only thirty-nine.

Years after Xi Kang's death, Xiang Xiu, a friend from the old days of the Seven Sages, wrote: "I was a close friend of Xi Kang and Lu An. Both men were indomitable. Xi Kang dwelled on his mind and lofty things. Lu An was unconcerned and carefree. The two were executed because they fell into trouble.

"Xi Kang excelled in all the arts and was an especially great musician. When his last hour drew near, he looked at the setting sun and took up his qin to pluck its strings.

"At that time, I traveled westward, but now I am returning, and I pass where he used to live. Night is falling. The darkness brings a piercing cold. A man plays a flute with sad and forlorn tones. I think of our friendship and the time we spent together. Moved by the tones, I sigh, and write this."

What does it mean to advocate being a Great Person? The Seven Sages of the Bamboo Grove gathered together thinking that their friendship and freedom from convention might save them from the dangers of society. But it did not. If we are to be Great Persons, if we are to soar beyond vastness without bounds, if we are to be thundering comets, what insight does that require?

You are a thundering comet, and yet, I fit you, you fit me.

Double Seven Festival

The **Double Seven Festival** (Qixi Jie) is also known as the Magpie Festival, Chinese Valentine's Day (Qingren Jie—literally, "Lovers' Festival"), the Festival to Plead for Skills, the Seventh Sister's Birthday, and the Night of Skills.

The Cowherd and the Weaver Girl

Once there were two brothers and a sister whose parents died. The older brother and sister were cruel day and night to the younger brother until they finally drove him away with only an old ox as a companion.

The boy's name was **Niulang** (Cowherd). Although he was strong, hardworking, honest, and handsome, he toiled all day in the fields and could barely support himself. The ox could not help but feel sorry, and one day he surprised the boy by speaking.

The ox said that he had once been a god in heaven. Long ago, he had seen humans suffering from famine and starvation. He stole a few seeds and secretly taught people how to cultivate crops. When the other gods discovered this, he was transformed into an ox as punishment and sent to work in the fields. The ox saw that the boy was of good character, and he told him to go to a secret place on a certain day.

The boy followed the ox's instructions, found a remote forest pool, and hid in the reeds. In a short time, the seven daughters of the Jade Emperor came to bathe. The cowherd hid the clothes of the youngest one, but the maidens caught a glimpse of him. Startled, they threw on their clothes and flew back to heaven. **Zhinu** (Weaver Girl) was left stranded. When she asked for her clothes back, the cowherd asked if she would marry him. She agreed.

They fell deeply in love and built a home together, and in time Zhinu gave birth to twins—Brother Gold and Sister Jade. The family was happy.

However, one year on earth is equal to a day in heaven. Although time passed on earth, it was only a few days in heaven before Zhinu's absence was reported to the palace. The Jade Emperor and Empress Huang Mu were upset that their daughter was living on earth and was married to a mortal. The Jade Emperor dispatched his imperial generals to bring Zhinu back to heaven, and when she was returned, the empress angrily sent her back to the loom to resume weaving clouds.

Niulang returned from the fields to find his young wife gone. The ox told him what had happened, and Niulang fell to his knees weeping. Seeing how inconsolable he was, the ox broke off one of his horns, and it became a boat big enough to carry Niulang and his two children to heaven.

As soon as Empress Huang Mu saw Niulang sailing to heaven, she pulled a golden pin from her hair and scratched a wide river into the sky, forming the Milky Way. Enormous waves beat Niulang's boat back, and he was unable to go any farther.

Even today, Zhinu must stay on her side, sadly weaving clouds at her loom day after day, while Niulang must stay on his side, caring for their two children. But once a year, all the magpies in the world take pity on the two lovers. They fly up to heaven and form a bridge (over the star Deneb in the Cygnus constellation) so that husband and wife can be reunited on the night of the seventh day of the seventh moon.

Others say that Zhinu became the star Vega and Niulang became the star Altair. Two adjacent stars are their children, and six other stars form the shape of an ox. Vega and Altair appear closest together on the seventh day of the seventh moon.

As with all Chinese legends, there are variations. In some versions, the Weaver Girl runs away to earth and finds the Cowherd. In other versions, it is the Jade Emperor who forms the river. Still others say that Huang Mu was touched by the pair's devotion and allowed the annual reunions. In the kindest version, the lovers are allowed to meet once a month rather than yearly.

Qin Guan (1049–1100), a student of Su Shi (p. 140), wrote this poem entitled "Immortal on the Magpie Bridge":

I weave clouds with nimble skill,
hating the flying stars that separate us.
The Milky Way is broad, long, and mysterious.

We meet like golden wind and jade dew.
A meeting better than all others, enthralling as others can't know.

Our tender love flows like water.
For one beautiful day, it's like a dream.
How can we bear to turn back to Magpie Bridge?

Two people's love can last forever.
What does it matter if we can't meet every day and night?

Other Traditions

In olden times, the Double Seven Festival was a notable celebration for women. They dressed in their best clothes to commemorate the meeting of the Weaver Girl and the Cowherd and built altars with incense burners and fruit offerings in their courtyards. Since the Weaver Girl is so skilled, women prayed to have her abilities in sewing, weaving, embroidery, and cooking.

There were a number of informal contests held at this time. Groups of girls and women gathered during the festival to make offerings and pray to Zhinu. Whoever could thread a needle with her hands behind her back would have any wish granted by the goddess. Women also competed in melon-carving contests or vied with one another to make fried pastries in different shapes. ▶

• The Double Seven Festival

Taoist Sex

Taoist sex practices are deeply rooted in ancient cultural concepts as well as internal alchemy. Understanding these practices begins with the concept of jing, the essence of the body. Positing that this essence was both limited and precious, three schools emerged:

Retaining of Essence This school aimed for complete celibacy. If the essence could be retained, then it could be circulated through the techniques of internal alchemy (such as the Exercises of the Twenty-Four Solar Terms) and used for spiritual practice.

Control of Essence This school aimed at restricting the release of essence during sexual climax. When the Yellow Emperor (p. 77) says, "Release your essence," he is referring to sexual release. However, he also says, "Cultivate storing your energy to stay young" (p. 214). When Qiu Changchun visits Genghis Khan (p. 25), he urges the ruler to sleep alone to preserve his health, echoing the very advice that the Yellow Emperor received from his tutor, Plain Woman. Taoists who practice this system regulate the frequency of intercourse by the season—allowing more frequency in summer, less in winter.

Exchange of Essence This school posits that two sexual partners exchange their vital essences with one another. Also called the Dual Cultivation School, its practitioners will have sex without climaxing, stimulating the release of some of each partner's essence through the prolonged sharing of pleasure. They will allow climax periodically to augment each other's energies.

I fit you, you fit me.
From two: a greater one.

The lover said: "You and I walk hand in hand as we follow the stream toward its headwaters. The sun flares unabated. Pausing in the shadow of a cinnamon tree, where the flowers are dazzling and each leaf is perfect in its greenness and shape, I break a lychee from a cluster I've brought with me and peel it for you. You bite into it, gaze steadily at me, take the juice as you delicately pull the soft flesh from the hard pit.

"Hold me. Breathe me in as I breathe you in, until our breaths intertwine and form helixes of energy encircling us, winding up our spines, binding them surely, rising up, heady and strong.

"Hold me. When you first touched me, I recognized that touch. I wanted it. I was grateful for it. It comforted me in a way that no one's touch has comforted me. It excited as no one's touch ever has. It pulled me as nothing had ever pulled me before. The first time we parted, I was despondent, weak, and could barely lift my head. When we said goodbye, the gulf of time that stretched ahead seemed monstrous. I forced myself to go on until I saw you again.

"Talk to me. Murmur to me in that voice that awakens me. What you say always surprises me, fascinates me, makes me drunk. Everything you say delights me. Once you tell me how you see the world, I instantly see the world that way too.

"Now, we are together again in the shade of this tree. You are a god. I am a god. We pull each other closer and the heat we have between us is hotter than the sun. We pull each other closer and a great cloud of stars falls into this valley, filling it slowly with dazzling light and rain."

From two: a greater one, delicate as butterflies joined.

188 | Two Butterflies

▸ Fasting day

The Butterfly Lovers

The legend of the **Butterfly Lovers** has been a theme for stories, plays, operas, ballets, and movies. Their temple, the Liang Shanbo Temple, is west of Ningbo. A violin concerto written in 1959 by Chen Gang (b. 1935) and He Zhanhao (b. 1933) has remained popular ever since.

During the Eastern Jin dynasty (317–420), the beautiful **Zhu Yingtai** convinces her father to send her to school. Since this was uncommon in those days, she disguises herself as a man. On her journey to Hangzhou, she meets **Liang Shanbo**, a poor scholar who is attending the same school. They are drawn to one another, apparently platonically, since Shanbo believes that Yingtai is a man. They take an oath of friendship together.

As the pair study together for three years, Yingtai falls in love with Shanbo. But he is too naive to realize what's happening, and though she hints that she's really a woman, he fails to understand her. When they part, she finally offers to be his matchmaker and marry him to her "sister." He happily agrees.

Months later, when Shanbo visits Yingtai in her home, he's overjoyed to learn that his beloved friend and classmate is also his love. However, their joy is shattered when they learn that Yingtai's parents have already betrothed her to a man from a rich and prominent family. The heartbroken Shanbo goes on to become a magistrate, but he soon weakens and dies of a broken heart.

Yingtai's wedding procession must pass Shanbo's grave. She asks to stop and pay her respects. When she goes to the grave, she begs for it to open. The earth parts with a clap of thunder and she throws herself in.

Two butterflies emerge from the grave—the reincarnation of the two reunited lovers.

Delicate as butterflies joined,
returning to the same tree.

How intangible love is! Where is its substance? Where is its solidity? When two people are in love, where is the evidence? There is none: there is only the resonance between two hearts, and yet no one who has ever been in love will deny that it's real.

Love is feared by priests, legislators, schoolteachers, and parents. Everyone recognizes that love will challenge all attempts to box it in and control it. From Romeo and Juliet to the Butterfly Lovers, no one can tame love.

Taoists have tried to impose celibacy, ritual, fasting, and all sorts of other practices. They end up the same as all the others who try to control love: frustrated.

The Butterfly Lovers even overcome the last frontier: death.

Love is intangible, fragile, delicate. Yes, it can be ruined, spent, wasted, and unrequited. Love can be tragic. Yet that doesn't lessen its value. It only illustrates how variable fortunes in this life are and how deluded people are to think life can be controlled.

Butterflies are delicate. They don't live long. Some live for just a week. Others live no longer than a year. People adore their delicacy, and understand their fragility to be the opposite of bombshells and the monuments of empires. However, even though individual butterflies die, butterflies always reappear. In the same way, love may be delicate in isolated moments, but love as a perennial force in human life is powerful and impossible to overcome.

Love is not gold, brick, or steel—and yet it will outlast all those things. Butterflies may be delicate, but they return every year.

Returning to the same tree, feel that waves are the sea breathing with us.

189 | The Sound of Waves

Code of the Devoted Woman

Meng Jiao (751–814) was a Tang dynasty poet who was unable to pass even the first stage of the examinations and so lived in poverty.

The wutong trees mentioned below are paulownias—the favored roost for the mythical phoenix and an excellent wood for musical instruments. Mandarin ducks are the symbol of marital fidelity because they mate for life.

This poem was also seen as a reference to chaste widows, and allegorically to those who killed themselves out of loyalty to feudal lords or kings.

The wutong trees grow old together,
mandarin ducks die side by side,
and a chaste woman honors her
    husband even in death.
If she gives her life in this way,
then swamping waves of passion won't
    rise,
and her heart remains still as a deep
    well.

Waves are the sea breathing with us.
We exhale to a farther shore.

The dearest one said: "The sound of waves is like breathing. With every sentence we say to one another, with every moment that we reach out to caress one another, the waves breathe in and out. Are the waves breathing us? Or are we breathing the waves? The waves and we breathe as one.

"The air is hot as a leaping fire. But only people who are outside this area call it tropical. We just talk of the weather, and we've come to accept that it's hot and humid. In the same way, only people outside of ourselves would want to analyze or describe what we share. They use words like attraction, love, desire. They use cardboard words because they cannot share our touch.

"The waves keep breaking on the shore. They don't go anywhere else, do they? If they go in a different direction, they're traveling to some other shore. A wave is not fully seen until it encounters the shore. Until then, the ocean heaves and rolls in search of a place to break, just as lovers search for each other.

"When we're apart, we keep trying to find one another. We attend to other business, declaring it to be important. That's what the mind says. The heart, like the waves, knows nothing of this. The heart is not beholden to right and wrong. It pumps with the same force that moves the waves.

"The heart is pure wanting, just as the waves are pure direction. The heart does not think, does not rationalize, does not budget, does not calculate. The heart only wants, and as the waves want the shore, I want you."

We exhale to a farther shore, for we need our body with its needs.

Needing a Body

‣ Birthday of Li Tieguai

Iron Crutch Li

Li Tieguai (Iron Crutch Li), one of the Eight Immortals (p. 124) is shown as a hideous, hairy, and deformed man dressed in rags. He carries a bottle gourd containing the elixir of immortality and leans on an iron crutch. Sometimes a mysterious vapor will rise from the gourd, and Li's soul will be inside it.

Originally named Li Yuan, he heard about Tao when he was a boy and began to practice the way of the immortals. He was so adept that Laozi himself came down to Huashan (p. 360) to teach him.

One day, Li was going to travel in spirit to meet Laozi. He told his student that he would be gone for seven days. If he had not returned after that time, his disciple should burn Li's body.

However, on the sixth day, the disciple got an urgent message that his own mother was ill. Thinking that the master was not going to return, the pupil burned the body. When Li returned on the seventh day, he was forced to enter the body of a nearby dying beggar.

In some versions of this story, Li then goes to heal the disciple's sick mother.

Iron Crutch Li is associated with medical professions. He is popular because he is irascible and eccentric. He fights for the rights of the poor and disabled, the downtrodden and needy.

We need our body with its needs.
We need a body to go on.

Li Yuan was a highly accomplished master—but he had to accept living in a beggar's body. Doesn't that alone show that no one can leave human existence prematurely? Doesn't that alone show that one needs a body to live in this world? True, the body, as well as earthly existence, is filled with contradictions. It is imperfect. Nevertheless, one needs a body, painful as it might be, to live.

The master had to take up an iron crutch. Doesn't that show that one must find any means of support necessary? That it's fundamental to the human condition to find a way out of one's limitations and miseries and try for something greater? Doesn't that show that self-sufficiency is not a matter of rejecting aid, but is a matter of using aid to be independent?

The master carries a gourd with the elixir of immortality. Doesn't that show that immortality and salvation cannot be compounded easily? That one needs the physical means to health and that sometimes those means are a matter of grace and not greedy coveting? Doesn't that show that we need the help of gods or heaven to fulfill what we must have?

The master accepted his fate and did not reproach his disciple. He did not cling to his old body. He accepted his new one, as ugly as it was, and cheerfully went on to help others. Doesn't that show that a certain equanimity, calmness, and compassion are the real keys to a bright future?

We need a body to go on, for we are a seed seeking lodging.

191 | Banyan Roots

The Tree and the Artisan

Zhuangzi tells the story of an artisan who walked by a tree that was used as an altar. It measured a hundred spans around. When his assistant called it a mass of beautiful wood, the artisan said the tree was useless. "A boat made from its wood would sink, a coffin made from it would rot, furniture made from it would fall apart, a door would leak sap, and a pillar would be riddled with insects. It is because it is useless that the tree has attained such an old age."

Later, the tree spoke to the artisan in a dream. "When hawthorns, pears, oranges, pomelos, and gourds ripen, their fruit is knocked from them and their branches broken. Their productiveness makes their lives bitter.

"Suppose that I was useful. Would I have reached the great size I am? Moreover, you and I are both living beings. How can one pass judgment on another? How can you as a useless man know anything about me as a useless tree?"

We are a seed seeking lodging,
with each root a generation.

Look at the banyan tree. How it sends out air roots. How those roots only know to drop as surely as any plumb line. How those roots nourish the central tree, how they draw up the earth's energy, how they reach for water, how they come to support an enormous limb.

We are like this banyan tree. A banyan can't grow in Himalayan altitudes, just as the heat of love avoids snowy purity.

The banyan starts life as an epiphyte—a plant that grows with the support of another tree. Its seeds are usually spread by fruit-eating birds. Once a seed germinates, it drops roots to the ground. Gradually, these fragile air roots thicken into larger roots, entwining upon one another until they will eventually merge with the original host tree.

We are the banyan tree. Each time we kiss, we send out roots into the ground of love. As we love further, the roots grow more plentiful and more thick. Soon the tree is supported by many air roots that look like rivulets made into wood.

And as we touch, our love grows. As our love grows, the supports become stronger and the nourishment richer. As our love grows, its circumference widens into a tree that lives for generations.

With each root a generation; with every love is a serpent traveling up the spine.

Lady White Snake

During the time of the Southern Song dynasty (1127–1279) a white snake named **Bai Suzhen** succeeds in taking on human form after centuries of self-cultivation and good deeds. She meets a green snake named **Qing** and the two become sisters.

They encounter a Buddhist monk named **Fahai** who believes that they are demons who must be destroyed. However, their magic and martial arts are too formidable, and he is unable to overcome them.

The two continue their spiritual practice and charitable work so that they might become immortal. When they try to save a town suffering from drought, Qing accidentally starts a flood and they lose their chance of success. However, Guanyin (p. 58) tells them that they may yet have a chance to redeem themselves.

Suzhen meets a handsome scholar named **Xu Xian**. The two fall in love and marry, and Suzhen is soon pregnant. The couple open an herb store where they treat all who come, regardless of their ability to pay. They heal so many people that fewer people go to the temple to pray for relief. The priest—the very same Fahai from before—goes to investigate and discovers Suzhen and Qing again.

On the fifth day of the fifth moon (p. 150), all supernatural creatures must revert to their original form for a day. Fahai kidnaps Xu Xian and tries to force him to renounce his wife. When he refuses, Fahai reveals Suzhen in her true form. Xu dies of fright.

Suzhen retrieves the mushroom of immortality to restore her husband. She gives birth and confesses that she is a snake. Xu Xian says he still loves her as his wife, but Fahai attacks again, imprisoning her under the Leifeng Pagoda in Hangzhou. Qing later battles with Fahai, forcing him to hide in the belly of a crab, where he is imprisoned to this day. Later, Suzhen's son visits the pagoda and frees his mother.

Love is a serpent traveling up the spine.
Love united destroys all barriers.

Love is a snake, coiled at the base of the spine. Once it is aroused, it coils up the spine, seeking its mate. That strength, that coil of sprung energy, that pure determination overwhelms the bounds of everyday reality. Those who oppose love are destroyed no matter how hard they struggle. There is no winning against this snake; it is the very power of being human.

Love climbs with the totality of its length. It does so to transform itself. Along the way, it breaks every blockage it encounters. The barrier of religion, the barrier of propriety, the barrier of learning, the barrier of society, the barrier of nature, the barrier of time, the barrier of even itself—it wants to destroy them all for the sake of uniting with what it desires.

Those who seek to imprison love even under the greatest of pagodas will fail. The pagoda will be overturned. If neither lover is powerful enough for the two to fulfill their destinies completely, it will be their offspring, living in the utmost devotion, that will win the freedom for love to finally be fulfilled.

Another lifetime happens in a day. Leifeng Pagoda is rebuilt, and we see it with nothing but heaven and earth behind it and all of West Lake before it.

The pagoda is a spine waiting for its coiling snake.

Love united destroys all barriers—as long as you know what's male but preserve what's female.

Limitlessness

Know what's male but preserve what's
female.
Be the watercourse for all under heaven.
By being the watercourse for all under
heaven, never separate from
constant virtue.
Return, go back to being like a baby.

Know what's white, preserve what's
black.
Be the pattern for all under heaven.
In being the pattern for all under heaven,
keep unerring and unchanging virtue.
Return, go back to the limitless (wuji).

Know what's glorious but preserve what's
humble.
Be the valley for all under heaven.
In being the valley for all under heaven,
let unchanging virtue be complete.
Return, go back to being a thicket.
A thicket can be broken, yet can be made
into utensils.

The sage uses these and therefore has
long leadership.
Therefore, the great plan is never divided.

You know what's male but preserve what's female.
Find your Other and complete the great plan.

Wuji is to have no limits (p. 64). Wuji, for Taoists, is the beginning of all things. In Taijiquan, we begin our movements from a state of wuji. In love, we can return to a state of wuji.

We understand who we are, we are used to doing things a certain way. We have cataloged our talents and our faults, and we know what our wealth is. We have aspirations and hopes, but they are only partially realized.

Then we meet the Other, the Lover, the one who is Mother, Father, Sister, Brother, all in one. We meet the Other and we are startled and delighted by how different the Other is from us. Yes, we search for compatibility, but really, the Other boldly leads us beyond our boundaries into new frontiers that we find breathtaking and heady.

But we are the Other to them too, and what a thrill it is to realize that our mere presence to them is like that of a god with a beacon. By our touch, our breath, our vision, our dance, we dissolve all borders for our Other and open a world so vast that a thousand caravans could never cross it, so wide that a thousand ships could never sail it, so high that even a bridge of birds could not span it. We are liberator to our lover, as they are emancipator to us.

Hand in hand we go into the future. Hand in hand, not bound, not coerced, not trapped. But when we put our hand lightly into the hand of our trusted Other, no fire, no steel, no rock, no flood can weaken that grip. Mere material things peter out, disintegrate, and fade. The simplest of touch, made with understanding, overcomes all limits.

Find your Other and complete the great plan: all is possible if we look with spiritual eyes.

194 | Foreign

‣ Fasting day

A Jesuit Becomes a Taoist God

Matteo Ricci (Li Madou; 1552–1610) was an Italian Jesuit priest who was part of the Jesuit mission to China.

He arrived in Macau, then a Portuguese trading post, close to Hong Kong, and learned the Chinese language. He completed a map of China using European cartographic techniques, compiled a Portuguese-Chinese dictionary, and translated the Confucian classics into Latin.

In 1601, Emperor Wanli (1563–1620) invited Ricci to become an advisor in recognition of Ricci's scientific and mathematical knowledge and his ability to predict solar eclipses (unless predicted by the court, an eclipse was considered an omen that the emperor had lost the legitimacy to rule). He was the first Westerner to be made a member of the court. When he died, the emperor ordered him buried at a Buddhist temple (now a part of the Beijing Administrative College).

Since Matteo Ricci also introduced Western mechanical clocks to China, he was forever linked with them in the popular mind. Accordingly, clock and watch makers regard him as the god of their trade.

If we look with spiritual eyes
there can be no foreign borders.

When people emigrate, they bring gods with them to ensure safe passage. Tin Hau (Mazu, p. 98) and Bok Kai (North God, p. 77) are two examples. After people settle, they establish temples and new altars. This process has continued for thousands of years, bearing gods throughout Asia and the world.

Similarly, Europeans brought Christianity to the Americas, and immigrants from the Middle East brought Islam to China. Buddhism, Hinduism, and Jainism came from India and spread throughout the world. Wherever people migrate, they bring their gods, and when they settle, they settle their gods too.

Matteo Ricci brought Catholicism to China, learning Chinese language and culture and becoming the emperor's advisor. Ricci argued that Christianity was the perfect manifestation of the indigenous Chinese religions and borrowed the title Heavenly Lord (Tianzhu) as the name for the Christian God. He also accepted the veneration of ancestors.

Millions of Chinese have become Christian without ever having been to Israel, just as millions are Buddhist without ever having been remotely close to Nepal. Taoism is spreading in the same way. Yes, it still is practiced in China, but it offers so much to those who have no ties to China at all. If you find something of value, Taoism offers it to you freely.

In time, there will be no "native" and "foreign." All will finally be seen as "under heaven." If we see this earth as one country, if we see all peoples as one country, if we see all the future as one country, then all our religious and spiritual practices fall into context: they are there to comfort and guide us and integrate us with a single greater whole.

There can be no foreign borders, so is feeding ghosts a waste?

Ghost Festival

Several observations occur on this day: the **Ghost Festival** (Gui Jie), the **Yulanpen Festival**, and the **Mid-Year Festival** (Zhongyuan Jie, p. 231).

Ghost Festival

A hungry ghost is the spirit of a dead person who has no descendants to care for it. In traditional belief, a dead person is still part of the family, to be remembered and cared for. A spirit tablet inscribed with that person's name is kept on the family altar, a light is kept on at all times, and incense and other offerings are given regularly. On days like the Clear Bright Festival (p. 72) the family sweeps and cleans the graves; offers food; and burns spirit money, paper clothes, and papier-mâché reproductions of important objects with which to supply their deceased in the afterlife. In turn, the ancestors continue to help in the progress of the family. However, if a person dies without a family or if the family is not devout, then that person becomes a hungry ghost—an abandoned spirit with no one to feed it.

The fifteenth day is significant because the gates of hell open and the deceased roam the earth. They do not leave the living world until the last day of the seventh moon. Some people therefore call this entire month the Ghost Moon.

There are many kinds of ghosts:

E Gui The hungry ghost who is the main focus of the Ghost Festival. Such a ghost suffers because of greed during his or her lifetime.

Diao Si Gui The ghost of someone who has died by hanging

You Hun Ye Gui A wandering ghost of someone who has died far from hometown or family without his or her body being sent home. Also known as a vengeful ghost.

Gui Po A ghost who takes the form of a kindly old woman

Nu Gui The ghost of a woman who has committed suicide because she has been wronged or sexually abused. Such a ghost returns to take revenge.

Yuan Gui A ghost who has died unjustly and roams restlessly to have grievances addressed

Shu Gui A ghost who has died by drowning. Such a ghost dwells by the water, waiting to pull a passerby into the water, drown the victim, and inhabit the body.

Wu Tou Gui A headless ghost (beheading was a common form of execution into the twentieth century)

Taoist and Buddhist ceremonies are aimed at relieving the suffering of the hungry ghosts. In addition to the normal offerings of incense and the burning of spirit money and supplies, there are often elaborate banquets held for the ghosts. Chairs at the table are left empty so that the deceased will have places.

When the Ghost Moon ends, paper boats and floating lanterns, often in the shape of lotuses, are set on the water to guide the ghosts home. If a lantern disappears, it means that a ghost took it. If the lantern stays afloat, it means that there are no ghosts in the area.

Yulanpen or the *Ullambana Sutra*

The Buddhist observation of Yulanpen (the Chinese name for the *Ullambana Sutra)* is about filial piety and saving ghosts. The origins of this story come to us through the *Ullambana Sutra (Rescuing Those Who Are Hanging Upside Down)* as well as a more elaborate account from the Dunhuang *Bianwen* Manuscript. These sutras tell us of one of Sakyamuni Buddha's two chief disciples, **Mahamaudgalyayana** (Mulian). This summary combines details from both writings.

When Mahamaudgalyayana had attained the status of an arhat (a highly accomplished Buddhist with supernatural powers), he thought of his deceased parents. Using his Tao Eye, he saw that his mother had been reborn as a hungry ghost: her throat was as thin as a needle but her head was as big as a mountain. She was being punished because Mahamaudgalyayana had once given her money to feed wandering monks, but she had kept the funds and had lied about it.

Seeing that his mother had neither food nor drink, Mahamaudgalyayana was filled with pity and sadness. He flew down to the underworld to feed her, but when she took his bowl, she first blocked it with her left hand so that other ghosts would not get any; then she grabbed the food greedily by the fistful. The food turned into burning coals, and she could not eat. Weeping, Mahamaudgalyayana rushed to Buddha.

The fifteenth day of the seventh moon happened to be the day when hundreds of Buddhist monks who had been meditating during the rainy summer months in the forest met together again. Buddha told Mahamaudgalyayana to prepare clean basins filled with hundreds of flavors, the five fruits, incense, oil, lamps, candles, bedding, and all the best in the world to give in offering to the gathering. Buddha instructed the assembly to recite mantras and vows for the sake of the donor's family and for parents of seven generations. Then the assembly received Mahamaudgalyayana's donations. His mother was able to attain rebirth, Mahamaudgalyayana's sorrow eased, and the assembly was greatly impressed.

Buddha informed his followers that if they continued this practice each year on the fifteenth day of the seventh moon, practicing filial piety and making offerings of hundreds of flavors of food in Ullambana basins, their parents' lives would extend to a hundred years without illness, suffering, or worries, and seven generations of hungry ghosts could be reborn. ▶

195 | Feeding Ghosts

- The Ghost Festival
- Inspection day of **Official of Earth–Great God**
- The **Mid-Year Festival**
- Fasting day

Official of Earth–Great God

This is the birthday of the Official of Earth–Great God (Diguan Dadi). He is one of the **Three Officials**, the other two being the Official of Heaven (p. 20) and the Official of Water (p. 336).

The Official of Earth presides over birth and death, controls the harvest, presides over places in the hereafter, and manages the forgiveness of sins.

Mid-Year Festival

The Mid-Year Festival is associated with the Official of Earth–Great God, and is one of the three festivals that divide up the year (p. 20). The Mid-Year Festival is now closely identified with the Yulanpen Festival (p. 230).

Bags of spirit money for the dead are prepared and burned during a ceremony for Taiyi Jiuku Tianjun (p. 365). © Photos by Saskia Dab

Is feeding ghosts a waste?
But who is being fed?

Many of us were taught the importance of caring in terms of self-interest: "Take care of others if you want others to take care of you." But the bodhisattvas and the immortals are not taking care of others because they want to be repaid one day. Their caring is the deepest expression of who they are.

Could you care about a ghost?

You scoff that the dead "don't know the difference." You say that you're not going to waste effort on superstition and meaningless ritual. But if you didn't have to worry about practicality or what others thought about you, would you be kinder?

Being spiritual may not be practical in an everyday sense; being spiritual is the essential expression of who you are as a human being. So feed others. Feed the ghosts. Feel your kindness for the weak, the oppressed, the helpless—and even the dead. Pray for the salvation of all.

You will end up feeding much more than the ghosts.

But who is being fed? Give all your inner feeling, as when water and fire are combined.

Exercise 14

This period signifies the ending of the summer heat and the beginning of drier weather and cooler nights. The cooler night air is actually beneficial to crops.

This exercise is best practiced during the period of 1:00–5:00 A.M.

1. Sit cross-legged and slowly turn your head to the left, return to the center and raise your head up, turn to the right, then return to the center and raise your head. As you do this, beat your fists on either side of your spine, up and down the back in a self-massaging action.

2. Inhale when you turn or raise your head; exhale gently between these actions. Each center–left–center–right–center movement is one cycle; repeat for thirty-five cycles.

3. Facing forward, click your teeth together thirty-six times. Roll your tongue between your teeth nine times in each direction. Form saliva in your mouth by pushing your cheeks in and out. When your mouth is filled with saliva, divide the liquid into three portions.

4. Inhale; then exhale, imagining your breath traveling to the dantian and then swallow one-third of the saliva, imagining that it travels to the dantian.

5. Repeat two more times until you've swallowed all three portions.

6. Sit comfortably as long as you like.

Through this exercise, ancient Taoists sought to prevent or treat rheumatism; pains in the shoulder, back, chest, ribs, and legs; cough, asthma, and shortness of breath; and thirst.

196 | Liquid Sunshine

Like a Dream

Li Qingzhao (1084–1151), a great poet of the Song dynasty, was born into a family of scholars. Her father was a friend of Su Shi (p. 140).

She was already famous when she married Zhao Mingcheng (1081–1129) in 1101. In a well-known story, he had awakened from a nap remembering three lines: "Well-ordered words are poetry. Removing a home's protection endangers a woman. Flowers without tops make a husband." His father said this meant Mingcheng would marry a woman poet.

This story depends on a wordplay that involves combining or taking apart ideograms. The last word in each line is formed by either combining or removing parts of the preceding words.

言 與 司 合 詞
Yan with **si** combine as **ci**
安 上 已 脱 女
An with its top removed is **nu**
芝 芙 草 拔 夫
Flowery **fu** with its grass top pulled is **fu**

The devoted couple composed poetry and collected art. They wrote the *Catalog of Inscriptions on Stone and Bone (Jinshilu)*, documenting over two thousand ancient works, and exchanged many love poems during Zhao's frequent travels as an official.

The Jurchens occupied Kaifeng in 1126 and burned the poets' home. Li and Zhao fled to Nanjing with their art collection. Zhao died while traveling to an official post in 1129. Li grieved the rest of her life.

"Like a Dream" is the designation of a poetic form and not necessarily the intended title of this poem; many such poems were untitled.

I constantly recall the river pavilion at
    sunset,
how we were so drunk we couldn't find
    our way home.
Excitement spent, we turned our boat
    back toward evening.
Mistakenly, we got stuck in lotus roots.
"Let's free the boat! Free the boat!"
We startled a marsh full of herons into
    flight!

When water and fire are combined,
it is pure illumination.

Have you ever been walking in the bright sunlight and rain? The drops fall as if all the stars in the Milky Way were suddenly around us. That is a beauty unimaginable in any other way.

This rain is fine. This rain is warm. This rain floats gently, for there is no wind to drive it, only atmosphere so thick that the progress of the drops is slowed, as if the very air was a sigh that wanted to hold the panoply of stars.

This rain soaks to the skin. It's so warm that dryness will come before one is even ready to complain. The drifting stars hit our bodies and become water.

Love is brilliance falling from the sky that soaks us completely.

Li Qingzhao's name means "Pure Illumination." She was someone who loved her husband deeply: theirs was the love that illuminated and permeated completely.

It is pure illumination when a man must dream he is a butterfly.

The Tao of Dreams

夢 The word for dream is *meng*. It shows an eye (the rectangle in the center of the word) being covered (by the hooked line below), thus implying both sleep and the visionary nature of dreams. The part of the word below the horizontal line represents a crescent moon, signifying night.

Dreams are prominent in tradition and stories. Emperor Taizong's dreams (p. 22) are part of the origin of the Door Gods. Zhuangzi's Butterfly Dream (p. 52) is famous for expressing relativity. The title of one of China's most famous novels is *Dream of the Red Chamber* (p. 66). Lu Dongbin decides to follow the Way after the Yellow Millet Dream (p. 125).

"No Sheep" from the *Classic of Poetry*

> Herdsmen will dream
> that the multitudes will have fish
> and that people's embroidered pennants
>   will replace war flags.
> The chief diviner will divine the dreams,
> hoping that the multitudes will have fish,
> as omens of abundant years;
> and that embroidered pennants in place
>   of war flags,
> are omens that our households will be
> as plentiful as the Qin River.

A man must dream he is a butterfly
if he is to be a man when awake.

All of us dream at night when the moon is out.

Scientists haven't determined all the reasons why we dream, but if a person sleeps poorly or has a disorder that prevents enough dreaming, then there are significant problems. Dreams are necessary. Our minds need to rest, they need to renew themselves, they need to prepare themselves for what is to come. All that is done by dreaming.

What are dreams but images and stories? That's how deep the need for stories is with us. Stories are an integral part of how we deal with reality. We use them to comprehend what we see around us. When we go to foreign places, we want to know the stories behind the places and people we see. When we meet new people, we want to know their stories.

We eagerly read memoirs and biographies. We read novels and go to theaters, even for the retelling of stories we already know. That's why we dream each night. The stories heal us from what we've grappled with the day before and prepare us for the day ahead.

We are active. We strive for greater awareness and accomplishment. We want to win accolades. As great as all this might be, none of it is possible without the complete letting go of consciousness for at least a third of our lives, a time when none of our everyday modes are in operation, a time when our bodies immobilize themselves and our minds soar into a netherworld.

At least a third of who we are, then, is made up of that which we cannot control with our conscious minds, of stories we create on a subconscious level, of dream perceptions, of what comes from the time when our souls free themselves to wander in a night that has no name.

Dreaming is a lunar Tao.

If he is to be a man when awake, he must go where the mountain's jagged profile is a key.

Queen Mother of the West

The **Queen Mother of the West** (Xi Wang Mu) is an ancient Chinese goddess who predates formal Taoism. Records of sacrifices to the Western Mother can be traced back to oracle bone inscriptions of the fifteenth century BCE. At first, she was a tiger goddess who brought the plague, but she was soon transformed into the benevolent and beautiful heavenly queen who lives in the Kunlun Mountains. Her palace is 333 miles in diameter, with ramparts made of gold and towers built from precious jewels. One side of the palace borders the Jasper River.

The immortals who live in the palace are divided into seven ranks, and are identified by the colors of their robes—red, blue, black, purple, yellow, green, and undyed. A magical orchard with the peaches of immortality grows within the palace grounds. These trees put forth leaves once every three thousand years, and it takes ten thousand years for the peaches to ripen. On her birthday, the queen gives an elaborate banquet for all the gods near a fountain built of jewels. Anyone who eats the peaches becomes immortal during a festive banquet with music from invisible instruments and songs in languages unknown to mortal tongues.

She is also known as the Golden Mother of the Tortoise, Golden Mother of the Shining Lake, the Primordial Ruler, the Perfected Marvel of the Western Florescence and the Ultimate Worthy of the Grotto Yin, Divine Mother, or simply Amah. She has nine sons and twenty-four daughters.

Her association with the direction west and her ultimate embodiment of yin makes her the opposite of the **King of the East** (Donghuang Dadi; p. 321). Just as the Queen Mother is the purest embodiment of the western yin, so is he the embodiment of the eastern yang. The Queen Mother's palace is in the Kunlun Mountains, and the King of the East's palace is in heaven. The King of the East was originally Emperor Mu, discussed below.

The Queen Mother of the West is the highest-ranking female deity and she protects all women. She was especially worshipped by women who did not wish to conform to the social norms. Significantly, the Queen Mother of the West is not subordinate to any god and she can confer the ultimate gift of immortality as she pleases.

A number of different stories relate how the Queen Mother of the West appeared to different Chinese rulers at various times throughout history.

She appeared to the **Great Yu** (p. 105) and taught him the techniques for being a good ruler.

When **Emperor Mu** (r. 976–922 BCE) of the Zhou dynasty set out with his charioteer, Zao Fu, and eight chargers to

inspect his realm, he encountered the Queen Mother of the West in the Kunlun Mountains. They began a love affair and the king gave her many earthly treasures. In turn, she taught him the secret of being a good ruler and of being immortal. However, when he returned to the human realm, he failed to follow her instructions and so died as a mortal.

In the same way, **Qin Shi Huang** (259–210 BCE, p. 159) also had the opportunity to meet the Queen Mother of the West. He likewise failed to follow her instructions, and so died as well.

Emperor Wu (156–87 BCE) of the Han dynasty received a visit from the Queen Mother of the West on the seventh day of the seventh moon. She shared a banquet with him, gave him special teachings, and then departed. Again, the emperor did not practice the techniques of immortality and so passed away like his predecessors.

There is a traditional custom of presenting an image of the Queen Mother of the West to a woman turning fifty, and making an offering asking for long life. Offerings are also made to the goddess at times of drought. ▶

- Birthday of the **Queen Mother of the West**
- Fasting day

鄉下 *Xiangxia* literally means "country" or "rural." However, many people use this term to mean "hometown." "Xiang" is a picture of two men (the left and the right sides) sharing food (the middle section of the word). "Xia" means "under" or "below."

Altar to Xi Wang Mu, Chang Chun Guan, Wuhan. © Saskia Dab

The mountain's jagged profile is a key.
Once your heart's door comes unlocked, you are home.

The returning traveler said: "Do you see this mountain against the sky? Our grandfather's generation was born and is buried in the shadow of this mountain. I saw this mountain all through my childhood.

"Then I went away to study, to work, and to travel. When I thought about home, I thought about my mother and father, my sisters and brothers, my friends, my home, my school—but I never thought of the mountain.

"The first time I came home after being away, I saw the mountain from the ferry. I recognized each peak, every contour, as if the jagged profile of those peaks formed a key that fit the lock in my heart. This is my home mountain.

"The sky reels overhead. Clouds and storms flash through. In the course of a year, the sky changes swiftly from day to night, from sun to cloud, from rain to wind to snow. The mountain stays still.

"Now, every time I go away, I don't feel I'm home until the mountain comes into view.

"Isn't that enlightenment?"

Once your heart's door comes unlocked, you are home; be a watercourse and channel the vast water to make a Way.

199 | The Canal

The Grand Canal

The **Grand Canal** (Da Yunhe), also known as the Beijing-Hangzhou Grand Canal (Jing Hang Da Yunhe), is the longest canal in the world. It begins at Beijing and ends at the city of Hangzhou. It is 1,103 miles long. Through the use of locks invented in the tenth century, the canal reaches a height of 138 feet. The oldest sections date to the fifth century BCE and the majority of its sections were finally joined during the Sui dynasty (581–618).

Watertowns

There are three watertowns in the Suzhou region—Zhouzhang, Touli, and Luzhi. They are crisscrossed with canals and feature picturesque bridges, and their older buildings and gardens have been preserved. The poet Bai Juyi (p. 273) ordered the construction of the Shantang Canal, and the poet and writer Fan Zhongyan (989–1052) founded a temple to Confucius in 1045 that became the site of imperial examinations.

Channel the vast water to make a Way.
Travel the road that is always alive.

How useful canals are. They cut through cities and farmland, carrying water for drinking, washing, transportation, and irrigation. To travel along this liquid road is to be on a journey that is always smooth, placid, and constant. The road leads to any point along its length, and its terminus is a grand destination.

We also build canals to regulate flooding. By cutting these channels, we save homes from becoming inundated, we distribute nature's largesse to the benefit of many, and we bring water closer to our lives. A canal is drainage, distribution, regulation. It doesn't wear like pavement. It is constantly renewed.

How like a canal love is. From the universal river of love, a couple begins to dig. As they find more mutual understanding and as they discover they can work together well, they gradually increase their efforts. Finally, they can open whole lengths, and let the waters of love flow in.

How long will their canal be? No one really knows at the beginning of digging. The work can be fortuitous, or the canal might cross barren land. Others might help, or others might hinder the progress. The waters might go dry, or they might flood, be poisoned, or hold hidden monsters. But if all goes well and the couple is lucky, the canal continues to lengthen day by day, until it is a beautiful canal like the Grand Canal.

Yes, we can learn a great deal about love from traveling a canal. Perhaps we're even sailing now to meet our lover: those who sail canals know best how to build a canal to join two distant places.

Travel the road that is always alive; go where you can feel the forest breathing.

200 | The Old Trees

Zhuangzi's Forest Breath

Nanguo Ziqi sat on his stool, looking up to heaven and breathing gently. He seemed to be in a trance.

In time, his disciple, Yan Cheng Ziyou, said, "What is this? Can the body become like a withered tree, and the mind become like slaked lime? I've never seen you before like this."

Ziqi said, "I was lost in myself, but how can you understand? You may have heard the notes of people, but not those of earth. You may have heard the notes of earth, but not those of heaven." Ziyou asked him to explain further, so Ziqi said:

"When the breath of nature comes strongly, it is called wind. When it comes, an excited noise rises from many openings. Have you not heard a prolonged gale?

"In a mountain forest there are great trees, a hundred spans around. The spaces between their branches are like the nostrils, mouth, or ears; now square, now round like a cup or a mortar; here like a wet footprint, and there like a large puddle.

"The sound may be like dropping water, or an arrow's flight, like stern command, or an inhalation, or a shout; a gruff note, a wail; or a sad, piping note. The first notes are slight, and those that follow are deeper, but in harmony. Gentle winds produce a small response; violent winds a great one. Once the fierce gusts have passed away, all the openings are empty.

"Have you not seen all this in the bending and quivering of the branches and leaves?"

Go where you can feel the forest breathing
and inhale understanding beyond words.

We climb the banks where the stream has rounded every rock to lapidary softness. We admire every plant for its health, achieved not by some gardener's fertilizer but by the sheer perfection of being in ideal surroundings. We can't help but notice the old trees. They are large, their branches twisting and spreading to catch the light perfectly, their canopies spreading to the sun and their roots firm in the trees' own cool shade.

The trees are silent and undeniably present. No other thing in the entire universe can take the place of a tree, and the way it's rooted is perfectly suited to its location. The legends say that these old trees have consciousness and wisdom. We can learn from that.

Behind is the whole of a forested ridge. Where the trunks are bare and the canopy thick, the shadows are as black as night and the silence is overwhelming. The sun is fierce, fiery, burning, but the millions of leaves absorb the blaze and leave only shadow below. They transform violent heat into peace.

In the forest, the trees may rustle with the breeze, but they make no words. We may see the outlines of the branches on the sky, but they form no image. The flowers may exude sweet scents, but they compound no perfume.

The old trees do nothing we would do. They are completely what they are, without the slightest veneer of the human, and yet they are supreme in the forest.

And inhale understanding beyond words as you swim, swim, and swim. Do nothing to oppose.

Confucius at a Waterfall

Zhuangzi tells us the story of Confucius visiting a waterfall that fell from an enormous height and produced a spray and turbulence near which no turtle or fish could swim. Thus he was startled to see an old man swimming in the pool.

Thinking that someone was about to take his own life, Confucius and his disciples rushed down to rescue him. But by the time they found him, he was singing and sunning himself on the bank, without even having bothered to dry or comb his long white hair.

Confucius looked at him. "I thought you must have been a spirit, and yet I see that you are a man. Do you have some great skill at treading water?"

"No, I have no particular way," the man replied. "However, I have been swimming since a young age. I go down in the center of the whirling water and simply follow it down. When it whirls the other way, I follow it up. I do nothing contrary, and that is how I swim."

Swim, swim, and swim. Do nothing to oppose,
and thus opposites will be united.

The supplicant said: "We've hiked up this valley, following the banks of the stream; admiring the flowering trees that are centuries old; marveling at enormous stands of philodendron with their air roots forming long brown lines around trees and rock. We've picked our way through patches where the sun singes our skin, and padded through places where tree shadows leave the earth cool and dark.

"Following a trail around boulders, we find the scene that the roar of water has already promised us: a waterfall. It is a stream suddenly turned vertical, it is a thousand frothing rivulets and cascades, it is splash upon splash leading to the loudest and largest splash at the bottom—where the water smooths into a deep pool.

"There is no one else here. This place is ours alone. Take off your clothes. Don't be shy. I'll take off mine. How beautiful you look in the sun. How I love to look at you. Take my hand and dive with me into the waterfall pool.

"How welcome the water's coldness is. How wonderful it is to be immersed in the pool, to float beneath heaven, to cavort with the fishes, to throw ourselves into the good fortune nature offers us.

"At the waterfall, there's a rocky ledge perfect for sitting. Ascetics sit and let the falling water run all over them. The stream, as it goes over the edge at the top, is like the moment of climax. The cascade is like the release and the trembling totality of those moments afterward. Only the waterfall does not stop. Its moments stretch longer and longer until it is liquid eternity. Let its waters cleanse, rinse away every element that would stop us from union, until we are pure and open only to each other.

"Swim with me in the waterfall pool, this womb. Birth me as your twin."

And thus opposites will be united, even though many lovers have been killed by tyrants.

Tears at the Great Wall

The story of **Meng Jiangnu** is the most famous legend associated with the Great Wall. It takes place during the Qin dynasty (221–207 BCE).

Shortly after their marriage, Meng Jiangnu's husband, Fan Qiliang, is conscripted for the building of the Great Wall. Winter comes and Jiangnu makes warm clothes and a quilt, and walks hundreds of miles over the mountains to the Great Wall. After many inquiries, she learns that her husband died of exhaustion and was buried in a mass grave inside the wall.

Meng Jiangnu's wails of grief move heaven itself, and the Great Wall splits open, revealing many dead bodies.

There are two versions of the ending of this story.

In the first, Meng Jiangnu cuts her own arm, and her blood magically flows to the bones of her dead husband. She buries him properly and then throws herself into the sea.

In the second, Qin Shi Huang (p. 159) has come to inspect the Great Wall and hears her wailing. When he sees how beautiful she is, he wants her for a concubine.

Meng Jiangnu agrees on three conditions: that they find the bones of her husband, that they give her husband a state burial, and that the emperor and all his officials walk behind the coffin during the funeral. After all this is done, Jiangnu throws herself off a cliff into the sea.

There is a temple to Meng Jiangnu on Fenghuang Mountain four miles east of the Shanhai Pass, adjacent to the Bohai Sea.

Many lovers have been killed by tyrants.
Yet lovers are remembered over kings.

How cruel kings are. In all of human history, how many are remembered as kind?

How stupid it is to build a wall, thinking that it will keep enemies at bay. The Great Wall succeeded in its purpose only for so long: the wall was repeatedly breached, the country invaded, and the empire conquered.

In the same way, walled have fallen everywhere. The Maginot Line failed. The Berlin Wall was torn down. The Iron Curtain rusted. The Bamboo Curtain decayed. And yet, even today, shortsighted people still want to erect walls across borders.

How ridiculous people are when they think that they can control love. They cannot. It is love that controls people, not people who control love. The king can issue his commands, but in the end, he cannot command the human heart.

Cruelty, walls, commands. These three things attack love in every generation, in every country, in every culture. They may win temporarily—one can always deface the beautiful, crush the delicate, belittle the romantic, mock the innocent, and imprison the carefree. But such barbarity never lasts. Love comes back time and time again.

Love is walking hundreds of miles with a quilt.
Love is wailing over one's lover buried in a mass grave.
Love is moving heaven to split stone.
Love is forcing a tyrant to honor those whom he has killed.
Love is keeping oneself from a tyrant's touch.
Love is tearing down walls.

Yet lovers are remembered over kings, just as a storm may not last for a day.

203 | The Typhoon

Wind and Rain

From the *Classic of Poetry*:

> Wind and rain, all is dark.
> The roosters crow without stop.
> I've already seen my lord.
> Why should I not be joyful?

Laozi on Storms and Rain

These lines are part of Chapter 23 of the *Daodejing*:

> A whirlwind doesn't last all morning.
> Sudden rain doesn't last all day.
> Who does this? Heaven and earth.
> If heaven and earth cannot last long,
> then what about people?

Jeff Schmaltz; NASA; The Visible Earth

A storm may not last for a day.
How much less are works of people?

Some time ago, a typhoon blew for twelve hours and all people could do was huddle in a shelter. Parents and children clutched one another. Pet owners abandoned dogs and cats to the storm. Residents who didn't evacuate were forced into their attics or onto their rooftops. People prayed and invoked the gods, but there was no turning back the violence of the storm. Ships capsized. Piers were destroyed. Seawalls crumbled. Valleys and lowlands flooded. Cars floated away. Home after home was destroyed and left under water. Some bodies were never found.

Afterward, the devastation was unimaginable. A steel bridge had washed away. Trees had been uprooted or stripped of their leaves. Debris piled into heaps twenty-five feet high. Red silt washed into swollen rivers left the land looking as if it was bleeding.

If the work of man is to mortar one brick atop another, the typhoon pulverized that ambition. If the work of man is to set a lintel atop two posts, the typhoon toppled such engineering. If the work of man is to manufacture goods, the typhoon mangled that production. If the work of man is to create civilization, the typhoon scraped the cities from the land and left miles of waste.

The typhoon was here years ago and people have rebuilt, even though we know that other typhoons will come each year. Our structures are engineered so most will survive another storm, but it's unavoidable that a devastating typhoon will come again.

The scars of the land have healed, but the scars inside us ache forever.

How much less are works of people—you see best where you stand highest.

▸ Fasting day

Floating on the Deep Blue Ocean

This passage is from the *Yangzi Fayan (Model Words of Master Yang)*, a Confucian text. The author, Yang Xiong (53 BCE–18), stressed the study of the Confucian classics in order to understand the Tao.

> Reading books is like looking at mountains and water: climbing the Eastern Mountain (Taishan), one knows how the many mountains wind and twist—isn't that even more so when viewing the many smaller hills?
>
> Floating on the deep blue ocean one knows how muddy the rivers and streams are—isn't that even more so when viewing dried-up marshes?
>
> Would you abandon a boat to cross a great river? Could you abandon the *Five Classics* and still reach Tao?

Climbing Crane Tower

This work by Wang Zhihuan (688–742) appears in the anthology *Three Hundred Tang Poems*.

> White sun sets behind the mountain.
> The Yellow River flows into the ocean.
> But if you want to take in a thousand miles,
> climb up one more floor in the tower.

Dr. Meierhofer

You see best where you stand highest.
Miracles are just good foresight.

This is a thin spit of land, a rocky wall narrow enough that one can look down the left and right sides just by turning one's head, and high enough that a fall would be impossible to survive. A lighthouse at the end guides ships from across the world. From this point, one can look across the horizon a full 180° for a hundred miles in each direction.

Ships sail by. Birds rise up in the air as they squabble over scraps of food. A storm comes and passes. The sun crosses the heavens and sinks into the sea. Isn't life like that too? One can appear to be prescient simply by gazing from the right vantage point. One can understand life simply by watching all that passes and fades into the horizon.

Do you wonder if another being is looking at us the way we look at the birds or the insects? Do you wonder if someone is caring for us, the way we try to be good stewards of the plants and animals? Do you wonder if our entire world is but a speck of sand on the beach of some other enormous ocean? Do you wonder if our generations upon generations, our kingdoms and nations, are contained in nothing more than a dust mote floating in the breeze?

Or do you wonder what becomes of the egg that the bird hatches, or the flower that blooms on a cliff no person can scale? Do you wonder about the feather that falls from the gull as it soars over the blue, or the eye of the whale that rises to the surface?

Are we simply in a world within worlds, and are we a life within many other lives?

It only takes finding the right vantage point to see.

Miracles are just good foresight: open your eyes and see the beginning.

205 | Seeing the Beginning

Laozi on the Beginning

In this excerpt from Chapter 52 of the *Daodejing*, Laozi compares the beginning of all things to a mother.

> All under heaven had a beginning, the
>   mother of all under heaven.
> Once one knows the mother, one knows
>   the children.
> Once one knows the children, one can
>   preserve the mother.
> Then, to the end of life, there will be no
>   danger.
> If one withdraws and closes one's door,
> Then to the end of life, there need be no
>   exertion.

All the Waters of the West River

Mazu Daoyi (709–788) was a Tang dynasty Chan Buddhist master. The West River (Xi Jiang) is a tributary of the Pearl River in Guangdong Province where Mazu Daoyi studied with the Sixth Patriarch, Huineng (638–713; p. 292).

Mazu Daoyi was once asked, "Who is not dependent upon the ten thousand things?"

The master answered, "I'll tell you when you swallow the waters of the West River in one gulp."

Open your eyes and see the beginning.
Close your eyes and see the beginning.

We see great glimpses of the ocean from the high bluff. The water is deep blue, the color of some memory we know but cannot articulate. We sense that we came from those waves untold millennia ago, not just in the sense of travelers coming across the ocean, but in the evolutionary sense: we crawled from those waves, and that memory is still there, deep in our very being.

Yes, all memories are still there—not just our memories, but our ancestors' memories and the memory of everything back to the first moment. That's why Laozi urges us to return to the source. He could not say this unless he knew that the source is still accessible to us today. He knew that we carry the source within us still.

We love to travel, to walk, to swim the rivers and lakes, to climb the high mountains, to sail the great seas, to fly the endless skies. Those outer journeys contain the pleasure of discovery and the thrill of learning. At the same time, we prize inner journeys as well, and such journeys are no less pleasurable or thrilling. When we glimpse the ocean from the high bluff, we are looking back to the beginning. When we close our eyes, we are also looking back to the beginning.

It's important to see the beginning because it makes our present all the more poignant and cherished. We talk about gaining perspective, but how can you have perspective without knowing where you stand? We try for a unique perspective, try to stand at the vanishing point and the vantage point at the same time, to look forward and backward, to be both of the beginning and of the present.

We stand on a high bluff and look out at the blue ocean, and we swallow the seas with one gulp.

Close your eyes and see the beginning: why wait for a god to write in the sand?

Planchette Writing

Planchette writing *(fuji)* is a method of spirit writing or automatic writing. A medium is seated by a tray of sand, holding a stick, and goes into a trance. When a god or spirit enters, the medium writes in the sand.

The medium is assisted by someone who levels the sand, a reader who interprets the words, and a scribe who records the messages. The history of spirit writing goes back as far as 420.

Spirit writing was supported by the Ming dynasty, especially by the Emperor Jiajing (1507–1567). He built a planchette altar *(jitan)* in Beijing. However, the subsequent Qing dynasty (1644–1911) outlawed the practice.

Planchette writing is still practiced in Taoist temples and folk shrines and is particularly associated with the Quanzhen (Complete Perfection) School of Taoism.

Why wait for a god to write in the sand
while heaven and earth write every moment?

Much is written on a beach, and therefore there is much there to read. There might be tracks or the footprints of a beachcomber. The high-water mark shows where the waves once reached, bordered by small bits of coral, seaweed, shell, and driftwood.

The debris of our civilization is evident too: worn pieces of plastic, fishing lines, shards of glass, pieces of signs with the paint half worn away, chunks of charcoal from past bonfires.

If coral is made from the colonies of marine organisms, entire chunks of cities are dead on the beach, abraded by the sand and water, thrown by the waves, tumbled by the wind, and bleached by the sun.

In the same way, every pebble was once part of some proud mountain. Now each one is rounded of its edges, drilled through with daylight and air, and perhaps cast thousands of miles away from its parent.

Small holes in the beach show where mollusks lie buried, where crabs have scuttled to shelter. Birds pick their way through the sand and rock looking for food.

There is so much to read in this narrow strip of sand, this interactive panoply that changes every minute, this combat zone of water against land. Walk the strip of sand and you walk an endless scroll, a story of waves from far away, pushed by the wind, pulled by the moon. The gods write this story in the sand to us without cease: all life is motion.

While heaven and earth write every moment, Zhuangzi's skull will speak but will not return.

207 | The Fish Skeleton

Perfect Enjoyment

Zhuangzi tells this story of a skull he found in the country of Chu. It had been bleached white but was intact. He tapped it with his horsewhip.

"Sir, were you greedy in life? Did you make a mistake in reasoning? How did you come to this? Did you lose in affairs of state? Were you beheaded by ax or halberd? How did you come to this?

"Did you do evil? Did you disgrace your parents, your wife, your children? Did you suffer from cold and starvation? How did you come to this?

"Or did you simply reach the end of your springs and autumns?"

After asking these questions, Zhuangzi used the skull as a pillow and went to sleep.

That night, the skull appeared to him in a dream.

"You speak with scholarly elegance. Your observations and words are about the troubles of people who are alive, but the dead don't have such problems. Would you like to hear about death?"

"I would," said Zhuangzi.

The skull said: "In death there is no ruler above and no minister below. There are none of the features of the four seasons, and yet we are with heaven and earth. Even the happiness of a king cannot surpass what we have."

Zhuangzi did not believe it, and asked, "If I asked the Ruler of Destiny to restore you to life with your bones, flesh, and skin, and to give you back your father and mother, your wife and children, and all your villagers, would you want that?"

The skull glared at him. "Why should I reject royal happiness and return to the toil of being a person again?"

Zhuangzi's skull will speak but will not return.
In life, know the bone. In death, leave the bone.

Here's a fish skeleton, ivory white in the moonlight. It's mostly intact, washed up by the waves, abraded by the sand and salt, whitened by the sun, lodged in the crevices of black rock. How perfect every part of it is: the skull to shelter the eyes and brain, openings for the nerves, a frame for a vanished body.

How many miles did this fish swim? Did it once twist and turn joyously with the waves? Was its death natural and inevitable, or was it injured or sick? Was it the victim of a predator or a fisherman who then lost it?

What is the value of such a skeleton? You might say it's worthless, since it can't be sold at a market. But should we measure all value by what someone wants to buy? That's only one kind of coarse valuation, and a grossly limited one at that. For us, this skeleton can be more valuable than a king's treasure if we can learn from it.

Within each of us is a design. This pattern determines who we are and what we'll become. Only when we can see to the bone of things can we penetrate the secret of existence.

Bone. It's fundamental. Bone. It's the solidity that stands behind our softness. Bone. When you see the bone, you see what's real.

In life, know the bone. In death, leave the bone, for the waves are relentless, the rock won't yield.

Nothing Is Softer or Weaker Than Water . . .

In Chapter 78 of the *Daodejing*, Laozi made one of his most famous observations:

> Under heaven, nothing is softer or weaker than water.
> Yet, in attacking the hard and stiff, nothing surpasses it
> because nothing can change it.
> The weak conquers the strong, the soft conquers the hard.

The waves are relentless, the rock won't yield.
Whatever destroys must also create.

The oceans swell and the rock tumbles. The waves crash and the rock stands intact. Only people worry about winning and losing. Does the wave care that it hasn't worn away the cliff yet? Does the cliff worry that another boulder has tumbled into the water? How many times have the oceans covered the land, and then how many times has the land risen up, drying up whole oceans? There is only the dynamic of balance, of yin and yang. What matters is not dominance or submission. What matters is balance.

Out of this process comes the sand. Out of this process comes the new. The sand and shore are constantly new, and yet they are always present. Is something being destroyed at the shore? If so, then something is being born too. Destruction and creation are in balance. Destruction and creation are the shore's living process.

We credit poets like Tao Yuanming and Qu Yuan with leaving behind a body of poems. Yet should we see this as some sort of conscious creation? Or the mere sand formed by the pounding of the waves on their shores?

Whatever destroys must also create: the sleeping lover dreams of her lover.

▸ Fasting day

The Peony Pavilion

The seventh moon is both the moon of romance and the moon of ghosts. Here is a story of both.

The Peony Pavilion (Mudanting), written by Tang Xianzu (1550–1616), is a famous **Kunqu** opera. Its full version is twenty hours long.

The story begins with **Du Liniang**, the sixteen-year-old daughter of Governor Du Bao. On a spring day when Liniang is in the garden with her maid, she falls asleep. The Flower God sends her a dream lover holding a willow branch—a handsome young scholar named **Liu Mengmei**. The two meet under a plum tree and consummate their love in the Peony Pavilion. After Liniang wakes up, she remains lovesick and dies during the Moon Festival.

In the underworld, Judge Hu is amazed by Liniang's beauty, hears her story, and rules that the couple are predestined for one another. Liniang is released.

Three years pass. Liu Mengmei finds himself in the garden, which has a plum blossom shrine. He had once dreamed of a beautiful woman under a plum tree and has changed his name accordingly—Liu Mengmei means "Willow Dreaming of a Plum." Liniang appears to him and they carry on an affair. After some time, she urges him to exhume her body. When he does so, she comes back to life.

Mengmei finds Governor Du Bao, who thinks he is a grave robber and a lunatic and orders him executed. Before that can happen, the results of the imperial examination are released; Mengmei is ranked first. He defends himself before the emperor, and Liniang shows that she casts a shadow—proof that she's real. The emperor intervenes. Du Bao relents and finally accepts the marriage.

The sleeping lover dreams of her lover.
The gazing lover is his lover's dream.

The admirer said: "How beautiful you look sleeping. All tension is gone from your face. There is nothing to be added. Nothing to be taken away. You're asleep, safe, secure, and at peace.

"People approach gods for their prayers, and the gods sit looking down, eyes open, holy implements in their hands, the symbols of celestial power swirling around them. Not so in the face of a sleeping lover. There is nothing to be done but to gaze.

"Artists wear themselves out sculpting and painting pictures of beautiful people. Poets exhaust language trying to describe lovers. Musicians sing themselves hoarse praising those who have entranced them. Yet art usually fails to capture the beauty of love. The artist is doomed to frustration. The lover has satisfaction.

"You open your eyes. You smile. Do you sense that you are admired, and does that please you? Do you sense that you've been guarded all this time, and does that reassure you? Do you sense that there has been a shared moment of exquisite privacy, and does that comfort you?

"With one touch, your weight balances mine perfectly. Until this moment, I was on a scale that teetered. Now the scale balances and there is graceful movement rather than jittery swinging.

"I want to see myself as you see me. I want to be as beautiful for you as you are to me. I want to feel heat the way you feel it, to be inside you, and for you to be inside me.

"You close your eyes and fall asleep again, and I—I am content to watch you forever and to be your mirror when you awake."

The gazing lover is his lover's dream, hearing the cry for the abandoned and drowned children.

210 | Crying for Dead Children

- Fasting day
- Ksitigarbha Bodhisattva Festival Day

The Earth Treasury

Ksitigarbha (Dizang Pusa), whose name means "Earth Treasury," is a bodhisattva who has vowed to care for all beings in the time between the death of Buddha (p. 117) and the coming of Maitreya, the Buddha of the future (p. 5). He has vowed not to accept Buddhahood until all hells are emptied. He is the bodhisattva of those who suffer in hell, the guardian of children, and the patron deity of deceased children and aborted fetuses. He is depicted as a Buddhist monk. In one hand he carries a staff to force open the gates of hell, and in the other a wish-fulfilling jewel.

In a previous incarnation, according to the *Sutra of the Great Vows of Ksitigarbha Bodhisattva (Dizang Pusa Benyuan Jing)*, Ksitigarbha had been a Brahmin maiden named Sacred Girl. She was deeply troubled when her mother died from slandering the Three Jewels— Buddha, dharma (teachings), and sangha (Buddhist community). Sacred Girl prayed every day and used all her money to buy offerings to save her mother. One day Buddha appeared to her and told her to meditate and repeat his name. She was transported to hell, where she learned that her mother had ascended to heaven because of her devotion. Sacred Girl was overjoyed, but she then saw the suffering of all the others still in hell, and she vowed to help them as well.

Jiuhua Mountain in Anhui is considered Ksitigarbha's dwelling, and it still has some ninety-five temples open for pilgrims. In time, Ksitigarbha was also adopted as a Taoist god. He is the protector of sorcerers and geomancers.

Cry for the abandoned and drowned children.
Stop all violence! Make this world paradise.

Every day, newborn children are abandoned. They are drowned in oceans, thrown into dumpsters, left on the streets. Some parents leave a child at a hospital and never return again.

Sadly, many of these dead infants are buried namelessly and in unmarked graves. No one acknowledges them, and no one cares for them. It may take decades to raise a child properly, surrounded with oceans of love. These children don't even receive ten seconds of care. Quite the opposite: they are subjected to a cruelty that could bring a hardened criminal to tears.

John Wigham

Ksitigarbha reminds us that we should care for all who are suffering in hell, and that we should take especial care to protect babies who cannot protect themselves.

Can we use our strength to open the gates of hell? Would we carry a wish-fulfilling jewel and let everyone in the world use it before we ever had one thought for ourselves?

Or is it the human lot simply to repeat the same behavior generation after generation? Are we that stupid?

Can we change? If we really are compassionate, can't we change instantly? Maitreya Buddha will come someday. Ksitigarbha is trying all that he can until then. Why shouldn't we join him and make this world a paradise before Maitreya ever appears?

It can begin with crying for dead children. It can begin with rescuing suffering children. It can begin with never allowing our own hands to commit evil. We can empty all the hells.

We can be Ksitigarbha.

Stop all violence! Make this world paradise. Let all war end today.

8

The Osthmanthus Moon

**Chancing Upon Old Friends
at a Village Inn**

It's autumn, and the moon is full again.
A thousand-layered night covers the towns.
We meet together south of the river.
I turn—it's like a dream to meet by chance!
The wind startles the magpies from their roosts,
insects tremble in the dew-covered grass.
We travelers linger and get deeply drunk—
each one tarries, fearing the morning bell!
—Dai Shulun (732–789)

The two solar terms within this moon:

WHITE DEW

AUTUMN EQUINOX

Exercise 15

WHITE DEW

The days grow dry. The sky is clear and the temperatures mild, but it grows cold enough that dew forms.

This is the beginning of the harvest season. The fields are golden, and farmers gather to reap grain, soybeans, and sorghum. Cotton is full.

Winter wheat is planted as well, so this is a busy time on the farms.

This exercise is best practiced during the period of 1:00–5:00 A.M.

1. Sit cross-legged and press your palms over your knees.

2. Slowly turn your head side to side as if you're trying to look behind you. Inhale when you turn your head to the side; exhale gently when you return to the center. Repeat fifteen times on each side.

3. Facing forward, click your teeth together thirty-six times. Roll your tongue between your teeth nine times in each direction. Form saliva in your mouth by pushing your cheeks in and out. When your mouth is filled with saliva, divide the liquid into three portions.

4. Inhale; then exhale, imagining your breath traveling to the dantian and then swallow one-third of the saliva, imagining that it travels to the dantian.

5. Repeat two more times until you've swallowed all three portions.

6. Sit comfortably as long as you like.

Through this exercise, ancient Taoists sought to prevent or treat rheumatism in the back and thighs; nosebleeds; dark coloring appearing in the lips and face; swelling in the neck; vomiting; and mental illness.

▸ Fasting day

Autumn and the Tragedy of War

Du Fu (p. 29) wrote this poem in 759 during the An Lushan Rebellion (755–763). Estimates of the death toll are as high as thirty-six million.

The goose is a symbol of autumn as well as letters from afar.

> Army drums cut off human travel.
> Along the autumn borders, a lone goose calls.
> Today is the start of White Dew;
> how bright the moon seemed in my home village.
>
> My brothers are scattered.
> No one's home to ask if they are alive or dead.
> The letters we send never reach them, and still the war does not stop.

Weapons Are Ominous Instruments

In one part of Chapter 31 of the *Daodejing,* Laozi writes:

> As for weapons: they are ominous instruments.
> All creatures hate them.
> Hence, those who have the Tao do not handle them....
> Weapons are ominous instruments.
> They are not the instrument of the noble person.
> They are used only when there is no choice.
> Quiet and calm are superior; victory is not beautiful.
> Those who consider it beautiful exult in killing people.
> Those who exult in killing people never find fulfillment under heaven.

Let all war end today.
Let peace bloom in our hearts.

The white dew in the morning can remind us powerfully that winter follows autumn. The weather will be cooling in time, the nights will grow longer, and winter will approach steadily.

White dew can look like tears, and it's a reminder that the world is still at war. Du Fu, writing more than 1,250 years ago, lamented how war was still raging in autumn when families should have been coming together to celebrate their bond and the bounty of the harvest. Today, we are still at war somewhere in the world. Families are still torn apart and scattered. Mad and selfish warlords still order gun and cannon fire and devastating explosions as expressions of their fiery ambitions. In a thousand more years, autumns will still come, but will humanity have given up war?

We should all eschew weapons, those ominous instruments. We should all take a bodhisattva vow to put all other beings ahead of ourselves. We should each do what we can to bring peace to everyone we meet. And yet, violence, oppression, and demonic cruelty continue as despots throw millions of bodies to the monsters of war. How do you change that?

If you say you will change it by sitting on a meditation cushion, you sound hopelessly naive. If you say you will change it by legislation, you are doomed to political struggle. If you say you will change it by social action, you are a swimmer fighting against the tides. In thousands of years, you say, the human condition has not changed. That is to be accepted. But good people have always been here too. Holy people have never stopped in their effort to bring peace. The only real question is, will you be good or evil? Choose good. That's the true test.

Let peace bloom in our hearts and strike the bell: ringing is instant.

Steve Evans

212 | The Bell

Song of Returning at Night to Deer Gate Mountain

Meng Haoran (689–740), anthologized in *Three Hundred Tang Poems,* was only partially successful as a civil servant—passing the examination at the age of thirty-nine and resigning his first and last appointment after less than a year. He wrote primarily about landscape, history, and legends. He was a close friend of Wang Wei (p. 174). Lumenshan—Deer Gate Mountain—is south of Xiangfan in Hubei.

> The mountain temple bell signals the coming of dusk.
> Noisy fisherman bustle onto the ferry, while others follow the sandy banks to riverside villages.
> I board a boat back to Deer Gate Mountain.
> The moon on Deer Gate shines on misty trees.
> Suddenly, I arrive at an ancient hermitage.
> Rustic door and pine, long in quiet: just a hermit returning alone.

Strike the bell: ringing is instant.
Open your heart: the Way is there.

The tower outside this metropolitan temple shelters a bronze bell beneath a peaked tile roof. A smoothed log hangs horizontally from a rope, aligned perfectly with the center of the bell.

The bell was cast by an old master far away. Esoteric symbols adorn every inch of it. Even a bell that was cast relatively recently wears the symbols from thousands of years ago on a shape so classic as to be timeless, so timeless that it appears as primordial as the mountains that rise in huge grooved crags far outside the city.

Pull on the rope. Let the striker slide back, then release it. The weight of the log is perfectly calibrated to strike the bell with just the amount of force to maximize its deep, sonorous reverberation. The bell sounds, and those hearing it cannot stop themselves from looking up.

They've been summoned. They notice that their hearts are still shaking from the sound, even though the bell hangs hundreds of feet away.

There is a saying, "The harder you strike the bell, the bigger the sound." How you strike the bell stimulates your enlightenment—and as soon as you strike the bell, the sound is instantaneous.

Open your heart: the Way is there. Then killing is good, if you kill all your faults.

• Birthday of the **Kitchen God**

The Kitchen God

Today is the birthday of the Kitchen God (p. 8). He watches all that a family does, and reports every detail to the Jade Emperor at the end of the year (p. 413). Offerings of food, wine, tea, and incense help celebrate his birth.

The Temple of Accumulating Fragrance

The Temple of Accumulating Fragrance (Xiangji Si) is south of the city of Xi'an. It was built during the seventh century in honor of the Buddhist monk Shandao (613–681), a major figure in Pure Land Buddhism (p. 91), by his disciple Huai Yun. The name is a tribute to the master, suggesting his great holiness. Wang Wei (p. 174) visited there and wrote this poem, "Toward the Temple of Heaped Fragrance."

I did not know Heaped Fragrance Temple was so many miles away in cloudy peaks and old forests few people cross.
It's the bell that guides me through the deep mountains,
where spring water gushes out a high cliff
from bright sun into cool green pines.
At twilight, by the bend of that deep pool, peaceful meditation tames the poison dragon.

When Wang Wei uses the word "meditation," it is the same as the name of Chan Buddhism.

Killing is good! If you kill all your faults.
Kneeling is good! If I kneel and find good.

The meditator said: "Let me take this as my daily meditation:

"I will pull all faults, regrets, inabilities, and shame out of myself. Each one is like a black basalt rock. I will stack these rocks day by day into a wall, so that they are outside of myself, mute, unmoving, having no place but to be dead in a wall.

Then I will go to a golden temple heaped with fragrance; I will kneel before the altar, open and without any doubt, and I will pray to be as pure as a god.

"I will pull all faults, regrets, inabilities, and shame out of myself. Each one is like a brick. I will fill a box with those bricks and send it off to some unknown destination, never to return and never to be opened. *Then I will go to a golden temple heaped with fragrance; I will kneel before the altar, open and without any doubt, and I will pray to be as pure as a god.*

"I will pull all faults, regrets, inabilities, and shame out of myself. Each one is a writhing demon. I will go to a place that is taboo and barren of all living things, and I will slay each one with the sword of mercy. I will go to a sacred pool and wash myself. *Then I will go to a golden temple heaped with fragrance; I will kneel before the altar, open and without any doubt, and I will pray to be as pure as a god.*

"Each day, I will resolve to eliminate my shortcomings and pray to be good, pray to be flooded with the divine. I will fear nothing. I will hurt no one. I will give myself over completely to the light of the divine.

"I meditate on this each day. I meditate to remove all impediments to Tao. I meditate to help every sentient being. I meditate for purity."

Kneeling is good! If I kneel and find good, I am at the center of the universe.

214 | The Circle's Center

I am at the center of the universe.
All depends on me, I depend on all.

The realized one said: "I sit here, radiant with light. The universe had no meaning until darkness parted. The stars, the sun, the very medium that gives us knowledge—all is light. I am light. I am alive.

"A circle of light surrounds me. The diameter of that circle is at once measured by the length of my arms and legs, and by the very edge of the universe, with an infinite diameter and an infinite circumference. However wide that circle of light is, it must have a center. I am its center.

"Let me breathe in, and all things come into me as the tide rushes to the shore. Let me breathe out, and all things sail away from me, like a thousand birds borne aloft on the trade winds. Let me think but one thing, and it exists. Let me forget one thing, and it is gone.

"When I move, it is the same force that turns the sun and the moon. When I am still, it is the same force that has existed since before the universe began.

"I am heaven. Every single cell of my infinite body contains myriad worlds, each one with myriad gods. My body is composed of gods. My body is divine.

"I sit here, radiant with light. I am all inside. There is no outside. There is nothing but the holy. There is nothing but the pure. There is nothing else."

All depends on me, I depend on all. Why ask where the road goes?

215 | Beside the Highway

"Song to Cherish Ancient Traces"

This poem is the first of a series of five written by Du Fu (p. 29). Yu Xin (513–581), the subject of the poem, died 131 years before Du's birth.

In 554, Yu was a poet and a diplomat sent as an ambassador from the Liang dynasty to the Western Wei in Chang'an. But the Liang fell in 557; Yu was imprisoned in Chang'an for the rest of his life, and three of his children were executed. Nevertheless, Yu is well known in literature for his accomplishments in the rhyme-prose form *(fu;* also called the prose poem).

Pulled from east to north in wind and
    dust,
cast adrift from south to west between
    heaven and earth,
he traveled where the Three Gorges'
    towers and terraces block sun and
    moon,
and where the five streams join to dress
    the cloudy mountains.

When the barbarian serving our ruler
    rebelled in the end,
our exiled poet grieving for the times did
    not return.
Yu Xin's whole life was bleak,
yet the poems and rhyme-prose of his
    twilight years moved rivers.

Why ask where the road goes?
Where are we rushing to?

Here are the ruins of an old fortress. Nothing is left but the foundations, and they are nearly lost in the overgrowth. A distant country once wanted to colonize this place, but it was too far from home, and the soldiers abandoned it hundreds of years ago.

Here are the ponds and fallen walls of the old imperial gardens. The gaily dressed women and proud aristocrats are now mere ghosts blown about in the breezes.

Here is a tumbled temple where devout people came to pray daily, now broken open to the rains, with vines hanging from the rafters.

We build things, and as soon as we stop maintaining them, they disintegrate. As skillful as we are as engineers, as solid as our materials are, nothing lasts. The monuments and palaces of olden times are now barely lines scratched into the dirt beside the highway. People speed by without stopping to match their footprints with those of long-gone kings.

Down the road is a cemetery. The older stones are worn, rounded. Some of the inscriptions are worn. Maybe the sharply etched memories are getting just as dim. The flowers are fresh, so we know people come to pay their respects.

Whether ruins or cemetery, people rush by and ignore them. Only the visits of the living make a place alive.

Where are we rushing to? A wheelbarrow works because of legs and hands.

Lake Namtso, Tibet. Peter Vigier

216 | The Wheelbarrow

The Wheelbarrow in Ancient China

The earliest wheelbarrows in ancient China that we know of are from a mural found in a second-century Han dynasty tomb. Wheelbarrows are also depicted in a carved stone relief in a Sichuan tomb.

A filial son named Dong Yuan is remembered because he moved his father from place to place in a wheelbarrow. The official Zhao Xi saved his wife from danger during the Red Eyebrow Rebellion (Chimei; c. 20) by disguising himself and telling the rebels that he was carrying his terribly ill wife in a wheelbarrow.

The *Records of the Three Kingdoms (Sanguozhi)*, compiled by the historian Chen Shou (233–297), credited Zhuge Liang (p. 410) with the invention of the wheelbarrow to help move military supplies.

There were two main types of wheelbarrows: those with a front wheel, and those with a large, centrally mounted wheel. This latter type could be sized to transport as many as six people. Some wheelbarrows were drawn by horses or mules, and there were even wheelbarrows with sails.

A wheelbarrow works because of legs and hands: someone still needs to grip it and push it.

The wheelbarrow sits there, ready. One wheel, two legs. It's stable. Once someone lifts it, though, there's a certain balance that's necessary, and learning to use a wheelbarrow takes a little practice—like learning to ride a bicycle. Why not use a cart with two, or even four wheels? It's because the mobility and simplicity of the wheelbarrow are better.

The handles are right where one can hold them with arms nearly straight and without stooping over. One can therefore move a great deal of weight: the wheelbarrow is not a rolling cart, but two levers and a wheel. It's a combination of two fundamental inventions. It's rough, improvisational, rocky, but efficient. The wheelbarrow is powered by a person's legs, body, and arms, but it greatly increases what that one person is able to do.

The wheelbarrow is the symbol of work. It's also the symbol of migration—so many times in old China, people would load their belongings, or perhaps a child or elderly person, into a wheelbarrow to flee from famine or invaders. One piles on as much as one can. We could say it has one personpower.

Today, we are smug, saying that we can do much more work than one person can. Our engines are measured in hundreds of horsepower, our computers hold entire libraries on our desks, and children hold mobile devices more sophisticated than once-gigantic mainframes. But we're still measuring work by one person, aren't we? Whether wheelbarrow or personal computer, it's the person doing the work, not the tool, that matters.

Someone still needs to grip it and push it, just as light cannot be seen without shade.

Yin and Yang

This is one of the most popular and well known symbols of Taoism. It is a modern derivation of the *Taiji Diagram (Taiji Tu)* shown in the *Compendium of Diagrams (Tushubian)* by Zhang Huang (1527–1608). Some scholars have found similar diagrams from as early as the Tang dynasty. Earlier, yin and yang were represented by the tiger (yin) and dragon (yang).

The diagram's meaning is that yin and yang interlock and cannot be separated: one cannot perceive one without the other. The dot of the opposite color within each area means that even in the most extreme cases of yin or yang, there is never totality—the beginnings of the opposite are generated even in the midst of seemingly complete yin or yang. The *I Ching* teaches us that when anything reaches its greatest point it inevitably begins changing toward its opposite.

 The words "yin" and "yang" themselves are another way to understand this concept. Pictorially, the ideogram for "yin" depicts the shady side of a hill. "Yang" is a picture of the sunny side of a hill. If one watches a hill all day, the sun and shadows will move. The sunny side cannot be seen without the shade, the shade cannot be seen without the sun.

Light cannot be seen without shade.
Shade cannot be seen without light.

By moonlight, we see in black and white. We cannot see colors. There is something fascinating and valuable about seeing the world that way. We see only what is essential. We see form emerging from a sea of blackness. We can appreciate shape and depth without the distraction of color or even meaning. We can look at the world so familiar by daylight and see it anew in the black and white of moonlight.

You see yin and yang.

If the door is not open, it's closed. If having it closed is what you want, then that's perfect. The closed door not only keeps two rooms separated, but may itself be something to look at as a handsome piece of handiwork.

You see yin and yang.

A good faucet in the bathroom is useful. You can have all hot water, all cold water, or a mixture of the two.

You see yin and yang.

The plug in the electric socket. The hinge pins holding the door. The top of a cabinet versus its drawers. What's on one side of a window and what's on the other side. Beyond our walls, the sun shining until it sets.

You see yin and yang.

Left and right. Up and down. The day warms, the night cools. The sun moves over a hill, changing the face from brightness to shadow. Stand in the middle of a bamboo forest and watch all the shadows and sunlight shift second by second.

You see yin and yang.

Shade cannot be seen without light; even when old, Du Fu could still wield his golden halberd.

218 | Growing Old

› Fasting day

Why Hurry to Ask About Me?

Du Fu's (p. 29) poem "Many People Bring Wine to See Me After I Fall Off My Horse Drunk" was written about 766. Xi Kang (p. 220) was one of the Seven Sages of the Bamboo Grove.

I, Du Fu, the duke's old guest,
finish my wine, sing drunkenly, and
    brandish my golden halberd.
Astride my horse, I am suddenly young
    again.
Hooves scatter stones tumbling down
    Qutang Gorge.
Out of White King City's gates above the
    water and clouds,
I lean forward and charge straight down
    eight thousand feet.
Whitewashed walls pass, I turn like
    lightning, my purple reins loose.
To the east, I reach a plateau, outlined
    against the sky,
gallop past rivers, villages, fields, halls.
I drop the whip, slacken my purple bridle,
and ride on, startling ten thousand
    people with my hoary head.
Confident, rosy-faced, I can still shoot
    arrows while riding.
It was hard to know, hard to judge by its
    winded steps
and its red sweat, that this black trace
    horse snorting jade
would suddenly stumble and fall injured.
In human life, quick thoughts lead to
    many humiliations.
Now I lie forlorn with quilt and pillow.
It's now late at dusk and I've added to
    your troubles and bother.
When I learned you were coming, I
    wanted to hide my face.
Using a pigwood cane, I get up and lean
    on a servant.
When we finish our talk, we laugh loudly
and, hand in hand, sweep by the bends
    of the clear stream.
Wine and meat stacked like mountains,
our feast begins with sounds of sad
    strings coupled with brave bamboo.
Together, we point to the western sun—
    there is no stopping it.
We exclaim and sigh and tip cups of
    strained wine.
You needn't have ridden your horse to
    ask after me;
don't you know that Xi Kang nourished
    life and was still killed?

Du Fu could still wield his golden halberd.
It was his horse, and not he, who stumbled.

If you're middle-aged or older, you can't help but notice the effects of aging. You might not be as strong, or as flexible, or as quick-witted as you once were, and you might find yourself troubled by pain and weakness that your doctor dismisses as "minor."

Everywhere people describe aging in disparaging terms. We fear growing old, fear being discarded, fear being ineffective. There aren't many good roles given to older people in today's fast-moving and youth-obsessed world. We admire the home run, the jumping splits, the multi-octave singing, the new speed record, the wild new idea from a college student that sparks a billion-dollar company. We don't admire a gray-haired person sitting quietly and sharing wisdom.

Even Taoism might be accused of fearing aging. After all, longevity and the search for immortality are central to so many Taoist beliefs. From the Queen Mother of the West's peaches of immortality to the God of Longevity, the Taoist could be accused of being as preoccupied with avoiding aging as anybody else is. Du Fu soberly reminds us that Xi Kang, for all his wisdom, creativity, flair, and Taoist alchemy, was still executed.

We need a new attitude on aging. Look at the words "growing old": growing is certainly positive, and there are so many things that get better with age—wine, antiques, redwoods. As we age, we have to recognize how we are still *growing*. We have to recognize that each stage of our lives is unique and valuable.

Bluntly put, we're all going to die, and we'll experience infirmity at the end as our bodies shut down. Accept that. Having accepted that, though, means that we embrace the unique features of each moment of our lives, accept that we are changing, find the growth in whatever stage we find ourselves in, take advantage of the insights that come to us, and use our wisdom to live healthy lives for our own benefit and the benefit of others.

Let us speak of aging not as a process of deterioration, but as a process of *growing* old.

It was his horse, and not he, who stumbled. Don't be hemmed in by destiny or place.

Going to Fusang

Fusang

Fusang was first described by the Buddhist Hui Shen in 499 as a country some 20,000 *li* east of the Great Han (one li is 415.8 meters; 20,000 li translates to about 5,167 miles, or 8,316 km). It is thought that Hui Shen traveled from China to Japan to Korea and then from the Kamchatka Peninsula to Fusang. The stipulated distance would mean he may have visited a place somewhere in British Columbia. There is no single agreement on where Fusang might actually be, only that it is a legendary place far to the east of China.

The Frog in the Well

This is a line found in the *Zhuangzi*: "One cannot speak to a frog in a well about the ocean." It has become an idiomatic phrase.

Don't be hemmed in by destiny or place.
Leap right through the air onto your new land.

Whether there was really a Fusang that Hui Shen found is not as important as the fact that Fusang fired the imaginations of people for over 1,500 years. We each need to have a Fusang in our lives. If we only thought of our world as where we travel each day, our world would be small indeed. We would remain like Zhuangzi's frog in a well.

So we travel. We go on long treks. We move across the country or even across the world. We are curious about everything. We read. We go to movies. We explore on the Internet. In every way, we challenge our boundaries every day. We might even take it farther: we could not survive if we did not think beyond our boundaries. We could not even stay sane.

When we think of gods, we are thinking of a world even farther away than Fusang was from China. When we meditate and open up the infinite world within us, we are pushing against the very shell of our normal references. We pass our mental borders and enter the world of meditation, which need not have any limits.

There is a passport that one can receive if one applies for it in person. Those issued by government agencies are automatically invalid. Merely saying that one has such a passport is as much folly as Napoleon crowning himself, and is worthless.

Every child began with a passport. Many are destroyed by parents and teachers. Others are lost. Some are put away in drawers and forgotten for years, while others sit in the trembling hands of those too afraid to use them. Most of us have to be reawakened and apply for a new one.

Those who use their passports find them stamped only when they cross a border.

Leap right through the air onto your new land. Otherwise, why climb the mountain? Just because it's there?

- Birthday of the **Great God of the Northern Peak**

The Great God of the Northern Peak

The Great God of the Northern Peak (Beiyue Dadi) is the god of one of the Five Sacred Mountains (p. 44), Hengshan (Permanent Mountain), in Shanxi. (Note that the southern mountain of the Five Sacred Mountains is also written as Hengshan, but this is a different Chinese word, and that mountain is located in Hunan.) Hengshan has been a place of pilgrimage and offering since the Zhou dynasty (1046–256 BCE), and the temple to the Great God of the Northern Peak dates to the Han dynasty (206 BCE–220). Li Bai's (p. 264) calligraphy of praise is still there—two characters, *zhuang guan*—"spectacular."

One of the Lesser Grotto Heavens (p. 49), Hengshan has a long association with Taoism. One of the Eight Immortals (p. 124), Zhang Guolao (p. 331), cultivated immortality there.

The Great God of the Northern Peak receives offerings; grants good fortune; presides over rivers, streams, all four-legged animals (especially tigers and leopards), reptiles, and worms; and guards one of the entrances to hell.

One of the most famous Chan Buddhist masters, **Mazu Daoyi** (p. 243), studied with his master Nanyue Huairang (677–744) on Hengshan. The Hanging Temple, a series of temples built onto the sheer side of the mountain, supported by narrow posts set into the rock, is one of Hengshan's most famous features.

Why climb the mountain? Just because it's there? We climb to make offerings to heaven.

In the past, being with nature was an integral part of Chinese culture. Emperors regularly visited Hengshan to make offerings and sacrifices so that the human world would stay in harmony with the heavenly one. There was a sense that people had to acknowledge heaven, that we were subordinate to heaven, and that only a sacred attitude toward heaven and our existence was right. What better place to go, then, than a high mountain where the vistas and beauty made the sense of a higher order obvious?

We still need sacredness today. There are still churches and temples. We still receive the bodies of soldiers killed in war with solemnity. We put up impromptu shrines for those killed on the street. We know to give thanks when we escape a bad accident. We are grateful when we manage a rare accomplishment. That all shows that we still need sacredness, and if we look further, we can find sacredness beyond our everyday means. We have to climb the mountain ourselves. Hengshan means the Permanent Mountain. The high mountain that is the ideal altar for worship will always be there. The path of the mountain will always be there. Heaven waits for us beyond the peak.

We climb to make offerings to heaven, for sunset is not death but serenity.

Priestess on Hengshan. © Saskia Dab

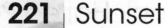

221 Sunset

"North in Qingluo"

This poem is by Li Shangyin (p. 149).

The sun sets in the west behind the
  mountain.
I call on the thatched hut of a solitary
  monk:
only fallen leaves—the man is gone.
Cold clouds cover the road in several
  layers,
A stone gong signals the start of night.
I pause and lean on my rattan staff.
This world is small as a grain of dust:
I'm at peace with love and hate.

Sunset is not death but serenity:
In this dark world at peace with love and hate.

The sun sets at the ocean's edge and people flock to watch it. Some light bonfires on the beach, as if they cannot bear to watch the sun go down, or as if they need to create their own fire to remember the sun. No, no—it's even more primitive than that. We are driven into a state without words, where we only know to go toward flaming light, and once we are there—unblinking, mesmerized, silent—we feel a fulfillment impossible to reach any other way.

The sun sets at the ocean's edge and we watch it, perched on a seawall, strolling hand in hand with a lover, romping with our children and dogs, or falling into a reverie that can only happen at twilight. In that slight space between day and night is a dream world that we dimly recall from childhood, a world where gods walk out of the oceans, spirits cavort in the trees and breezes, and our memories unfold before us in fables no storyteller can recount.

Are our memories only the record of what we ourselves did at one time in our lives? Or can we have memories that are not our personal history, but the history of a people? After all, we are not just ourselves, not just tiny people with fragile stories; we are part of a long line of people that were once here and a long line of people that will be here, and we, in the middle, can remember all that those before us and all that those after us can know.

We know all that at sunset, when the world pauses around a flaming orb plunging into the waters, setting the sky in a pattern that our minds don't comprehend but our hearts read. We sing those lyrics long into the night.

In this dark world at peace with love and hate, remain unblinded by today's needle.

© andelieya

Mencius (p. 63) refers to a good country where "persons of seventy wear silk and have meat to eat, and the black-haired people suffer neither from hunger nor cold."

In the *Classic of History*, the Great Yu (p. 105) says of the sovereign who knows how to rule wisely: "When he appoints the right officials, brings peace to the people, and confers kindness, then the black-haired people cherish him in their hearts."

In a lament from the *Classic of Poetry*, a poem about a terrible drought has the line, "Of the black-haired people of Zhou, few will be left behind."

Black Heads and Millet People

There are two sets of words translated as "black-haired people."

 Qianshou means "black heads." Notice how the second word, "shou," is part of the word "Tao" (p. xx).

The words for "black-haired people" are *limin*, and their meaning is instructive. "Li" combines words that mean "millet" with the symbol for a knife, an old coin, or measure. The modern meaning of the word is "numerous," "many," or "black." The second word, "min," means "people," "subjects," "citizens." It was once a symbol of an eye being pricked by an awl—meaning a slave—but the modern meaning is positive and is a part of terms such as "public," "popular," "citizen," "democracy," and "nationality." (It's possible that this word originated thousands of years ago when people were regularly captured during wars and made into slaves. The needle in the eye may have been a threat or a direct method of enslavement.)

Remain unblinded by today's needle.
See that all people are the same as you.

In China's past, the populace was called "the black-haired people" because everyone had black hair. Today, though we live in a global community where hair color varies, the idea of complete commonality among all humanity is still relevant. We might need a new term that transcends race or outer features. Maybe we need a term like "the breathing people" or "the heart people."

It's harder to see the similarities between ourselves and others in this multicultural world. After all, systematic dehumanization of another group is behind racism, sexism, and oppression. For centuries, people have refused to see their commonality with others. Nations have justified invasion, enslavement, and genocide by claiming that it was their right and that the others were less human. Even today, labels like "other tribes," "other countries," and "other skin colors" divide us. But as we move to a more enlightened world, we can make the leap to seeing what is really there: commonality with all other people. If you look deeply at people, they all look like you.

If you look at others deeply, how can you miss having compassion and consideration for them? The man who collects your garbage, the mechanic who fixes your car, the waitress who takes your order—all these people serve you. And all these people look like you.

You're going to keep moving through your world, accepting the services of others. If you remember, however, that they are just like you, there will be more compassion in the world, and the payments, gratitude, and recognition you accord to others will be paid back to you.

See that all people are the same as you: crossing to the other side is the task.

The Couple's Bridge

There have been many suspension bridges in Chinese history, but one of the most famous is the **Anlan Bridge** in the Dujiangyan Irrigation System (p. 208) near Chengdu.

The Anlan Bridge was constructed in 1803, during the reign of Qing Emperor Jiaqing (1760–1820), replacing two earlier bridges. The construction was led by He Xiande and his wife. However, local officials misappropriated the funds earmarked for the bridge's construction, and when He Xiande reported this, he was killed. People rose up and asked He's wife to direct the construction of the bridge. When it was finished, the bridge was named Anlan, meaning "couple." The bridge was replaced in 1975 by a steel and concrete structure, but the Couple's Bridge stood in its earlier form for 172 years.

Anlan Bridge. Prince Roy

Crossing to the other side is the task.
Even if the bridge sways, we have to cross.

Here is a footbridge that is barely wide enough for one person. It's suspended over a ravine, green water running far below it.

The bridge sways from side to side. It bobs up and down. The planks flex and pull at the ropes from which they're suspended. Each step is fearful, and the person's mind starts wondering whether retreating or sprinting would be possible if the tenuous span were to snap. Five feet in, it's already obvious that there is only crossing—or plunging fatally into the river below if the bridge were to break.

The bridge does not break. It moves with a rhythm so frightening and unpredictable that gracefulness is impossible. Instead, a drunken stumbling emerges, the feet pushing against sinking floorboards or struggling against abrupt heaving. Only by staggering, pitching, and rolling is it possible to reach the other side.

This bridge is made of wood, iron, and rope. People cross it every day, and those who cross it all the time no longer notice the swaying; they don't even break their conversation as they stroll across.

We don't remember the names of those who first pinned the ropes. We don't know the names of those who cut and planed the timbers. But their service makes it possible for generations of people to carry on their lives.

Be the sage that is the footbridge.

Even if the bridge sways, we have to cross—why care if you drunkenly spill your wine?

▸ Fasting day

The Wine Immortal

Li Bai (701–762) is often named as China's best poet. He's admired for his unconventional stance and the deep emotions that his poetry conveys. He is also known as Li Taibai, "Great White," in reference to the planet Venus, in addition to various extravagant titles: Householder of the Green Lotus, Poetry Immortal, Wine Immortal, Exiled Immortal (meaning exiled from heaven), and Poet-Knight Errant. Li Bai confirms this last title: "When I was fifteen, I was fond of swordplay, and challenged many great men with my skill."

Li Bai never sat for the imperial examinations, but his brilliance was admired by Emperor Xuanzong (685–762), and he was named to the Hanlin Academy. He leaves behind about one thousand poems. According to legend, he drowned trying to embrace the moon's reflection in a river.

One of his most famous poems is "Drinking Alone Under the Moon."

A pot of wine among the flowers;
drinking alone without companions.
I raise my cup to invite the bright moon:
we two and my shadow make three.
While the moon cannot drink
and my shadow only follows my body,
we are quick friends—the moon,
    shadow, and me.
On with joy all the way to spring!
I sing as the moon lingers.
I dance with my shadow, staggering.
While sober, we share our joys.
Thoroughly drunk, we each wander off,
never again to be lonely in our travels—
next time we'll invite the distant clouds
    and stars.

Why care if you drunkenly spill your wine?
"What's poured on the table drenches the world!"

That's an old drinker's expression. You might say it's merely a means of consolation, but within it is the assumption that what goes on in us also moves the world.

Most of the time, we say that human beings must learn to sublimate themselves to nature and to heaven. We speak philosophically of how we must follow Tao.

However, Tao also follows us. It's a difficult and subtle point. After all, we are part of Tao too. If we say we are not, it's a huge philosophical mistake. Speaking as though we are outside of Tao would be to separate ourselves from it, and if there's any definite mistake, it's alienation. So we are part of Tao. Therefore, what we do and think is also Tao.

There is a line in Li Bai's poem "Singing on the River" that captures this attitude. "Inspired! Intoxicated, my moving brush shakes the Five Sacred Mountains." The emperors believed that the world would fall apart without devotion; Li Bai declares that his will could move mountains.

Perhaps that's why these poets loved wine so much: they sought to release themselves from the constraints of conventions, and with their power so unleashed, they could accomplish great things. So if alienation is the primary sin, here's the second one: to be squeezed by conformity and convention. Taoism is the antithesis of Confucianism, and wine is the symbol for Taoism's wilder side. We are Tao and we want to remove all that interferes with that.

We must remember that wine in itself is not the real means any more than there's an elixir of immortality. Any mature person knows that there is no single secret ingredient to spirituality. In fact, before you know it, anything you believe or practice can become a trap. That's why the masters of old challenged their students with seemingly irrational behavior, with shouts and contradictory pronouncements: they knew that every means of liberation could also backfire.

It's funny, isn't it? Drunkenness helps us transcend our limitations, but the ultimate drunkenness is to be drunk without wine.

What's poured on the table drenches the world: that's how we might celebrate all under the sun.

Moon Festival

The **Moon Festival** is also known as the **Mid-Autumn Festival** (Zhongqiu Jie) or is simply named by its date, "Eighth-Moon-Fifteenth." This day is the autumn equinox, and this is the month in which the moon looks the largest in the night sky. It's one of the most popular festivals and has a history dating back to the Shang dynasty, three thousand years ago.

The moon's round shape symbolizes completion and wholeness, and for most Chinese people, this means a family reunion. Family members gather to enjoy the full moon, which is the symbol of abundance, harmony, and luck. After nightfall, families will go for a walk or enjoy picnics to view the moon. If some family members are away, it's natural to think of those who may be far from home. The Mid-Autumn Festival is also a romantic night for lovers, who sit holding hands on riverbanks and park benches beneath the brightest moon of the year. Su Shi (p. 140) wrote this poem in 1076 while drunk and missing his brother, Ziyou. It expresses the feelings of those missing loved ones during the Mid-Autumn Festival.

> When will the bright moon appear?
> Holding a wine cup, I question the blue sky.
> I don't know what time of year it is tonight
> in the palace towers of heaven.
> I would ride the wind and go there,
> but fear those elegant buildings and jade eaves,
> and that I couldn't last in the height and cold.
> I rise to dance with my pale shadow—
> better to stay in the human world.
> The moon around the cinnabar pavilions
> comes low through silk-draped doors
> to shine on the sleepless.
> There should be no regrets for anyone,
> so why are we separated for so long?
> People have sorrow and joy, parting and reunion.
> Like the moon waxing or waning or going from full to crescent,
> since ancient times nothing has ever been perfect.
> Nevertheless, I wish you long life,
> so we'll share a thousand kinds of grace and beauty!

The last five lines have entered the culture as idiomatic phrases. "People have sorrow and joy . . . nothing has ever been perfect" expresses an acceptance of the human condition. The last two lines have become an expression of good wishes to others.

The Moon Goddess I

We retell the story of Hou Yi and Chang'e every year during the Moon Festival. They lived on earth during the time of the legendary Emperor Yao (p. 94) around 2200 BCE.

Hou Yi was an archer in heaven. Chang'e was a young attendant to the Queen Mother of the West (p. 235). They fell in love and were married. However, the other gods were jealous of Hou Yi, and they slandered him before the Jade Emperor (p. 13). The emperor banished Hou Yi and Chang'e

to earth. Hou Yi used his skill to hunt for food and eventually became famous for his archery.

At that time, there were ten suns. Each one was a three-legged bird, and they roosted in a mulberry tree across the sea. Each day, one of the birds sat in a carriage driven by Xihe, the mother of the suns. One day, however, all ten birds rushed out together, drying up the lakes and burning the earth. Emperor Yao commanded Hou Yi to shoot down all but one of the suns, which is why we only have one sun today.

As a reward, Hou Yi was granted a pill of immortality that might restore him to heaven. Emperor Yao advised Hou Yi to prepare himself by meditating and fasting for a year before taking it. Hou Yi hid the pill in the rafters of his house.

Later, Hou Yi was again summoned by Emperor Yao. While he was gone, Chang'e noticed beams of light coming from the rafters and found the pill. She swallowed it and floated into the air. Startled and ashamed when she heard her husband come home, Chang'e flew across the sky. Hou Yi followed her, but strong winds blew him back. Chang'e landed on the moon and coughed up half of the pill. She asked the rabbit who lived on the moon to help make more elixir for her husband. People can still see the shadow of the Jade Rabbit in the moon as he pounds herbs.

In the meantime, Hou Yi lives in the sun far from his wife. Only once a year, on the fifteenth day of the eighth moon, is Hou Yi allowed to see his wife, which is why the moon is at its fullest and most beautiful on the night of the festival.

Li Shangyin (p. 149) wrote this poem entitled "Chang'e."

> The candle casts deep shadows on a mica screen.
> The endless river of stars falls, the morning star sets.
> Chang'e must regret stealing the divine elixir:
> in an azure sky over the green sea—she ponders night after night.

The Moon Goddess II

There are many versions of this story, but this one is significantly different in adding a villain and a bitter ending.

In this version, the gods sent Hou Yi to earth to save it from the errant suns. Chang'e was a beautiful mortal, and when she met the divine archer, the two fell in love immediately. Hou Yi loved her so much that it pained him to think that she could not live with him forever as an immortal.

Accordingly, he traveled to the Queen Mother of the West to ask for the elixir of immortality. Since Hou Yi had saved all of earth, she gave him two doses so that Chang'e could become immortal and Hou Yi could return to heaven. Overjoyed, Hou Yi returned home, and he and Chang'e made plans to take the elixirs on the fifteenth day of the eighth moon.

However, an evil man named Feng Meng had followed Hou Yi and was spying on the couple from outside. He wanted the elixir for himself. When Hou Yi went out hunting, Feng Meng confronted Chang'e and demanded the elixir.

Determined to prevent Feng Meng from gaining the elixir, Chang'e hurriedly swallowed both bottles and immediately rose to heaven. Unable to bear the thought of being separated from her husband, she managed to divert herself to the moon.

In the meantime, Hou Yi returned and learned from a maid what had happened. He fought with Feng Meng and killed him, then tried to find Chang'e. He saw that the shadow in the moon looked exactly like his wife. Running with all his might, he rushed toward the moon, but with every step, the moon seemed to rise farther away.

Finally, Hou Yi built a palace inside the sun, and the couple continues to long for the day when they might be reunited.

The Red Thread

Once a boy walking home at night met an old man in the moonlight. His name was **Old Man Under the Moon** (Yue Xia Lao). The old man said that he had tied the boy to his destined wife by a red thread and showed the girl to him. Being young and immature, the boy threw a rock at the girl and ran away.

Many years later, when the boy had grown into a young man, his parents arranged for a marriage. On the wedding night, his wife waited in the bedroom with a red veil over her face, as was the tradition. The young man lifted the veil, and was delighted to see that his wife was beautiful—even with the faint scar on her forehead. When he asked about the scar, his wife told him the story of a boy who once threw a rock at her.

This legend persists in a folk practice: if you want to stay together as a couple all your life, tie two juniper branches together with red thread and put them under your bed. You can also go to the **Longshan Temple** in Taipei, where you can pray to the Old Man Under the Moon.

Wu Kang and the Cassia Tree

The shadows of the moon might also be a magical cassia tree. There was once a woodcutter named Wu Kang who wanted to become immortal. When the Jade Emperor heard of such audacity, he banished Wu Kang to the moon, telling him that he had to chop down the cassia tree before he could become immortal.

However, no matter how much Wu Kang chops day and night, the cassia tree regenerates with each blow. He can still be seen in the full moon, chopping at the tree.

Jade Rabbit

There is a reason why Chang'e found an immortal rabbit on the moon.

In the distant past, three immortal sages traveled the earth disguised as three aged and weak old men. Meeting a fox, a monkey, and a rabbit, they asked for something to eat.

The fox and the monkey had food and gave it to the men to eat. But the sages were still hungry. The rabbit had nothing

to give. Offering itself, it jumped into the fire so it could be roasted and provide food for the old men.

Impressed by its selflessness, the immortals restored the rabbit to life and sent him to live in the Moon Palace.

Mooncakes

Mooncakes are central to the Mid-Autumn Festival. These pastries are about three inches in diameter and about one and a half inches thick. Mooncakes are round and golden, like the ideal harvest moon. They have a thin crust and a variety of fillings, such as lotus seed paste; sweet red, black, or green bean paste; egg yolks from salted duck eggs; jujube paste; the Five Kernel *(wu ren)* combination of walnuts, pumpkin seeds, watermelon seeds, peanuts, and sesame seeds; and many more variations.

A mooncake is dense and rich, so it's often cut into wedges. Served with tea, it's eaten while people gather to admire the moon.

There are other kinds of mooncakes, depending on local customs, availability of ingredients, and historical differences. A Beijing-style mooncake has a light and foamy dough; a Cantonese-style mooncake can have rich fillings of ham, chicken, duck, roast pork, and up to four egg yolks; and Yunnan-style mooncakes might combine rice, wheat, and buckwheat flour for the dough. Mooncakes have spread beyond China, with Indonesia, Japan, Vietnam, the Philippines, and Thailand developing their own versions.

Businesses have contributed to the mooncake market as well. Innovative mooncakes have been made with chocolate, taro, coffee, fruit, seaweed, and ice cream. It's customary for families and businesses to give mooncakes as gifts during this time, and the sales of mooncakes are tracked in Asia as an economic indicator.

A folktale associates mooncakes with the overthrow of the Mongol Yuan dynasty and the establishment of the Ming dynasty in 1368. The Ming revolutionaries used mooncakes to smuggle secret messages to one another. Zhu Yuanzhang, the leader of the Ming (and eventual first emperor), and his advisor, Liu Bowen, began a rumor that a deadly plague was spreading. The disease could only be prevented by eating a special kind of mooncake. This prompted the distribution of more mooncakes—with a message that the revolt would begin on the fifteenth day of the eighth moon.

A more complicated method entailed embossing a message baked into the decorations on top of the mooncakes and packaging the cakes in groups of four. Each mooncake had to be cut into four parts and the resulting sixteen wedges was then reassembled to reveal a secret message. Once the message was decoded and understood, the mooncakes were eaten, thereby destroying the message. ▶

225 | Moon Tao

• Fasting day
• The **Moon Festival**

The Mid-Autumn Moon

Su Shi (p. 140) wrote the following poem for this day:

> Sunset clouds gather in the distance: it
>   is clear and cold.
> The Milky Way is silent and has become
>   a jade plate.
> The goodness of this life does not last
>   long.
> Where will I be next year to see the
>   bright moon?

Taoist Moon Meditation

1. Sit in meditation facing the moon.
2. When you're calm, imagine that the moon descends until it is over your head.
3. Imagine that it's inside your head.
4. Gradually let its light fill your entire body, eradicating all illnesses and blockages.
5. Hold that image as long as possible.

Sun- and Moon-Faced Buddha

The *Blue Cliff Records* tells of Mazu Daoyi (p. 243), who was indisposed. When the head monk asked how he was, the master replied: "Sun-faced Buddha, moon-faced Buddha."

We might celebrate all under the sun,
but also honor all under the moon.

All our great accomplishments are made under the sun (including by artificial light). We celebrate that which is yang: technology, government, warriors, champions, money, and all that is patriarchal. In the meantime, all that is yin—women, mothers, emotion, creativity, intuition, art, love of nature, gentleness, mysticism, and the pure miracle of life itself—we fail to comprehend or honor.

The Moon Festival is a time for women to celebrate. It is the time of poets. It is the time to remember that all that is yin also makes the world function. The Lunar Tao comes down to this: can you comprehend the Way that is dark and yet is as vital and powerful as what we celebrate in the light? This day is close to the autumn equinox: a reminder that yin and yang are equally important.

The Mid-Autumn moon is the harvest moon. At this time, the fields we planted and labored over during the preceding moons show their results. Yes, we must work—yang. Yes, we must make decisions about what to plant and what to grow—yang. Yes, we must go out with tools to weed and then harvest what we grow—yang. What we cannot do is make the plants grow any faster. We cannot do more than give them what they need and then invest the time that it takes for everything to ripen. In that, it is all yin. We can engage in agricultural science, but after a certain point, we can do nothing more than let nature take its course. That is yin.

No plant ever grew upside down. No season but autumn came after summer. No pear trees bear apples. Nature is true, time after time. Follow that path to truth. Give yourself completely to the Lunar Tao.

But also honor all under the moon as we are all journeying to see Buddha.

Exercise 16

The night and day come to equal length. From this point on, the nights will grow longer. The weather is colder, and rain comes.

This exercise is best practiced during the period of 1:00–5:00 A.M.

1. Sit cross-legged and press your palms gently over your ears.
2. Slowly bend from side to side as if you're trying to touch your elbows to your knees. Exhale when you bend; inhale when you return to the center. Repeat fifteen times on each side.
3. Facing forward, click your teeth together thirty-six times. Roll your tongue between your teeth nine times in each direction. Form saliva in your mouth by pushing your cheeks in and out. When your mouth is filled with saliva, divide the liquid into three portions.

4. Inhale; then exhale, imagining your breath traveling to the dantian and then swallow one-third of the saliva, imagining that it travels to the dantian.
5. Repeat two more times until you've swallowed all three portions.
6. Sit comfortably as long as you like.

Through this exercise, ancient Taoists sought to prevent or treat rheumatism in the ribs, legs, knees, and ankles; distension in the abdomen; incontinence; thirst; and asthma.

Monkey King

The **Monkey King** is one of the most popular, beloved, and accessible characters in all of Chinese culture. Known also as **Sun Wukong** (Realizing Emptiness) and the Great Sage Equal to Heaven (Qitian Dasheng), he is a superhero and the focus of novels, operas, dramas, songs, movies, television series, comic books, and children's books, and he will undoubtedly be featured in media to come.

We know him best through one of the four great classical novels of Chinese literature, the epic *Journey to the West (Xi You Ji)*. This book was first published anonymously in the 1590s during the Ming dynasty; the author has since been identified as Wu Cheng'en (1505–1580). People love the Monkey King because he is mischievous, gleefully overturns every social convention, triumphantly defies heaven, and in his own way is more wise than nearly everyone except Buddha and Guanyin.

The Actual Journey to the West

Journey to the West was inspired by a Chinese Buddhist monk named **Xuanzang** (c. 602–664), who journeyed from China to India in the early Tang dynasty to study Buddhism and to bring back as many sutras as possible. His pilgrimage took him seventeen years. He returned in 645 to considerable honor, declined all offers to enter imperial service, and devoted himself to teaching and translation for the remainder of his life. In addition to his religious work, Xuanzang wrote an autobiography and account of his trip, *Great Tang Records of the Western Religions (Da Tang Xiyu Ji)*. Along with a biography by the monk Huili, such factual records of the journey must have inspired Wu Cheng'en to embellish the events into his fantastical tale.

In *Journey to the West*, Xuanzang makes his famous pilgrimage with the supernatural help of the Monkey King, Pigsy (Zhu Bajie—Pig of the Eight Precepts), Sandy (Sha Wujing—Sand Enlightened to Purity), and Jade Dragon, a dragon prince transformed into a white horse. The group encounters eighty-one trials before they complete their quest and return to China. The Monkey King is clearly the star of the epic.

The Story of the Monkey King

The Monkey King was born from a stone formed by the primal forces of chaos. Finding a band of monkeys, he becomes their king, naming himself the Handsome Monkey King (Mei Houwang). However, he realizes that he is still mortal, so he journeys until he finds the Taoist Patriarch Subodhi. His master names him Sun Wukong, and the Monkey King learns a variety of magic arts, including shape-shifting in the form of the Seventy-Two Transformations, cloud somersaulting that covers more than 33,554 miles (54,000 km) in a single flip, and the ability to transform any of the 84,000 hairs on his body into an object or living being. However, the Monkey King's boastfulness offends the master. Patriarch Subodhi sends the Monkey King away, telling him never to reveal where he learned his arts.

The Monkey King returns to his monkey clan at Flower and Fruit Mountain, but he grows restless. He wants a weapon truly fitting to him. After more searching, he eventually acquires a marvelous staff from the Dragon King of the Eastern Sea. It weighs more than eight tons and can change from an ordinary staff to an enormous pillar. It was originally used by the Great Yu (p. 105) to measure the ocean's depth. In the Monkey King's hands, it is a light and versatile weapon—and he is able to shrink it to the size of a sewing needle and hide it behind his ear when he doesn't need it. He also wins golden chain mail, a phoenix-feather cap, and cloud-walking boots from the dragons.

When death comes to collect the Monkey King, he goes to hell itself and wipes his name from the *Book of Life and Death*, thereby removing himself from the cycle of reincarnation. The Dragon Kings and the Kings of Hell complain to the Jade Emperor (p. 13), who dispatches troops to arrest the Monkey King.

However, after many battles, the Monkey King and his followers defeat all of heaven's armies. He steals the peaches of the Queen Mother of the West (p. 235), Laozi's elixir of immortality, and the Jade Emperor's wine, and he defeats the great general Erlang (p. 208). Through combined Taoist and Buddhist forces, the Monkey King is eventually captured and put into Laozi's Eight Trigram (p. 184) furnace to reclaim the elixir of immortality. After forty-nine days, however, the Monkey King emerges stronger than ever and with the added ability to see evil in any form. The Jade Emperor appeals to Buddha (p. 117), who imprisons the Monkey King under a mountain for five hundred years.

When Guanyin searches for heroes to protect Xuanzang, the Monkey King eagerly offers to help. In order to control him, Guanyin gives Xuanzang a golden hoop that magically stays on the Monkey King's head. Whenever he misbehaves, the monk chants and the band constricts, causing much pain. Together with Pigsy, Sandy, and Jade Dragon (the white horse), the Monkey King escorts Xuanzang to India, where they receive an audience with Buddha before they all return safely to China.

Temples to the Monkey King

There are temples to Sun Wukong in Hong Kong, Macau, Taiwan, Singapore, Malaysia, and Indonesia. In the past, monks at a Buddhist temple in the Sai Mau Ping area of Kowloon were possessed by the Monkey King and performed feats that only Sun Wukong could do—walking on fire or climbing ladders of steel blades—as they reenacted the story of the journey to bring back sutras. ▶

Taming the Monkey

▸ Birthday of the **Monkey King**

Monkey Mind

Monkey mind *(xinyuan)* means the mind that is unsettled, restless, capricious, whimsical, inconsistent, confused, indecisive, and uncontrollable. This mind is also brilliantly creative, smart, and inventive.

The term was originally Buddhist, dating from as early as the fifth-century phrase "mind like a monkey" in the Chinese translation of the *Vimalakirti Sutra* (p. 113). The phrase has been adopted by Taoism, Confucianism, poetry, drama, and literature.

The common phrase we have today, "monkey mind or horse thought" *(xinyuan yima),* still means a mind that is hyperactive, adventurous, and uncontrollable. The expression is rooted in the Buddhist description of the mind being as restless as a monkey and the will galloping like a horse.

Remember that the word translated as "mind" is the same as the word for "heart" (p. 148).

We are all journeying to see Buddha,
all while trying to tame the monkey mind.

We each must find Buddha. We are all pilgrims. To reach Buddha is to reach ourselves, the spiritual core that in itself will be a fountainhead of wisdom. Once we reach that Buddha, we need no other deity: we become Buddha, the Enlightened One. To reach Buddha is to be enlightened.

Then comes the long path back. We have to return,

bringing the scriptures, spending the rest of our lives processing and sharing. That journey requires the taming of the monkey mind. Notice that the monkey cannot be destroyed. It can only be given the proper role, a true place in our lives, and finally, the honor of having brought us to Buddha and back.

All while trying to tame the monkey mind, we light fire to share warmth.

Wisher of Warmth

The Red Emperor

Wisher of Warmth, or Zhu Rong, is also known as the Red Emperor (Chidi), the god of fire and deity ruling over southern China. He wears armor, wields a sword, and rides a tiger.

In the distant past, Zhu Rong battled his own son, Gong Gong, a water demon who was flooding the earth. Gong Gong attempted to seize control of heaven itself, but his father fought with him for days until both fell to earth. Gong Gong was defeated and Zhu Rong returned to heaven.

In another version of his origin, Zhu Rong was named Li and was the son of a tribal chieftain who learned how to make and store fire and taught primitive people how to cook food. The Yellow Emperor invited him to join his court and appointed him Fire Administrator, giving him the title Zhu Rong.

When a tribal chief named Chiyou attacked, the Yellow Emperor named Zhu Rong the head of an army against Chiyou's eighty-one brothers—all of whom could spew smoke from their mouths. But Zhu Rong armed his men with torches and bombs, and they won the war.

The Yellow Emperor sent Zhu Rong to Hengshan (p. 44), to oversee the south. People came to offer him tribute each autumn, and they began to call him the Red Emperor.

Zhu Rong lived to be over one hundred years of age and was buried on the tallest peak of Hengshan. A hall in his honor is still there.

We light fire to share warmth
on the cold granite heights.

Fire made civilization possible. Until we had fire to cook and boil water, to light the darkness, to clear land, to melt and forge metal, and to dispel the cold, we were unable to progress. Beginning an estimated 400,000 years ago, human beings were able to use fire to improve their lives.

Wisher of Warmth is surrounded by myth and legend, but he personifies the human need for and use of fire. That's worth honor and worship. Without fire, we would revert to primitive levels very quickly.

We think nothing of flipping a light switch, turning on the furnace, or lighting the stove. It's worth pausing and thinking about these things, and being grateful for them. Fire is fundamental to our lives, and it's important to remain aware of what's fundamental.

According to legend, Wisher of Warmth had a red face, was highly intelligent—but had a bad temper. Without our internal fire, we would not be human either. Sometimes, anger and ferociousness are necessary. In the same way that we have to control fire to keep it from destroying us, we have to control our tempers if we are to move forward. In English, "temper" also means to moderate and control. The tempering of our emotions makes the difference between Wisher of Warmth and destroyer with fire.

On the cold granite heights, we see that every river flows back in time.

228 | Flowing Backward

‣ Fasting day
‣ Qiantang Tidal Bore

The Tidal Bore

A tidal bore is a wave that travels up a river from the ocean against the river's current. The water is turbulent and audible, churning sediment and air in a powerful roar. The Qiantang tidal bore is the largest in the world. It can be as high as thirty feet (nine meters) and travel up to twenty-five miles per hour (forty kilometers per hour).

The tidal bore occurs each full moon, but it's particularly powerful around the spring and autumn equinoxes. Crowds gather to watch it. Occasionally, the surge has been powerful enough to top the embankments. People get too close and perish.

Su Shi (p. 140), who was vice prefect of nearby Hangzhou from 1071 to 1073 and prefect from 1089 to 1090, would have had many opportunities to see the tidal bore. Here is the third of five quatrains, "Watching the Tidal Bore." The Qiantang River normally flows east, which gives Su Shi's last line its resonance.

> On the riverbank, I'm a person so much at odds with the world.
> I've long been as white-headed as the waves.
> The creator knows how easily we grow old,
> So he teaches the river to flow west.

Every river flows back in time.
When waves flow upstream, remember.

High on the mountains, the snow melts—first in a trickle, then in a gathering stream, then in rivulets joining as headwaters. Springs deep in rock fissures gush from some mysterious source and add to the flow. The waters run down the slopes and become a river that is young, new, fresh—tumbling, rushing, surging with a power that can overturn rocks, uproot trees, and flood plains. After many miles, it reaches the mouth, having grown old, flowing to the sea to join a far larger body of water, churning sand and earth and mixing with the salt of the sea, stirring the stuff of new land, new cells, new life. Then the waters rise into the air, free of their particulates, as if their work is done and they must go into heaven as a sacred vapor. Eventually, the waters become rain and snow—and then they become the river again.

Is a life like that too? Coming to birth, running with the power of youth, flowing with full maturity, joining in an ending that is not a negating death but a fulfillment, then rising to heaven purified—only to cycle back again? Is that what's called returning to our source?

If so, does knowing that bring peace? For then, life is no prize and death is no penalty. In fact, there is only life, turning, turning, turning. Thinking only of our "life span" is like identifying only the course of one river as the sole existence of water—when we know that course is only part of a much greater cycle.

The water reaches the sea, the sea rises in the clouds, the clouds rain on the mountain, and the river continues to run. So let us not be worried about what comes after death: we know.

When waves flow upstream, remember that all is possible if you choose the right place and know how to build.

| # The Spring-Fed Barrel

The Thatched Hut on Lushan

Bai Juyi (772–846), a famous poet of the Tang dynasty, was a successful official and a member of the Hanlin Academy—the elite group of scholars founded by the Emperor Xuanzong (p. 136) and charged with secretarial and literary responsibilities (Li Bai and Ouyang Xiu were two other members). Bai was demoted and exiled when he remonstrated with Emperor Xianzong (778–820) over the failure to find the murderer of two high officials. He was later restored to office, serving as the prefect first of Hangzhou, and then of Suzhou.

During his exile, he began traveling to Lushan, a mountain famous for its beauty, in Jiangxi Province. He fell in love with the scenery and resolved to build a thatched hut there. As a devout Buddhist, he also visited the nearby temples to meditate. In his essay, *Record of the Thatched Hall on Lushan (Lushan Caotang Ji),* Bai Juyi describes the hut as having unpainted beams and rustic plaster walls left without whitewash. Slabs of stone formed the steps, sheets of paper covered the windows, and the bamboo blinds were left natural. The furnishings were simple: four wooden couches; two plain screens; a qin; and Confucian, Taoist, and Buddhist books.

He built a trough of split bamboo from a waterfall east of the hut and made a network of bamboo gutters so that water would splash from the hut's eaves like a string of pearls. In this way, he could delight in the sound and sight of water.

If you choose the right place and know how to build
nature will come to you in abundance.

There is an enormous barrel on a hill, made by a cooper who died some years ago. The barrel has never leaked or rotted in all this time, and that alone is more than enough to marvel at. How can mere wood and copper, rivets and workmanship, keep a barrel from leaking?

Beyond its mere existence, however, the barrel is impressive for its place in a greater design. The barrel is filled by a spring—how blessed we are to have this land that is abundant with water—and from there, the water runs in a system of pipes to supply all that is needed for house, fountains, and ponds. The excess drains into the river.

There is no pump, and yet if we were to open any valve fully, the force of the water would create a geyser that would shoot up twenty-five feet. We have more than enough. Nature is generous. Gravity never fails. The water, filtered through the mass of an entire mountain, is always cool, fresh, and clear.

Bathe in this water, and wounds seem to heal faster. Drink tea with this water, and the purity of the rains and stone seem to enliven the cup. Listen to the sound of water as it trickles over stone, and heart rates slow and people want to linger forever.

Best yet, kneel down, cup your hands, and drink. Everything you need is right there.

Nature will come to you in abundance, even if autumn winds blow with unexpected frost.

Chenyun

Red Leaves

The anthology *Three Hundred Tang Poems* includes this piece written by **Xu Hun** (fl. 830–850), a man who loved both Buddhism and Taoism before he became an official. Since he never achieved a high position, he gradually became more reclusive. His view on the Taoist life is contained in this couplet:

> With elixirs, the body is ever healthy.
> Without calculation, one's mind is
>   naturally tranquil.

As the title indicates, the following poem was "Inscribed in the Inn at Tong Gate during an Autumn Trip to the Capital."

> Red leaves; the dusk is mournful,
>   mournful.
> I'm at a roadside pavilion with a wine
>   ladle.
> Storm clouds blow toward Great Flower
>   Mountain,
> a shower crosses the Middle Ridge.
> Forests color the distant hills,
> one hears the river flowing to the remote
>   sea,
> I will go into the capital tomorrow—
> Yet I dream of being a woodsman or
>   fisherman.

Autumn winds blow with unexpected frost
To live forever is such useless talk.

Sip clear rice wine and sit in moon-cast shadows beneath the arbor. Dragons soar to the fountains of heaven. Phoenixes lead the hundred birds sunward. We need no palace—just a stone stool near a shrine where red candles lean, blackened. Who can be a wild sage of the mountains? A "banished immortal"? What a big laugh. Ice drops from branches into this wine cup and chills the earth to its very root.

The garden this morning was covered with leaves. It was just swept yesterday. And the day before too! In the trees above, more leaves are yellow. That means that there is even more work to come.

Sweep up all the leaves and put them on the compost pile. The leaves fall. It is inevitable, the way of things. It's our choice whether we work with that, or whether we try to be graceful about it.

The dead matter. Death is ubiquitous, so constant, so much a part of the Way, that there's no choice but to accept it. People die all the time, and we must recognize that.

The trees above have some green leaves, some yellow, some brown. One by one, the leaves will fall until the branches stand bare against the chilly skies. Our time to face death will come too. We don't know where we are in the sequence, just as we can't tell which leaf will fall next. We only know that it will happen.

What truth can be glimpsed before we wither and fall? Can we be the leaf that knows which branch it's on? Can we be the leaf that knows where its root is?

To live forever is such useless talk—and the wine that can be drunk is not the true wine.

231 | The Wine Bowl

Facing My Wine

Here is a poem by Li Bai (p. 264) entitled "Diversions."

Facing my wine, I did not feel the dusk,
or the falling petals cover my clothes.
Drunk, I stand, step, see the moon in the stream;
birds are distant and people are few.

Wine that can be drunk is not the true wine.
Bowls that can be smashed are not the true bowls.

This wine bowl is antique porcelain, with remarkably thin walls. The rim was once edged in gold that has mostly worn away. Delicate polychrome symbols decorate the sides: a vase with a peacock feather, coral, a flag with the word "command," a container with a lotus blossom, another vase with peony flowers, a tray with peaches, two fish made to look like a yin yang symbol, an incense burner. The inside of the bowl is pure white.

The bowl may have been used in a home or in some fine inn during the imperial days. It was meant for delicious meals and lingering enjoyment, but also, as the flag with the word "command" implies, it was made for people in authority.

Although the bowl is over one hundred years old, it is not chipped. It has outlived its maker, its first owner, and whoever tossed it into the uncertainty of overseas trade. People are merely custodians, temporary in this world, who may well die before this bowl shatters.

Some of us grew up in households with addicted parents. Some of us may be struggling with addiction itself. Some of us may be enabling others to continue their addiction. Some of us may be trying to recover. Almost everyone recognizes that addiction is bad, including the addicts themselves. The addiction, the struggle against it, and the effort to establish a positive life without it are triply consuming. It's one thing to say you're against addiction. It's another thing to know what to do instead. This wine bowl is beautiful. But what does someone do who sees the reflection on the wine's surface and finds him- or herself ugly?

The Tao of wine is not a Tao of addiction. It is a Tao of freedom from limitations and acceptance of who we are. Both the addict and the Taoist are faced with pain, but their responses differ.

One is like this wine bowl: one cannot take the shape of someone one is not. Let people live according to their nature, though, and they will have great and lasting accomplishments.

If you feel polluted, wash out your bowl. Don't break it.

Bowls that can be smashed are not the true bowls: just be an old person in a courtyard.

232 | Old Man in the Courtyard

An Autumn House

We read "Autumn House on the Ba River Plain" by Tang dynasty poet **Ma Dai** (799–869) in relation to his disappointment over repeatedly failing the imperial examinations. The Ba River is near Xi'an: Ma is in the countryside, far from the glorious capital, and his alienation and sense of failure are clear. In the third line, he describes the trees with a term that means "foreign," "nonnative," or "far-off"—the trees aren't like the ones in his hometown, emphasizing his estrangement and uncertainty.

> After the wind and rain on the Ba River,
> I see a flock of geese cross the night;
> dead leaves drop from trees not like my
>   homeland's;
> a lone man with a frozen lantern in the
>   night;
> an empty garden, white with dripping
>   dew;
> the solitary walls of a neighbor—a rustic
>   monk.
> Lodging so long in a small house on the
>   outskirts . . .
> How will the years send me on?

On Courtyards

A courtyard is a *yuan,* and the predominant kind is the Four Combinations Courtyard, or *siheyuan.* The history of these courtyards dates back at least two thousand years. Four buildings surround the courtyard with the gate usually at the southeastern corner with a "spirit wall" to block evil spirits.

According to feng shui, a house should face south. Therefore, the northern and south-facing main house is for the owner of the home, the eastern and western buildings are for children or less important family members, and the southern building is for the reception area and servants' quarters.

A courtyard is prized for its space, comfort, privacy, and tranquility. There are usually plants, rock arrangements, and flowers, integrating house with nature in the Taoist ideal.

Just be an old person in a courtyard,
savoring peace in a bustling city.

Close to midnight. The streets are still. The day's demands are at an end—or at least temporarily at bay. An old man returns to his courtyard. A stonecutter laid out the pattern centuries ago, and the old man admires the workmanship each night. He feels right returning to the center of his universe.

His heart soars free. He notes where the moon is, to mark the journey ahead and to shape memories for years to come—memories that will well up in the quiet of future nights like this one.

Just outside, an old pear tree bursts into beautiful white blossoms at the end of winter. Weeks later, the petals fall to the ground in a fragrant snow. By early autumn, the tree hangs heavy with sweet, full fruit.

The old man sweeps the courtyard, thinking of monks who sweep their courtyards and recite sutras every day. The old man is willing to sweep, and in the sweeping find understanding and peace.

Wild monks of old wandered cloud-battered ridges in their search for enlightenment. Courageous sailors crossed thousands of surging waves to find routes to new lands. Nomad warriors galloped across continents to extend the will of their khans. The old man retreats to this little patch, studying what he sweeps away each week. That is good enough.

In the quiet, he listens to his heartbeat.

Savoring peace in a bustling city, the Great Immortal turned stones into sheep.

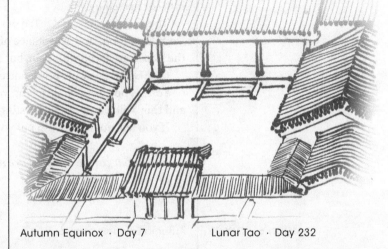

233 | Immortal Shepherd

▸ Fasting day
▸ Birthday of **Great Immortal Wong**

The Great Immortal

Great Immortal Wong (Huang Da Xian)—commonly spelled **Wong Tai Sin** according to its Cantonese pronunciation—first became popular in Hong Kong, and his cult has spread throughout Asia and into the United States.

Great Immortal Wong's original name was Wong Cho Ping (Huang Chuping), and he was born in 338 in Lanxi, Zhejiang. Other sources put his dates around 284–364.

Poor, Wong became a shepherd at the age of eight. He began practicing Taoism at fifteen. Forty years later, he was able to turn stones into sheep.

In 1915, a man named Leung Renan (Liang Renan) arrived in Hong Kong. He opened an herb store in Wan Chai, a district in Hong Kong. Customers could pray as well as have their prescriptions filled. When the shop burned down in 1918, Leung received a message from Great Immortal Wong, guiding him to where the Wong Tai Sin Temple now stands at Lion Rock Mountain in north Kowloon.

The busiest times for the temple are the New Year period (the first to fifteenth days of the first moon) and this day, the twenty-third day of the eighth moon. Worshippers come at other times as well, observing all the other holidays.

The temple offers a divination process called *kau cim* (*qiuqian;* "Asking the Sticks"). A worshipper lights incense and kneels before the altar with a bamboo cylinder filled with fortune sticks. The worshipper shakes the cylinder until one stick works its way out of the bunch and falls out. A number on the stick will match a printed piece of paper with the same number, and a soothsayer will discuss the problem and interpret the divination.

The Great Immortal turned stones into sheep— even the stones wanted to be herded.

According to one story, Great Immortal Wong reached his enlightenment while he was tending sheep. He fell backward onto the grass with the blue skies and white clouds above him, his arms and legs spread to form the word "heaven."

The shepherd boy cared for sheep, and a livelihood came to him. The shepherd boy practiced Taoism, and heaven responded to him. The power of Tao filled the shepherd, and stones came alive like more sheep and wanted him to care for them.

On festival days, the Wong Tai Sin Temple in Hong Kong is mobbed with people. It's impossible to get close enough to make offerings or to get a response from the Great Immortal through the divining power of kau cim. So people just drop to their knees in the crowd with their offerings of fruit, cooked chickens, whole roast pork, and flowers. They pray fervently, lighting incense and burning paper offerings. Temple attendants are nearby with hoses, trying to control the enormous burning heaps. Clouds of incense rise into the air, and the prayers of the devout mix with the sounds of traffic and the city's noise.

Leungchopan/Shutterstock

People need new gods, even in the twentieth century, and the shepherd responded to them. Great Immortal Wong rescues the dying, heals the wounded, punishes evil, and has the power to grant requests made to him. Heaven, the gods, and this world are not fixed. They are constantly changing. Thus, our needs change too. Our religions and our spiritual practices are not static and unvarying: they are alive and move with us.

The sheep must have wanted Great Immortal Wong to herd them. The worshippers are confident that Great Immortal Wong has heard them.

Even the stones wanted to be herded, to imagine and be different.

234 | Imagination

• Fasting day

Four Questions from Laozi

In Chapter 10 of the *Daodejing*, Laozi refers to the innocence and purity needed to be spiritual, an innocence also indispensable to imagination.

> In carrying and managing the soul, can you hold it as one without any separation?
> In concentrating your energy for softness, can you be like a baby?
> In cleansing and contemplating the profound, can you remain flawless?
> In loving the people while ruling the country, can you act without acting?

Statue of Laozi, Quanzhou. Thanato

Imagine and be different.
Be different to imagine.

Something happened to the world, and an imaginative person became the king. "Everything is music," he whispered to his aides one day. The aides nodded politely. The king valued each noise as surely as the cry of a newborn baby was the sound of life. Then he had an idea: he decreed that musical instruments be set on cliffs to be played by the wind. Soon, there were different instruments, different tones, different keys. The musician king heard not a cacophony but a wonderful stream of music.

Witnessing all this, others began to question the order of things. The architects saw that the palace and other important government buildings were stone and steel, and had the same arches and columns first invented three thousand years before, and they asked themselves, "Why are we doing the same thing today?" They made buildings with pivots, springs, loosened joints, and gyroscopes that didn't stand straight or try to resist earthquakes, but instead swayed and bent with the wind. As new movement came into their lives, people realized that the stiffness of their static buildings meant they were similarly rigid about their desks, and therefore their deskwork; about their computers, and therefore their computer work; about their beds, and therefore their sleep and lovemaking. There was more lovemaking.

Not to be outdone, the poets tried to bring poetry everywhere. They attached words to birds and by tracking the words that flitted by, they let poetry compose itself. They added up the words from all the signs all over the city. They invented new data-mining programs so that with each day that passed on the Internet, new words appeared, and people read them each day as eagerly as others looked at the stock market data, because, after all, what is the real meaning of accumulation? Suddenly, the curricula of schools began to change, so that people weren't so much looking back on what dead poets had written in long-past times, but were following where language—and thinking—was going.

You see what could happen, don't you, if we allowed new ideas? That's why the imaginative are not allowed to be kings.

Be different to imagine; remember that in childhood, we all found the window.

The Taoist Priest of the Lao Mountains

This is a short version of a story that appears in **Strange Tales from Liaozhai** *(Liaozhai Zhiyi)* by Pu Songling (1640–1715).

Wang approached a Taoist priest in the Lao Mountains hoping to learn the ways of immortality. The master predicted that Wang could not put up with the hardships, but Wang insisted.

One night Wang saw the master drinking with two men. The master cut a piece of paper into a circle and pasted it on the wall. Bright moonlight filled the room. The master passed a jug of wine, and there was always more to fill the cups no matter how much had been poured out. One of the guests threw a chopstick into the moon and summoned Chang'e, who sang and danced for them before turning back into a chopstick. The master and his two guests left their seats and walked into the moon, and Wang could see their profiles as they drank and feasted.

After a while, the three men returned. The moon dimmed and became a piece of paper again. Everyone went to bed.

Another month passed, but Wang was not allowed to do anything but collect firewood. Growing tired, he told the priest that he wanted to leave—but he wanted the priest to teach him something to compensate him for his work. "Didn't I say you couldn't endure the hardships?" asked the priest. But when Wang pressed him again, the priest taught him a magic spell. He told Wang to run into a wall, and it was as if it was not there. Wang was delighted.

"Remember that your heart must remain pure, or it won't work," advised the priest, giving Wang money and sending him home.

Wang immediately bragged to his wife of his new power. He ran straight at a wall, but struck his head and fell down with a swollen lump on his forehead.

In childhood, we all found the window.
Will you be the adult, searching for it?

There was a boy who found a window floating in midair.

He wasn't old enough to know that this was unlikely, impractical, unrealistic, or wrong.

He merely knew that there was a window there. So he went up to it and looked through it.

The window was well lit, with a field of green grass and a forest beyond it. Sunlight warmed the glass.

The boy put his hands on the sill and the window opened.

It was big enough to crawl through.

So he did.

He romped in the forest for a day, then found his way back to the window into his own world.

The next day, the window was gone. He never saw it again.

Years later, as a man, he would remember the window at odd times, and lament that such things never happened for him anymore.

But when his own son told him of a window, the man smiled, and there was one less parent to crush a boy.

Will you be the adult, searching for it, and never regret being outside the gates?

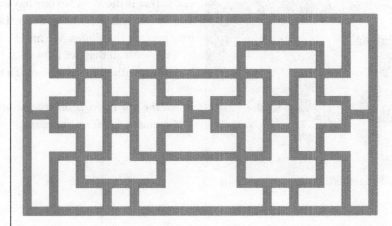

236 | Outside the Gates

What Use Is the Trap of Fleeting Fame?

When Du Fu (p. 29) wrote this poem around 758, the government had recaptured Chang'an. This poem is the first of a pair of poems entitled "Winding River." A *qilin* is a mythical creature said to appear when a great sage appears or passes away; qilin appeared in the garden of the Yellow Emperor (p. 4) and at the birth of Confucius. According to one description, a qilin has the head of a dragon, the antlers of a deer, the scales of a fish, the hooves of an ox, and the tail of a lion.

> One flying blossom petal diminishes all of spring.
> When ten thousand dots whirl in the wind, it saddens me deeply.
> I wish I could see each one as it passes; to escape such sorrow, I pour wine through my lips.
> Kingfishers nest on the little halls by the river.
> Qilin crouch in the flowers bordering the grand tombs.
> If you carefully investigate the reason for things, you must seek joy.
> What use is the trap of fleeting fame?

Statue of a qilin, Ming Tombs, north of Beijing.

Never regret being outside the gates.
All the snares are inside the palace walls.

We have such an odd cult of perfection in today's world! We take athletes who win by thousandths of a second and make them famous for life, casting the runners-up into obscurity. We idolize movie actors who fight cinema armies with swords and guns, ignoring the veterans who return wounded and with disabilities. We laud the businessmen who create the right products for market, mocking the owners of small stores and restaurants for naive doggedness and failure.

We drive our children to train assiduously as champions and to aim for the validation of crowds. We hold glamorous role models up for them, trumpeting success, success, success. That's what counts in life, we tell them, ignoring the fact that heroes first had to be true to themselves. In other words, the hero's success is a by-product of his or her total being. We forget to help our children be themselves, especially if it does not arouse the adulation of millions or bring gold ringing through the doors.

Even among the gods, there are high and low, great and small. Surely it is grand to be the Jade Emperor, but what if one is an immortal stable boy sweeping up dung? The Jade Emperor has his frustrations, and the stable boy has his satisfactions. The answer has to be in finding contentment with one's place in life.

The road is a highway of missteps, pitfalls, disasters, and dead ends. That is the Way. No one has walked the road ahead before, and no one will walk the same road after us. We may stumble. We may pant on the slopes. We may be confused by what we see.

Even with all that, we know that the beauty of the Way cannot be known without passing through the gates of trial.

All the snares are inside the palace walls: go back inside, where Confucius holds up one corner.

237 | Holding Up One Corner

Kong Fuzi

Confucius (Kong Fuzi, 551–479 BCE) was a philosopher and one of the most influential men in Chinese history. The predominant moral, ethical, scholarly, and governmental standards came out of his school and have lasted to this day. Every Chinese person is, in some way, a Confucian, and nearby countries such as Korea and Japan also adopted Confucian values. The name "Confucius" was a Latinization of his name by Matteo Ricci (p. 229). Kong Fuzi means "Master Kung." His given name was Kong Qiu.

Although Confucianism is highly complex, it is based on the idea that the worship of the emperor and his subjects integrates society with nature, that filial piety is essential, and that there are a set of feudal relationships to be maintained at all times: ruler–subject, father–child, elder brother–younger brother, husband–wife, friend–friend. The superior person in the relationship is expected to be benevolent to the other, and the subordinate is expected to be obedient.

Three concepts are key to Confucianism:

> ren benevolence; a humane attitude toward others and oneself
>
> li propriety; following prescribed roles and duty, obeying social order
>
> yi righteousness; morality, justice, and fairness

Philip Lange/Shutterstock

Confucius holds up one corner.
We still search for the other three.

The historian Sima Qian (p. 46) wrote in the *Records of the Grand Historian* that Confucius emphasized four things in his teaching—culture, conduct, loyalty, and honesty— and that he avoided foregone conclusions, arbitrary views, obstinacy, and egotism. He advocated caution in times of sacrifice, war, and illness; seldom spoke of profit, fate, or goodness; and would only help those who were earnest. Is that advice enough? Sima Qian said that if Confucius held up one corner of a square and the pupil could not infer the other three corners, he would not continue teaching.

Confucius was humble and deeply interested in learning and improving himself: "When three walk together, there must be one who can teach me. I am only worried about four failings: failure to cultivate virtue, failure to perfect my knowledge, failure to change when I hear what is right, and failure to correct my faults."

According to Sima Qian, Confucius and Laozi met one another. Some scholars consider this encounter fictional, and there's no way to know the truth with any certainty. However, Sima was writing history, and because he considered this story credible, it's worth considering.

As Confucius was departing, Laozi said: "I have heard that the rich offer farewell gifts of money, while the good offer advice. I am not rich, but while I am unworthy of it, I have been called good. Let me offer you a few words of advice. A shrewd observer who criticizes others risks his own life. A learned man who exposes others' faults puts himself in danger. Neither a filial man nor a good subject should thrust himself forward."

Confucius has been venerated. He's been vilified by governments when it suited them, then revived when it was thought profitable. Best to go directly to him, ignore the scholarly and political wars, and treat him as the man of wisdom that he was. He was not a god. He was an important thinker. He held up one corner. Let's seize the other three.

We still search for the other three corners, no matter how often we get knocked down.

238 | Get Back Up

‣ Fasting day

Confucius's View of a Righteous and Accomplished Person

In the *Analects,* Confucius's words on satisfaction are quoted as:

> The Master said, "Even with coarse rice to eat, with water to drink, and my bent arm for a pillow, I am still happy to be alive in the midst of such things. Riches and honors acquired unjustly are like floating clouds to me."

In discussing his idea of an accomplished person, Confucius is quoted as having said:

> One sees an advantage, yet thinks of what's right; sees danger but is willing to commit one's life; and, no matter for how long, one does not forget one's word. Then one can be called an accomplished person.

No matter how often we get knocked down
Get back up again! Get back up again!

Don't we all try? Don't we all try as hard as we can?

Then, though we try our hardest, we still experience great disappointments. We work long hours of overtime, only to have someone else take credit for our work or to be laid off ruthlessly. We work for months to create a strong love relationship, only to have our lover turn from us without remorse. We put all our hearts into teaching or rearing young people, only to have them fall into drugs and promiscuity. We try. We try. We try. And still it seems that our skills are inadequate. Why do we keep trying? What makes us keep going no matter what the obstacles?

We keep working in the face of overwhelming discouragement because we stubbornly refuse to give up our ideals. We believe that to be ethical in the face of great temptation is important. We believe that to be compassionate in the face of great cruelty is essential. We believe that faith itself will be rewarded, and that the reward is not for us, but comes in the affirmation that good will triumph over bad. We glimpse that the good we do yields dividends a hundredfold, and those flashes are enough to make us labor over years of adversity.

So how often can we keep getting back up? There is no one watching, no one applauding. It's strictly a personal issue. Can you get back up again? Sure, you've been hurt. Sure, you've been crippled by all the battles you've fought on behalf of someone else. But you'll do it again and again.

You'll go on, the warrior, holding up the standard when others let it fall. You'll do it as long as you have to, until someone else has to pry that standard from your closed fist.　　　　✦

Get back up again! Get back up again! Before you withdraw into silence.

239 | The Wisdom of Silence

• Fasting day

Zhuangzi on the Substance of Tao

In describing Tao, Zhuangzi gives silence a prominent place. He uses the following qualities to describe the substance of Tao, but he could just as easily be describing the qualities a person should have:

Calm, cheerful, silent, solitary, empty, action without action: these qualities maintain the level of heaven and earth and are the character of Tao and its power.

Withdraw into silence
and you'll find all you need.

The essence of wisdom is to work hard and persevere when it's right. Wisdom is also knowing when to withdraw. Knowing the difference between these two ideals is the crux of the matter. How do we know when to continue, and how do we know when continuation is impossible?

Silence is the indispensable condition for making important life-changing decisions. By all means, collect all the opinions you want from others, and tally all the contradictory feelings and thoughts you have about the situation as well. Stand them all up around you. Then, after you've reviewed each one and are thoroughly sure that you understand them, put them aside. When the situation is one where all possibilities seem good, and when there is no clear future down any one path, then it's time to check with yourself. You are the best source of truth.

No divination will substitute for looking within. No system of logic will tell you what to do about your future. No statistics or probabilities can perfectly predict what will happen if you choose one possibility over another.

Call it what you know in your heart. Call it a gut check. Call it how you feel deep down inside. This is the only valid way to make a decision. It has to be the individual who makes the final choices. Make your choice, and make it in silence, when all other voices, including the disparate ones inside you, have been quieted. There is a source of wisdom in you that has nothing to do with your intellect or your emotions. If you quiet yourself, if you allow that wisdom to well up in the solace that time and darkness provide, then you cannot go far wrong.

And you'll find all you need, even though nine stars to the north seem untouchable.

- Fasting day
- The **Nine Emperor Gods Festival**

The Nine Emperor Gods

The Nine Emperor Gods Festival (Jiuhuangye Jie) is a nine-day celebration that begins on the eve of the ninth moon. It is observed primarily in Myanmar, Singapore, Malaysia, Thailand, and the Riau Islands of Indonesia.

The nine emperors are star gods and the sons of Big Dipper Father (Doufu Zhouyu Guowang) and Big Dipper Mother (Dou Mu Yuan Jun; p. 296). They are the seven stars of the Big Dipper combined with two invisible stars thought to be on either side of the Dipper.

Ceremonies invoke the nine emperors, and since the emperors are believed to arrive via waterways, they are met at the shore. Devotees dress in white and carry incense and candles to welcome the gods near midnight. Other celebrants wear traditional costumes and perform music, acrobatics, and lion dancing. Flags and drums are prevalent. Statues sitting in sedan chairs receive the spirit of the gods and are carried through town to give their blessings before going to their local temple. A carnival atmosphere reigns for nine days.

In some communities, spirit mediums become possessed by one of the Nine Emperor Gods and respond to questions. Other mediums show their invulnerability to boiling oil and fire, allow themselves to be pierced by hooks or stabbed with spears, or walk on fire.

At the end of the nine-day celebration, an elaborate procession returns to the waters to send the gods back to heaven.

Nine stars to the north seem untouchable.
Meeting nine gods at the shore makes them ours.

Gods who come to earth make for a much richer and more intimate world. If the gods stayed in heaven, it would make conceiving of them or trying to be holy too remote. The fact that the Nine Gods as well as other gods come to earth is essential.

Now, there are already gods on earth—the Kitchen God (p. 8), the God of the Local Land (p. 40), and the City God (p. 160) reside on earth, and other gods such as the Eight Immortals (p. 124) wander around and even interact with people. But to have lofty gods like the Nine Gods come down from the Big Dipper to visit helps us feel closer to them. The gods are not somewhere "up there." They are with us. They hear us. They see us.

Thus, all is continuity. From the living, to the dead, to the divine, there are no divisions in these cosmos. All three levels are treated the same. All are offered food, tea, flowers, wine, and gifts. All are subject to the same rules and consequences. All are a part of Tao.

The nine stars of the Big Dipper are far away and untouchable. Meeting them at the ocean shore makes them an intimate part of our world. Many fear gods because they seem remote and disinterested. Instead, those who celebrate the Nine Gods would have us see the joy and involvement that they represent. These gods belong to the people.

Celebrating their descent to our world and hosting them for nine days removes all doubt. Heaven and earth flow continuously into one another.

Meeting nine gods at the shore makes them ours—then, if pillars tumble, are we sad?

9

The Chrysanthemum Moon

To My Brothers and Sisters

Times are hard: a year of famine leaves the fields bare.
You, brothers and sisters, are strewn from east to west.
Few tend the fields after shields and spears have gone
and war spilled bone and flesh all over the roads.
Dangling shadows burst like thousand-league geese in flight,
old roots were ripped, scattered in ninth moon's autumn ash.
When we each view the bright moon, how our tears will fall.
From five places, let one night unite homesick hearts.
—Bai Juyi (772–846)

The two solar terms within this moon:

COLD DEW

FROST DESCENDS

Exercise 17

COLD DEW

It is cold in the morning and cold in the evening as well. The weather is unstable, with cold air colliding with any lingering warm air. In northern latitudes, frost can appear already.

This exercise is best practiced during the period of 1:00–5:00 A.M.

1. Sit cross-legged and raise your hands overhead, palms pointing upward.

2. Maintaining that position, jerk your body up gently as if trying to keep something overhead. Relax your joints between movements, but keep your arms overhead. Inhale when you jerk; exhale gently when you relax. Repeat fifteen times.

3. Facing forward, click your teeth together thirty-six times. Roll your tongue between your teeth nine times in each direction. Form saliva in your mouth by pushing your cheeks in and out. When your mouth is filled with saliva, divide the liquid into three portions.

4. Inhale; then exhale, imagining your breath traveling to the dantian and then swallow one-third of the saliva, imagining that it travels to the dantian.

5. Repeat two more times until you've swallowed all three portions.

6. Sit comfortably as long as you like.

Through this exercise, ancient Taoists sought to prevent or treat swelling, cold, and damp feelings in the limbs; pains in the body; headache; bulging eyes or yellow eyes; and nosebleeds.

241 | The Moon Is Like a Bow

- God of the **Southern Pole Star** (Shou Xing) descends to earth to review deaths of people
- Fasting day

The First Three Nights of the Ninth Moon

Bai Juyi (p. 273) wrote "Song of Sunset on the River" for this time of the year.

> The sun sets straight away into the water.
> Half the river trembles; half the river turns red.
> How we cherish the first three nights of the ninth moon:
> the dew like pearls, the moon like a bow.

If pillars tumble, are we sad?
Look at the moon that's like a bow.

We've passed the summer solstice, the time when the days are at their longest and the sun is at its most ascendant. We're heading toward the Ninth Moon, Ninth Day, also called the Double Yang or Double Yang Festival. Again, the sense of yang being at its strongest is clear. Yet we have to remember the philosophy of the *I Ching:* what is highest must descend, and what is brightest must dim. That must be why Bai Juyi wrote with such melancholy during this time of the year: he sensed winter approaching. More than that, he bore witness to how all things were descending: like the sun heading into the sea (the line is literally, "With one Tao, the setting sun spreads into the middle of the water"), the year is three-quarters over. Spring, summer, and autumn have passed. In addition, he must surely have been thinking of his own life and the life of people in general: late in life, what is there but descent? Are we not each like the setting sun, plunging on a single path into the sea, setting the water half trembling and half red?

Even at this sad moment, Bai Juyi reminds us of a response beyond grief: "The dew is like pearls, the moon is like a bow." His images—selected with a poet's sensitivity, tenderness, and insight—draw us to the dew that always returns, and that glistens with beauty. Dew indicates life, shows the earth's respiration, and is a reminder that the plants on which it clings will come back to life again, even if the poet is grieving over the ninth moon's first three days.

"The moon like a bow" is the crescent moon. The moon seemingly "suffers" its decay each moon, and yet it returns regularly to full brightness. How delicately Bai Juyi leads us to consider the philosophical implications of this moment. Yes, everything may seem to be in descent, but the poet reminds us to take a longer view of things, to remember again how brightness leads to darkness— but also how darkness must again rise into brightness. Each time we feel sad over the nature of this cyclical existence, we only need to see "the dew like pearls, the moon like a bow."

Look at the moon that's like a bow. When the sun comes up, that is truth.

Morning Truth

 In one religious calendar, this day is designated by the name Zhaozhen, which combines the words for "morning" and "truth." It is a forgotten day for worshipping the eternal.

On the left side of *zhao* is a rectangle with a horizontal line. This represents the sun. The crosses above and below the rectangle stand for the number ten, meaning "perfect and complete." On the right side is the sign for the moon.

The second word, *zhen*, means "genuine," "true," or "real." The top portion alludes to something hidden, mysterious, secret, and minute; other sources say that it represents transformation. The rectangle below represents an eye, and the L-shaped bracket below it symbolizes what might block one's sight. At the bottom are the two diagonal strokes of the number eight, meaning that an eye must look in all directions.

When the sun comes up, that is truth.
With the light, look past what blocks you.

We don't know what the future holds. We are called upon to make decisions that are little more than educated guesses. Our scientists, whether physical, social, political, or economic, are honest when they say that they can only speak in terms of probabilities and not certainties. When all is said and done, we're still required to make decisions in the face of uncertainty.

Perhaps that's why some people throw up their hands and become gamblers. If everything can be taken away in a moment and by chance, it would seem logical that we might also get everything back in a moment by chance. Alas, things don't seem to work that way: there are people actively working to take advantage of us, just as the odds in a casino are stacked in the house's favor.

But the sun still comes up each morning. The moon is in the sky each night. Day follows night, night follows day. Spring, summer, autumn, and winter follow each other in an unvarying sequence. The word "zhen" alludes to seeing something mysterious, secret, and minute. Can it be that the reliability of these sequences is truth?

This is a day that was once set aside to worship the eternal. Who can conceive of the eternal? In our naivete, we just think of a calendar that never ends. One day will be stacked onto the next. Whatever number we have, we will simply add one to that. Yet it's important to look at this in a more subtle way. The eternal is not "out there"— the tail end of a long train that is always having one more car added on to it. The eternal is here and now. The eternal is why the sun comes up each day.

Do you want to know the truth of the eternal? It is in the morning song.

With the light, look past what blocks you: each thing resonates at its frequency.

"Mantra" is a Sanskrit word meaning a sound, syllable, or group of words chanted as part of a spiritual practice. A number of utterances that serve an equivalent function in Chinese practice are *nianjing*—to recite the scriptures; *koujue*—mnemonic chant; *tuoluoni*—religious chant, and a transliteration of the Sanskrit *dharani*; *zhenyan*—literally a "true statement," and also a transliteration of dharani; and *zhouwen* or *zhouyu*—an incantation, spell, or enchantment.

Taoist qigong includes the **Six Healing Sounds** *(Liu Zi Jue),* single syllables one utters in conjunction with exercises to heal and stimulate the organs.

Both Taoism and Buddhism use mantras believing that they will attune a person to the purpose of that mantra. Confucianism emphasizes the memorization and chanting of texts, which in itself becomes a mantra practice, and even poetry is meant to be recited and chanted.

In Taoist temples, the chanting of scriptures—nianjing—is an essential function of the priest and devotees, and each god is worshipped through complex ritual and chanting.

Each thing resonates at its frequency.
Chanting joins our resonance with others.

We don't yet have instruments to measure or detect such things on a spiritual level—we don't even have scientific agreement on what spirituality is—but a person can sense subtle resonances. Being attracted to certain kinds of music, certain colors, people, or places are all a matter of sensing resonance. Pushing a child back and forth on a swing, ringing a tuning fork, the movement of the many machines around us, the impulses of our own heart and nerves—all is frequency. All light and sound is frequency. The accumulated perception of those frequencies is resonance.

Thus, it's reasonable that frequency can be moderated, that we can select frequencies and make use of them. We need to tune ourselves to our own frequencies, adapt to new ones, or investigate other patterns. The point of identifying with a god, for example, is to attune ourselves to the frequency that god represents. Many of the gods are star gods—the light coming to us at night is another reminder that the gods are frequencies.

When we feel "out of touch," "inharmonious," "out of sync," we are subconsciously acknowledging that there are frequencies we are not attuned to at that moment. Likewise, when we feel a part of things, we subconsciously use the language of frequency too. We talk of "resonating" with things, feeling "in sync," and "attuned." All this means that we understand on a subtle level that Tao is a matter of resonance, and that being one with Tao is a matter of tuning in to the subtle vibration felt with the soul.

Chanting joins our resonance with others, no matter how you strike the bell.

God of Music

The **God of Music** (Ling Lun) was a member of the Yellow Emperor's court and is the legendary founder of music. According to the *Annals of Lu Buwei*, the Yellow Emperor commanded Ling Lun to establish a standard pitch for the nation. Ling Lun traveled to the northern slopes of the Kunlun Mountains and selected bamboo that was straight and even. Cutting between two nodes, he blew on it and made that sound the pitch standard. He then cut twelve more lengths of bamboo and carried them to the foot of the mountain.

The calls of six male and six female phoenixes inspired him to designate twelve standard pitches, and he cut the bamboo to the lengths that allowed him to preserve these sounds. He combined the pitches into scales and keys, and he called the tonic note the root of the male and female pitches.

The Yellow Emperor commanded Ling Lun and Rong Jiang to cast twelve bronze bells tuned to the twelve bamboo pipes so that the standard pitches would remain fixed.

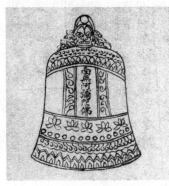

No matter how you strike the bell,
the bell sounds with only one tone.

How long does the music of life reverberate? It began with the first moment and goes on forever, sometimes at frequencies we cannot hear. Yet, each dawn as the sun rises, we see the golden hills shimmer with the rising heat, we see the forests swaying in the breeze, the sparkling streams, the dew trembling on the shaded leaves. All is movement, all is life, and all life shimmers with the intensity that is unique to it.

A bell cannot lie. It vibrates according to its shape and material. That is a certain kind of truth, a truth that is reasonably constant, a truth that can be relied upon. The truths that lawmakers legislate, the truths that academics propound, even the truths that are written in scriptures are made by people and are fallible. They do not have the "ring of truth" that a bell has.

Taoists rely on nature as their template for truth. We walk the hills along the meridians and feel the energy from the earth. We feel the ongoing vibration set in motion by the feet of our ancestors. The Taoists feel the shimmering music of the hills. They feel the truth directly, not through words and writing, which are easy to manipulate or misinterpret, but through direct resonances.

One bell can set off another one. Nature's vibrations set off our inner bells. When we feel that, we know truth: what we receive from the land we feel in our ringing bones.

The bell sounds with only one tone. Answer quick: does every person matter?

245 | Every Part of the Pattern

Heaven's Robe Is Seamless

The *Extensive Records of the Taiping Era (Taiping Guangji),* first published in 978, describes this story:

Guo Han was a handsome young man who lived during the Tang dynasty (618–907). Orphaned at an early age, he lived alone.

Unable to sleep one summer night, he set up his bed in the garden. The moon was bright above him. Just before he fell asleep, he felt a cool breeze and he saw a beautiful girl fly down from the moon.

She introduced herself as an immortal, sent by the heavenly emperor to accompany Guo Han in his loneliness.

Naturally Guo Han could hardly believe his good fortune. Looking at the girl, he saw that she was beautiful and that her clothes were just as alluring as she was. He was astonished that he could not see a single seam in her clothes. He asked her about it.

"Heaven's clothes are not made with needle and thread," she replied. "Heaven's robe is seamless."

Ever since then, the phrase has been used to describe the flawless.

Answer quick: does every person matter?
How about every person who's ever lived?

The answer has to be yes. Every person matters. The bodhisattva vow is to help every sentient being reach enlightenment. That can only mean that every living creature matters.

Every living creature occupies a space and a time in this world. That space and time cannot be occupied by anyone or anything else. There are many strange things in the world, but you can't have two living creatures in one place at one time. They occupy different places.

Every person is special. It has always been so. Therefore, every person in history has been important: the pattern that brings the world to this very moment could not have been achieved in any other way. So let us not say that anyone has been forgotten, because every person played a part in bringing us here today.

The dead matter. The dead are still with us. The dead must be honored. They must not be forgotten, because to forget them is to make ourselves ignorant of huge patches of our past. Each person who walked across this earth had a role. Each of us helps to make this world. Each one of us is essential.

An ongoing pattern is being formed at every moment—and every thought, every movement, every presence alters the world. The universe may have started from one point, but now it is a pattern of nearly infinite complexity. Never mind that our human minds cannot comprehend the pattern. That in no way negates the pattern. It's there, and it's real.

How about every person who's ever lived? Search! Even if, while the storm rages, it obscures.

246 | The Storm

Two Views of Dust

This poem, entitled "Do Not Push the Great Wagon," appears in the *Classic of Poetry*.

> Do not push the great wagon:
> the dust remains dark and deep.
> Do not ponder your hundred worries;
> if you do, you won't escape into light.

One of the most famous Chan poems is the retort to another posted by a more conventionally learned monk. The answering poem was significant enough that the author, **Huineng** (638–713), an uneducated Cantonese woodcutter and rice-pounder in the temple kitchens, became the Sixth Patriarch.

The Fifth Patriarch, **Daman Hongren** (601–674), asked the monks of his temple to express their learning in a poem. The one who wrote with the greatest insight would be ordained as his successor.

The chief monk, Shenxiu (601–674), wrote a poem on the temple wall:

> The body is the bodhi tree.
> The mind is like a bright mirror on its
>   stand.
> Always wipe it diligently
> so that no dust will land.

All the monks thought that this poet should surely become the next patriarch. Huineng was illiterate, but he asked a fellow monk to write what he dictated:

> The bodhi, at root, is not a tree,
> nor does the bright mirror have a stand.
> At root, there is not a single thing.
> What is there for dust to sully?

Huineng used a significant pun on the word "root." In the first line, the word "root" is used both in relation to the tree and to mean the more abstract "originally," or "at the source." In the third line it is usually translated as "originally," or "from the first," but the use of the word "root" continues the image of the bodhi tree (under which Buddha achieved enlightenment).

While the storm rages, it obscures.
When the storm clears, it will reveal.

If everything in the world matters, if all people and all events combine to make the whole of this Tao, then the same is true about what's inside us. Every part of our bodies matters, every part of our mind matters. That's why Taoists lay such an emphasis on health. Everything matters and everything is connected.

The dead are still with us. Our memories are with us too. All of us have pasts that have influenced who we have become. We need to embrace that, acknowledge that our past makes us who we are today. Even if we've seen war. Even if we've been assaulted. Even if we've glimpsed horrors that sliced our hearts open. Even if we suffered at the hands of someone close to us. Yes, that's a part of us too. It cannot be denied. Deny it and you begin a war with yourself.

You exist as an embodiment of a unique order. You are the consciousness created when pure spirit enters this dusty world and is shaped by it. The dust swirls around you. You cannot see past it. It coats you, sticks to you. You don't know where you are. You cannot do anything but strike out in a direction and call that "right." When the dust storm eases a bit, you see that it has abraded your skin, cut you, left red welts and painful scars. The pattern of those marks is unique to you. You accept them. They erode you, revealing the more fundamental form that is within you, the form that can't easily be worn away: the form that is your root.

The storm begins again. Storm, scars, and your blind stumbling are all you. You will never be able to negotiate the storm if you deny them. If you accept them, you turn the storm into your Way.

So accept who you are, as painful as it is, because you have more pain coming, because you need to go out in the dust storm, because you do understand what this is all about.

Go until you realize that there is no body, no dust, and nothing to be sullied.

When the storm clears, it will reveal two fishermen, saved by different gods.

247 | For the Pilgrims

Kusu Island Tua Pek Kong Temple

Kusu Island, only 101,659 square yards (85,000 square meters) in size, is situated off the southern coast of Singapore. Its name, Turtle Island, recalls two fishermen, a Chinese and a Malaysian, who were caught in a thunderstorm and thrown overboard. Each of them prayed to his god for help, the Chinese to Tua Pek Kong (Dabo Gong) and the Malaysian to Allah. Just as they were about to drown, both were saved by a giant sea turtle that carried them to the island. Each fisherman vowed to build a shrine in gratitude. Tua Pek Kong Taoist temple (housing both Tua Pek Kong and Guanyin) and the Kramat Kusu Muslim Shrine stand near one another on Kusu Island. People travel there during the ninth moon to pray for good fortune.

Big Uncle (Dabo Gong) is regarded as a god of prosperity, a curer of disease, and a god who can calm stormy seas and prevent danger while sailing. Meanwhile, people come to Guanyin to ask for children. The temple has a wishing well in the shape of a lotus. People making a wish throw coins at one of three bells inside the well. There is also a wishing tree. Pilgrims write their wishes on a piece of paper, fold it, tie it with red string, and throw it into the tree; the higher their paper lands, the greater the chance that their wishes will come true.

Mosques in China

The Great Mosque of Xi'an (Xi'an Da Qing Zhen Si) was founded in 742 and marks one end of the famous Silk Road. The Chinese-style building that stands there now was built in 1392, with frequent reconstruction after that.

There are other mosques throughout China, including those in Beijing, Guangzhou, Kowloon, Quanzhou, Harbin, and Jinan.

Two fishermen, saved by different gods,
leave one island for pilgrims to find.

Every religion is worthy of respect. All of them can coexist, just as Taoism and Islam coexist on Kusu Island. As we listen to the story of the two fishermen, we can understand that both men called upon their respective gods, both gods responded and saved them, nature—in the form of the turtle—also responded, and each man expressed his gratitude and devotion by building a shrine. No one has ever felt compelled to attack the other shrine, no one has spoken out against two shrines of two different religions being in the same place. Instead, people make peaceful pilgrimage there by ferry and by walking. Many people visit both shrines.

Another mosque stands in Xi'an, a city over two thousand miles away. The mosque was built in 742 during the Tang dynasty, and it has welcomed anyone who wished to understand Islam better. Standing as it does at one end of the Silk Road, it symbolizes the exchange of religion and the communication of peoples across thousands of miles—long before there was any instantaneous technology to facilitate it. People want to exchange ideas peacefully, they want to worship the gods to whom they're drawn, they want to be able to offer comfort to others, and they want to exalt their religions in surroundings that are tolerant and dignified. What more is there to say? We must accept everyone's religious beliefs: we ultimately all want the same spiritual values.

The Taoist pantheon includes thousands of gods to suit different worshippers. In the same way, we need different religions to suit different people. We may never have a time where the whole world has a single religion. For the moment, let us respect each other's gods and each other's religions.

Leave one island for pilgrims to find, just as each flower is born beautiful.

248 | Chrysanthemums

‣ Fasting day

A Courtesan and Taoist Nun

Yu Xuanji (c. 844–869) was a late Tang dynasty poet from Chang'an (now Xi'an). The name "Xuanji" means "Mysterious Principle," a special term in both Taoism and Buddhism. At the age of sixteen, Yu was married as a concubine to an official named Li Yi.

Li abandoned her three years later, and Yu lived as a courtesan before becoming a Taoist nun. A published and famous poet in her own lifetime, she reportedly had a liaison with the poet Wen Tingyun (812–870), is thought to have lived a scandalous and promiscuous life, and was executed for allegedly beating a maid to death. She was only in her mid-twenties at the time.

Forty-nine of her poems survive, collected during the Song dynasty (960–1279) in an anthology of odd poems (including poems purportedly by ghosts and foreigners) and in the seventh-century anthology, *Complete Tang Poems (Quan Tang Shi)*.

This is one of her seven-character poems, "Delayed by Rain on the Double Nine Festival."

> The courtyard is full of yellow chrysanthemums plucked near the fence.
> Two clusters of hibiscus "mirror" as they open.
> At the Terrace of Windblown Hats, delayed by wind and rain,
> I don't know where I can get drunk on golden cups.

There are ambiguities in this poem. In "mirror", do the flowers mirror one another, or are they reflected in the puddles, or does she mean both? Are the golden cups wine cups, or are they the yellow chrysanthemums, or does she mean both?

Each flower is born beautiful.
Why must we insist on the vase?

The imagery of Yu Xuanji's poem is ambiguous. Is the courtyard festively filled with blooming chrysanthemums and hibiscus, as we might expect during this time of year? Or is it strewn with picked flowers or blooms knocked down by the storm? Are the hibiscus mirrored in puddles? Or are some knocked down to mirror ones still standing?

We love flowers, and the chrysanthemums are at their best during this time of year. We call them beautiful, pick them to give to our lovers, show them off to friends, place them on our altars. What we cannot seem to do is to leave them alone to bloom naturally, and to let them play out their lives without interference.

The same was true of Yu herself. Married as a concubine and then abandoned (according to some accounts because of the jealousy of the primary wife), forced to be a courtesan, and finally trying to find refuge as a nun, Yu endured the constraints her society imposed upon women. Like the flowers she observed in this poem, she was unable to live a peaceful life. The rain that detained her was emblematic of the deluge that thwarted her throughout her life. Like the flowers, she was undoubtedly gaped at by ugly faces. Who can blame her for seeking out golden cups—yet, in the poem, even this satisfaction is denied her. Du Fu may drink more cloudy wine (p. 296). Yu Xuanji, the woman poet, cannot even have one sip as she stands blocked by the wind and the rain.

So let us consider the lot of women, and the lot of flowers, and the violence we do to them. Why chant at rosewood altars, fingering jade beads and savoring pear-scented incense, while ignoring the bowed heads of the nuns and the withering chrysanthemums?

Why must we insist on the vase? Let us not trap others, for if disease approaches, we evade it.

Double Nine Festival

The **Double Nine Festival** (Zhongjiu Jie) is a long-established festival, with written records extending to the Han dynasty in the year 25. It is also called the Chung Yeung Festival in Cantonese communities.

The number nine is significant in several ways. It is one of the key numbers of the *I Ching* (designated as a yang number). It is also a homophone for "forever," so double nine symbolizes the doubling of forever—an allusion to long life. Traditional activities for this festival are climbing high mountains, drinking chrysanthemum wine, wearing the dogwood plant *(zhuyu—Cornus officinalis),* and visiting the graves of ancestors.

There are at least two explanations of the festival's origins. The first dates back to the practices of the Han dynasty (206 BCE–220) emperors. They ate rice cakes, drank chrysanthemum wine, and wore the dogwood plant to dispel misfortune and to pray for longevity. This practice was passed to the common people through a woman named Jia Peiling, the maid of Concubine Qi.

Lady Qi (d. 194 BCE) was exceptionally beautiful and was the favorite concubine of Emperor Gaozu (202–195 BCE), the first ruler of the Han dynasty. Upon the emperor's death, Empress Lu (241–180 BCE) poisoned Lady Qi's son to keep her own son on the throne. She then imprisoned Lady Qi, chopped off her arms and legs, blinded her, cut out her tongue, forced her to live in a toilet, and dubbed her the Human Swine. Her maid, Jia Peiling, was dismissed from the palace and married a commoner, Duan Ru. She introduced the palace customs of the Double Nine Festival to the outside world.

A far less bloody explanation is related to a man named Huan Jing. After his parents died from the plague, he went to Zhongnanshan to learn how to combat the disease. A Taoist immortal named Fei Zhangfang gave him a blue dragon sword capable of destroying demons. Huan Jing practiced diligently.

Fei Zhangfang predicted that the plague demon would arrive on the ninth moon, ninth day. He gave his student a bag of dogwood leaves and a bottle of chrysanthemum wine, and urged him to gather people into the hills to escape the disaster.

Huan Jing led his wife, children, and fellow villagers up a mountain. He gave them dogwood leaves to drive off the demon, and sips of wine to keep them from getting sick. When the demon attacked, Huan Jing fought with the blue dragon sword and killed him.

Today, the Double Nine Festival is an occasion to go hiking, appreciate chrysanthemums, eat rice cakes (the word for "cake" is a homophone for "heights"), drink chrysanthemum wine or tea, wear the dogwood plant (still believed to ward off disease), and recite poetry—much of it having to do with the festival of chrysanthemums.

The Republic of China has reshaped the festival into Elders' Day in honor of seniors.

Two Poems Associated with the Double Nine Festival

Li Qingzhao (p. 233) wrote this poem, set to the tune of "Drunk Under the Flower Shadows," and titled "The Double Nine Festival." In the body of the poem, she refers to the festival as "double yang." She knows that the term implies great energy and heat, so the juxtaposition of the burning incense stick and the midnight cold is significant. The word "dissolve" is used to refer both to incense in the second line and to the soul in the eighth. The word "way" in the eighth line is the word "Tao."

> Light mists; thick clouds; melancholy all day,
> The burning incense dissolves in the gold censer.
> It's the good time of double yang.
> Jade pillow, silk curtains, the furniture—
> all are pierced by the midnight cold.
> After drinking wine at the eastern hedge during the yellow dusk,
> some hidden fragrance overflows my sleeves.
> There is no way that does not dissolve the soul.
> The curtain swirls in the west wind:
> I'm wasting like the yellowing flowers.

Another well-known poem, associated with this day is "Double Nine, Missing My Brothers in Shandong," by Wang Wei (p. 174).

> Alone in a strange land as a strange traveler.
> At each holiday, I miss my family even more.
> I'm far away, knowing that my brothers have climbed the heights
> and are placing dogwood everywhere without me.

Tao Yuanming: from Poet to God of Chrysanthemums

The poet Tao Yuanming (p. 106) loved chrysanthemums so much that he grew them in large gardens both in front and in back of his house. People associated him with the flowers and the Double Nine Festival to such a degree that he was made the God of Chrysanthemums. This poem is entitled "Drinking Wine."

> If I wanted to build a hut away from people
> and the clamor of carts or horses—
> let me ask you, sir, can this be done?
> I set my heart in this remote place.
> Picking chrysanthemums below the eastern fence,
> leisurely viewing the southern mountains.
> Mountain and fresh air are beautiful day and night.
> Flying birds gather together.
> In all this, there is true meaning
> not for deliberation—and beyond words.

▶

249 | From the Terrace

- The **Double Nine Festival**
- Festival day for **Dipper Mother**

Wine from a Terrace on Double Nine

This poem, "Climbing High," was written by Du Fu (p. 29) around 766 for the Double Nine Festival.

> Under high heaven, apes wail against
>   the rushing wind.
> White birds circle an islet clearing.
> Leaves drop endlessly, rustling after
>   rustling.
> The Yangtze River surges endlessly on.
> Traveling ten thousand miles through
>   sad autumns, always a wanderer.
> A hundred years with too many illnesses,
>   climbing to the terraces alone.
> So many difficulties, sufferings, and
>   regrets made my temples white.
> Dispirited, I pause again for a cup of
>   cloudy wine.

Dipper Mother

Dipper Mother (Dou Mu Yuan Jun) is the goddess of the Big Dipper. According to legend, she was bathing one day when seven lotuses appeared. A star emerged from each lotus, forming the seven stars of the dipper. She is venerated by both Taoists and Buddhists. Dipper Mother has four faces and eight arms. She represents the universe, gave birth to all the stars, was the mother of Tao itself, and grants protection, safety, and fortune to all who worship her.

If disease approaches, we evade it.
Fate is only what cannot be escaped.

Belief in predestination permeates traditional culture, and yet that does not make it real. Otherwise, why would people ascend the heights on the ninth moon, ninth day, wear dogwood, and celebrate triumph over pestilence? Yes, we're all mired in circumstance every day, but we don't know what can be altered until we challenge it and test it. When the hero Huan Jing destroyed the disease monster, he was not accepting fate, he was challenging it. We must keep pushing against circumstance. We must seek health over disease. We must always try to escape disaster.

So on the Double Nine Festival, we climb the mountains in an outing that is more celebratory than it is urgent, more charming than harrowing, more enjoyable than anxious. We recite poetry, wear dogwood, picnic, admire the chrysanthemums, and drink chrysanthemum tea or wine. We toast one another and wish each other good health. By doing that, we signal our deep belief that we can challenge fate.

There is no better way to see the future than to climb the heights. The place that helps you see disaster coming is also a good

Dipper Mother. Dr. Meierhofer

place of refuge. Throughout thousands of years, people have escaped to the mountains, knowing that the remoteness of those places would slow or prevent pursuit. The Double Nine Festival is a good time to find that mountain in your life—a place of both celebration and escape.

Fate is only what cannot be escaped: ignorantly, I once worshipped with many objections.

Beholding

The Statement of Hexagram 20 in the *I Ching* depicts a person at an altar who is about to begin a ceremony. A crowd watches this sacred moment:

Behold! The hands have been washed,
but the offering has not yet been made.
Be sincere and dignified in appearance.

The commentary of the *I Ching* states that this moment should transform all who see it, and that when we "behold the spiritual Tao of heaven, we see how the four seasons proceed without error."

Wise words have always been cherished. The *Triword Classic* (p. 216) says:

Recite them by mouth,
and keep them in your heart.
Do this in the morning.
Do this in the evening.

Ritual in Changchun Guan, Wuhan.
© Saskia Dab

I once worshipped with many objections.
Now I worship with many agreements.

The doubter said: "When I was young, I was devout. Then I became cynical after I saw holy people doing the very things they preached against.

"So I had nothing but objections when I went to worship. Did the priest believe his words? Were these words really divine? Weren't the building and the altar nothing but wood, metal, plaster, and paint? How could one priest I knew to be an alcoholic really bless someone else? How could a monk seen lurking surreptitiously with pornographic magazines say anything authoritative about purity? How could the teacher who stuttered and made mistakes and failed to answer questions about the scriptures awaken Tao in students? Oh, yes, when I was young, the poor way that spirituality was taught meant that every moment of worship shredded my heart with doubt.

"I'm older now. I've been on a long journey, wanting to feel and perceive Tao for myself, away from the monks and priests. I've been on decades of pilgrimage. As Du Fu says [p. 296], it's been 'a hundred years with too many illnesses,' of 'many difficulties, sufferings, and regrets.' I can feel Tao for myself. I don't have to rely on priests and monks.

"Reluctantly, I went back to the temple for the funeral of an old friend. Unexpectedly, I felt the spirit enter into the building—yes, that old building of wood and plaster. I felt not a single objection to the priest's words—yes, those same words I had heard since childhood. I looked at the architecture, and realized that it was a three-dimensional metaphor for the inner journey. I looked at the worshippers who had come—the same ones that I had once judged as deluded, old, and weak—and now only saw the devoted. I felt the power of the spirit rise in me with the same force that I had learned to feel on my own.

"Running away from the temple meant I discovered that Tao could be found within oneself and in walking by the rivers and lakes. I still see the imperfection in the temple, outrageous, perhaps even criminal, but I feel compassion and acceptance now."

Now I worship with many agreements—even at the funeral as we say goodbye.

251 Gone but Still Here

Cultivate It in the Family

The *Classic of Rites* was first compiled by Confucius (p. 281) but took its current form during the Han dynasty (206 BCE–220).

> Affection for parents leads to respect for ancestors. The respect for ancestors leads to the honoring of the lineage. Honoring of the lineage leads to the unification of the clan. Unification of the clan leads to the rigor of the ancestral temple. Rigor of the ancestral temple leads to reverence for the land and grain. Reverence for the land and grain leads to love for the Hundred Family Names (meaning, all people).

In Chapter 54 of the *Daodejing*, Laozi writes:

> What is well constructed cannot be lifted.
> What is well surrounded cannot be taken.
> Children and grandchildren sacrifice without cease.
> Cultivate that in the individual, and his virtue will be true.
> Cultivate it in the family, and their virtue will be plentiful.
> Cultivate it in the village, and its virtue will be lasting.
> Cultivate it in the nation, and its virtue will be abundant.
> Cultivate it among all under heaven, and their virtue will be universal.
> Therefore: use the self to observe the self, and the family to observe the family.
> Take the village to observe the village, and the nation to observe the nation.
> Take all under heaven to observe all under heaven.
> How do I know about all under heaven? By this.

There is a parallel sentiment in the *Classic of Filial Piety (Xiaojin)*, which dates from about 400 BCE:

> The average man uses the family to examine himself. The worthy person uses the state to examine himself. The sage uses all under heaven to examine himself.

At the funeral as we say goodbye
we see how one returns to family.

Many families have family burial grounds, and in old families, the most recently dead join those who have died centuries earlier. Two people who were never alive at the same time are now together for centuries to come. Individuals come and go, but the family survives.

We realize that we are not alone, that we come from a long and unbroken line of people. We realize that we cannot live for ourselves alone, because we must give and help the next generation. In time, we can come upon a great truth: we are not single people; each of us is one in a line between people that have been here and those yet to come. This line is impossible without us.

There is no need, then, to fear alienation. There is no need to scramble for meaning. We have known the simple truths for thousands of years: birth, a good life working on this earth, death, and a rebirth in those who come after us. We come from the dust of this earth, fashioned by our parents out of nothing, and when we die our bodies go back to the earth, scattered into countless particles. However, not a single particle goes out of existence. They all flow back into the great mass of movement that is this world, and they combine, and recombine, and become part of everything, refashioned, made to live again. In time, every speck of ourselves will be reborn.

So we are one person in our family line. On a larger level, we are one among all the particles of this world. We are temporarily assembled in this form, and then we are miraculously reassembled into other forms. Every part of us comes back.

We see how one returns to family: just begin from yourself. Count outward.

252 | Counting Outward

Begin from yourself. Count outward.
Know the world that turns around you.

You're here, yes? What is the next most important thing after that?

Maybe you'll say your health and your mind. After all, few of us want to be kept alive in a coma.

You might pick your spouse and children next.

Then maybe your house and the rest of your family—siblings, parents, grandparents, uncles, aunts, cousins.

And your friends.

Your work. Your city. Your state. Your country. Soon, you're at the entire globe. In your mind, you leap off this planet. This solar system, this galaxy, yes, you can now see the entire universe with its countless stars. You're holding the undefined limits of this universe in your mind.

You can put this all together in spiritual equations:

you + family + community + country + world = 1
heaven + earth + you = 1
body + mind + spirit = 1
life + death = 1

Understanding Tao is as easy as understanding that all is an equation, and the sum is always *one*—meaning wholeness. If we subtract from one side, then we diminish the whole. Ignore the body, for example, and the whole should be diminished. Ignore death, and the whole must be affected.

And if we subtract you from the world, then the entire world should be affected. In the same way, when you ignore your place in your family or community or even the world, then you miss out on the one whole.

Whether you count from yourself outward, or whether you count inward to understand the central equation of your life, you matter. You are the one.

You counted. And because you did that, you know you count.

Know the world that turns around you. Give. Some give gold, but to give blood is precious.

© Ying Fry

• The day Guan Yu became a god

Giving Up One's Life for Loyalty

This day marks the naming of Guan Yu (p. 17) as the God of War.

Guan Yu was in charge of Jing Province. Sun Quan (182–252) formed a secret alliance with Cao Cao (p. 88) and sent troops to seize Jing Province while Guan Yu was fighting elsewhere. The two generals that Guan had left to guard the province surrendered.

When the troops with Guan Yu heard that Jing Province had been seized by Sun Quan, they begin deserting. Guan retreated to Maicheng. Sun Quan's forces surrounded him.

Guan Yu tried to break through the siege but was ambushed and captured. He was executed on Sun Quan's orders after refusing to renounce his loyalty to his sworn brother, Liu Bei (p. 17).

Some give gold, but to give blood is precious.
Some give blood, but to give love is precious.

Guan Yu represents the epitome of the warrior: loyal, intelligent, strong, skilled, heroic. In his day, a general did not stay in the rear: he battled the other general in a duel, or sought him during the clashes. Each warrior fought for what his flag represented, and he did it personally.

It seems obvious to say that a warrior puts his or her body at risk during battle. Nevertheless, it's an important place to start this inquiry: what do we have to give?

A warrior gives dedication, courage, bodily strength, and, if necessary, life itself. How truly precious that life is.

A farmer gives dedication, patience, and strength to grow the food we eat. Although farming is not as risky as warfare, a farmer nevertheless commits to growing food year after year. How truly precious that life is.

A mother gives dedication, courage—her very body to give birth and to care for her child. A mother will give her life for her child. How truly precious that life is.

When we want a measure of what's valuable in life, we do not use gold or fame. We use body and life. We respect those who sacrifice for others. For life is the greatest value we know. Those who fight to protect it are honored.

It is life that is the greatest measurement for life.

Some give blood, but to give love is precious. How impressive when the man in the news says, "I'm no hero."

254 | Why Do We Rescue?

· Fasting day

More Important than Propriety

For the Confucian scholars, propriety was nearly absolute. However, this exchange between Mencius (p. 63) and Zhun Yugun illustrates an exception:

> Zhun Yugun said, "Is it the rule that men and women shall not allow their hands to touch in giving or receiving anything?"
> Mencius replied, "It is the rule."
> "If a man's sister-in-law is drowning, shall he rescue her with his hand?"
> "He who would not rescue a drowning woman is a wolf. For men and women not to allow their hands to touch in giving and receiving is the general rule; when a sister-in-law is drowning, to rescue her even with one's hand is a special necessity."

Who Else Will Go There to Save You?

A man asked the Chan Buddhist master **Zhaozhou Congshen** (p. 15): "Where will you go after this life?"

"I will go to hell," the master replied.

"How can that be? You've led such a virtuous life! How could you go to hell instead of paradise?"

"If I don't go to hell, who else will go there to save you?"

The man in the news says, "I'm no hero."
He is beyond heroes—he is a saint.

What does it mean to save someone? We have firefighters, police, search and rescue teams, paramedics, doctors. We have priests and religious people. We have counselors, teachers, social workers. All of these people, in one form or another, dedicate themselves to saving others. It's worth considering what "saving" means. There can be no saving unless there's agreement that there are dangers and there is life to be saved.

We indulge in many philosophical speculations, saying that we must all find our own way, that no one should interfere with how we want to live, that we each want to be free to create our own paths in life. Yet we have all these people who are there to save others when there is trouble—and people in trouble rarely refuse help. That means that people who save others are truly blessed, and that we agree that people should be saved.

We all understand that life should be saved.

We all understand that people should be saved from injury.

We all understand that people should be saved from suffering.

If we agree that we should save people from death, injury, or suffering, then why should we ever threaten to inflict such trouble ourselves?

Whenever we see someone in trouble, we should do the simplest and most human of acts—we should extend our hand.

He is beyond heroes—he is a saint who shows you the mountain has many trails up.

255 | One Religion from Many

‣ Fasting day

Three Laughing at Tiger Brook

This Song dynasty painting depicts Taoist Lu Xiujing (406–477) on the left; Buddhist monk and First Patriarch of the Pure Land Sect, Huiyuan (334–416), in the center; and poet (and therefore Confucian scholar) Tao Yuanming (p. 106) on the right.

Huiyuan never went beyond a certain brook on Lushan for fear of a tiger that lived on the other side. One day, however, he was so deeply engrossed in conversation with his two friends that they crossed the brook without realizing it. They heard the tiger's roar, but they were not attacked. They shared a good laugh together, and the story became a symbol of the harmony between Taoism, Buddhism, and Confucianism.

"Three laughing at Tiger Brook" is also an idiom referring to deep friendship and laughter at the world's troubles.

The mountain has many trails up—
but all trails lead to the summit.

People fight for country, for family, for honor, to defend themselves and their loved ones from danger. It's instinctive, and it's even necessary at certain times. But we should not fight over religion.

Fighting is awful, filled with contradictions and excess. It is impossible to control. Violence is the opposite of religion. Violence is never sacred, never holy, never right. If we're called upon to defend what we love, we do so with sadness: we must fight, wrong though it is, but the violence demeans what we love.

How is another religion a threat? Unless a religion has madly declared war on us or others, what is there to resent about it? If another religion has more adherents than ours, is that any reason for alarm? If another religion worships a god that is not ours, is that any cause for rancor? If another religion has rules that we bridle against, is that any cause to seek its destruction?

Every religion seeks the sacred. Every one of them advocates moral living, kindness and generosity, triumph over our faults, and a journey toward the divine. We have different religions because we start out from different places. It's important that we do not fall into squabbling and fighting along the way. Contests between religions or persecution of those of other religions only destroys everyone's journey.

The holy belongs to no nation, no king, no people, no clan. The holy does not power or profit. The holy has no skin color. It has no gender. It is eternally present. Every religion is to be respected. Every religion is to be honored.

Honor your own religion. Honor yourself. Honor tolerance and humility. Then, all religions will reach the holy summit that much more directly—and with no fear of the tigers along the way.

But all trails lead to the summit. How the world's lines radiate from us.

Exercise 18

FROST DESCENDS

Areas prone to frost now experience it in earnest. Farmers are concerned about freezing and frost damage to their crops.

This exercise is best practiced during the period of 1:00–5:00 A.M.

1. Begin by sitting with your feet stretched out before you. Bend your knees and grasp your feet. Slowly and gently push your legs straight, stretching all parts of your body. Relax and pull your knees toward your chest.
2. Exhale as you push; inhale as you bend your leg. Repeat thirty-five times.
3. Sit cross-legged and face forward. Click your teeth together thirty-six times. Roll your tongue between your teeth nine times in each direction. Form saliva in your mouth by pushing your cheeks in and out. When your mouth is filled with saliva, divide the liquid into three portions.
4. Inhale; then exhale, imagining your breath traveling to the dantian and then swallow one-third of the saliva, imagining that it travels to the dantian.
5. Repeat two more times until you've swallowed all three portions.
6. Sit comfortably as long as you like.

Through this exercise, ancient Taoists sought to increase flexibility and prevent or treat swelling in the leg; joint pains; headache; muscular or nerve dysfunction; swelling in the lower body.

256 | Our Web

• Birthday of the God of Looms

Gods of Weaving

This is the birthday of the now-forgotten God of Looms (Jishen). The worship of two gods of weaving and looms—Zhinu, the **Weaver Girl** (p. 221), remembered on the Double Seven Festival, and **Silkworm Mother** (Cangu Nainai)—are more contemporary and show the centrality of making cloth.

Silkworm Mother was a legendary empress and the wife of the Yellow Emperor (p. 4). According to tradition, she discovered silk and invented the silk loom in the twenty-seventh century BCE.

In one account, a silkworm cocoon fell into her tea and expanded from the heat. Leizu (her given name) unwrapped the silk and was able to stretch it across her garden. She eventually invented the silk reel to join the filament into threads for weaving, as well as the loom.

Archaeological explorations have uncovered a cut silk cocoon that dates to between the thirtieth and fortieth centuries BCE. Scraps of silk have been found dating back to 2700 BCE.

The Happy Insects

Spiders were called *ximu*—"happy insects"—in ancient China. It was believed that they brought happiness in the morning and wealth in the evening. Spiders in paintings are thus symbols of happiness. Here is one story explaining what the spider augurs.

One morning, an official woke to find that a chestnut-sized spider had woven a web in the door frame. "This is a happy insect!" he exclaimed. "Happy insects drop from Heaven, happiness drops from Heaven!" A few days later, good news came: the emperor issued an order of general amnesty and promised advancement to all officials.

The world's lines radiate from us
like the silver webs of spiders.

The spiders build webs in the bamboos, flowers, and eaves. Even in ruined doorways or on broken railings, they suspend silvery lines. The gossamer strands are nearly invisible to us, but their every length is known to the spider. The slightest trembling along any line is instantly communicated to the spider, that lord of the web. Everything that the spider needs will float by; the spider builds its web in Tao and Tao provides everything—just as Tao provides for each of us.

There are twelve regular meridians and eight extra meridians in the human body. These are pathways of energy.

There are lines in the earth where energy travels. Traditionally, Taoists wandered the land, walking these lines, absorbing the power of the earth in the process.

If one studies Tao deeply, then it's possible to see that the glowing lines of light in the body connect to the glowing lines of the earth;

that the glowing lines of light in the body connect to the glowing lines of our family;

that the glowing lines of light in the body connect to the glowing lines of every person in this world;

that the glowing lines of light in the body connect to the glowing lines of the spirit body;

that the glowing lines of light in the body connect to the glowing lines of heaven;

that the glowing lines of light in the body connect to the glowing lines of all events, past, present, and future;

that the glowing lines of light in the body connect to the glowing lines that lead back to the Source.

When you move, the world moves with you. When the world moves, your body moves. This world would not be the same without you. You are unique, important, and vital in all that happens. Therefore, who you are, what you think, what you feel, and the aspirations you have flow into the world instantly.

Like the silver webs of spiders, we are connected, even as each person is a container.

Three Treasures

The **Three Treasures** (Sanbao)—also called the Three Jewels, Three Refuges, or Three Gems—are the three things in which a Buddhist takes refuge:

Buddha (Fotuo) The historical Buddha; one's individual Buddha nature

Dharma (Fa) The teachings of all Buddhas

Sangha (Seng) The community of Buddhists

Each person is a container
hiding three jewels you can't see.

Each person is a container with jewels inside. When we go through life in our ordinary ways, we only see the outsides of the containers—wrapped by resumes and social networking, accents, colors, and shapes. We know that there are three jewels inside every container, but we don't normally look for them. We look at the outside of the containers, sometimes making life-or-death decisions based solely on those perceptions.

If you've ever bought jewelry, you've set aside the box or wrapping it came in, no matter how fancy it might have been. You know that what's important is the jewelry inside. Why don't we do the same thing with each other?

The Three Treasures that each human being has inside are as priceless as the Three Treasures within any other person. We cannot discard the containers that represent us, but it is important to know that the jewels are there, and that we should cherish and help one another accordingly.

Hiding three jewels you can't see, no part that makes the whole can be removed.

Reclining Buddha, Jade Buddha Temple (Yufo Chan Si), Shanghai, depicting the moments prior to Buddha's physical death. Steve46814

▸ Fasting day

Zhuangzi's Hunchback

He was a hunchback. His five viscera were squeezed upward, his chin was pushed into his navel, and his shoulder was higher than his crown. An ulcer on his crown pointed to the sky. His breath came and went in gasps.

Yet his mind was at peace, and he was untroubled. He limped to a well, saw his reflection, and exclaimed, "Look how I'm made!"

Another person asked, "Do you hate your condition?"

"No, I am not bothered. If my left arm were transformed into a rooster, I'd herald the time of night. If my right arm were transformed into a slingshot, I'd find an owl to roast. If my rump were transformed into a wheel and my spirit into a horse, I would ride away."

No part that makes the whole can be removed:
from genitals to brain, heart to spirit.

A belief that seeks to deny any part of a person can never succeed, and yet accepting all parts of ourselves is a challenge. We must be the people who eat and go to the toilet, and we must be worthy enough to take Buddha's place on the altar itself. We must be the one who wants a mate, who lusts, who craves—and yet we must be holy enough to be a Taoist recluse on the mountain.

We must be the people who make mistakes, stumble, forget, and get tangled in confusion, and yet we must have the intellectual clarity of the greatest Confucian scholar. We are all these at once: the foundations of our temple stand in filthy muck even as our spires touch heaven. There is no top without the bottom.

We can never be holy denying who we are. Yes, Taoists speak of purification, but this is not the purification of denial. It is the purification of cleaning what will get dirty again. It is the purification of letting things die and be reborn. It is the purification of letting the wheel of all things turn, turn, turn—understanding that for a wheel to be perfectly round is to keep every single point of its circumference equidistant from the center.

From genitals to brain, heart to spirit—to hear a cry arouses
compassion.

259 | Awakening Compassion

• Commemoration day for **Guanyin**

The Lotus Sutra

In Chapter 25 of the *Lotus Sutra* (*Miaofa Lianhua Jing;* translated from Sanskrit into Chinese by Zhu Fahu in 268), titled "The Gateway to Every Direction," Buddha explains why Guanyin (p. 58) is called the Hearer of Sounds:

If innumerable hundreds of thousands of myriad sentient beings who experience suffering hear of Bodhisattva Guanyin and wholeheartedly chant her name, she will hear them immediately and free them from their suffering. As long as people call upon her, they will find that:

one who enters a great fire but calls upon her will not be burned.

one who is caught in a storm on the ocean will not be drowned.

one attacked with sticks and swords will find them broken to pieces and will be rescued.

one bound with fetters and chains will find their bonds broken and will be freed.

one subject to sensual desires will become free from those desires.

one who is overwhelmed with anger will be freed from such anger.

one who is confused will be freed from confusion.

a woman wanting a baby boy will bear a baby of merit and wisdom.

a woman wanting a baby girl will bear a beautiful baby of merit and wisdom who will be loved by all sentient beings.

anyone who holds the name of Guanyin, pays homage to her, and makes offerings even for a moment, earns merit that will never be extinguished even after hundreds of thousands of myriad eons.

To hear a cry arouses compassion.
To arouse compassion brings forth healing.

Guanyin is the bodhisattva who hears the cries of the suffering. If, as Buddha observed, all of life is suffering, then all of us cry out at one time or another.

Those who cry alone are unheard and plunged into even greater misery. It brings us some relief to know that someone hears us. It would be even better if our sufferings were alleviated immediately. But even if our pain continues, we want to know that someone hears, and, we hope, that someone will help us.

Guanyin is such a being. She listens to the cries of everyone in this world, discerning those cries with the clarity of someone in a sealed chamber hearing only one person. It is said that the other gods are too lofty, too involved with their cosmic roles, too reluctant to come in contact with the polluted human world. Only Guanyin, in her holiness, is willing to listen to the cries of anyone.

She does not judge. She does not condemn. She does not reject. Who among us, in our wretchedness, does not need such understanding and compassion? Who among us does not long for such gentle kindness? Who among us does not wish to be accepted simply for who we are?

If we pray to Guanyin, we are her devotees. If we are her devotees, then we cannot help but want to emulate her. She is a noble paragon of what we could be too. We can listen to the cries of others. We can accept others for who they are. We can eschew being judgmental, cruel, and cold.

We can each take the vow to relieve suffering, to help all other people become Buddhas. There is no magic to it. Simply listening and being kind transforms even hell into paradise.

To arouse compassion brings forth healing when a goddess loses a drop of blood.

Guanyin, Lu Dongbin, and the Lady at the Water's Edge

The **Lady at the Water's Edge** (Linshui Furen) is the patron deity of spirit mediums, ritual masters, and lesbians; she protects women during pregnancy and childbirth and protects all children. She is most popular in Zhejiang, Fujian, and Taiwan. Her birthday is celebrated on the fifteenth day of the first moon (p. 20).

When the people of Quanzhou were unable to raise the money to build a bridge, Guanyin (p. 58) appeared as a beautiful maiden and stood on a boat, offering to marry any man who could throw a silver ingot from the shore and hit her. A large number of ingots missed her and landed in the boat, until Lu Dongbin (p. 125) gave supernatural power to a merchant's attempt. A speck of silver powder severed a strand of Guanyin's hair, which fell into the water and floated away.

Guanyin bit her finger and vanished. A drop of blood fell into the river. The distraught merchant hung himself.

The drop of blood was swallowed by a woman washing clothes in the current, and that woman, Lady Ge, gave birth to Lady Linshui in 767. The hair became a female white snake that ravished handsome men and devoured beautiful women. The dead merchant was reincarnated as a man named Liu Qi and was destined to marry Lady Linshui.

At first, the beautiful Lady Linshui refused marriage, fleeing to Lushan to study Taoism with the Immortal Xu Xun. However, she eventually obeyed her parents and married Liu Qi.

At that time, the people of Quanzhou suffered from a terrible drought, and they asked her to perform rituals to bring rain. During the effort, she suffered a miscarriage. The snake ate the fetus, but Lady Linshui's blood became the life-giving rain that saved the people. She killed the snake with her sword just before she died.

Lady at the Water's Edge

When a goddess loses a drop of blood,
years must pass before the river runs clear.

A bodhisattva like Guanyin enters into the popular imagination, becomes mythologized and mixed with local superstitions and beliefs, is borrowed for whatever the community needs, and, above all, becomes a center of imagination. The Lady at the Water's Edge reflects a need to see Guanyin in both magical and heroic modes. That the Lady at the Water's Edge is destined to die fighting the snake that was originally born from a part of Guanyin expresses the idea of the yin-yang struggle between good and evil, and the conflicts we all carry within ourselves.

In the meantime, the Taoist, Lu Dongbin, is the agent of change, of mischief and disruption. Had he not interfered, the people would have gathered enough silver to build the bridge, and it would have only been a charming story. But instead, it turns into a struggle that transcends reincarnation, consumes the lives of several people, and leads to considerable pain and suffering. Is the Taoist, then, the troublemaker? Or is he merely fulfilling a duty that only he perceives and that Guanyin secretly understands?

Finally, notice the direction of the story. The people want to build a bridge across a river. However, all the story takes place downriver. The drop of blood and the hair float downstream, and that is where Lady Ge is washing. With the inevitability of water flowing downstream, the merchant kills himself and is reincarnated, just as water goes through its cycles; the female white snake, whose form is analogous to the river, kills people; and Lady Linshui must marry the reincarnated merchant. That momentum, accompanied by rain—more water—brings the final climax, during which the lady suffers a miscarriage—more water, more blood, more loss of life—until she kills the snake and her sacrifice brings life-giving rain.

But what about the original need of the story, the need to cross the river? In other words, what about the direction perpendicular to the thrust of the tale?

No matter how much life involves us, we must not forget the original direction we want to take.

Years must pass before the river runs clear. Those who are skeptical must keep searching.

261 | Skepticism

Laozi on Skeptical Reaction

The first part of Chapter 41 from the *Daodejing* reads:

> When superior persons hear of Tao, they
> implement it diligently.
> When middling persons hear of Tao, they
> take some of it and leave some of it.
> When inferior persons hear of Tao, they
> laugh loudly.
> If they did not laugh without stop, it
> would not be Tao.

The word Laozi uses for "person," *shi,* also means "scholar," "ranking official," and "gentleman."

The Great and Small from Zhuangzi

A bird named the *peng,* which has a back as great as Taishan (p. 44) and wings like clouds, flew upward on a whirlwind as if it were pushing the very skies upward.

A quail laughed and asked, "Where is it going? I spring up and come down in a few fathoms, and fly about the brush and bushes. This is perfect flying. Where is that bird going?"

Zhuangzi comments: "This shows the difference between the small and the great."

Those who are skeptical must keep searching.
In time, all searching must end in belief.

It's all right that people are skeptical of Tao. There isn't any one path that is right for every person. Each path is meant to be walked. Could you and another person walk in exactly the same place? As soon as one person moves aside for the other, a new path is created.

In the same way, beliefs must be tailored to each person. Assertions that there is one true god, or one true doctrine, or one true path are only true if we add, "For you." There is one true god, one true doctrine, and one true path—for you. Once you find it, you will know, and no one else's belief or path, no matter how glamorous or powerful, will make you want to abandon your own.

Many people don't believe that a human being can be spiritual. They don't believe that someone wants to take the raw material of the words, numbers, and images we use in daily life and transform them into worship of the holy. They would rather dismiss all this.

Charlatans and corrupt leaders don't help. Each day, there is some new revelation that a trusted leader has abused followers. Each day, it turns out that money is the root of poor spirituality. Aren't we used to that? We all try to shop shrewdly, realizing that there is hype and deception in the marketplace. How much more true that is of the spiritual path.

Yet the presence of corruption and deception does not negate the possibility of purity and truth. We must still strive for purity and truth each day—with complete faith.

In time, all searching must end in belief—only then can we wield four treasures to be expertly handled.

262 | Ink Drop

The Four Treasures of the Study

The Four Treasures of the Study *(wen fang si bao)* are brush, ink, paper, and inkstone.

Four treasures to be expertly handled:
ingredients combined make one treasure.

If you've never had the chance to try Chinese ink painting, it's worth considering the challenges.

The brush is flexible and pointed. It's as a fine an instrument as a superb violin: in the hands of a master, it produces beautiful work that looks effortless—but in the hands of someone inexperienced, the brush will not produce beauty by itself. It will splay frustratingly in all directions, it will run dry, or it will flood the paper. A brush well wielded is usually held perfectly plumb—just as the spine of the person holding the brush must be perfectly straight and plumb. Only this righteous attitude makes good strokes. Only a straight brush centers perfectly.

Well-prepared ink has an opaque and tactile presence that poor ink does not have. The ink must be of good ingredients, and then it must be properly ground on an inkstone. We grind our ink ourselves, all the while contemplating what we're about to paint, mixing our very intention into the black. Used correctly, the best-quality ink will express every tone and color that we may need.

Good paper is a necessity. Without it, the ink sinks dully into short and broken fibers. If the paper is good, the ink flows into it: the ink is the lifeblood, the paper is the waiting tissue. Just put good paper next to a sheet of bad paper and brush the same thing onto each sheet: you'll see for yourself.

The inkstone should be fine-grained and even in texture. Perhaps some of the stone's molecules go into the ink, giving it that much more body. A bad inkstone receives the ink poorly, robs the ink of moisture, and leaves uneven particles. A good inkstone brings one into direct contact with the smooth rock. One can even feel the river from which it came and the maker who selected it. All this goes into the ink.

Four treasures make one drop of ink. But that drop lands in the heart of the one who uses the four treasures.

Ingredients combined make one treasure—but even then, must a good painting "look like what it is"?

263 | What Is It?

Why Should I Worry Whether It Shows Likeness or Not?

Ni Zan (1301–1374), also known as the Hermit of the Cloud Forest (Yunlin Jushi), was considered one of the Four Great Masters of the Yuan dynasty (1271–1368). His work differs from most Chinese paintings in that the human figure is minimized or nonexistent. Ni Zan was more attracted to landscape and trees.

The Yuan dynasty was Mongol, and the indigenous Chinese had little place in the government. Unable to find success, many scholars turned to Taoism and its renunciation of worldly pursuits. Art historians feel that the great landscape painting of Ni and his many contemporaries inspired people to become mountain hermits.

In 1364, Ni Zan said: "Bamboo painting releases the untrammeled feelings in my breast; that is all. Why should I worry whether it shows likeness or not?" In saying this, Ni Zan was echoing Su Shi (p. 140), who had written: "Anyone who talks about a painting in terms of likeness deserves to be classed with children."

At another time, Ni painted bamboo during a drunken night. The next day, someone criticized the painting as not resembling bamboo at all. "Ah, but a total lack of resemblance is hard to achieve!" he laughed. "Not everyone can manage it!"

Must a good painting "look like what it is"?
A painting's itself. Don't ask, "What is it?"

It's the vulgar phrase that continues to be uttered in museums and galleries: "What is it?" How can one really ask that question? The answer is obvious: it's a work of art.

Art does not need to be a depiction of anything. In fact, that's a ridiculous role for art in a post-photographic world. Now that we can upload videos and cell phone images from anywhere in the world in a matter of seconds, we don't need painting to depict events.

We need painting to show us what a photograph cannot. It's not the job of a painting to be something else. It's the job of a painting be a painting.

Chinese painters solved this problem hundreds of years ago with landscape painting. While some paintings were depictions of recognizable places, many were imaginary travels through an improvised landscape. In other words, to those who might ask again, "What is it?" the answer is that it is an artist's mental journey.

A painting's itself. Don't ask, "What is it?" Even you can put one stroke after another.

- Fasting day

Painting Legs on a Snake

"Drawing a snake and adding legs" is an idiom indicating misplaced cleverness, unnecessary embellishments, and superfluous additions.

According to the story from *Strategies of the Warring States (Zhan Guo Ce;* compiled third to first century BCE), a family in the state of Chu gave a pot of wine to the stewards after a memorial ceremony for ancestors had been concluded. However, there was not enough wine for all the stewards, so someone suggested that each of them draw a snake on the ground. The first one to complete a good likeness would win the pot. They all agreed.

One man finished first and grabbed the wine. However, when he saw that the others were still working, he decided to continue drawing, and ended up adding legs to his snake. While he was still working, another man finished his drawing and took the pot.

"A snake has no legs," the second man said. "It's not a likeness, and you're still drawing." With that, he drank the wine.

You can put one stroke after another, but you cannot take back even a dot.

Traditional ink painting has this one crucial dynamic: nothing can be corrected. Drop ink onto paper as absorbent as any tissue paper and you know that you cannot ever erase or paint over that mark. Life is that way too: every stroke you make is indelible. What will you paint?

At first, it seems like a simple thing. Anyone can pick up a brush, hover over a piece of paper, and drop the brush down, pulling it and twisting it here and there.

Oddly enough, the central task for even an experienced artist is no different on the ten thousandth painting than the first one. Pick up a brush, load it with ink, and put it to the paper. The child's painting reflects a child's mind. The mature artist's painting reflects the mature artist's mind. True, the mature artist may have learned quite a bit of art technique—the words "art" and "artifice" are related—and all of that is on display in the work. At the same time, the artist's mind is no less exposed than the child's mind is in the child's painting.

In the Asian style of ink painting, there is no taking things back. One acts with all the force of one's personality and the results are there to see. Painting in this way is a tremendous tool of self-discovery, a way of externalizing one's inner state so that one can really learn about oneself. One puts down one stroke after another, not to correct, erase, paint over, or patch, but really just to *be* during that act of creation.

But you cannot take back even a dot, especially when the artist is the audience.

265 | The Artist and Audience

Laozi on Dimness

This is a portion of Chapter 21 of the *Daodejing*:

> The form of great virtue is to follow Tao only.
> As for Tao's substance, it is shadowy and faint.
> Faint, shadowy, yet within it there is an image.
> Shadowy, faint, yet within it there is substance.
> Deep and dark, yet within it there is essence.
> Its essence is very real—within it is something to be trusted.

The artist is the audience.
The actor, the judge, the learner.

"Oh, I just want to paint for myself," the sincere amateur might say, embarrassed to show his or her work for scrutiny. Doesn't that mirror how so many of us think about ourselves? We fear that others will really discover us to be bumblers despite fine clothes, a fancy car, or an impressive bank account. We are afraid because we've grown up brutalized, mocked, belittled, and humiliated at every turn. Therefore, to pick up a brush and to display oneself on a piece of paper is an act of courage. If you don't believe that, try it for yourself. Make a painting and show it to someone.

There is not a single artist, living or dead, who has escaped criticism, derision, or—the most dreaded of all reactions—indifference. Yet the dedicated artist goes on for years, enduring the reactions of the audience, striving to realize a vision often sensed dimly and waveringly. Praise and fame come fleetingly, and to only a few artists in each generation. Most artists end up searching for a niche, whether it's painting scenes for tourists, becoming a factory worker decorating pottery, or decorating theater sets.

Every artist wants an audience. Some get it, some don't. But there's one member of the audience that every artist has. That's the artist, him- or herself.

Now, one doesn't simply paint to please one's audience. One paints to communicate. One doesn't go look at art simply to be entertained or pleased. One looks at art to observe and learn.

"I just want to paint for myself." Every artist does. Every artist paints to communicate, above all, with a single person who is there to observe and learn.

The actor, the judge, the learner: it takes a lifetime to be an artist.

266 | The Old Artist

The Eccentric Artist

Bada Shanren (c. 1626–1705) was born as Zhu Da, the son of a Ming dynasty prince, Zhu Quan. He is regarded as one of the great painters of his time, and among the great painters in all of Chinese history.

Bada Shanren was raised in an aristocratic family and learned painting and writing in his childhood. However, a number of disasters led to the collapse of the Ming dynasty before Bada Shanren turned eighteen. There was a monetary crisis, unusual cold weather in the time now known as the Little Ice Age, and widespread famine and poverty. During a rebellion and invasion of Beijing in 1644, the last Ming emperor hung himself. Seizing that moment, the Manchus invaded China from the north and declared the Qing dynasty. Bada Shanren fled and took shelter in a Buddhist monastery.

In the following decades, the Qing dynasty gradually consolidated its control of China. Confident that it was firmly established, the Qing became tolerant of former members of the Ming. Bada Shanren cautiously left the monastic life after forty years, became a professional painter, and adopted his pseudonym that is hard to explain: it literally means "Mountain Man of the Great Eights," but he signed his characters so that they looked like the words "laugh and cry." He suffered several mental breakdowns—perhaps at least one of them feigned.

Bada Shanren is known for the unusual quality of his brushstrokes, his eccentric use of large expanses of blank space, the expressive splashing of ink for lotuses, and unusual calligraphy.

This poem is entitled "No One, No Two."

There is no One that can be separated.
No Two that can be doubled.
If you suck up all the West River,
he can explain Tao to you.

It takes a lifetime to be an artist, and no artist ever truly retires.

"How long did it take you to paint that?"

The correct answer is: "All my life."

The individual piece of art is one in a sequence of many pieces. It could not have been made one work earlier, and the next work could not exist without this present one. A painting takes all the skill of an artist to make, and that skill develops year after year.

In addition, an artist often spends years trying to comprehend what it means to be an artist. What do you do with the visions you have? How faithful will you be to them? Will you trust them? Being wildly successful is not necessarily a help—it's one more non-art factor to balance. Being a neglected failure is not necessarily a deterrent—it, too, really has nothing to do with the art. All that matters is understanding what it means to be an artist over a lifetime.

Therefore, artists continue to see and pursue the possibilities of life. They may not even see looming death as a narrowing of their future. They only know that they want to keep creating, and they spend every day looking beyond limits. An artist doesn't ever accept or preserve the status quo, for that is artistic stagnation. An artist only thinks of transcending limits. An artist forever lives outside the boundaries.

Artists search for order, meaning, and a future exactly in all the places ordinary people won't go. That's why it takes a lifetime to be an artist. That's why artists never really retire: you can't get them to come in from the limitless expanse to tend a tiny flame by the hearth, no matter how old they might be.

And no artist ever truly retires from the thought, "I can't draw."
Then nobody can.

"I Can't Draw"

Using a Finger to Illustrate a Finger

This passage is from Zhuangzi. The complicated and confusing language is his mocking of philosophers who make their points by logical argument:

> Using a finger to show that a finger is not a finger is not as good as showing what a finger is not by using what is not a finger.
>
> Using a horse to show that a horse is not a horse is not as good as showing what a horse is not by using what is not a horse.
>
> Heaven and earth: one finger. The ten thousand things: one horse.
>
> Is this so? Is what is not so, not so? Tao moves and gains completion. Things are named and thereby defined.... Everything has its substance and place.... whether we take a stalk of grain and a pillar, or take grit and compare it to Xi Shi, the immense changes unfathomably.
>
> Through Tao all is made one.

Xi Shi (b. 506 BCE) was one of the famous Four Beauties of Ancient China. It was said that fish in a pond were so dazzled by her beauty that they forgot to swim, and sank.

"I can't draw." Then nobody can.
"I can draw." But few truly do.

People say, "I can't draw."

However, everyone *can* draw. Most people don't draw because of arrogant criticism inflicted in childhood. Discouraging a child from drawing should be added to the list of abuses hurled at the innocent.

Drawing at a professional level is another matter. While every drawing is a valid act for that moment in time—and is the sincere expression of exactly who that person is at that moment in time—drawing in the context of the art world presents many more difficulties. It is competitive, it is a dialogue with all other art that has gone before, it is a tension among the many issues of skill, technique, materials, criticism, formal consideration, psychology, and artistic vision. The ground becomes not just a place to depict an image but an arena for all the issues with which an artist must struggle.

People say, "I can't draw." That fear happens to everyone, even professional artists as they pick up the pencil.

Everyone can draw.

Few overcome all the issues facing an artist who finally says, "I can draw."

"I can draw." But few truly do, asking, "How many strokes to complete a painting?"

▸ Fasting day

If People Speak of Destiny . . .

Mozi (c. 470–391 BCE), was a Chinese philosopher who argued against both Confucianism and Taoism. His work emphasized each person's thought and action over the Confucian sense of ritual and propriety, and he believed that true self-knowledge came from reflecting on one's own successes and failures. His school of thought, called Mohism, was suppressed in the Qin dynasty (221–207 BCE) and had largely died out by the Han dynasty (206 BCE–220). However, much of Mozi's thinking had been absorbed into mainstream thought.

In his book, the *Mozi*, he declared that he would judge whether fate existed by whether people testified to it. He asked if anyone had seen such a thing as fate since the beginning and concluded that no one had. The records of neither feudal lords nor sage kings recounted observations of fate.

Mozi noted that there was significant social change whenever a new king came to power, and that people had to make great adjustments. Sometimes the results were good, sometimes bad. He concluded: "By what method can we call this fate? If people speak of destiny, it's false."

How many strokes to complete a painting?
Prefer your hand to a soothsayer's words.

Answer quickly as you are about to make a painting: is it predestined?

Some people might say it is: that every stroke is already known in some other dimension and that you're merely painting as you were meant to paint.

If that painting is bad, or if you spoil it by a mistake, was that "meant to be" too?

Maybe we're thinking about this the wrong way. The future is certainly determined in a general fashion—once you get all the materials for a painting, set up a place for them, and think about a painting, then you really ought to make a painting to make all the effort worthwhile. Even so, the painting you're going to make isn't already existing somewhere else and merely waiting to be reproduced.

Pick up the brush, then. Put down one stroke. Look at it. Add something to it afterward. Two lines make an image. But when you add a third line, it changes the appearance of the first two. And so on. As the painting progresses—even if it's being made over months or years—each subsequent stroke changes how we see all the strokes that went before it.

We only know that the painting is done when we know we've laid down the last stroke. No one knows in advance how many strokes it will take to get to that last one.

Prefer your hand to a soothsayer's words, because the mind determines everything.

269 | A Mind, Used Correctly

▸ Fasting day

A Mind Set on Learning

One of Confucius's most famous reflections is recorded in the *Analects:*

> At fifteen, I set my mind on learning. At thirty, I stood firm. At forty, I had no doubts. At fifty, I knew heaven's commands. At sixty, my ear obeyed the truth. At seventy, I followed what my heart desired—without transgressing what was right.

The mind determines everything—
if it accounts for everything.

The mind is powerful. What you concentrate on, what you meditate on, what you fix your mind on, will come true.

But a snake won't become a crane no matter how much it concentrates. An apple seed won't become a pear tree no matter how much you wish it to be so. And an old man won't become young again no matter how much he wishes for it.

However, an athlete can become a better one. A scholar can become a better one. All of us can be better than we are if we set our minds to it.

The artist is used to imagining what's never been imagined before. The work is the expression of that imagination. Perhaps, in the beginning, it can "be anything you want it to be," but in the end, it will take more and more concrete form. It goes from being "anything" to being "something." Artists have to learn to live with that. Sometimes, the result is joyful. Many times, the result is disappointing. So we try again.

The mind determines everything. As soon as the painter begins painting, that mind must be fully engaged: it will view and must accept what it makes.

If it accounts for everything, the mind opens when a strand of cold, pale blue parts the gray mist.

270 | A Cold Hue

› Fasting day

Xue Tao

Xue Tao (768–831; her name, "Tao," means "wave") was one of the most popular female poets of the Tang dynasty. About one hundred poems of a known 450 survive.

Xue was a courtesan early in her life, attracting admirers through poetry and music. When she became the hostess for Wei Gao, a local military governor, her popularity grew even more. Wei died, but his death became an unexpected opportunity: he left her a substantial inheritance. Xue bought her freedom and became a Taoist nun.

She remained highly regarded for her poetry. It was said that any poet completing a new work wanted to first show it to the emperor—and after that, to Xue Tao. Poets such as Bai Juyi (p. 273) and Du Mu (p. 75) eagerly collaborated with her on poetry and music.

In addition to these accomplishments, Xue Tao made her own artisanal calligraphy paper with a pink tint and fine texture, so calligraphers, artists, and poets had a reason to seek her too. The well Xue used and a memorial to her are in Wangjiang Park, Chengdu.

The following poem is "Autumn Spring" (as in, a spring of water).

Cold color opens a strand in the mist.
Mysterious tones of ten silk strings flow
    from afar,
and with them, sentimental thoughts
    weigh me to my pillow.
For someone anxious, not even half a
    night's sleep.

A strand of cold, pale blue parts the gray mist.
The chill air stills: angle of crying geese.

The air is colder, and the snows will be coming in the weeks ahead. The year is three-quarters gone. The blazing sun of summer has given way to a wan disk hidden by gray haze. Passions that blazed like forest fires across thousands of acres are only kept alive in a stone hearth to wait for the joy of another season. Poets write of such times with drooping chins and fingers trembling around the wine pot. But today, it's different.

As a cold strand of blue opens, it's possible to see that there's relief to the stilling of passions. There's peace now that the harvest is done. Good or bad, the course of this year is known and can be accepted. We have had to unpack the winter clothing from trunks, we have prepared stacks of firewood, we've checked our homes to ensure that they will withstand the winter ahead. Outside, squirrels and mice bury caches of food. With little left in the way of fruit or insects, the fox begins to hunt small rodents. Yes, the branches are turning bare, and much of the brush has died into thickets rattling in the wind, but we understand that. We accept it. We are grateful for it.

One person in the night may be playing on silken strings, sending music into the black air. Another may toss on her pillow, worrying about the coming day.

The clouds cross the sky and the moon is dark. Summer sun has its charms, but winter darkness can be a time to rest, a time to store and heal.

The chill air stills: angle of crying geese. Kneel at the sacrifice, where no one confuses money and paper.

10

The Excellent Moon

Moonlit Night

Surely the moon shines in Luzhou tonight;
you will watch it alone from your chambers
far from me. Our beloved boy and girl
will wonder why you can't forget Chang'an.
The fragrant dew will have soaked your chignon,
your jade arms will be cold in bare moonlight.
When will we lean in an open window
paired in brightness, traces of our tears dry?
— Du Fu (712–770)

At the time of this writing, 756, the poet was imprisoned by the
An Lushan rebels in Chang'an (the ancient name for Xi'an).

The two solar terms within this moon:

WINTER BEGINS

SLIGHT SNOW

Exercise 19

WINTER BEGINS

The leaves have withered, yellowed, and fallen. Migrating birds fly south, and insects crawl into holes. Animals prepare for hibernation. Storms come, bringing strong gusts of wind and biting cold.

Metabolism slows down for human beings too, and the body's energy can become dormant. People take care to eat nutritiously and build their resistance to the cold.

Huangdi on Winter

In the three moons of winter,
all nature stores and conserves.
Water freezes, the earth cracks.
Nothing moves; there is little power.

Go to sleep early, wake up late.
Wait for daylight.
Keep your will hidden and restrained.
In hiding, stay solitary.
In hiding, reach near-cessation.
Once winter passes, warmth will come
    again.
Don't release your essence, keep your
    skin covered.

In the winter season, follow the Way of
    conservation.
Act against it and you will injure your
    kidneys
and spring will bring impotence.
Cultivate growth to stay young.

This exercise is best practiced during the period of 1:00–5:00 A.M.

1. Sit cross-legged and hold your outstretched hands in front of you, palms facing forward.

2. Slowly turn your neck to one side as if you're trying to look behind you. Repeat on the other side. Inhale when you turn; exhale gently when you return to the center. Repeat fifteen times on each side.

3. Facing forward, click your teeth together thirty-six times. Roll your tongue between your teeth nine times in each direction. Form saliva in your mouth by pushing your cheeks in and out. When your mouth is filled with saliva, divide the liquid into three portions.

4. Inhale; then exhale, imagining your breath traveling to the dantian and then swallow one-third of the saliva, imagining that it travels to the dantian.

5. Repeat two more times until you've swallowed all three portions.

6. Sit comfortably as long as you like.

Through this exercise, ancient Taoists sought to prevent or treat illness caused by toxins; feelings of fullness in the torso and limbs; lack of limberness; insufficient saliva; pallor; nausea; hiccups; poor digestion; headache or swelling in the face and head; hearing problems; and vertigo.

- The **Ancestor Sacrifice Festival**
- Birthday of the **King of the East**
- Birthday of the **God of Oxen**
- **Fasting day**

Ancestor Sacrifice Festival

The Ancestor Sacrifice Festival (Minsui La) is a time to offer grain and the harvest to one's ancestors. Ceremonies are held at home and at cemeteries. Beyond giving thanks and sharing the harvest, people also burn paper offerings of symbolic money, clothes, and other goods so that their ancestors will be well provisioned as the weather turns cold. This is also a day of atonement when Taoists propitiate 36,000 evil spirits.

The King of the East

The King of the East (Donghuang Dadi or Dong Wang Gong) is the deification of **Emperor Mu** (p. 235). In addition to representing the yang, or male, element in relation to the Queen Mother of the West's (p. 235) yin or female element, he is the keeper of the register of all the immortals.

God of Oxen

The God of Oxen (Niuhuang) is also called the Golden Ox (Jinniu). Sixteen feet tall, with two large horns, a twisted mouth, and pointed ears, he wears a red gown, golden helmet, and armor and carries a three-pointed sword. Farmers hang his image in stables and make offerings to him to protect their herds from pestilence.

Vmenkov

No one confuses money and paper:
true value lies in heartfelt offering.

Cai Lun (c. 50–121) invented paper. A folktale explains how his brother, Cai Mo, and his sister-in-law, Hui Liang, took his method and opened their own paper-making factory. Unfortunately, their product was inferior. No one bought it, leaving them with a factory and warehouse filled with bad paper. Hui Liang thought of a plan.

The couple staged Hui Liang's death at midnight. Cai Mo burned money made from his paper (in those days, money was usually gold or silver ingots or copper coins) over her coffin and wailed, "My paper was no good, and so you became ill and died. I must burn it all to ease my sorrow." His neighbors rushed to him and tried to comfort him as he burned stack after stack.

Late in the night, however, Hui Liang's voice came from the coffin: "Raise the lid! I'm home!" She frightened everyone when she leaped out, but she quickly explained, "People in the underworld use paper as money. My husband sent me a fortune. I gave it to the officials and the King of Hell released me."

"But how could I have sent you money?" asked Cai Mo, pretending not to understand.

"The paper you burned here turned into money in the underworld! They never saw so much!"

"If that's so, then we can help our ancestors too!" Cai Mo picked up more paper and burned it, announcing that it was now going to his relatives in the afterlife.

Believing that Hui Liang had come back to life, and eager to send money to their own ancestors, the people bought paper from the couple's factory. Within two days, the stock was completely sold, and their business thrived.

This story took place on the first day of the tenth moon, and people still go to the tombs to burn paper money. While the deception was wrong, the story does show that a product that is bad in one context might be perfect in another. Today, one can still buy paper offerings in many Chinese markets and in any Chinese community.

True value lies in heartfelt offering to better gods who began human.

272 | Gods Once Human

▸ Birthday of Cao Guojiu

Cao Guojiu

Cao Guojiu, one of the Eight Immortals (p. 124), is an old, bearded man dressed in royal robes and carrying a pair of clappers. The younger brother of the mother of a Song emperor, he was ashamed of how the nobility killed the common people so lightly and so often. Disillusioned, he retreated to a mountain cave to practice Taoist austerities.

Eventually, he happened to meet Han Zhongli (p. 126) and Lu Dongbin (p. 125), who tested him immediately.

"Sir! We hear you are cultivating yourself. What are you cultivating?"

"I am cultivating Tao," replied Cao.

"Where is Tao?" Han and Lu asked.

Cao pointed upward.

"Do you mean heaven? Where is heaven?"

Cao pointed to his heart.

The two immortals laughed. "Your heart is one with heaven and heaven is one with Tao. You have indeed arrived at a profound understanding."

Then they imparted the Taoist secret of being in perfect harmony with nature and invited him to join them.

Better gods who began human
instead of gods who rule supreme.

Many Chinese gods began as human beings. Laozi himself was a historical person who became deified. Mother Ancestor (p. 98); Guan Yu, the God of War (p. 17); Lu Ban, the God of Carpenters (p. 193); and all the Eight Immortals (p. 124) are just a few of the many others who are worshipped today as gods.

Perhaps this is just a macro- and communal extension of ancestor worship. Perhaps it happens because seeing how people became holy encourages us to believe that there are higher levels to human existence.

Cynics will say that this only proves that religion is fantasy, and a use of myth to shape societal attitudes. Others may object to the idea that humans can become gods: they want gods who are supreme, who sprang from stars rather than mud, or better yet, who themselves created all we know. They will say that only gods who are all-powerful, not limited to a skill like carpentry or weaving, are good enough.

In general, the Chinese and Taoist attitude is not to proselytize. If you're curious about the gods and temples, people will happily invite you in. If you're not interested, people will hardly thrust pamphlets in your face or invade your house with their gods. So the right way to understand the gods is simply to meet them and see if their stories resonate with you. If they do, then you've gained something, as you would from any other happy encounter with another. After all, we walk by thousands of people a day, meet hundreds at social gatherings, and probably have contact with dozens in the course of business, shopping, and recreation. How many of those people become friends?

Gods who were once human demonstrate that everyone is fallible. Gods who were once human show us that it's important to accept our role in life, embracing our powers and understanding our limitations. Gods who were once human encourage us to think of ourselves in terms beyond the ordinary. Can we be people who are willing to help every other person as a god would?

Instead of gods who rule supreme, be a god yourself— for no one claims a body lives forever.

273 | Living Forever

• Celebration of the **Three Mao Brothers**

The Three Mao Perfect Sovereigns

The Three Mao Perfect Sovereigns (Sanmao Zhenjun) were the brothers Mao Ying, Mao Gu, and Mao Zhong (c. second century BCE; p. 93). All three learned the ways of Taoist cultivation, settling on Juqushan to cultivate Tao, pass on their teachings, and heal the sick. The mountain's name became Maoshan because it was so strongly associated with them.

Over the centuries, Maoshan became an important Taoist center, with Shangqing, Lingbao, Zhengyi, and Maoshan (p. 93) sects building temples there. War heavily damaged the temples during the first half of the twentieth century, but many have been extensively rebuilt.

No one claims a body lives forever.
Immortality lies in memory.

We should not cling to this body. It ages. It declines. It can be invaded by disease. It can be destroyed.

Although there are some legends of people ascending to heaven bodily, they are legends only. Philosophically, it does not make sense. It is the spirit, not the body, that lives forever. It lives forever because we are all aspects of the one holy spirit and we rejoin that one spirit. Laozi says, "Return to the source."

So even someone who is an immortal or a god eventually must surrender his or her body and enter Tao. Wasn't that very thing hinted at in the story of Li Tieguai (p. 225)? In a more spiritual state he was outside his body. Eventually, his spirit could have merged with Tao, and then he would not have returned to this mortal world.

Some believe that all three Mao brothers attained immortality. Each of them was supposed to have risen into heaven, but then they returned to teach and heal others. Like Li Tieguai, they had to be here physically. But they're gone now, and no one claims to have seen them: their immortality, then, is only made possible by the memory and reverence of others. Their bodies are gone, but they live on in the minds of those who learn about them.

Therefore, there are only two ways to "live forever": by being remembered for generation after generation, or by returning to Tao.

Immortality lies in memory: belief is powerful.

The Buddha Before the Empress

According to one religious calendar, this incident happened on this day in 460.

Empress Wenming (442–490) visited a temple for the dedication of an important statue. She had been one of the concubines of Emperor Wencheng (440–465) of the Northern Wei dynasty, but became empress dowager and regent when the emperor died.

We do know that she was responsible for the imperial shrines at the Yungang Grottoes, and the statue reportedly showed a bodhisattva seated on a white elephant. Such iconography suggests that the statue might have been **Samantabhadra** (Puxian Pusa), who is depicted in the *Lotus Sutra* (p. 307).

During the ceremony, one of the priests unexpectedly went forward from the crowd and sat before them like a god. All were astonished by his bearing and believed that he was a Buddha.

Yungang Grottoes

The Yungang Grottoes are a series of Buddhist temples near Datong. They are part of a long tradition of temples cut from live rock. Other examples in China are Longmen and Mogao, and there are still earlier examples of rock-cut architecture in India, such as the Barabar Caves, Ajanta, and Ellora temples.

Belief is powerful.
Belief is vulnerable.

Why did that priest go forward during the dedication ceremony? Surely breaking rank and boldly striding before the empress was improper, even a crime. However, because of his bearing and, apparently, his beauty, the assembly was awed. Perhaps the spirit really did act through him as its corporeal instrument. In that case, it was a grand confirmation of devotion.

On the other extreme, it could have been a political ploy. Although Empress Wenming was considered devout, and was eventually buried in a mausoleum with honors extraordinary for any empress in Chinese history, she was also ruthless. She overthrew the regent Yifu Hun to become regent herself over her stepson. When her stepson, as emperor, executed her lover, she had him assassinated in turn and assumed regency over his son, the new emperor. Certainly, an orchestrated show of "divine presence" would have been in her favor.

But let us take the tale at face value. Let's say that the priest went forward for some mystical reason. Let's say that the empress and her retinue were astonished and moved, as the story holds. All the religious feeling that the empire could muster had been brought to bear on the Yungang Grottoes, beautiful temples carved out of live rock rather than constructed. Such belief demanded a supernatural event.

What is belief, then? Is it necessary for religious feelings? Is it open to manipulation, to our "seeing what we want to see?" Do we make it happen, out of our sheer desire?

The Yungang Grottoes were carved out of live rock. How the belief of the rock carvers must have contrasted with the belief of the empress.

Belief is vulnerable, so use eyes that never close.

Bodhidharma

Bodhidharma (Putidamo) was an Indian Buddhist monk who traveled to China during the fifth to sixth centuries. He is called the First Patriarch, because he was the first person to bring Chan Buddhism to China. The sect would eventually spread to Japan, where it became known as Zen.

Bodhidharma is also credited with initiating the physical training of monks in the **Shaolin Temple,** the eventual source of Shaolin martial arts. Little is directly known about him through reliable documentation. Most of what is said is traditional belief and legend. Nevertheless, he was a real person and an important part of the Chan–Zen lineage.

Bodhidharma was a Tamil prince from southern India's Pallava Empire, and his probable place of birth was Kanchipuram in Tamil Nadu. His arrival in China is uncertain, but he was active during the years of the Northern Wei dynasty (386–535).

The *Record of the Buddhist Monasteries of Luoyang (Luoyang Qielanji),* compiled in 547, mentions Bodhidharma traveling to the temple Yongning Si. Tanlin (506–574) wrote a biography of Bodhidharma stating that the master was a southern Indian and the third son of a great king of the Pallava dynasty. Tanlin also mentions two disciples, Daoyu and Huike.

Bodhidharma and Chan Buddhism

While Bodhidharma is called the First Patriarch, he is also regarded as the twenty-eighth patriarch of a lineage that goes back to the first transmission of an unspoken understanding from Buddha to **Mahakasyapa** (p. 82). Therefore, every person initiated in Chan or Zen Buddhism, even today, can trace his or her lineage back through a long line of masters to Bodhidharma, and from there back to Buddha himself.

Famous stories of Bodhidharma are embedded in the *Blue Cliff Records*:

When Bodhidharma first came to China, he visited Emperor Wu of Liang (464–549).

"What is the first principle of the holy teachings?" asked the emperor.

"Emptiness and no holiness," replied Bodhidharma.

"Who stands before me?"

"There's no knowing that."

Since the emperor did not grasp his meaning, Bodhidharma departed for the neighboring kingdom of Wei.

In another version of this story, the emperor says, "I have ordained many Buddhist monks, built monasteries, had sutras copied, and commissioned images of Buddha. What merit do you think I have accumulated?"

"None," Bodhidharma answered. "Good deeds done with worldly intent may bring good karma, but no merit."

"So what is the highest meaning of the noble truth?"

"There is no noble truth. Only void."

"Then who is standing before me?"

"Your majesty, I do not know."

Legend holds that when Bodhidharma traveled to Wei, he crossed the Yangtze River on a reed. He settled outside the Shaolin Temple near Songshan (p. 93), where he faced a wall in meditation for nine years.

Although the date of his death is uncertain, his legend describes Ambassador Song Yun of Wei seeing Bodhidharma holding one shoe some three years after the monk's death. The ambassador asked Bodhidharma where he was going, and he replied, "I'm going home." Song asked why Bodhidharma only had one shoe.

"You'll know why when you reach the Shaolin Temple, but don't say you saw me or you'll meet with disaster."

The ambassador promptly informed the emperor, who had him arrested for lying. Exoneration only came when Bodhidharma's grave was exhumed: it was empty except for a single shoe. ▶

• Birthday of **Bodhidharma**

Mythical Origin of the Tea Plant

Bodhidharma (Putidamo) is known as the Wall-Gazing Brahman because of his meditation method of quieting the mind *(anxin)*.

A popular legend depicts Bodhidharma falling asleep while meditating. Angry at himself, he cut off his eyelids; tea plants sprang up from the ground where the eyelids fell. This was used to explain the wakefulness that comes from tea and why monks drink tea to help their meditation.

Bodhidharma in Brief

Bodhidharma is said to have given the *Lankavatara Sutra (Lengqiejing;* first translated into Chinese in 443) to his disciple Huike. This sutra sounds the keynote to Chan and Zen Buddhism's "transmission outside the scriptures":

> Anyone who teaches a doctrine that is dependent upon letters and words is a mere prattler, because truth is beyond letters, words, and books.

Bodhidharma declared that there were two ways of entering Tao: reason—learning through study—and conduct—consisting of four rules:

1. Requital of hatred: suffering in this life is the result of misconduct in previous existences.
2. Adaptation: the mind does not increase with gain and does not decrease with loss.
3. Nonattachment: all suffering springs from attachment, and true joy springs from nonattachment.
4. Dharma (Buddhist teaching): understanding the dharma so there is no stain from sentient beings and one is free of the stain of the self. (Others do not affect you, and you aren't partial to yourself or a burden on others.)

Use eyes that never close
and rock walls become glass.

Bodhidharma sat in meditation while facing a wall for nine years. The usual assumption is that he had iron-strong discipline, and that he refused to be distracted by anything worldly. Yet, as with so much received tradition, it's worth reconsidering and contemplating this story. Are there other meanings?

First, let us assume that Bodhidharma found this practice deeply rewarding. Most of us would go mad sitting before a wall for nine hours, let alone nine years. The Wall-Gazing Brahman, however, must have found this fulfilling. What did he feel and what did he see that made his activity worthwhile? Surely he was looking inward at an inner universe more compelling than the world outside his cave.

Second, we know that this was a method called anxin—bringing peace to the heart and mind. Again, tradition teaches that when we withdraw from the clamor and turmoil of the outer world, then the inner mind can be at peace. Bodhidharma's rock walls smothered all sound and light. The cave remained at a constant temperature. Sunlight, rain, wind, and snow could not bother him. As soon as the slightest stimulation is felt—even if it's the slightest breeze—the mind and body must react. Bodhidharma allowed his mind to find peace by staying in a quiet place.

Third, why was this man, who was the twenty-eighth person in an unbroken line leading back to Buddha, still meditating? He was already a master when he came to China. He had—at least according to legend—the ability to cross the Yangtze on a reed. But he still practiced. Doesn't that show that there is always more to experience, no matter what our abilities and accomplishments?

Bodhidharma sat facing a wall for nine years. During that time, the wall was no impediment to him. But it blocked the outer world while he sat on the brink of the infinite. He could see boundlessness where we can only see a boundary.

And rock walls become glass: who can see the mountain of books' summit?

‣ Festival of the heavenly teachers

The Heavenly Teachers

Listed in one religious calendar, this day honors those who teach in heaven. The presence of such teachers in the iconography is significant, showing that beings who are supreme must continue to learn. Even the Jade Emperor (p. 13), who governs all the cosmos, should continue to learn from those disinterested in power. Laozi is named as one of the foremost of heavenly teachers.

The Mountain of Books, the Ocean of Knowledge

Couplets are often posted on both sides of doors, expressing cherished beliefs. A famous couplet is:

The mountain of books has a road, but it takes diligence to climb.
The ocean of knowledge has no shores and it's bitter work to sail the boat.

The couplet has been attributed to Han Yu (p. 55). A similar idiom is "Mountain of Tao, sea of learning," meaning that learning is as high as a mountain and as wide as the ocean.

Who can see the mountain of books' summit?
What boat can sail the ocean of knowledge?

The mountain of books keeps growing, thrusting up higher with the pressure of the knowledge that builds beneath it. It heaps up as new books are published at an increasing pace, and it spreads until it blots out every horizon of understanding. Yet the sheer daunting height of this mountain does not deter people. It inspires them to climb the slopes, each step a rewarding thrill, each pause yielding a new vista, each ledge a place of memory and perception. We can't see the summit. We don't know how long the climb is, and in some ways, we neither care nor want to reach the top. All we know is that every day on that mountain satisfies our longing to know, and every day on that mountain promises to reveal more the next day. Yes, it take diligence to climb the mountain of books, but the mountain itself rewards such diligence.

Just as the summit of the mountain remains unseen, the ocean of knowledge has no shores. How can any one person truly find every shore of a great ocean? It's bitter work to sail the boat, and yet the waves have their own hypnotic allure. The thrill of learning with one's entire body and mind is a delight unequaled anywhere else. Something akin to madness drives us to the shores and compels us to hoist the sails.

How blessed we are to have teachers to show us how to climb the mountain and sail the ocean. We must do this ourselves, and yet without their guidance, we might fall off a cliff or be swamped and drowned.

Apparently, as the festival to the heavenly teachers shows, even the gods want to climb the mountain and sail the ocean. In spite of their powers and their exalted immortality, they still want to learn.

Isn't this the most important of godly virtues to emulate?

What boat can sail the ocean of knowledge, no matter how clever our plans and work?

277 | Explaining Meaning

Zhaozhou's Oak Tree

Chapter 37 of the *Wumenguan* records a monk's question to **Zhaozhou Congshen** (p. xxix):
"What is the meaning of Bodhi-dharma [p. 325] coming to China?"
Zhaozhou's answer: "The oak tree in the garden."
Wumen Huikai (p. xxix) adds this comment:

If one sees Zhaozhou's answer clearly, there is no Sakyamuni Buddha before him and no future Buddha after him.
Words cannot describe everything.
The heart's message cannot be delivered in words.
If one takes the words literally, one will be lost.
If one tries to explain with words, one will not attain enlightenment in this life.

No matter how clever our plans and work,
we keep building and rebuilding meaning.

Every culture has tried to explain existence. Some of those explanations are so good that we continue to study them today. Yet in each culture, and in each generation, we continue to adjust the explanations. Some reduce everything to a biological explanation: we exist to pass on our genes. Some explain misfortunes as spurs for us to seek the divine.

Taoism, Buddhism, and Confucianism have no shortage of ideas either. Some Taoists find meaning in seeking immortality. Some Buddhists find meaning in the Four Noble Truths (p. 117), the drive to become Buddhas, and the desire to save all sentient beings from suffering. Confucians find meaning in moral order, filial piety, governmental service, proper rule, and reverence for nature.

All of these ideas must be honored, but one cannot help but notice that we go on tinkering with the explanations. Clearly, we have not found an explanation that satisfies everyone.

In the past, we assumed that there was a supreme being, a supreme emperor, a supreme spiritual master. Today, we honor each person's individual experience. There is no one to dictate the absolutely "right" way, because there isn't one way that is right for every person in this world.

Every person builds his or her own meaning in life, just as we each live in our own homes. We tinker, we remodel, we adjust. Sometimes we tear the house down altogether or just move to another one. Some live in palaces, some live in schools, some live in huts. Some are "homeless."

Is there an alternative?

We keep building and rebuilding meaning, and still mystery will happen to you.

278 | What Can You Keep?

▸ Fasting day

The White Horn Cup

According to an old religious calendar, a scholar named Zhang Yu noticed something odd in his courtyard on this day in 818. The air first filled with a strange fragrance. Soon, several men dressed in dark clothes appeared, leading seven or eight beautiful girls to a feast in the courtyard. A group of musicians sang and played on both string and wind instruments.

Zhang Yu cried out, "Fox spirits or demons!" The entire assembly vanished with his cry, but Zhang rushed forward and managed to grab a wine cup that he tied to his clothes. Then he lost consciousness.

In the morning, there was no sign of the assembly—but he awoke to find the white horn cup still tied to himself.

Mystery will happen to you,
but what will you keep of it?

We can't explain everything that happens to us. Sometimes mundane or insignificant events are later revealed to be pivotal points in our lives. At other times, we strive with every bit of ourselves, only to collapse at the foot of the monument we hoped to create. One day we meet a person who will be our friend for life, but most days we pass through the crowds on the street, never to see them again.

Old stories of fox spirits, demons, and supernatural music may seem remote, but if we really examine this day, we are reminded that we cannot really understand everything that happens to us. However odd the events that happen to you, what will you keep?

Some spiritual people declare: "You cannot hold onto anything permanently!"

The Taoists agree, but then they ask, "Can we make a difference holding onto some things temporarily?" This is where Taoists and other spiritual people part ways, because the Taoist is willing to make use even of what we ought not to do. We are taught not to hold on to things in life, but when life is odd, you might still wrest something from it.

Strange things can happen in this life. When they do, what will you rush forward to grasp?

But what will you keep of it when you can't know the outcome of every act?

279 | Living with Mystery

Like Cooking Small Fish

Chapter 60 of the *Daodejing* addresses the ruling of a nation, but whether one is governing a country or simply trying to govern oneself, the principle is the same:

> Ruling a great state is like cooking small fish.
> Use Tao to govern all under heaven and demons will have no supernatural power.
> It's not that the demons have no supernatural power,
> It's just that their supernatural power will not harm people.
> Just as their supernatural power will not harm people,
> neither does the sage harm people.
> When neither demons nor sages harm people,
> virtues merge, and all return to the Way.

You can't know the outcome of every act,
but you can learn to accept mystery.

We cannot always predict the outcome of our actions. Even a physicist can only state probabilities, not certainties. If you count up all that you do in a day, it's hard to judge the results. Can you incorporate mystery into your life and still be functional?

We face the unknown every time we act. Some people try to use theories or procedures. They think that the right philosophy or the right method will guide them. That becomes slow, clumsy, artificial. If we act from the spirit, however, we can go beyond the intellect and intuit the probabilities.

That means not relying on prayer. Not relying on gods. Not relying on guessing. Not relying on luck. Not relying on fatalism. Not relying on superstition. Not relying on the words of others. Not relying on tradition. Not relying on education. Not relying on fads. Not relying on friends' advice. Not relying on habit. Not relying on calculation. Not relying on society.

That doesn't mean those things are unimportant. It means we can't depend on them exclusively to solve our problems.

Then what does one rely upon? One relies upon oneself. That's the reason for all the practice and meditation when there is quiet. When the time comes, one simply acts.

And one acts as one.

But you can learn to accept mystery if you accept that aging is Tao: the river's mouth.

280 | Aging Is Tao

• Birthday of **Zhang Guolao**

Zhang Guolao

Zhang Guolao represents the elderly in the symbolism of the **Eight Immortals** (p. 124). He carries a musical instrument called a "fish-drum," a bamboo cylinder with a piece of fish or snake skin stretched over one end accompanied by two long sticks of bamboo that are struck together. Zhang is frequently shown riding a white donkey—which he can fold up like a piece of paper to store in his cap-box at the end of the day. The next morning, he only needs to spray water from his mouth, and the donkey reappears.

Zhang learned the arts of immortality, knew how to regulate the breath, and could go for days without food—but he also drank wine potions frequently. When the Emperor Xuanzhong (712–756) of the Tang dynasty summoned Zhang to court, his envoy was told that the master had recently died—but when his coffin was opened, it was empty.

Aging is Tao: the river's mouth,
always older than headwaters.

The river rushes from its headwaters to its mouth. The mouth never becomes the headwaters again.

The sun rises in the east and sets in the west. The east never becomes the west.

Winter follows spring, summer, and autumn. The trees do not flower in winter.

The moon is new, waxes, then wanes. The moon is never new and full at the same time.

In the same way, each of us ages. Our aging in this lifetime is a one-way process, but oh, what a powerful process that is! Any parent can observe that the care, feeding, and protection of a child is paramount—and yet, after a certain point, there is nothing to be done except to let natural growth occur.

By contrast, we do not marvel at the developmental stages of an adult. We don't often consider that there might be natural advantages to each decade of an adult's life. But they are surely there: each decade of your life might lose the advantages of the previous one, but you might gain new insights and abilities. We have to recognize and celebrate the aging process.

While it's common to be sad over growing old, and while we often describe our senior years with adjectives like "infirm," aging is itself a powerful Tao—a Way. We simply need to follow it, accepting all that is natural in our lives.

The essence of being Taoist is to seek the advantage in every moment and to minimize or eliminate the disadvantages. Do that every day, and you will not be far from the secret of immortality.

Always older than headwaters—it's through age that life gains meaning.

281 | Choices

Take That and Leave This

In Chapter 38 of the *Daodejing,* Laozi sums up the issue of choice with the simple, "take that and leave this."

> Superior virtue is not virtue: thus it is virtue.
> Inferior virtue never departs from virtue; thus it is not virtue.
> Superior virtue does not act, but there is nothing that is not enacted.
> Inferior virtue does not act, and it always acts.
> Superior benevolence does not act, but there is nothing that is not enacted.
> Inferior benevolence does not act, and it always acts.
> Superior ritual acts, but when there is no response,
> it bares its arms and forces things.
> Therefore, after Tao is lost, virtue remains.
> After virtue is lost, benevolence remains.
> After benevolence is lost, righteousness remains.
> After righteousness is lost, ritual remains.
> For those who emphasize ritual inspire little trust,
> but this is the beginning of disorder.
> Diviners make Tao flowery,
> and this is the beginning of foolishness.
> This is why the superior person deals with the profound and does not dwell on the superficial
> He deals with the solid, and does not dwell on the flowery.
> Therefore he takes that and leaves this.

We Are What We Think

The Buddhist sutra *Dhammapada (Fajujing),* translated from Pali into Chinese in 223, contains this verse:

> We are what we think.
> All that we are arises with our thoughts.
> With our thoughts we make the world.
> Speak or act with an impure mind
> And trouble will follow you
> As the wheel follows the ox that draws the cart.
> We are what we think.
> All that we are arises with our thoughts.
> With our thoughts we make the world.

Life gains meaning
through our choices.

Meaning is not to be found outside. It cannot be discovered, because there is no objective, freestanding meaning. You make meaning through your choices. Nobody is out there waiting for you to find yourself or the true "purpose" of life. Neither is the purpose of life written in books. Others have found and have set down their own purposes, but none of them can be your purpose.

If we woo another person with words not our own, we consider that phony. If we publish a paper with plagiarized passages, we call that a lack of integrity. If we serve a meal that someone else cooked as if we had made it, we call that dishonest. Now, when it comes to spirituality, why in the world would we try to adopt something wholesale from someone else? Although we need to learn from others, it's what we do ourselves that matters. So too with spirituality. We need to do it ourselves, we need to shape it ourselves, we need to experience it for ourselves.

That is honest spirituality. It is the path that we are walking, the path that we are discovering and creating at each moment. That path is ours, and we make it by making our choices.

A way requires movement. We could stand in one place forever, but we would not be living then. We need to move, just as everything else moves. As soon as there is movement, then there is direction. As soon as there is movement and direction, then there is a path. What's up ahead? We don't know, but in order to get there, we need to take steps now. And these steps now must be the steps we *choose* to take.

Through our choices, we learn how the weaver is perfect.

The Weaver's Daughter

Verse 174 of the *Dhammapada (Faju-jing)* reads: "This world is dark, few can see here; only a few go to heaven, like birds escaped from the net." Here is an abbreviated telling of the story of the weaver's daughter, which is attached as the commentary to this verse.

During a discourse, Buddha saw that a sixteen-year-old weaver girl was one of the few who understood his message: that one who was ever aware of death would face death mindfully and leave the world for a good destination.

Three years went by before Buddha returned to that area. The girl again wanted to hear Buddha's discourse. However, her father also wanted her to wind spools of thread for him. She did so promptly and, on the way to deliver the spools, stopped on the edge of the assembly to listen.

Buddha saw that the girl was about to die, and he wanted her to hear the right words of wisdom. He asked four questions, which she answered:

"Where have you come from?"
"I don't know."
"Where are you going?"
"I don't know."
"Do you not know?"
"Yes, I know."
"What do you know?"
"I do not know, venerable one."

The assembly thought that the girl was giving rude and nonsensical answers, but Buddha asked her to explain. She replied that her answers meant that she did not know her past existence, she did not know her future existence, she did know that she would die someday, but she did not know when. Buddha then uttered the words of verse 174. Having gained this wisdom, the girl went to her father, who had fallen asleep at the loom. When he awoke, he accidentally pulled on the shuttle, which struck the girl and killed her. Heartbroken, he went to Buddha, who admitted him into the order, and in a short time, the father became a luohan (arhat, p. 341).

The weaver is perfect,
to know the perfect whole.

A weaver is truly admirable. Passing the shuttlecock through the loom, building fabric little by little, she creates what might be yards of material. With each thread, she can't possibly see the whole, and yet, she has confidence in her plan.

The whole is created by the interweaving of threads. There's no glue, no tying, no attachments—nothing extra. All the benefits and the beauty of cloth are achieved simply by design, and the natural strength of the thread determines the strength of the whole.

Imagine that there's a gambling parlor across the street from the weaver's workshop. People go in there haphazardly, at all hours of the day. Instead of planning each movement of their lives carefully, they stumble in. Instead of meticulous concentration, they thrive on boisterous drive. Instead of a certain outcome, they're willing to take a chance on a single big win. In the end, how many of them end up with whole cloth?

The weaver has no need to be anxious. She takes what nature provides, confident that even and constant work will yield a pattern and a whole.

The course of each day is like a thread, and the cloth that is being made is like our life. If one concentrates on the perfect arrangement of each day's thread, then the whole is ensured.

To know the perfect whole, you must sometimes go back.

© andelieya

283 | Going Back to Go Forward

Returning Home

He Zhizhang (659–744) was one of the Eight Immortals of the Wine Cup (p. 124), a group that also included Li Bai (p. 264). "Returning Home" is one of his most well-known poems.

> When I was young, I left home; old,
>   I return.
> My accent hasn't changed, yet my hair
>   is thin.
> Children see me, but don't recognize me.
> They smile and ask, "Stranger, where do
>   you come from?"

You must sometimes go back
to see where you're going.

If all of life is cyclical, you'll inevitably end up at the beginning of a cycle again. These completions sometimes take decades, so patience and observation are helpful. If life seems to take you back somewhere, then go with great interest. There is a secret there, an answer, an ending to one story and a beginning of another.

The possibility of resolution is inherent in this. Who among us does not have "unfinished business"? We went away to war, waving at our family through the bus window. We kissed that boy and then never saw him again after that summer. We buried our father. We took a chance, drove away, and never went back even though we promised ourselves we would. We remember the texture of the sand underneath us as we boarded the ship to take us past the distant clouds.

Then, unexpectedly, life pulls us back. The letter. The phone call. The change of plans that suddenly transports us back to the place we never thought we would see again.

Who knows what our reaction will be? Will the place seem small, as we so often read about? Will we view those we left behind with pity—and will they have the same reaction to us?

Or will we feel the rare flow of energy because of something special about that place? Will we find something deep and unnamed that has been waiting, just for us?

To see where you're going, rely on neither design nor divine agency.

- Birthday of **Fuxi**
- Fasting day

Fuxi

Fuxi (c. mid-twenty-ninth century BCE) is one of the Three Legendary Emperors of China (note that while Fuxi is always a part of this group, there is no widespread agreement on the other two members), and he is a semi-mythological figure. On the one hand, he is supposed to be the brother of Nuwa (the goddess who first created humans) and in some accounts is supposed to be half-human and half-serpent. On the other hand, his mausoleum stands in Huaiyang County, Henan.

Fuxi is credited as an inventor of writing, fishing, and trapping and is said to have established a patriarchal society over a matriarchal one, ruling for over one hundred years.

The tradition of the *I Ching* traces its beginnings to Fuxi. According to legend, Fuxi was meditating on the banks of a river when a "dragon-horse" emerged from the waves. From the pattern on its back, Fuxi perceived the "River Chart," and tradition holds that he derived the eight trigrams of the *I Ching* from that experience.

The chart can be understood by the numbers of circles grouped around the square (which represents the Five Phases, p. 422). The scholar Shao Yong (1011–1077) showed how the numbers were combined to create Fuxi's pattern of the Eight Trigrams (p. 184).

Neither design nor divine agency:
only constant mixing of light and dark.

Is any moment of the day more important or "better" than any other? Is meaning, or holiness, or enlightenment more likely to come at a particular time of day than at another? Are you vital and completely centered at the same time each day?

Any moment of any day is a good time for spirituality. Any moment can also be banal, ordinary, dull. However, any of these states has to do with you, not the day. In the meantime, millions upon millions of events are happening each moment to innumerable beings across innumerable worlds. All we can say with certainty is that there is constant movement and constant transformation.

What makes this happen? Is there a divine operator directing it all, willing to suspend the laws of nature to intercede on our behalf? Or does the cosmic motion have its own momentum, with enough energy to keep the universe moving—expanding even—without the need for anyone to be working at it? When you think about it, the idea that we need superbeings to pull the levers is primitive and pitifully needy.

Light and dark interact. Heat and cold interact. Hard and soft are transformed from one another constantly. All is change, all is transformation, all is exchange.

All is Tao.

Only constant mixing of light and dark teaches this truth: Be water. Be lake spreading. Be chasm drain.

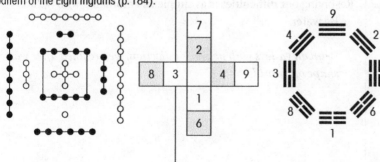

285 | Be Water

- Inspection day of **Official of Water–Great God**
- **Xiayuan Jie** (The Later Year Festival)
- Fasting day

Official of Water–Great God

This is the birthday of the Official of Water–Great God (Shuiguan Dadi). He is one of the **Three Officials**, the other two being the **Official of Heaven** (p. 20) and the **Official of Earth** (p. 231). The Official of Water presides over the last four moons of the year. Like the other two officials, the Official of Water brings good fortune, punishes wrongdoing as a divine judge, and is responsible for all things watery, from the rain to the streams and oceans.

Soft as Water

The first portion of Chapter 78 of the *Daodejing* carries the preeminent Taoist statement about water—and an entire philosophy of life as well:

> Under heaven, there is nothing as soft
>   and as weak as water,
> yet for attacking the strong and powerful,
>   there is nothing better—
> for there is nothing that cannot be
>   changed.
> The weak overcomes the strong.
> The soft overcomes the hard.
> Beneath heaven, everyone knows this,
> but no one can put it into practice.

Be water. Be lake spreading. Be chasm drain.
Brim all valleys with heaven's reflection.

One drop of water. Like every other drop, and yet, for that moment, an individual drop, with its own role to play. Whether it's a tear or a raindrop, a nearly invisible sphere rising to the clouds, or part of the froth of a waterfall, it is a singular drop.

One drop of water. Clear, spherical, with no head, no tail. It's not made for its own direction—it takes any direction. It has no intention to go anywhere. It's not concealing anything.

When that drop of water runs with other drops, greater and greater forms emerge. First a trickle, then a stream. In time, a river, or roaring rapids. The lake, the flood, the sea. Yet even if we consider the vastness of all the world's oceans combined, the drops are still there. Water is still there: quantity does not change its character.

What humans fear—the chasm, the abyss, the dark hole, the jagged fall—water fills completely. What humans make in the name of civilization and profit—the levee, the canal, the seawall, the dam—water deluges completely. What humans make to raise the towers of their empires—the skyscrapers, the pagodas, the holy spires—water erodes completely.

All the creatures on this land crawled out from water. All of us were surrounded by water in the womb. All of us need water to live. Breathing air may be a marker for life, but so is water. Water is life. Water births us all.

We are 65–95 percent water. Why keep up the pretense that some narrow membrane of self-aware consciousness is what makes us human? The sages tell us to abandon our sense of self, our sense of separateness. They are only hinting at what is real: we are water. Resolving our difficulties is as simple as embracing who we are.

Be water.

Brim all valleys with heaven's reflection, we are filled after we shape our world.

Exercise 20

SLIGHT SNOW

Winter is complete everywhere. There are frosts, cold spells, and severe cold weather. Snow comes to the north, rainstorms come to southern latitudes, and sunlight lessens.

This exercise is best practiced during the period of 1:00–5:00 A.M.

1. Sit cross-legged. Press one palm to your knee and grasp the elbow of that arm with your other hand.

2. Slowly turn your torso and your neck to one side as if you're trying to look behind you. Repeat on the other side. Inhale when you turn; exhale when you return to the center. Repeat fifteen times then change to the opposite position and repeat another fifteen times. Move slowly, but with strength.

3. Facing forward, click your teeth together thirty-six times. Roll your tongue between your teeth nine times in each direction. Form saliva in your mouth by pushing your cheeks in and out. When your mouth is filled with saliva, divide the liquid into three portions.

4. Inhale; then exhale, imagining your breath traveling to the dantian and then swallow one-third of the saliva, imagining that it travels to the dantian.

5. Repeat two more times until you've swallowed all three portions.

6. Sit comfortably as long as you like.

Through this exercise, ancient Taoists sought to prevent or treat swelling and dampness; abdominal distension; incontinence; joint pain and muscle stiffness; diarrhea; feeling of fullness in the chest; and fearful feelings.

286 | We Make Our World

▸ Birthday of Pan Gu

A Taoist Creation Myth

In the beginning, all was formless until primordial chaos coalesced into a cosmic egg. During a period of 18,000 years, yin and yang slowly came to balance inside the egg. Finally, a hairy giant hatched. He had two horns on his head, a hammer in his right hand, and a chisel in his left. His name was Pan Gu.

He separated heaven and earth, created the sun and the moon, and began to sculpt the world as we know it. He died after 18,000 years of labor.

As his body dissolved, it animated the rest of his world: his breath became wind; his voice became thunder; his blood formed rivers; his muscles made the land; his beard became the stars of the Milky Way; his body hair scattered and became plentiful forests; his bones sank into the ground as minerals; his sweat became rain; and the fleas in his body hair became animals, fish, and human beings.

After we shape our world,
the next world will take form.

We make our world. As we become more aware, make decisions, and explore what is around us, we shape the environment around us. We are each our own Pan Gu, emerging from the chaos of our birth and childhood, trying to balance yin and yang.

When we die, our bodies dissolve and go back into the world. Just as Pan Gu's breath became the wind and his bones sank into the ground, what we've done in our lives gets used by others. No matter who we are, we benefit others by becoming their raw material.

The beginning is not really the start of anything; it's merely transformation. Death is not really an ending; it is also transformation. We cannot remember what we were before we were born, why are we worried about what we might be after we die? Between those two passages, there is still a rich and great world. Pan Gu didn't question who he was. He did not resist what he had to do. He simply acted, and labored, and then transformed. There was no other Pan Gu. There is no other you. We make our world, and that is joy enough.

The next world will take form after you learn what's possible.

287 | What's Possible?

A Dialogue with No Beginning

Zhuangzi imagines a dialogue between Grand Purity and No Beginning. In a passage that echoes the opening lines of the *Daodejing* (p. 53), Grand Purity asks No Beginning:

"Now then, is not-knowing actually knowing? And is not-doing then doing? What is, and what is not?"

No Beginning replies, "The Tao cannot be heard; what can be heard is not it. The Tao cannot be seen; what can be seen is not it. The Tao cannot be described; what can be described is not it. Do we know the form which gives form to form? Tao cannot be referred to by name."

After you learn what's possible,
you will know all that's possible.

There's a widespread belief: you can be anyone you want to be. Usually this is voiced by athletes from the winner's podium or entertainers accepting awards. That leaves the unfortunate conclusion that the rest of us have not wanted intensely enough.

Then there are spiritual people who urge us to bring our minds to the fore. We become what we imagine, they tell us. Pray intensely enough and what you want will come true. That leaves the unfortunate conclusion that the rest of us are not devout enough.

No wonder other spiritual people urge us to give up everything. Empty yourself, they say, and then all will unfold naturally. That leaves the unfortunate conclusion that the rest of us are simply too overloaded to be empty.

Each of these viewpoints—that we can be whoever we want to be, that a strong mind makes its own reality, and that there is a great advantage to emptying oneself—has a kernel of truth. They are subtle understandings, but they cannot be simply plugged in to work automatically.

You have to know what's possible. The mountain is high, but no mountain grows downward from the sky. The river is long, but no ocean flows upstream. Don't search in the wrong directions. Make use of what's at hand. Play with what is in your life today. Assemble pieces into a new sculpture. Collect sounds into a new song. Choreograph movements into a new dance.

All things are possible if you consider all things that are present.

You will know all that's possible, because meditation will make you powerful.

▸ Fasting day

Polishing a Mirror

This story is from the *Treasury of the True Dharma Eye (Shobogenzo)*, composed by the Japanese Zen master **Dogen Kigen** (1200–1253), who traveled and trained in China.

One day, the Chan Buddhist master Nanyue Huairang (677–744; p. 260) saw his disciple, Mazu Daoyi (709–788; p. 243), sitting in meditation.

"What are you trying to do by sitting like that?"

"I want to become a Buddha," replied Mazu.

The master picked up a piece of tile and began rubbing it.

"What are you doing?" asked Mazu.

"I'm trying to make a mirror."

"How can you make a mirror by polishing a tile?"

"How can you become a Buddha by sitting like that?"

"What do you mean?"

"Think about driving a cart. If it stops moving, do you whip the cart or the horse?"

Mazu said nothing.

Nanyue explained: "Do you want to practice sitting in meditation or do you want to practice becoming a Buddha? If you understand sitting meditation, then you know that meditation is not about sitting or lying down. If you want to learn to become a Buddha, remember that being a Buddha is without any fixed form. Do not use discrimination in the dharma. If you practice sitting as a Buddha, you must kill Buddha. If you cling to the form of sitting, then you have not mastered the essential principle."

Meditation will make you powerful—
but you can't change into somebody else.

Meditation is so subtle that we might wonder if anything is happening. If this occurs to you, think back to a time when you were interrupted during meditation, or just stop abruptly the next time you're meditating. You'll notice a difference. Perhaps even your breathing and heartbeat will be different than normal. It isn't ever comfortable being interrupted during meditation, but that's a sign that something is indeed going on. Meditation is powerful.

However, meditating to try to get somewhere or be someone you're not is not true meditation. Meditating to get rich, or to try to be more beautiful, or to become more calm—none of this is true meditation. True meditation is simply being yourself. You don't need special techniques, or gods, or some mystic destiny. Sit with nothing extra—not even the "extras" of ambition or desire—and you will have true meditation.

You may sometimes think, "I have been meditating for years and I'm still a mess." Consider this: meditation doesn't make you someone you aren't. Meditation is to be wholly who you are.

If you don't like who you are, then meditation won't fix that. Indeed, accepting yourself with all your foibles and your limitations is the great challenge—and the great work.

"Think about driving a cart. If it stops moving, do you whip the cart or the horse?"

But you can't change into somebody else, even if five hundred luohans preach the law.

289 | Five Hundred Luohans

▸ The day that the **Five Hundred Luohans** preached the law

Luohans

"Luohan" is the Chinese word for the Sanskrit "arhat." A luohan observes the 250 moral precepts, is unfailingly pure in behavior, and continues to practice assiduously. A luohan can fly through space and time, can assume different forms, and is immortal. However, a luohan has not yet attained the status of a bodhisattva or a Buddha.

Traditional stories tell of various groups of luohans—sixteen, eighteen, or five hundred—whom Buddha commanded to await the coming of **Maitreya Buddha**—Budai Luohan—the Buddha of the Future (p. 5). Other stories describe the luohans as a group of monks chosen to protect the faithful until all sentient beings can be liberated.

Some of the temples with statues of the Five Hundred Luohans are Longhua Temple, Shanghai; Qiongzhu Temple, Kunming; Guiyuan Temple, Wuhan; Baodu Zhai, a village in Shijiazhuang; and Biyun Temple, Beijing.

Five hundred luohans preach the law
because there's still room for one more.

Several temples in China have life-sized statues of the Five Hundred Luohans, and it's quite an experience to walk down row after row, marveling at how each one is different from the next. Most have shaved heads and wear Buddhist robes, and they are either gilded or painted realistically. Sometimes, shawls are draped on them. Some scowl fiercely, while others smile benignly. One's magic power is shown by a terrifically long arm stretching twelve feet in the air. Another holds important symbols—a begging bowl, a lotus flower, a drum—and many are gesturing in benediction.

The statues show the diverse forms and possibilities that spirituality can take, and they also show that appearances from the beautiful to the ugly make no difference when it comes to being holy. Remember, too, that these adepts, as skilled and powerful as they may be, are still on their journeys too. They are maturing into Buddhas, but they are not there yet. No matter who you are, you can be spiritual. No matter how arduous the path, others are there to show the way.

In the end, the reason that there are five hundred luohans is that there is room for one more—you.

Because there's still room for one more if you were on the threshold of heaven.

The Hall of Five Hundred Luohans, Baodu Zhai, Shijiazhuang.

- The day dogs and chickens rose to heaven

Once Someone Finds Tao . . .

"Once someone finds Tao, even his dogs and chickens rise to heaven."

The story behind this idiom involves the Prince of Huainan and ardent Taoist, **Liu An** (p. 50). He invested a considerable amount of money and effort to find the method of achieving immortality. The **Eight Immortals** (p. 124) heard of his interest, visited him, and imparted the secret recipe.

It took Liu An years of effort to create the elixir. Just as he was on the verge of success, he was accused of a conspiracy against the throne, and the emperor issued an order for his arrest. The Eight Immortals told Liu that this calamity proved that there was no reason to stay in the mortal world. They urged him to take the elixir.

Liu An wanted all his relatives to go to heaven with him, so he prepared the elixir and shared it with them. Once they all ascended to heaven, the dogs and chickens smelled the delicious elixir and gobbled what was left. They too rose up into heaven as immortals!

Today, the idiom refers to friends and relatives benefiting from a person's promotion or rise to prominence.

In actual history, Liu An was a prince and advisor to Emperor Wudi (156–87 BCE). He was responsible for the philosophical work the *Huainanzi*, (p. 50) composed by the Eight Immortals of Huainan (p. 124), a group of scholars. Instead of the elixir of immortality, Liu An is credited as the inventor of soy milk (some worship him as the God of Bean Curd).

Liu An was indeed involved in a plot to overthrow the emperor. He committed suicide when his effort failed—and all his relatives were executed.

If you were on the threshold of heaven,
would you stop and ask if others could come?

If you were trapped in ignorance, poverty, or some nightmare dilemma and you suddenly had the chance to escape, would you stop and think of others?

Many people who come from poverty and who find themselves wealthy go back and try to help others. As soon as we have the chance to have a significantly better life, may we all stop and remember those less fortunate than ourselves and ask, "What about them?" That is the essence of holiness.

Are we really alone? Are we really just individuals with our own record? Do benefit and damnation alike accrue to us alone? Or are we more than that, part of a larger collective?

Do we take pleasure solely in fulfilling our daily desires, content to be satiated as expediently as possible? Or is there some greater pleasure in sharing with others, in seeing them have happiness too?

Living solely for our own gratification can be accomplished relatively easily. Yes, there will be some satisfaction, but then there is a question of whether there is more.

It's exactly at the point when you reach success that you can arrange for the happiness of others. You already know what it feels like. Knowing this pleasure can motivate us to help others find it. That is fulfilling in a way that the original pleasure no longer is.

Stopping on the threshold to heaven means that you already know that liberation is yours. Asking for others to come with you means that you are also liberated from your own selfishness. At that point, taking that last step is a mere formality: in that moment, you've already achieved the real heaven.

Would you stop and ask if others could come, before you show yourself as you were before your birth?

Pure Simplicity

The Master and the Wizard

Zhuangzi tells the story of a mysterious wizard called Jixian. He could accurately predict the destiny of any person just by looking at him.

Liezi (p. 65) went to see him and was fascinated. Returning, he said to his teacher, Huzi: "I thought that your doctrine was perfect, but I have found a better one." Huzi was not upset but asked to meet the great wizard.

The next day, Liezi escorted his master on the visit, but as soon as the wizard saw Huzi, he said, "Alas! Your master is a dead man. He will not live—not even for ten days more! I saw something strange about him. He was like ashes slaked with water."

Liezi wept until his jacket was wet, and he told Huzi what the wizard had said. Huzi said, "I showed myself to him like the form of what's beneath the earth. There were sprouts, but they were still dormant. He saw me with my vital powers closed. Let's visit him again."

The next day, the wizard thought that Huzi would recover his health fully. The master replied that he had merely shown himself as earth and sky.

The day after that, the wizard said he could not determine anything. The master replied that he had shown as a person with yin and yang in complete balance.

On the subsequent day, the wizard became frightened and ran away. The master commented that he had shown himself as he was before he had been born—pure emptiness.

Liezi went home and did not leave for three years. He practiced until he was like a clod of earth, standing in the silence of pure simplicity.

Show yourself as you were before your birth.
Stand like a solitary clod of earth.

If you want to be happy, then just be simple. Preserve yourself and limit your ambitions, and all will be well.

Liezi thought that he had found a master better than his, because the wizard could seemingly tell anyone's destiny. Significantly, Liezi's master was open-minded and mild. He did not express indignation when his student announced that he had found someone better. Perhaps he knew his superiority anyway and simply wanted to arrange for a lesson both for his student and for the wizard. But notice the contrast between the wizard—someone who had learned to discern and use natural forces—and the master, someone who had learned to *be* the natural forces.

The story goes on to tell what happened to Liezi. Realizing that his master's teaching was great, and understanding that he had not gained enough proficiency in it, he withdrew from the world in order to perfect himself. This is a wonderful strategy that any of us can use. Sometimes we have to go out and work widely among others. Sometimes, we need to withdraw and work on ourselves. Liezi wanted to work on himself. The story says that he cooked for his wife. He fed the pigs as if he were feeding people. He took no part or interest in worldly affairs. He was like carved jade. He returned to simplicity. He was like a solitary clod of earth.

Again, this is not the power of wizardry. It is the power of being fully and naturally human. Remove all art and wizardry and you open the way to simplicity. You don't transform yourself magically into anything. You shed complications until you are most fully yourself. That, in the end, is the ultimate state of being human.

Stand like a solitary clod of earth, for you must not change the sages' words.

292 | The Scribe's Lament

Chinese Scripts

There are different Chinese scripts:

1. **Oracle Bone Script (Jiagu-wen)** Dating back to at least 1500–1000 BCE, symbols were incised onto turtle shells and ox bones. These pieces were part of the historical documents of the Shang dynasty (1600–1046 BCE).

2. **Great Seal Script (Dazhuan)** This script is found mainly on cast bronze vessels made primarily between 1100 and 700 BCE.

3. **Small Seal Script (Xiaozhuan)** This script was formalized by Li Si and was the script of the Qin dynasty (p. 159). It has a more pictorial character and uses strokes of even thickness.

4. **Clerical Script (Lishu)** This script was also developed during the Qin dynasty so scribes could write more quickly with the pointed Chinese writing brush.

5. **Regular Script (Kaishu)** Attributed to Wang Xizhi (p. 85), this script became the basis for printed books.

6. **Cursive Scripts** Running Script (Xingshu) is a cursive script. Grass Script (Caoshu) is an eccentric form that departs from normal rules.

Chinese Tones

Chinese is a tonal language. For any given basic sound in official Chinese, there are four different tones plus a neutral tone, all signifying unrelated words. Cantonese, the dialect of southern China spoken by many immigrants, is even more complicated, with six tones for any given sound.

You must not change the sages' words.
But what words will you add yourself?

The scribe said: "The prince asked my temple to make a copy of the *Daodejing*. Seven of us gathered, while the eighth one slowly read each chapter aloud. The reading was a precaution. I'm over sixty years old. I've recited the *Daodejing* since I entered the temple as a boy of nine.

"Since there are eighty-one chapters, we stopped every ninth chapter to compare. Each one of us read our version aloud, and if it agreed with the others, we went on. Man makes errors only when he varies from the truth.

"We were about a third of the way through the project when I was ordered to travel to another temple to teach transcription to the monks there, delaying our own project by two weeks.

"Before I left, I realized that I had not packed my brushes. Afraid that the abbot would accuse me not only of being inattentive but of being eager to travel, I rushed to the transcription room. There were the seven versions, open on the tables. I went to retrieve my brushes.

"Something caught my eye. What was that word? That could not have been what I wrote. I hurried to my copy. The strokes were even, the rows were straight, but my version did not match the first copy I saw. I checked the others. Four of the scribes had put down a different word—although each word had the same pronunciation. Just then, I heard other monks coming, and I rushed out.

"In the other temple, I demonstrated with the *Daodejing*. I broke into a sweat as the reader came to the passage. Now, the word he read wasn't even pronounced the same as it was in our version! During a break, I casually asked to see his copy. He handed it to me and then went into the courtyard.

"The abbot of the temple saw me reading, assumed that I was devout, and praised me. 'Tell me,' he inquired, 'after all your years of study, what is your insight into Tao?'

"I did not speak.

"I was afraid of saying something wrong."

But what words will you add yourself? Or will you merely burn paper, burn trash, burn bodies?

293 | Burning

• Fasting day

Simplicity in Funerals

Burial of the body, rather than cremation, was the major funerary practice in ancient China. There were some instances of cremation, encouraged by Buddhism, but otherwise, only burial was practiced. Here is Mozi (p. 316), who happens to mention cannibalism and cremation in passing:

In ancient times, east of the state of Yue there was the tribe of Kaishu.... When the father died the mother was abandoned, because one should not live with the wife of a ghost.... Was this good and right? No, because habit affords convenience and custom carries approval.

South of Chu there was a cannibal tribe. Upon the death of the parents the flesh was scraped off and the bones were buried. By following this custom one became a filial son.

West of Qin there was the tribe of Yiqu. Upon their death the parents were burned on a bonfire and the smoke was said to be ascension to the golden clouds. In this way one became a filial son....

Now, the practice of these three tribes is too heartless ... there should be rules for funerals and burials. Even regarding clothing and food, which are the necessities of life, there are rules. How then can there be none regarding funerals and burials, which are the necessities of death?

Outlining the rules for funerals and burials, Mozi said:

The coffin shall be three inches thick, sufficient enough to hold the rotting bones. There shall be three shrouds, just enough to hold the rotting flesh. The pit shall not be dug so deeply that it strikes water, nor so shallowly that it allows odor to escape. The mound shall be high enough to be identified. There may be weeping on the way to and from the burial. But upon returning the family shall engage in earning its livelihood. Sacrifices [rituals to ancestors and to nature] shall not be neglected in order to express filial piety.

Burn paper. Burn trash. Burn bodies.
Be clear what you put to the torch.

Here's a strange contrast. We burn papier-mâché offerings (p. 230) and spirit money in order to support the dead. We also burn effigies, objects, and flags in protest. One act of burning is devout transmission. The other is disdainful destruction.

Let's say someone pulls up dead roots—like Tao Yuanming clearing his "tangled brush" (p. 107)—and then burns them to enrich the newly cleared fields—like Bai Juyi's ninth-moon's autumn ash (p. 285). How is the garbage heap that much different than the heaps of incense hosed down at Great Immortal Wong's temple (p. 277)?

In one case, we pull out what was once living but is no longer wanted, and destroy it to fertilize the soil. In the other case, our devotion goes flaming beyond all bounds, has to be swept into great heaps on the temple grounds, and is then desperately hosed down so it will not consume the very building that houses our worship.

Then we have the funeral pyre. The very vessel of an entire human being, representing decades of life; representing a parent and leader; representing hopes and dreams, disappointments and heartaches; representing beauty that the world will never know again—that person is burned and the ashes scattered. Contrast that today with people undergoing self-immolation as their one final sacrifice to change the course of all under heaven.

It's so strange to ponder the differences between all these types of burning.

Be clear what you put to the torch if you want things to grow.

294 | Hold It Close

‣ Fasting day

Mencius's Mother

"Mencius's mother moved three times" is a popular idiom.

The young Mencius (p. 63) and his mother lived near a cemetery. Since he saw mourners constantly, he began to imitate them in his play. Alarmed, Mencius's mother found a new home near a marketplace.

The vendors in the stalls were boisterous, boasting of their stock and shouting for customers to buy their goods. The young Mencius imitated them in his play. Again, his mother was not pleased, and she moved to a house near a school.

Mencius began to attend school, and his manners and education improved. Only then did his mother think that they had found a suitable home, and they settled there for good.

If you want things to grow,
hold them close to yourself.

A chicken sits on her eggs to incubate them. A kangaroo carries her joey in her pouch. Peasant women still strap their babies to their backs and go out to work in the fields. Urban mothers and fathers carry their children in slings. When children are sick, hurt, or tired, we hug them. All over the world, parents prefer a family bed. We all know this: whatever we want to grow, we hold it close to ourselves.

We can give time, we can give labor, we can give money, we can give food, we can give shelter, we can give advice, we can give knowledge, we can give a ride, we can give what we make with our hands. Certainly all these acts are generous. But the most primal and most precious thing is to give ourselves. We reserve this gift only for what is most precious to us, and the marvelous part of it is that there is nothing to do, nothing to decide, nothing to make. Just us. Just our presence, our life force, our being. We embrace what we want to nurture and charge it with the force of who we are.

Having understood that, there is no reason to interfere with what others want to hold close, or to destroy those who give their very presence to others. Honoring that would eliminate most of the violence in the world.

So for the moment, let us not worry about grand policies, the economic engine, the scale of empires, or the exploration of other planets. For now, let us think about what we hold close to ourselves, and how love given wordlessly grows many times over.

Hold them close to yourself, even if you move like a thunderbolt in shock and fury.

295 | Keep Moving

The Sword of Lady Gongsun

This first section of a poem by Du Fu (p. 29), "Watching the Student of Lady Gongsun Wielding the Sword," describes a sword demonstration that reminds the poet of the beautiful master. The Archer is a reference to Hou Yi (p. 265).

In the past lived the excellent Lady
    Gongsun.
As soon as she wielded her sword, she
    moved the four quarters.
The awed onlookers were motionless as
    mountains.
Heaven and earth dipped and rose.
Sudden as the Archer shooting down the
    nine suns,
bold as gods before the wings of
    dragons,
she came like a thunderbolt with shock
    and fury,
and finished like a river meeting the sea
    in serene brightness.

Like a thunderbolt in shock and fury,
    then a river meeting the sea brightly.

We all experience the extremes of life. We relish heavenly joys and face hellish dilemmas. No one escapes this process.

One minute we can be experiencing the greatest pleasure; the next, we can be plunged into the deepest despair.

Don't let misfortune immobilize you. One of the most common exhortations you will hear from a boxing coach is "Keep moving!" You might get hit four or five times in the face and you'll become so confused that you don't move until you hear your coach yelling: "Move! Don't just stand there!"

People don't understand how martial arts can be spiritual, but they are. They train you to think under awful pressures and to believe in yourself enough to survive. When the weight of life threatens to crush you, remember: you don't have to stand there. Move. Look at what the situation offers you and take it.

The metaphor of martial arts is also helpful in this way: there are winners and losers in a match. However, losing is not the greatest problem. We all have to die. What good is it to worry about when? In combat sports, we learn from our "deaths," just as we learn when we are "reborn" for the next match.

It's not bad to lose; it's bad not to try. The greatest shame in life is not to be mowed down by death. The greatest shame in life is to not move.

Then a river meeting the sea brightly—revealing whatever is at the stone's core.

Cutting Rocks

Confucius said this about jade in the
Classic of Rites:

> Zigong asked Confucius: "May I ask why
> the superior person sets a high value
> on jade, but little on soapstone? Is it
> because jade is rare and soapstone
> plentiful?"
>
> Confucius replied: "It is not because
> the soapstone is plentiful that a person
> thinks little of it, nor because jade is
> rare that a person values it highly. The
> superior person of old found that virtue
> was like jade: soft, smooth, and glossy—
> like benevolence; fine, dense, and
> strong—like intelligence; angular but
> not cutting—like righteousness; hanging
> down in ranks—like propriety; when
> struck it yields a clear and lasting tone
> without going on forever—like music; its
> flaws do not conceal its beauty, nor does
> its beauty conceal its flaws—like loyalty;
> its radiance shines from every side—like
> trust; bright as a rainbow—like heaven;
> of energetic spirit seen in mountains
> and streams—like the earth; a symbol
> of rank—like virtue. Beneath heaven
> nothing is more valuable—like Tao."

Whatever is at the stone's core,
the carver will cut something good.

Jade merchants live high-stakes lives. When they buy boulders, they cannot see into them. They must get a rock to the workshop to open it. The first cut reveals everything, and it can make the difference between fortune and failure. A stone purchased for tens of thousands of dollars can turn out to be worthless.

This process is a metaphor for each of us. When we are first confronting a situation, we cannot tell what value may be there for us. We must look for it, even work to reveal it. Our first cut—like the first word we say in a meeting, or the first date we have with someone, or the first stroke we lay down in a painting—is critical. It is the first omen for all other efforts.

Taoists never shy away from the bad, the adverse, the ugly. They realize that unpleasantness and ill fortune are unavoidable. They work with what they get. Good things happen in time, and bad things happen in time.

Taoists know that when things are good, there is nowhere for them to go but toward the bad. And when things are bad, there will be some reaction that must become good. The Taoist is not passive. The Taoist engages this process.

Just as stonecutters work with the rocks they have collected, the Taoist accepts all that comes. But just as the cutters look for the cut that will show the rock off to the best effect, the Taoist reveals the truth of every situation.

*The carver will cut something good by asking: where is true
north?*

• Festival of the Northern Pole Star

The Northern Pole Star

Early Chinese astronomers imagined that the night sky was a dome that rotated clockwise over the earth on an axis centered around the pole star. The sun, moon, and five visible planets were believed to rotate counterclockwise around the same center. Since the earth makes a full revolution around its axis each day, the imagined dome of stars appeared to rotate 360° each day. At the same time, the dome appeared to shift 1° each day (because of the earth's orbit around the sun). Thus, over the course of a full year, the sky appeared to also go through a greater full rotation.

Using the shifting positions of the sun and moon throughout the year, the sky was divided into twelve sections, called the **Earthly Branches** (Dizhi). Due to the gradual rotation of the stars, the handle of the Big Dipper seemed to point to the Earthly Branch of that month. Thus, the handle of the Big Dipper represented the cyclical nature of heaven and became a significant focus of astronomy. The Northern Pole Star, being a relatively fixed point in the night sky, naturally took a prominent place in Taoist belief, symbolizing the center of cycles.

Shen Kuo

Shen Kuo (1031–1095) was the head official for the Bureau of Astronomy, and he was accomplished in many subjects: mathematics, inventions, finance, poetry, and music. He discovered the magnetic declination of true north while experimenting with a compass. He also improved the design of the astronomical sighting tube, allowing him to fix the position of the pole star, which had shifted over the centuries.

Where is true north?
Where is your heart?

The North Star had true utility for ancient sailors. They traveled thousands of miles and were able to return. While the star's position has shifted over thousands of years, it can still be used for navigation today.

Whether the stars in the sky or the beauty of the mountains and streams, nature has always been present. By contrast, human speculation is variable and temporary. Scientists declare that a theory stands until it is proven wrong and replaced by another. That is the rightful method of science, but spirituality must concern itself with the eternal. The stars remain above us, the mountains still stand, and the waters keep flowing to the oceans.

Human knowledge fluctuates against the constant presence of nature. We revise our understanding to fit how the skies have shifted. We adjust to nature. Nature does not adjust to us.

Our knowledge of nature changes; so too does our self-knowledge. Unless we "stargaze" into ourselves, we won't know how we are changing. Unless we adjust our charts, we won't know how to traverse the vastness of our own personalities.

Where is our own true north?

Where is your heart, once you accept that we regret that we can't live forever?

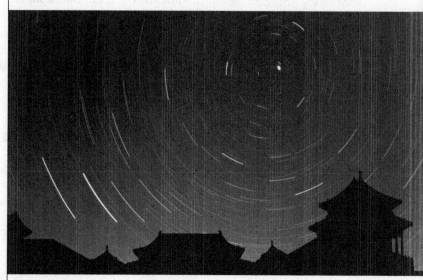

298 | Lifelong Creation

The Magic Brush

A folktale tells of Ma Liang, a poor youth who tended cattle for a rich man. Ma liked to draw. One night, he dreamed that an old man gave him a magic paintbrush and asked him to help poor people. The next day he awoke with just such a brush.

Whatever Ma imagined and painted became real. The people had no water in the fields, so Ma drew a river, and there was water. He saw that the people had difficulty plowing, so he drew a water buffalo to pull the plow.

Hearing this, the rich man took the paintbrush. He planned on painting great riches for himself. But nothing he painted became real.

Angrily, he had Ma Liang brought to him and demanded that Ma draw a mountain of gold for him.

Ma drew an ocean.

The rich man was furious. "I told you to draw me a mountain of gold!"

Ma added a mountain of gold on the other side of the sea. The rich man was happy now. "Quickly! Draw me a ship!" Ma drew a big ship. The rich man boarded with all his family and friends and set sail.

When the ship reached the middle of the ocean, Ma drew a big wave that destroyed the ship.

From that time on, Ma Liang continued to help the poor with his magic paintbrush.

We regret that we can't live forever,
but things from our hand can last beyond us.

Literal physical immortality is impossible. But the works of a person—whether physicist, official, or artist—can live on beyond that person. The poet, for example, can create a body of work that lives for centuries.

Creative works can reach an audience far away, in different times, across the world. Such works often have the ability to transcend personal and cultural boundaries. A person might make a poem in the United States in the twenty-first century, but that poem may well find a response among people in other countries and in later times.

Taoism has certainly perpetuated the myth of immortality, with its white-haired hermits wandering the mountains and its alchemists compounding elixirs of immortality. Immortality is easy. You never have to face an end. You avoid an accounting. You avoid limits.

Yet everything in life has limits. An atom has a certain number of particles, and those particles follow certain pathways. If we combine oxygen and hydrogen, we will get water—H_2O. What happened to the atoms that were there prior to the reaction?

We cannot aspire to individual consciousness surviving death, but we can leave something behind that can go on with its own separate life. We can pour our souls into our work. That takes a lifetime and the result can be superb—something only a master could create.

If we're clear on that, we are free. We choose to involve ourselves in this creation. We aren't afraid of death. We keep trying. As long as we remember that this sense of living past our death is not meant to perpetuate a narrow sense of ourselves, then all will be well. Art may live past our death, but the purpose is to make the human spirit tangible. That is always precious, and that will be a great boon to all who come after us. Anything else is folly.

But things from our hand can last beyond us, and we never regret cutting off dead branches.

299 | Pruning

▸ Fasting day

Regret for Peonies

A poem by Bai Juyi (p. 273):

> Sadly I stand before the red peonies.
> By evening, only two remain.
> They won't withstand the bright
>   morning's wind.
> I'll gaze all night to cherish the fading
>   red.

Never regret cutting off dead branches,
but bear through winter to look for new buds.

We prune the peony so that new growth will come. As we do, we remember how glorious the blossoms were in early summer. The color was brilliant, the petals uncountable at a glance, the edges perfect and unbroken, the sense of glory and grandeur unmatched. We enjoyed it at that time, perhaps even arranged a viewing party while sharing fragrant wine with good friends. We recited and wrote poetry, we played music.

In the course of time the flower withered and spent the subsequent months green and growing. Then came fall and withering. From the outside, the plant looked ill, in the irreversible pull of death's gravity.

Then, quite unexpectedly, we one day see the beginnings of magenta buds. Already? Before the heavy snows? When there are still so many months to go until we can anticipate a glorious celebration again? We prune the dead branches and broken leaves. The stalk seems gray, withered, weather-beaten. Yet the buds show that the plant is resurrecting.

We may wander in the garden, regretful that the reveries of past days are no longer with us. We may wander in the garden, reeling from the disappointments that have struck us. We may wander in the garden, anxious for our loved ones and feeling unable to protect them in a harsh world.

In the meantime, the peonies in our garden fulfill their destinies—flowering as much a part of the cycle as withering, green leaves as much a part of the cycle as bare branches.

Do we feel the poignancy of life?

Then go out and prune the garden.

But bear through winter to look for new buds, and if you must scale a mountain, take small steps.

300 | Think Small, Think Big

▸ Fasting day

Thinking Small

"Grinding an iron pestle into a needle" is a common idiom. When the Tang dynasty poet Li Bai (p. 264) was a boy, he was often truant. One day, he saw an old woman by the side of the road, grinding an iron pestle on a stone. When he asked why, she said: "Even though the pestle is big, it will become a needle if I keep at it long enough." Li Bai thought about it and saw that anything could be achieved through perseverance. He was never truant again.

Thinking Big

"Made of courage" is an idiom referring to General Zhao Yun (d. 220) and Cao Cao (p. 88). Cao Cao had stockpiled grain and fodder. When General Huang Zhou tried to burn the stores, Cao Cao's men surrounded him.

General Zhao came to Huang's rescue. Cao Cao in turn led an army to attack, forcing Zhao to retreat to a garrisoned town. With Cao Cao's armies closing in furiously, Zhao's soldiers rushed to close the gates. But Zhao stopped them.

He ordered the gates opened, kept his flags furled, and ordered the drums stilled. Cao Cao's army, fearing a ruse, pulled back. Only then did Zhao Yun's drums sound and his armies charge, utterly defeating Cao Cao's troops.

If you must scale a mountain, take small steps.
If you must build an empire, take huge strides.

A traveler at the foot of the mountain peers at a summit hidden in clouds. The trail is steep through closely packed fir and pine, rocks turn under foot, and even handholds are few. What is there to do? There is no way to leap to the top of the mountain; there's no way but to climb. All the traveler can do is take one step, and keep taking steps.

A leader who wishes to build an empire can be guilty of many things, but the worst one is thinking small. If the leader is meek and of little ambition, success is unlikely. Building empires is only for those of great vision and will. The horizon must be seen as a mere threshold to cross rather than an unreachable limit. Unless one is bold and daring, unless one sees enormous possibilities, then there will be no victory.

Both those who know when to think small and those who know when to think big must have one quality: courage. In both cases, the future is tenuous, unpromised, and overwhelming. Having the wisdom to know what to do is crucial, but having the courage to persevere is greater still.

If you must build an empire, take huge strides, and yet bow when clear sunlight drives away the year.

Wudangshan. © Bernard De Poorter

11

The Winter Moon

Bamboo Grove

Sit alone, hidden in bamboo.
Pluck the qin and whoop with joy.
Forest so deep no one knows it:
the bright moon comes to shine on me.
—Wang Wei (699–759)

The two solar terms within this moon:

GREAT SNOW

WINTER SOLSTICE

Exercise 21

GREAT SNOW

The temperature drops even more and snow is plentiful. Farmers actually welcome heavy snow, because the ground then stays at a constant temperature, insulating it from even harsher cold spells. The snow also keeps the ground moist and kills many pests.

However, since snowstorms and blizzards can become significant disasters, people must take the proper precautions.

This exercise is best practiced during the period of 11:00 P.M.–3:00 A.M.

1. Stand with feet shoulder-width apart. Push your hands out to each side, palms facing outward. Slowly and rhythmically stamp your feet.

2. Exhale each time you stamp, inhale between stamps. Repeat thirty-five times on each side.

3. Sit cross-legged and face forward. Click your teeth together thirty-six times. Roll your tongue between your teeth nine times in each direction. Form saliva in your mouth by pushing your cheeks in and out. When your mouth is filled with saliva, divide the liquid into three portions.

4. Inhale; then exhale, imagining your breath traveling to the dantian saliva, imagining that it travels to the dantian.

5. Repeat two more times until you've swallowed all three portions.

6. Sit comfortably as long as you like.

Through this exercise, ancient Taoists sought to prevent or treat swelling in the feet and knees; dry mouth; swollen throat; hunger without being able to eat; cough; vision weakness; and feelings of fear, as if about to be seized.

301 | Sitting Alone

▸ Fasting day

Returning to a Broken Hut

Here is a poem by Meng Haoran
(p. 252), "Returning to Nanshan at
Year's End." As the poem begins, he's
been rejected by the emperor and is
contemplating the ending of his career.

No more petitions at the north gate;
I return to a broken hut on Nanshan,
cast aside by an enlightened ruler for
    lacking talent.
Sick too much, I don't see old friends.
My white hair shows my speeding age,
clear sunlight drives away the year.
Always pondering and worrying, I can't
    sleep:
Pine. Moon. Night. Window. Graves.

Clear sunlight drives away the year:
the brightness can show what's coming.

Sitting alone after ten moons—or has it been a lifetime? We've
spent a long time in contemplation and exploration: what do we
know? Perhaps we've been successful as we've thought about
Tao, or perhaps, like Meng Haoran, we've been disappointed and
rejected. In either case, it's right to ask what we've gained from our
efforts.

Let us turn back in our minds, harvest what we've discovered,
store up what we've decided, hold what we value, and look forward
to spring. Yes, the clear light burns away the year, but a new year
must come afterward. We sit alone, to make sure we have a pure
signal from the great expanse within us, and to make sure that
there is nothing between us and the great Way.

But we are not simply alone, are we? We are among the pines in
the mountains, and the moon comes to shine on us. That light represents our insight: spiritual guidance is always there, as it has been
for every generation before us, as it will be for our children and our
children's children, as it is even when the clouds of disappointment
and violence obscure it temporarily. Why should we fear? The light
is there, even if it too goes through its cycles of waxing and waning.

*The brightness can show what's coming: a time when most will
profess to value the spirit.*

302 | Why Are We Spiritual?

Turning to the Spiritual

Sakyamuni Buddha (p. 117) lived the first twenty-nine years of his life as Prince **Siddhartha** in Kapilavastu. His father commanded that his every desire be fulfilled. One day, the prince left the palace to meet his people, but he saw the sick, the aged, and the suffering. Later, Siddhartha went on more excursions, and he saw a diseased man, a corpse, and an ascetic. Siddhartha then turned to the spiritual life and left the palace to be a mendicant.

Confucius's father died when he was three. His mother raised Confucius in poverty. It's said that he loved to play with the ritual vases on the altar, a traditional explanation of his inherent spiritual bent. Confucius worked as a shepherd, cowherd, clerk, and bookkeeper and eventually entered the civil service, rising to the position of minister of justice in the state of Lu. However, he did not last long in that position and spent the rest of his life trying to find a lasting patron.

Laozi grew weary of the moral decay and decline of the empire. He mounted a water buffalo and made his way to the wilderness beyond China's borders.

All three of these sages' great spiritual work was accompanied by disappointment and wandering.

Most will profess to value the spirit,
while few confess to actual practice.

Most people profess to value the spiritual. Churches and temples stand in every city and in every country. Places that people deem sacred are all over the world. Yet in our popular culture, few want to go to a religious or spiritual movie. Few say that they read spiritual books, or go to lectures by spiritual leaders. No one wants to be lectured about spirituality, nor will anyone accept being offered spirituality on the street.

That's odd because we want to know about so many subjects that affect us. We try to be smart. No one wants to be cheated when buying things. Everyone understands the need to know enough math to get by and not be swindled. We want to be smart enough to understand contracts. We want to be informed enough to comment on our political leaders. Most of us want to know what's going on in the world. While we may cheerfully allow ourselves to be distracted by the latest video or celebrity gossip, we do want to be serious about things at least some of the time. But spirituality is perhaps the least popular of the serious topics.

Thus, one of the most important of endeavors receives the least acknowledgment in our lives. We don't want to think about it. We want someone else—a priest, a holy person, an author, even a fortune-teller—to tell us what to do. We don't have enough attention to practice for half an hour, let alone half a lifetime. If someone says that he or she practices spirituality deeply and sincerely, most people will politely move to the other side of the room.

Why are we spiritual? We are, at the very least, because we still have questions.

While few confess to actual practice, sky and mountains awe us, and death scares us.

303 | The Spiritual Impulse

Heaven Is Exalted, Earth Is Humble

Zhuangzi gives the order and sequence of all under heaven:

> Heaven is exalted, the earth is humble. Spring and summer lead, fall and winter follow, and the four seasons have their order. The ten thousand things change and flourish. Every bud has its proper form, first thriving, then withering, and decaying. Change and transformation is ongoing.
>
> Heaven and earth are spiritual. If they can be exalted and humble, if they can lead and follow, if they can have order, then that should also be the Tao of people....
>
> There is order to the Great Tao. If we speak of Tao but not of its order, then how can we call it Tao?

The Altar of Earth and Harvests (Shejitan) built in 1421, Zhongshan Park, Beijing. Used for soil and grain ceremonies in imperial times. Yongxinge

Sky and mountains awe us, and death scares us.
We continue the search that will free us.

Our spiritual impulse comes from three directions. First, we are awed by this world, and, sensing that there is an order far greater than us, we react with reverence. This is natural. Primitive people and children all know that they are surrounded by wonder, and when they respond with solemnity, joy, care, and trust, they are showing that reverence is natural to us.

Second, we are frightened by all that is wrong with this world. Sickness, death, scarcity, natural disasters, human cruelty, and our own foibles mark our world with misfortune. Again, the reaction against this is natural. We want to find medicine to ease suffering. We want to find enough for everyone to eat. We want to help others when hurricanes, blizzards, tidal waves, and drought strike. We want to help those victimized by others, and we question whether we want a world where one person can prey on millions. We worry when we make mistakes that lead us into accident or wreck all we have worked for. Thus, we search for some greater overall way of life, a way of seeing beyond the immediate problems of the world.

Third, we want to know what truth is. This is inherent in us too. Truth might be as primitive as knowing not to eat poisonous plants or to avoid snakes. It might lie in the realm of education, from simple arithmetic to the ability to accurately convey our needs and understand others. It might be emotional: we want to know if someone really loves us. It might be scientific, from the geneticist wanting to understand the structure of our DNA to the origins of the cosmos. It might be artistic, such as the novelist trying to capture the veracity of life in fiction, or the artist trying to make the purest painting. Above all, we want to know the truth of who we are, why we are here, what made this world, where we are going, and whether death is truly final.

The spiritual impulse is great, and it is part of being human. Whether one calls oneself a Taoist or any other name is immaterial. What's important is to recognize the impulse, which is as fundamental to us as our heartbeat.

We continue the search that will free us, but why study the words left by Confucius?

• Festival for **Confucius**

King Wen and Two of His Sons

King Wen (1099–1050 BCE) was the founder of the Zhou dynasty. He was initially the Prince of Zhou, a vassal state to the Shang dynasty (1600–1046 BCE). Di Xin, the king of the Shang, imprisoned him for seven years, and it was during this time that King Wen revised the *I Ching*. Other officials and states worked to free him, and even after he returned to Zhou, King Wen planned the overthrow of Shang carefully, aided by his sons and Jiang Taigong (p. 169). However, he died before the dynasty could be fully established, leaving his son, King Wu, to complete the task.

King Wu (d. 1043 BCE) was the second son of King Wen and led the armies that finally overthrew the Shang dynasty. However, he died three years later. His son, King Cheng (r. 1042–1021 BCE), was too young to rule at first. King Cheng's uncle, the Duke of Zhou (d. 1105), served as regent for seven years and was also a contributor to the *I Ching*.

The God of Dreams

Confucius, who lived roughly five hundred years after the beginning of the Zhou dynasty, made this rueful statement recorded in the *Analects:* "Great is my decline! For so long, I have not had another dream where I saw the Duke of Zhou." In folk legends, the duke will appear to a person if an important event is about to happen. The Duke of Zhou is therefore known as the God of Dreams.

Why study the words left by Confucius?
Why hope that the Duke of Zhou will appear?

King Wen, one of the main shapers of the *I Ching*, suffered in prison for seven years and died before he could establish the nation he had dreamed about. His fourth son, Ji Dan, the Duke of Zhou, served as regent and led a war against two of his brothers to preserve the dynasty. Confucius revered the Duke of Zhou—he once lamented that he had not dreamed of the Duke in a long time, taking it as a sign that heaven no longer favored him. Indeed, Confucius never realized his own dream: he never held an office through which he could truly establish the utopia he envisioned, and many competing philosophers and rulers ridiculed him.

Many great people have suffered to hold their views of life while they have pursued their dreams. There is no finishing in life. There are no permanent accomplishments. One is only as good as one's last work. In spiritual terms, that means that there is never a day where you can say, "I've made it." Taoists do not believe in a permanent and total enlightenment that spares a person from the vicissitudes of life. This is made explicit by the stories of gods exiled from heaven.

Therefore, there is only the journey. Every place—even if it is in heaven—is only a temporary way station. No matter how enchanting the place may be, one has to travel on. Thus, if one must speak of being a "good" Taoist, it means having an appreciation of the journey, helping others along the way, and being true to oneself. One is never a burden to others, but one is willing to lighten the burdens of others. There is no other life than this one, and this one is meant to be lived to its fullest.

We will meet many people ahead, not just the Duke of Zhou, not just Confucius. They are not ghosts, but spirits. In their benevolence, they have left brilliant lights to guide our way. It is what we see by their light that so brings us joy on the road.

Why did Confucius dream of the Duke of Zhou, and why do we still dream of Confucius? We still have an ear for their words.

Why hope that the Duke of Zhou will appear, when in the garden, all you see is the wall?

305 | Our Beliefs Must Change

A Story from the *Classic of Rites*

Confucius held an archery contest in a garden. Many people gathered outside, wanting to enter. Confucius told his disciple Zilu to take up his bow and arrows to address them: "No general of a defeated army and no officer who's lost a country may come in. The rest may enter."

Half departed and half entered.

Then Gongwang Qiu raised a horn cup: "Are the young and strong and the elderly all firm in propriety? Do you avoid following licentiousness? Are you resolute to death? If so, take your honored places."

Half departed and half remained.

Finally, Xu Dian raised a horn cup: "Are you excellent in learning without tiring? Are you excellent in propriety without wavering? Do you who are old expound Tao without confusion? If so, take your honored places."

Only a few remained.

Know That You Don't Know

Laozi wrote in Chapter 71 of the *Daodejing*:

Knowing that you don't know is superior.
Not knowing wisdom is sickness.
The sage is not sick
because he knows that his sickness is
    sickness.
Since he knows that his sickness is
    sickness, then he's not sick.

In the garden, all you see is the wall.
Looking up, you see the limitless sky.

Studying the lives and works of others is important, but we must also assess them and allow our beliefs to change. This process has been a part of spiritual life for thousands of years. It's happening now: gods being forgotten, legends being combined, new forms of worship being adapted to what people need today.

Every garden wall we build also blocks the view. Every temple we build limits our view of the sky. In the same way, the philosophies we construct may benefit us immensely, but they can also wall off the openings to new and further immensity.

If you ask ten people and they can't agree on the exact date of a festival, if you hear ten different versions of the old stories, if you hear arguments that "it was never done that way where I came from," then that is all good. It exposes the process of adaptation that is crucial to a living spiritual tradition. If the purists shudder that there are combined Confucian-Buddhist-Taoist practices, let them keep trembling, because in a hundred years' time, our spirituality will have evolved even more. There may be people who argue for doing it "just like the masters," but any examination of the past thousand years will show that no one in any given generation did everything just like the preceding one.

The crucial thing is that one learn thoroughly before one changes and adapts. This is true of anything—science, music, art, literature, government, business. There's a vast difference between an ignorant pretender and an enlightened master. We must all take the trouble to master tradition, and then afterward, we must be free to improvise something new.

Looking up, you see the limitless sky—and there is only one trail up the mountain.

306 | Climb the Mountain

- Birthday of the **Great God of the Western Peak** (Xiyue Dadi)
- Festival day for the **Jade Emperor**

Huashan

Huashan (Splendid Mountain), Shaanxi, is the western mountain of the Five Sacred Mountains (p. 44) and the fourth of the Thirty-Six Lesser Grotto Heavens. Its guardian is the Great God of the Western Peak (Xiyue Dadi), whose statue is in the Mountain Guarding Temple (Zhenyue Gong). The god receives the offerings of the people, grants wishes, and guards an entrance to hell.

A cluster of five peaks, with the highest being 7,087 feet high, Huashan has been a retreat for generations of Taoist hermits. Legend places Laozi there as he compounded the elixir of immortality, suggesting that it was a Taoist place even in the sixth century BCE. Legends and history abound about nearly every turn of the trail up the mountain, and it has inspired painters as well as poets such as Li Bai and Bai Juyi.

On the Eastern Peak, the Losing at Chess Pavilion memorializes the story of the Taoist **Chen Tuan** (920–989) playing a game of chess with **Taizu** (r. 960–976), the first emperor of the Song dynasty (960–1279). The emperor staked Huashan on the game, and when he lost, the mountain was given to the Taoists.

Chen was credited with creating the martial art Six Combinations, Eight Methods (Liuhebafa). He is also known for his qigong, most famously his Sleeping Qigong, where he slept continuously for one hundred days at a time.

Chenshiyuan

There is only one trail up the mountain:
the way is steep for all who seek heaven.

Huashan is a place of many stories and fables. Its beauty is so ethereal that anything seems possible there. And it is remote—the popular saying is that there is only one path up the mountain. All in all, it's been a place of retreat for countless Taoist practitioners.

Those of us who want to understand spirituality better may despair that we don't have a Huashan to climb or to retreat to. While there's no doubt as to the wonderful quality of being in Huashan, we must find our own way in our own place and time. Each of us has a mountain to climb—the mountain of our own life. Like Huashan, that mountain has only one path, and we should trudge it every day.

Will we stay on the slopes? Will we find a little plot somewhere off the trail and be content to work it each day? Will we lack enough curiosity to see what's further ahead? Each of us must make his or her own choice, but the mountain is always there.

Every mountain climbed leads upward toward heaven. The arrangement and the possibilities of life are simple to understand.

The way is steep for all who seek heaven—learn, but don't fully trust teachers or gods.

307 | Don't Trust Teachers Fully

Visiting the Gods

There was once an old teacher who set his students to their lessons while he slept at his desk. Each time he excused himself by saying that he had been visiting the gods.

There came a day when one of the students fell asleep at his desk, and the teacher angrily woke him with a stick in his hand.

"I was visiting the gods," claimed the boy.

"Is that so?" the teacher replied furiously. "And just what did the gods say?"

"I asked if my teacher ever came to visit, and they said that they had never heard of such a fellow."

Learn, but don't fully trust teachers or gods.
Stay independent and true to yourself.

If life were as simple as listening unquestioningly to your teachers and parents—as thousands of years of Confucian training would have us do—don't you think we'd all do it? Instead, everyone goes through a period of disappointment at the failings of teachers and parents, sometimes with a bitterness that is difficult to overcome.

If spirituality were as simple as memorizing scriptures, chanting to gods, and abdicating critical thinking for a painted idol, don't you think we'd all do it? Instead, the scriptures turn out to be misinterpreted, the chants vary from school to school, and no one comes to protect us when evil appears.

If knowledge were as simple as applying everything our teachers taught us, don't you think we'd be finished learning upon graduation? Instead, knowledge keeps changing; the important part of a theory is later proved wrong; our teachers turn out to be mistaken or no smarter than we are, or they turn out to be ardent subscribers to crackpot theories.

There are no persons in the world to whom you can fully trust your spiritual life. They are fallible, they can make mistakes, they are corruptible, they are doomed. Why cling to someone on a flaming mountain? At best, they might be able to point you to some way out, but you still have to decide whether to take it.

So if teachers and, by extension, gods are unreliable, what are we to do with the grand tradition we have inherited? We have to sift through all of it and find what works for us. We have to be careful not to be infected by outmoded ideas. Yes, we have to do this even with a spiritual tradition. Spirituality is not finished once one has acquired membership, made vows, memorized holy words, understood history, and even absorbed the mistakes that have been made. Nor does spirituality dwell in a group of adoring disciples and a smug guru. Spirituality consists of the hardheaded exploration, the honesty with oneself, the commitment to act with integrity and morality, and the determination to face death with dignity and calm. Trust yourself.

Stay independent and true to yourself when both belief and gods
are forgotten.

308 | Do We Still Need Gods?

▸ Fasting day

Some Gods Who Are Rarely Worshipped Today

There are many gods who have been forgotten or are rarely worshipped. The list below is not exhaustive, but merely gives some examples taken at random.

- The God of Basketmakers
- The Barefoot Immortal
- The Goddess of Brothels
- The Centipede Spirit
- The Goddess of Wig Sellers
- The God of the Bowels
- The God of the Lungs
- The Frog Spirit
- The God of the Brain
- The Thunder God of the Ninth Heaven
- The God of the Classics
- The Goddess of the Corner
- The Goddesses of the Corpse
- The God of Cruelty
- The Duke of the Bed
- The Earl of Wind
- The Grabbing Commissioner
- The Goddess of Grasshoppers
- The Cup-Boat Monk
- The God of the Road
- The God of Scorpions
- The President of the Ministry of Time
- The Gods of the Tongue
- The Tortoise Spirit
- The First Princess of the Azure Clouds
- The God of the Ribs
- The Servant of the White Lotus
- The God of Lust, Sin, and Death
- The Solemn Emperor of the Golden Palace
- The God of Drains and Ditches
- The Spirit of Pustules
- The God of the Stomach

When both belief and gods are forgotten, why should we still preserve and revere gods?

We are watching the pantheon of Taoist gods changing before our eyes. The Nine Emperor Gods (p. 284) are primarily worshipped in Southeast Asia, outside of China. Mother Ancestor (p. 98) has a powerful following, but it's concentrated in coastal areas and overseas communities. All sorts of gods are no longer worshipped nor remembered. Who remembers the Spirit of Pockmarks, Ma Shen? Or the God of the Left Kidney, Chuan Yuanzhen, who is exactly 3.70 inches in height and whose body can be any one of five colors? When we see gods being forgotten or changed, and we see legends overlapping one another, it shows how people are subconsciously revising and combining their beliefs.

Altar to Mother Ancestor (Tian Hou, Mazu), Hong Kong. FlyingToaster at en.wikipedia

Offerings to ancestors have kept up with the times, and people burn effigies of computers, cell phones, iPads, and the like, leading some people to ask mockingly whether wireless services have been installed in the underworld. "I don't know," one man shrugged when asked this question. "All I want is to do my best for them." Indeed, the Asian Funeral Expo held in Hong Kong featured paper effigies of designer homes, gyms, spas, nightclubs, and yachts.

Why do people continue to worship even as they are completely involved with the primarily materialistic and rationalistic world we live in today? Is it stupidity? Or is there a basic need to be fulfilled?

Why should we still preserve and revere gods when we find a priest may be lustful beneath his holy robes?

309 | Is Abuse Refutation?

Taoist Mistakes

Throughout the history of Taoism, there have been grand theories, grand experiments, and grand failures. Here are some of them:

The Three Worms Some Taoists believed that every person is born with three worms that feed on grains. When the worms become strong enough, they consume the person and cause death.

External Alchemy Believing that physical immortality was possible, alchemists tested numerous substances in a search for the right formula. Many of these were toxins such as mercury and lead, and the experimenters died (although their followers hid these results by claiming that they had become immortal).

Penglai (p. 49) An isle of immortals was believed to exist somewhere in the Pacific Ocean east of China. Qin Shi Huang (p. 159), the First Emperor of China, sent numerous unsuccessful expeditions to find the mythological island.

Taoist Scams

Scams by Taoists, or people purporting to be Taoists, have existed for a long time. In the time of Qin Shi Huang, for example, it was shown that many of the so-called Formula Doctors (*fangshi*) could not show any benefit to their prescriptions, and they were executed.

Many scandals have involved sex. Some Taoist nunneries were actually brothels. Taoist theories of sexual cultivation (p. 222) were exploited. Even today, people offering Taoist "sexual empowerment" are arrested and convicted for sexual abuse.

Then there are all sorts of scams involving fake feng shui, clearing of karma, exorcism, immortality, and even the granting of divinity. All of these scams are in some way based on distortions of traditional practice.

A priest may be lustful beneath his holy robes,
but the sacred symbols on his robes will not change.

Taoism—just like every other spiritual tradition in this world—has struggled with people who exploit it to abuse others. From promises of divine healing, extraordinary wealth, and sexual ecstasy to spirit possession, demon enslavement, and consorting with hell, there have been plenty of corrupt Taoists throughout the centuries—and they exist even today.

Anyone interested in Taoism has to be forewarned that such people must be avoided—and that, sadly, such abusive figures are far more likely to present themselves to sincere seekers than are the true masters.

However, the existence of abuse and evil is no invalidation of the core value of Taoism. The philosophy of Taoism; the health exercises; the appreciation of nature; the deep entwining with art, poetry, and music; the scientific attitude; and the centering on great reverence are important and powerful. Yes, bad people have victimized others while dangling Taoism as bait, but that doesn't make Taoism wrong.

It seems that every month there are new revelations of innocent people abused by those in power. The worst thing is to be silent about it. We must speak out against the use of religion and spirituality to deceive and injure others.

The *I Ching* gives us the perfect test. In Hexagram 27, Nourishing, the Statement reads: "Watch the jaws and what one seeks to fill one's mouth." In other words: watch what a person says, and look to see what that person really wants. If it's power, money, fame, adoration, or sex, then that person must be avoided, no matter what he or she promises you. If you apply that test, though, you'll find that there are very few true teachers in this world.

We have to learn for ourselves and not be beholden to any one school or teacher. The masters don't have all the answers, the scholars don't have all the answers, and certainly the fortune-tellers and magicians are even less likely to have the answers.

No tricks! Don't go for smoke and mirrors. Look for Tao. And do the looking yourself.

But the sacred symbols on his robes will not change when confronted with the ridiculous.

Selling iPhones in the Underworld

When Steve Jobs, the founder of Apple, died in 2011, a temple medium in Penang, Malaysia, held a ritual at Pulau Jerejak, near a statue of Mother Ancestor (p. 98), so that Jobs could be reincarnated. The medium also announced that he was authorized as a general agent for iPhones in the underworld. He added that Yama, the King of the Underworld, would use an iPad to access the records of the living and dying.

The ritual asked participants to take a bite from an apple and observe three minutes of silence before throwing the apple into the sea. Some people ate their apples before the ritual was completed.

Other Taoists spoke out against the ceremony, saying that the dead could only receive items that were burned. One declared: "Taoist believers burn only traditional items like houses and maids."

When confronted with the ridiculous,
will you choose a fantasy or belief?

As is so often the case, both sides in the story of the temple medium have muddled the situation. However, there are some traditional elements to be affirmed here. The idea of helping someone be reincarnated comes from Buddhism and has been adopted by some Taoist sects. Trying to make contact with the deceased is a ritual that brings comfort and acceptance of death. Unfortunately, everyone involved in this situation has distorted the tradition nearly beyond recognition. Anyone mildly interested in Taoism could understandably lose all enthusiasm after reading such a story.

We often seem to believe most stubbornly in what we know the least about. Let us ask then, is belief simply what we do to fill in the gaps of what we don't know? Are we mere children, making up stories of demons in the closet, or reasons why a fairy star will come down and help us? This is the kind of belief that we must try to outgrow. Fantasy-as-belief is not reliable.

Life is a mystery, and belief is an essential ingredient of sanity. This is not the belief that is fantasy, but the belief that is faith.

This faith is the sense that the world is inherently good, that people are inherently good, and that our values are essential to living in harmony with nature, others, and ourselves. It is belief in ourselves, that we are capable of meeting life's challenges, and that we have integrity, honesty, and kindness. It is the faith that we will work toward the good whenever there is the evil of disaster.

As Laozi says, knowing that you don't know is superior (p. 359). Belief is necessary, but choose the belief of faith and not the belief of fantasy—even if the fantasy has the name of your favorite religion. We need to move beyond telling ourselves stories to comfort ourselves and instead try to perceive the truth directly.

Will you choose a fantasy or belief? Why not choose the ultimate sum? "One."

311 Great One, One Great

- Festival for the **Great One Heavenly Ruler**

The Great One

The Great One Heavenly Ruler (Taiyi Jiuku Tianjun) personifies a complex philosophical concept. Here are some of the many beliefs about him:

Emperor Wudi (156–87 BCE; p. 46) of the Han dynasty was not succeeding in his search for immortality, and he was told this was because his sacrifices had omitted Taiyi. Ceremonies to this god began from that point.

Taiyi was an immortal with medical knowledge, invited to the banquet of the Queen Mother of the West (p. 235).

He listens to those who are suffering and saves them, sending a boat of nine lotus flowers to ferry them to the shore of salvation.

He represents cosmic matter before it congealed into material shape.

The Great One as a Philosophical Concept

In Chapter 39 of the *Daodejing,* Laozi writes:

Since ancient times, these things gained the one:
Heaven gained the one and became pure.
Earth gained the one and became serene.
The gods gained the one and became divine.
The valley gained the one and became full.
All things gain the one and grow.

Ceremony to Taiyi to save all souls.
© Saskia Dab

The ultimate sum? "One."
The ultimate goal? "One."

How do we understand a world of gods, demons, ghosts, and humans? How do we comprehend unlimited heaven and earth?

Heaven gained the one and became pure: without oneness, heaven would be complexity without order.

Earth gained the one and became serene: without oneness, earth would be multiplicity without sequence.

The gods gained the one and became divine: without oneness, the gods would be immortal without purpose.

The valley gained the one and became full: without oneness, there would be receiving without fullness.

On this one day, the eleventh day of the eleventh moon, the eleventh day of the Great Snow, think back to the one. You came from one and need only return to one for all to be—one.

The ultimate goal? "One." We kneel as pilgrims to the temple gods.

The Evolution of Gods and Myth

The role of gods continues to evolve to adapt to people's needs.

Lesbian, gay, bisexual, and transgender issues will be among the fundamental civil rights issues of the early twenty-first century. Accordingly, the Lady at the Water's Edge (p. 308) has become a protector of lesbians, and the Rabbit God (Tuershen) has been established in Yonghe City, Taiwan, as the patron god of homosexuals.

China launched its first moon probe in 2007, naming the mission after Chang'e (p. 265). In 2011, China completed its first successful docking of its space lab module Tiangong-1 (Heavenly Palace) with the unmanned spacecraft Shenzhou-8 (Divine Vessel). The names and the numerology are quite Taoist. Furthermore, many citizens saw it as the romantic reenactment of the Cowherd and the Weaver Girl from the Double Seven Festival (p. 221), proclaiming the docking to be a long "space kiss."

Taoist and Buddhist figures appear every year in films from Hong Kong, Taiwan, and China. They also appear in novels, manga, and computer games. Chinese operas, many of which preserve folktales, legends, historical events, or religious themes, are regularly staged.

Many contemporary martial arts and exercise classes have Buddhist and Taoist heritages. Shaolin martial arts comes from the Shaolin Temple at Songshan (p. 93), Taijiquan is based on a Taoist idea, Baguazhang is based on the *I Ching,* and qigong is almost completely Taoist in origin.

Finally, Taoism and Buddhism continue to be live religions, with priests still presiding over marriages, births, and funerals, and with individuals worshipping gods according to their professions—police have statues of Guan Yu (p. 17), and sailors have images of Mother Ancestor (p. 98).

We kneel as pilgrims to the temple gods
and we see the world as if through their eyes.

The gods are archetypes and role models. Just as children go through predictable fantasies—the warrior, the princess, the mommy and daddy, the hero, and so on—each generation needs gods to worship. Our values of compassion, ethics, loyalty, courage, and faith are passed on.

The very fact that the gods are divine—meaning that we believe them to be above the foibles of mortals—shows that we want to celebrate our ideals. Objecting to gods because they are impossibly mythologized or that we don't think they exist is illiterate. The gods represent ideals, and we need ideals.

We are entangled with the cult of personality more intensely than at any other time in history. Gossip magazines, memoirs, reality television shows, social networking, microblogging, real-time video uploads of every significant event—we're more involved with people than ever. Yet, we quickly spin raw history into stories. We mythologize everyone from singers to boxers, athletes to national leaders. They become the ideals we idolize.

That ideals such as peace and love, honesty and integrity, loyalty and courage, learning and improvement, good government and social justice are hard to achieve does not negate their value. We want people to embody those ideals. We want Taoist gods to embody them, too.

When a physicist tries to explain a complicated concept, mitigating factors are often set aside to facilitate communication: "Now let's look at this first in two dimensions," or "For the moment, let us assume that there's no air friction." Our ideals and our gods are the same way. We set aside difficulties—although we don't forget them—until we can reach the right conclusion. Then when we add back the difficulties, we still keep in mind the basic principles we were trying to affirm.

And we see the world as if through their eyes. We want to stand in peace at stone altars.

Stances in Chinese Martial Arts

Stance is crucial in martial arts. Without a stable stance, all other actions are impossible. The basic stance is called the horse stance, because it's the posture of someone riding a horse. All other stances are derived from it,

and when people admire someone's "horse," they mean that they admire the stability with which the person stands.

Confucius on Reverence

This passage is from the *Analects*:

> The noble person holds three things in reverence: Reverence for heaven's command. Reverence for great people. Reverence for the words of the sages. The inferior person does not know heaven's commands and doesn't know to revere them. Such a person does not respect great people and ridicules the words of sages.

We want to stand in peace at stone altars.
All is shifting—where do we stand today?

This table has stood in a Suzhou garden for years, impervious to the rain and the sun. It's made of solid granite, with a top that is nearly a foot thick. It's a bridge on three trestles, mighty, permanent, unmoving, and undoubtedly having outlived its makers and its owners. What was this table used for? Maybe it was merely used for a child to set down her toy, or for someone to set out tea during a charming garden party. On the other hand, this looks like the kind of table to use for sacrifice, for observations of the moon, for offerings. It is more altar than garden table.

Such was the sensibility of the past. The tombsite chosen by the best geomancer was meant to bring a thousand years of glory. Neither rain, nor snow, nor sun dulled the edges of those granite memorials. If you talked to the old man who moved a mountain (p. 65), he would not have whispered even a moment of doubt that his family line would continue the work that he set out to achieve.

Now we live in a world where the tabletop is virtual, bodies are burned into nearly weightless ash, and the will of one is sublimated to crowd-sourcing. This table in Suzhou was a place to make vows in reverence. Where do we stand today?

All is shifting—where do we stand today? How can you keep belief and reverence?

314 | No Magical Thinking

314

• Fasting day

Stationed at a Stump to Wait for a Rabbit

This is a famous idiom that originated with the philosopher **Han Fei** (280–233 BCE). His text, the *Han Feizi*, is a core book of **Legalism** (Fa Jia), which focuses on advice to a ruler.

Once there was a farmer in the state of Song who was working in his field when he saw a rabbit dash by. It collided with a stump, broke its neck, and fell down dead. The farmer got a rabbit without having to catch it or buy it.

From that day on, he abandoned his farming and waited by the stump each day for the next rabbit to appear. But none did, and in time his fields were overgrown with weeds.

How can you keep belief and reverence without the trap of magical thinking?

Spirituality can degenerate into superstition. We must avoid that. No magical thinking.

Belief is good. For example, we need to believe in ourselves. We say that to encourage our children, cheer our favorite sports team, support a political candidate, or make a commitment to a spiritual path. Yes, we need to believe in ourselves—but mere belief alone does not carry the day.

How do we keep all the good of belief while avoiding the pitfalls of magical thinking? How do we support ritual, prayer, offering, and sacrifice without falling into superstition? How do we avoid compulsive behavior because we long too much for miracles?

Magical thinking is done to get a reward. We act as if we are manipulating some supernatural physics. Perhaps this is one reason why the Chan Buddhists and Taoist masters emphasize practicing with no thought of reward. By removing any expectation of a result, they remove the basis for magical thinking. On a deeper level, they assert that we practice for the sake of realizing emptiness. Now, encountering the void is surely not what most people expect from magical thinking. That is no obvious "reward." But it leads to the truth that transcends belief.

Without the trap of magical thinking, can you see that self-knowledge is enlightenment?

315 | The Right Self-Knowledge

‣ Fasting day

The Boxer Rebellion

Between 1898 and 1901, China had a corrupt and weak imperial government faced with foreign imperialism, a debilitating opium trade, unequal treaties, and resentment of Christian missionaries. The **Righteous Harmony Society** (Yihetuan) arose in response. This movement originated with peasants of Shandong Province who had lost their livelihoods to imperialism, opium addiction, and national disasters. Thousands embraced martial arts, spirit possession, and incantations to Taoist and Buddhist gods. They believed that they could fly and resist bullets, and that millions of spirit soldiers would descend from heaven to help them. They were tragically mistaken, but the conflict became known in the West as the **Boxer Rebellion**.

Knowing Yourself

Laozi gave one of the wisest pronouncements about self-knowledge in Chapter 33 of the *Daodejing*:

> To know others is wise; to know yourself
>   is enlightenment.
> To conquer others is strength; to conquer
>   yourself is power.
> To know what's enough is wealth.
> To move resolutely is will.
> Those who do not lose what they have
>   will go a long way.
> Those who do not die will have longevity.

Self-knowledge is enlightenment
and self-control is great power.

Disaster tempts us into magical thinking. When life seems uncontrollable, when our ambitions fall apart, when our loved ones die, when our country is overrun, then we become desperate to comprehend. If we panic, we may make up reasons rather than search for understanding.

If we're too overwhelmed, we may even long for rescue. We may call on the bodhisattva and the immortal, the Buddha and the god to save us. When we feel helpless to lift ourselves out of terror, we will turn to any source for salvation.

However, Taoists strive to stay aware no matter how terrible their fates. They strive to save themselves rather than expect others to rescue them. They try to learn from each experience, but they know that they cannot change the past. They walk resolutely into the future.

No external power substitutes for inner spirituality. Nothing is better than walking your own path. You need to do that with eyes wide open, powered by your own heartbeat and breath.

Laozi states: "To know others is wise; to know yourself is enlightenment. To conquer others is strength; to conquer yourself is power." For Laozi, self-knowledge is enlightenment, and self-control is power.

Trust in your understanding and walk the Way. No matter what the hardships, understand yourself, conquer yourself, and find your power. Then you will not be trapped in the past, and your future will be ever open.

And self-control is great power—if you know that every year has its darkest day.

Exercise 22

This is the shortest day and the longest night. From this point on, the days will gradually lengthen again, although the weather will still be cold for weeks to come.

This exercise is best practiced during the period of 11:00 P.M.–3:00 A.M.

1. Begin by sitting with your legs stretched out straight before you. Grasp your knees. The thumb squeezes the side of the knee; the index and second fingers push into the indentation on either side of the lower leg, just below the patella.

2. Squeeze your knees and press the points. Exhale as you clench, hold momentarily, then inhale as you relax. Repeat fifteen times.

3. Sit cross-legged and face forward. Click your teeth together thirty-six times. Roll your tongue between your teeth nine times in each direction. Form saliva in your mouth by pushing your cheeks in and out. When your mouth is filled with saliva, divide the liquid into three portions.

4. Inhale; then exhale, imagining your breath traveling to the dantian and then swallow one-third of the saliva, imagining that it travels to the dantian.

5. Repeat two more times until you've swallowed all three portions.

6. Sit comfortably as long as you like.

Through this exercise, ancient Taoists sought to prevent or treat cold and dampness in the hands; loss of sensation or excessive heat in the feet; pain in the lower ribs, between the shoulders, in the navel, or in the middle thighs; pain in the torso and limbs; diarrhea; and excessive longing.

Winter Solstice Festival

The **Winter Solstice Festival** (Dongzhi) is celebrated when the sunlight is at its weakest and the days are the shortest. Therefore, it is deeply tied to the observation of yin and yang: yin is at its greatest, and yet people know that yin must recede as yang becomes ascendant with each subsequent day. Like all the other festivals, the Winter Solstice is a time to gather as a family, and naturally, food and visits to one's ancestral temple are involved.

One central custom, especially for southern and overseas Chinese, is the making and eating of *tangyuan* (soup with spherical dumplings). Tangyuan are balls of glutinous rice flour. Their diameters vary according to the tradition of the maker. Some make the balls up to a few inches in diameter and serve them with smaller sizes, while others make the balls the same size and about an inch in diameter. The balls can be plain or stuffed, and the dish can be sweet or savory. The entire family is expected to gather—*tangyuan* sounds like *tuanyuan,* which means family reunion.

Some people make a dish of glutinous rice and red beans in the belief that this will drive away evil spirits. According to one story, **Gong Gongshi** had an evil son who died on this day, but came back as a malignant spirit who made people ill. Knowing that his son was afraid of red beans, Gong taught everyone how to cook this dish to repel his evil son.

The white spheres symbolize the completeness of cycles, that there is returning, and that all will be smooth.

In the north, dumplings rather than tangyuan are eaten. This practice is tied to the Han dynasty physician, **Zhang Zhongjing** (150–219). Seeing poor people suffering from chilblains on their ears, he ordered his apprentices to make mutton dumplings to distribute to the poor. The dumplings themselves were shaped like ears, and he named the soup "Expelling-Cold Tender-Ear Soup" *(quhan jiao'er tang).*

Another northern Chinese custom is to eat a dumpling soup called *huntun.* During the Han dynasty, the Huns, led by two leaders, Hun and Tun, invaded China. The *huntun* dumplings became a way to show anger for the enemy. Some people believe there's a connection between the huntun and the wonton dumpling soup popular today, but this is difficult to establish with certainty.

In the old days, those clans that still maintained family temples had reunions of all members at the ancestral shrines for ceremonies and sacrifice, followed by lavish meals.

The Solstice in the *I Ching*

 Some hexagrams of the *I Ching* are associated with the seasons. Hexagram 24, **Returning** (Fu), is specifically linked to the winter solstice and the eleventh moon. Understanding the graphic structure of this hexagram can help make the philosophy and symbolism of the solstice clear.

The bottom of the hexagram is the early stage of a situation; the top is the ending of a situation. Viewed as a diagram of time, the top five lines of the hexagram's split lines, representing yin, show a situation of nearly complete darkness (one of yin's attributes). Only one yang line, represented by an unbroken line, has appeared at the bottom, the traditional "entrance" to the hexagram. Therefore, this hexagram is seen as a graph of light returning to nearly complete darkness.

Commentators on the *I Ching* have explained that all movement is analyzed according to the six stages represented by the six lines of the hexagram. The seventh stage brings return. Corresponding to this, the winter solstice occurs in the seventh moon after the summer solstice, as sunrise occurs in the seventh double-hour after sunset.

Three texts accompany each hexagram of the *I Ching.* One of the three texts is called the Image, reputedly written by Confucius himself.

> Thunder in the center of the earth: returning.
> The ancient kings closed the borders during the solstices.
> Traveling merchants did not journey.
> Sovereigns did not tour the provinces.

This means that the winter solstice was seen as a time of rest and renewal. During winter, life energy is dormant and nature is resting. The movement that will bring a restoration of life is underground. If one looks at the hexagram spatially, the yang line that represents the return of life is still under the earth. The sages extrapolated from this to suggest what we should do whenever there is darkness in our life: we rest and renew ourselves. Whether this means the return of health after illness, the return of understanding after conflict, or the return of good fortune after disaster, the return of good has to be allowed to come in its own time, and it must be strengthened by rest and care.

The Statement, contributed by King Wen (p. 358), emphasizes the forbearance necessary to accept the cyclical nature of life. Since the *I Ching* is partially a book of divination, the profundity of how it would have us accept cycles and to work with returning is of vital importance:

> Returning. Continue.
> In coming and going, there is neither sickness nor distress.
> Companions come without fault.
> Returning is its Tao.
> In seven days, returning comes.
> Gain by having a place to go.

The Winter Solstice Festival is the time to reunite with our families, enjoy good food that will aid in renewal, and to contemplate the truth of the seasons. Whenever we are oppressed by darkness, light is sure to return. ▶

316 | The Darkest Day

Visiting the Temple of Auspicious Omen Alone on Winter Solstice

Su Shi (p. 140) goes to the temple with no other visitors present. The weather is cold and rainy, and it isn't the season for the lovely flowers that attract people at other times of the year. Perhaps musing to himself, he asks who else would go to the temple on such a frigid and rainy day.

> Wan sunlight cannot warm the well's bottom,
> and cold, sighing rain soaks the withered roots.
> Is there anyone more like Mr. Su?
> This is not the season for flowers and still I come alone.

Every year has its darkest day;
each dark day is followed by light.

Who among us goes through three hundred days without any misfortune or trouble? All of us experience trials. Trouble can often drive us to madness and leave us staring bewildered through our windows at the dark.

For all of us, then, winter solstice is a reminder that darkness comes to its greatest extreme—for exactly one day. On this day, as on all the others, there is a dynamic and precise proportion between dark and light. It is measurable, it is complete. It is, for one day, immutable. The darkness of the solstice cannot be avoided—but human beings can outlast it and live to see the next day.

The people of the past have left us many hints about what to do: families come back together, nourish themselves, give thanks to their ancestors, and, in looking at the round balls of glutinous rice in their round bowls sitting at round tables, reaffirm that all of life is a smooth cycle. Taoists observe the day precisely, aligning themselves with the greater cosmic cycles of sunrise and sunset and the turning of the earth. They also celebrate the Three Pure Ones, worshipping and turning to faith at a time when the sky is dark and the cycles of life so profoundly change. The lunar calendar is calibrated by the winter solstice, so this day is the reference point for the year to come.

At any time of your life, you may find yourself in a winter, and you may feel that you are in the darkest of times. Think back to this day then and do what has been done for thousands of years: unite with your family, nourish yourself and others, fix your mind on the truth of cycles, and take refuge in reverence for the holy.

Each dark day is followed by light—remember that if you want a happy future.

317 | The Calico-Bag Luohan

If you want a happy future,
just use your skill to serve others.

It's clear from the transliterated names that the luohans had their origin in the Indian arhats. However, like the rest of Buddhism, the arhats became sinicized.

Angida or Yinjietuo, the Calico-Bag Luohan, became one of the most popular of the group. Whether he simply appealed to people

or, as we will see in a moment, he got combined with Maitreya Buddha, people love him because of his message: the future will be good and filled with plenty. While obesity may be a problem today, it was virtually unknown in ancient times. Drought, flooding, famine, and daily effort without machines guaranteed that most people were thin. Even today, the polite way to compliment someone who might confess to being overweight is to say, "You've had more good luck."

According to one legend, Angida was a snake catcher who wanted to prevent snakes from biting people. Once he caught a snake, he carried it in his bag, removing its venomous fangs before releasing it in the mountains. This led to his enlightenment. He's been combined with Budai Luohan, or Maitreya, the Buddha of the Future (p. 5). In any event, he represents the wishes of the people for plenty and happiness.

Angida, and the other luohans, certainly represent an eclectic and odd grouping. But the message is that there is room for everyone and a need for each person's talents. Angida had the impulse to use his snake-catching ability for good. In the same way, we can each contribute to the holy cause by being who we are, and by finding a way to use that for compassionate service. If we find our place in life that way, there is no reason for doubt.

Just use your skill to serve others as we wish each other long life and good health.

318 | Finding Solitude

River Snow

Liu Zongyuan (773–819) was a Tang dynasty poet and writer, and one of the Eight Great Prose Masters of the Tang and Song. While he was initially successful as an official, he was exiled first to Hunan Province and then to Guangxi Province, where he eventually became a city governor. He wrote poems, fables, essays, and travelogues, and his writings combine elements of Taoism, Confucianism, and Buddhism.

> A thousand mountains, with no birds
>   in flight,
> ten thousand paths, with no one's tracks.
> Old man in bamboo raincoat and hat,
>   alone on a boat,
> the only one fishing in the cold river
>   snow.

We wish each other long life and good health.
While alone, our tears run from our torment.

When we gather with our friends, we wish them long life and good health. They wish us the same. The value of good health is unquestioned, and long life is one of the major goals of Taoism.

At the same time, we all endure the torment of life. We have our anxieties, our pains, our poverty, our frustrations. When Buddha said all of life was suffering, he was stating a truth as much emotional as philosophical. Why, then, if life is so awful, do we urge each other to have more of it?

Today, we are no different than the ambitious Confucianists of imperial China. We exhort our children to study harder, to find careers of great power and wealth, to find cures for cancer or become world leaders. We worship fame and accomplishments, lavishing more attention on the logo of a champion's water bottle than we give to someone thirsty on the street. We climb over one another for money, elbow others aside for gleaming cars, and trample anyone for the sake of getting ahead. Then, when it all collapses in the cross fire of greed and corruption, of impossibility and selfishness, of exploitation and sheer incompetence, we fall apart with it. We cover it up with makeup. We cover it up with grins and touched-up photographs. We cover it up with excuses. We cover it up by blaming others. And then we wish each other long life and good health so we can do it all again.

Li Zongyuan knew the antidote to the poison of ambition when he composed "River Snow." In winter, when all the color of growth and ambition has been bleached away and only the most vital needs are being met, it's a good time to contemplate. The old man on the boat knows why he's fishing, knows why he's old, and knows what sustains him as he fishes alone in the cold river snow.

While alone, our tears run from our torment: we see that light has no form, form has no light.

319 | Light Has No Form

• Worship of the Sun God

The Sun God

The **Sun God** (p. 39), along with the Moon Goddess, brings hot and cold weather. He is impartial, shining on good and evil alike; he brings increase to the earth, and he protects people from misfortune. Since the sun itself can suffer misfortune—in the form of clouds, storms, and eclipses (referred to as being eaten by the Heavenly Dog)—the ancients burned incense and lit firecrackers to frighten off malignant influences.

Light has no form. Form has no light.
Truth comes from light and not from form.

All that we see around us, we see only because light has been reflected off forms. Only then do we perceive shape.

However, we can't fully perceive light itself separate from its striking some object. The sun may be blinding, but we can't see its beam as having shape unless it passes through smoky air.

Light has been taken as a constant. We measure both time and distance in light-years. Physics has found light to be one of the most significant areas of study. We can still see light from billions of years ago, leaving us the possibility that we can see almost to our beginnings. Light reveals something of the immense and the near infinite.

The light from the sun is imperative to our survival. To be imprisoned away from light for any significant amount of time leads to swift deterioration. We may have bodies composed of a little earth and a vast amount of water, but we need the light of the sun to live and be whole.

Spirit is universally described as radiant. The sages assert that there is a light inside us—the light of the soul. Just as cosmologists tell us that the beginning was a sudden burst of light, so too do many spiritual teachers agree that the beginning was light. Therefore, the central goal is to reopen ourselves to the light within.

When you find the light within, then you find the soul.

When you find the soul, then you find that it is light.

When you find the light, then you find that the soul is not divided from all other souls, just as light forever remains light.

When you see yourself as light, then you are enlightened.

When you are enlightened, then you see that all is light, you are light, and that all is you and you are all.

Truth comes from light and not from form: belief is nothing but focus.

On Concentration

The *Classic of History* describes the sovereign using his own person to concentrate power on behalf of his people:

> The sovereign builds himself to the highest degree. He concentrates the five kinds of happiness, and spreads them to all the people.

Zhuangzi also gives a description of concentration that depends on gathering powers together in a person. Only in this case, the subject is a hunchback—a far different kind of person than the magnificent sovereign mentioned in the *Classic of History*.

As Confucius was on his way to Chu, he passed through a forest and saw a hunchback catching cicadas with a sticky rod. "What is this?" he asked. "Do you have a method?" (For the word "method," he uses the word Tao.)

"I do," replied the hunchback. (He literally says, "I have Tao.") "For five or six months, I tried balancing two pellets on my rod without them falling. When I could do the same with three pellets I missed catching only one cicada out of ten. Once I could balance five pellets without dropping them, I caught cicadas as if I were grabbing them with my hand. My body is like a broken stump, my arm is like a withered branch. Heaven and earth are great. The ten thousand things are many. I only notice cicada wings. I don't turn, I don't lean. Nothing distracts me from the wings; how could I not succeed?"

Confucius turned to his students: "Use an undivided will and you concentrate the spirit. That is what this venerable hunchback is telling you."

Belief is nothing but focus,
just as the glass narrows the sun.

If we focus the sun's rays with a magnifying glass, they have the power to burn. All we did was take the sunlight and direct it to a pinpoint. Belief in ourselves is like that. This is the belief that says we are strongly determined to reach a goal or overcome a problem. This is the belief that is the result of our focused attention.

Belief in gods is the same thing. By focusing on a god, the story, the devotion, and what we're trying to do, we sharpen our energy. Worship is a magnifying glass.

Meditation is the same. By focusing on meditation—the sitting, the breathing, the concentration, and the opening to our own inner powers—it sharpens our minds. Meditation is a magnifying glass.

One of the strongest goals we can have is to understand ourselves. This process requires great courage and perseverance. And like all great ventures, it takes belief. Again, we are at the metaphor of the magnifying glass, but here, we can do one more thing with it. We can look through it to understand ourselves.

In the focus that is belief, then, the two aspects of the magnifying glass are merged. The glass becomes both the means to concentrate our minds and the means to examine our minds. When those two functions unite, then true enlightenment is possible.

Just as the glass narrows the sun, why resent the sages' wisdom?

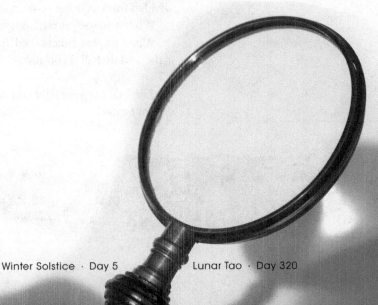

321 | Advice

An Essay by Han Yu

Han Yu (p. 55) was exiled in 803 for opposing a reform movement, and was only recalled when the group declined.

In 815, Han was demoted from the head of the Supreme Academy to the lowest academic position when he allegedly offended the emperor. In response, he wrote the essay "Explanation upon Entering the Academy" ("Jinxuejie"), describing a scene in which his students challenge him. He was clearly alluding to the Confucian duty to criticize one's superior—be it teacher or ruler—a principle the emperor did not bear graciously.

> Teacher, you never stop reciting the Six Arts. Your hands never leave the books of the Hundred Schools. . . . you refute heresies, you rebut the Buddhists and Taoists. . . . yet in public affairs you are not trusted by others, and in private you are not helped by friends. . . . fate colludes with your enemies, and you have met defeat several times. . . . you don't know to worry about this and instead teach others how to act.

Instead of punishing the student, Han Yu says, "Oh my! Come forward!"

> In the past, Mencius was good at debate and clarified Confucianism, but he trekked through all under heaven and died of old age on the road. Xun Qing held to what was right, giving great discourses on profound truths, yet ended up fleeing slander at Chu and died rejected at Lan Ling. . . . yet every month I get a salary and each year eat government grain. . . . I act and get slandered, but fame also follows.

When this essay was read, Han was promoted to a higher office.

In 819, Han Yu wrote a memorial in protest of the emperor's fascination with a relic, supposedly a finger bone of Buddha. The memorial also opposed the government's overinvolvement with Buddhism in general. This again aroused the emperor's anger. Han was nearly executed but was sent into exile instead.

Why resent the sages' wisdom
when you still read advice columns?

One piece of advice often given to writers is this: "Don't be didactic."

The very definition of "didactic" is tinged with suspicion. The word means: "intended to teach; having moral instruction as an ulterior motive." The very definition implies that someone is trying to trick us, to slip morality into our subconscious under the guise of entertainment.

We also use "didacticism" to mean treating someone in a patronizing way. We speak of the tedium of slow, plodding, didactic lecturing. There's no doubt that we resent teaching, we resent morality, we resent being lectured. Certainly, those charged with teaching morals don't do the subject any favors. They couch their lessons in warnings, stories of foolish and doomed people, or dry proverbs tethered to some dusty story from the remote past. Worse, many of these pedagogues prove themselves unable to even hold up their own standards out of weakness or hypocrisy.

Most people would say we should be ethical and moral. We just don't want to talk about it. It's left practically to accident, in the same way we leave a couple to figure out how to have sex, or throw people helplessly into a crowd to get to know others, or leave it to parents to find their own way in raising children. In so many vital aspects of our lives, we are left untaught.

In the meantime, people avidly read advice columnists. They want to know how to use their technology. They want to try new recipes. There's no shortage of people eager to learn and no shortage of information to help them. Why is it bad to be didactic? How can we learn about ethics, morality, religion, and spirituality if we don't listen to teachers?

When you still read advice columns, do you see that body, instinct, and mind are officials?

Advice to the Ruler

"When the ruler excels in propriety, the people respond easily," said Confucius, according to the *Analects*.

"When a ruler practices benevolent government, nothing can hold out against it," said Mencius.

"The ruler's duty lies in making his people abundantly wealthy, making Tao clear, and upholding righteousness," stated the *Model Words of Master Yang* (p. 242).

The Statement of Hexagram 15 in the *I Ching* reads:

Mountains in the middle of the earth: humility. The wise person takes from the ample to add to the meager, weighing and balancing fairly.

In Chapter 66 of the *Daodejing*, Laozi begins by observing that the rivers and oceans act as kings of a hundred valleys because "they are adept at being below them."

That's why the sage who wants to rule the people
must speak as if he were below them.
If he wants to lead the people, he must stand behind them.
That is why, when the sage rules, the people do not find it heavy.
The ruler leads, but the people are not harmed.
All under heaven gladly support him and do not despise him.
He does not contend, so nothing under heaven can contend against him.

Body, instinct, and mind are officials.
Our one soul within us is the ruler.

Many of the classics are couched as advice to a ruler. From the *I Ching* to the *Daodejing*, the authors are addressing the emperor and urging enlightened rule over the people. These books were radical for their day and remain so today: they assume that the emperor is not perfect and needs teaching, and they ultimately urge selfless and kind governance over a nation.

In fact, a ruler has always needed advice. The Yellow Emperor (p. 4) was guided by advisors. Every dynasty has had officials who dared to remonstrate with the emperor, sometimes dying for it, like Bigan (p. 148), or merely being exiled, like Su Shi (p. 140). This assumption that the ruler always needs advice, balance, and teaching is incorporated into the Three Pure Ones: the Jade Emperor rules, but Laozi, as the Great Supreme Old Lord, and the Heavenly Lord of the Primal Origin (p. 12) advise and support him.

We play the part of the ruler in our own lives, and all the classic advice can be taken for our own use. Who are our officials and our subjects? They are all the different aspects of ourselves: our priorities, our ambitions, our thoughts, our minds, our subconscious, our health, and so on. All these have to be kept in harmony and ruled in an enlightened way if the nation of our personality is to prosper continually.

Every nation needs a leader, and every leader makes a difference in the progress of a country. Good governance is essential. In the same way, we as individuals must rule ourselves and our worlds with kindness and understanding—and never allow any one aspect of ourselves to overrun the others.

Our one soul within us is the ruler: whether dreams or thoughts, our minds make their shapes.

323 | Words and Pictures

The Ten Stone Drums

In the days before paper, carving in stone was the means of preserving words. A famous set of ten stones inscribed with poems shows characters in the Great Seal Script (p. 344). These stone drums were discovered in a field during the Tang dynasty (618–907), and poets such as Du Fu, Han Yu, and Su Shi praised the inscriptions as models of both poetry and calligraphy. Archaeologists have dated this set of stones to at least the fifth century BCE.

Song of the Stone Drums

Han Yu (p. 55) wrote a long poem about the stone drums that is preserved in *Three Hundred Tang Poems*. Someone had given him tracings of the inscriptions. Han wrote an emotional paean to the drums. He describes the inscriptions as being like:

> fast swords chopping live crocodiles,
> *luan* birds and phoenixes soaring as a
>   host of immortals descend,
> coral and jade trees in interlocking
>   branches,
> golden cords and iron chains locked
>   together tight,
> ancient *ding,* leaping water, soaring
>   dragons.

Han Yu goes on to urge that the drums be rescued from the field to preserve them, but he laments that he cannot get the academy president to fund moving them, leaving them for "herd boys to strike . . . for fire, and for cows to polish their horns on them."

Luan birds are mythological companions to the phoenix. The *ding* (p. 41) are three-legged bronze vessels from the Zhou dynasty (1046–256 BCE) that were considered emblems of the legitimacy of rule.

The stones are worn and damaged, but still preserved today in Beijing. They are the oldest known stone inscriptions in China.

Whether dreams or thoughts, our minds make their shapes using nothing more than pictures and words.

We communicate through words and pictures, and we go about this in complex and sophisticated ways. The very Chinese language, for example, has many words that are word *and* picture, combining sound, meaning, and depiction in a single ideogram. Poets use clusters of words to form images, similes, and metaphors. And on an entirely different level, we can hardly digest the daily news without photographs, diagrams, charts, tables, and animations to show what is happening.

What faith it takes to put words down. Specifically, what faith it took to have the words carved in stone, as in this photograph taken over one hundred years ago in the Temple of Confucius. Surely the carvers wanted the stones to survive long after they died.

Such words are completely dependent on the reader, not the writer. First, someone has to find them. Second, someone must be able to read and interpret them. Third, someone has to find them useful. Finally, we hope that someone will preserve them for others. The wisdom of the past has been set down for us to find and to use, and we should do so.

Ultimately, this reflects how we think: our minds work in words and pictures. What will we inscribe today?

Using nothing more than pictures and words, we take all colors beamed together to make white.

324 | White Light

‣ Fasting day

Newton and the Prism

Prior to Isaac Newton (1642–1727), scientists believed that white was the natural color of light and that colored light occurred by an additive process. Newton passed white light through one prism and then through another. No colors were added. Instead, the light was refracted back into a single color, demonstrating that white light is the combination or presence of all colors.

Newton's work was eagerly adopted in China. When he published *Theory of the Moon's Motion* in 1702, showing how to find the moon's longitude to determine universal time and find longitude at sea, imperial China quickly seized upon the work. It allowed the more accurate prediction of lunar eclipses. This was a cultural imperative, since unpredicted eclipses were regarded as signs that heaven was displeased with the emperor.

White, Plain, and Su'nu

Some explain that the word "white," *bai*, is a picture of a burning candle, while others say it's the rising sun. In either case, the idea of white light is inherent in the pictogram.

The word *su* (shown at right) depicts the shining threads of silk and also means "white."

Su'nu, whose name means Plain or White Woman, was the legendary teacher of the Yellow Emperor (p. 4). She instructed him on the importance of yin and yang in sexual union, and her book, the *Classic of Su Nu (Su'nujing)*, is a frank and fundamental book on sexuality in the context of health, longevity, and spirituality. While the book is framed as a dialogue with the Yellow Emperor, current scholarship places the book no earlier than the third century.

All colors beamed together to make white:
you make the brightness a unified self.

When all the colors of the rainbow are added together, the result is white light. By extension, true brilliance of character is only possible when we have combined all our different sides. Just as no color of the spectrum can be eliminated without tinting the combined rays, we can never be successful denying or suppressing any part of ourselves. Rather, we bring our different aspects into balance. The key to this is to adjust the amounts and proportions of our different "colors" until the result is—colorless.

There are different systems of color symbolism. In one, white represents purity, plainness, and simplicity. The Yellow Emperor learned about health from Su'nu. The word "su" means "raw silk," "white," "plain," "unadorned," and more. The implication that white is pure, natural, and essential is unmistakable. Metaphorically, the *Yellow* Emperor learned of balance from the *White* Woman—color balanced becomes colorless.

If we unify all our aspects, keeping them in harmony with one another, then the result is pure radiance. This reminds us of the sun, of the light that spiritual people mention in their experiences, of the light that one is supposed to perceive when one reaches higher spiritual centers, of the light that one is supposed to merge with upon death. This light is the light of the spirit, and in it there are no distinctions and therefore no conflicts.

In winter, the snow gradually covers the world in its whiteness. The trees lose their leaves, the fence posts become black lines, and the flowers and shrubs are crushed under white. The world becomes drained of color. Most of the time, we consider winter death. By the metaphor of white light, the world approaches wholeness in winter.

Live your life by the pure light.
Open the pure light within you.
When the pure light appears, go into it without hesitation.

You make the brightness a unified self, if you collect, cover, and store.

325 | Bank and Store

Storing in Winter

The *Classic of Rites* emphasizes the essential activity of storing for the winter.

> The breath [qi, the vital energy] of heaven flies upward, and the earth's energy sinks downward. Heaven and earth do not commune. All is shut and sealed by the eleventh month. The hundred officials are ordered to cover things and store them. The minister of instruction is ordered to check that the people have made their stores, and that nothing is left ungathered.

If you collect, cover, and store,
you can weather any winter.

If it's the essence of Tao to live in harmony with the seasons, then what does winter mean for us? Traditionally, winter is the symbol of storage. All of nature stores its energy and goes dormant in the cold months. The trees drop their leaves, insects and other small animals burrow into the ground, bears hibernate. That makes sense, for the bursting of spring will show the energy and potential that was stored during the winter.

In the same way, we are urged to follow the wisdom of storing. Where people depend on firewood for fuel, it is prudent to chop and stack enough wood to last through the winter months. We need to keep our houses in good repair, prepare warm clothes, and bank food in the cellar to provide for the entire family.

We store at the grander levels of our lives, too. Saving money is one aspect of such storing. A good education in our youth is another. But spiritual storing is also important: we practice when times are calm so that we have the stamina and resources to bear the calamity that will inevitably come.

The full blizzard of disaster can come at any time, so we have to be wise enough to accumulate when times are good. Hopefully, most of your life is peace. If so, then commit yourself to spirituality. Only then can you endure all that you must.

You can weather any winter. Just remember: what is the beat of the world that you feel?

326 | Find Your Own Rhythm

Drums

This passage is from the *Classic of Rites*. The word "wen," or "culture," has multiple meanings. It also means "language," "writing," "formal," "literary," "gentle," "civilian" (as opposed to military), and is an old measure word for "coins."

> The sage is concerned with culture [wen], displaying it in carts and robes; brightening it in splendid colors; praising it in song and music; and illuminating it in poetry and writing.
>
> However, if the ritual vessels are not set out, the jade and silk not properly distributed, the zither and harp not struck, or the bells and drums not beaten, then I do not see a sage.

© Saskia Dab

What is the beat of the world that you feel?
Why shouldn't your heartbeat be the one heard?

You get tired each day. You discharge all your energy, and then you need to sleep. Unless you do that, you cannot recover from the day, your mind cannot process your experiences, and you cannot rest.

But during that rest, you are not only repairing damaged and exhausted parts of yourself, you are also learning. Whatever happened to you that day cannot be mastered until you spend one or more nights resting. The alternation of the active days and restful nights is one example of the rhythms of our lives.

Each day, then, is meant to be challenging enough so that you must adapt and change. You change daily. You aren't a static person going through the years. You're always changing, always preparing yourself for the challenges that will come.

All this forms a beat, a rhythm. It's a regular response to each day's stresses and rewards, each day's questions and insights. That beat is constant and steady: it is your own personal structure.

You're the drummer. This is not a passive process. It's one of participation. Hear your beat. Hear your timing. Drum along with it. What greater joy is there than to be on the beat?

Why shouldn't your heartbeat be the one heard if you are sitting under a boulder?

327 | The Boulder

Utilizing the Energy of Stones

The *Art of War* (*Sunzi Bingfa;* p. 200) is a superb book of military strategy that has been used by military leaders the world over, including Mao Zedong, Douglas MacArthur, Napoleon, and American Gulf War generals Norman Schwarzkopf and Colin Powell. The text has been taught at West Point and other military academies. It has also been popular as a guide to management and business.

> When the right energy is used, warriors move like rolling logs and boulders. The nature of logs and boulders is to be still when level and to move heavily when precarious; to stop when square, and to move when round. Thus good warriors know how to use natural energy, traveling like a round boulder down a thousand-foot mountain. That is energy.

If you are sitting under a boulder,
it would be fitting to move to one side.

You can do many things with a boulder. You can use it to build a wall, to put in your garden, to carve a memorial, to shore up a roadway, or to make a seawall. But there's one certainty for a boulder on a hillside: loosen it and it will roll downhill.

It seems obvious that the riskiest place to sit is beneath such a boulder. There's no question that it will roll. The only real question is when. Do you want to be there when that happens? If so, you will want that rolling to be useful to you, and you will not want to be in the way.

The thief found dead beneath a safe at the foot of the stairs might be laughed at for being dumb, but how many times do we play with forces equally ponderous, thinking that we'll "get away with it"? Luck won't hold a boulder back.

It's not very hard being a Taoist. Certainly not as long as you know where to sit, know what to loosen, and know the right timing.

It would be fitting to move to one side. Avoid two blades, two levers joined.

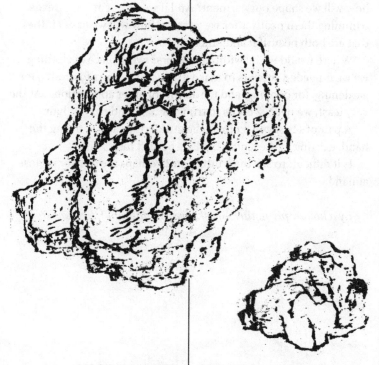

328 | The Scissors

Zhang Xiaoquan Scissors

Zhang Xiaoquan of Hang-zhou set out to make scissors in 1663 with the motto, "Good steel, excellent workmanship." He became noted for a wide range of scissors: some were utilitarian, while others were carved with motifs such as the West Lake landscape, birds, and animals. Their making involved as many as seventy-two distinct processes, including repeated forging of different kinds of iron and steel and hand sharpening.

Emperor Qianlong (1711–1799) adopted the scissors for the imperial court. According to one story, he secretly came to Zhang in person in 1781, buying scissors for all the concubines in the palace. Zhang Xiaoquan scissors won prizes outside of China at the Southern Coast Industrial Exposition in 1910, the 1915 Panama Pacific International Exposition, and the 1926 Sesqui-Centennial International Exposition in Philadelphia.

Two blades. Two levers joined
by a hollow pivot.

Scissors are so simple and admirable. Two blades that are equals are joined together by the emptiness of a pivot. We concentrate so much on what the cutting edges are doing that we don't always notice that they are levers too, increasing our hand strength for cutting. Depending on how one uses the scissors, sometimes both blades cut, and sometimes one is anvil for the other. The scissors do their job with nothing extra needed.

Isn't this a wonderful metaphor for everything else we need to do in life?

Can we uphold the same principle as the scissors—working with another as two equals joining to do a simple job, each one faithful to the agreed-upon direction?

Can we have the sharp eyesight to see the line we must follow, and then cut straight down that line?

Can we be the scissors that both destroy and create? If we don't cut, say, an armhole in the jacket we're making, how will the garment function? If we don't cut the cloth according to the pattern, how will we shape our garment? And if we don't cut the threads, trimming them neatly after we've sewn, how will we have clothes that are both beautiful and functional?

Where would we be without scissors? Every piece of clothing we wear needed scissors to make it. We use scissors for crafts, for gardening, for cooking, and for dozens of other applications. At the very least, we need scissors to trim our nails and cut our hair.

A pair of scissors becomes a beautiful companion, fitting the hand, existing in the length of blade perfect for its task.

Is it difficult to see the truth of life? Perhaps the answer is close at hand.

By a hollow pivot, turn to ask: are you dancer of the dance?

329 | The Dance Is the Dancer

• Fasting day

Method of Walking the Earth's Pattern and Flying Through the Heavenly Net

The diagram below shows the **Steps of Yu**, a way to shamanistically integrate oneself with the cosmos. The spiral shows the path to the North Star and the Big Dipper. The steps on the right lift a dancer to heaven, and the diagram at the bottom shows steps in the pattern of the Big Dipper.

The Great Yu (2200–2100 BCE; p. 105) was one of the legendary rulers of China and famous for his work to control flooding. According to mythological beliefs about him, Yu was able to change into a bear and could travel to the stars and learn from the gods. The Steps of Yu are the dance of power that made such journeys possible. Preserved in Taoist texts, the method is still practiced by Taoist priests, mediums, and sorcerers.

Some people believe that the idea of a pattern of steps that leads to transcendence is part of the foundation of Chinese martial arts and dance.

The dance starts with a spiral inward and in the center takes the zigzag pattern of the Big Dipper.

Are you dancer of the dance?
Or is the dance dancing you?

Dancing is thrilling. There's nothing quite like spirit, breath, mind, heart, and body all working together. When the dance is expertly performed, it transcends what the dancer does even in practice. It's quite common for a dancer to describe a performance as the "best one yet" and "far beyond what I dreamed I could do." Those privileged to watch good dance will use words such as "extraordinary," "ethereal," and "superhuman."

Another common description is of the dancer becoming totally lost in the dance. The dancer's everyday mind is somehow suspended, and he or she is so absorbed in the dance that there is no separation between dancer and dance.

The Great Yu had a dance that took him to the stars and the gods. That may be beyond most of us, but if we dance well, then we are just as uplifted, just as transcendent, as if we were with deities. We can be the dancer who is the dance—on a spiral that first turns inward and ends in the stars.

Or is the dance dancing you to show: what is the best way to learn Tao?

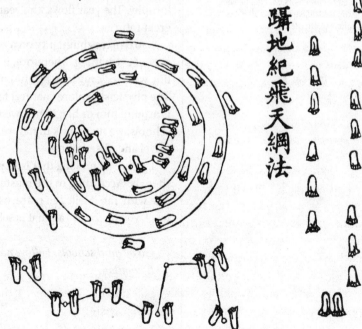

蹋地紀飛天網法

330 | Follow Nature

The Four Greats in the World

In Chapter 25 of the *Daodejing*, Laozi takes us from the beginnings of the universe to a simple basis for our laws and principles:

> There was something chaotic yet
> complete
> here before heaven and earth were born.
> How silent and still it was, how singular
> and unaltered,
> turning without stop.
> Perhaps it was the mother of all under
> heaven.
> I do not know its name,
> but if it must be given a word, call it Tao.
> If a name must be made for it, call it
> great.
> The great flows.
> What flows goes far.
> What goes far returns.
> Therefore, Tao is great.
> Heaven is great.
> Earth is great.
> Humanity is great.
> In this world, these four are great,
> and humanity is one of them.
> People pattern their law after the earth.
> Earth patterns its law after heaven.
> Heaven patterns its law after Tao.
> Tao patterns its law on itself.

What is the best way to learn Tao?
Go beyond schools. Follow nature.

Within Taoism, we have different schools of thought. Within each school of thought, we have various subjects and teachers. When we're still learning about Tao, it makes sense to find a good school and a good teacher. There isn't one school or a single teacher right for everyone. It's the *combination* of school and student that matters. As long as you find the school of thought that fits who you are, then it's right.

Every school has its advantages and its limitations. Every teacher has abilities and shortcomings. In time, when you have absorbed the best of what can be taught and have also confronted the limitations, then what do you do?

Laozi is an excellent guide here. First he establishes the very root of what we are looking for: the beginning of all that we know. If we can find the beginning, then our understanding is grounded in the most fundamental way possible. This beginning is mysterious, enormous, beyond definition. As a label, we call it Tao. Just as we are at the end of the eleventh moon and heading toward the end of the year and therefore the beginning of a new one, so too must we go back to the beginning whenever we want to validate our philosophy. The year flows, the year returns. The great flows, and the great returns.

Laozi places humanity on a par with heaven and earth. We are a part of everything. Therefore, if we want to know more about this life, we need only look around us. The astronomer gazes at stars. The physicist explores natural forces. The poet writes about what is around him or her. When we want to continue learning beyond schools, we must look to nature. Tao is ultimately to be found by travel and observation.

Is there a knowing that is beyond learning from nature? Yes, there is. According to the masters, our goal should be to become one with Tao itself. Tao patterns its law on itself. At the highest level, you become Tao that is self-defined.

Go beyond schools. Follow nature. But ask: why do all ships carry lifeboats?

The Last Moon

Night Mooring at Maple Bridge

The moon sets, birds cry, and frost fills the sky.
River maples, fishing torches—can't sleep.
From Cold Mountain Temple outside Gusu:
the midnight bell sounds to this traveler's boat.
—Zhang Ji (d. 780)

Gusu was the ancient name for Suzhou.

The two solar terms within this moon:

SLIGHT COLD

GREAT COLD

Exercise 23

The year enters its period of greatest cold, and if low-temperature records are set, it's commonly during this time.

This exercise is best practiced during the period of 11:00 P.M.–3:00 A.M.

1. Sit cross-legged and raise one hand overhead, palm facing upward. Press the other palm on your foot.

2. Alternately change position, pushing upward with the raised hand, but with force, and press downward with the other hand. Inhale when you push; exhale when you change sides. Repeat fifteen times on each side.

3. Facing forward with your hands resting on your lap, click your teeth together thirty-six times. Roll your tongue between your teeth nine times in each direction. Form saliva in your mouth by pushing your cheeks in and out. When your mouth is filled with saliva, divide the liquid into three portions.

4. Inhale; then exhale, imagining your breath traveling to the dantian and then swallow one-third of the saliva, imagining that it travels to the dantian.

5. Repeat two more times until you've swallowed all three portions.

6. Sit comfortably as long as you like.

Through this exercise, ancient Taoists sought to prevent or treat blockages in the circulatory system; vomiting; stomach pains and abdominal distension; loss of appetite; sighing; feelings of heaviness; diarrhea; problems in urinating; and grief.

331 | Lifeboats

- Fasting day
- Festival of the Eight Immortals Crossing to Penglai

The Eight Immortals Cross the Sea

This festival commemorates the story of the Eight Immortals (p. 124) as they cross the ocean to Penglai (p. 49), the legendary island of immortals.

When the Eight Immortals arrive at the shore of the Eastern Sea, they find the waves turbulent. Lu Dongbin proposes that each immortal help cross the sea through his or her special skills. Li Tieguai throws his crutch; Han Zhongli tosses his palm-leaf fan; Zhang Guolao sends his paper donkey, and so on. In this way, all the immortals cross the sea.

This story lives on in a number of ways. First, Penglai City, Shandong, has a scenic area with gates, buildings, and sculptures based on this very legend. Second, a popular idiom, "The Eight Immortals cross the seas," symbolizes overcoming difficulties or accomplishing marvelous feats using one's own skills. Finally, the story has inspired a luxurious banquet dish featuring the eight ingredients of shark fin, sea cucumber, abalone, shrimp, fish bone, fish maw, asparagus, and ham. In this version of the story, there is a luohan as well, represented by adding chicken. The dish was often prepared for the families of Confucius, officials, scholars, and the emperor.

Why do all ships carry lifeboats?
We want to have another chance.

The answer to the lifeboat question seems obvious. However, sometimes the obvious can be overlooked, and sometimes discovering what we overlooked can tell us something important. Even the sailors who pray to Mother Ancestor (p. 98) carry lifeboats. They may worship the Mother, but they are prepared to save themselves. The sinking of a boat in a storm may be terrible, but we no longer ascribe it to devils and monsters. We know accidents happen, and we know accidents happen impersonally.

When a ship begins to sink, we go to the lifeboats. We have prepared, and we understand that there are no guarantees: our lifeboat could still be capsized, or we might not be rescued. But it's necessary. Without it, we wouldn't even get another chance. When the rescued sailor reaches land, thanks will be expressed, but being prepared was crucial.

What about each of us in the sea that is this lifetime? Do we have lifeboats? When our flesh-and-blood hull breaks apart for the last time, will there be a lifeboat and will there be a sailor in that boat?

Taoist alchemists wanted to make the Golden Embryo that would carry the human soul away from the body upon death. Other Taoists wanted to cross to the island of Penglai and thereby join other immortals. The Chan Buddhists and the philosophical Taoists would scoff: there is no ship, there is no lifeboat, there is no passenger, and there is no one to rescue and nothing to be rescued from.

What's your answer? Whether you're sailing to Penglai or whether you're just trying to navigate the stormy events of ordinary life, must you have a lifeboat?

We want to have another chance, and we can: the word "Tao" can simply mean "road."

332 | Is It Just a Road?

Believable Words Are Not Beautiful

Laozi begins the *Daodejing* with an immediate play on words. The first three words can be read as "The Tao that can be spoken" because "Tao" has so many meanings: direction; way; road; path; principle; truth; morality; reason; skill; method; Dao (the central term of Taoism); to say; to speak; to talk; measure word for long, thin stretches, rivers, roads; province (of Korea and formerly Japan).

In Chapter 70, Laozi writes:

My words are very easy to understand
and very easy to practice.
Yet no one under heaven can
understand them or put them into
practice.
Words have a lineage; all matters have
their ruler.
Since people don't understand, they
don't know me.
Those who understand me are few, those
who follow me are rare.
That's why the sage wears coarse cloth
but holds jade.

Chapter 78 ends with the line: "Straight speech seems contradictory," and in Chapter 81—the final chapter of the *Daodejing*—Laozi declares:

Believable words are not beautiful.
Beautiful words are not believable.

The word "Tao" can simply mean "road"—
as plain and yet profound as that.

If you know what the word "Tao" looks like, you might be startled to see it on the street signs in Chinese communities, where it simply means "road." In that context, the term means nothing more. It's not religious, it's not a reference to history, and it's certainly not meant to be poetic. So you could be walking down a road, carrying books in which "Tao" means the movement of the universe and the natural principle upon which all human law should be based while talking with a friend about a Taoist immortal, and then look up and see that you are on such-and-such a *road*. You could see the two meanings as strictly separate. In fact, literate people probably see the same word as so completely distinct in its meanings, they might strain to even put the two meanings together.

(Incidentally, this isn't the only case like this. The first hexagram of the *I Ching* is named Qian—meaning "heaven" at its most profound. The same written word is pronounced differently—*gan*—in ordinary life, and so one might be startled to see the word on a package of *dry* biscuits.)

So to say that Tao is profound, yet ordinary, is wrong—and also right.

—to say that Tao is the movement of the universe is wrong—and also right.

—to say that Tao is the invisible is manifest right here in front of us is wrong—and also right.

—to say that Tao should be followed in our everyday life as unconsciously as we travel on roads is wrong

—and also right.

As plain and yet profound as that, do you laugh at the road up Cold Mountain?

333 | The Narrow Path

Cold Mountain

Little is known about **Hanshan** (c. ninth century; p. 60), whose name means Cold Mountain. He presumably took his name from the Hanyan Cliffs in Zhejiang, where he lived as a hermit. He is especially popular in Chan Buddhism, and is represented in paintings as a wild eccentric dressed in tatters and grinning crazily. However, his poems reveal a recluse who grappled fiercely with the ardors of spiritual life, and they attest to his individualistic response.

The title of this poem, "You Might Laugh at the Road Up Cold Mountain," can also be read as "Laughable Cold Mountain Road." Here, Hanshan uses the word "Tao" for "road."

You might laugh at the road up Cold
   Mountain,
no track for cart or horse.
Ravines after ravines, it's hard to
   remember all the turns.
Cliff upon cliff rises as if weightless.
Dew weeps from a thousand kinds of
   grass.
Sighing winds always in the pines.
For a time, I'm so confused by such a
   mysterious maze
that I ask my shadow
   which way to go.

Do you laugh at the road up Cold Mountain?
Climb up to laugh over your own reasons.

Morning traffic, car horns honking. Riders shout for the bus to stop. Between parked cars, toes over the curb and shoulder to shoulder, two guys grin. One has a commuter mug in hand, the other holds a canvas bag. With bristle-urchin hair, they could be our modern Hanshan and Shide (p. 60)—drunk, even though it is early morning. Are they the silly ones, or is it the business of the streets that's silly?

You will never know who they are, but they've already done their jobs if they've made you think about an alternative to the serious business of society. That's what we need Hanshan for, to remind us that all our rushing to and fro on our well-planned streets is not the same path as his.

The road up Cold Mountain is not like our everyday thoroughfares. The way is twisted and too narrow for cart or horse. It's barely a foot trail, passing through linked ravines that are turned back on themselves between cliffs that rise up like shadowy towers. Unlike our crowded streets, it is empty of other people. This is a place no one ever comes; it's a place of recluses.

Seeking Tao is not for everyone. Perhaps that seems like madness in this world where "best-selling" seems like the only real measure. When people are celebrated for how many contacts they have in their address book, it's a radical thing to walk a barely trodden path to a mountain where nobody else lives.

Yet in every generation, there will always be people who understand that the path leads to all that they truly want. With each step, everyday involvements grow more distant and the spiritual glows with increasing brightness.

You might laugh to look at the arduous path up Cold Mountain, but are you someone who wants to know why Hanshan grins?

Climb up to laugh over your own reasons—or do you sing a song the world's heard?

334 | A Song Few Know

A Lofty Song with Few Singers

Song Yu of Chu (third century BCE) was a scholar and may have written some of the poems in the *Songs of Chu* (p. 151). One day, King Xiangwang (232–202 BCE) summoned him and said, "Your conduct is quite reproachable, and people are whispering about you."

"That may be," Song Yu conceded. "But I ask your majesty to hear me out before condemning me. A few days ago, I saw someone singing in the street. He first sang a folk song called 'Song of the Rustic Poor.' Several thousand people joined in. Then he sang a more sophisticated song, 'Song of the Spring Snow.' Less than a hundred people joined in. Finally, he sang the most unusual and sophisticated of songs, and only a half dozen people could sing with him.

"This shows that the more unusual the song, the fewer people know it. Therefore, how can the average person understand what I do?"

This incident is remembered in an idiom, "A lofty song with few singers."

Do you sing a song the world's heard?
Or do you sing a song few know?

We admire the singers with best-selling recordings, who play in stadiums to fifty thousand people or more at a time. We want to know who has a hit, how many times the song has been recorded by others, how emotional it makes everyone in a generation. We laud the chart toppers, looking with pity at the "where are they now" programs. We search for the video that has the most hits. We watch television shows where people compete to be the best singers, and we reward the winner with what can be a lifelong career.

Taoism is the inverse of that. There are few people interested, it is hard to fathom and to quote, and no one competes to be a Taoist. It's practically secret knowledge, not because adherents want to hide it but only because Taoism is fundamentally anti-conformist, individualistic, and oriented toward the patterns of nature over the patterns of society. The song of Taoism is not the song of society.

Will you be that kind of person who does not follow others? Will you sing the song that few people know, a song that cannot be packaged and sold to others?

The song of Tao is the song of the universe. If you are to sing its song, you must hear it first.

If you would hear that song, you must turn away from the crowd. For the song is powerful, but subtle, easily obscured by the raucous shouts of commerce, the siren drone of people trying to seduce one another, the endless prattling of millions offering their self-confessions, the devilish xenophobia of demagogues, and the endless sentences pouring from bad journalists and poor poets alike. If you want to hear the song few know, you must first withdraw into silence. Only when you are deeply familiar with silence can you hear the song of Tao.

Or do you sing a song few know, understanding why serenity will be found in the world?

The Bell over the Monastery's Deep Pool

Su Manshu (1884–1918) was a writer, poet, painter, revolutionist, and translator. He was the son of a Cantonese merchant and a Japanese woman. Born in Yokohama, Japan, he returned to China when he was five years old. As a student, he was a revolutionary opposing the fading imperial government, then went on to become a journalist. Eventually, he abruptly left all worldly activities and became a Buddhist monk. Despite his vows, he feasted often in the company of singing girls, although he reportedly remained celibate. He suffered from illness and poverty until his death.

This poem, "Staying at White Cloud Hermitage," places him in a Chan Buddhist monastery in Hangzhou. The Thunder Peak Pagoda mentioned is the famous site of the legend of Lady White Snake (p. 227).

White clouds surround Thunder Peak
　　Pagoda.
A few trees of winter plum girdle the
　　snow with red.
In a screened study, I sink, sink into
　　meditation
as the bell sounds over the monastery's
　　deep pool.

Serenity will be found in the world.
It can't be found by negating the world.

There are plenty of problems in the world. Getting a perspective on them and finding a way to feel Tao requires periods of peace and silence. But it doesn't follow that we should reject and negate the world.

Even the mountain sage lives in a cave. Even the greatest monastery still has brick walls and is built on the ground. When we hear that worldly entanglements impede us from finding Tao, it's easy to assume that merely abandoning worldly entanglements will immediately reveal Tao.

Unfortunately, it's not that easy.

We cannot divorce ourselves from this world. No matter what, we still have to walk on this ground, breathe the air, drink the water, and eat the food harvested from this earth. Denying ourselves air, water, and food and not providing a livelihood for ourselves will not make us holy. True, Buddha went through a time of living in the forest as he sought enlightenment, but as the story of the upcoming Laba Festival (p. 396) shows, even he needed food and drink.

Su Manshu had an odd and unusual life. He certainly tried to make his way as a worldly person, and he obviously struggled with the monastic lifestyle. If he wrote the poem "Staying at White Cloud Hermitage" because he was there, then he had to have traveled to reach it from his home province. Traveling means that one is not above this world. One is literally traveling through the world to arrive at a destination still on this earth.

Once there, though, he sank into meditation. In the same way, we have to take the time to meditate even as we establish and maintain a worldly life. Serenity is essential. But it can never be found by denying the world.

Where in the world can you go that is not still of this world? Thus serenity must be found in this world.

It can't be found by negating the world, and Tao does not require a special person.

336 | Plain and Ordinary

One's Spirit Is Pure, Clean, and Simple

Zhuangzi describes the pure, clean, and simple soul of a sage in this way:

The life of a sage moves like heaven. Death is like the transformation that all things undergo. Calm, yin qualities are at one with virtue. In action, one's yang qualities are like waves. One need not strive to be happy. One need not struggle solely to avoid calamity.

One responds as seems necessary, and moves when force seems to compel it. One need not strive to get what will come later by itself.

Wherever one goes, the cause can be known—one only wishes to conform to heaven's law. Then there will be no calamity from heaven, no entanglements from other things, no blame from others, and no reproach from ghosts.

One's life is like floating, death is like resting. There is nothing to think about, no reason to worry, no facile scheming. One is bright, but not flashy, truthful without end, sleeps without dreaming, and awakens without melancholy. One's spirt is pure, clean, simple, and one's soul does not tire. Open, tranquil, yet cheerful, one will be united with the virtue of heaven.

Tao does not require a special person.
How could that be? Everyone has a soul.

There have been masters in the past who declared that spirituality was only for the qualified. Perhaps you had to have been someone extraordinary in a past life. Perhaps you had to be beautiful, or to have talent, or to be extremely learned. Certainly, if you look at the example of the luohans (p. 373), each one with his special powers, you might be tempted to think that you have to be someone unusual to be holy. But what kind of doctrine is that?

We already live in a society of hideous discrimination. The beautiful, rich, talented, powerful, and ambitious try to raise themselves over everyone else. Clubs are selective in whom they admit. Corporations only want the best employees. Schools reject any student below lofty admissions standards. Then there are the more subtle kinds of selectivity—when you're not striking enough, or funny enough, or well connected enough to be of interest to others. In every one of these cases, you're rejected because you don't offer something to be exploited. So as painful as it is, understand that your rejection means that you've escaped being cannon fodder for other people's greed.

The pursuit of Tao must be open to everyone. It must not require that you be a special person. Tao must be plain and ordinary, something anyone can gain access to, something that anyone can embrace.

Isn't that true of all the really valuable things in life? The air, the sky, water, a place to live—these are fundamental and you don't have to have any special quality to receive them. They are part of your birthright. Tao is just like that—as open to you as the air you breathe. In fact, perhaps that's why breathing exercises like qigong are one beginning approach to Tao. It's that plain and ordinary.

Tao is open to everyone because everyone has a soul. If you were able to pull out dozens of souls and line them up, you could not see anything different about them. There are no "pretty" souls and no "rich" souls. There are only souls. Everyone has a soul. Thus, the way to that soul is open to everyone.

How could that be? Everyone has a soul. There is no chosen one, no chosen race.

337 | No Chosen One

The Hunchback of Shu

Zhuangzi tells the story of the hunchback of Shu. His chin was in his navel, his shoulders rose over his head, the vertebrae of his neck pointed at the sky, his five viscera were crammed into the upper part of his body, and his thighs seemed to emerge from his ribs.

By sewing and washing clothes he earned just enough to afford porridge. By winnowing and sifting grain, he was able to feed ten other people.

When the government called for soldiers, he came and went without having to hide. When great public works were undertaken, none of the work was assigned to him because he was an invalid. When the government distributed grain to the sick, he received triple portions along with ten bundles of firewood.

If such a poor man with a strange body was able to support himself and complete his natural life, how much easier it should be for others with all their faculties!

There is no chosen one, no chosen race.
Who would do such choosing when all are one?

There is no chosen one, no special person that the gods have raised above all others. How outrageous that would be.

Some have asserted that there is a chosen race—usually meaning that they, their families, and their friends are in the chosen race and that everyone else is not.

Honestly: look at everyone in this world. Can anyone truly say that one person is "better" than the next, or that someone is worth really following as if he or she is divine? There is no such person, and there never will be. There will never be a chosen race, because all humans are of one race. There will never be anyone chosen, because there's no divine authority to do the choosing. Like it or not, we are all on this earth, equals, with no person having a cosmic advantage over the others. True, we may choose leaders whom we regard as wiser or more skilled, but they are human beings, struggling with the same life as everyone else, aging like everyone else, and heading toward death like everyone else.

Really, this is a cheerful and reassuring thought. Society may have created and sanctioned hierarchies and pecking orders and there may be ranking in Taoism, Buddhism, and Confucianism, but there cannot be any ranking on a spiritual level. Once you strip away the body and the history, there is still the soul, and the soul of one person is no more superior than the soul of the next.

Every culture implicitly believes this, because everyone's account of the soul is freedom from the bounds and troubles of this world—and that includes rank. Who knows where people are going after they die? But they are not going to some deity who's going to choose them over others and who is going to sequester them in a divine realm where they can sneer at others for eternity.

Who would do such choosing when all are one? When we offer what we receive?

Laba Festival

Year-End Sacrifice on the Eighth Day, or the Laba Festival (Laba Jie), is a vestige of an old day of offering. *La* means "the year-end sacrifice" and "the twelfth moon." *Ba* means "eight" and is a reference to the eighth day of the twelfth moon. The festival is also known as the Laji Festival, meaning the end-of-the-year festival. It originated more than three thousand years ago as a sacrificial ceremony in which the game captured during great hunts was offered to ancestors and gods.

By the Song dynasty (960–1279), Laba had also become an occasion for farmers to express their gratitude for good crops. Especially when the harvests had been good, the farmers showed their appreciation by making sacrifices to heaven and earth. In time, the Laba Festival's main culinary symbol became Laba porridge.

Laba porridge consists of glutinous rice simmered with sugar for one hour and a half, with additional ingredients such as red beans, millet, sorghum, peas, dried lotus seeds, dried dates, mung beans, jujubes, peanuts, chestnuts, walnuts, almonds, or lotus seeds. In the north, Laba porridge is a sweet dish, but in the south it is a savory dish with soybeans, peanuts, broad beans, taro, water chestnuts, walnuts, vegetables, and diced meats. People tend to select eight ingredients to add to the rice and sugar, probably as a reference to the eight of Laba, and also because eight is considered a lucky number.

There are two traditional explanations for the origins of Laba porridge.

The first story recounts a poor peasant boy who eventually became the Ming Emperor Zhu Yuanzhang (1328–1398). While he was herding cattle, one of the cows broke its leg. His employers punished Zhu by starving him. Hungry, he found a rat hole, dug out the beans he found there, and boiled them in porridge to create a delicious dish. After he became emperor, he missed the taste of this simple food and asked for it to be prepared for him. He also ordered the porridge cooked with a mixture of several grains and sugar to feed hungry citizens, and the recipe eventually passed from the palace to the populace. Zhu Yuanzhang also features in the story of mooncakes (p. 266).

The second story recalls Sakyamuni Buddha's attainment of enlightenment on the eighth day of the twelfth moon. Sakyamuni meditated so deeply and practiced such extreme asceticism that he was close to dying of starvation. A girl named Sujata saved his life by feeding him rice porridge and milk, enabling him to continue meditating and to attain enlightenment on the day of the Laba Festival. Thus, the eating of porridge on this day commemorates Buddha's breakthrough, and the festival is also known as the Day of Enlightenment.

In ancient China, before the advent of refrigeration and especially in the north, the cold winters meant that much of the food could be stored in coolers without spoilage. Pickled garlic and cabbage were also popular in the north.

With the cold weather, hearty and warming dishes like porridge are great comfort foods. Another popular dish is Laba soup noodles, made with eight different shredded ingredients. Hot rice wine makes the perfect accompaniment to both dishes.

Soaking of Laba garlic is a custom associated with this festival. Garlic is soaked in vinegar for twenty days beginning on the day of the festival. The garlic and vinegar are served alongside the dumplings (jiaozi) for Chinese New Year.

Rice Porridge

Also known as congee (a word adopted from the Tamil *kanci*) or *baizhou* (white rice porridge), rice porridge is also served outside of the Laba Festival as a common breakfast dish. Its base is simple to make, with a handful of rice cooked in a pot of water yielding a dish that can feed many. Rice porridge is therefore served frequently in monasteries, where a little has to be stretched among many, and it was also used to help feed the hungry in times of famine.

Even this simple usage has added to the lore of rice porridge. According to one legend, Emperor Yongzheng (1678–1735) of the Qing dynasty ordered rice porridge distributed to the starving  people during a famine. The corrupt officials distributed only a watery gruel, which displeased the emperor. From that day forward, he decreed that rice porridge must be thick enough so that a pair of chopsticks would stay upright when inserted into a bowl of porridge. That should give some idea of the proper consistency of the porridge (it is also the only time that chopsticks can be stuck in a bowl, since this is considered a rude thing to do at the table).

Rice porridge is also a therapeutic dish because it is easy to digest, hydrates the patient, and can be customized with different foods to combat the illness. In the *Compendium of Materia Medica (Bencao Gangmu),* the Ming dynasty physician **Li Shizhen** (1518–1593) stated that rice porridge "increases the life force, produces saliva, nourishes the spleen and stomach, and resolves sweating due to a weak constitution." ▶

Bonchan/Shutterstock

- Fasting day
- The Laba Festival

In the Time of Slight Cold, Spring Is Already on Its Way

Zong Lin (c. sixth century) wrote about festivals in a book entitled *Festivals and Seasonal Customs of Jingchu (Jingchu Shuishi Ji):* "The eighth day of the twelfth moon is the day of the year-end sacrifice. There is a saying: Beating drums on the day of the year-end sacrifice means that spring has set in and grass will grow again."

Accordingly, villagers paraded with drums and wore masks as the Buddha or other deities to celebrate and to chase away pestilence, bad luck, and devils.

We offer what we receive
to be worthy to receive more.

What does it mean to sacrifice today? Without falling into primitive superstition, is there a place for it?

The desire to sacrifice is a real emotion. It is a true and genuine expression. When we feel reverent, when we feel humbled by our experiences, when we feel that we have received more than we deserved, when we feel that the extraordinary has happened to us, when we are grateful for our lives, then we naturally want to make an offering. This has nothing to do with movie images of savages throwing a virgin into a volcano. What we're referring to begins within, with sacrifice being the only way to express how we feel.

However, ruining something we love or hurting ourselves to appeal to the unseen is unnecessary and akin to guilt and self-destruction. We can move beyond that. We don't hurt what we have to express ourselves properly. Rather, true sacrifice is an expression of unselfishness.

The earliest participants in the Laba Festival were grateful for their hunt and so wanted to *share* their success with the gods. It's as if they were saying, "We are grateful that we were able to catch game to feed our community. You, the gods, made this possible, so we would like to give you some of what we have in return."

Sacrifice is a real expression. In order to discern it clearly and to keep it from degenerating into superstition or selfish quid pro quo, we need to make sure our sacrifice conforms to these standards: it's unselfish, it's an act of sharing, and it's a gift. As long as sacrifice has these qualities, it's a positive and perfect way to be devoted and reverent.

Beating drums on this day means that the spring has set in and grass will grow again: of course spring is already approaching. Of course the grass will come again. It's our *attitude* that makes all the difference.

To be worthy to receive more,
ask: which one do you prefer?

339 | Confucianism or Taoism?

- Birthday of Han Xiangzi
- Begin preparation for end of the year

Han Xiangzi

Han Xiangzi was born during the Tang dynasty (618–907). He is one of the Eight Immortals and a student of Lu Dongbin (p. 125). He is shown holding a flute, a pair of castanets, or sometimes a small crucible as a reminder of his skill as an alchemist. A peach tree in the background of some depictions is a reference to his falling from such a tree, killing his body but beginning his immortal life. He is identified closely with his uncle, the scholar Han Yu (p. 55).

At a banquet that Han Yu hosted, Han Xiangzi urged his uncle to give up the life of a scholar-official to study Taoism. But Han Yu insisted that Han Xiangzi should dedicate his life to being a Confucian official instead. Han Xiangzi responded by filling every wine cup from a small gourd without it ever running dry. He then sprayed water into a clay bowl filled with soil: a bud sprang up immediately and continued growing until there was a peony tree in full bloom.

Which one do you prefer?
Society or Tao?

Taoism might not exist in its present form were it not for the tremendous social pressures Confucianism caused. The Confucian emphasis on the rites was unmitigated, the demand for conformity—reinforced on a daily basis by familial and peer pressure and on a grand level by absolute imperial rule—was unrelenting, and the system of great advancement solely through the examinations and the scholar-official life was unforgiving. There almost needed to be Taoism to relieve the strictness of Confucianism.

Taoism advocated a carefree life, a life of nonconformity, an appeal to nature as the ultimate authority beyond any emperor. It was the life prizing joyous mysticism over solemn duty. Therefore, Taoism was the particular favorite of those who were already inclined to follow impulses beyond society. Artists, poets, musicians, mystics, alchemists, herbalists, recluses, and seekers of all types took refuge in Taoism because it offered a way out of the immense pressures of the sanctioned social life. The conflict between Han Xiangzi and Han Yu symbolizes the tug between two polarities that people experienced in the past. Even today, many face the question of whether to fulfill the expectations of their parents and society or live lives of nonconformity. Thousands of years of Taoists show that there is a life there, with rewards every bit as rich as the gold and the titles that the Confucianists pursued.

Han Xiangzi plays the flute. He is carefree. He communes with nature, as the leopard represents. The gourd by his side can pour wine to fill every cup in a banquet hall, or it can dispense the elixir of immortality. If you listen, you can still hear his fascinating melody. He's beckoning you down a path, and as you walk it, your steps will fall in time to the clicks of his castanets. If you choose the path of the nephew over that of the uncle, you will find friends, beautiful vistas, and travel in the clouds.

Society or Tao? Whatever you do: know.

Enough Is Enough

Chapter 46 of the *Daodejing* concludes with the declaration: "Therefore know when enough is enough, that will always be sufficient." Laozi uses *zu,* which shows a leg and foot—meaning "enough, sufficient, ample."

Beginning of Housecleaning

From the end of the Laba Festival to the day before New Year's Eve, people clean their homes thoroughly. This is supposed to dispel ghosts and bad luck, prepare the Kitchen God (p. 8) for his journey back to heaven, and ready the home for the new year. Every part of the house is cleaned and washed, and the couplets and decorations from the old year are taken down. Fresh couplets and decorations for the new year are put up. The altar is cleaned, and new offerings are made.

All necessary provisions are bought and stored. Some businesses will close for the first two weeks of the new lunar year, so people don't want to be caught short of supplies. The heads of families prepare a number of large meals during the Spring Festival, so it's important to have plenty on hand. Children get new clothes and receive firecrackers to drive away evil spirits.

Although it's traditional to begin preparation following the Laba Festival, there are still thirteen days until efforts begin in earnest. The signal for these efforts is the sending off of the Kitchen God on the twenty-third day. A popular saying gives the basic schedule: "Eat sticky candy on the twenty-third; sweep the house clean on the twenty-fourth; fry tofu on the twenty-fifth; stew mutton on the twenty-sixth; kill a rooster on the twenty-seventh; set dough to rise on the twenty-eighth; steam bread *(mantou)* on the twenty-ninth; stay up all night on New Year's Eve; pay holiday visits on New Year's Day."

Whatever you do, know
when enough is enough.

Enough. It's really a marvelous concept. Know when enough is enough. As the year comes to an end, it's a reminder that all things have their endings and their limits. At other times, endings and limits are frustrating. "Enough" means that endings and limits can also be positive. You've done enough.

Whether this past year was good or bad—and chances are it was a little of both—it's coming to an end and you've done all that you can. Now it's time to begin cleaning up, clearing out the excess, and getting ready for a new time. The custom of cleaning up because it clears away "bad luck" is true in this sense: once a time period has passed, it's best to do away with all the leftovers that will encumber your future. No baggage. No dead weight. Get rid of it so you can move on as freely as you can.

In this sense, wuwei (p. 215), or "not-doing," has additional meanings: do just enough. Do no more than necessary. Act without extra ramifications. And when you're finished, really be finished, with no lingering regrets, no sloppy excess, no reason for matters to come back again uglier and messier. This is why Laozi says that we should know when enough is enough, and that if we do, we will still have sufficiency. There is nothing to fear, because when you know enough is enough, then you also know that you *have* enough.

The word "zu," "enough," is a picture of a leg and ankle. The illustration shows some of the many ways to write "zu" (showing a different kind of "enough!"). Sit down and rest. Then, when it's time to walk the road again, you'll be renewed and hopeful.

When enough is enough, the constant present is so vast.

341 | Past, Present, and Future

The Poet Lu You

Lu You (1125–1209) was a prominent Song dynasty poet. At the time of his birth, northern China had been invaded by the Tartar Jin dynasty, forcing the native Chinese government to continue as the Southern Song. The dynasty fought during Lu's entire life against the Jin, and Lu is known as one of China's most patriotic poets.

His love life was tragic. He married his cousin, Tang Wang, when he was twenty. However, his mother did not like his wife and forced them to divorce. Lu You, obligated to obey his mother, reluctantly complied. Eventually, each remarried.

Eight years later, he chanced upon Tang and her husband in Shen's Garden. She asked her new husband to send wine and food to Lu, and when she offered a cup of wine to him, Lu saw tears in her eyes. Draining the cup, he turned away and wrote his famous poem "Phoenix Hairpin" on a wall with the clear rant, "Wrong! Wrong! Wrong!"

Tang Wang later read the poem, wrote one of her own in response, and died less than a year later. A year before his own death at eighty-five, Lou wrote a poem called "Shen's Garden," commemorating his first love. Their tragic story became so famous that it was made into an opera.

This poem, "Sharing a Drink with the Taoist of Qingyang Gong," speaks of Lu's attraction to Taoism.

The Taoist of Qingyang lives among
    bamboo
and plants flowers like those of Xuandu
    Retreat.
When the light rain clears, he sees the
    dancing cranes.
Through a small, dim window, he hears
    the bees hum.
The fire of his alchemy stove glimmers
    and glows warmly.
Drunkenly, his sleeves flutter in the wind
    at a slant.
Though old, this official is really free
    and easy,
and has come to share a simple life.

The constant present is so vast
that it straddles past and future.

Green Ram Palace (Qingyang Gong) stands in the western portion of Chengdu, Sichuan, and is the oldest and largest Taoist temple in southwest China. Originally built in the early Tang dynasty (618–907), the temple has been restored many times; the current buildings dates from the Qing dynasty (1644–1911).

According to legend, Qingyang Gong marks Laozi's birthplace and the location of his first discourse on Taoism. This is hard to confirm, since Laozi lived at least 1,200 years earlier. It's a mystery that can probably never be fully addressed. Laozi would probably be delighted. "The Tao that can be told is not the constant Tao." We can never arrive at anything completely through words, and this applies to niceties like birthplaces and first sermons.

Laozi is gone. Lu You is also gone. Tang Wang is gone. And the Taoist of Green Ram Palace with whom Lu You spent a pleasant day is also gone. If we go to Green Ram Palace in Chengdu, we can't really say that we are going back to Lu You's time, and we certainly can't say that we can even trace our feelings back to Laozi's time. We go for ourselves.

There is past, present, and future. What's important is that we live in all three. Conventional wisdom would have us live in the "here and now," and we praise someone who can exist in the "eternal present." This is not a negation of that, but is a different view of what the present means. We can live in a present that activates the past and the future.

We look back at people who have been dead thousands of years because they show us the very roots of human experience, revealing what is archetypal and therefore true on a deeper level than what we might experience today. Taoists are clever not because they depend on fate but because they formulate strategies so thoroughly that the future takes place as if preordained.

If we go to Green Ram Palace, we go in the eternal present to embrace the past and the future. Then we will know the free and easy simple life that Lu You went to find.

That it straddles past and future may be, and yet the mountain pine may be wind-pruned.

342 | Evergreen

The Pine

The pine is the symbol of long life and hardiness. It's especially admired because it doesn't drop its leaves in the winter, and because it lives a long time.

Pines and cypresses are planted around graves not only because their evergreen branches are a comfort all year long, but because they are believed to repel the *wangxiang,* legendary creatures that eat the brains of the dead. Pines and cypresses are also the symbol of friends who stand together through hardship.

The *Classic of Rites* compares a person's character to the pine and cypress:

> . . . the pine or cypress have hearts. Both have extreme greatness under heaven. They can go through the four seasons without altering their branches or changing their leaves.
>
> This is how noble persons behave with propriety, harmonizing with outsiders and having no conflict with anyone in their inner circles. When there is never a lack of benevolence for all, then even ghosts and spirits acknowledge such virtue.

The mountain pine may be wind-pruned,
but it stays an unaltered pine.

The pine stands on the mountainside. It does not need a grove to survive. It may be assaulted by rain, snow, wind, and harsh sunlight, but it endures. Where rock splits from the baking afternoons of summer or the ice wedges of winter, the pine maintains its heart and living bark.

The maple may shed its leaves in winter, withdrawing into itself. The pine maintains its needles, even under the weight of snow.

However, what old pine retains all its branches for its entire life? When the *Classic of Rites* says "without altering their branches," it means that the pine doesn't do anything to change itself. It is true to its character, and so it has "extreme greatness under heaven." However, the pine does not escape danger. It is battered by storms and can be burned by lightning and fire.

The ancient pines on barren mountainsides all show the scars of branches sheared away, or trunks and bark roughly split. Yet the pine lives. It finds a way to heal. It continues to stand. It remains evergreen.

But it stays an unaltered pine,
even when the arrow strikes the
sphere's center.

343 | To Be Balanced

Centered

The word *zhong* has many meanings: within; among; in; middle; center; while (doing something); during; China; Chinese. The ideograph is a picture of a circle on a flagpole. But it has also been interpreted as a spherical target on a pole or tree pierced by an arrow. Perhaps there's something to that because "zhong" also means to hit the mark; to be hit by; to suffer; or to win (as in a prize or lottery).

"Zhong" has also been interpreted as "balance," and you can look at the word as two halves balancing on a central axis.

The arrow strikes the sphere's center,
but what is pierced remains empty.

There are many orthodox ways to think of being centered. There are many ordinary ways to invoke balance in our lives. Thinking more about the word "zhong" can take us to another level of understanding.

Imagine a brass sphere high on a pole. Warriors on horseback compete to show their skills. Each one draws back an arrow and shoots at the target. The one who pierces the target perfectly through its center wins the highest rank.

Our spiritual practice can be compared to that. In aiming for the truth, we try to get right to the heart of the matter, and success is greatest when our perception is most on target. But the target remains hollow—and is not even the prize itself.

If we hit the center, if we understand ourselves thoroughly, then, like the hollow brass target, we discover that our minds are empty. This is a metaphor for our minds being completely dynamic. In other words, if we are truly centered in our perception, we will discover that our minds are not material—they certainly aren't just our brains, and they aren't any sort of static substance. Furthermore, our minds cannot be stilled, they cannot be stopped in a single state. Every person's mind is movement.

How wonderful then if we can find the center of a constantly shifting infinity. Once we find that center, we can also realize balance. Only knowing the center of a circle can bring a sense of proportion. Only knowing the center allows us to divide the circle into two halves, and only two halves yield balance.

The mind is infinite. Any point and every point in one's mind is the center. The mind has no shape and no limits to its size, and yet it is also a circle with a circumference that is everywhere. The mind stretches endlessly, and yet it can also be balanced around its center. All this is possible to understand: just look at the word "zhong."

But what is pierced remains empty, even after you take care to stretch the string neither too loose nor too tight.

344 | Hold the Middle

Examples of the Middle Way

In Hexagram 11, Prospering, of the *I Ching,* the reading for line 2 states:

Encompass the wasteland by crossing the river without a boat, but do not advance so far that you abandon comrades to perish. Win honor by a middle course.

"Encompassing the wasteland" and "crossing the river without a boat" are metaphors for attempting ambitious, nearly impossible things. However, no matter how great one's actions, one wins honor through a middle course.

Another example of the importance of the middle comes from the *Analects:*

Yao said: "O, you, Shun. Heaven's order rests with you. It grants you the responsibility of holding the center. All around the four seas are in need. Let heaven's prosperity be forever established to the end."

Emperor Yao (2333–2234 BCE) was a legendary Chinese emperor who passed the throne on to Shun (twenty-third to twenty-second century BCE). The word "order" literally means "calendar and numbers."

Buddha's Middle Way

Buddha's understanding of the middle way—avoiding the excesses of sensuality as well as asceticism—is captured in a traditional story. The story has many variations, but here is a representative one:

When Buddha was sitting by the river one day, he heard a lute player tuning his instrument.

Buddha realized that a lute string must be tuned neither too tightly nor too loosely to be in tune, and at that moment, he understood the Middle Way.

Stretch the string neither too loose nor too tight,
to find the middle way that stretches right.

According to the example of Buddha hearing the lute player, the right way to live is to be neither too loose nor too tight. Should we talk in terms of too loose or too tight? If you've ever tuned a string instrument, you know that there is only one tension to sound the perfect note; there is only "just right."

There aren't many one-stringed instruments. The *erhu* has two strings, played with a bow. The average modern grand piano has over 230 strings. We should not be "one-stringed" in our spiritual outlook. Yes, the middle way means to have a string tuned just right, but if you have many well-tuned strings, you can make great harmony—and always be able to vibrate to the tune of whatever comes your way.

Anyone who plays an acoustic instrument will tell you that it varies every day. Changes in temperature and humidity alter the tone immediately. The instrument has to be tuned frequently: before we can have the harmony of music, we have to be in harmony with heaven and earth.

If you recall how much Laozi valued emptiness, it's worth seeing that every musical instrument requires emptiness. The stringed instruments have sound boxes, the woodwinds and brasses are hollow tubes, and the drums are skin stretched over big cylinders or kettles. Bells and cymbals have hollows, and sticks and triangles need to have the air around them to produce sound. Furthermore, the musical instruments need the emptiness of the chamber or concert hall to sound their best—a lute played in the middle of the desert can hardly be heard well.

Isn't all of creation stretched across heaven's expanse? All of existence is ongoing music. Stretch and tune our strings and let heaven play us.

To find the middle way that stretches right, the swan geese fly in autumn and spring.

345 | The Flying Geese

- Birthday of the **Great God of the Southern Peak** (Nanyue Dadi)
- Fasting day

The Southern Sacred Mountain

Hengshan in Hunan is the South Great Mountain of the Five Sacred Mountains (p. 44) and is a mountain range of seventy-two peaks. The southernmost peak is Huiyan, meaning Wild Geese Returning, because geese come back to it every year. The highest peak is Zhurong, named after the God of Fire (p. 271). Du Fu (p. 29), Han Yu (p. 55), and Cai Lun (p. 321) were all born in Hengyang, just to the south of Hengshan.

The Grand Temple of the Southern Mountain (Nanyue Dai Miao) has a history that dates to the Tang dynasty. It was rebuilt in 1882 during the Qing dynasty.

Buddhism, Taoism, and Confucianism all coexist at Hengshan in the Eight Temples of Buddhism, the Eight Temples of Taoism, and the Imperial Library Tower.

The Great God of the Southern Peak (Nanyue Dadi) presides over the south, receives the prayers and offerings of the people, and guards an entrance to the underworld. In the past, emperors traveled to make sacrifices to him along with the gods of the other sacred mountains.

The swan geese fly in autumn and spring:
they follow the Tao of season and place.

The southern Sacred Mountain of Hengshan is known for its gods, temples, history, and beauty. It is also known as a place where swan geese stop during their migration. Geese represent yang, because they follow the sun south in the winter: they are honored because they know the seasons. Since they often fly in pairs, they were also recognized as the symbols of fidelity in marriage.

The swan geese are models for us. Could we spend part of the year in one place with the delicacy of a guest, not worrying about leaving when we felt it was time? Could we then have the energy to fly thousands of miles, following our own instincts, navigating by the stars, and the rivers, and the mountaintops? Could we find where we belong, with a memory that was imbued in our very bodies? The ancients thought that the swan geese demonstrated faith, because they were never lost; duty, because they were never deterred from their destinations; and propriety, because they arrayed themselves in a formation for orderly flight.

The swan geese are not afraid. The expanse of heaven is enormous; the risk in migration is ever present. Through some ability that human beings still cannot comprehend, the swan geese are rarely lost. Heaven and earth are vast, the swan geese are tiny, but they are not afraid to fly with single-minded determination to follow their Tao.

The swan geese cross rivers many people never cross during entire lifetimes. They fly over mountains no human has ever climbed. Even the great sacred mountain of Hengshan is but a way station for them. They are unafraid to transcend limits, and yet they know the path that they must follow, and for that, they evince a natural brilliance.

If only we could fly like the swan geese.

They follow the Tao of season and place, and ask, "Have you heard the breath of heaven?"

Exercise 24

Extremely cold weather marks this period. Crops and livestock must be protected and people must be cautious—even as they go about their celebration at the year's end.

This exercise is best practiced during the period of 11:00 P.M.–3:00 A.M.

1. Begin from a kneeling position, supporting yourself by pressing your hands on the floor behind yourself. Raise one leg and kick it forcefully forward. Then switch positions to kick with the other leg.

2. Exhale as you kick; inhale as you change positions. Breathe normally as you change sides. Repeat fifteen times on each side.

3. Sit cross-legged and face forward. Click your teeth together thirty-six times. Roll your tongue between your teeth nine times in each direction. Form saliva in your mouth by pushing your cheeks in and out. When your mouth is filled with saliva, divide the liquid into three portions.

4. Inhale; then exhale, imagining your breath traveling to the dantian and then swallow one-third of the saliva, imagining that it travels to the dantian.

5. Repeat two more times until you've swallowed all three portions.

6. Sit comfortably as long as you like.

Through this exercise, ancient Taoists sought to prevent or treat circulation problems; pain or inability to move the tongue or the body; difficulty standing; swelling in the torso or limbs; abdominal distension; diarrhea; and difficulty walking.

The Wind Through the Openings

This passage from Zhuangzi compares the stillness of meditation to the stillness of the earth when the winds have calmed down.

Nanguo Ziqi sat leaning on a low table, gazing up at heaven, and breathing gently. He appeared to be in a trance. His disciple, Yan, was standing beside him and exclaimed, "What is this? Can your body become like dry wood and your mind like dry ash? The man leaning on the table is not the one who was here a moment ago."

"Yan, it's good that you ask. Just now, I lost myself. Do you understand? You may have heard the music of people, but not the music of earth. You may have heard the music of earth, but not of heaven."

"Can you tell me more?" asked Yan. Ziqi replied: "There is a great cosmic breath. We call it wind. Sometimes it's not active, but when it is, it howls fiercely through ten thousand openings. Have you ever heard a roaring gale?

"In the mountain forest, mighty and awesome, great trees a hundred spans around have gaps and hollows like nostrils, mouths, and ears; like a corral, or mortars, or pits. The sounds burst out like geysers, or an arrow, or like scolding, shouting, wailing, moaning, or gnashing. The first sounds hiss, and then come enormous fusillades. Small breezes make small harmonies, cyclonic winds make great harmonies. When the ferocious gusts have calmed, all the hollows are again quiet and empty. Have you not seen this phenomenon so marvelous?"

The word rendered here as "phenomenon" means both "change" and "tune," so there's a double meaning in that Ziqi is simultaneously talking about sound and great transformations. The word translated as "marvelous" means "artful," "tricky," or "cunning," so here the meaning is that these sounds and transformations reveal a greater, "crafty" order.

Have you heard the breath of heaven?
Is it any different from you?

There is a breath of heaven. Nominally, we call it wind, but it isn't just wind.

There is a breath of the human. Nominally, we call it inhalation and exhalation, but it isn't just inhalation and exhalation.

The breath of heaven moves in gales and howling storms—but the subtlest of forces create the more obvious wind.

In just the reverse of that, the coarse breathing of a human being can help us discover a more subtle, invisible force associated with that breathing. Our mind commands our bodies to move. How does it do that? Do you say it's just nerves and chemicals? If you say that, you are not wrong—but you're not completely right either. It's the breath—our own internal energy—that moves in us at the command of the mind to achieve all that we wish to achieve.

So if you stop the coarse outer breath—when, as Ziqi puts it, the hollows are again quiet and empty—why do you continue to live? There has to be a more subtle life force that continues on between breaths. Then, from the outside, we will look like the master—all dry wood and dry ash. But from the inside, we will be able to discern a far more subtle and refined energy.

When the wind stops, nature does not stop. When our breath stops, life does not stop. It is just at that moment that you must go inside, that you must go into the gaps, hollows, and pits. There, in the stillness, is what is to be sought.

Is it any different from you, when you hear how great is the one with faith, courage, and strength?

Tending Sheep

Su Wu (140–60 BCE) was a diplomat and statesman during the Han dynasty (206 BCE–220) known for his faithfulness and forbearance.

In 100 BCE, Emperor Wu of Han (156–87 BCE; p. 235) sent Su Wu, Zhang Sheng, and Chang Hui on a goodwill mission to the Xiongnu, a confederation of tribes to the north of China. They were received by Chanyu Qiedihou, who had just come to power.

However, Zhang Sheng conspired with the Prince of Gou and Yu Chang to kill the chief advisor, Wei Lu, and kidnap the chanyu's mother while the chanyu was hunting. Chanyu Qiedihou learned of the plot, rushed back, killed the prince, and captured Yu.

Su knew nothing of the plot, but tried to commit suicide with his sword. Impressed, the chanyu and Wei ordered Su's life saved. Zhang and Chang were captured. After Su recovered, Yu was executed and the Han mission was ordered to surrender. Though still weak, Su refused.

The chanyu tried to starve Su into submission. But Su survived by eating the lining of his coat and drinking snow melting into his dungeon. Su was then exiled to Lake Baikal (in present-day Russia) and ordered to tend a flock of rams, while the Hans were told that Su was dead. However, the Han ambassador told the Xiongnu, falsely, that the Han emperor had shot a goose while hunting—and that a letter from Su had been attached to its leg. Surprised, the Xiongnu released Su. Nineteen years had passed.

Great is the one with faith, courage, and strength,
who fulfills duty against ice and death.

Su was caught in a horror not of his own making, and yet he maintained his honor and determination. He tried to kill himself, and having already nearly died once, was unafraid of death. First Wei Lu put a sword to his neck, but Su would not surrender. The chanyu tried to starve him, but Su would not surrender. Then he was exiled for years to a frozen wasteland. The chanyu sent General Li Ling (p. 46), who had been defeated by the Xiongnu in 99 BCE, to visit Su. Li told Su that both his brothers had been accused of treason and had committed suicide, that his mother had died, and that his wife had remarried—but Su would not surrender. Li was sent again some eight years later, to inform Su of Emperor Wu's passing—but though Su wept and vomited blood, he would not surrender. He kept his hand on his imperial staff, the emblem of his office: in his years in exile, the hairs of the decorative tufts all fell off, but his grip on his staff never weakened.

When Su returned home, he was given a high-ranking post and lauded for his faith and indomitable loyalty. When we look at ourselves and do we suffer as important than lament the way that fate seems to test us, much as Su Wu? There is nothing more unwavering determination.

*Who fulfills
who will*
*duty against ice and death, and
never stop seeking Tao?*

348 | Seeking

› Fasting day

An Official's Leniency Leads to Friendship

Jia Dao (779–843) was a Buddhist monk who gave up the religious life for poetry. He was deeply intent on his art, which the following anecdote shows.

One day, Jia Dao was composing a poem while riding his donkey. He was thinking about the lines:

> Birds return to their nests in the trees by the pond.
> A monk knocks on a door at midnight.

He couldn't decide between the words "knocks" and "pushes." As he rode along, acting out the movements, he didn't notice that he was headed for an official entourage, and he did not give way as he should have. He was immediately arrested and brought before the official.

Fortunately, the official was Han Yu (p. 55). He asked Jia Dao to explain himself, and Jia explained that he was trying to choose between two words. This intrigued Han Yu, who considered for a long time before suggesting "knocks" as the better word. The two became friends from that day on.

This is one of his poems, "Seeking a Hermit and Not Finding Him," preserved in *Three Hundred Tang Poems*.

> I asked the child under the pine tree.
> "My teacher went to gather herbs," he answered.
> "But in the midst of these mountains, deep in the clouds, I don't know where."

Never stop seeking Tao
no matter the hardships.

Even though Jia Dao renounced the life of a Buddhist monk and tried to make a career as a poet and scholar (he failed the examinations several times), he evidently never stopped seeking Tao. This poem tells the story of his seeking a hermit and being unable to find him. The master had gone into the cloud-covered mountains to look for herbs.

This is the way it is. The masters of Tao are never easy to find. If one is fortunate enough to encounter them, then there's the question of how to communicate with them and understand them. And yet, there's no other way to learn the philosophy and techniques of Tao except through the words that the teachers leave for us. Both Laozi and Zhuangzi emphasize that words alone cannot lead us to Tao. But they are useful markers to point us in the right direction.

When you are a sage some day, remember that others will seek you. Be kind to them. It's easy to be lost in the mountains.

No matter the hardships, the older I get, the faster time goes.

Straight Timber Is Cut Down First

Zhuangzi writes of slowness in the story of a bird called the *yidai*. The name could be interpreted as "idle thought," or "loose intention."

In the Eastern Sea there are birds called yidai. They fly low and slowly, almost as if they were incapable of it, and as if they were leading and helping one another. When they roost, they press against each another. No one dares to lead going forward, or to be the last to turn. No one ventures to take the first mouthful in eating, but prefers what is left by others. This is why their movements are blameless, people cannot harm them, and they avoid worry.

Straight timber is chopped down first; a sweet well is exhausted first. Your aim is to embellish your wisdom so as to startle the ignorant, and to cultivate your person to show the ugliness of others. You shine as if you were holding the sun and moon—and that causes all your problems.

In the past, I heard a highly accomplished man say, "Those who boast have no merit. Merit achieved will fade. Fame and success will fail. Who can rid himself of merit and fame and live with the common person?"

The older I get, the faster time goes,
and yet I've learned to move fast and not rush.

The old man said: "I'm old now. Actually, I don't feel much different than before, but others startle me by calling me that. I admit that my hair is white, but inside, I am unbowed.

"I seem to go to funerals and memorials more often. I don't even bother putting my dark suit away because I know I will have to wear it again soon. Most of the people precious to me are gone—certainly the generation before mine barely has one or two left to light candles at the altars—and I have to support them as they walk, shooing away the children cheerfully offering to help *me*. I'm sure the day will come when I will be desperate for someone to offer me a hand.

"There is a line of people waiting to die, and I reluctantly accept I'm in that line too. At the moment, I can't see the end of it. Someday, nobody will be blocking my view. I say that because it's my duty to tell you of these things. I'm not looking for sympathy, and I'm not complaining.

"The ghosts live with me. I hear them every day. I see them floating in the sky, challenging me: 'Can you live as we did? Can you die as well as we did?' Yes, those who went before me were heroes, who lived their lives fully, who proved that integrity could be made real in a vessel of flesh and blood, who demanded that all around them were the best that human beings could be, who never tolerated excuses, who died smiling quietly. I wonder if I can be so strong.

"I am happy to receive these ghosts with their silent demands. I know the time for me to reach for their upraised flags is short. Each moment, I ask myself, 'Is what I'm about to do worthy of the precious time I have left?' If the answer is yes, then I go ahead. I am a fool, and I have so little time left to perfect my unique foolishness.

"I don't waste time as I did in my youth. Doing something completely and correctly the first time is better than fixing mistakes.

"Old age does not slow me down. It is experience and care that make me go slower. True, the older I get, the less time I have."

And yet I've learned to move fast and not rush: that is the greatest good fortune.

Zhuge Liang

Zhuge Liang (181–234) was a chancellor of the state of Shu during the Three Kingdoms period (220–265). He is known as the quintessential Taoist strategist, an inventor—and a scholar of exceeding intelligence. Since he lived in seclusion for a time without its diminishing his fame, he earned the nickname Hidden Dragon (Wolong). He is also known by the style name Kongming. Zhuge Liang is often depicted in flowing robes and holding a fan made of feathers.

Many of Zhuge Liang's deeds have been mythologized. Here are three:

General **Zhou Yu** (175–210) was jealous of Zhuge Liang and ordered him to make one hundred thousand arrows or be executed. Zhuge Liang agreed to do so within three days. He made a few arrangements but otherwise waited in his tent, drinking wine. On the dawn of the third day, there was a great fog. Zhuge Liang sent boats with decoy soldiers across the river, ordering loud drumming and shouts to simulate the attack. The frantic enemy fired volley after volley into the fog—where the arrows stuck in hay bales on the boats. The boats returned to camp with more than enough arrows.

An attack by fire was prepared, but Zhou Yu realized he'd need an easterly wind to succeed, and there was no breeze at all. Zhou collapsed and became ill. Zhuge Liang visited him and offered to pray for the wind—but he had already determined that the weather would shift. Days later, the eastern wind came. Zhou Yu thought Zhuge Liang was supernatural and sent men to kill him—but Zhuge Liang had already escaped.

When a city Zhuge Liang was protecting was attacked, he ordered the city gates opened and the soldiers disguised. The enemy would not enter, fearful of an ambush.

The greatest good fortune
is your preparation.

As the new year approaches, we will be wishing each other good fortune, happiness, and long life. But what does good fortune really mean? Are we waiting for something good to come our way? Yes, there is such a thing as good luck, and it's a valuable gift. It's something entirely different to stake your life on waiting for such luck.

Good fortune is as simple as finding a place to live that sustains you, surrounding yourself with good friends, making prudent decisions, and cultivating yourself. As a comparison, you can certainly have bad fortune—but if you choose to live in a dangerous place, associate with bad people, are careless with your decisions, and make no effort to discipline or calm yourself, then it's certainly not "bad luck" that is visiting you. You're living a toxic life. You maximize your chance of returning to good fortune by choosing to live in good places, choosing good relations, and choosing good work.

We can't know the future, but we can certainly arrange many things in the future. We make appointments, schedule visits to people and places, begin new ventures with others. If, for example, you buy a farm, then a farm is certainly "destined" to be in your future. This is good fortune that we engineer. The kind of fortune that brings rain or sunshine, or that might spare your farm when others are attacked by disease, is luck.

So we have to be careful about fortune. What we do when we arrange things in advance, follow through on initiatives, and arrange to meet with others is the fortune we create for ourselves. The circumstances that occur during the time that we're carrying out our plans—those are luck. Likewise, sometimes accident is just that. It's bad luck, but not the bad luck of divine intervention.

We wish each other good fortune. But really, shouldn't we simply be wishing each other the wisdom to arrange our lives properly in advance? What will happen in the new year is built on what you've done this year.

Is your preparation in knowing which phase of the moon is most important?

351 | Yin, Yang, and the Moon

The Phases of the Moon

In the illustration below, the sunlight is coming from the left. The earth is at the center. The moon is shown at eight stages during its revolution around the earth. The middle circle is the moon as it's actually illuminated by the sun; the outer circle is the moon as it appears to us.

Half of the moon is always lit by the sun. We often see both the sunlit portion and the shadowed portions simultaneously, and that creates the various moon phases.

The new moon occurs when the moon is between the earth and the sun, and the illuminated portion of the moon is on the side away from us.

In contrast, during a full moon, the earth, moon, and sun are in approximate alignment, and the moon is on the opposite side of the earth. The sunlit part of the moon faces us and the shadowed portion is hidden.

The first-quarter and third-quarter moons, called half moons, occur when the moon is at a 90° angle in relation to the earth and the sun.

After the new moon, when the sunlit portion is increasing but is less than half, it is waxing crescent. After the first quarter, the sunlit portion is more than half, so it is waxing gibbous. After the full moon, the light continually decreases, and this is the waning gibbous phase. After the third quarter is the waning crescent; the moon wanes until the light is completely gone and a new moon occurs again.

Which phase of the moon is most important?
Which shifting takes longer than the others?

No phase of the moon is more important than the others. Each phase is the same length; each transition from one phase to the next takes the same amount of time as all the others. The moon has circled us steadily for millions of years, and it will continue for millions more. Each night, it is the perfect lesson in yin and yang.

We know that the moon's light is a reflection of the sun's, but the amount of light that we see simply depends on the moon's position. If we want to follow the lunar Tao, we simply have to remember to be ourselves—just as the moon never really changes shape—and we simply have to reflect the light of heaven in the orbit that is our life. What could be easier?

Which shifting takes longer than the others? Only one prepared can find a teacher.

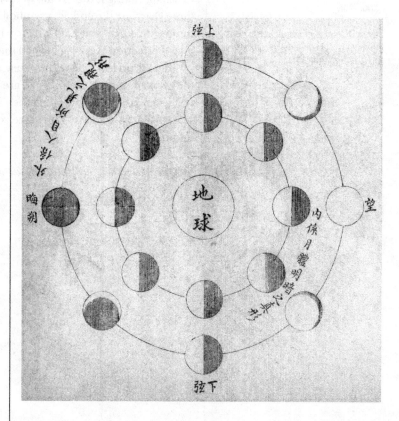

> • Birthday of **Wang Chongyang**

Wang Chongyang

Wang Chongyang (1113–1170) was one of the Five Northern Patriarchs of the Quanzhen (Complete Perfection Sect of Taoism). According to traditional beliefs, he met **Han Zhongli** and **Lu Dongbin** of the Eight Immortals (p. 124) in 1159, and they initiated him into the inner traditions of Taoism. Already an accomplished martial artist, Wang undoubtedly adapted to the techniques quickly.

Following this, he went to Zhongnanshan near Xi'an to practice and teach others. This was the same mountain where Laozi is believed to have written the *Daodejing* and that became an important retreat for both Taoist and Buddhist hermits. Chongyang Palace and other buildings on that mountain honor Wang.

Wang had seven disciples, the **Seven Disciples of Quanzhen**. One of the most best known of this group was **Qiu Changchun** (p. 25).

© Peter Pynchon

Only one prepared can find a teacher.
Only a teacher makes other teachers.

Unless Wang Chongyang was prepared by being intelligent, familiar with Taoism, and knowing martial arts, how would he even have been worth the notice of Han Zhongli and Lu Dongbin? The immortals are looking for others to join them, but they are looking for candidates who are ready.

According to legend, Wang intended to begin a rebellion against the Jin dynasty (1115–1234), established by the invasion of Jurchen tribes from Manchuria. However, his life shifted when he met the immortals. Was he seeking Tao, or was Tao seeking him?

Once he was initiated into the inner traditions, Wang progressed quickly. He went into seclusion for some time on the same mountain where Laozi passed down the *Daodejing*. Surrounded by other recluses and the beauty of nature, he practiced sincerely and deeply. According to one account, he built a tomb on Zhongnanshan, calling it the "Tomb of Living Death," and stayed in it for three years. At the end, in a symbolic rebirth, he emerged, filled the tomb with earth, and built a hut on top of it, naming it the "Complete Perfection Hut." He burned the hut in 1167.

There is no learning without teachers. There are no teachers if others do not teach them. There are no new teachers if no teachers will teach others. If you would seek Tao further, prepare yourself so that the teachers can recognize you. If you learn well, then teach others.

Only a teacher makes other teachers: when you're alone, always act like a guest.

353 | The Inner Kitchen God

- Kitchen God reports to heaven
- Fasting day

The Departure of the Kitchen God

This is the day that the Kitchen God (p. 8) leaves the family and flies to heaven for his audience with the Jade Emperor. Having sat in the kitchen, hub for all activity, for nearly an entire year, he's had ample opportunity to observe the good and bad deeds of the family. He makes his report to the court so that all of a family's activities are known to heaven. The Jade Emperor will punish or reward the family based on the Kitchen God's report.

In order to ensure that the Kitchen God will say only good things—or perhaps to glue his mouth shut if there aren't many good things to say—the family smears his mouth with honey. Then they burn his picture so that he can be sent to heaven in the smoke. The family will install a new picture of him on the day he returns.

When you're alone, always act like a guest—
as if the Kitchen God lived in your heart.

Whether or not you believe in the Kitchen God, you recognize his true function: conscience. If you understand that, you don't need his altar on your floor. Far better to have a Kitchen God inside you. Far better to have a conscience and to heed it.

Conceiving of a supernatural tattletale is really missing the point. It's better not to have a conflict with our conscience. In other words, it's better to act correctly in the first place. Maybe your response is that this is hard to do. It isn't really. Why not simply act correctly and dispense with the guilt, the conflict, the vacillations, and the stress?

By this analogy, you invite the Kitchen God up from his place on the floor and ask him to speak to you on a daily basis. Make him your advisor. Involve him before you have to do something. Surely after centuries of watching people do good and bad, right and wrong, he has a worthwhile opinion.

When you're alone, act like a guest. Act like someone is watching you. After all, most misdeeds are done in the dark and away from others. Most misdeeds are kept secret. However, if you're watching yourself, or if you manage to make your conscience an integral part of your decision making, then you are unafraid for your actions to be known.

If that's the case, then you'll put the Kitchen God out of business. That's a worthy goal. Then he—not you—can just be a guest in your house.

As if the Kitchen God lived in your heart, make the wish: "Will my dear friend return next year?"

› Fasting day

Poems of Parting

Poems of parting are virtually their own subgenre of Chinese poetry. Here is one from Wang Wei (p. 174).

> We accompanied each other into the
>   hills until we had to stop.
> As day becomes dusk I shut the timber
>   door.
> The spring grass will be green next year.
> But will my honored friend return or not?

Meng Haoran (p. 252) wrote this poem, "Parting from Wang Wei." While we don't know that this is a direct answer to Wang Wei's poem, it fits well. The sixth line is a reference to the story "High Mountain, Flowing Water" (p. 16).

> When will my loneliness end?
> I must go home, where day after day will
>   be empty.
> I could seek other worthy people,
> but I'm reluctant to part with an old
>   friend,
> Who will keep me company on this
>   road?
> Few in this world know the same music.
> All I can do is keep my solitude,
> go back, and close my
>   old garden gate.

Will my dear friend return next year
and break the silence with music?

The ghost of the poet said: "Dear friend, I've walked with you to see you off, and now we've ventured deep into the hills. Here, at the edge of the county, we must finally say farewell."

"Each day spent with you was joyous, and yet each day hastened the moment of parting."

"Where will you go?"

"I'll search the village markets for some herbs to strengthen myself. The road is long and icy, and I won't have a companion like you to depend on. But I feel guilty that I took so much of your time. Go back to your work—your music, your painting, your poetry, your official duties, and your practice with the abbot."

"But who will read my poetry as you do, or listen to my music as you do, or appreciate my paintings as you do? Make sure you stay busy yourself. Go to the capital. Give my letter of introduction to the prince. He'll recognize a worthy man like you! Don't just hide behind the garden gate!"

"Why talk that way? You know I'm a man of ambition. If I can find the right opportunity to work with others, I'm sure I can make a great contribution. You needn't worry about me—as I hope that I needn't worry about you! May your door swing constantly with honored guests and patrons!"

"But none of them can take your place in the garden, exchanging couplets with me, or performing duets."

"Stop frowning! Throw open your doors. Go out and light up the world!"

"Good-bye, dear friend. Will you come in the spring?"

"Only if you promise to be merry in my absence!"

"And only if you promise to go straight to the capital."

And break the silence with music, though nothing lasts. But long or short, we're still here.

355 | Nothing Lasts

The Dream Within a Dream

Zhuangzi wrote of two people who were discussing why the sage avoids worldly affairs. One of them, Chang Wuzi, said:

> The ordinary man labors and labors; the sage seems stupid and foolish. But the sage simply blends ten thousand years into one, and makes the ten thousand things a complete whole.
>
> How do I know whether or not the love of life is a delusion? Or that the hatred of death is like a young person's losing his way, and not realizing that he's really going home? The ruler of Jin captured Li Ji, the daughter of a border guard of Ai. She wept until she soaked the front of her dress. But when she was brought to the king's palace, shared his luxurious couch, and ate grass-fed meat, she regretted her weeping.
>
> How do I know that the dead do not repent their former craving for life? Those who dream of drinking may wail in the morning; those who dream of wailing may go out hunting the next day. While they were dreaming they did not know it. They may even have tried to interpret their dream while asleep, but only when they awoke did they realize that they had been dreaming. There will be a great awakening, and we shall know that this life was a great dream.

Zhuangzi further addresses this concern in another passage:

> Human life between heaven and earth is like a white colt's passing by a canyon opening and then suddenly disappearing. With a plunge and effort all leaves; easily and quietly all enters again. By one transformation all lives, and by another transformation all dies.
>
> Although living things may feel sad and people may grieve, all that is happening is the removal of the bow from heaven's sheath. It confuses us when the soul and spirit depart and the body follows. Yet that is the great returning!

Nothing lasts. But long or short, we're still here.
Good or bad, all things pass—and still return.

Nothing lasts. By now, we don't need the sages to tell us that. Living long enough, we know. The glorious might of youth stumbles, the highest tower of civilization tumbles, the loveliest piece of carved jade crumbles. Nothing lasts.

Nothing lasts. All things are impermanent, the sages tell us, so it's foolish for us to place value on anything as if it will stand for all time, or will always be dependable, or that it can never be taken away. But that lesson has always been here for us to see. Every winter sees the leaves fall from the trees. Every epoch sees whole dynasties trampled under pounding hooves.

Realizing that we ourselves are just as impermanent is difficult, because it strikes at the very assumptions and reflexes that keep us alive. Perhaps that's why we're supposed to count our breaths, because it helps us see the crux of the matter: that we continue living while we realize this is all temporary.

All must change, but we should find comfort in that. When we go through trauma, we must know it cannot last forever. When we have happiness, we treat it as the valuable but rare occurrence that it is. And no matter what we think, whether good or bad, genius or mistake, we understand that our very thoughts arise and fall.

We all die. Yet each day, we awake and we are still here. We must work each day. We must eat each day. We must breathe each day.

We are the dreams that must yet work within a dream.

And yet, here in the middle of winter, the bare, black branches of the plum and quince are already starting to bud. Impossibly, dead wood springs back to life with living red and green. All things pass, and yet all things return.

Good or bad, all things pass and still return: there's no end.

Don't Disturb the Transformation

This story from Zhuangzi tells the story of Li going to visit Lai, a dying friend.

Lai lay panting and gasping, while his wife and children stood around him wailing. Li entered and said, "Hush! Step back! Do not disturb the transformation." Leaning through the door, he said to Lai, "Great indeed is the Maker! What will he make you now? Where will he send you? Will he make you into a rat's liver, or an insect's leg?"

Lai whispered, "Wherever a parent tells a son to go—east, west, south, or north—he must follow that command. Yin and yang are like my parents. If they bring me near death and I do not obey, then I am disobedient, with no one else to blame.

"There is the great mass of nature. I find support for my body in it; I've spent my life toiling in it; in my old age I seek ease on it; in death I will rest in it. Whatever made my life good will also make my death good.

"Compare this to a great founder casting metal. If the metal were to leap up and say, 'Make me into Moye [a famous sword],' the founder would surely consider it disastrous. So if I were to say, 'I must become a man, I must become a man,' while my form is being refashioned, the Maker would surely consider it disastrous.

"Once we understand that heaven and earth are like a great melting pot, and the Maker a great founder, where can we go that isn't right for us? We are born as from a quiet sleep, and we die to a calm awaking."

No end.
Go on.

There are no endings. Only transitions.

This year is dying. But a new year will begin in a moment that is neither longer nor shorter than any others. In truth, it can't even be distinguished from any other moment. It's only our record keeping that gives it a label. Today is the twenty-sixth day of the twelfth moon, just an arbitrary number. When New Year's Eve comes and we move into a "new" year, nothing will have changed with the moon, the earth, or the heavens. They have been there eternal and they will continue on eternal. That the heavens too will end is barely within the borders of our comprehension. On some great cosmic scale, where all of human history would not even equal a grain of dust, our universe might end, but there would still be continuation. The totality of that boggles our minds so that they go blank: that's why Taoists and Buddhists speak of void.

One of the major goals of Taoist practice is to have a graceful, dignified, and conscious death. We try to prepare ourselves long in advance. When will that day come? We don't know. Each day we wake up, take stock of ourselves and the tasks before us, and are grateful that we can continue. Some day, we will slow to the point that there is no coming back as ourselves. We will be dying and then there will be nothing to do but to prepare ourselves for that moment. We need not go out sniveling and complaining. We should go forth, and face what is coming.

Though our bodies will stop, and they will decay, every single part of our bodies will become something else. Although our spirit will no longer have a body in which to dwell, it returns to Tao. This is one reason why Laozi and Taoism speak of returning.

We human beings mark death with great solemnity, and that is right. It is emotional for us, spiritual for us, profound for us. Our very identities are tied up with the idea of birth and death. While we mark death as enormously significant, however, it is not an ending—just as one year rolls into the next.

Go on: do you see your breath blow clouds in winter?

The Face You Had Before You Were Born

When Daman Hongren decided to make Huineng (p. 292) the Sixth Patriarch of Chan Buddhism, he knew that the other monks would object. According to legend, he secretly gave Huineng the bowl and robe that were the emblems of his position and told him to flee the temple. However, the other monks found out and angrily chased after Huineng.

This koan, "Do not think of good or evil," is recorded in the *Wumenguan* and portrays the moment that a monk catches Huineng. (Ironically, the name of the monk is Ming, a name that could be interpreted as "enlightened.")

Monk Ming pursued the Sixth Patriarch to Taiyu Mountains.

Seeing Ming, the patriarch laid the robe and bowl on a rock and said, "This robe represents our faith. It should not be taken by force. If you want it, take it."

Ming tried to take the robe and bowl but found them as heavy as a mountain. Stunned and frightened, he said, "I came for the dharma and not the robe. I only want to receive your teaching."

"Don't think good. Don't think evil. Right now, at this moment: what was Monk Ming's original face?"

Ming was immediately enlightened, and sweat poured all over his body.

This phrase, "original face," is a key idea in Chan Buddhism.

Do you see your breath blow clouds in winter?
It comes from the face you had before birth.

Spirituality is easy. It only takes looking and acceptance. Following Tao is easy. It only takes walking.

If you go out on a cold day, you'll see your breath fog up before you. What a miracle! Only living creatures breathe! You have the miracle of life, and with such a miracle, it's ridiculously wasteful to use the perfect mind you have to complain. Yes, life can be challenging, but there is no "good" and "bad." There's only the yin and yang that animate all that we know. An artist does not complain about white paper and black ink: it's the very basis of painting.

Look further at your breath. It moves at the volition of the mind—and a subconscious part of it at that! In other words, just to live, you barely need to do anything except feed yourself and sleep. Life is given to you. You don't need cleverness or learning to live it. It came with your birth. If you inquire further into this, you will discover the mind that is the very basis of your existence. That, in itself, is spirituality.

Our breath is autonomic and yet can be controlled consciously. We can, to some extent, control the length of our breath, call on ourselves to breathe deeply, or briefly hold our breath. When we swim, for example, we need to control our breathing. If we smell smoke, we can hold our breath for a time until we get to safety. In the same way, living is a matter of melding our conscious mind with the subconscious mind. Neither side can take over completely: spirituality is a matter of comprehending this yin and yang.

Why are we alive? The reason lies in why we breathe. Once you find that reason, you find life itself.

It comes from the face you had before birth; rejoice to hear a baby's cry.

358 | The Crying Baby

▸ Fasting day

Laozi's Infant

Laozi speaks of the intact vitality of an infant in Chapter 55 of the *Daodejing*. While this chapter refers to a boy baby, the words "vitality," jing (p. 222), in line 6, and "energy," qi (p. 63), in line 12, apply to both genders.

> One who holds substantial virtue can be
>   compared to an infant.
> Poisonous insects will not sting him,
>   savage beasts will not seize him,
> birds of prey will not strike him,
> although his bones are fragile and his
>   muscles soft, his grip is firm.
> He has not known the union of female
>   and male, yet he can become erect
> because he has full vitality.
> He can cry all day without becoming
>   hoarse
> because he has full harmony.
> To know harmony is called "constant."
> To know the constant is called "bright."
> Call increasing life propitious.
> Call the heart controlling energy
>   powerful.
> Then things will be strong even into old
>   age.
> What do you say about what is not with
>   Tao?
> What is not with Tao meets an early end.

Rejoice to hear a baby's cry.
It is truly the sign of life.

In the smothered quiet of a snowy morning, you might hear the sound of a baby crying. Her mother might hurry to shush her, and bundle her up to soothe her. Perhaps the baby keeps crying until the right comfort is found.

All parents learn to be mortified at their baby's cry, not only because that response is biological, but because so many people frown when a baby cries in public. It's common to describe being stuck on an airplane with a crying baby as a nightmare. But how can a baby cry "privately"? By its very nature, a baby's cry is a loud demand to the world at large. All under heaven should be moved by a baby's cry.

The cry of a baby is the sound of life.

That alone means it should be treasured. There's time enough for the unwavering silence of the graveyards. There's indulgence enough for the eerie quiet of the scholar's study. There's excess enough of the stunned choking whenever tragedy strikes. Hold that baby, and hug her, and let her know she's loved, and that she is the hope for our future. For however old we are, our days grow fewer. We give our all to the baby, because she will walk the living road after we falter.

The cry of a baby is the sound of life.

A baby's cry is affirmation that life is worth living, that a being can come into this world that has battered us into bitterness and cynicism and cry for life, cry for food, cry for love, cry for comfort, cry to be cared for, cry for us to try and make everything perfect out of a big pile of imperfection and contradiction. She wants life, she wants to add beauty to the world, she wants to overcome all the cruelty and corruption. It is because she wants it that we still want the same—years after we abandoned such goals as impossible.

We rejoice when we hear a baby cry, and we rush to help. That alone opens the way to all that is good.

The cry of a baby is the sound of life.

It is truly the sign of life—yet who wants to be goddess of latrines?

359 | The Violet Lady

- Fasting day
- Ceremony for the **Violet Lady Spirit**

The Goddess of Latrines

The Violet Lady Spirit (Zigu Shen) was born as He Mei in Shandong. After having studied successfully in her youth, she was married as a concubine to Li Jing in the period 684–705. (In other versions, she is an orphaned peasant girl sold to a man named Wei Zixu.) However, the primary wife was jealous of her beauty and intelligence. She forced He Mei to live in a shed by the outhouse and eventually murdered her, burying the corpse by the latrine.

According to legend, the gods took pity on He Mei and made her the spirit of latrines and patron of concubines. In real life, she was canonized by Empress Wu Zetian (p. 80) of the Tang dynasty—herself the concubine of two emperors and the only ruling empress in Chinese history.

In ancient times, women, never men, offered sacrifices to the Violet Lady. On this night, a basket decorated with earrings, hairpins, and flowers was brought to the latrine. A young girl of about ten was selected to hold it before an altar table topped with candles, incense, and pounded rice. When the ceremony began, all prostrated themselves. Then someone drew outlines of household objects such as scissors, knives, and flowers in the rice, using a silver hairpin, while everyone prayed for abundance and good fortune in the new year. The basket was supposed to become heavier or to make sounds in answer, a sign that the Violet Lady had heard them.

Who wants to be goddess of latrines?
Yet she is honored who still follows Tao.

There is no predestination. We are not condemned before birth to walk a certain path. Yet in the course of our lives, a destiny unfolds that is a mix of circumstance, our own actions, the actions of others, and pure chance. In the case of the Violet Lady, every strike seems to have been against her: married as a concubine, forced to live beside a latrine, murdered, buried by the latrine. Even rescued and deified, she is forever associated with wives, concubines, and latrines. Some of this reflects the wretchedness of women's treatment over the centuries. Empress Wu Zetian, who canonized the Violet Lady, also suffered as a concubine and resisted many intrigues. Although some historians have judged her harshly, she wielded power no differently than other emperors in Chinese history—few of whom are judged to have been enlightened. Her reign is known as having been peaceful and culturally diverse, with good foreign relations and exceptional freedom for women. She commissioned biographies of prominent women, and women in those times could walk outdoors without chaperones or fear of being bothered. "Fate" was unkind to both the Violet Lady and the Empress Wu Zetian, but they each made the best of who they were and what their lives gave them. For that, each one attained power, and each one inspires us today.

No one wants to be a concubine, or to use an outhouse—let alone be the spirit of one. Times change. But each one of us wants to have a better life and to inspire others to have better lives. The empress used her power to help others. The Violet Lady uses her position as a goddess to help others. They accept who they are, unjust though it may be, and make something better of it.

By that same analogy, the year that is nearly over took the form it did. There is no changing it, just as there's no changing the lives of these two women. But like them, we can look forward to the future, still unmade, for something better. May the basket become heavier with good fortune and peace.

Yet she is honored who still follows Tao, who knows that the last day is the eve of the first day.

New Year's Eve

The central focus of New Year's Eve is a big family banquet to celebrate the completion of one year and to look forward to the new one.

Preparation is therefore essential. If the banquet is going to be cooked at home, the house must be cleaned and all the groceries bought early. The cook prepares as much in advance as possible.

Even if the banquet will be held elsewhere, every home is cleaned so that anything unneeded from the old year is thrown away. Anything that was bad or unlucky is swept out too. Needless to say, only what is wanted and lucky remains, a good way to ready oneself for a new year. Important maintenance should also be taken care of, and all one's tools, equipment, and possessions should be cleaned and repaired. After you clean up, put away all the brooms and cleaning supplies. They should be out of sight for the duration of the Spring Festival.

People rush to settle their debts. Merchants are loathe to enter the new year with lingering debts, and anyone who has unfinished business of any kind tries to resolve it. This extends to relationships and emotions too. Is there anything you've left unsaid? Are there lingering conflicts between you and a friend or relative? Is there someone you've neglected this year? The traditionalists would urge you to resolve all of this prior to New Year's Eve.

Jiaozi

Many families in the north gather together to make dumplings called jiaozi. Each person rolls out thin, round pieces of dough (about two to three inches in diameter), puts a small ball of ground meat or vegetable filling in the center of each, and then folds the dough and crimps the edges to make the dumpling. The dumplings are boiled, steamed, or panfried, and they are usually eaten with a soy-vinegar dipping sauce.

Claudio Zaccherini/Shutterstock

Typical fillings are pork, mutton, chicken, fish, and shrimp, often mixed with vegetables such as cabbage, scallion, leek, or garlic chives.

Cantonese, or southern Chinese cooking, has all sorts of variations on the dumpling, or *jiao*. Most dim sum dumplings are variations on minced meat folded inside translucent skins of dough.

The dumplings resemble ancient Chinese gold ingots or horns. The word "jiaozi" also sounds like an early name for paper money, so people like to think that eating jiaozi brings prosperity. The idea that the semicircular dumplings, pointed on both ends, look like horns recalls another word, also pronounced "jiao," which means "horns"—and this is what the dumplings were called until they got their own word.

The dumplings also recall the story of Zhang Zhongjing (p. 371), who used dumplings that looked like ears, called jiao'er (tender ears), to feed to people whose ears were frostbitten.

New Year's Items

Here are some of the things people buy before New Year's Eve:

- **Red envelopes** These envelopes are decorated with good wishes stamped in gold foil. The usual wishes are for prosperity, success, many children, smooth sailing, and all things going as you wish. Red envelopes with money inside them are given to all unmarried relatives. Crisp, new bills are best.
- **Oranges, tangerines, and pomelos** These citrus fruits are popular decorations. The seeds signify the wish for many children. The oranges and tangerines also symbolize wealth because of their golden color. Oranges are given to all visitors.
- **Candy** Especially a New Year's tray of candy. This symbolizes sweet words and sweet success. Pieces of chocolate wrapped in gold foil to look like coins are also popular.
- **Flowers** Popular flowers that are just beginning to bloom are quince, plum, narcissus, and orchids.
- **New clothes** Especially for children. Red, orange, and purple are favored colors. Black and white are never used.
- **New Year decorations** Couplets, New Year's wishes, or decorations of auspicious subjects express one's hopes. ▶

360 | Eve

› Fasting day

Waiting for the New Year

Su Shi (p. 140) wrote this poem, "New Year's Watch," as he spent New Year's Eve with his children.

I wish I could understand how the year's end approaches:
it seems to slither like a snake into a hole—
those patterned scales are nearly gone!
Who could stop a snake determined to leave
even if they wanted to tie its tail?
No matter how hard we try, we can't do it.

The children force themselves not to sleep,
each guarding the night with joyous clamor.
Roosters: don't sing the morning in just yet;
night-watch drums: don't beat just yet.
Let's sit until the lamps sputter and dim,
and we get up to watch the Northern Dipper tilt.

Will next year be good or not?
I worry that my heart's ambitions might go amiss.
But take strength! Let's send off this night with all the boisterousness of youth!

The last day is the eve of the first day
One year ends so the next one can begin.

The moon is dark tonight. The year is ending. Think back over the year. In the end, you must evaluate yourself, judge yourself, and reward yourself, and that is far more important than whether the Jade Emperor does so.

We often fear endings. We don't want our love relationships to end, we don't want good fortune to stop. But endings also apply to conflict, drudgery, misfortune, and toil. We certainly don't mind if those stop.

So on this last day of the year, say goodbye to the bad things. Give thanks that your health is as good as it is, that your material blessings are as abundant as they are, that your family life is as close as it is. Sweep the house, as is the prescribed action for this day. Sweep away the misfortunes and regrets of the old year and arrange all that you have so that it is new and as ready as you want it.

The cycles begin again. We are blessed that they do. We follow the seasons, we follow Tao. The way is endless and so too is the fullness of the spirit.

One year ends so the next one can begin—that's why you must know wood, rising force that remains rooted.

The Five Phases

The **Five Phases** (Wuxing) is the name of an ancient Chinese philosophy that views all phenomena as parts of a constantly shifting whole. It's crucial to understand each phase—as complicated as the descriptions are—but it is also critical to remember that no one phase can be isolated from the others.

This emphasis on unity rather than separation puts the philosophy at odds with the normal scientific approach of distinguishing one system from another and breaking the universe down into its constituent parts. That is not an attack on science, but a note that fundamentally different assumptions must be used to comprehend the message of the Five Phases.

The makers of the Five Phases took their observations of nature and formulated them into a unified system. Instead of asking what inner components were responsible for movement and change, they asked how they could *describe* and *systematize* them. Instead of seeing all things in isolation from one another—for example, a bear having nothing to do with a rock—they asked what common forces animated the universe. It is an inclusive rather than an exclusive process.

The Five Phases theory sought to expand the model of yin and yang—which describes the universe in terms of two polar forces—into a more subtle method of analysis. Today, both models are still in use, most notably in Traditional Chinese Medicine (TCM), which views both health and illness through these frameworks. In the context of philosophical Taoism, the Five Phases theory is a vital way to comprehend the inner forces of the universe and yet not lose track of the whole.

In terms of this book, the Five Phases are an excellent way to round out the number of days from the 360 of an idealized lunar calendar to the 365 of the solar calendar. The lunar calendar of any given year is adjusted to reconcile with 365 days by adding the five days during the year. The reader matching this book to a lunar calendar can add one of the following five pages as needed to expand the 360 entries of this book to 365.

The Five Phases Generate and Control One Another

The Five Phases are wood, fire, earth, metal, and water. Each one has its own attributes, detailed on the pages that follow. As an introduction, a few basic attributes are listed below. Full lists are with each phase.

- **Wood:** Expansive; east; windy; sprouting
- **Fire:** Ascending; south; hot; blooming
- **Earth:** Stabilizing and harmonizing; center; damp; ripening
- **Metal:** Contracting and solidifying; west; dry; withering
- **Water:** Descending; north; cold; dormant

It should be immediately clear that the Five Phases describe movement, forces, direction, and functions, and are not strictly confined to the material aspects of their labels.

The Five Phases were formulated to articulate the relationships among phenomena. Each phase is thought to generate another (parenthetical phrases below are mnemonic, and should be taken metaphorically). The sequence is:

Wood generates—
Fire (wood burns to make fire), which generates—
Earth (fire turns to ash), which generates—
Metal (ore from earth makes metal), which generates—
Water (metal melts into liquid), which generates wood (water is needed for wood to grow), beginning the cycle again.

However, each element also controls another (parenthetical phrases below are mnemonic, and should be taken metaphorically). That sequence is:

Metal controls—
Wood (an axe chops wood), which controls—
Earth (trees uproot the earth), which controls—
Water (earth dams water), which controls—
Fire (water extinguishes fire), which controls metal (fire melts metal), beginning the cycle again.

Thus, each phase can generate another phase, and each phase can destroy another phase. This is summarized in the illustration below, where the clockwise circle shows the phases generating one another, while the star shaped lines show the phases controlling each other.

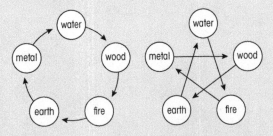

The Secondary Relationships of the Five Phases

The description above of the generation and control aspects of the Five Phases gives basic examples. However, it's believed that two cycles of generation and control operate simultaneously, and a secondary set of relationships between the phases occurs. For example, water controls fire, but fire can indirectly control water by generating earth which in turn controls water. Such secondary reciprocal relationships between phases describes a cyclical relationship between any three particular phases. These relationships are summarized as follows:

When **Wood** controls earth, then fire is also promoted, which could then control Wood

When **Fire** controls metal, then earth is also promoted which could then control Fire

When **Earth** controls water, then metal is also promoted which could then control Earth

When **Metal** controls wood, then water is also promoted which could then control Metal

When **Water** controls fire, then wood is also promoted which could then control Water

The Five Phases make up a closed system. No one phase can be "removed" from consideration. Thus, when viewing any situation in this framework, all of the phases must be identified.

Imbalances occur when one phase is more active than it should be, overwhelming another phase and generating more power in its successor phase. Similarly, if one phase is weak or deficient, then the other phases will become dominant, and imbalance will occur.

Whether one's setting is philosophical or medical, the proper use of the Five Phases theory lies in assigning each detail to its correct phase, and analyzing the primary and secondary relationships between them.

The Five Phases and Traditional Chinese Medicine

The Five Phases are an integral part of the theory of traditional medicine. Learning TCM takes years of study and clinical experience. This brief introduction illustrates how the Five Phases theory has a practical, real-world function.

Within the human body, the Five Phases have two major roles. First, the body as a complete system can be understood through the Five Phases. Second, the body's interaction with the environment can be understood. The weather, the seasons, the locale, and the presence of agents such as viruses, bacteria, or toxins—all these factors' effects on the body are also analyzed according to the Five Phases. For example, hot and dry weather will affect the body, causing an imbalance of fire in a body unable to regulate itself. A healthy person achieves balance within the body and in relation to the environment.

On a structural level, TCM focuses on five major organs, and each of these is assigned one of the phases: wood–liver, fire–heart, earth–spleen, metal–lungs, and water–kidneys. The proper balance and functioning of these organs is vital. If one of the organs weakens, then the others may overwhelm it. Or if one organ becomes overactive, it will suppress others.

Liver (wood) stores blood and supplies the heart

Heart (fire) produces heat and warms the spleen

Spleen (earth) transforms and conveys the essence from food and replenishes the lungs

Lungs (metal) help provide the kidneys with water through its descending movement

Kidneys (water) store essence and nourish the liver

The controlling relationships of the Five Phases manifest in the function of the organs:

Metal controls wood: solidifying lung energy controls upward-moving liver energy

Wood controls earth: the ascending movement of liver energy can overcome stagnation of the spleen

Earth controls water: the transporting and harmonizing function of spleen energy can check kidney deficiency and edema

Water controls fire: the moistening action of kidney energy can neutralize excessive heat in the heart

Fire controls metal: the heating heart energy can control too much solidifying lung energy

TCM uses various therapies, including acupuncture, herbal medicine, massage, and exercise, to moderate the energy of each organ or of the body as a whole, thereby keeping the body in good health.

Emotions and the Five Phases

Traditional doctors and Taoists recognize five emotions, each keyed to one of the five organs: anger (wood–liver), joy (fire–heart), worry (earth–spleen), sadness (metal–lungs), and fear (water–kidneys). Under the Five Phases theory, it is impossible to eliminate any emotion—we need to experience them all and to keep them in balance. In addition, since the emotions are rooted in the organs, balancing the organs may help emotional healing, just as an emotional imbalance may cause a physical ailment. In this way, Chinese medicine establishes a continuum between the emotions and the body.

The Gods of the Five Planets

Like so many aspects of Chinese culture, the Five Phases have been anthropomorphized. According to this belief, Emperor Zhuanxu (c. 2514–2436 BCE)—known for contributions to the calendar, astrology, establishment of patriarchy, and the forbidding of marriage between kin and who was one of the sons of the Yellow Emperor (p. 4)—appointed princes to govern the five regions of the universe. These gods reside on their respective planets: Jupiter (wood), Mars (fire), Saturn (earth), Venus (metal), and Mercury (water). ❱

361 | Wood

Know wood, rising force that remains rooted,
the green sprout that becomes the ancient tree.

What is the secret of wood? Wood is to know the beginning. The beginning is a seed. But a seed is useless without a place to be planted. Hence, the seed of heaven is impotent without the bed of earth. The fundamental power of wood cannot be understood without remembering that heaven and earth must combine, that power and place must unite, that there is no whole unless both yin and yang are present and intermix.

The seed does not sprout without rain. The seed will burn to death unless it's kept underground. Rain and sunlight are imperative to the coming plant, but if the seed is exposed to rain and sunlight unremittingly, it will die. Life is miraculous, but the miracle can be thwarted simply by a failure of arrangement and timing.

The sprout shows the beginning power of wood. It grows upward. The seed may send roots downward, but the tree never confuses root with sprout. Wood understands direction.

Unless thwarted, wood grows straight upward, as if it knows heaven and seeks it. Upright, true to its character, content in where it's rooted, branching out to accept the rain and the sun, the breezes and mists, the tree needs nothing else. The tree never tries to be anything but a tree, and heaven and earth give all that the tree needs to sustain itself.

Wood has grain. The tree trunk has rings. The tree's colossal size is scaled from tiny fibers and cells that join together in a perfect wholeness. The tree is efficient. No matter how mighty its girth, the circulation of the tree takes place in its thin bark. Thus the tree is modest and yet effective in how it lives.

The tree absorbs carbon dioxide and produces oxygen. It takes our waste—a gas that would kill us if we breathed it in large enough quantities—and it gives back air that helps us live. Isn't that alone a tremendous service and an example of how integrated we are with the life cycle of wood?

Wood is growth. Wood is rising. Wood is the humility to accept the sustaining power of heaven and earth from one place. Wood is breathing out the very air we breathe in. Know wood.

The green sprout that becomes the ancient tree teaches us to know fire—crackling, explosive heat and light.

362 | Fire

FIRE

Color:	red
Shape:	triangle
Material:	heat, light, fire
Direction:	south
Season:	summer
Climate:	hot
Planet:	Mars
Time:	9:00 A.M.–1:00 P.M.
Heavenly Stem:	*bing, ding*
Phase:	full yang
Development:	blooming
Energy:	ascending
Creature:	vermilion bird
Livestock:	chicken
Fruit:	apricot
Grain:	millet
Flavor:	bitter
Organ:	heart
Body system:	circulatory system
Body part:	blood
Part of the face:	tongue
Emotion:	joy
Quality:	politeness

Know fire—crackling, explosive heat and light,
transforming the solid to smoking flame.

What is the secret of fire? It consumes the solid. It cannot exist
without something to cling to—even the sun is feeding on its own
core. Did wood come from a seed? Then fire comes from a spark.
Did wood grow from earth? Then fire grows from what it feeds
upon. And in that consumption, it transforms. It breaks apart all
that holds the tangible together, breaking the bonds that make
material solid, and frees it as dancing brilliance. It bursts the form
of what it burns in raging, soaring, dancing combustion.

Fire rages, and its power is so great that it births all life by its
light. The sun doesn't exist for our sake, but we cannot live without
it. The sun doesn't exist to grow plants, but the plants green in profusion beneath it. We need fire. In every culture, the story of civilization has the same beginning: fire.

Every home has a stove. Every home has fire in the form of light.
We cannot have our homes or our work without fire. The flicker of
our computer screens is the light of fire refined.

How do we know that we are alive? We feel for warmth. Fire. We
speak of the warmth of a person, of kindling a friendship, of someone lighting up our lives. We are fire. It is the very energy of living.

That which expands, that which is brilliant, that which dances
and moves without set form, that which blasts the sheer power to
turn entire planets, that is fire. Know fire.

*Transforming the solid to smoking flame, the light of heaven
shows how we can know earth—flat, expansive, endless, and
broad.*

363 | Earth

Know earth—flat, expansive, endless, and broad,
where all things grow and where they all return.

Know earth. The earth has been home to every human being and will be home to every human being to come. It is the ground for all our foibles and our ambitions; for our marauding and conquering campaigns and our quiet days of eking out crops in the fields; for our play in the dirt and our lying with mates in mossy nests; for our first steps and our last fall.

All that grows on this planet grows from the earth. All that dies on this planet falls to earth. And in that mysterious power that is both womb and grave, all that is ruined is taken, and all that grows again is brought forth.

Just as the ground is support, acceptance, and the basis for all that we are, so too is the force of earth a vital force in the way of all the universe—for the power of earth is gravity, and gravity is fundamental to the universe.

Earth is the harmonizing force, the force that takes every extreme and makes it level. Earth is gravity, attraction, a connection without there being anything solid, a tether more powerful than any rope, a force for an allegiance more powerful than any kingly demand.

The four seasons have their distinct characters, but who is subtle enough to see what is between the four seasons? Look there, and you will see. Know earth.

Where all things grow and where they all return, they must change to know metal poured from the earth's crucible.

364 | Metal

Color: white
Shape: round
Material: lightning, metals, rust, blood
Direction: west
Season: autumn
Climate: dry
Planet: Venus
Time: 3:00–7:00 P.M.
Heavenly Stem: *geng, xin*
Phase: new yin
Development: withering
Energy: contracting
Creature: white tiger
Livestock: horse
Fruit: peach
Grain: rice
Flavor: spicy
Organ: lungs
Body system: respiratory system
Body part: skin
Part of the face: nose
Emotion: sadness
Quality: renown

Know metal poured from the earth's crucible,
from ingot, to gold coin, to glinting blade.

Know metal. Thousands of years ago, the ancients poured bronze to create enormous legged vessels—to hold the offerings to the gods, to hold tribute to emperors, and to feed the people. They understood that metal was the culmination, the solid presence of their devotion. They understood that metal was the refinement of the earth, one of earth's great gifts, and marvelous because it could be refined; smelted; poured into a shape that would accept the hottest fires and yet outlast dynasties; hammered, worked, and polished so that it reflected the sun. There were many metals, each one with properties that never failed, each one potentially a lasting benefit to anyone who knew how to use it. The lesson of alloy was the lesson of community.

Metal is beauty. Golden spires, golden coins, golden jewelry. We compare people to metal: sterling character, iron will, steely strength, golden kindness.

Metal is the sword. That blade with an edge that tapers to nothingness and a spine that swells to be unbreakable. That edge that parts. That point that thrusts. Mighty is the blade, mighty is the one who wields it—wise is the one who turns the blade inward to slay delusion.

Metal forged into a sword pares away ignorance. That is why it has such a vital place. Know metal.

From ingot, to gold coin, to glinting blade, all must melt, all must dissolve and know water—the liquid that all becomes.

the five phases

WATER

Color:	blue
Shape:	curve
Material:	seas, storms, rain, ice, mist, flood, salt, time, moon
Direction:	north
Season:	winter
Climate:	cold
Planet:	Mercury
Time:	9:00 P.M.–1:00 A.M.
Heavenly Stem:	*ren, gui*
Phase:	full yin
Development:	dormant
Energy:	conserving
Creature:	black tortoise
Livestock:	pig
Fruit:	chestnut
Grain:	beans
Flavor:	salty
Organ:	kidneys
Body system:	elimination system
Body part:	bone
Part of the face:	ears
Emotion:	fear
Quality:	gentleness

Know water—the liquid that all becomes,
the clear liquid from which all life must come.

Know water. The waterfall drops a thousand feet and is not hurt. The rain scatters from lofty black clouds and gathers as a lake. Winter turns water to ice, the sun turns water into clouds. Yet, no matter how the outer world works on water, water is still true to itself.

Water does not hesitate to go where humans are afraid to go. Water does not disdain any opening: it seeks the lowest point and runs there without effort. No matter how jagged the cavity it fills, the top is always smooth, sleek enough to mirror heaven.

Leave water alone and it calms. Impurities fall to the bottom and the inherent clarity of water becomes manifest. The silt never truly sullied the water. It was water that diluted the filthy, not the filthy that oversaturated water. The river runs into the shallows, the shallows become pools, and in time the mud settles to the bottom. Water was clear all along. It was only temporarily carrying the dirt.

Water is soft, and yet it can slice mountains in half over time. Water is soft, and yet it can wipe an entire island away in one wave. Water is soft, and yet what it floods may never be seen again.

A woman holds water in her womb. We all crawled out from water. We need water to live. We need water to bathe. We purify ourselves in water. We are mostly water. We sometimes commit our dead to the sea, or scatter their ashes on the waves. We come from water, we are water, we return to water.

Liquid, never fixed in form, flowing, cold, downward-moving, always seeking level: water is substance, form, force, power, universal energy. If you would want to be spiritual, there is no better place to start and end than this. Know water.

The clear liquid from which all life must come, you cup in your hands and you drink: you hold the old and hold the new.

Dynasties and Republics

The following list is intended to give the reader the relative sequence of dynasties and their rough duration. Some dates, especially the ones in the distant past, are approximate or not fully agreed upon. There are some overlaps because one dynasty began while a previous one was still struggling for survival, or because there was more than one dynasty in different territories.

Three Sovereigns and Five Emperors Period	2852–2070 BCE
Xia Dynasty	2070–1600 BCE
Shang Dynasty	1600–1046 BCE
Western Zhou Dynasty	1046–771 BCE
Eastern Zhou Dynasty	770–256 BCE
Spring and Autumn Period	771–476 BCE
Warring States Period	475–221 BCE
Qin Dynasty	221–207 BCE
Han Dynasty	206 BCE–220 CE
Western Han Dynasty	206 BCE–9 CE
Xin Dynasty	9–23
Eastern Han Dynasty	25–220
Three Kingdoms Period	220–265
Western Jin Dynasty	265–316
Eastern Jin Dynasty	317–420
Southern and Northern Dynasties	420–589
Sui Dynasty	581–618
Tang Dynasty	618–907
Five Dynasties and Ten Kingdoms Period	907–960
Liao Dynasty	916–1125
Northern Song Dynasty	960–1127
Western Xia	1038–1227
Southern Song Dynasty	1127–1279
Jin Dynasty	1115–1234
Yuan Dynasty	1271–1368
Ming Dynasty	1368–1644
Qing Dynasty	1644–1911
Republic of China	1912–
People's Republic of China	1949–